THE FOUNDING FATHERS

BY

Nathan Schachner

South Brunswick and New York:
A. S. Barnes and Company
London: Thomas Yoseloff Ltd

New edition published 1970.
Library of Congress Catalogue Card Number: 54-5497

A. S. Barnes and Co., Inc.
Cranbury, New Jersey 08512

Thomas Yoseloff Ltd
108 New Bond Street
London W1Y OQX, England

ISBN 0-498-07497-8 (cloth)
ISBN 0-498-07645-8 (paper)
Printed in the United States of America

Foreword

THE FIRST YEARS of the United States—the years comprised in the administrations of George Washington and John Adams—were the most crucial as well as the most exciting in the history of the country. That short decade was to determine whether the novel experiment of a new form of government, of a new vision of the democratic way, was to survive or perish.

That it survived and did not perish may be considered as something of a miracle. The outlook was dark and the difficulties seemingly insuperable. A world of predatory powers, locked in mortal combat, daily threatened its existence; conflicting ideologies, sectionalisms, social and economic antagonisms, and personal passions nearly tore it asunder.

In large part, the miracle may be laid to a happy conjunction of men of talents and genius on a scale perhaps unexampled in the history of the world. Washington, John Adams, Jefferson, Hamilton, Madison, Monroe, Gallatin, Fisher Ames, John Jay, Aaron Burr, Rufus King, the Pinckneys (Charles Cotesworth and Thomas), John Marshall, Edmund Randolph, George Cabot, Oliver Wolcott, John Taylor—the list can be endlessly extended. From their internecine struggles, from their clashing philosophies, came a middle course that steered safely between the extremes of right and left. To them, rather than to the earlier group (of which indeed many of them were members), the appellation of the Founding Fathers may properly be given.

Today, more than ever, that period merits study and understanding. For once again the United States is groping its way in hitherto uncharted seas, and amazing parallels may be traced between the two eras.

Yet, for all the wealth of monographs on particular themes and biographies of individual leaders, no modern study in extenso has been made of the period as a whole, its panorama of men and events, its social, cultural, religious and political forces. It has been with that in mind that this book has been written.

The list of the author's obligations to institutions and their staffs from coast to coast is enormous. The latter range from the huge manuscript depositories of the Library of Congress near the Atlantic to the magnificent collections of the Huntington Library within sound of the Pacific. It would require pages to list them all, and his indebtedness to them for aid, comfort and facilities. To each and every one of them he extends his grateful thanks; but special mention must be made of Mr. Ivor Avellino and Mr. Edward B. Morrison of the New York Public Library, of Mr. Wayne Andrews and Mr. Wilmer Leech of the New York Historical Society, for unwearied friendliness and helpfulness over the years, not only on this book but on all previous ones.

Certain abbreviations have been used in the notes: LC for Library of Congress; ASP for American State Papers. The others should be immediately obvious, or readily decipherable from the full texts in the bibliography.

NATHAN SCHACHNER

Contents

THE FOUNDING FATHERS

CHAPTER 1

The Nation Is Born

ON THE SIXTEENTH DAY of April, 1789, at ten in the morning, George Washington embraced his wife, Martha, entered his carriage and, with a heavy heart and many a backward glance toward his beloved Mount Vernon, set out for New York to become the first President of the United States.

Two men accompanied him. One was Charles Thomson, who in his official capacity as secretary to Congress had brought the news of the election. Thomson was now a settled man of sixty, deeply interested in such diverse matters as the books of the Bible, science and philosophy. In earlier days, however, he had been a violent radical who had done as much as any man to inflame his adopted city of Philadelphia with revolutionary fervor.

The second man was Colonel David Humphreys, Washington's confidential aide. Tall, handsome and florid of complexion, Humphreys had been a member of the general's official family during the Revolution and had faithfully adhered to him ever since. But his talents were not limited to military correspondence. In his salad days he had made a name for himself as one of the little band of Yale literati known as the Connecticut Wits, and had written creditable classical, patriotic and satiric verse.

As the three men journeyed northward, the newly elected President's thoughts held no tinge of exultation. On the contrary, they were marked with anxiety and pain.[1] The fact that his choosing had been unanimous did nothing to lighten his mood. Indeed, the accolade merely added to the general feeling of oppression under which he labored.

For Washington in some respects was a humble man, despite that massive outer shield of dignity which served to freeze the overfamiliar and even to awe his closest friends. He knew his own limitations. He had a sufficient faith in his powers as a military strategist

3

and commander in the field; he had no such confidence in his abilities as a statesman in time of peace.

It was true he had sat in elective bodies and presided at the Constitutional Convention. But in neither case had his role been active. He had listened silently if attentively to the speeches and ideas of others; he had rarely, if ever, come forward with a speech or proposition of his own. His ideas neither moved with quicksilver swiftness nor dazzled in exposition as did those of many of his compeers, like Hamilton, Patrick Henry, John Dickinson or Sam Adams; nor were they clothed in the impeccable logic of a Madison or a George Mason.

Instead, he came to conclusions slowly; yet when he did they were solid, fixed and tenacious. For him to write a speech or compose a document was an agony; to deliver it before an assemblage a dreadful experience. Why then, he wondered, had he been chosen to fill a post unprecedented in scope and demanding just those qualifications which he sincerely believed he did not possess?

He had told his countrymen again and again that he wished for no further public office; that his highest felicity would be to end his days at Mount Vernon managing his estate, cultivating his farms and dwelling in domesticity and a happy obscurity. They had refused to listen. Or rather, they had pleaded the urgent necessity which imperatively required his hand at the public helm.

Of the urgency and the necessity Washington was only too well aware. Therefore he had loyally if reluctantly obeyed the summons. He had small hope, however, of being able to live up to the universal expectation that he could bind together in "a more perfect union" the disparate and quarrelsome sovereign states that had been cajoled, threatened and even bullied into the compact of the Constitution. Two states, in fact, still remained aloof. North Carolina might perhaps with proper political jockeying be induced to join the union; but tiny Rhode Island, notorious for her intransigence, had already declared she could never be compelled to do so.

It had been one thing for the thirteen colonies to unite in the common rebellion against Great Britain—though even then they did not always co-operate with touching unanimity; it was another for them now to submit their pride and dissolve their rooted suspicions in the fiercer if more subtle conflicts of peace. What, for example, had Calvinist, clergy-dominated Connecticut in common with slave-holding, easy-mannered South Carolina? What the self-righteous, penny-prudent merchants and shipowners of Massachusetts with the feckless planter-aristocrats of Virginia? Or even the stolid Dutch patroons of New York with the Quakers of Philadelphia and the pioneer settlers of backwoods Pennsylvania?

That the Constitution would not have smooth sailing, that the newly contrived United States was headed for stormy seas, was universally acknowledged by even their stoutest defenders. Young Alexander Hamilton, whose brilliant contributions to the *Federalist* papers had helped make both a reality, privately considered the Constitution to be "a frail and worthless fabric" that would not last over ten years.[2] Others, like Governor George Clinton of New York and Patrick Henry of Virginia, who had fought ratification to the bitter end, could be counted on to exert all their powers to sabotage and emasculate the new government.

No one, in fact, was wholly satisfied with the Constitution. It was a patchwork of compromises, a delicate adjustment of checks and balances, a devious course between Scylla and Charybdis. It had sought to placate the extremists at either end: the nationalists and the states'-righters, the big states and the little ones, the rich and the poor, the creditors and the debtors, the merchant industrialists and the tillers of the earth, the conservatives and the radicals, the North and the South.

To some extent it had succeeded; but the embattled forces subsided in uneasy truce rather than in permanent peace. Suspicions refused to be quelled; and the mutterings of monarchism and tyranny on the one hand and demagogic leveling on the other were an ominous portent for the future.

Besides these fundamental ideational and economic conflicts, the new nation was also faced with concrete problems of almost insuperable magnitude. Both the national government and the states of which it was composed were saddled with a crushing load of debt—the sad heritage of years of revolution. The currency was depreciated and shifting in value. Taxes were a necessity, yet the very thought of taxation was anathema to most Americans. Indian troubles impended, deftly exacerbated by England and Spain, the two great European powers whose American possessions abutted on the United States. The peace treaty with England, breached by both parties, remained a dangerously open sore. Foreign trade moved with difficulty under a complex of strangling regulations. A machinery of government, novel in many of its aspects, had to be established.

No wonder then that the prophets of doom were almost as numerous as the proclaimers of future utopia. No wonder that Washington's heart was oppressed and his mind harried as his coach plowed its muddy way toward New York, the temporary capital of the United States.

If considerations such as these may have caused Washington some sleepless nights, they did not seem to bother in the slightest the plain people who flocked to welcome him along the road. To them he was the magnificent architect of their victory, the symbol of their hard-won freedom. At every crossroad, in every hamlet and town, they cheered his passing and flung their hats into the air.

The President-elect stopped first at Alexandria in Virginia to attend a public dinner, to listen gravely to flowery addresses and to speak in turn to the assembled citizenry. His next pause was at Georgetown, where the bells clamored, the cannon thundered, the military paraded in full dress, and the populace pressed eagerly to gaze upon the countenance of their hero. Crowds poured out of Baltimore to meet his carriage. On the Pennsylvania border waited Governor Thomas Mifflin and a troop of cavalry to escort him all the way to Philadelphia. And miles before he came to that historic town, twenty thousand citizens swelled his entourage to accompany him to the City Tavern for further banqueting and further solemn oratory.

But the high point came at Trenton. There a triumphal arch composed of thirteen flower-bedecked pillars straddled the road. In front of it stood thirteen maidens in white, each with a flower basket on her arm. As the great man, now astride a white horse, rode into view the maidens burst into song.

> Virgins fair and matrons grave,
> Those thy conquering arm did save,
> Build for thee triumphal bowers;
> Strew, ye fair, his way with flowers!
> Strew your hero's way with flowers! [3]

As they sang, they suited action to words. It was all very charming, and no doubt it touched the hero's heart.

On the morning of April 23rd a committee of Congress met him at Elizabethtown Point on the New Jersey coast. Headed by John Jay, holdover Secretary of Foreign Affairs, the committee ceremoniously escorted Washington to a resplendent barge, specially built for the occasion and manned by thirteen master pilots in white uniform under the command of Commodore James Nicholson of New York.

Washington stepped in and took his seat. So did the members of the committee. The pilots raised their oars, dipped, and the barge glided across Newark Bay. Behind came two other barges, laden with dignitaries. From the receding shore troops in line fired volley after volley to speed them on their way. Boats in New York harbor, gay with welcoming flags, fell into procession. At Bedloe's Island, a sloop crowded with choristers raised a joyous paean. The trail of accompanying boats lengthened endlessly. Porpoises, so it is solemnly averred, rose to gambol about the consecrated barge.

But one large ship, lying at anchor, seemed indifferent to the general rejoicing. Her masts and rigging were bare of bunting and her decks deserted. The fact that she was a Spanish warship made the lack more striking. Brows on the approaching barges knit, and scathing comments passed. An international incident was in the making. As they pulled directly alongside, however, the somber vessel suddenly burst into life. Flags blossomed miraculously from the rigging; the crew sprang on deck and cheered, while thirteen guns boomed a salute.

On the approaching shore, as far as Bowling Green and beyond, thousands were packed into a solid, seething mass while hundreds more clung to vantage points on the surrounding buildings. Shore guns flamed a welcome. Loud huzzahs rent the air. On the steps of the ferry slip, crimson-carpeted, stood Governor Clinton of New York and a group of officials.

Washington mounted the steps to a formal greeting. Then a cortege formed, in which officials, troops, bands of music, representatives of foreign powers and plain citizens joined to honor the President of the United States. The procession wound up Broadway and then turned east to the corner of Cherry Street and Franklin Square, where the house of Samuel Osgood, a member of the Treasury Board, had been tendered for Washington's use.

It commenced to rain in the evening, but the ardor of the populace refused to be dampened. Brilliant illuminations transformed night into day, transparencies glowed with patriotic themes, and a chorus sang enthusiastic, if not exactly inspired, new verses to the old tune of "God Save the King":

Thrice welcome to this shore,
Our leader now no more,
But ruler thou;
Oh truly good and great!
Long live to glad our state,
Where countless honors wait
To deck thy brow.[4]

With adulations such as these resounding in his ears and the
smoke of incense pungent in his nostrils, Washington might well
have been forgiven the vanishment of his earlier fears and the growth
of confidence in his fitness for the post to which he had been called.

John Adams of Massachusetts, Vice-President-elect, was already
in New York. He had departed for the capital from his native town
of Braintree on April 12th. At Roxbury a troop of horse met him
and escorted him to Boston. There the bells pealed, the people
cheered and Governor John Hancock—whose signature had been
affixed to the Declaration of Independence large enough for King
George to read without spectacles—entertained him in his home.
From Boston, Adams proceeded to New Haven in Connecticut,
where some forty horse and sixty carriages formed an entourage.
Then on to the border of New York, where the Westchester Light
Horse met and brought him down in state to the city limits, there
yielding their charge to a motley of troops, officials and congressmen
who accompanied him on the final journey to John Jay's house in
the lower town.[5]

The enthusiastic receptions along the route ought to have gratified
Mr. Adams's somewhat overdeveloped love of ceremonial and display,
yet they only partly served their purpose. For the new Vice-President
was a trifle peeved. Unlike Washington, his own election to the
second post had been anything but unanimous. Whereas his chief
had received all sixty-nine accredited ballots, Adams had been given
a paltry thirty-four, less than half of the total cast. The balance was
distributed among a scattering of favorite sons in the several states.

John Adams thought highly of himself, as indeed he had a right.
He had done as much as any man to further the cause of the Revolution; he had been a tower of strength in his native state and in the
Continental Congress on behalf of the nation. Short of stature,
with a large head and stout body surmounting rather diminutive

legs, irascible and quick to take offense, stubbornly independent yet wholly honest, perhaps the most widely and deeply read man of his generation in the classics, in political and in moral philosophy, he was not the type to excite personal veneration to the same degree as Washington.

Nor were his philosophic views, which he had rashly committed to print, such as to endear him to the commonalty of men. Though a convinced republican, his republicanism had an aristocratic cast to it. Perhaps he would have felt most comfortable in the days when Rome rose to glory under the tutelage of an all-powerful and stable Senate.

For both his readings in history and his own reflections convinced him of the essential instability of a democracy unrestrained by discipline, laws and the governance of the best minds. Only a month previous, he had tartly observed that "the People of our united America find it much easier to institute Authority than to yield Obedience. They have Smarted Severely under a total oblivion of the two first Principles of Liberty and of Commerce, that Laws are the fountain of Freedom and Punctuality the Source of Credit." [6] Americans, indeed, had never been notable for their slavish adherence to either of these principles.

The date of the inauguration was set for April 30th. For two weeks before, the city's taverns had been filled to capacity with visitors come to see and behold. The overflow took to private homes and even to tents hastily erected in fields and lots.

The citizens of New York were determined to make the inaugural ceremony a lavish and memorable event. They were well aware of the fact that Congress had chosen their town merely as a temporary abode, pending a final determination of the site of the permanent capital. They were also aware that powerful influences were at work to place that site elsewhere. Therefore they exerted themselves to the utmost to retain the coveted honor for themselves.

Several men of wealth contributed a purse of $32,000 to remodel the old City Hall at the corner of Wall and Nassau Streets for the use of the new federal government. The renovations were extensive. The basement floor was redecorated in ornate Tuscan with four stout pillars to support the heavy arches above. Over these rose four Doric columns, to which a series of broad stone steps led from the street level. Through the columns passed officials and visitors into a public room which in turn led into the chamber of the House of Representatives. On either side stairways climbed to the upper story, where the Senate sat; and galleries ringed the well of the House beneath.

The number *thirteen* figured extensively, if as yet optimistically, in the general decorative scheme. Thirteen stars glittered in the metopes; thirteen arrows, encircled by twining olive, surmounted the windows. Only an eagle remained solitary in the pediment. Within, the two congressional chambers had been lavishly fitted out with an eye to the comfort and well-being of the lawmakers. It was hoped thereby that they would refrain from removal to realms as yet untried.

The day of the thirtieth dawned ominously overcast; fortunately, the skies soon cleared. All through the preceding night boats had plied the Hudson and Long Island Sound to bring new hordes of spectators into town. The volunteer companies turned out in their finest, with blue, yellow and gold lace furnishing the predominating color scheme. There were also Highland kilts and bagpipes, while bear shakos nodded everywhere.

The inaugural procession formed early before Washington's quarters. The order of march had been planned with great precision and doubtless caused many an angry mutter from those who felt their importance had been slighted.

In the van rode a company of cavalry, followed by three companies of foot. Then came the sheriff of New York resplendent on a horse. Behind him rolled carriages holding the welcoming committees from Congress. Then came three mounted masters of ceremony.

At a decent distance behind appeared the prime mover and sufficient cause of all the hubbub—the President of the United States seated solitary in a carriage drawn by four horses and attended by three men in livery. Immensely tall, austere and rugged of countenance, reserved to the point of grim immobility, gray of eye and boldly Roman in nose, Washington acknowledged the wild plaudits of the massed spectators with stiff and uncomfortable little bows.

Amid the prevalent gold lace and ornate uniforms his dress showed plain and drab. He wore a dark-brown suit of homespun cloth relieved only by the white of his silk stockings. The coarse homespun —instead of the fine imported broadcloth or silk he ordinarily affected—was a concession to the importunities of the domestic manufacturers and later led to favorable newspaper comment.[7] John Adams and several members of Congress from the manufacturing states prudently wore the same.

After the presidential carriage came three more masters of ceremony; then followed the two presidential secretaries, John Jay as Secretary of Foreign Affairs, the three commissioners of the Treasury, General Henry Knox of the War Department, the chancellor of the state of New York, the mayor of the city, the aldermen, representatives of foreign powers, clergymen and a vast concourse of plain people.[8]

The procession moved to the blare of bands to the newly named Federal Hall, where Congress waited in dignity. Washington descended from his carriage, mounted the steps and shortly thereafter reappeared to the popular view on the outside gallery leading from the Senate chamber. There Robert R. Livingston, chancellor of New York, administered the oath of office and Washington in turn solemnly promised to perform his duties in faithful accordance with the Constitution. When he had ended Livingston cried out in a loud voice: "Long live George Washington, President of the United States!" To which the great assemblage in the streets below raised a mighty shout and cannon roared antiphonal thunder.[9]

The newly installed President now entered the Senate chamber to address both Houses of Congress. He had labored long on the inaugural speech, knowing how carefully it would be scrutinized and each word weighed. Yet in spite of lengthy preparation and diligent practice in the privacy of his own home, in spite of the sympathetic and respectful faces that met his gaze, when the time came for delivery he shook and trembled so he could scarce hold the papers on which it was written.

Two members of Congress have left records of the embarrassing scene. Young Fisher Ames, member of the lower House and already attracting attention as one of the most brilliant men in Congress, was perhaps the kinder of the two. Time, he noted with pain, had made its havoc on Washington's face since the heroic days of the Revolution; nevertheless, Ames gazed up at him with a feeling of veneration and awe. The President's aspect, he observed, was "grave, almost to sadness; his modesty, actually shaking; his voice deep, a little tremulous, and so low as to call for close attention."[10]

Senator William Maclay was more critical. He had learned politics the hard way in the back country of Pennsylvania, and had come to New York breathing radical ardors and prepared to sniff monarchical and aristocratical tendencies on every tainted breeze. Thus accoutered, he naturally found what he sought. Only a few days before he had

triumphantly confirmed that "we have really more republican plainness and sincere openness of behavior in Pennsylvania than in any
other place I have ever been"; and that "no people in the Union
dwell more on trivial distinctions and matters of mere form" than
"the gentlemen of New England." [11]

Laden with these preconceptions, Maclay was prepared to view
Washington with a compound of veneration for his services to the
Revolution and suspicion of his Virginia gentility. What he now
saw disturbed him mightily and planted the seeds of further revulsion.

He noted with approval the brown homespun dress and the plain
metal buttons embossed with eagles. With perhaps less approval he
took in the white stockings, the bag and the ornamental sword. What
astounded him, however, was the obvious fact that "this great man
was agitated and embarrassed more than ever he was by the leveled
cannon or pointed musket. He trembled, and several times could
scarce make out to read."

Washington's stage fright might have awakened his sympathy, had
not the President attempted certain unfortunate flourishes and gestures. These, thought Maclay, were both ungainly and unnecessary.
"I sincerely, for my part," he wrote with considerable asperity, "wished
all set ceremony in the hands of the dancing masters, and that this
first of men had read off his address in the plainest manner, without
ever taking his eyes from the paper, for I felt hurt that he was not
first in every thing." [12]

The address itself was innocuous enough and leaned heavily on
generalities and religious sentiment. He had answered his country's
call, said Washington, with reluctance and a feeling of disqualifica-
tion. However, he trusted to the guidance of the Almighty who had
already shown His hand in the affairs of the United States. "Every
step," he was convinced, "by which they have advanced to the character of an independent nation seems to have been distinguished by
some token of providential agency." The Revolution itself, the united
government they had just achieved without the usual convulsions
that had attended the birth of other nations, all pointed to such supernatural intervention. It awoke sentiments of "pious gratitude, along
with an humble anticipation of the future blessings which the past
seem to presage."

Only once did Washington descend into the arena of concrete
human affairs, and then only by indirection. He was certain, he con-

cluded gravely, that "no local prejudices or attachments—no separate views, nor party animosities, will misdirect the comprehensive and equal eye which ought to watch over this great assemblage of communities and interests." [13]

It was the same note which he was to develop more frankly and at greater length in his Farewell Address. Unfortunately, in both instances the warning was not heeded. The local prejudices and attachments were only too plainly visible in the deliberations of Congress.

CHAPTER 2

Its Diverse Parts

THE UNITED STATES over which George Washington came so reluctantly to preside was as yet neither a nation nor even a geographical entity. It was, rather, a philosophic idea and a dream for the future, embodied in a phrase and engrossed on a sheet of parchment.

Some 3,929,000 people (including 757,000 Negroes) inhabited a long, curving seaboard strip that stretched for almost fifteen hundred miles from the British Canadian frontier on the north to the Spanish possessions of the Floridas in the south.

Westward the Alleghenies and the backbone of the Appalachian range acted as a natural barrier, though trappers and hunters as well as land-hungry settlers had pushed through the various gaps into what was known as the Northwest Territory. At the southern end, where the mountain ridges subsided into mere foothills, other adventurers sought to penetrate the Indian country in spite of treaties and the stern commands of the national government.

Hemming in the legal and illegal advance and hostile to both were powerful Indian tribes, the British astride the Great Lakes, and the sprawling empire of Spain stretching west to the Pacific and south to the inhospitable reaches of Patagonia. There were visionaries who peered into the future and foresaw an expanded America bounded on the west by the Mississippi and extending to the Gulf of Mexico; but not even the boldest gave more than a passing thought to the interminable plains and savage mountains beyond the Father of Waters.

Even on the inhabited Atlantic strip the population clumped into dispersed areas, islanded by numerous rivers and separated by stretches of still primeval forest. A bare hundred miles or so inland from the sound of the sea, the forest reigned triumphant, with widely scattered vents through which the carrier pigeon might have seen

14

ragged clearings and the smoke pluming upward from isolated settlements.

Communications were spotty and poor. There were few regular roads, and these chiefly connected the larger cities. The best were in New England and the Middle States; but even these excited bitter comments from foreign travelers. As for those below the Mason and Dixon line, no adjective was too gross to describe their condition. In rainy weather they were almost impassable; in dry, the dust rose in clouds and the ruts jolted and jarred. Luckless passengers either helped push the stagecoaches out of wheel-deep mud or swayed in unison from side to side at the command of the driver to avoid overturn on the ridges.[1]

All the roads leading into Philadelphia were in deplorable condition, broken or churned according to the weather by the heavy wagons employed to bring provisions into the city.[2] The Boston post road which led to New York was not much better. It was not until 1794 that a private company built a toll turnpike between Philadelphia and Lancaster, a distance of sixty-two miles, and maintained it in a state of tolerable repair. Thereafter other companies added many miles of private road to fill the lack of public improvements.

Men preferred to travel on horseback wherever possible; where not, stagecoaches were the only means of transportation. On the arterial road between Boston and New York the coaches ran twice a week and took from six to seven days to make the trip. In 1797 a faster service was installed, an extra coach was added, and the time of passage shortened to five days in winter and three days in summer. Passengers paid five cents a mile, baggage extra.[3]

Between Philadelphia and New York, perhaps the most heavily traveled road in America, the stages ran daily. They accommodated nine to twelve persons, uncomfortably perched on backless benches. The drivers, so it was said, were almost always slightly drunk from the potations imbibed at every stop. As a result they drove fast and recklessly, and spills and accidents were frequent. Two full days were required to make the journey. But in 1799 "The Swift-Sure" line promised that its stages would leave Philadelphia at 6 A.M. and reach New York at noon of the following day, at a charge of five dollars a head.[4]

Wherever possible, however, and particularly in journeys between the Deep South and the Northern Seaboard, travelers went by packet boat; though weeks might elapse before the happy combina-

tion of a departing ship and favoring winds permitted the conclusion
of the voyage.

Conceived as separate units and settled by diverse groups animated
by diverse motives, the thirteen colonies had originally felt no common bond other than their similar allegiance to an England across
the sea. The inhabitants had come to these shores for political, economic and religious reasons which had no common denominator and
only too often clashed in practice. The Puritans of New England
tolerated no other sects; while the Anglicans of Virginia in turn
surveyed them with a cold contempt. Both joined in condemning the
Catholics of Maryland and in despising the backwoods Baptists and
Methodists.

To the original religious divergences were shortly added ethnic
ones. The first settlers had been overwhelmingly English in origin,
(with a sizable enclave of Dutch in New York and a smaller group
of Swedes in Delaware); but the later emigration poured floods of
Irish, Scotch-Irish, German and even French into the colonies. Except for the French, these pushed largely into the interior of highlands, mountains and beyond to hack out new lands for themselves
and establish manners, customs and forms of political thought that
differed sharply in many instances from those of the settled communities closer to the sea.

Geography and climate played potent roles in widening the original
diversities. Thin-soiled and rock-embedded New England could
maintain only small farms from which backbreaking toil elicited
scanty crops. But the neighboring sea, so they said, was their natural
farmland. The long, indented coast, the icy waters and the famous
Newfoundland Banks yielded a fertile tillage of valuable fish; while
the straight, tall pines and hemlocks of the mountain forests provided the materials for proud ships to sail the seven seas.

The Middle States, blessed with a temperate climate and good
soil as well as vast interior stretches still open to settlement, yielded
a ready growth of wheat, maize, rye and barley, the staple food
crops of the American economy. Cattle grazed the pastures, and pigs
and fowl commingled in the barnyards. Though farms were larger
than those of New England, their size was limited by the area culti-
vable by the proprietor, his family and perhaps a few hired hands.
The valley of the Hudson and the eastern reaches of the Mohawk
were exceptions to the general rule. Here the Dutch patroons had

established a semifeudal type of manorial holding on which tenant cultivators paid heavy dues in kind for the privilege of eking out a meager living.

Tapping these resources and making them available for foreign and domestic consumption were the seaport and river towns of New York, Philadelphia, Wilmington and Baltimore. In these marts of trade flourished a merchant class, rivaled in wealth and influence only by the merchant adventurers of Boston, Salem, Portsmouth and Providence in New England, and Charleston in the South.

The Southern States were a different world. They depended almost wholly on the produce of the earth. But their economy was sharply limited, with a few exceptions, to a small number of specialized crops. Because of a historical accident, most of tidewater Virginia was devoted to the single staple of tobacco, largely for export and therefore dependent on world conditions. It is true that certain planters saw the fallacy of the single crop and sought to diversify their land with the more durable grains; but their neighbors and even they themselves were tempted too easily by the ready market for tobacco in good years and were prone to forget the lean years in between.

Rice was the chief crop of the steamy marshlands of South Carolina and Georgia; while cotton was coming in slowly, impeded as yet by the laborious toil required to separate the seeds from the clinging strands.

The Southern climate was generally hot, ranging from the milder temperatures of Virginia to the almost insupportable summer heats of lower South Carolina and Georgia. Only in the western highlands could white men labor on the fields, and these were peopled with a different breed from the dwellers of the tidewater—chiefly Scotch-Irish moving down along the backbone of the hills from Pennsylvania and the North.

The cultivation of tobacco, rice and cotton lent itself readily to large plantations and the employment of gangs of laborers. The heat, the ease with which white servants, indentured for a term of years, could take up piedmont and highland lands after their terms had expired, plus the plying slave ships of the earlier days, helped fasten Negro slavery and Negro labor as a fundamental institution in the economy of the South.

It was true there were also Negro slaves in the Northern states, but they were few in number and tended to be domestic servants rather than tillers of the soil. Neither climate nor existent conditions favored their large-scale use; and those in bondage eventually gained freedom by manumission, money payments or by law. By 1789 slavery had been legally abolished in the New England states, while Pennsylvania had enacted a system of gradual emancipation. New York yielded to the mounting pressure by the turn of the century, New Jersey did likewise, and only in Delaware and Maryland did slavery continue to exist well into the nineteenth century.

The art of manufacturing was still in its infancy and the home supplied most of the rough products required for local use where importation was expensive. There was good reason for the lack of regular industrial establishments. England, in accordance with the prevailing philosophy of colonization, had rigorously prohibited the manufacture of any articles that might compete with her own industries. Colonies, so ran the theory, existed for the benefit of the mother country. They furnished raw materials and foodstuffs to the homeland, and in turn presented an exclusive and profitable market for the manufactured wares of their begetter.

Even after independence, the American states found it extraordinarily difficult to institute manufactures. The great continental powers, solicitous of their monopolies, threw every impediment in the way of the possible rival across the seas, and went so far as to prohibit under stringent penalties the export of machinery, of parts and even of the artisans themselves. So that, aside from a few weak and as yet largely futile ventures, the United States lagged behind in the initial stages of the Industrial Revolution that was soon to transform the face of the earth.

For all that the country was essentially devoted to the pursuit of agriculture, the methods of tilling the soil were quite primitive and differed negligibly from those employed in antiquity. The plow, the hoe and the rake were clumsy and inefficient; man and horse provided the only motive power; and soil butchery was rampant.

Though men like Washington and Jefferson in Virginia, and Dr. George Logan in Pennsylvania, advocated proper manuring, crop rotation and, in some instances, deep plowing, the great majority of farmers preferred to skim the fat off the soil and, after its exhaustion, to move on to virgin lands. Foreign observers were constantly amazed at the agricultural ignorance of the Americans. One Englishman called them downright "slovenly" in their practices and estimated that a British farmer could produce as much on fifty acres as an American on two hundred. A French traveler declared that such was the American indolence and indifference that they failed to employ procedures "which in Europe are considered as the ABC of husbandry." [5]

Nor did Americans believe in the European tradition of rootedness in the soil where one was born. Why should they? They had originally crossed the Atlantic to better their lot, and if expectations failed in the first settlement, they sought their fortune elsewhere. The interminable forests, the land across the mountains, lush with the mulch of centuries and swarming with game, held an irresistible lure. Already the westward movement was well under way, the harbinger of further migrations hitherto unparalleled in the history of the world.

The march of settlements to the west followed a general pattern. First came the man of broken fortunes—often compelled to flee to escape the debtor's jail. He piled his earthly belongings in a cart drawn by a scrawny horse, seated his wife and smaller children on top, gave his older children the driving of a few cows and, mounted on another spavined nag, took off over rutted trails for the ever-receding frontier.

If he had soldiered in the army, he was entitled to a grant of land in specified sections of the wilderness; if not, he could obtain a number of acres from state or federal government on a small down payment and a long term of credit for the balance. In too many instances, however, he did not bother with such idle formalities but squatted wherever he pleased and thereby created untold headaches for the future.

Once he had found a good site, usually a natural clearing in the woods contiguous on a stream, he proceeded to build a rude log cabin of split logs, left the native earth for a flooring, provided openings for door and window, and dug a pit in the center of the earthen floor for his hearth fire. He rarely bothered to construct a chimney, allowing the smoke to find its way through chinks and openings into the outer air. A similar, though smaller, structure furnished a barn to house his livestock.

The habitation completed, he next plowed the clearing and planted Indian corn. Until the crop matured the family lived on the grain they had brought with them, fished the neighboring streams and hunted the game in the surrounding forest.

Gradually the clearing was extended by the process of girdling trees to keep the sap from rising. Once the trees were dead, corn could be planted around the shadeless trunks, and the trees themselves awaited the settler's leisure for felling and conversion into logs, rails and firewood.

Thus remotely ensconced, the family took on the manners and protective coloration of the Indians. Hardships, backbreaking labor and disease took their toll. Civilization fell away. Rags and dirt abounded. Crudely distilled corn afforded a too ready solace.

Within a few years other settlers moved into the area, the game was killed off or vanished into remoter areas, and law and government, scant enough in their beginnings, caught up with the settlement. Unable to brook these limitations on his livelihood and hitherto lawless state, the settler sold his land if he had held it by legal grant, or simply abandoned it if he did not, and repeated his trek into the farther west.

The second settler, the man who followed him and took over the land with its improvements, was of a different sort. He paid for possession, either to the original holder, a land company or the government. A rough log cabin did not content him; as soon as possible he built a substantial dwelling of sawed logs, clapboards or even stone. He dug a cellar and cleared a meadow on which he pastured cows, planted orchards and raised wheat and rye, as well as the ubiquitous Indian corn.

In spite of his industry, however, he too generally failed as a settler. Either he knew little of the art of agriculture or his ambitious schemes led him into debt. Thereupon he took to drink, quarreled with both church and government as the putative authors of all his ills, and was lucky if he sold out before his creditors foreclosed.

The third and final settler was a substantial, moneyed citizen. Like entrepreneurs in other fields, he came into the picture late enough to take advantage of the spadework of his predecessors and build success on their failures. A prosperous farmer in the East, he also prospered here. He employed modern techniques of cultivation, added additional wings to the buildings, erected fences, a milkhouse and a smokehouse for curing meats, increased the variety of his crops with oats, buckwheat and garden vegetables, and transported furniture by wagon or muleback from the East.

Eventually he commenced an even finer dwelling, which usually was left for his heirs to complete. His table groaned under an abundance of food; he upheld the government, paid his taxes regularly and contributed to the upkeep of churches and schools. In short, he was that solid citizen, that sturdy, independent yeoman, that back-bone of democracy, concerning whom the pamphleteers and philosophers were wont to wax lyrical.

Dr. Benjamin Rush, in his pungent description of these three stages of settlement, did not hesitate to sound the lyric note. The third migrant, he asserted, had instituted "a new species of war. . . . The weapons with which he achieves his conquests are the implements of husbandry, and the virtues which direct them are industry and economy. Idleness, extravagance, and ignorance fly before him. Happy would it be for mankind if the kings of Europe would adopt this mode of extending their territories." [6]

Society in the United States was still fluid, particularly on the frontiers. Even on the seaboard, where a century and a half of settlement had achieved a certain stability and given rise in special groups to a discernible aristocratic temper, the awareness of the frontier with its supposedly limitless opportunities prevented that crystallization into classes which marked the landscape of Europe. The farmer, the petty tradesman, the artisan, unable to make a decent living where he was, could always pull up stakes and depart for the free, or semifree, land of the West.

Furthermore, the concepts engendered by the Revolution—that all men are created free and equal, and endowed with certain inalienable rights—were not allowed to molder on paper. They were taken seriously by the ordinary American, and prevented him from bowing and crooking his knee to those who assumed to be his betters. That peculiar optimism and faith in the possibility of a quick and easy material success which has since characterized him were plainly visible during this period. Timothy Dwight, president of Yale and an acute observer when his prejudices were not involved, described the phenomenon.

"In certain stages of society," he wrote, "the expectations of enterprising men may, with little difficulty, be raised to any imaginable height. Fortunes, they will easily believe, may be amassed at a stroke; without industry or economy; by mere luck; or the energy of superior talents for business. These talents every sanguine man will arrogate to himself; and on this luck he will rely without a fear. The prize, he is assured, will fall to *him*; and the twenty thousand blanks, by which it is ominously surrounded, will be drawn by others." [7]

The most common outlet for this itch for easy riches was speculation in land. Almost everyone with some money, or audacity, or influence, entered the grand sweepstakes. Both the states and the national government granted princely domains to individuals or groups with unseemly haste and sometimes under the most corrupt influences. Even where the grants were legitimate, and for a supposedly proper consideration, the official donors were too often prone to overlook long-term considerations.

Among such lavish cessions were the Macomb grant of 3,635,200 acres in northern New York; the Western lands of the Ohio Company that, with its associated Miami and Scioto Companies, totaled 7,000,000 acres; and the notorious Yazoo Company which corrupted almost the entire legislature of Georgia to gain a fabulous empire in the Southwest. Even foreign groups, like the Holland Land Company, succumbed to the lure and joined in the scramble for speculative lands, nor did they balk at the means required to gain special favors.

However, few if any of these numerous ventures brought the hoped-for pot of gold to their initiators. Poorly financed, viewing with an apprehensive eye the eventual necessity of meeting installment payments, the speculators sought quick turnovers rather than holding for long-term appreciation in values. Nor did they adequately take into consideration the factors required for successful settlements.

Surveys were of the sketchiest, local conditions were disregarded, and planning consisted in drafting glowing prospectuses which superimposed whole cities complete with public buildings and schools, surrounded by thriving farms, on the pathless wilderness. These were displayed to the unwary purchaser as though they were realities and not mere figments of the entrepreneur's imagination.

Since such purchasers were chiefly sought abroad, in England, France and elsewhere, where silver-tongued agents were prone to promise more than could possibly be substantiated, disillusionment was inevitable. Some few boatloads of emigrants whom these blandishments induced to voyage to America found themselves plunged unprepared into savage forests, the promises unkept, their boundaries ill-defined and even their titles suspect. Such was the case with the attempted settlement of Gallipolis under the aegis of the Ohio Company by a group of sanguine but tragically unfit French refugees.[8]

The peculiar restlessness and readiness to pull up stakes which characterized the Americans was evident even in the settled cities. Moreau de St. Méry, resident in New York, noted with astonishment the strange "mania" of the Yorkers for moving from one rented house to another, no better, on the first of every May. "This moving," he exclaimed, "must be seen to be believed. No one was able to tell me the reason for it." [9] Nor, for that matter, has anyone since been able to explain the phenomenon.

The great metropolises—by American standards—were Philadelphia, New York, Boston, Charleston and Baltimore. By European standards, however, they were barely medium-sized towns. Philadelphia, the largest, boasted a population in 1790 of 42,444. New York crowded the Quaker town with 33,131 inhabitants; while Boston, Charleston and Baltimore trailed with 18,028, 16,359 and 13,503 respectively. America was not as yet urban-minded; and Thomas Jefferson prayed devoutly that it never would be. Cities, he thought, tended to become dens of iniquity and haunts of vice. Only in the country could virtue and independence flourish, or a true democracy become possible. "Those who labour in the earth," he wrote, "are the chosen people of God, if he ever had a chosen people, whose breasts he has made his peculiar deposit for substantial and genuine virtue." On the other hand, "the mobs of great cities add just so much to the support of pure government, as sores do to the strength of the human body." [10] Many influential Americans of the day agreed with him. The outstanding dissident was Alexander Hamilton.

Nor were the cities beautiful by European standards. They had no palaces, no magnificent buildings, public or private, no formal parks and gardens, no museums, no monuments. Culture and tradition had not yet imprinted their marks. Time had not yet rubbed down the rawness with its gentle patina. The smell of the land and the forest still penetrated the innermost cobbled squares.

Philadelphia already possessed that boxlike appearance of rectangular streets and uniform houses which still characterizes her. A censorious Englishman thought the houses mean and undistinguished, and called her public buildings, with the single exception of the State House, "heavy tasteless piles of brick." The waterfront was kneedeep in filth, and the stench that came from it offended the strongest nostrils.[11] No wonder the yellow fever was endemic!

New York, thought a somewhat friendlier Frenchman, had a few beautiful homes, but the streets were narrow and too often unpaved. Cows and pigs were a not uncommon sight on even the main thoroughfares; while dead dogs, cats and rats lay untouched in the streets until natural decay or a supersensitive householder removed them. Familiar though he was with prerevolutionary Paris, the number of prostitutes who plied their profession with brazen candor in New York amazed him. So did the size of the red-light district, which some wit had labeled the "Holy Ground." The appellation puzzled the chronicler, who neither understood the appropriateness nor appreciated the humor.[12]

Boston's winding streets were a hopeless maze, as they still are; and the legend that they had merely followed ancient cowpaths sounded quite plausible to the visitor. But her State House and Faneuil Hall obtained admiring glances even from those accustomed to the architecture of London and Paris.

Perhaps the most gracious of American towns was Charleston. The aristocratic homes with their white columns, fanciful grillework and lovely gardens already prefigured the glories of the next century. Williamsburg, however, had fallen into decay; while Norfolk had never emerged from its original crude and makeshift appearance. Her streets were unpaved and laid out without any visible plan. Open sewage ditches lined the main thoroughfares, nor did the planks for crossing always save the pedestrian from an unsavory ducking. The houses, of soft pine and a single story in height, so it was said, were never put in repair because ten years represented their life expectancy and it was cheaper to tear them down at the end and rebuild.[13]

But fine homes, soundly constructed and well-proportioned, were already dotting the American landscape. These were usually built in the prevailing English modes, with such modifications as the taste and ingenuity of American craftsmen suggested. Simplicity and grace were their keynotes, as they were of the churches and meeting houses whose white steeples dominated every village.

Another and different style was shortly to compete with this Georgian simplicity. Thomas Jefferson, freshly returned from Europe, where he had become enamored of the Graeco-Roman Maison Carrée at Nîmes and had fallen under the spell of Andrea Palladio, initiated neoclassical forms in America. His home at Monticello, the cluster of buildings that make up the University of Virginia, and the Capitol at Richmond, exemplify them at their best.

In New England the young architect Charles Bulfinch created his own modifications; while Benjamin Henry Latrobe, who designed the Bank of Pennsylvania in 1798 in the form of a Grecian temple, was

largely responsible for the rash of Attic banks, churches, public buildings and even jails that later broke out across the country.

The traveler who sought to encompass the length and breadth of
America in a single journey might well find it difficult to believe that
the people he met actually belonged to the same nation.

In New England, it was true, they seemed largely fashioned out of
the same cloth. They were Calvinist in the main (with a sprinkling
of burgeoning Unitarians), sober in habits, drab in dress, industrious
and with a keen eye to the main chance. They plowed their stubborn
acres and sailed the seven seas with equal energy and persistence, and
they followed the maxims of *Poor Richard's Almanac* as closely as
possible.

They believed devoutly in the efficacy of education and in the divine origin of law and order. The tenets of religion and morality were
sternly preached, if not always practiced. Gaming and idle sports were
anathema, and the theater proscribed as an invitation to immorality.

Massachusetts, in 1750, forbade by law all dramatic performances;
and it was not until 1793 that persistent agitation gained its repeal.
Such a figure as Sam Adams denounced the stage in terms reminiscent
of the English Puritans. The rural districts viewed the glitter and
tinsel as part of the corruption of the cities and their works as born
of the Devil.

Even before repeal, however, the prohibitory law was evaded in
Boston. *Romeo and Juliet* was billed as a "Moral-Lecture"; so was *All
the World's a Stage*.[14] The "lectures" raised a storm of indignation
from the puritanical forces; the newspapers teemed with denunciations
of the "band of detestable miscreants" who produced them. Nationalist
rancor played its part in the proceedings, for most of the actors were
British. "If we have any laudable pride remaining," cried one correspondent, "let us teach these EXOTICS, that the same spirit *now*
animates the people of Massachusetts, to resent the insults offered our
government by individuals from Briton [*sic*], as actuated us during
the war, to oppose the attempts of the whole nation." [15]

Nor did the agitation die out with repeal. Five years after, when
one of the two theaters in Boston burned down, it was solemnly proposed to demolish the other, in the light of the clear warning thus
vouchsafed from Heaven.[16]

Literacy was high. There was scarcely a child, rich or poor, who had
not been taught at least the elements of reading, writing and arith-

metic. In Connecticut, declared Timothy Dwight with pardonable pride, "there is a school-house, sufficiently near to every man's door . . . to allow his children to go conveniently to school throughout most of the year." [17] Harvard and Yale, already venerable, pointed the way to the higher reaches of education.

In some aspects, the eastern fringes of the Middle Atlantic States resembled their New England brethren. The Dutch inhabitants of New York partook of some of their sober traits, though they did not take their religion quite so seriously. The Yorkers of English descent, on the other hand, interpreted their Anglicanism and way of life in much more liberal fashion. They liked the good things when they could obtain them, and enjoyed the theater, balls and other entertainments. Plays were freely performed in New York, Philadelphia, Williamsburg and Charleston. The first professional companies were of English origin. So were the plays. The fare was good, and included Shakespeare, Dryden, Steele, Sheridan and Otway. To lighten such heavy drama, however, a straight farce was usually given as a curtain raiser. George Washington, during his presidency, regularly attended the theater and by such public approval did much to obviate objections.

Tumblers, acrobats, riding exhibitions, recitations and comic songs were in even greater demand. The illuminati flocked to hear Signor Trisobio, direct from Italy, present such musical tidbits as the rendition by his single voice of a trio in "imitation of three Italian nuns" as well as "the favourite comic song of the Cats." [18] Transparencies and dioramas extracted their share of shillings from gaping crowds; so did traveling zoos and exhibitions of animal oddities—elephants, bears, tigers and "learned pigs." Thomas Jefferson did not consider such entertaiment beneath his dignity to attend.

In Pennsylvania, the Quakers easily outdid both New Englanders and Dutch in the somberness of their dress and the strictness of their morals; while they proved worthy rivals in the realms of business and finance. Mingled with them was the recent influx of Irish, Catholic in religion and turbulent by nature. Since most of them had fled famine and the political oppression of the English overlord, it was only natural that they were animated with a fierce hatred of all things English and helped inject their animosity into Pennsylvania politics.

Once the seaboard fringe was penetrated, however, and the Alleghenies surmounted, a new and different order of being seemed suddenly to emerge. The pioneer, the forest dweller, has never been noted for his polished manners or the amenities of more settled folk.

Nor does he admire the same virtues. Strength of limb, dexterity with gun and knife, boundless energy, the ability to outfight, outdrink and outroar his fellows, these are the targets for admiration. In a rough society where legal forms have not yet fully penetrated, each man must be self-reliant and ready at all times to protect what he conceives to be his natural rights. Violence is king, and personal combat the accepted procedure for settling disputes.

Among those who considered themselves gentry, the combat took the form of the duel. Among those who neither had nor claimed such pretensions, the rough-and-tumble fight held sway. This curious mode of exercise, prevalent not only on the frontier but in certain Southern states, invariably horrified the foreigner who witnessed it. A passing remark, or even the mere exuberance of drunken spirits, was sufficient to set it off. No holds were barred, no brutality or inhuman practice held amiss. They wrestled and traded blows, they bit fingers and noses to shreds, they twisted ears, legs and arms, they gouged out eyes with powerful thumbs, they ground heavy boots into helpless faces and kicked in ribs, they were even known on occasions to seize an unfortunate opponent by his private parts and tear them bloodily away.[19] All that hindered final extermination, at least in the presence of an audience, was the practice of desisting when the victim cried he had had enough.

Just as the Central states were divided into two sections, so were the Southern. Their frontier folk possessed the same characteristics as those farther to the north and west. They stemmed from the same roots and adhered to the same sects. These were chiefly revivalist in nature: Presbyterian, Baptist and Methodist.

Itinerant preachers would proclaim a camp-meeting day, and the people would converge on foot, by horse or wagon from great distances around. The pattern was usually the same. The revivalist preached hell-fire and brimstone for the unregenerate, prayed and exhorted, gesticulated and thundered, rising to greater and greater heights of frenzy until it seemed that human lungs and human frame could bear no more.

In one notable Kentucky instance, ten thousand attended and harkened to a number of preachers performing simultaneously. As the frenzy rose and the contagion spread, one after another in the assemblage would jerk in every limb, shout, scream, fall to the ground and roll convulsively, to subside into an epileptic trance. Others ran aimlessly, barked like dogs, or raced shrieking into the neighboring woods, where enthusiasm occasionally vented itself in a final sexual act.[20]

Nor were such strange practices wholly confined to the revivalist sects. Jemima Wilkinson, a Rhode Island Quakeress, migrated to central New York, where she proclaimed herself not only possessed of prophetic powers but to be the literal bride of Christ. She managed to attract a worshiping following until one day, or rather night, some skeptic discovered that the regular visitant to her bed was a certain Squire Parker, her chief assistant and the alleged incarnation of the Prophet Elijah.[21]

The tidewater gentry of the South, however, had little or nothing in common with their fellow citizens to the west. The flat littoral lent itself to great plantations, single-crop cultivation and a slave economy. These in turn colored the character, manners and mode of life of their possessors. Some of the largeness of their domains entered their spirit, and, in addition, some of those vices which seem an inevitable concomitant of absolute power over land and men.

They despised trade and industry as much as any English country squire, though their continued existence depended on the marketing and sale of their produce. They loved hunting, horse racing, gaming and ostentatious display. Their hospitality was proverbial, their manners gracious, yet their tempers hinged on a hair trigger, and a word or a look might easily lead to sudden death. They lived in the grand style, spent recklessly what they did not have, and ran up staggering debts without a thought as to how they would be paid. Even their own contemporaries asserted that the alacrity with which they took up arms against the British was due in part to their heavy indebtedness to British merchants.[22]

At the same time they were keenly, even passionately, political. They held statecraft to be a responsibility and a duty, nor was self-interest the sole factor that induced them to participate in the functions of government. In religion they were Anglican, and when that term fell into disrepute, Episcopalian. But their religion was not fanatical. It was part of the gentleman's code to uphold the church, and though most of them opposed the disestablishment advocated by such members of their own class as Jefferson and Madison—and enthusiastically endorsed by the dissenting groups—they yielded gracefully and without too much rancor when disestablishment triumphed.

They believed in education; that is, the education proper to a gentleman. When they could, they sent their sons to England and to the Continent for the grand tour; when they could not, William and Mary in Virginia, Princeton in New Jersey, and later Columbia College in South Carolina afforded them the necessary classical veneer. But free or universal education at the lower levels was not to their taste, and they were able to stave off Jefferson's persistent campaign for its introduction.

Even on the growing question of slavery, the foundation stone of their economy and way of life, they were not as yet fanatical. A substantial number of their leading men saw and deplored its inherent evils and sought for some moderate solution that would eventually end in emancipation. Such efforts were not too bitterly resented, but two factors were soon to put an end to their complaisance. One was the invention of the cotton gin, which made the cultivation of cotton on a large scale with slave labor hugely profitable; the other was the increasing agitation for abolition by Northern groups. The cry of outside interference is always effective as a means for solidifying home sentiment, even in the case of native doubters.

It is true that America in 1789 might be considered a new country, in the sense that the oldest settlement was less than two hundred years old, and the vast majority of the population was of much less recent date. It is also true that the land itself created new problems and new opportunities which necessarily modified the character of the people, submerging certain traits and bringing others to the fore. But people, individuals, can never be said to be *new*, in spite of St. John de Crèvecoeur's famous query: "What then is the American, this new man?" The emigrants brought with them from their native lands an inheritance, a tradition and a culture which left their mark in spite of later modifications. The Pennsylvania Dutch (Palatinate German) still clung to many of their original customs and modes of thought. The Anglo-Saxon heritage continued to influence those who revolted against the mother country. The New World creeds, for all their diversity, stemmed from those of the Old. The same classics were read with equal diligence in both worlds. Even the political philosophies under whose banners the Americans had proclaimed their freedom from kings and tyrannical institutions had been first pronounced abroad—by Locke, Harrington, Montesquieu, Vatel, Burlamaqui, Grotius and a host of others.

At the same time, differentiation and modification had already set in. What had been mere theory in the Old World, or confined to a favored few, was now being put into practice by the many. Freedom, equality, opportunity, had become more than slogans or philosophic ideas. They were incorporated into written constitutions, and the great experiment of making them viable had begun. The Old World itself felt the repercussions, much to the astonishment as well as delight of those who had set them in motion.

"The Revolution in America, it was very early predicted," commented a newspaper, "would have a great influence upon the publick affairs of the European World—but the most sanguine advocate for the Liberties of Mankind, could not have anticipated those Surprising Events, which have already transpired to distinguish the annals of the present age. Our generous, and magnanimous Allies, the French nation . . . discover a noble ardour in the best of causes." [23] This of course was in the initial stages of the French Revolution.

The concept of political equality soon spilled over into the field of education. Most Americans understood that representative government could not flourish without a responsive and well-informed electorate. Since the franchise base was steadily widening, this implied a system of education that embraced even the poorest and most humble. Knowledge, at least in its fundamentals, could no longer be confined to the wealthy few.

Massachusetts had already gone a long way toward achieving this goal. Connecticut and the other New England states were not far behind. Elsewhere the problem had not yet been solved, and in some cases not even admitted. But the advocates were eloquent and persistent. Benjamin Rush called on the citizens of Philadelphia to support a system of free schools for the children of the poor. "Where the common people are ignorant and vicious," he exclaimed, "a nation, and above all a republican nation, can never be long free and happy." [24] Jefferson was later to demand a similar system for Virginia.

If this was a departure from the general European idea, the crusade for a utilitarian instead of a classical education was even more so. Yet it followed logically from the nature of the American scene and the proposed universalization of knowledge. All the reformers agreed that reading, writing and arithmetic were essential studies. Most assented to Rush's dictum that a truly American education ought to be based, not as in Europe "upon the ruins of Palmyra and the antiquities of Herculaneum, or in disputes upon Hebrew points, Greek particles, or the accent and quantity of the Roman language," but "in acquiring those branches of knowledge which increase the conveniencies of life, lessen human misery, improve our country, promote population, exalt the human understanding, and establish domestic, social, and political happiness." [25]

Noah Webster was even more radical and thoroughgoing than Rush. He proposed a new American language, flexible and alive, and breaking sharply with English and European traditions in spelling, grammar and modes of literature. In the preface to his revolutionary *Speller* he set forth his views. "This country must in some future time be as distinguished by the superiority of her literary improvements, as she is already by the liberality of her civil and ecclesiastical constitutions. Europe is grown old in folly, corruption and tyranny—in that country laws are perverted, manners are licentious, literature is declining and human nature debased. For America in her infancy to adopt the present maxims of the old world, would be to stamp the wrinkles of decrepid age upon the bloom of youth."

The same strain of exuberance and youthful disdain for the old impelled the poet Joel Barlow to issue his own manifesto: "My object is altogether of a moral and political nature. I wish to encourage and strengthen, in the rising generation, a sense of the importance of republican institutions; as being the great foundation of public and private happiness, the necessary aliment of future and permanent ameliorations in the condition of human nature. This is the moment to give such a direction to poetry, printing and the other fine arts, that true and useful ideas of glory may be implanted in the minds of men here, to take place of the false and destructive ones that have degraded the species in other countries." [26]

Americans, indeed, had convinced themselves that they were the only true children of the Enlightenment, that they alone possessed the natural virtues hymned by the philosophers, and that the indefinite perfectibility of man depended on their sole efforts. In these naïve beliefs they were abetted by many a European who, despairing of his native surroundings, saw Utopia building in the New World.

CHAPTER 3

The Foundation Is Laid

THE PROBLEMS WHICH confronted the first Congress and the first President of the United States were staggering in the extreme. A new nation had to be created within a novel framework—a federated republic of thirteen sovereign states suspicious of one another and of the national government in which they were joined, touchy in their pride and swayed by local and often mutually contradictory interests. The Constitution, written though it was, meant all things to all men; and the general clauses therein were susceptible of differing interpretations even by those who had helped in their formulation. Antifederalism was still rife, and the fear of eventual monarchy haunted the minds of many.

On every side the problems rose hydraheaded: the installation of administrative machinery, the liquidation of the public debt, the provision of an adequate revenue, the government and disposition of the public domain, the creation of a legal system, the regulation of trade and commerce, relations with hostile Indians at home and powerful nations abroad.

Precedents were few and points of irritation many; yet solutions had to be found with speed and dispatch if the new nation was to survive and be secure.

It was Congress that first assumed the burden. As its members gathered slowly in New York, the eyes of the country fastened on them with a certain degree of distrust. Would the alarm of the antifederalists prove well-founded, and Congress attempt to arrogate to itself and to the national government too much power?

Old Sam Adams, stormy petrel of the Revolution, was skeptical. He hoped that they would not, but was prepared for the worst. "Few men," he observed sagely, "are contented with less power than they have a right to exercise. The ambition of the human heart grasps at more." [1]

On the other hand, there were those who feared just the reverse: that Congress would fritter away its time in theoretical discussions and vain quibbles on constitutional limitations, and end by failing to adopt essential measures. "Speculative men," asserted an anonymous writer, "seldom give energy or success to their operations." [2]

James Madison, who had barely managed to win a seat in the House after being defeated for the Senate, thought the prospect not at all flattering. Few of the members, he commented acidly, could be expected to share "in the drudgery of business." He foresaw also sharp lines of cleavage; "first between federal and anti-federal parties, and then between Northern & Southern parties." [3]

Few members of the first Congress, indeed, were fully aware of the responsibilities they had assumed. The date for their assemblage had been set for March 4, 1789; and until they met, the country was practically without a government. A handful of administrative officials, holdovers from the old Continental Congress, barely functioned in the semivacuum; while Washington and Adams had not yet been officially informed of their election or installed in office.

Yet March 4th came and went without a Congress. The members straggled into New York at a leisured pace and with an infuriating nonchalance. The faithful few who arrived promptly, met in the chambers of the newly decorated Federal Hall—each House a law unto itself—surveyed the empty seats, noted the lack of a quorum, and adjourned. Day after day the same procedure was followed, while urgent letters went out to the absentees demanding their immediate presence. Fisher Ames, representative from Massachusetts, detected in the general tardiness an ominous portent for the future. "I am inclined to believe," he wrote gloomily, "that the langour of the old Confederation is transfused into the members of the new Congress." [4]

At long last, however, a sufficient number of latecomers trickled in to provide quorums in both Houses, and they were able to settle down to business. [5]

It was by no means an outstanding Congress in the sense that the best and ablest minds of the country were represented in it. Even the old Continental Congress, hampered though it was by lack of power and subservient to the will of the states, had attracted a far greater proportion of the nation's leaders.

The reasons for the discrepancy are not far to seek. Those who were skeptical of or even opposed to the new government preferred to remain in official positions within their own states, where they could maintain a vigilant watch on the proceedings of the national government and block, through appropriate legislative and executive action, any attempts to go beyond the strict limits of the Constitution. On the other hand, those who favored the new government were either too busy with their private affairs to desire public office or preferred the executive arm as a larger and more congenial field for their activities.

Yet it was not a mediocre Congress, either. Two first-rate men took their seats in the House of Representatives and found themselves almost at once the leaders of opposing parties whose outlines were slowly sharpening into clarity. They were James Madison of Virginia and Fisher Ames of Massachusetts.

Madison had already achieved fame. Small, dry and scholarly, with inconspicuous features and a shy, retiring manner, he made no immediate impression. Yet during the years of the Confederation he had come steadily forward in the public view. In his own state he had helped write some of its most important laws. The cause of civil and religious liberty had no greater champion anywhere; and Jefferson, now in France, was happy to call him friend. He had labored diligently and well in the Continental Congress. His role in the Constitutional Convention was such that he has since been claimed as the intellectual father of the Constitution. His important collaboration with Hamilton in the *Federalist* papers was known to the right people. Almost singlehanded he had turned the tide of antifederalism in Virginia, beat down the redoubtable Patrick Henry and brought that influential state safely into the Union. With Virginia recalcitrant, New York would probably have remained out too; and the United States might have been delayed indefinitely.

Yet that very triumph almost sealed his own political destruction. Enraged at their defeat and rightly conceiving Madison to be the author of their woes, the opposition revenged itself by passing over his candidacy for the United States Senate and elected Richard Henry Lee and William Grayson, moderate antis, instead.

To retrieve his fortunes, Madison was compelled to hasten back to Virginia and stand for the popularly elected House of Representatives. Only by a vigorous campaign, by circulated letters and private explanations, was he able to modify the general impression that he was too extreme a nationalist and win the suffrage of his neighbors.[6]

It had been a close call; and the knowledge that he had proceeded beyond the sentiments of his state was perhaps responsible for the shift that gradually took place in Madison's public views. Indeed, the minister from France discerned a direct connection between the measures advocated in Congress and the pressures exerted by the home constituencies.

"One of the great vices in the exercise of power by Congress," he reported to his government, "comes from the local spirit disclosed by the majority of the members and which they must follow if they would conserve their popularity in the district which appointed them." Even the President, he was convinced, would be unable to resist such local influences.[7]

Underneath his dry exterior, Madison was a complex individual. A profound student of ideas, he was capable of translating them into action. A bold and original thinker, he proceeded with deliberation and caution. Though able on occasion to restrain his friends from rushing to political destruction, he could not prevent the lightnings of hatred from descending on his own political head. Apparently timid and retiring though he was, his industry made him the terror of the opposition. Happiest with pen and paper, he spoke incessantly on the floor of Congress. His command of facts was impressive, and his logic pure; yet he convinced no one but those who already were convinced.

Fisher Ames, his leading opponent in Congress, was puzzled how to appraise him. In the beginning at least, he characterized Madison as "a man of sense, reading, address, and integrity," though "very much Frenchified in his politics." He thought his speeches in the House "pure, perspicuous, and to the point," but that the effect was lost by his low, almost inaudible voice. Himself a man of action and bold in debate, he considered Madison "a little too much of a book politician, and too timid in his politics." Yet even Ames was compelled to admit that "he is our first man."[8]

Ames, on the other hand, was as yet no national figure, though he had already made his mark in Massachusetts. There he had practiced law, taken a prominent part in the ratifying convention, and gained the respect of conservative leaders and businessmen by his national views and ability. Like Hamilton, he believed that only the rich and the well-born were fit to rule, and that that government was best which possessed both power and the will to employ it. He despised what he called the "mob"; and he sincerely believed that should it ever gain control of the government there would be an end to religion and property. The example of the French Revolution merely served to deepen his convictions and narrow his vision. Though strongly nationalist, he vigilantly safeguarded New England's interests; and tended in his own mind to equate the two. Possessed of great personal charm, a ready, eloquent and persuasive speaker, knowing precisely what he wanted and how to obtain it, contemptuous of theory and unshakably secure in his prejudices, he rose rapidly to leadership and became one of Hamilton's most trusted lieutenants. He was only thirty-one when he began his career in Congress.

The first order of business in Congress, once the essential organizational matters had been disposed of, was obviously the procurement of a regular and sufficient national revenue. On this rock the Confederation had foundered; on this reef the new United States might equally come to destruction.

Accordingly, the House of Representatives, as the constitutional initiator of money legislation, voted itself into a committee of the whole to consider this and kindred matters. The committee of the whole was a euphemism which permitted them to shut their doors against public scrutiny and debate freely without the necessity of cocking a wary eye at the gallery. The Senate, which forbade spectators as a matter of principle and allowed no report of its deliberations, required no such subterfuge.

Barely had the doors been closed when Madison rose. He wished, he said, to propose two measures as a means of revenue. The first was a tariff on imports; the second was a tax on all ships entering American harbors from abroad, calculated on the basis of their tonnage.

Both measures were standard methods for raising money. But both could also be employed to further special interests. What items were rendered dutiable, and in what amounts, involved directly and variously the vital economic interests of the different classes, groups and sections of the country. Similarly, ship-tonnage taxes could be so manipulated as to favor a specific class or even a nation against all others. This was precisely what happened to Madison's proposals.

In the first category—a general tariff on imports—Madison purportedly wished for revenue only. He asked for specific duties (the actual amounts to be determined later) on such "luxury" items as liquors, wines, molasses, sugar, tea, cocoa, coffee and pepper; and ad valorem duties on other items. The New England members stirred uneasily at the classification of molasses as a luxury; it was a fundamental cornerstone of their foreign trade. Other states showed an equal unease, but for other reasons: either because certain articles appeared on Madison's list, or because they did not.

In the second category—the tax on ship tonnage—Madison discarded his first announced principle of tariff for revenue only. He now demanded discriminations. He would, he said, divide shipping into three classes. The first, comprising American-built and owned ships, would pay the least duty per ton. The second, consisting of the ships of those nations which had entered into commercial treaties with the United States, would be subject to an intermediate tax. The third and final class, which included the ships of all other foreign powers, would pay maximum amounts.

A startled buzz rose all over the House. The calm, low drone of Madison's voice could not obscure the explosive consequences of his proposal. It meant war—commercial war now, and a shooting war in the not too distant future. For only three foreign pow s were substantially engaged in the American carrying t these, two (France and the Netherlands) had entere mercial treaties with the United States. The third, wh ot, was no other than the ancient enemy, Great Britain.[9]

Barely had Madison r ed his seat when the storm broke. From all sides angry con nen rose to attack both prongs of Madison's program, while others jumped to his defense. For weeks the debate raged furiously, with section arrayed against section, just as Madison had earlier predicted, and state against state. Strange alliances were formed, and as quickly broken; while the specter of parties, deplored by most, rose to haunt both participants and the country at large.

The first assault was directed against the conception of a tariff for revenue only. Thomas Fitzsimons of Pennsylvania spearheaded the attack. What about our "infant manufactures"? he asked. Should they not be protected against foreign competition? Place heavy duties, he demanded, on the following articles; and he read off a long, impressive list. Many of them were Pennsylvania products, as might have been expected; others were cannily added in order to gain the support of certain Southern states.[10]

Fitzsimons's speech opened the sluice gates. Member after member took the floor to plead for similar protection for the goods and produce

of his particular constituency. Petitions were read from the tradesmen
and mechanics of Baltimore, New York, Philadelphia and Boston,
demanding relief from foreign competition on a bewildering variety
of articles: ships, iron wares, copper, tin and brass manufactures,
clocks, combs, furniture, coaches, mathematical instruments, jewelry,
clothes, stays, etc., etc.[11]

In vain Madison sought to allay the storm. Personally he would
have preferred a system of complete free trade, and considered a
tariff for revenue only as a necessary evil. But a protective tariff was
anathema. Who else would pay the bill for the advancement of
Pennsylvania and New England industries but the agricultural states
of the South?

Yet he was caught on the horns of a dilemma of his own making.
What, after all, were his proposed tonnage differentials but a form
of protective tariff, not only to American shipping but to that of
France as well, and directed against England? But this he would not
give up; indeed, it was the hard core of his system. He wished to use
it as a bludgeon to compel an arrogant England to sign a treaty of
commerce with us which would grant our shipping and exports special
favors in her ports and those of her colonies.

With this in mind, Madison wavered midway in his arguments and
half surrendered. Perhaps, he admitted, some products of domestic
manufacture ought to be placed under protection; and, he added hastily, some agricultural produce as well.[12]

This strategic retreat aroused the ire of both sides. Boudinot of
New Jersey and Bland of Virginia promptly protested. Bland called
a protective tariff "a tax upon the whole community, in order to put
the money in the pockets of a few." He even opposed Madison's pet
measure of retaliation on England. He saw clearly what righteous passion had prevented the leader of Virginia's delegation from noting:
that there was not, and would not for a long time to come be, sufficient
American shipping to carry their huge agricultural crop overseas. This
meant that the extra tonnage duties paid by foreign carriers would
merely be added to the freight charges.[13]

But the clamor for protection proved too overwhelming. As one
item after another came up for consideration, each member sought a
high or low rate, or placement on the free list, in strict accordance
with the interests of his constituency. Sitting behind closed doors, the
lawmakers were frank in their avowals. Tucker of South Carolina

wanted to know which of the articles under consideration came from
his state, and why therefore she should be taxed in their purchase.
When Clymer of Pennsylvania demanded a heavy duty on steel (a
Pennsylvania product), Lee of Virginia protested that it would really
be a tax on agriculture. This brought on him the sanctimonious wrath
of Fitzsimons (also of Pennsylvania). "If gentlemen did not get rid
of local considerations," he exclaimed, "the committee would make
little progress. Every State will feel itself oppressed by a duty on particular articles, but when the whole system is perfected, the burden
will be equal on all." [14]

Eventually agreement was reached by a process of give and take.
Virginia was mollified with a prohibitive tariff of six cents a pound
on tobacco. Pennsylvania obtained protection for her steel and allied
products. New England was given a heavy duty on ships and cordage.
On salt, where the South threatened shipwreck to the country and
the detachment of the Western territories if a tax was imposed, it was
agreed to provide drawbacks on salted provisions in exchange for the
general duty.[15]

On two items, however, no compromise seemed possible. These were
molasses and rum. By an ironical turn it was now the South—the fervent proponent of free trade—that demanded a heavy tax; while pro-
tectionist New England clamored for none, or one for revenue only.
Madison took the floor to insist on a tax of eight cents a gallon on
molasses. The New England members retorted angrily. If there must
be a duty on this "necessity" of the poor, they shouted, let it be set at
two cents and no more. Fisher Ames very frankly declared the true
reason for New England's concern. Her very existence, he pointed
out, depended on her ability to import molasses from the West Indies.
If we do not take their molasses how, he asked, can we sell them our
fish? And if we cannot sell them our fish, not only that important
source of revenue but our navigation will decay.

Unperturbed by these arguments, Madison placed the issue on
moral grounds. The imported molasses, he said, was used here to
manufacture rum; and the consumption of rum was the curse of the
people. Ames's reply to this new tack was blistering.

"I treat as idle," he cried out in scorn, "the visionary notion of
reforming the morals of the people by a duty on molasses. We are not
to consider ourselves, while here, as at church or school, to listen to
the harangues of speculative piety; we are to talk of the political

interests committed to our charge." Warming to this theme, he continued: "The present Constitution was dictated by commercial necessity more than any other cause. The want of an efficient Government
to secure our manufacturing interests, and to advance our commerce,
was long seen by men of judgment, and pointed out by patriots solicitous to promote the general welfare." [16]

Frankness could go no further. In the heat of debate and beyond
the popular hearing, the veneer of fine phrases concerning the Constitution and the Union was ripped away, and the naked economic
interests underneath fully displayed.

Goaded to unwonted exasperation, Madison retorted in kind. "Are
the Northern people made of finer clay?" he demanded. "Do they
respire a clearer air? . . . Are they the chosen few? Are all others to
be oppressed with accumulated burdens, and they to take their course
easy and unrestrained?" [17]

Thus early was the issue drawn, and sectional lines made their
dreaded appearance. But this time the South had allies. Pennsylvania
and some New Yorkers joined with her, and New England went down
to ignominious defeat. (In western Pennsylvania and the back country generally, the farmers did not use molasses for distillation. They
made whiskey out of home-grown corn.)

Angry and embittered, it was now the turn of the New Englanders
to talk privately of disunion. Ames, now their acknowledged leader,
quickly scotched the incipient mutterings.

"I am displeased," he wrote in sharp rebuke, "to hear people speak
of a State out of the Union. I wish it was a part of the catechism to
teach youth that it cannot be. . . . I wish to have every American
think the union so indissoluble and integral, that the corn would not
grow, nor the pot boil, if it should be broken." [18]

Yet his patriotic fervor did not prevent Ames from continuing to
consult New England's special interest. He argued, pleaded and
stormed until the House grudgingly lowered the rate on molasses
from six to five cents a gallon. Beyond this it refused to go; and the
embattled New Englanders were compelled to turn to the Senate for
aid and comfort.

That august body proved most obliging. Against the shrill protests
of the South and her ally, Pennsylvania, it whittled away at the duty
until it was reduced to two and a half cents a gallon. Ames, who had
closely followed the proceedings, gave vent to a fervent hallelujah.

"The Senate," he exulted, "God bless them, as if designated by Providence to keep rash and frolicsome brats out of the fire." [19]

Concurrently a second debate was in progress—on Madison's proposed discriminatory tonnage duties.

The first section, which concerned American ships only, met only with minor opposition from some of the Southern members; and a nominal tax of six cents a ton was swiftly agreed on.

The second section, relating to ships of nations in commercial treaty relations with the United States, ran into much more trouble. Proposals for the tax ranged from twenty to sixty cents a ton. New York and New Jersey, in conjunction with Southern members who foresaw that their own constituents would have to pay the bill, plumped for the former. New England, seeking to discredit the entire business, called for the latter. But Madison's cohorts withstood the assaults from either side and managed to push through their own figure—thirty cents a ton.

The real struggle, toward which the rest had been preliminary maneuvering, came on with the consideration of the third section, which dealt with the ships of nations *not* in treaty relations. This section, for all its apparent universality, was aimed directly at Great Britain. So too was a conjoint proposal by Madison—to discriminate by a heavy differential between British and French West Indies rum.

In a speech of unprecedented bitterness, Madison threw down the gauntlet to England. "I wish," he cried, "to teach those nations who have declined to enter into commercial treaties with us, that we have the power to extend or withhold advantages as their conduct shall deserve. . . . Let us review the policy of Great Britain towards us. Has she ever shown any disposition to enter into reciprocal regulations? Has she not . . . plainly declared . . . she will shut us out from her ports, and make us tributary to her? Have we not seen her taking one legislative step after another to destroy our commerce? . . . Have we not reason to believe she will continue a policy void of regard to us, whilst she can continue to gather into her lap the benefits we feebly endeavor to withhold?"

As he spoke, Madison grew increasingly belligerent. "We shall soon be in a condition," he declared, "we are now in a condition, to wage a commercial warfare with that nation. The produce of this country is more necessary to the rest of the world than that of other countries is to America. . . . Let us but show that world that we know justly how to consider our commercial friends and commercial adversaries. Let us show, that if a war breaks out in Europe, and is extended and carried on in the West Indies, we can treat with friendship and succor the one, while we can shut the other out of our ports." [20]

This was not merely a challenge; this was a plain intimation that we would side with France in the event of a war between her and England; if not with military arms, at least with an embargo against British ships and goods.

What had caused this sudden upsurgence of belligerence? The answer lay in the disposition of the immensely profitable West Indies trade; or, rather, in the nationality of the ships that were engaged in it.

As long as the American colonies remained within the orbit of the British empire, that trade was open to them on equal terms with the mother country. But once they revolted, they found themselves outside the charmed circle, and subject to the same onerous restrictions that applied, under the navigation acts, to the ships of other nations. This swift removal from the lucrative carrying trade naturally, if somewhat illogically, annoyed the Americans. They wanted their cake of independence, but at the same time they wished to continue to eat of the dish that had been theirs while in servitude.

England, with more logic though perhaps with a lack of foresight, refused to grant special privileges to her errant offspring. Why should she treat them better than any other nation? Why enter into a commercial treaty with them which, so the Americans were insisting, must open the West Indies to their ships and thus provide a formidable competition to her own?

At the moment, indeed, England's position seemed impregnable. As Phineas Bond, her American-born consul stationed in Philadelphia, was prompt to point out, her "bcneficial" regulations had given her ships an almost complete monopoly of the American trade and driven all competition from the seas.[21]

Furthermore, so Bond advised his home government, any threats of American retaliation in the form of discriminations and embargoes might safely be dismissed as impotent. American agricultural products must, he reported, find a vent abroad or the American farmer must perish; and the British empire was by far the largest customer. Any attempt to cut off that outlet would, so the consul was convinced, "shake the foundation [of] their new Constitution." Besides, to permit New England into the West Indies would immediately revive their dormant shipbuilding (the cost of which was much cheaper than in Great Britain) and enable them to monopolize the trade.[22]

If such British reasoning was well-founded, why then did Madison, the representative of the agricultural South, fight so pertinaciously for retaliation on England, when the net result would be to cut off its most valuable outlet and advantage only the maritime North? And why, even more amazingly, did the merchants and shipowners of New England, who on the surface would appear to benefit most by discriminations against English shipping, oppose them desperately and to the last ditch?

Two considerations may have animated Madison, and particularly his native state of Virginia. One of these was acknowledged; the other was imputed to them by Northerners.

The acknowledged motive was simple, even though there were those who quarreled with its premises. If American shipping could be built up at the expense of the British, it could move Virginia's huge tobacco crop at a substantial saving over current British rates. This would prove even more substantial during the wars in which England was so frequently involved. Thomas Jefferson, from his vantage post in France, calculated that the insurance differential alone during wartime—as between belligerent bottoms and neutral American ones—cost the United States the tidy annual sum of $3,250,000. He also noted with disfavor that British ships carried American exports to the value of $10,000,000 out of an annual total of $25,000,000.[23]

The unacknowledged motive—if there was such—stemmed from two roots: the deep and abiding hatred of England that resulted from the wanton damage done by British raiders in the South during the Revolution; and the prewar debts still due from Virginia planters to British merchants. Though the peace treaty had called for immediate settlement of outstanding accounts, Virginia's legislature and courts persistently connived with the debtors to prevent collection.[24]

New England, on the other hand, believed that retaliation on England would prove a boomerang. As her merchants and shipowners appraised the situation, even with the current hampering restrictions on their commerce, they still throve and grew wealthy. England absorbed half of all American exports; while ninety per cent of all imports originated in her factories and on the plantations of her colonies. The American people preferred English goods to any other, including their own domestic manufactures. They were superior in quality and cheaper in price. And on all this trade, export and import alike, the merchants took their profit; while American shipping managed to find enough cargoes to keep it busy.

What would happen if Madison's discriminatory measures were enacted into law? Certain commercial war with their best customer, and perhaps even a shooting war which would, by virtue of England's control of the seas, put a stop to *all* foreign commerce.

It must not, however, be assumed that New England was happy over the British restrictive regulations. She was not. But she preferred peace on the present status, with the prospect of an eventual amelioration through amicable diplomacy, to the disaster of another war. Another consideration lurked in back of her leaders' minds—war tended to bring out radical sentiments and raise the mob to the seats of the mighty. The "Liberty Boys" of the Revolution still rankled in their thoughts, and the late uprising of Daniel Shays in Massachusetts still filled them with retrospective terror.

So that, in the struggle over Madison's resolution, the lines were sharply drawn. Pennsylvania, in spite of her commercial interests in Philadelphia, joined with Virginia. Her course was determined by her backwoods radicals and by Virginia's assistance in the matter of the protective tariff. In fact, it was Fitzsimons who assumed the doubtful honor of proposing a tax on ships in the third category—that is, British ships—of sixty cents a ton. Strangely enough, a New England man, Benjamin Goodhue, deserted his fellows to second the motion. Perhaps the fact that he was a shipowner had something to do with it.

The rest of the delegation, joined by members from New York and by a small group of Southerners who persisted stubbornly in the belief that a tax on the boats that carried their agriculture would eventually come out of their own pockets, opposed the motion bitterly. They insisted that there must be no distinctions drawn between the ships of other nations. They pointed out that Great Britain, in spite of the fact that she had no treaty with us, voluntarily admitted our goods on the same footing as those of the most favored treaty nations of Europe; that the enactment of the motion would lead to instant retaliation and the loss of such privileges as we already possessed; that we did not have enough shipping of our own to carry our exports; and, finally, that we were neither strong enough nor united enough to enter into a commercial war that might end in a fighting one.

In spite of these arguments, Madison's coalition pushed through a tonnage tax of fifty cents. Indeed, the original figure of sixty cents resulted in a tie vote which was broken in the negative only by the casting vote of the Speaker of the House.[25]

Once again, in their extremity, the opposition turned to the Senate for succor; and once again the upper House did not fail them. Senator Maclay, the backwoods Pennsylvania radical, fought valiantly to keep the discriminations imposed by the lower House on both British shipping and British rum intact; but an angry chorus shouted him down. Plain speaking was the order of the day. What necessity was there for commercial treaties altogether? demanded the senators. Self-interest governed all nations, treaty or no treaty. If we discriminated against Great Britain, she would strike back, and we would be fast in the grip of a commercial war. We could not afford such a war.[26]

The offending articles were stricken out, and the revenue bill sent back to the House. There chaos reigned. On the one hand, Pierce Butler of South Carolina ranted against the entire tariff act as calculated to ruin his state and threatened, should it pass, that the Union would dissolve. On the other hand, John Page of Virginia swore he would rather lose the bill than yield to the Senate amendments. Madison pleaded with the House to stand firm and not recede. But other members were not as intransigent. Second thoughts prevailed. Pennsylvania and the dissident sections of the South quietly broke ranks, and when the vote was taken, the House concurred with the Senate by 31 to 19.[27]

The final revenue bills, as signed by the President on July 4th and July 20th, laid the foundations of the tariff policy of the United States. In reality it deftly mingled two guiding principles. In general, it hearkened to the philosophy of a tariff for revenue only, imposing an ad valorem tax of five per cent on most items. At the same time, specific duties were levied on a limited number of articles; some of which, such as those on steel, boots, indigo, wool and cotton cards, were made sufficiently high to give protection against foreign competition.

The principle of discrimination among foreign nations, so persistently advocated by Madison, was temporarily thrown into the discard. Neither on British as against French rums, nor on the vital matter of the tonnage tax, was any distinction permitted. American-owned ships paid six cents a ton; American-built but foreign-owned vessels paid thirty cents. All other ships, no matter where built or owned, were taxed at fifty cents a ton.[28]

The first great debate had been won by New England. The battalions of the South, weakened by internal dissension, had been defeated. But Madison did not despair. At a later date he was to return to the fray, armed with a wealth of new data which England by her further conduct most obligingly furnished him.

If the struggle over tariff and discriminations was the most spectacular of this first session of Congress, it was by no means the only one. The Senate managed to become engrossed in a fight of its own which, trivial and absurd though it might sound, aroused as angry and as partisan emotions as the debate on the tariff.

It was touched off by no less a person than John Adams, Vice-President of the United States and, by virtue of his office, in the chair of the Senate.

The strong opposition to his election had rankled in his proud and touchy spirit. He brooded over it and exaggerated its meaning until it became to him a world-shaking wrong. "Is not my election to this office," he demanded of his friend, Dr. Benjamin Rush, "in the scurvy manner in which it was done, a curse rather than a Blessing? Is there Gratitude? Is there Justice? Is there common sense or decency in this Business? Is it not an indelible stain on our Country, Countrymen and Constitution? I assure you I think so, and nothing but an apprehension of great Mischief, and the final failure of the Government from my Refusal and assigning my reasons for it, prevented me from Spurning it." [29]

Filled with such a sense of the intolerable slight that had been put upon him, and theoretically convinced that the heads of state must be furnished with the ceremonial indicia of office and surrounded with an aura of authority if the general populace were to respect and obey them, he now advocated an amazing series of titular forms grounded on English court practice.

A Senate committee gravely considered the matter and brought in a mouth-filling formula with which to designate the head of the state. They proposed to address George Washington as "His Highness, the President of the United States of America, and Protector of their Liberties." [30]

Adams was delighted, foreseeing that a somewhat similar title would necessarily be joined with the office of vice-president. But elsewhere the recommendation met with a mingled rage and ridicule that threatened to sink all other business.

Maclay, the sharp-tongued and acidulous democrat, filled the pages of his private diary with vehement comments. Adams, he wrote, "may go and dream about titles, for none will he get." He objected to the Vice-President's lecturing members from the chair and treating them like so many schoolboys. He noted with glee Senator Izard's malicious reference to the somewhat corpulent Adams as "His Rotundity." [31]

The lower House also rose in arms. Madison declared that it would stand adamant, even though "the friends of titles in the other branch are headed by the vice-president who is seconded with all the force and urgency of natural temper by R. H. L.!!!" [32] The initials stood for Richard Henry Lee, whose defeat of Madison for the Senate seat from Virginia still rankled.

The House of Representatives did stand fast, and forced the Senate to concur in the simple address "To the President of the United States." But the democrats inside Congress and the people outside never forgave Adams for his advocacy of titles and honors. The hue and cry was to follow him all through his political career, and hounded him even after he retired.

The seriocomical affair had even more far-reaching consequences than the vilification of a single individual. The penchant for honorific titles was taken by many as conclusive evidence that certain groups in the Eastern states were aiming to establish a monarchy in the United States.

"Is it not strange," wondered Senator William Grayson of Virginia, "that monarchy should issue from the East? Is it not still stranger, that John Adams, the son of a tinker, and the creature of the people, should be for titles and dignities and pre-eminencies, and should despise the Herd and the ill born?" [33]

Even Washington was compelled to disavow any leanings toward titles, and to reply to violent criticisms of his Vice-President's use of a carriage drawn by six horses. Adams, he wrote to an excited correspondent, "though high toned has never, I believe, appeared with more than two horses in his carriage; but it is to be lamented that he and some others have stirred a question which has given rise to so much animadversion, and which I confess has given me much uneasiness lest it should be supposed by some . . . that the object they had in view was not displeasing to me." [34]

From such small seeds sprang a situation that probably made the

office of Vice-President into the innocuous thing it is today and its
occupant the forgotten man. On several occasions Washington had
asked Adams, in conjunction with the heads of departments, for
advice on questions of state. Now he refrained from submitting any
further questions; and the office and the man became, in Adams's
disgusted phrase, "the most insignificant . . . that ever invention of
man contrived, or his imagination conceived."

With the lamentable matter of titles finally disposed of, Congress
once more settled down to serious business. In rapid succession a
series of important measures were passed providing for a framework
of government.

First came the judiciary. A Supreme Court was created with a Chief
Justice and five Associates. The country was divided into thirteen
judicial districts, each with a court and with carefully defined powers.
The nature of those powers, however, elicited considerable debate;
particularly the right to review cases initially brought up in the state
courts which involved federal laws or the Constitution.

The state sovereignty men became alarmed. This was an attempt,
they cried, to swallow up the state courts and make them a part of the
federal system. We need no district courts and district judges subservient to the federal government, declared Livermore of New Hampshire and Jackson of Georgia. Let the state courts handle national
cases.[35]

Such an extreme position, however, ran into the opposition of
Madison himself. He calmly replied that the state tribunals could not
be trusted to enforce federal laws that might be obnoxious to their own
states, and supplemented his contention with specific examples.[36]
Whereupon Livermore's motion to strike the district courts from the
bill was defeated, and the Judiciary Act went to the Senate for
approval and to the President for signature.

The next step was to create the great administrative departments.
There was little dispute over the Department of Foreign Affairs (later
renamed State), War, the Attorney General and the Post Office.

Nor was there any doubt as to the necessity of a Treasury Department. To most congressmen, in fact, this department was the most
important of all. For that very reason its composition and powers were
scrutinized with exceptional care. During the Confederation it had
been headed by a board, and it was now suggested that such a board

nued. In the end, however, a single responsible head was
decided on.

rimonious debate took place, however, over a proposed section
nabling act which made it the duty of the Secretary to "digest
rt plans for the improvement and management of the revenue,
support of the public credit."

of Virginia saw in this a dangerous invasion of the constitu-
ght of the House to initiate fiscal legislation. "It would," he
"create an undue influence within these walls, because mem-
ht be led, by the deference commonly paid to men of abilities,
rt the minister's plan, even against their own judgment."

argument was finical, his next went to fundamentals. The
word *report* in the bill, he pointed out, gave the Secretary
sury the right to appear before the House to explain and
lans. And if the Treasury were granted such a right, the
ventually be yielded to all other departments. But this,
was the essence of the British Cabinet system; and
said, lay the foundations "for an aristocracy or a dete..
." 37

l conclusion seems far-fetched, it did not appear so to
ginations of those who hated the English system root
honestly believed that there was a secret and con-
to introduce it into the United States. Ames, Good-
Sedgwick, all from Northern states, pooh-poohed
red, with a show of reason, why the House should
he specialized ability and information of the Secre-
only when Madison declared that he personally de-
danger as Page had professed to see in the offending
he latter's motion to strike it out went down to defeat.
ss, the agitation and general uneasiness continued, until
proposed a compromise: instead of the phrase "digest and
o substitute "digest and *prepare.*" The compromise was ac-
and the section was passed by a large majority.38

he heat of debate, it is doubtful whether the members of Con-
ealized the full implications of their action. By eliminating that
c word *report* they turned away from a system of responsible
t government in which Congress would have had a measure
rol over the heads of departments, and forced them into the
and dependence on the single will of the President. Unwit-
Congress had yielded a vital source of power and gratuitously

handed it over to the Executive branch. Present-day attempts
dy that initial misstep by requesting members of the Cabinet to
before select congressional committees have failed to reverse th
of long-established custom.

If Congress thus failed, in the face of an imaginary fear, to
powers for itself in its eternal duel with the Executive arm of
ment, it tried hard to establish them in another direction. Un
Constitution, the President required the advice and consent
Senate in making appointments to office. Nothing was said, h
as to his power of removal.

In both Houses it was argued that the consent of the Ser
equally essential when it came to removals as in appointments
view was violently controverted, and the first great debat
interpretation of the Constitution was on.

Madison led off with a powerful statement of constitu
that what the Constitution had failed to specify in so
could not now be read into it, or added to it by congre
ment.

For once Ames agreed with him; so did others wh
posed Madison at every step. They even quoted from
cussion of constitutional powers in the *Federalist* p
of their common stand. Not everyone, however, was
citations; some insisted that appointment and remov
site sides of the same medal, and that any power ov
a similar power over the other.[39] In the end, M
adopted in the House.

Madison, at this stage, still believed in strengthen
government, and particularly in a strong Executive.
indeed, that the President ought to have more power th
ingly possessed. "I see, and *politically feel*," he wrote at
time, "that that will be the weak branch of the Government
much more concerned to curb the power of the Senate, which
sidered an essentially aristocratic body.[40]

In the Senate, where self-interest might have been conside
controlling factor, the debate was even more furious than in the
and ended in a draw when the question came to be put to
John Adams decided the issue by his casting vote as chairm
first he had been called upon to make—and tipped the scale
of the President. By this time every move of poor Adams was

and it was insinuated that he had been swayed by his expectation of the presidency in the future; a charge which he explosively denied.[41]

The Constitution of the United States had been ratified by several of the states and had received the grudging approval of many Americans only on the express agreement that a series of amendments would be immediately proposed and incorporated into its framework. These amendments were intended to cure two defects which it was generally agreed existed in the original document.

The first looked to safeguards against encroachments by the federal government on the rights and liberties of the people. Following the pattern of the state constitutions already in effect, guaranties were insisted on against federal interference with religious beliefs, free speech, press, assemblage and petition; and a positive grant of the right to bear arms, trial by jury and habeas corpus; as well as other privileges and immunities which had become part of the Anglo-American heritage.

The second sought to reserve to the people and the states all powers not specifically delegated to the United States by the Constitution nor prohibited by it to the states.

On June 8th, in conformity with the pledges previously made, Madison brought the matter of such amendments to the attention of the House. Instead of the smooth sailing he had expected, however, he found himself confronted with cries for delay. Let us first finish the pressing business of organizing the government, it was argued; the amendments could wait. Indeed Jackson of Georgia, though one of the most vehement advocates of states' rights in Congress, saw no reason for present action at all. The Constitution ought first to be given a fair trial, he said. After its structure had been fully tested, then and then only was the time to offer cures for such defects as had become apparent.[42]

But Madison persisted. He had a mandate, he believed, from his own state of Virginia and from the people of the United States to insure them against possible tyranny; and he refused to be sidetracked by impatient members who thought other business of more vital concern. Yet it was not until August 13th that a wearied House finally agreed to debate on the list he presented. After modifications in phrasing and sequence, most of the amendments were passed by both the House and Senate, and submitted to the states. By 1791 the ten we now know as the Bill of Rights had received the ratification of the requisite number of states and went into effect.

One amendment, however, which Madison offered with the remark that he considered it the most valuable one in the entire list, was quietly mislaid in Congress; probably because it was felt that it would never pass the states. It proposed a similar prohibition on the states as on the United States against infringements of the rights of conscience, freedom of speech, press and trial by jury in criminal cases.[43]

Had Madison succeeded in effecting its passage and ratification, much of the constitutional history of the country would have had to be rewritten, and certain disastrous consequences might have been avoided. The Fourteenth Amendment, ratified in 1868, purported to perform the same duty; or at least so the Supreme Court has decided within recent years.

By the end of September 1789, Congress had completed its major business and both its members and the country could appraise its initial accomplishments. In spite of the constant clash of interests, bickerings and violent debates, those accomplishments were impressive. The government had been organized and placed on a firm foundation. A regular source of revenue had been established, powers had been defined and limited, a system of administration had been arranged, and a Bill of Rights added to the fundamental framework. It is doubtful whether any Congress since ever accomplished so much in so little time.

It was inevitable, of course, that the measures which passed into the law of the land should be viewed with mixed feelings by the members themselves and by political leaders in the various states. Nor was the Constitution, on which they were based, immune from criticism.

That homespun democrat, Senator Maclay, took time out from sessions to write bitterly in his journal: "My mind revolts, in many instances, against the Constitution of the United States. Indeed, I am afraid it will turn out the vilest of all traps that ever was set to ensnare the freedom of an unsuspecting people." [44]

John Adams, on the other hand, surveyed the same Constitution and found that it was good. It contained the very elements which he considered all-essential to good government: a system of checks and balances whereby neither could the rich dominate over the poor, nor the poor over the rich. To him the Senate represented the rich, while the House of Representatives watched over the interests of the poor. In order to keep these two eternally warring classes under control, however, "an intermediate power, sufficiently elevated and independent" was essential.[45] This power to Adams was personified in the presidency; and it was with that in mind that he had been so insistent on investing it with dignity and splendor.

There was similar disagreement over the measures of Congress. Fitzsimons thought that the sessions had been bathed in an atmosphere of the "most perfect harmony"; a belief based, as he frankly admitted, on the fact that he had been able to obtain protection for Pennsylvania's manufactures.[46]

The Virginia delegation took a different view. To them the sacred rights of the states, particularly the Southern states, had been bled on the altar; and they were ready to concede that the warnings of the antifederalists had proven only too true—that the South "would be the Milch Cow of whom the substance would be extracted" by a maritime and manufacturing North.[47]

To Madison, Congress had been dilatory and prolix in discussion; though he was willing to attribute the oratory and the fumbling to the novelty and complexity of the matters on which they were legislating. "We are in a wilderness," he confessed, "without a single foot step to guide us. Our successors will have an easier task." [48]

They did not. Nor did the cleavages, already visible, become narrower. The split between the North and the South, with their totally different economies, was already an accomplished fact. Time was not to heal the divergence; even the horrors of a civil war failed to eliminate it.

CHAPTER 4

The Executive Begins to Function

WHEN GEORGE WASHINGTON took office on April 30, 1789, as
President of the United States he found himself confronted
with an even more difficult situation than that which Congress had
faced. At least the duties of a legislative body were fairly well defined, and many of the members had gained experience in their own
state legislatures and in the Continental Congress.

But the presidency was a novel creation; the first of its kind, aside
from the title, in the history of the world. Its incumbent was neither
king nor archon nor doge nor prince nor podesta. He possessed powers
never before attached to an elective office; at the same time he was
hemmed in with unusual limitations. The full stretch of his powers
and the contraction of his limitations had yet to be explored; and to
this day neither the one nor the other has been fully mapped or
bounded.

It is small wonder then that Washington, inexperienced, diffident,
was at first reluctant to accept the post; and after accepting, sought
advice at every turn from those whom he deemed competent to
give it.

The first question to which he addressed himself immediately after
the inauguration was a seemingly trivial one—the matter of presidential etiquette. How should he conduct himself, for example, in
his relations with callers and those who sought to engage his time?
How could he steer a safe course between unrestrained accessibility
and the total seclusion of an absolute monarch? Was one day a week
sufficient for visits of compliment? What hour of the day should he
set aside for those with business? Ought he to give four great entertainments a year? Was it proper for him to visit informally whomever he pleased? [1]

If these queries, solemnly propounded, sound somewhat ridiculous,

54

it must be remembered that the course of history has on occasion been changed by the breach or observance of matters of etiquette. The failure of Charles Evans Hughes to shake hands with Senator Hiram Johnson of California probably cost him the presidential election of 1920.

Washington sent his questions in writing to John Adams, the Vice-President, to John Jay, the holdover Secretary of Foreign Affairs, and to Alexander Hamilton, the forthcoming Secretary of the Treasury.

All three men would have preferred, as did Washington himself, to surround the office of President with a certain dignified aloofness and ceremonial investures. But Hamilton and Jay understood better than Adams that the American people would resent such trappings and raise the cry of monarchy.

"The notions of equality," warned Hamilton, "are yet, in my opinion, too general and too strong to admit of such a distance being placed between the President and other branches of the government as might even be consistent with a due proportion." [2]

Adams proposed that all applications for interviews be first processed by an authorized minister of state; while the actual system of etiquette should gradually develop itself in practice, helped perhaps by occasional "unauthorized" paragraphs in the public prints. Yet he was willing to confess that his "long residence abroad may have impressed me with views incompatible with the present temper and feelings of our fellow-citizens." [3]

By and large it was Hamilton's detailed instructions, complete with morning levees for the reception of visitors, which Washington decided to follow. But even this innocuous "middle course" was too monarchical for rigid republicans like Maclay. The Pennsylvania senator took a jaundiced view of the levees.

"Nothing is regarded or valued at such meetings," he exclaimed, "but the qualifications that flow from the tailor, barber, or dancing-master. To be clean shaved, shirted, and powdered, to make your bows with grace, and to be master of small chat on the weather, play, or newspaper anecdote of the day, are the highest qualifications necessary." [4]

Even when he was invited to dine at the President's house, his backwoods puritanism sniffed taint in every course, monarchical trappings in every table decoration. Though compelled to admit that it was the best dinner he had ever eaten, Maclay thought the atmos-

phere too solemn, the service too formal; while the ceremoniousness
with which Washington drank everyone's health in turn roused his
wrath. "Such a buzz of 'health, sir,' and 'health, madam,' and 'thank
you, sir,' and 'thank you, madam,' never had I heard before." At
least, he hoped, when the ladies retired, the men might unbend and
become convivial. Alas, they did not. It was true that Washington
tried his hand at a joke, and the table dutifully laughed. But Maclay
thought the story feeble, and those which followed even worse. For
a while the President toyed with his fork; then the company trooped
upstairs to drink coffee. But Maclay had had enough. He took his
hat and went home.[5]

It must be admitted that Washington took his pleasures somewhat
solemnly, and that boisterousness and convivial jollity fled when he
was present. Yet he loved the theater, stately balls and shows of
every kind. He went regularly to the theater in New York and later,
when the capital shifted, in Philadelphia. He sat in a box, attended
by his wife and flanked by a considerable retinue. His appearance
was always the signal for loud applause from the audience, deep
bows from the actors and the playing of the "President's March" by
the orchestra.

His patronage of the theater did much to counteract the incessant
propaganda against it, and to insure a profitable season. But it also
aroused angry mutterings from unreconstructed Puritans, to whom
New York was already a sufficient combination of Sodom and Go-
morrah.

"Our beloved PRESIDENT," sneered the Boston Gazette, "stands
unmoved in the vortex of folly and dissipation, which the city of
New-York presents." [6]

Some of the alleged "folly" of New York was concentrated in its
great cotillions and balls. A week after Washington had assumed
office, all society flocked to the Assembly Rooms on Broadway, just
above Wall Street, to see and be seen at a ball given in honor of
the President. The ladies outdid one another with the costliness of
their gowns and the lavishness of their headgear. Blue satin dresses,
full-swept, shimmered on every side; with Italian gauze handker-
chiefs draped delicately so as only partly to conceal bare necks and
bosoms. But the most tender care was expended on the headgear.
Hours of painstaking effort and the services of hairdressers and maids
went into achieving the right effect with a *pouf* of gauze shaped like

a globe and adorned with a *créneau* or headpiece of white satin, double-winged and plaited, and trimmed with artificial roses.[7]

A week later Count de Moustier, the French minister, dedicated another ball to the President. This proved to be even more splendid and lavish. There were such truly Gallic touches as the appearance of two sets of cotillion dancers dressed in full military costume—one set American and the other French—who intertwined their evolutions to symbolize the happy alliance between the nations. Perhaps more to the taste of the assembled company was the refreshment room, where a long table and bracketed shelves sank under the profusion of wines, cakes, fruit and ice cream.[8]

Martha Washington arrived in New York on May 29th, too late to participate in these festivities in honor of her husband. But she lost no time in instituting her own levees. While the President received visitors every Tuesday afternoon, Madame President held her audiences on Friday evenings. If the President's levees were solemn, *hers* were positively glacial. Formality of manner was stressed equally with formalism in dress; while those who were fortunate enough to be invited to the sacred precincts had been screened with the utmost care. There was no place at these soirees, remarked a complacent entrant, "for the intrusion of the rabble in crowds." [9]

Small wonder then that "the rabble" looked askance at the whole institution of levees and mocked them derisively in newspaper squibs and doggerel verse. No wonder that Jefferson, attentively noting action and reaction, determined later when he became president to mollify "the rabble" and transfix "society" with his informal, undress, Devil-take-the-hindmost *pêle-mêles*.

More weighty matters also engrossed Washington's attention. He found himself a general without an army, a head of state without assistants to set the wheels of government in motion. His first task was to choose heads for the various departments.

There were six major posts to be filled: State (Foreign Affairs), Treasury, War, the Attorney General, Postmaster General and Chief Justice of the United States. All these offices had been created by act of Congress, with the exception of the Chief Justice, who held under the Constitution. In addition, five Associate Justices, United States marshals, district attorneys, collectors of revenue and a motley array of subordinate officials required consideration and appointment.

The War Department posed the simplest problem. General Henry

Knox of Massachusetts, Washington's old friend and comrade in arms, already acted in that capacity and the President merely continued him in office.

Knox had commenced life as a Boston bookseller to the officers of the British garrison and Tory ladies. On the side he studied manuals of artillery practice. When the Revolution came he quit his shop and his haughty customers, entered the Army and rose rapidly as an artillery officer to the rank of major-general. His war service may not have been spectacular, but it was fairly competent; and it was generally conceded that he knew the technical side of guns better than anyone else in the Army.

In person Knox was extremely large and corpulent; and his wife matched him with ample dimensions of her own. The wits proclaimed them "the largest couple in the city." [10] Florid of hue, with small gray eyes deep-set and rather brilliant, somewhat bowlegged, cane invariably tucked under arm, he marched along with such an air of grandeur and complacency as further to excite the risibility of the wits. He was a hearty, sociable man, given to gusts of laughter and good living, and sensitive of but one thing—his mutilated hand (a war casualty), which he usually hid from public view by a black silk handkerchief wrapped around it.[11]

Knox's career in the Cabinet has generally been overshadowed by that of his more brilliant associates, and there has been a tendency to dismiss him with the contemptuous phrases of Jefferson—that he was a fool and a docile echo to Hamilton. Actually, he handled his department with considerable ability, and took a broad, humanitarian and statesmanlike view of the Indian problem which the country would have done well to adopt. Most of the difficulties that arose in the War Department were not of his making.

For the office of Attorney General, Washington chose Edmund Randolph of Virginia. Randolph was a handsome, portly man with a good reputation as a lawyer and orator. He had elected while still a boy to remain in the colonies and take the rebel side when his father, John Randolph, then the Crown attorney in Virginia, fled to England never to return. Young Randolph embraced the radical cause with great ardor, entered the legislature and became governor shortly after the end of the war. He did well in both offices and fought sturdily for the measures advocated by his friends and compatriots, Jefferson and Madison. These latter were therefore happy to see him in a Cabinet post; but Jefferson, after a year of close association, turned vehemently against him and condemned him, with some injustice, as a straddler and a trimmer. On Jefferson's departure from the State Department, Randolph took over but soon became involved in a cloud of accusation that has never been fully lifted, and spent the rest of his life shrilly seeking vindication.

The Post Office was still considered as a minor division of government and not worthy of Cabinet rank. It went to Samuel Osgood of New York.

The two most important departments, of course, were State and Treasury. Foreign affairs and finances—these were at once the danger points and the life lines of the new republic.

For the State Department, John Jay was the logical candidate, since he had held that office during the Confederation and was actively holding over during the interregnum. But Jay, a conservative New York leader of much rectitude and a concomitant stiffness of manner, was happy to relinquish the arduous post and preferred to accept what he deemed a dignified sinecure—the office of Chief Justice of the United States.

With Jay removed from consideration, there were but few left with sufficient experience in the intricacies of foreign relations. Benjamin Franklin was old, ill and soon to succumb to his infirmities. John Adams was Vice-President of the United States. That narrowed the field to Thomas Jefferson, the incumbent minister to France.

Jefferson was well known to Washington, to his fellow Virginians and to all Americans. His talents had been amply displayed in the legislature of his own state, in the Continental Congress, in his polemic writings against England and, above all, in his drafting of the Declaration of Independence. The immortal phrases of that document had sunk deep into the hearts and consciousness of the people; his ardor in the cause of the Revolution had been unquestioned; while all classes paid tribute to his person and abilities—the aristocratic planters because he was one of them, the political leaders for his contributions to the common cause, the intellectuals for his diversified interests and scientific inquiries, and the ordinary man for his advocacy of human rights and his deep sensitivity to human needs and problems.

If his governorship of Virginia during the war years had been somewhat less than glorious, the passage of time had caused adverse recollections to fade. For the five years just past he had been minister to the French court, where he was privileged to witness and be consulted on the initial stages of the French Revolution and to hail it as the dawn of a new era for European man. Smitten with the French, their rubbed-off edges, their manners and way of life, and impressed with the principles of their Revolution, which he believed to be modeled on the earlier American one, Jefferson steadfastly and against all hazards adhered to their nation.

To him too as to many Americans, France was the ally who had helped them win their freedom; while England was still the enemy whose course since the war had done nothing to eradicate the memory of ancient wrongs.

Jefferson's long absence from home during the crucial period of Constitution making and ratification made him acceptable to both sides in that heated struggle; and each could claim him as their own. Viewing the finished product from afar, Jefferson on the whole approved of it; criticizing however the failure to prohibit repeated re-elections of the president, and the omission of personal safeguards against the possible tyranny of the federal government. The first objection had to await the administration of Harry Truman before it was corrected; the second was placated by the passage of the amendments collectively known as the Bill of Rights.

A complex individual, sometimes inconsistent but always steadfast in his passionate devotion to mankind, and America in particular; a man who had sworn on the altar of Almighty God to wage eternal warfare against every form of tyranny, mental as well as physical, and who kept his oath; a universal genius in an age of highly talented men—Jefferson's place in history is secure.

To Jefferson, therefore, Washington made overtures to accept the State Department post while he was still in France. But Jefferson, on the eve of a leave of absence to Virginia, was loath to give up his observation point abroad. The President bided his time until Jefferson came home, then renewed his offer late in 1789 with such insistence that the reluctant minister finally acceded to it as in the nature of a command. It was not until March 22, 1790, after the lines of government had already been solidly laid down, that Jefferson quit his home at Monticello and arrived in New York to assume his duties.

The other major office of government—the Treasury—underwent similar if not as long-drawn-out vicissitudes. Here the logical man was Robert Morris, who had been Financier under the Confederation; but he too was reluctant to reassume a job which he had been only too happy to end. He recommended Alexander Hamilton instead.

Born in the West Indies under the bar sinister, Hamilton had come to the mainland at an early age to seek knowledge and a career. He found himself in the midst of a fermenting revolution, and entered upon its headlong course with an ambitious ardor that outran even the course of events. With great rapidity he came to a lieutenant-colonelcy and an honored place in Washington's military family. And there he stuck, except for one brief interlude, much to his disgust, writing letters and composing reports instead of galloping gloriously on the field of battle.

From earliest boyhood, when he had wished there was a war in which he could participate, Hamilton had dreamed of himself as the man on horseback. Yet throughout his life he was condemned forever to grasp at the sword and see it always slip from his hand. His true métier, though he refused to admit it even in the privacy of his own mind, was the pen. One of the greatest controversialists of all time, he dashed off pamphlets, reports, forensic documents and many-paged letters with a facility and wealth of illustration and argument that was the envy of his friends and the despair of his opponents.

Obscure in his origins, and perhaps because of it, he assumed the role of leader to the aristocratic, the rich and the wellborn. A romantic in private life and in his secret dreams, he was a thorough realist in politics and economics. Of the mass of the people he took the most cynical view, referring to them as a "great beast" against whom the only bulwark was a strong central government, supported and controlled by a self-interested group of "the rich and the well-born."

Throughout the Revolution, Hamilton had clearly foreseen that economic and financial problems would bedevil and eventually sink the nation if they were not properly solved. He proposed remedies then, and continued unweariedly to offer them with an Isaiah-like intensity to all who would listen until the time arrived when Washington gave him the chance to put them in operation.

Though he thought the Constitution a milk-and-watery thing that could not possibly last, and though he exhorted a silent Convention to adopt the British form of government, retiring in disgust when they failed to do so, he nevertheless took the completed document as the best thing available and penned its most eloquent defense in the *Federalist* papers.

With Hamilton ensconced in the Treasury and Jefferson in the Department of State, the Cabinet which Washington had gathered around him possessed two titans of a stature the country was not to see in any future Cabinet. Yet no two men could have been more diametrically opposed in every respect.

Jefferson was tall, loose-limbed and somewhat gangling, with reddish sandy hair, a mild, open countenance and a thin skin both literal and figurative. Hamilton was short and wiry, compensating for his limitation in inches by an erect, precise military bearing. Every accent was positive, every gesture sharp and to the point. Both men were brilliant; but Jefferson was the more universal man, while Hamilton concentrated with greater intensity on the administration and the mechanisms of government.

It was perhaps inevitable that between two such giants, opposed in every thought and concept, conflict would develop. And it did, of a nature and intensity as both to dominate the times in which they lived and reverberate through succeeding generations. To this day the echoes of their dispute and the ideas which they engendered have not yet died away; and Jeffersonian principles and Hamiltonian policies have almost as much pertinence now as in the decade when they were first formulated.

The salaries of government were not large, except that of the President, which was set at the surprisingly high figure of $25,000 a year. Out of this sum, however, Washington had to maintain his own quarters, pay for his servants and the upkeep of the levees, balls and entertainments, and serve his visitors food and French wines on a gargantuan scale. So that there was little enough left at the end of the year; and a later president, Jefferson, found himself steadily in the red even though he inhabited rent-free the President's House in the new capital of Washington.

If the President could barely get along on his salary, the other officers of state were virtually on the dole. The sum of $5000 was deemed sufficient for the Vice-President; while the Cabinet heads had to manage on $1500 to $3000 a year. Their offices were either in their homes or placed in small near-by rooms, bare of all but essential furniture and staffed with a clerk or two. As for Congress, its members received six dollars a day during actual service, and there were many who thought that amount too much for the work they did and a dreadful burden on the taxpayer. An attempt was made to differentiate between senators and representatives by a dollar per diem, but the latter repelled the insinuation of their lesser worth to the nation with such indignation that the idea was dropped.

Certainly no one was overpaid, and all officers of government were forced to dip into their private fortunes to maintain themselves in what was alleged to be the most expensive city in America.

With his chief offices finally filled, Washington settled down to the task of making himself acquainted with the complex of problems which confronted the nation. With painstaking care he perused mountains of documents and requested from his department heads general reports to help guide him in his conclusions. On specific questions he sent officers short notes listing the points which troubled him, and calling on them for written replies. Nor did he hesitate to query outsiders whom he deemed competent in any field. In the beginning he asked Madison for his opinion; and he relied on John Jay even after he was appointed to the Supreme Court.

Indeed, the "Cabinet" in its modern sense was not yet in existence. Its members did not meet regularly and were usually polled separately on important matters. Not until later did Washington get into the habit of convening them at his house to discuss general or specific issues in concert. At that point the Cabinet as such might be said to begin. Yet neither the departments themselves nor their presiding officers were mutually exclusive, with that sharp differentiation of function to which we are at present accustomed. The lines of demarcation were blurred, and spheres of influence without precise delimitation. As a result there was a considerable overlapping of powers and many conflicts that might otherwise have been avoided.

In general, Washington conceived himself to be the chairman of a board in which his four major officers—State, Treasury, War and Attorney General—were the members. In most cases he adopted the views of his board as expressed in written or oral opinions. Only when they clashed or stalemated did he, after lengthy consideration, cast a deciding vote. Not once did he proceed against his Cabinet's unanimous decision; rarely, if ever, did he go counter to the majority.

He surveyed his Cabinet with justifiable complacency. All were men of ability, and two were men of genius. With such as these, he wrote, "I feel myself supported by able Co-adjutors, who harmonize extremely well together." [12] How was he to foresee the irreconcilable differences that were shortly to develop?

In the midst of his arduous preliminary labors Washington sickened with what appears to have been anthrax, accompanied by high fever and a large and painful tumor in his thigh. After some weeks of suffering, he called in Dr. James Craik, who made an extensive incision in the swelling. For six weeks more Washington lay in agony on his side, while the open wound healed with exasperating slowness. Unable to turn on his back or to sit up, the President was compelled to receive visitors half reclining and twisted to one side. Even when he finally emerged into the open air, it was in a carriage fitted with a bed. Six horses hauled the great vehicle, and four servants attended him; just such a number of men and animals as had been imputed to John Adams and summarily denied by Washington.[13]

The President grew despondent over his long illness, attributing it to lack of exercise and the burdens of an office which, he feared, would hasten his departure "for that country whence no Traveller ever returns." [14] Nevertheless, in spite of pain and despondency, he persisted in his duties until the wound healed and the disagreeable symptoms disappeared.

One of the very first matters to engage the attention of the government was the state of the frontier—that amorphous, elastic area to the west in which Americans, Indians, Spaniards and English formed an immiscible mixture whose enforced contiguity threatened disaster to the peace of the continent.

Three problems were closely interrelated in any consideration of the frontier: the disposition of the Western lands ceded by the states to the nation; relations with the Indian tribes; relations with Spain. Not one of these could be resolved without a similar resolution of the others; not a single move could be made to cope with one without the most careful consideration of its immediate effect on the other two.

The so-called Northwest Territory had long been a bone of contention among the states and between them and the national government. Conflicting claims, complicated by the land hunger of determined squatters and the money hunger of equally determined speculators, made that vast area into a witches' cauldron of intrigue, corruption and bloodshed. The only matter on which states, squatters and speculators could agree was the method by which to get rid of outside claimants; i.e., the original Indian inhabitants. This was to shoot on sight and inquire afterward. Only the Continental Congress took a long view and sought by treaties to settle land rights with the Indians and to obtain national control from the states. One by one the states acceded, though not without many delays and mutual recriminations. However, when North Carolina, one of the last to yield, finally ceded her claims, even her own citizens heaved a sigh of relief. As one of them exclaimed: "The cession of the Western territory is at last completed, so that we are rid of a people who were a pest and burthen to us." [15]

Troubles indeed in plenty harassed the government of those distant wildernesses and the turbulent people who inhabited them. General Arthur St. Clair, the newly appointed governor of the Northwest Territory, audibly doubted "whether the peopling that Country will ultimately be of advantage to the Union." It drew off the population of the East, and the influence of the national government on them was slight, if at all existent.

Whatever happened in the future, he continued gloomily, the United States would be faced with a dilemma. On the one hand, if the navigation of the Mississippi were opened to them by Spain, they would tend to become economic and political rivals of the East. If it were not, then the people "will become idle, restless and dissatisfied." In either event, the first outbreak of war with either Spain or England would tempt them to join the enemy against their parent nation.

In fact, both these powers were busy with intrigues among the Kentuckians. Spain actually sought to lure the settlers into her own dominions, offering them substantial grants of land free of charges and future taxes, and promising them freedom of religious worship, at least in private.

The only solution that St. Clair could suggest was to have Washington prevail on Congress to open a part of the Western territory "for those who want land and cannot pay for it immediately." [16]

Even before St. Clair's ominous report reached the seat of government, and while Kentucky was still under the suzerainty of Virginia, Madison had received similar confidential reports of Spanish intrigues. One of these, relating to the presence of a Spanish emissary in Kentucky, he forwarded to the governor of Virginia, "in order that regular steps may be taken, if sufficient ground be afforded, for apprehending the incendiary." [17]

Another was in the form of a "handbook" which one George Morgan, an American turned Spanish agent, was distributing to "confidential people" in Pennsylvania and New Jersey. The prospectus dangled tempting bait. He would, said Morgan, lead a group of settlers across the Mississippi into Spanish territory, where he had authority to lay out a complete township, to be called New Madrid. The emigrants would receive 320 acres each at a nominal price of twelve and a half cents an acre, and numerous privileges, including the navigation of the Mississippi, a free market in New Orleans, free transportation and long-term credit for their land, provisions and livestock.[18]

Why was Spain so anxious to entice American settlers into her territories? And why, on the other hand, did the American government view the proceedings with such intense alarm and consider any acceptance as tantamount to treason?

Spain proceeded from impeccable premises: that her vast and empty possessions offered a constant invitation to invasion and seizure by an ambitiously expanding United States. The corollary that a string of well-established settlements along the frontiers, prosperous and content, would constitute an effective barrier to neighboring designs was equally valid. But the conclusion to which she came as a result contained a fatal error: that her new citizens, once they repudiated their old allegiance, would resist any attempt at aggrandizement by the country of their birth.

Thomas Jefferson, for one, was quick to perceive the flaw in this reasoning. When, as Secretary of State, he was confronted with a similar attempt by the Spanish governor of Florida to entice Americans into his domains, Jefferson pretended public indignation but expressed private satisfaction. Let but enough Americans settle in Florida, he wrote, and the plum will drop into our laps without a struggle.[19] This actually happened much later in the case of Texas.

At the time, however, the American government saw eye to eye with Spain on both premises and conclusions. Remembering how its own land was peopled by Europeans who repelled with arms their old allegiance, it could only foresee the same course of events: the irrevocable loss of its most valuable and enterprising citizens, and an eventual war of brother against brother.

Indeed, as matters stood, it seemed only too probable that the Western country would separate from the East. Worse still, the Westerners might seek either the protection or actual sovereignty of Spain or

England; a denouement in which both powers would have been only too happy to concur.

Already there existed a carefully planned conspiracy in Kentucky for joinder with Spain. Men of prominence were involved; many more, perhaps, than the present records disclose. When the tide finally shifted, there was haste to disavow and to hide all evidence of complicity.

One figure, however, must remain forever tarred with the conspiratorial brush, in spite of later denials and the continued favor of the country he had sought to betray. This was James Wilkinson, brigadier and clothier general during the Revolution, the confidant and eventual betrayer of Aaron Burr, and inglorious commander of the American Army in the War of 1812.

This "finished scoundrel," as John Randolph of Roanoke termed him, was now seeking his fortune in Kentucky and trading down the Mississippi with the Spaniards. To further both trade and fortune he took a secret oath of allegiance to Spain in 1787, and thereafter became her paid spy, *agent provocateur* and seducer of the West. In the end, however, when he found it to his advantage to do so, he betrayed his new employer with the same aplomb with which he had betrayed his country and his friends.[20]

England similarly was fishing in the troubled waters. A certain Colonel Connolly, from the British posts on the Great Lakes, was currently offering Kentucky if and when she seceded from the Union such English aid as would be necessary to help her "assert her rights." [21]

This alarming information and more to the same effect came to Madison through his confidential correspondents. He forwarded it promptly to Washington with the hope that Congress would act on the situation with wisdom and dispatch.[22]

Wisdom and dispatch were indeed called for. The Western folk had substantial grievances that could not be fobbed off with words alone. Geographically they faced south and southwest rather than east, where the rest of the nation lay. The ridges of the Appalachian chain interposed an almost insurmountable barrier between East and West, traversed by a handful of wagon trails that twisted steeply over narrow passes and through interminable forests. The cost of transporting goods to the Eastern markets and the difficulty and danger of the route were such as to make regular commercial ties impossible.

But a broad and easy highway led to the Gulf of Mexico and the ocean lanes to Europe. This was the river system of the Ohio and the Mississippi, down which flatboats and barges could be floated to New Orleans for sale or transshipment by sea. Tobacco, hides, grain, whiskey and game comprised their exports; and furnished the hard money with which to purchase manufactured goods.

Unfortunately, for most of its lower course the Mississippi ran through Spanish territory. By treaty at the end of the Seven Years' War, England and her subjects had been given the right of free navigation; a right which was summarily terminated when Spain in 1779 joined France in the new war against England. Though the Americans were in effect their allies, Spain refused them the privileges they had formerly possessed as British subjects. Difficulties, imposts and downright prohibition hampered the Western country's access to the sea and to the all-important station of New Orleans.

From the very first, the Western settlers had clamored to the Continental Congress for a resumption of free and unhampered navigation. But the Northern states were lackadaisical about the Western grievances. They feared the growth of a countervailing power to themselves, both political and economic; and they were alarmed over the probable drain of their population should the West be made too attractive.

In fact the Continental Congress, seeking Spanish recognition of their newly won independence, had authorized their plenipotentiary in Spain, John Jay, to yield the navigation. Jay disapproved, writing home that such a yielding would "render a future war with Spain unavoidable, and I shall look upon my subscribing to the one [the cession of the rights of navigation] as fixing the certainty of the other." [23]

Nevertheless he obeyed his instructions; but Spain delayed so interminably that the entire matter was dropped. In 1785, after Jay returned home to take over the post of Foreign Affairs, he changed his mind. He was willing now to forbear the alleged right for a period of years provided Spain would agree to a settlement of boundaries and enter into a commercial treaty. By this time, however, the Southern members of Congress, alarmed at the serious unrest in the West, were clamoring against the "betrayal," and prevented further negotiations. But the West and the South never forgave Jay for his afterthought; and the business rose to plague him in 1795 during the excitement engendered by his treaty with England.

One of the first matters on Washington's agenda, therefore, was this matter of navigation. In a careful précis he came to the conclusion that it ought "delicately and tenderly" to be conveyed to Don Diego de Gardoqui, the Spanish envoy to the United States, that there was no chance of our yielding the navigation of the Mississippi "which is so tenaciously contended for by a large part of the Union, and the relinquishment of which, or the fear of which, founded on appearances, would occasion certainly the separation of the Western territory." [24]

John Brown, the Kentucky delegate to Congress (without a vote) expressed satisfaction with the President's stand, and expected a majority of the Senate to back him up. He feared, however, that the Eastern manufacturing interest would oppose any insistence on the right.[25] But Senator Grayson of Virginia, though he believed Washington to be sincere, demanded "active exertions" to gain the right instead of mere passive refusal to yield it. Should Georgia surrender *her* claims to the lands contiguous to the Mississippi as Virginia had done with hers, he added slyly, perhaps the general government might find it profitable to become more interested in the fate of the river.[26]

Actually, there was little that the national government could do at the moment to force a decision upon Spain. A full-scale war was unthinkable, in spite of Western hothead and no other course would have sufficed. The business had to wait for more favorable times.

Concurrent with the controversy over the navigation of the Mississippi, and intimately interconnected with it, was the grave state of relations with the Indian tribes within and beyond our borders. The Revolution had left them restless and in many instances hostile; a condition which England and Spain diligently exploited. From the far Northwest to the extreme Southwest the Indians were aflame. In the North, British agents were active; in the South, Spanish emissaries assumed the congenial task of stirring the tribes to plunder and rapine. Both nations had a special interest in keeping the Americans and the red men constantly embroiled; powerful and warlike Indian tribes would provide a substantial buffer against American aggrandizement on their own possessions and weaken the upstart nation vis-à-vis themselves.

Some progress had been made in settling the vexed Indian question, at least in the North, by the Treaty of Fort Harmar concluded with the Six Nations and their allies. Disputed boundaries were settled,

causes of controversy removed and matters of trade meticulously regulated.[27] But nothing as yet had been done with the powerful tribes of
the West and South.

As soon as General Knox received his appointment to the War
Office (and even before the Senate confirmed), he devoted his attention to the Indian problem. Knox, as has been previously suggested,
has been generally underrated. He approached the knotty question in
a wise and statesmanlike fashion, tinctured with justice and a readiness to admit faults wherever he found them. The reports which he
submitted to Washington surveying and reviewing the long history
of Indian relations merit much more study than they have hitherto
received. They rise on occasion to eloquence and are always imbued
with dignity and fairness to a much-wronged race. Could his recommendations have been heeded by the people and the border states,
much unhappy Indian history might have been avoided.

To him—and he cited chapter and verse for his conclusions—the
burden of guilt lay generally on the whites. In most instances, he
reported, Indian raids and aggressions were in retaliation for white
outrages and illegal invasions of their territories.[28]

He took up the cases of the various tribes. To the west and northwest contiguous to Kentucky dwelt the Wabash Indians and associated
tribes. While it was true that on occasion small bands of the Wabash
had murdered white settlers, the whites had offered ample provocations. To such sporadic killings the men of Kentucky had retaliated
heavily, not on the Wabash, but on peaceable Piankeshaws; possessing,
as Knox put it, "an equal aversion to all bearing the name of Indians."
Unless decisive measures were immediately taken, he warned, the entire West would flame into a general war.

The same situation existed farther south. There lay four great Indian tribes—the Creeks, the Cherokees, the Chickasaws and the Choctaws. They stretched in a solid line along the borders of the United
States from Virginia through Georgia. They too had suffered from the
irresistible movement of the whites into their territory, driven by a
compulsion for land and sharp trading that refused to bow to concepts
of rights, either of person or property, in the abstract or fortified by
government order.

Of these the Creeks were the largest and most warlike nation. Technically their lands were within the borders of the United States
(chiefly Georgia) and of Spain (the Floridas); actually and by several
treaties, then currently in issue, they were independent. A remarkable

half-breed influenced their policies and welded them into a formidable weapon. This was Alexander McGillivray, whose father had been a Georgia loyalist and whose mother was a Creek. The father had fled to the Creeks after the confiscation of his property by revolutionary Georgia and instilled into his son his own undying hatred for the state that had treated him so badly. Able, unscrupulous, ambitious and fortified by an excellent English education, young McGillivray swiftly rose to power among the Indians, allied himself with the Spaniards against the Americans and sought to weld all the tribes of the South into a vast confederacy whose avowed purpose was to drive the Georgians from their encroachments on its territory.

Georgia insisted that her inhabitants had a right to enter the border lands of the Creeks by virtue of previous treaties. Outrages on either side brought swift retaliations. Rapine, torture and murder swept the entire frontier. Armed bands swooped at will and left a trail of smoking chaos behind. The state militia was called out, and the Indians mustered in strength. A full-scale war developed, and a clamor rose for immediate armed assistance from the general government.

The Cherokees, lying along the frontiers of Virginia, the Carolinas and Georgia, had supposedly settled all boundary disputes with the Americans by a treaty signed in 1786; but the terms had been wholly disregarded by encroaching whites. Fleeing outrage and the violent dispossession of their lands, the Cherokees sought refuge with the Creeks; welcome grist for McGillivray's mill.

The Chickasaws and the Choctaws, inhabiting the lands between the Creeks and the Cherokees, were also in treaty relations with the United States. Knox described them as "candid, brave, and honest." But neither treaties nor character prevented land-hungry whites who saw no distinctions among Indians from invading their territories. If the invasions continued, Knox warned, it would be relatively easy for McGillivray and the Spaniards to convince the embittered tribes that their only hope of salvation lay in joining the contemplated confederation of the Creeks and placing themselves under the protection of Spain.

As he surveyed the entire explosive situation, Knox determined that it could be handled adequately only by a strict adherence to certain fixed principles. The Indians, he maintained, had a prior right to the soil which "cannot be taken from them unless by their free consent, or by right of conquest in case of a just war. To dispossess them on any other principle, would be a gross violation of the fundamental laws of nature, and of that distributive justice which is the glory of the nation."

He firmly opposed any yielding to the clamor of the frontier that an army of federal troops march immediately against the Indians. Let us first, he insisted, seek to negotiate on an amicable basis with the tribes, and once agreements are reached, adhere to them rigorously. "When the impartial mind of the great public sits in judgment," he rebuked the clamorers, "it is necessary that the cause of the ignorant Indians should be heard as well as those who are more fortunately circumstanced."

A wise and humane Indian policy, a sedulous respect for Indian rights and treaties, a guardianship by the general government based on law and justice, and the use of force only to repel unprovoked aggression—these were the cardinal points in Knox's proposals to solve the Indian problem.

At the end of his reports, the Secretary of War gave way to philosophic reflection. "It is painful to consider," he wrote, "that all the Indian tribes, once existing in those States now the best cultivated and most populous, have become extinct. If the same causes continue, the same effects will happen; and, in a short period, the idea of an Indian on this side the Mississippi will only be found in the pages of the historian. How different would be the sensation of a philosophic mind to reflect, that, instead of exterminating a part of the human race by our modes of population, we had persevered, through all difficulties, and at last had imparted our knowledge of cultivation and the arts to the aboriginals of the country, by which the source of future life and happiness had been preserved and extended." [29]

Even as Knox penned these moving reflections, he must have known that the cause of the Indians was lost, that the forces he opposed could not be restrained by appeals to abstract principles and a sense of justice. Yet he convinced Washington, if the latter required convincing, that his ideas were correct.

On Saturday, August 22, 1789, accompanied by General Knox, Washington entered the Senate chamber. He intended, he announced, to lay before the members the facts relating to the Indian troubles and to obtain their advice and consent on the procedures he proposed for handling them.

Just how to obtain such advice and consent, as specified in the Constitution, had already agitated both the President and Congress.

In a previous written communication, Washington had suggested that he appear in person to discuss all matters relating to treaties and the nominations of foreign envoys; all other nominations to be submitted in writing. The Senate, still feeling its way through uncharted waters, had agreed, though not without some mutterings.[30]

The scene that followed in the Senate chamber held elements of drama and comedy. Adams politely vacated his chair and Washington assumed it. Knox sat next to him, his vast bulk overflowing the confines of his seat. Washington pulled a paper from his pocket and handed it to the Vice-President.

The message was in essence a summation of Knox's report. It was important, wrote Washington after reviewing the ominous situation, "to conciliate the powerful tribes of Indians in the Southern District amounting probably to fourteen thousand fighting men, and to attach them firmly to the United States." Such a measure "includes not only peace and security to the whole Southern frontier, but is calculated to form a barrier against the Colonies of an European power [Spain], which in the mutations of policy may one day become the Enemy of the United States."

In the case of the Creeks, war already raged on the frontier. Georgia claimed that the Creeks had yielded to her by three previous treaties the lands in dispute. The Creeks denied the validity of the alleged treaties, insisting they had been negotiated and signed by unauthorized individuals and obtained through trickery. Washington now proposed that a commission of the United States proceed to the frontier to investigate these conflicting claims. Should they find against Georgia, then they would negotiate anew with the Creeks for a proper and just conveyance of the territory in dispute.[31]

Adams read the message in hurried and half-audible tones, made more inaudible by the noise of carriages rattling outside as citizens took the summer air. Few of the senators heard more than that the document had something to do with the Indians.

After Adams had mumbled his way to the end, Robert Morris of Pennsylvania rose to ask that it be read again. With a gesture of annoyance Adams did so. After the repeat performance, Maclay called for additional information; while James Gunn of Georgia angrily demanded that consideration of that part of the message which referred to Georgia be postponed. Morris moved that the entire matter be turned over to a select committee, and Gunn promptly seconded his motion. Maclay rose to speak in favor.

Throughout these proceedings, Washington's face assumed the aspect of a thundercloud. By the time Maclay had finished, the storm broke. He started out of his seat, so Maclay reported, "in a violent fret" and burst forth with great vehemence: "This defeats every purpose of my coming here!" Later, however, his wrath cooled and he agreed to a postponement until Monday. Then he stalked out of the chamber (Maclay again reporting) "with sullen dignity."

The Pennsylvania senator hurried home to confide to his journal: "I cannot now be mistaken. The President wishes to tread on the necks of the Senate. Commitment will bring the matter to discussion, at least in the committee, where he is not present. He wishes us to see with the eyes and hear with the ears of his Secretary only. The Secretary to advance the premises, the President to draw the conclusions, and to bear down our deliberations with his personal authority and presence. Form only will be left to us. This," Maclay exclaimed, "will not do with Americans." [32]

The period of honeymoon was over so far as the suspicious backwoods democrat was concerned. Yet, though his comments were exaggerated and over-touchy, they contained an element of truth. Opposition always annoyed Washington, who in this instance conceived himself in a situation somewhat similar to that of the English monarch appearing before a silent and respectful Parliament that listened and acceded without much ado.

On Monday, however, the President was "placid and serene" and manifested "a spirit of accommodation."

The discussion was resumed on the message under the vigilant eyes of Washington, whose presence, so Maclay thought, inhibited debate and promoted a shamefaced timidity among those senators who disagreed with his proposals. The President, Maclay wrote sourly, got most of what he wanted.

Maclay erred. On the crucial question of the Georgia claims to Creek territory, the Senate, after agreeing to a commission for treating with the Indians, voted resoundingly that Georgia had a good and equitable title to the disputed lands.[33]

This time Washington lost his iron control. His placidity vanished. He stormed out of the Senate chamber and down the stairs. He would be damned, he cried out angrily, if he would ever go back there again.[34]

He never did; and a pattern was set for the future fraught with momentous consequences. Never again did a President discuss in advance the details of a proposed negotiation with the Senate. There-after, treaties were first made and then submitted for ratification or rejection. Though the *consent* of the Senate was still necessary, the *advice* envisaged by the Constitution quietly slipped into the discard.

In the lower House, another constitutional question reared its head when it came to vote an appropriation for the commission's expenses. John Page of Virginia enunciated the doctrine that the House had the right to determine for itself the advisability of granting funds; in other words, that it could interpose a veto if it disliked what the Executive had negotiated and the Senate had approved. By a narrow majority the House evaded the fundamental question and voted the requisite expenses; though Jackson of Georgia demanded strong measures against the Indians. Let the commission, he exclaimed, carry an olive branch in one hand and a sword in the other.[35]

But the root question would not down, and rose again full-panoplied and terrible in the great debate over Jay's treaty.

It required the utmost skill and tact of the commission and of the administration to smooth over the ruffled feelings of the Creeks on one side and Georgia on the other. At many points the negotiations were on the verge of breaking down. In the beginning the Creeks refused even to treat; and their obstinacy goaded Knox into proposing an army of five thousand men and a string of border posts to punish any future aggressions on their part; though he hastened to add that they would also be employed to prevent incursions of lawless whites into the territory of the Indians.[36]

At length McGillivray sullenly consented to negotiate; and after endless conferences finally came to New York, accompanied by twenty-three blanketed chiefs, to sign a treaty which drew a boundary between the embattled forces. Unfortunately, the boundary was sketchily described, and a provision was made for a later definitive survey.[37]

The treaty at least provided a breathing space, though the survey in futurity naturally paved the way for further troubles. With the Indian tribes to the north, however, not even that breathing space intervened.

CHAPTER 5

Party Press and Financial Reports

WHEN CONGRESS RECESSED at the end of September, Washington heaved a sigh of relief. The critical initial stages were over and the federal government seemed firmly established. Fundamental measures had been taken by Congress, including the provision of a revenue, and the future was perceptibly brighter than when he had first taken office.

One flaw in the picture, however, remained to be rectified. The two recalcitrant states—North Carolina and Rhode Island—had still not joined the Union. Of North Carolina, Washington had no doubts. As a matter of fact, she ratified the Constitution on November 21, 1789, though not without a sizable minority of protest within her borders.

Rhode Island was another matter. That tiny state carried a perpetual chip on her shoulders and seemed to enjoy setting herself at odds with her larger neighbors. Washington thought irritably that her people had long since bid adieu "to every principle of honor, common sense, and honesty." [1] It took considerable pressure and hints of worse to come to make Rhode Island finally and reluctantly see the light.

If the administration of the government appeared to be in a fair state, what about the country at large and its people? How were they disposed toward the new government after some six months of operation? How were their crops progressing, and their manufactures? The only way to find out, decided Washington, was to go in person and see for himself. He was familiar enough with the South; but he had not been through the Eastern states since the days of the Revolution. When he consulted Hamilton about it, the Secretary of the Treasury agreed that it was an excellent idea. Whereupon the President made his preparations for the grand tour. [2]

On October 15, 1789, he started out from New York in his "chariot and four," accompanied by his private secretaries Tobias Lear and Major Jackson on horseback.[3]

Slowly and majestically the cavalcade entered Connecticut, meeting with enthusiastic receptions, welcoming addresses and parades wherever it went. But the President kept a sharp eye open for the contours of the land, the state of the crops, the hum of business, and cocked his ear to catch the undertones of the people's sentiments. These were what he had come to observe.

In Hartford he visited a woolen manufactory and fingered the cloth. Though not of "the first quality," it was fairly good. To encourage the operators, he ordered a suit of broadcloth to be made for him.[4]

Turning northward, he crossed the border into Massachusetts, where he was pleased to discover "a great equality in the People of this State. Few or no opulent men—and no poor."[5]

But this was in the central section. In Boston, where his coach next rolled, there was a greater disparity of classes. Opulence was plainly visible, and an aristocracy which John Adams considered equal to any in Europe was in the making. Yet even here there were few if any poor.

A huge parade marched endlessly in his honor. Grouped as the participants were by trades and professions, their mere enumeration perhaps gives a better picture of the economic strata of Boston than any census. In the procession marched officials, clergy, lawyers, doctors, merchants, soldiers; bakers, blacksmiths, boat builders, cabinet and chair makers; carvers, chaise and coach makers; clock and watch makers, coopers, coppersmiths and braziers; cordwainers, distillers, duck manufacturers, glaziers and plumbers; goldsmiths and jewelers, hair-dressers, hatters and house carpenters; leather dressers, lemon dealers, limners and painters; masons, mast makers and makers of mathematical instruments; paper stainers, pewterers, printers and bookbinders; riggers and rope makers, saddlers, sail makers, ship joiners and shipwrights; sugar boilers, tallow chandlers, tanners and curriers; tailors, tinplate workers, tobacconists, truckmen and wharfingers; wheelwrights, sailors and—scholars.[6]

An amazing variety of tradesfolk, artisans and mechanics that w required to keep the wheels of a town in motion; not to speak of t vast additional number of farmers, agricultural laborers, cattle dea rs and raisers, and similar producers of essential foods.

Washington, however, was annoyed in spite of the huge tu out. John Hancock, the governor of the state, had not come to visit m in his quarters. Instead, Hancock invited the President to his own home for dinner, pleading the gout as an excuse. Washington suspected that the governor really wished to force him to pay the first visit as a token of his official superiority to the President of the United States. Hancock, indeed, had been a leading malcontent with the proposed Constitution and had battled valiantly against its adoption by his state.

With some asperity, therefore, Washington turned down the invitation; and Hancock was compelled to come to him the next day in a litter, his body swathed in bandages from what the President insisted on calling a "pretended gout." [7]

Actually Hancock was ill. He suffered intensely from the disease, and his hands as well as his legs were so swollen that he found it almost impossible to hold a pen for writing.[8]

Thus somewhat appeased on the knotty question of etiquette, Washington inspected a duckcloth factory where twenty-eight looms were employed and fourteen girls spun the flax, assisted by small children to turn the wheels. The girls and children labored from eight in the morning until six in the evening, and were paid by the piece. "They are," commented the President, "the daughters of decayed families, and are girls of Character—none others are admitted." He was more enthusiastic about a card manufactory where machines were in use to produce cards of such good quality and low price that they were even smuggled into England to undersell the domestic product.[9]

Everywhere that Washington traveled, through all the states of New England (with the exception of Rhode Island, which was outside the pale), he observed the commercial and manufacturing life. At Marblehead he noted 110 ships and 800 sailors employing in fishing; at Salem thirteen ships plied the seas to distant India; at Lynn 400 workmen made 175,000 pairs of shoes annually; at Beverly the prosperous and politically powerful brothers John and George Cabot ran a cotton manufactory employing the newly invented carding and spinning machines.

Returning through Connecticut, the President came afoul of the notorious "blue laws." On Sunday, "it being contrary to law and disagreeable to the People of this State to travel on the Sabbath day," he obediently went to church instead, where he was compelled to listen to some "very lame discourses." [10]

On November 13th he was back in New York, well satisfied with what he had heard and seen. Everywhere he had found an increasing good will toward the new government and a complete recovery from the ravages of the Revolution. He was realist enough to attribute this benevolent attitude in part at least to economic factors. The wheat harvest had been excellent and the abundant grain found a ready market abroad. Commerce boomed in every port, while the number of new manufactories which had sprung up in a single year, he wrote, was "astonishing." Even the agricultural South, so came the reports, was teeming with a similar abundance.[11]

But a different picture of Virginia was painted by Jefferson. "Antifederalism is not yet dead in this country," he said. "The gentlemen who opposed [the Constitution] retain a good deal of malevolence towards the new government. Henry is its avowed foe." Even the amendments, he feared, would have hard going in the state senate.[12]

But no one disputed Washington's observations on the Northern or, as they were usually called, the Eastern states. Everywhere were the visible signs of the coming Industrial Revolution that was to transform the economy of the nation. Washington saw the first stirrings; and each month showed marked advances. In every New England town ambitious entrepreneurs were establishing factories, chiefly for the production of textiles and shoes, and were experimenting with machinery run by water power. If the initial results were meager, and sometimes downright discouraging, no one seemed dismayed or was prevented from persisting.

The markets abroad for American grain were excellent. England and France took practically everything that was offered—wheat, rye, barley, rice and flour. France alone, so Jefferson estimated, purchased 5,000,000 bushels during 1789; while England of course imported considerably more.[13]

The great Boston merchant, Stephen Higginson, was confident that "we could easily supplant other countries like Ireland in all open markets, for our beef, pork, butter and pickled fish," if we saw to it by strict inspection that the quality was uniformly good. There was but one flaw in the general scheme of our prosperity, he added. That was the restrictive system which Great Britain interposed as a barrier against our shipping. Yet how could we fight it effectively? By retaliation, as Madison proposed in Congress? That remedy, Higginson was convinced, would prove worse than the disease. It would lose for us all markets, instead of a few. He could see only one answer to the problem; a settlement by "calm negotiation."[14]

As the event was to show, much more was required than calm negotiation. For the British had become uneasily aware of the possibility of successful American competition in what had hitherto been their semiprivate domain. From New York came the report of their consul with disturbing evidence of the rapid strides the Americans were taking. "All kinds of Cabinet work, Carriages, Saddlery, Men's and Women's Shoes, etc.," he wrote, "are so made here, as that the duties laid upon such Articles from Europe will put an end to any Importation of them. Carriages are here made so well and so much cheaper than from Europe that the Count Moustier [the French minister] has a coach building to take with him to France." And in general, "a Spirit of Temperance and Industry hath taken place with the generality of the people in the Eastern and Middle States, within two or three years past, that can no way be accounted for, it seems almost Supernatural!" [15]

The newspapers boasted exultantly of the new American prosperity, and their columns teemed with items tending to prove that we were becoming self-sufficient in manufactures as well as in agriculture. On the whole, the press at this time was well disposed toward the new government. It was not until the following year, after Hamilton published his famous Reports, that cleavages made their appearance.

There had been newspapers in the colonies from the beginning of the eighteenth century. Their life had been a continual struggle for existence. Circulation was limited, and subscribers notably delinquent in paying up. Hardly an issue came off the press without some anguished outcry from the publisher over his financial troubles.

By modern standards the papers were small and badly printed. A single sheet was folded over to make four pages; the type was small, uneven and eye-wearyingly solid. Exclamatory capitals and italics were strewn liberally over every page. The front page was devoted almost exclusively to advertisements (how else could the publisher hope to survive?), though sometimes a lead article threaded its solitary way down the right-hand side to be continued on the inside pages.

These articles, usually from the pens of prominent political figures who masqueraded thinly under a variety of classical pseudonyms, ran to astonishing lengths and endless numbers. Close-knit in argument and strewn with learned allusions, they presupposed in their readers a standard of intelligence, a familiarity with history and a fixity of attention which no modern editor would dare to rely on.

A surprising amount of space was devoted to foreign news; indeed, world affairs outweighed by far in actual lineage items of domestic import. But there was a sufficient reason for the seeming disproportion. Without reporters or news-gathering agencies, relying for information on an occasional private letter that came into their hands, the editors found it much simpler to obtain foreign intelligence than an account of what was taking place in a town fifty miles away. Every incoming ship brought packets of foreign newspapers, while the captain, crew and passengers were only too happy to discharge their budgets of personal information.

In addition to the advertisements, lead article, foreign and local intelligence, the newspaper editor filled up his space with squibs, fillers, ship news, commodity prices, reprints from other papers, proceedings of Congress—and personal billingsgate.

Since the average circulation wavered between five hundred and two thousand copies—not all of which were paid for—the struggling printers did not wax fat. To eke out a bare living they were compelled to do general printing and sell supplies on the side. It was no wonder that their tempers frayed and snapped, or that their political and personal animosities took on an envenomed character perhaps unsurpassed in the history of the American press. Canings and whippings from their victims were not uncommon; and rival editors breathed blood and mayhem against one another in print, though rarely condescending to more intimate encounters.

The *Gazette of the United States*, in spite of powerful political and governmental support, complained bitterly of its 650 subscribers whose contributions of three dollars a year (when paid) could not begin to cover expenses.[16] It was only from advertisements that the printer could hope to obtain a modicum of income; hence he could not afford to be too straitlaced in censoring what was offered.

The advertisements were sometimes of a nature that would not be permitted through the mails today. Yet, because of their frankness, they throw considerable light on the manners, habits and mores of the time. Quack nostrums for the cure of venereal disease fill the columns in such profusion as to give unmistakable testimony to its prevalence in the country;[17] while the following announcement veils with the merest gauze the trade of the abortionist:

Mr. B., Man-Midwife.—His fidelity, secrecy and discretion, may be relied on. He has few scruples to interrupt him in his calling, and will chearfully wait on *any person*, for a very moderate *fee*. He has lately made some *surprizing* attempts in the course of his business, in which

he is free to acknowledge that he has not been so successful as he expected; but he flatters himself that the *discerning* public will impute
the miscarriage to the peculiar and very difficult circumstances of the
case, than to any fault or mismanagement on his part.[18]

Yet, in spite of limited circulation and blatant advertising, the
American press was amazingly influential. Its vaporings and political
attitudes received the careful scrutiny of the highest public officials,
including the President himself; and a squib or article which appeared
in one paper, by virtue of likeminded editors reprinting from one
another, achieved an astonishing spread over the entire country.

The new government had not yet got under way when John Fenno
of Boston decided to venture to New York and start a newspaper "for
the purpose of disseminating favorable sentiments of the federal constitution, and its administration."[19] Under such circumstances he
found no difficulty in obtaining the proper introductions or a warm
welcome at the seat of government, together with more substantial
tokens in the form of official advertising.

The son of a Boston alehouse-keeper, Fenno had started his career
as an usher in a writing school and then had gone into trade. The business failed and he departed for New York to begin his newspaper.[20]
Later, when the seat of government was shifted to Philadelphia, he
moved with it.

The *Gazette of the United States* was never financially profitable,
and at one time Hamilton was compelled to raise $2000 to keep the
paper and its editor alive; but as the semiofficial organ of the administration and of the Federalist party it became a power in the land.
Industrious, fairly likable and with a small poetic talent, Fenno started
off mildly enough; but the exigencies of political controversy and the
attack of rival papers forced him into a heavy bludgeoning style and
a wide command of vituperation.

His chief and most inveterate opponent was Benjamin Franklin
Bache, better known as "Benny" Bache, the grandson of the famous
Dr. Franklin. Bache began his Philadelphia *General Advertiser* in
October 1790 as the organ of the antiadministration party. Through a
series of transformations the *Advertiser* finally became known as the
even more notorious *Aurora*.

Bache immediately became a thorn in the side of Hamilton, Washington and Federalists everywhere. His arsenal of billingsgate was
enormous, and his talent for poisonous innuendo even more formi-

dable. Only Philip Freneau, who at a later date published the *National Gazette,* got under the skin of the Federalists to the same extent that he did. Eventually, however, he met his match in the redoubtable William Cobbett, whose aptly named *Porcupine's Gazette* darted poisoned quills in every direction.

Two newspapers presented the opposing political views of Boston. The Federalists patronized the *Columbian Centinel,* while the Republicans read only the *Independent Chronicle.* Toward the end of our period more newspapers sprang up, if they did not exactly flourish, throughout the country. Almost every one of them was politically inspired, and equally envenomed. In New York, there were Noah Webster's *Minerva* (Federalist) and Thomas Greenleaf's *Argus* (Republican); in Hartford, the *Connecticut Courant* (Federalist); in Richmond, the *Examiner* (Republican). Each quoted extensively from the others, and attacked with a right good will opposing papers and opposing parties.

Objective news as such there was none, unless it happened to be a fact of nature like a fire, a nonpolitical death or an epidemic. And on occasion even these were made the subject of political animadversions. Most items were partisan in character and editorially inspired. The truth was not in them, unless it fitted with the preconceived political slant. The general stock in trade was epithets, abuse, violent reiterations of charges, attacks—and more attacks.

Yet these ink-stained, starveling hacks, at once the biters and the bitten, portrayed in their close-packed columns an unrivaled picture of the superheated times and of the storms that periodically swept the new nation from end to end.

Alexander Hamilton assumed his office as Secretary of the Treasury on September 11, 1789. Ten days later the House of Representatives called on him to submit a plan for the "adequate support of the public credit."

That the public credit needed support was patent to everyone; but how it was to be done baffled the imagination. No nation can long survive unless its finances are in tolerable order. There must be a steady and adequate income; debts must be paid or placed on such a basis that creditors are reasonably assured of eventual payment; and credit facilities must be such that money to meet emergencies may be readily borrowed at low interest rates.

Congress had already provided a means of revenue, but it was intended as a temporary stopgap until a more permanent and settled arrangement could be arrived at. And Congress had made no provision for the payment of the old public debt.

That debt had a long, sad history. The revolutionary colonies had neither money nor the means to raise the sums necessary for fighting a war. Paper tokens of money indeed were issued as fast as they could be printed, but their value, already depreciated in the moment of issuance, dropped with frightening rapidity from day to day. Only from amenable foreign governments could funds in the form of loans be obtained. The French were the chief lenders; later on, the Spanish government and private Dutch bankers added substantial sums.

These, however, proved insufficient as the war dragged its weary way. Tax collections were lamentably small, and both the Continental Congress and the several states were compelled to depend on notes of hand or promises to pay for supplies, food, military weapons and the soldiers' monthly stipend. While these were supposed to bear interest, that too was rarely met; and indents were issued—more promises to pay, and again bearing interest—in order to delay the day of judgment.

During the years the value of this compounded and undigested mass of paper money, certificates of indebtedness and indents kept on depreciating. Payment of any part of it seemed a long way off, or never. Those who were financially secure and possessed faith in the eventual stability of America placed the seemingly worthless paper in their strongboxes. The others—lacking faith or ready money —sold their holdings at tremendous discounts to hopeful or farseeing speculators.

There is no question that those who still clung to their certificates, the speculators who had purchased for a song, and the foreign lenders were unanimously in favor of the several moves to cement the nation by a written Constitution. A strong, enduring central government meant eventual payment in full. There is also no question that it was to the advantage of speculators to know in advance what plans were being made, once that government was established, to settle the debt.

One of the most active of their tribe, Andrew Craigie of Boston, stated his position with engaging candor. "The public Debt," he declared, "affords the best field in the world for speculation—but it is a field in which strangers may easily be lost. I know no way of making safe speculations but by being associated with people who from their official situation know all the present and can aid future arrangements either for or against the funds." [21]

Suiting action to words, Craigie made it his business to become intimate with William Duer of New York, a member of the Treasury Board during the Confederation and later to become Hamilton's Assistant Secretary of the Treasury. Duer was a fantastic character, whose life and checkered career deserves a full length biography.

Related by marriage to the powerful Schuyler family of New York, into which Hamilton had also married, Duer leaped from speculation to speculation with the agility of a mountain goat. Huge land schemes and far-flung financial operations alike were grist for his mill. He was a prime mover in the ill-fated Scioto Company and used his business and family connections to obtain tremendous land grants from a complaisant Congress. He and his wife, the so-called "Lady Kitty," set themselves up as the *bon ton* in New York, lived on the most lavish scale and entertained with princely munificence. No less than fifteen kinds of wine graced their dinner parties, nor would "Lady Kitty" dream of venturing into the street unless attended by two footmen in complete livery. [22]

Such a style of living obviously required a constant influx of money, and Duer found the wherewithal by buying and selling the Continental certificates of debt and their numerous progeny: indents, loan office certificates and evidences of final settlements. From his vantage points in the Treasury Board and the later Treasury Department, he occupied an incomparable position for gaining advance information through which to calculate nicely on his private operations. No wonder that Craigie was happy to associate himself with such a man; especially one whose business morals were notoriously easy and whose official probity was conspicuous by its absence.

Why Hamilton chose to appoint this known speculator as second to himself can be explained only by family connection, personal friendship and his philosophy of government. Hamilton's cardinal aim was to create a strong, vigorous centralized government which could provide order and stability to the domestic scene and earn the respect of nations abroad.

But to obtain such a government, he was convinced, he must gain the support of the moneyed class. That support, he realistically perceived, could be obtained only through self-interest. It did not matter to him, therefore, that the speculators profited by the fluctuations of the governmental debt, or that they were able to obtain advance information of his plans for paying it off. Rigorously honest in his own personal and public dealings, he viewed with a too tolerant eye the financial legerdemain of others. It was only, as later happened, when unrestrained speculation endangered his entire financial system that he publicly denounced it; and then on practical, not moral, grounds. Even when Duer's outrageous machinations finally brought him crashing to earth and Hamilton was compelled to cast him adrift, he did so with regret and without further denunciation.

Craigie, as an agile businessman should, had more than one string to his bow. He had watched the fall of the Continental certificates during the dark days of 1788, when it appeared most probable that the states would not ratify, to a low of two shillings six-pence on the pound (in modern currency, twelve and a half cents on the dollar). Yet he had hesitated to buy, fearing that New York would associate herself with the dissentients. When New York, because of Hamilton's superhuman exertions, placed herself under the Constitution, he lamented his indecision and determined he would not be caught napping again for lack of inside knowledge. He intended, he told a group of Dutch bankers, to "cultivate and improve such official connections as shall give me the best opportunity for acquiring information and forming just opinions respecting the finances and politics of the United States and it will give me pleasure if I should be able by any communication to serve your views." [23]

Craigie did cultivate his official connections, both then and later. When assumption hung in the balance, he obtained lodgings in the same quarters with Caleb Strong, Fisher Ames and Theodore Sedgwick, all leading congressional figures. They kept him regularly informed of the innermost workings of the legislative body, so that he could guide his private operations accordingly.[24]

As a result, he was able to send brokers down to the hinterlands of South Carolina to buy up certificates from the original holders. From these poor ignorants he purchased state paper at seven cents on the dollar; and sold it almost immediately at double the amount.[25]

Nor was Craigie the only one to foretell, by appropriate means, governmental moves before they were made. Joseph Barrell, another Boston speculator, put out feelers of his own. He wrote to a friend who was also a friend of Hamilton: "You know I have a considerable sum in indents, and as you are intimate with Mr. Hamilton, the man to whom we look for the resurrection of the Public Credit, I wish you would find out how his ideas [are] upon that matter. . . . I can then judge whether I had best dispose of them at the present price, or purchase more." [26]

This at least was getting knowledge at a remove. But the Dutch agent Theophile Cazenove was introduced to Duer in very plain terms by a mutual friend. "He [Cazenove] is to settle himself in America, and I believe to make some speculations in your funds. I am sure, knowing your obliging temper you'll give him good informations about his speculations; and I'll be much obliged to you to do it." [27]

Duer was indeed most obliging, not only to Cazenove, Craigie and others, but to himself as well. While in office, he continued to deal actively in certificates, and his private firm of Duer & Flint was able to purchase $30,000 of South Carolina paper early in 1790, at a time when the outlook for assumption in Congress, at least to the public view, was exceedingly dark.

His other dealings, while connected with the Board of Treasury, were even more shady, and are still wrapped in a fog of his own making through which only an occasional gleam of light manages to penetrate. One such was his successful attempt to foist himself on another speculator, James Jarvis of New York, in connection with a contract for the sale of copper to the United States. Jarvis at first refused to pay the *douceur* of $10,000 which Duer demanded for permitting the contract to go through; but second and more prudent thoughts prevailed. As the blackmailed speculator complained: "Tho I did not want his assistance, I wished him not interested against me." [28]

Though this transaction took place prior to his appointment by Hamilton, Duer did not hesitate to continue his larcenous practices under the aegis of his friend and benefactor. One in particular brought Hamilton more private and public humiliation than any other in all his tempestuous career.

Duer abstracted warrants on the Loan Office which were on deposit in the Treasury as already paid, and used them as collateral security for his personal engagements. When he was forced to default on the latter, the collateral warrants were sold by the creditor to Andrew Fraunces, a minor Treasury clerk who knew of their origin, and were boldly presented by him for repayment. Hamilton, becoming suspicious, conducted a quiet investigation, discovered they had been paid before, and refused to honor them. Yet he held his peace over Duer's part in the transaction.

But Fraunces was not so easily to be disposed of. He had hoped to make a tidy profit of $1500 on the deal; instead, he lost his original purchase price. Vowing vengeance, he bided his time until Hamilton himself departed from the government and became involved in an intimate relation with a certain Mrs. Reynolds. It is probable that Fraunces and his confederates may have instigated the tawdry romance for their own ends; in the course of which Hamilton was compelled to pay blackmail to an allegedly aggrieved husband.

When Hamilton had finally been mulcted of all he was able or willing to pay, Fraunces came up with a tale of himself as go-between in a joint series of speculations by Duer and Hamilton in which the latter obtained $30,000 from the Treasury. The stolen warrants and Hamilton's checks to Mr. Reynolds were produced as evidence. To extricate himself from the web of circumstances, Hamilton was compelled to lay bare to a snickering world the sordid story of his adulterous relations with Mrs. Reynolds.[29] Though the charges were thus disproved, Fraunces had had his revenge.

The demand of the House of Representatives on Hamilton for a plan to support the public credit found him eager to respond. He set to work immediately. It was a momentous task, one on which the future of the country might well depend. Yet the difficulties involved in any scheme he might suggest were truly enormous. Whatever was proposed was certain to arouse fierce opposition from groups which believed their interests jeopardized as a result.

Lacking in any financial training, guided only by precedents, extensive economic readings and years of thought devoted to theoretical solutions of the difficulties which had arisen during the Revolution and the period of the Confederation, Hamilton labored long into the nights gathering the requisite material, marshaling his facts and arranging his proposals in serried ranks.

He sought Madison's advice.[30] They had been collaborators in the initiation and final ratification of the Constitution; they had made one of the most successful partnerships in history in the writing of the *Federalist* papers. As an influential figure in Congress, Madison could do much to smooth the thorny path which any scheme of revenue must inevitably face when it came up for consideration before that argumentative body. As yet there were no signs that their paths were soon to diverge; though Hamilton certainly did not approve of his friend's proposals for retaliatory measures against England.

Nor was there any sign of divergence in Madison's reply. In essentials it agreed with Hamilton's own scheme. The foreign debt must necessarily be funded and placed on a sound interest-bearing basis, wrote Madison. On the knotty question of the domestic debt he was more cautious, though still not in disagreement. It would be "viewed in different lights by different classes of people," he said. "It might be a soothing circumstance to those least favorably disposed, if by some operation the debt could be lessened by purchases made on public account; and particularly if any impression could be made on it by means of the Western lands." [31]

If the response on the domestic portion was vague, it held no evidence of Madison's later clear-cut proposals either for partial repudiation or for differentiations. These followed suspiciously on the public reaction in Virginia and elsewhere after the publication of the plan.

By the beginning of 1790, Hamilton's First Report on Public Credit was ready for submission. It was a brilliant tour de force, bristling with facts, figures and arguments, discursive in tone yet compact in final effect, interlarded with ingenious analogies and perhaps too rich in intricate calculations that served only to bewilder the reader.[32]

It began with a series of almost platitudinous propositions. The debt, Hamilton asserted, "was the price of liberty," to the payment of which the national faith had been repeatedly pledged. Even the wealthiest nations on occasion found it necessary to borrow money. How much more did this necessity arise in a country possessing "little moneyed wealth." Hence a sound public credit was the first essential. How could this happy state be achieved? "By good faith; by a punctual performance of contracts. States, like individuals, who observe their engagements, are respected and trusted, while the reverse is the fate of those who pursue an opposite conduct."

On these elementary propositions Hamilton proceeded to erect a formidable structure. The country was faced with a dilemma. It could not, in any reasonably near future, liquidate the mass of the debt. It was impossible, however, to let it drift on its present uncharted course. But Hamilton cut the Gordian knot with a single bold stroke. He declared that the entire debt must be funded and put into a more usable, manageable form. Call in all the outstanding paper of whatever kind and issue in its place to the holders new certificates of indebtedness bearing interest and guaranteed by the establishment of a regular revenue devoted to the payment of the interest and the eventual extinguishment of the principal.

The new certificates—or governmental bonds, in the modern term —would be negotiable and legal tender in the payment of taxes and other public obligations. Indeed, as in England and elsewhere, once these certificates were firmly established in the public confidence, they would answer "most of the purposes of money. Transfers of stock or public debt are there [in England] equivalent to payments in specie; or, in other words, stock, in the principal transactions of business, passes current as specie." In a country like the United States where hard money—gold and silver coins—was scarce, such an issue would increase enormously the available amount of negotiable funds and enlarge the scope of business and financial transactions. Thereby trade would be extended, agriculture and manufactures promoted, interest rates lowered and land values increased.

With these general principles established, Hamilton next moved to the root of the matter. Who among the present holders of the old paper should be paid, and how much on the dollar?

There was no dispute over the holders of the foreign debt. Everyone agreed that eventually it must be paid in full. That accounted for some $11,700,000 of the total. The rub came on the domestically held debt, which amounted to over $49,000,000. Many of the original holders had been compelled through financial necessity or because of lack of faith to sell their certificates at prices as low as twelve cents on the dollar. They and their sympathizers would resent—and they said so plainly—any scheme that would reward the speculative purchasers at their expense. Would it not be better, they argued, to adopt one of two courses. Pay *all* holders at the current market value of the paper and thereby save the government considerable sums; or, in the alternative, differentiate between original holders and later purchasers. Pay the first class in full; pay the second class only what *they* had paid, with accrued interest, and turn over the balance to the original holders.

As Hamilton ticked off these propositions, he set them aside as unethical, impractical and subversive of all financial axioms. The argument for repayment at current market prices only, he dismissed as bad faith and ruinous of future public credit. The proposal for differentiation constituted a repudiation of the terms of the original contract. The Continental Congress had specifically made the original certificates assignable and negotiable; to change the terms now to the disadvantage of those who had bought in good faith would run counter to every view of fair dealing. And how, he asked, was it possible to determine the respective equities of those who had sold and those who had bought? In a considerable number of cases the certificates had changed hands many times. How adjudicate between the various holders in the line of title? What about those who had purchased and then sold at a loss? Who would be satisfied with any decision in the thousands of individual claims?

There was only one answer, Hamilton concluded. All claims must be paid in full to the current holders, with accrued interest, in accordance with the plighted word of the government.

So far, Hamilton had been concerned only with the *national* debt. But the states had also issued certificates and other evidences of debt for their own obligations. On these, Hamilton estimated, about $25,000,000 was still due.

Here the situation was even more complicated than in the case of the national debt. Thirteen separate states were involved, each with its own system of bookkeeping. Each had paid off some part of its obligations, though in varying degree. There had been no uniform or general system employed.

As a matter of fact, few anticipated that Hamilton would take the state debts into consideration. They seemed outside the purviews of the national government, and any attempt at interference an unwarranted intrusion on the sovereignties of the states.

Yet among those few were men of influence. Six months before, Christopher Gore of Massachusetts had declared that the federal government *ought* to take over the state debts, if only because such action would help consolidate the Union.[33] And, more recently, Fisher Ames hoped that Hamilton's report when issued would contain such a provision. "I am positive," he wrote, "there cannot be a safe and adequate revenue while the States and the United States are in competition for the product of the excises, etc. Wherefore the [state] debts must be assumed." [34]

Hamilton agreed with both men as to the basic idea and the reasons for its adoption. Every argument, he now reported, which had held good for the funding of the national debt, was equally valid for the assumption by the federal government of the state debts. Both must be intermingled in a common pool and consolidated in a single fund. The final certificates which would be issued in exchange must contain no internal evidence of the original obligation, whether it derived from the states or the nation.

With the fundamental base thus laid, Hamilton next considered the actual mechanics of funding, and provisions for payment of interest and principal. Here he unfortunately allowed his love of ingenious expedients and intricate alternatives to run away with him. He set up a system of complicated classes of stock, a sliding scale of rates of interest and a choice of straight repayments, annuities and "tontines" (annuities or lump sum payments based on survivorships) which was so complicated and undigested as to give rise to well-merited complaints.

Yet the acrid comment of Joe Jones of Virginia, who opposed all phases of the plan, was decidedly unfair. "I think," he wrote, "it well calculated to keep us all in the dark excepting those . . . who thrive on speculation." [35]

To this and other complaints of a similar nature, John Fenno replied in doggerel verse:

> The Secretary makes reports
> Whene'er the House commands him;
> But for their lives, some members say
> They cannot understand him.
> In such a puzzling case as this
> What can a mortal do?
> 'Tis hard for ONE to find REPORTS
> And understanding too.[36]

Actually, the opposition understood only too well the main features of the Report, and promptly mobilized their forces to defeat it at any hazard.

CHAPTER 6

Discriminations or No Discriminations

O N THE MORNING OF January 8, 1790, Washington entered his coach and six and set out for the Federal Hall. His journey took on the formidable appearance of a state procession. Before him rode his aides, Colonel Humphreys and Major William Jackson, dressed in full military array and mounted on white horses. Behind him rolled a chariot in which sat his secretaries, Tobias Lear and Thomas Nelson, Jr.; and bringing up the rear came Robert Lewis duly mounted. In back of the official family stretched a line of carriages, each with a solitary passenger: John Jay, Chief Justice of the United States; Alexander Hamilton, Secretary of the Treasury; and Henry Knox, Secretary of War.

The stately entourage wound its way through narrow streets to the entrance of the Hall, where doorkeepers handed them out and escorted them ceremoniously to the Senate chamber, in which both Houses were assembled. They led the President to the chair in which John Adams was wont to loll his short, stout body. As Washington mounted the platform, all rose to their feet; then, as he put on his spectacles and began to read, they sat down again.[1]

With such pomp and ceremony the Congress, in session assembled, greeted the first annual address of the President of the United States.

It was a short speech. The country, so the President declared, was in a satisfactory state. North Carolina had finally joined the Union, leaving only Rhode Island still outside the fold. Both credit and respectability were on the rise, and there was a general and increasing good will among the people toward the federal government.

Perhaps the first part of the statement was true; the second was doubtful. But annual addresses are given to generalizations and soothing phrases.

Not so soothing, however, was Washington's reference to Indian troubles on the frontier. In calling for a proper establishment of troops to cope with them, the President delivered himself of an apothegm. "To be prepared for war," he observed, "is one of the most effectual means of preserving peace."

He asked for a uniform rule of naturalization, and for a standard system of currency, weights and measures. He spoke of the necessity for the improvement and extension of the post office and post roads; and recommended in general terms the encouragement of science and literature, and the establishment of a national university.[2]

His speech finished, Washington bowed stiffly, sat down a moment, then arose and quit the chamber, leaving Congress to its own devices.

The House of Representatives certainly had much to engage its attention. On the Speaker's desk lay a short communication from Hamilton. He had, he said, prepared a plan for the support of the public credit which he would like to deliver in person before the assembled lawmakers. Would January 14th be satisfactory for his appearance?

Immediately Elbridge Gerry of Massachusetts was on his feet. It would *not* be satisfactory, he asserted, then or any other day. Let the Secretary submit his report in writing. The request should be granted, protested Elias Boudinot of New Jersey. "It is a justifiable surmise that gentlemen would not be able clearly to comprehend so intricate a subject without illustration."

But Boudinot stood almost alone. Even Fisher Ames thought that the propositions ought to be in writing; "in this shape they would obtain a degree of permanency favorable to the responsibility of the officer, while, at the same time, they would be less liable to be misunderstood."[3] And so it was voted.

Once again Congress had taken the decisive step in severing all personal relations with the members of the Cabinet. Gerry had feared the persuasive powers of the brilliant Secretary of the Treasury; Boudinot had welcomed them. Neither one realized that he was equally wrong; that the personal appearance of a Cabinet officer before the legislature, compelled to explain his ideas and to reply to questioning from the floor, thereby rendered him amenable to, and in a sense the creature of, that body. Once more Congress had unwittingly isolated itself from the Executive branch and given to the latter, powers it might not otherwise have possessed.

Thus rebuffed, Hamilton sent over his written report, coupled with proposals for increasing the revenue so that the interest charges on the funded debt might be met and the principal eventually extinguished. These included additional taxes on wines, spirits, teas and coffees, and the use of the postal revenues.

Incautiously he dropped a phrase which rose to haunt him again and again. "The proper funding of the present debt," he said, "will render it a national blessing." It was immediately hailed by the opposition as clear proof of his intention to fasten a permanent debt load on the United States. They failed, however, to quote also the qualifying statement: that Hamilton wished to "see it incorporated as a fundamental maxim in the system of public credit of the United States, that the creation of debt should always be accompanied with the means of extinguishment." [4]

The reaction to the report, in Congress and out, was immediate and acrimonious. If all the complexities of Hamilton's provision for payments were not wholly understood, the principles of the funding operation itself were. Men ranged themselves for and against on the basis of their previous convictions, economic status and belief in the desirability of a strong or a weak central government.

Another line of cleavage disclosed itself. There were those who could see the logic and necessity for funding the national debt; but refused to accept the thesis that the state debts should be taken over also. The plight of the "old soldier" who had been compelled to sell his certificates at a fraction of their face value excited the sympathy of many; the orgy of speculation which followed the first rumor of Hamilton's report aroused the indignation of others. A score of crosscurrents prevented any impartial consideration of the report on its merits.

The spotlight was first thrown on the initial half of Hamilton's program: the funding of the *national* debt. The right of foreign holders to be paid in full was agreed to as involving the national honor. But on the domestic debt passions, self-interest, sympathy and discordant philosophies of government had a field day.

In the markets of New York, Philadelphia and Boston the price of the old Continental securities was jumping daily. Accusations filled the air. It was loudly asserted that members of Congress, friends and relatives of Hamilton, and business associates of William Duer, all possessed of advance information, had hastened to feather their nests.

Now he understood, exclaimed Senator Maclay when Hamilton's

report was laid on his desk, why the public securities had been rising so rapidly. He saw members of Congress from his own state deep in speculation. Robert Morris of the Senate and Thomas Fitzsimons of the House were buying furiously. Jeremiah Wadsworth of Connecticut sent two small vessels, loaded with smooth-talking agents and money-bags, to Southern ports to buy up the precious certificates before their holders got wind of the proceedings up north. Others rushed expresses by land to the back country of North Carolina for the same laudable purpose. This would, wrote Maclay indignantly, "in all probability damn the character of Hamilton as a minister forever." 5

Maclay even suspected Washington of having a hand in the direful proceedings and darkly suspected the motive when the President invited him to dinner. "Yet he knows," he brooded self-righteously, "how rigid a republican I am. I cannot think that he considers it worth while to soften me. It is not worth his while. I am not an object if he should gain me, and I trust he can not do it by any improper means." 6

Madison had been observing the conduct of his colleagues and of less public speculators with similar if less naïve misgivings. Even before Hamilton issued his report, Madison had written to Jefferson, still down in Virginia, that "the avidity for stock had raised it from a few shillings to eight shillings or ten shillings in the pound, and emissaries are still exploring the interior and distant part˙ of the Union in order to take advantage of the ignorance of holders." 7

The full-throated cry spilled over into the newspapers, and a cascade of bad verse inundated their hapless subscribers.

The semiofficial *Gazette of the United States* rushed to the speculators' defense:

> Says JOE to JEM, this speculation,
> Will prove the ruin of the nation.
> Gods! that these fellows thus should thrive,
> When you and I can scarcely live.

> Says JEM to JOE, this speculation,
> Has sav'd the *credit* of the nation;
> For when fate stop'd the new emission,
> *Their cash* preserv'd us from perdition. 8

Not to be outdone, an opposition paper came up with its own masterpiece:

> 'Pay the poor soldier!—He's a sot.'
> Cries our grave ruler Boudinot.

'No pity, *now*, from us he claims,'
In artful accents, echoes Ames:
'In *war*, to heroes let's be just,
In *peace*, we'll write their toils in dust;
A soldier's pay are rags and fame,
A wooden leg—a deathless name.
To Specs, both *in* and *out* of Cong,
The four and six per cents belong.' [9]

That Hamilton had disclosed in advance the main outlines of his report to a favored few cannot be denied; that they rushed to take advantage of the information for their personal benefit is equally true.[10] But the widely believed accusation that he hastened to feather his own nest cannot be sustained. At no time did he own a single share of the debt; even later, when it had been transmuted into funded obligations of the United States, he never possessed more than a few hundred dollars' worth. When he quit his post he was actually poorer than when he went in.

Unfortunately, the same cannot be said for the members of his immediate family. Both his father-in-law, General Philip Schuyler, and his brother-in-law, John Barker Church, traded heavily in the certificates and made substantial profits when they were funded.[11] Hamilton even went so far as to act as agent for Church, then in England, in the purchase and sale of the certificates.

A storm of anger was gathering inside the walls of Congress. Those who took no part in the rampant speculation resented the activities of those who did. The flood of rumors, charges and dark tales of chicanery, plus the avalanche of indignant letters from back home, swayed even those who had at first agreed in principle with the leading ideas of Hamilton's plan.

On January 28, 1790, under the eyes of a crowded gallery, James Jackson of Georgia took the floor. He was already known as one of the most vociferous and passion-tearing members of the House. At one time, he cried, he had tended to agree with Hamilton's thesis of no discrimination between original holders and their assignees. But circumstances had changed his mind. "Since this report has been read in this House," he shouted, "a spirit of havoc, speculation, and ruin, has arisen and been cherished by people who had an access to the information the report contained. . . . Three vessels, sir, have sailed within a fortnight from this port, freighted for speculation; they are

intended to purchase up the State and other securities in the hands
of the uninformed, though honest citizens of North Carolina, South
Carolina and Georgia. My soul rises indignant at the avaricious and
immoral turpitude which so vile a conduct displays." He therefore
demanded that the report be laid over until May.[12]

Boudinot retorted that the longer the delay, the more chance it gave
speculators to pick up certificates. Roger Sherman of Connecticut
called for immediate consideration at least of the national debt. But
the first member to rise to the defense of speculation as such was
Elbridge Gerry.

Gerry's politics changed with such chameleonlike rapidity that it
is sometimes difficult to follow him in all his divagations. He commenced his public career as an extreme antifederalist and refused,
while in the Constitutional Convention, to sign the finished document. As a result he narrowly escaped defeat in Massachusetts for a
seat in the current Congress. As if to disprove the charges circulated
against him, he now became an ardent federalist. Later on he
switched again, disrupted the unity of the American mission to France
during the notorious "XYZ" affair and joined the Jeffersonian Republicans.

Just now he was in his Federalist phase. Speculation, he insisted,
was a good thing, particularly on the part of foreign-money men. It
raised the value of the debt and helped the credit of the United States.
However, since the delegation from the newly joined state of North
Carolina was momentarily expected, he was willing to postpone consideration until March. Boudinot, who agreed with Gerry on the uses
of speculation, opposed any lengthy adjournment; and so did other
members of what came to be known as the Hamiltonian "phalanx."
They mustered sufficient strength to postpone only to February 8th.[13]

But Hamilton became alarmed. He had not anticipated any such
concerted opposition. He scurried from member to member, employing
all his arts to hold the faithful in line and to convert the skeptical. He
was moving heaven and earth, observed the dour Maclay, and engaging even the Cincinnati (a society of the officers of the Revolution)
as well as the merchants of New York to further his cause.[14]

If Maclay might be dismissed as a prejudiced witness, the testimony
of the Reverend Manasseh Cutler, himself an archspeculator, must
be believed. He asserted that "the friends to the assumption depend
more on management out of doors than within, and I believe, will out-
general their opponents." Fisher Ames was another one whose outdoor
missionary work was most effective.[15]

But though the postponement gave the Hamiltonians a chance to align their forces, it helped the opposition as well. Jackson veered from an "almost" to an unqualified dissent. Madison, who initially had not mentioned discriminations, now decided definitely in their favor. Hamilton's report, he now declared, was "faulty in many respects." What particularly grated on him was that unfortunate phrase of Hamilton: that a public debt might become a public blessing. On the contrary, complained Madison, "a Public Debt is a Public curse, and in a Representative Government a greater than in any other." [16]

As for the proposed assumption of the state debts, he disliked it altogether. It was, he avowed, "particularly unfriendly to the interests of Virginia." [17] Indeed, of all that state's numerous delegation, only one, Colonel Bland, supported the proposal, and he died of the influenza before the matter came to a crucial vote.

While both sides were thus busily engaged in strengthening their lines, Congress took up other pending matters. Madison had proposed that the census ordered for 1790 be much more than a mere enumeration and counting of heads. In order to legislate properly, he argued, it was essential to "know the various interests of the United States" and its great divisions and classes. But Livermore of New Hampshire objected on the ground that people might be afraid the additional inquiries were intended "to learn their ability to bear the burden of direct or other taxes." [18] The House, however, agreed to Madison's amendment.

The next question involved the right of aliens to become naturalized citizens of the United States. Several plans were offered, ranging from a residential requirement of fourteen years to none at all. The radical Jackson of Georgia expressed his unalterable opposition to any rule that might encourage immigration. "Rather than have the common class of vagrants, paupers and other outcasts of Europe," he stormed, "we had better be as we are, and trust to the natural increase of our population for inhabitants."

In this ultrarestrictionist policy he was abetted by the conservative Theodore Sedgwick of Massachusetts, who thought that future immigrants might be so steeped in monarchical and aristocratical principles as to deprive them of any "zest for pure republicanism." [19]

This curious switch of radical and conservative, coupled with other utterances based on religious differences, exasperated John Page of Virginia into making the greatest speech of his otherwise not outstanding career. "We shall be inconsistent with ourselves," he thundered, "if, after boasting of having opened an asylum for the oppressed of all nations, and established a Government which is the admiration of the world, we make the terms of admission to the full enjoyment of that asylum so hard as is now proposed. It is nothing to us, whether Jews or Roman Catholics settle amongst us; whether subjects of kings, or citizens of free States wish to reside in the United States, they will find it their interest to be good citizens, and neither their religious nor political opinions can injure us, if we have good laws, well executed." [20]

Eventually a compromise was reached, and a term of two years' residence was set for free white aliens, with the provision that they must first obtain proofs of good character from competent persons in the community where they resided.[21]

On February 8th the House returned to its main theme—Hamilton's report. Boudinot led off with a long historical argument to prove that funding was essential for gaining the confidence of "moneyed men" in the government; and Fitzsimons followed with a series of resolutions intended to put the report in effect.[22]

The first resolution, for the payment of the foreign debt, met with no opposition; though Jackson inveighed against the whole idea of a "permanent funded debt." Why should the productive tiller of the soil, he demanded, stagger under a heavy burden of taxes so that "the indolent and idle creditor" might be able to take his ease in the large cities? Why should there be taxes altogether? Why could not the Western lands be sold to meet all debts and the expenses of the government?[23]

If Jackson stood alone in this vision of an untaxed nation, he had plenty of company when the domestic debt came up for consideration. Here the floodgates of oratory and of wrath opened to let out the deluge. But the Northern men received unexpected aid from a solitary Virginian. Bland, with the shadow of death imperceptibly upon him, disregarded the black looks of his colleagues to argue sturdily that he could see no difference between foreign and domestic creditors. In turn, Livermore of New Hampshire plumped with the embattled South. The domestic creditors, he asserted, were mainly of two classes: original holders who had profiteered during the Revolution, or speculators who had purchased from needy soldiers at tremendous discounts. If we paid them off at current market price, he cried, they still would be making an excellent profit on their investment.[24]

Ames rose in hot anger. "What is the object for which men enter into society," he wished to know, "but to secure their lives and property. . . . Shall it be said that this Government, evidently established for the purpose of securing property, that in its first act, it divested its citizens of seventy millions of money, which is justly due to the individuals who have contracted with Government!" [25]

Livermore punctured his rhetoric, however, with a counterquery. If the claims of property were so sacred, why did no one advocate payment in full to the holders of the old Continental paper money which, in truth, had become "not worth a Continental"? But, continued Livermore, he was willing to see the domestic creditors paid, and in full, *provided* the proposed rate of interest on the funded certificates was reduced from six to either three or four per cent.[26]

As Livermore doubtless knew, any such reduction was certain to meet with violent opposition from the creditors and their supporters. The Boston merchant Christopher Gore described their attitude very plainly. The creditors here, he wrote, "are numerous and important, and are so attached to property that we have reason to fear they would change sides rather than lose any share of the blessing—a less rate of interest than 4 per cent you may rest assured will never be acceded to by nine tenths of the creditors in Massachusetts. Consider the great holders in this town, Bowdoin, Phillips, Breck, Mason and Moses Gill; and think if they will accede to anything less than 4 per cent— and if this pill must not be gilded to insure success, farewell." [27]

Farewell indeed, to patriotism, to government, to national security. Of such was the "interest" of these gentry compounded.

Gore again returned to the congenial theme, in phrases that might have been penned by Hamilton himself. The "solid" men of Boston, he wrote, were exclaiming against the idea that funding of the national debt be held up until the state debts were similarly funded. "They say this money is taken from their pockets, and from trade in general, to be locked up in the chests of the treasury, or spent by the immediate officers of Government." Unless, therefore, Congress put the revenue money speedily in circulation again—in the form of interest payments —"the collection of duties will be as unpopular, as under the British government." [28]

Still harping on the same theme, Gore reported that the importing merchants of Salem were openly preaching resistance to the payment of duties. "For what purpose," they growled, "do we pay our money into the Collector's chest—none of it returns—and what can oblige us to visit the Customs House, on an arrival?"

But Gore had a simple solution for quelling such revolutionary talk, and he passed it on to Senator King of New York. In Hamiltonian accents he declared that it was necessary "that some men should be bound to this government by strong pecuniary ties, and which ties are not obvious to the public view. . . . What other chain so binding as that of involving the interest of the men of property in the prosperity of the Government?" [29]

Whatever else may be said of the men of this era, it cannot be said that they were not plainspoken in their avowals among themselves.

With the mercantile class thus patriotically willing to resort to smuggling and evasion of duties if the debt were not funded at par, with a good rate of interest attached; and with the gentleman plantationers and farmers, animated by an equal patriotism, refusing to be saddled with taxes to meet the obligations of government at face value, it was obvious that matters had come to an impasse.

At this point of extreme delicacy the Quakers of Pennsylvania and New York saw fit to petition Congress to stop "the abominable commerce" of the slave trade. And abolition societies, claiming such influential members as Benjamin Franklin, Dr. Benjamin Rush, John Jay, and later Alexander Hamilton, followed suit.

Even in the slaveholding South, thinking men like Jefferson, Madison, Washington and others were convinced that slavery was a curse and were cautiously advocating some system of eventual emancipation. Certainly the stopgap remedy of the discontinuance of the slave trade met with the approval of many Southerners.

Nevertheless, the presentation of the petitions at this particular time, and particularly from Northern groups, caused the tempers of an already irritated Congress to explode. The immediate question before the House was merely one of procedure—that the petitions be referred to a committee for study and possible report. Under ordinary circumstances debate was purely formal; but in this instance it rapidly widened to engulf the House for over a week in acrimony, insults and retorts ad hominem that pushed aside not only funding but all other business.

In a sense Northern members were responsible. They rose not only to speak in favor of commitment, but to avow their hearty support of the petitions themselves. Even Madison and John Page, both of Virginia, expressed their readiness to restrict the nefarious trade.

But the overwhelming mass of Southern members, sensitive to any probing of their "peculiar institution," reacted with extreme violence. Stone of Maryland opened fire with a savage attack on the Quakers themselves. "It was an unfortunate circumstance," he shouted, "that it was the disposition of religious sects to imagine they understood the rights of human nature better than all the world besides; and that they would, in consequence, be meddling with concerns in which they had nothing to do."

Aedanus Burke, the firebrand of South Carolina, was even more direct. These meddling Quakers, he sneered, thought they had more virtue and religion than other folk. Perhaps, if the truth were known, they had less "if they were examined to the bottom, notwithstanding their outward pretenses." [30]

Northern men promptly rose to the defense of the abused Quakers, but could not stop the infuriated Southerners. "Is the whole morality of the United States," cried Jackson, "confined to the Quakers? Are they the only people whose feelings are to be consulted on this occasion?" [31]

As members glared at one another, and tempers rose, the portent of future civil war cast its lengthening shadow over the contestants. As insult was compounded on injury by the presentation of still another petition—this one by the Pennsylvania Society for Promoting the Abolition of Slavery, signed by its president, Benjamin Franklin —the shadow thickened into visible form. Though the petition made no mention of emancipation, but echoed the Quaker request for the discontinuance of the slave trade, Tucker of Virginia promptly declared that any attempt at emancipation would touch off civil war; while Burke averred that even a commitment of the petition "would sound an alarm, and blow the trumpet of sedition in the Southern States." [32] As for the aged Franklin, already on the verge of death, intimations were freely spread that he had lost what little wits he had ever possessed.

With such angry charges and violent distortions emanating from their representatives in Congress, it was no wonder that the people of the South gave ready ear to the wildest rumors. Congress was intending, so it was said and believed, to emancipate all Negro slaves immediately. Even in Virginia, more sensible than her neighbors to the south and not averse to regulation of the slave trade, people took alarm and rushed to sell their slaves for the "merest trifle." [33]

Madison sought vainly to spread oil over the troubled waters. As he pointed out to Southern hotheads, "had they permitted the commitment of the memorial, as a matter of course, no notice would have been taken of it out of doors," and it could never have been blown up into a full-dress debate not only on the slave trade but on abolition as well.[34]

The South refused to be pacified. Jackson came up with a lengthy defense of slavery as an institution; and Baldwin of Connecticut retorted that the South had been willing even to break up the Constitutional Convention unless they got their way on it.[35]

Stung by the taunt, Smith of South Carolina shouted back: "When we entered into this confederacy, we did it from political, not from moral motives, and I do not think my constituents want to learn morals from the petitioners. I do not believe they want improvement in their moral system; if they do, they can get it at home." [36]

As the debate threatened to burst all bounds, the more levelheaded Northerners, assisted by Madison and Page, finally gave assurances that neither emancipation nor any other unconstitutional measures would be discussed in the committee. As a result, the tumult subsided and all the petitions were referred.

This was not the end, however. Later on the issue was once again dragged out for further astonishing displays of rancor that held up essential business for days at a time. By March 21st it still was going full tilt and Jonathan Trumbull of Connecticut, thoroughly alarmed at the disastrous effect it had on Hamilton's entire program, reported disgustedly: "The whole of the past week has been wasted with the Quakers and the Negroes. The South Carolina and Georgia members have taken up the matter with as much warmth and zeal as though the very exist ?nce of their States depended on the decision on the Committee Report. . . . In the mean time all discussion on [Hamilton's] Report is at a stand." [37]

Hamilton's business had indeed been momentarily spiked by the interposition of the petitions. It moved tortuously and with exceeding slowness through the obstacles which the Quakers in all innocence had raised.

Madison had been strangely silent through the initial stages of the funding debate. Perhaps he had not yet fully decided on his stand; perhaps he waited to hear the repercussions from Virginia. On

February 11th, however, he rose in the House to deliver one of his greatest efforts. The members strained to hear his low, even tones.

He declared first that the national debt was a full and valid obligation, both as to principal and interest. Thereby he laid to rest the proposal that only the original holders be paid in full; that all others receive at most the current market price of the securities.

Then, having made his obeisance to the Hamiltonians, he proceeded to his own principle of differentiation. Let the creditors be divided into four classes, he said: first, the original holders still in possession; second, the original holders who had sold their certificates; third, current holders who had purchased from them; and fourth, intermediate holders no longer in possession.

As to the first class, there was no dispute. All agreed they must be paid in full. Nor was there any question on the fourth class; they had no rights, either legal or moral. The whole difficulty came in the consideration of the second and third classes—the original assignors and the ultimate assignees. Both, he argued, had claims which must be taken into account on a final settlement. Why not, then, come to an equitable compromise? Pay the final holders a sum representing the highest price of the certificates in the open market; and pay the difference between that price and face value to the original holders.[38]

Madison's plan, embodied in a resolution, satisfied neither party. The Hamiltonians accused him of a denial of his position as outlined in his earlier letter to Hamilton. He was now attempting to play politics, they charged. The accusation troubled the sensitive Madison. He defended himself to his own conscience in a memorandum which he attached to his private notes. It read: "This explains the apparent change in Mr. Madison's opinion from his previous one opposed to discriminations. At that time the debts were due to the original holders." [39]

This was not so. The certificates had been sold, assigned and traded in even during the Revolution, and on an ever-increasing scale thereafter. The final burst of speculation during and after the period of Constitution-making was a mere capstone on a structure already well erected.

Nor did the plan meet with the approval of Madison's usual associates. The sharp-tongued Maclay thought him obstinate, peevish and selfish; and his scheme even more dangerous than Hamilton's because it tended to hoodwink Congress into accepting the funding plan as such. Funding, he exclaimed, was the "political gout of every government which has adopted it. With all our Western lands for sale and purchasers every day attending at the Hall begging for contracts! What villainy to cast the debt on posterity!" [40]

But Maclay's vanity had been touched when Madison refused to heed his advice or use resolutions which he had drawn. "It hurt his *Littleness,*" wrote the Pennsylvanian in some spleen.[41]

He was not the only one who believed in the Western lands as the cure-all for every financial ill. But he failed to note, or noting did not care, that the ones who were clamoring for contracts were just as much speculators as those who traded in the certificates of debt; that they demanded princely grants for a pittance; and that present alienation of the lands would mean the future mulcting of individual and legitimate settlers.

In his native state, Madison received acclaim for his solution; though the conservative Edward Carrington pointed out that it had been the first holders of the certificates who had insisted they be made negotiable, and therefore could not now equitably take another tack.[42]

From the militant Dr. Rush came warm praise. Hamilton's plan, he told Madison, would place "a stain upon our Country which no time nor declamation can ever wash away." In a burst of fuddled thinking he saw the funds eventually falling into the hands of foreigners and at the same time laying the foundations of an aristocracy here.[43]

Henry Lee, better known as Light Horse Harry Lee, informed Madison that his stand had received the general approval of Virginia's landed interest, but was "disrelished" by the town merchants.[44]

But the Hamiltonians in Congress fell on Madison *vi et armis.* One after another rose to riddle his arguments and demolish his premises— Boudinot, Sedgwick, Ames, Gerry, Smith of South Carolina and Lawrence of New York. Even Aedanus Burke and Samuel Livermore, originally in favor of discriminations, now deserted to the enemy. Only Jackson and Page came to Madison's assistance in a vain attempt to stem the tide.

On February 22nd, Madison's motion was decisively beaten by a vote of 36 to 13. Only nine Virginians and four scattering votes from the South stood firm. Thereupon the triumphant Hamiltonians pressed to final passage all of Fitzsimons's original resolutions.[45]

The first round had been won. The second, and more decisive one, was now to begin. This related to the assumption of the state debts by the national government.

CHAPTER 7

A Bargain Is Made

IF THERE HAD BEEN dissension and bitterness in connection with the funding of the national debt, it was as nothing compared to the storm over the second phase of Hamilton's plan: that the national government assume the payment of the debts which the states had incurred during the Revolution and intermingle them with its own.

A seeming paradox developed. The devotees of the national government were most strongly in favor of taking over the staggering load; the advocates of state sovereignty were bitterly opposed. Yet the reasons were logical and clear.

Hamilton made no secret of his intentions. He frankly asserted that assumption would strengthen the Union and make it a matter of self-interest both for the states and the creditors for the central government to endure and be able to pay. It would also provide the government with a powerful argument for asking authority to lay uniform and general taxes and to seek the exclusion of duplicating levies by the states.

The states were equally frank in setting forth their point of view. New England, though, wished for a strong Union. Its component states had as a whole not met their debts or made adequate provision for their payment, and were only too happy to unload them on the national government. In the South the case was different. Those states which, like Georgia, had incurred very few obligations during the Revolution saw no reason why their citizens should be taxed to meet the obligations of the others. Virginia, whose debt load had been heavy, had already paid off a substantial portion and now inquired why she should be penalized in taxes to meet the debts of her less diligent sisters.

Overriding all financial considerations, however, was the fear of the very thing which Hamilton desired: that assumption would so strengthen and centralize the national government as to make the hitherto sovereign states its mere appendages. What further com-plicated and bedeviled the issue was the spectacle of Northern men of wealth seeking out holders of state certificates in the remotest areas and buying them up at tremendous discounts.

Even such a staunch federalist as Edward Carrington of Virginia took alarm when it came to assumption. Though the principle itself might be wise, he wrote, "as matters *actually* stand among the States, it is truly iniquitous unless each state were considered as a creditor for so much of its debts as it has already redeemed; some states have discharged considerable parts of their debts, whilst others have paid not a farthing of theirs. An assumption by the General Government of none but the outstanding debts of the states, would in becoming a common burthen, operate grievous oppressions upon those who have already burthened their people with taxes to reduce the amount of their debt." [1]

Madison was literally bombarded with letters from home avowing unalterable opposition to assumption. He was told that its passage would mean the return to power of the antifederalist Patrick Henry who had predicted just such encroachments from the ratification of the Constitution. [2]

It is small wonder then that Madison fought the plan tooth and nail in Congress. It would have been worth his political life had he done otherwise.

Only Washington in his presidential aloofness resisted the home pressures. He replied to a complainant with unaccustomed asperity. Virginia, he declared, was "more irritable, sour and discontented" than any other state in the Union except Massachusetts. The trouble was, he continued, that the enemies of the government always placed "malignant constructions" on every move; and even its friends, if defeated on any measure, hastened to write home imputing "the worst motives for the conduct of their opponents."

By this time the President was angry and sore over a number of other and more personal imputations. From Virginia had come mali-cious criticisms of his "day" for "the reception of idle and ceremonious visits." What was wrong with it? he fumed. How else could he get business done on the other days? People came and went during a single hour on Tuesdays. "At their *first* entrance they salute me, and I them, and as many as I can talk to I do. What pomp there is in all this, I am unable to discover."

What touched him even more to the quick was a reported remark of Colonel Bland disparaging the "stiffness" of his bows. These were, retorted the President rather pathetically, "the best I was master of. Would it not have been better to throw the veil of charity over them, ascribing their stiffness to the effects of age, or to the unskillfulness of my teacher, than to pride and dignity of office, which God knows has no charms for me?" [3]

In Pennsylvania, a Middle State, there was also considerable opposition to assumption. Some national creditors were against the idea, fearing that the addition of the state debts would, by sharing in the federal revenues, impede or delay the payments on their own certificates. The antifederalists were naturally open-mouthed in their opposition. They cried up "the old demon, *consolidation*, which they raised up as a bugbear to prevent the adoption of the Constitution," Tench Coxe reported. There were even federalists against the idea, as in Virginia. For Pennsylvania owed little on its debt and its citizens held a considerable amount of the national securities. [4]

And in rock-ribbed Massachusetts, too, there were rumblings. The antifederalists there were so alarmed over the thought that they were tempting the state creditors to fight assumption by offering them any terms they wished for the payment of their certificates. The only way to hold the state creditors in line, wrote Gore, was to guarantee them a minimum of four per cent interest on their funds. [5]

In such an atmosphere of conflicting political and economic interests the great debate on assumption began on February 23, 1790.

The opponents of the measure sought to delay consideration, but the Hamiltonians pressed for immediate action, expatiating at length on the manifold advantages of assumption both for the nation and the component states. Stone of Maryland, on the other hand, heaped ridicule on the idea. "A greater thought," he ironically exclaimed, "could not have been conceived by man." It was quite true, he said, that assumption would make the federal government impregnable. If it took over "the payment of all the debts it must, of course, have all the revenue; if it possesses the whole revenue, it is equal, in other words, to the whole power; the different States will then have little to do." And in that case, they must wither away and leave the federal government solitary and supreme. [6]

But this appeal to state patriotism ran on a hidden shoal in the form of South Carolina. That state lay under a heavy load of debt and had made little or no attempt to pay her creditors. So that Aedanus

Burke, ordinarily amenable to the slightest hint of an encroachment on state sovereignty, now went over to the assumptionists. He was quite frank in the avowal of his reasons. His state, he declared, would otherwise be forced into bankruptcy; she is "no more able to grapple with her enormous debt, than a boy of twelve years is able to grapple with a giant." [7]

The Virginia delegation had thus far sat in silence, permitting their friends to bear the burden of debate. But South Carolina's defection impelled them to step into the breach. Madison had already led off in cautious vein. From the trend of the argument he foresaw that an outright general attack might end in disaster; he therefore, while accepting in part the principle of assumption, proposed a series of qualifying amendments. Let us first, he said, arrange for a final settlement of accounts between the states and the United States; after that was done, then the general government could take over the balances. In that way those states which had paid off most of their debts would not be burdened with taxes for the benefit of states which had been delinquent. [8]

Richard Bland Lee went a step further. Such a settlement, he insisted, must take into account only the war debts of the several states, and not those incurred in time of peace. John Page, on the other hand, opposed assumption altogether on the ground that it would give the general government the power to levy direct taxes and thereby tend to "consolidation." [9]

Jackson of Georgia was more violent. He was opposed to assumption "not only in its original form, but in every possible modification it might assume." We must not, he cried, "run ourselves enormously in debt, and mortgage ourselves and our children, to give scope to the abilities of any Minister on earth." [10]

This was a direct slap at Hamilton. But it was as nothing to the insults heaped on him by Aedanus Burke, for all the latter's ending up in his camp, or perhaps because of it. The insults were so cruel that everyone was certain it must end in a duel. Maclay thought that the general agitation "may really make the fools fight." [11] But the matter was settled without a personal encounter.

Alexander White of Virginia moved that Hamilton inform the House just how he intended to pay the state debts should assumption pass. On this first test vote an equal balance of parties was disclosed. It stood at 25 to 25, and was broken only by the casting vote of the Speaker in favor of the motion. Hamilton immediately reported that he would propose further duties on imports to provide the necessary funds.

The equal vote, however, alarmed his supporters. Some of their most active men were absent, and Ames deemed it wise to mark time until they returned. Fortunately the lengthy uproar created by the Quaker petition intervened to permit this strategic delay.[12]

Even when the missing members resumed their seats—Fitzsimons and Clymer of Pennsylvania and Wadsworth of Connecticut—the issue continued to hang in the balance. Wadsworth himself wrote gloomily: "I almost begin to despair of the assumption of the State debts, and with that I shall despair of the National Government."

John Quincy Adams, the youthful and brilliant son of the Vice-President, viewed the situation prophetically from afar. "It appears to me," he said, "that the hostile character of our general and particular governments each against the other is increasing with accelerating rapidity. The spirit which at the time when the Constitution was adopted, it was contended would always subsist of balancing one of these governments by the other has I think almost totally disappeared already, and the seeds of two contending factions appear to be plentifully sown. The names of Federalist and Anti-federalist are no longer expressive of the sentiments which they were so lately supposed to contain, and I expect soon to hear a couple of new names, which will designate the respective friends of the national and particular systems. The people are evidently dividing into these two parties."[13]

In the Senate, too, behind closed doors, a bitter and partisan fight was raging. Senator Maclay watched with ironic satisfaction the despair of Hamilton's "Senatorial Gladiators" over the issue. "Ellsworth and Izard in particular," he confided to his journal, "walked almost all morning back and forward. Strong and Patterson seemed moved, but not so much agitated. King looked like a boy that had been whipped, and General Schuyler's hair stood on end as if the Indians had fired at him."[14]

On April 12th came the climax. The issue of assumption was put to a vote in the lower House, and the senators quit their own chamber to witness the result. It was close, but seemingly decisive. By a count of 31 to 29, assumption went down to defeat.

The world appeared to crash for the Hamiltonians. Sedgwick rose to pronounce what the sardonic Maclay called "a funeral oration." In bitter tones he warned that his state of Massachusetts would not submit tamely to the verdict. "We have demanded justice," he cried, "we have implored the compassion of the Representatives of the People of America, to relieve us from the pressure of intolerable burthens; burthens incurred in support of your freedom and independence. Our demands and entreaties have both been ineffectual." [15]

When he had finished he clapped his hat on his head and stalked out of the room, leaving the members in an uproar. A little later he returned, his eyes red and his face displaying "visible marks of weeping."

The ensuing scene almost defied description. In Maclay's colorful if partisan reporting it mingled elements of high tragedy and wildest burlesque. "Fitzsimons reddened like scarlet; his eyes were brimful. Clymer's color, always pale, now verged to a deadly white; his lips quivered, and his nether jaw shook with convulsive motions." The usually resourceful Ames "sat torpid, as if his faculties had been benumbed." Elbridge Gerry shouted that the Massachusetts delegation would take no further part in the business of the House, but would send to their state for instructions. Wadsworth "hid his grief under the rim of a round hat. Boudinot's wrinkles rose in ridges and the angles of his mouth were depressed and assumed a curve resembling a horse's shoe."

Only Fitzsimons was able to think coherently. He hoped, he said, that "the good sense" of the House would lead them to reconsider their vote and adopt the proposal with proper modifications. At this suggestion, Maclay noted, "the Secretary's group pricked up their ears, and Speculation wiped the tear from either eye." [16]

Fitzsimons's calmer counsels prevailed. The Massachusetts delegation remained in their seats; and two days later new motions were being made for the adoption of assumption, with sufficient modifications to have them technically constitute new bills. Madison, perturbed at "the uncommon perserverance with which the advocates for an assumption adhere to their object," now attacked the entire measure as unconstitutional; a question which had not previously been raised in debate. [17]

Meanwhile the cause of all the hubbub, Alexander Hamilton, exuded to the outer world a calm confidence that assumption would pass; if not at the current session, then the next one. [18] But the speculators were skeptical. One in particular, Andrew Craigie, lamented later that only a few days before assumption did finally triumph he had unloaded his certificates of the South Carolina debt, purchased at three and six to the pound or under, at an insignificant profit of four-pence on the pound. A canny Dutch agent snapped them up and made a large fortune for his principals in Holland.[19] Craigie should have had more faith in the resourcefulness and mental agility of the Secretary of the Treasury.

For some time Hamilton had been observing the, to him, unac-countable passions that had been aroused in Congress over the choice of a permanent site for the capital of the United States. The New England states wanted it placed, with some degree of reason, at a geographical midpoint. Either New York, the temporary residence, or Philadelphia was acceptable to them. New York naturally wished it to remain where it was; while Pennsylvania asked for Philadelphia or, as the representatives of the Western counties demanded, some-where in the interior of the state. But the Southern delegations vehemently asserted that the capital rightfully belonged to them; that it be set either in Baltimore (so said the Marylanders) or on the banks of the Potomac, as the powerful Virginia group insisted.

To Hamilton the whole contest over the placement of the capital was a tempest in a teapot. What did it matter where it was, except insofar as it catered to local vanity and local profit? Assumption, how-ever, was a different matter. Without it, the nation would forever remain a mere congeries of quarreling states, ready to fly asunder at the slightest divergence of interest.

His most faithful lieutenant, Fisher Ames, echoed his views. "I care little where Congress may sit," he wrote with cold disdain. "I would not find fault with Fort Pitt, if we could assume the debts, and proceed in peace and quietness. But this despicable grog-shop contest, whether the taverns of New York or Philadelphia shall get the custom of Congress, keeps us in discord, and covers us all with disgrace." [20]

A brilliant idea flashed on Hamilton. Why not connect the two? Let the South have their trumpery capital as a sop for assumption. Placate Pennsylvania by giving her a temporary residence for a term of years. As for deserted New York, General Schuyler and other political friends would find the proper arguments to assuage her grief. Ames and his followers would convince New England.

The problem was—how to approach the South? Madison, Virginia's titular leader, had committed himself irretrievably against assumption. To what other man of equal influence could he broach the subject?

Irresistibly his eyes turned toward the recently arrived Secretary of State, Thomas Jefferson.

Thus far Jefferson had remained aloof from partisan passions and congressional wrangling. Fresh from France, pressed into office against his will, he had arrived in New York only a few weeks before to find himself immersed in a seething cauldron of politics, passions and horse trading.

In later years he was to cry out bitterly that he had been "a stranger to the ground, a stranger to the actors on it, so long absent as to have lost all familiarity with the subject"; that by Hamilton's trickery he had been "most ignorantly and innocently made to hold the candle." [21]

But this was after the event, when the consequences rose to bedevil him. At the time he had been sufficiently familiar with the dispute over assumption, and discussed its complexities at length in letters to his friends.

Indeed, during the Confederation period both he and Madison had favored some form of assumption; but this was before Virginia had managed to pay off most of her own debts. Now, during the great debate, he delicately balanced the pros and cons. "It appears to me," he declared on April 18th, after the initial defeat in the House, "one of those questions which present great inconveniences whichever way it is decided: so that it offers only a choice of evils." [22]

Before he approached Jefferson, however, Hamilton first tried his blandishments on the Pennsylvania delegations as less likely to make onerous demands. Their Western representatives, coming from the farming, whiskey-distilling and frontier counties, were voting steadily against assumption. If he could offer them the permanent capital, perhaps he would not need the South at all. One additional vote in the Senate and five in the House would bring assumption in, and Pennsylvania could furnish these.

The first Pennsylvanian whom his emissaries approached, Senator Maclay, righteously refused. The second, Senator Robert Morris, was more amenable. But he preferred to discuss the business with the principal rather than with underlings. He would, he wrote Hamilton, be taking the early morning air on the Battery the following day. If Hamilton had any proposition to make, they could meet there "as if by accident."

Hamilton hastened to sniff the harbor breezes beforetimes. As Morris strolled casually up, Hamilton walked with him. He would, he said, see to it that the capital was placed either at Germantown (just outside Philadelphia) or at the falls of the Delaware River, in return for the requisite votes for assumption. Morris agreed to consult with the other members of his delegation. They assented to the proposition—though Maclay violently objected. But they demanded an additional concession: that the temporary capital be removed immediately to Philadelphia.

In their greed the Pennsylvanians overreached themselves. Hamilton replied coldly in effect: "Do not bother. My friends won't hear of such an arrangement." [23]

For Hamilton had not been idle while Morris and his group were deliberating. It would be wise, he thought, to have several irons simultaneously in the fire. Taking a cue from Morris's Battery walk, he strolled idly one morning in front of Washington's house. As Jefferson came along to visit the President on business, Hamilton's manner changed. A seated despair beclouded his countenance as he stopped the astonished Secretary of State and walked him up and down the street for half an hour. In vivid colors he painted for his companion a picture of the confusion into which all business had been thrown by the fight over assumption, discoursed on the anger and disgust which its loss had occasioned in "the creditor states" and the possibility that they might secede from the Union. Why could not Jefferson, himself an officer of the administration, speak to some of his Southern friends in Congress and induce them to change their votes?

Jefferson was impressed, or so he later wrote, by the reference to a possible dissolution of the Union, and agreed to arrange a private dinner party where the business could be discussed at greater leisure.

A group of Virginia congressmen met with Hamilton at the festive board and some of them assented to the deal, provided that, since "this pill would be peculiarly bitter to the Southern States . . . some concomitant measure should be adopted to sweeten it a little to them."

Hamilton was only too happy to furnish the requisite "sweetener," knowing exactly what they were hinting at. He would, he said, have his friends vote the permanent capital to Georgetown, on the banks of the Potomac in Virginia. In the meantime, he added with an eye toward placating the double-crossed Pennsylvanians, they would move the temporary capital to Philadelphia for a period of ten years—about the time it would take to erect the permanent seat.

The Virginians agreed to the bargain, though not (so Jefferson reported) without some "convulsive" revulsions of the stomach.

Alexander White and Richard Bland Lee were to change their votes
on assumption in the House, and Hamilton engaged to get his followers to do the same on the capital. And so, commented Jefferson
many years later, Hamilton "effected his side of the engagement; and
so the assumption was passed, and 20 millions of stock divided among
favored states, and thrown in as a pabulum to the stock-jobbing
herd." [24]

Hamilton hastened to notify his confidential lieutenants of the
bargain he had made. Ames in turn cautiously told a friend that
"every instrument of influence" had been employed to put the assumption through.[25] King was a little obdurate at first when Hamilton spoke to him. The latter argued that the funding system was "the
primary national object—all subordinate points which oppose it must
be sacrificed." King remonstrated that "great and good schemes ought
to succeed on their own merits and not by intrigue or the establishment of bad measures." But he quickly receded from this somewhat
naïve point of view, grumbling that if others proceeded on state and
local views, so would he.[26]

Maclay was furious when he heard of the deal, both because it
brought in assumption and because the Pennsylvanians had been
outmaneuvered. He attributed the Southern surrender, however, not
to Jefferson but to Washington. "He has become," he noted venom-
ously, "in the hands of Hamilton, the dishclout of every dirty speculation." [27]

All Maclay's veneration for his former idol was rapidly vanishing.
Several months later he was to burst out: "If there is treason in the
wish, I retract it, but would to God this same General Washington
were in heaven! We would not then have him brought forward as the
constant cover to every unconstitutional and irrepublican act." [28]

The honeymoon was over. Party passions and national cleavages
were making personal enemies of former friends and comrades. The
luster of Washington's name was already tarnished; if not with the
mass of the people, certainly with the leaders of the South, who felt
that the President was betraying his own section. To them as to
Maclay, Washington had become Hamilton's puppet, obeying his
will and furnishing a convenient cloak for his devious operations.
Though this was by no means the truth, they sincerely believed it
and acted accordingly.

Henceforward Washington was no longer sacrosanct or untouchable;

the journalistic pack was let loose to snap and snarl at his heels until, bewildered and enraged, the President was only too happy to retire from the public scene.

Muhlenberg of Pennsylvania, who still did not know that his state had been bypassed, was willing to employ a little trickery of his own. Just as Hamilton had turned to the South, so would he. Let us, he advised, deal with the South instead of Hamilton. Let us give them the permanent capital, taking for ourselves the temporary seat for twenty years. Then, by our united efforts, we can kill assumption.[29]

Meanwhile Jefferson was busy trying to convince his friends that his bargain had been a good one. The peace and continuance of the Union, he declared, required a mutual sacrifice of opinion and interest. All proceedings in Congress were at a standstill; and should they separate without funding the public debts, there would be an end to the government. Besides, as he was careful to point out, if Virginia had not taken the capital in exchange for assumption, "something much worse" would have happened: "to wit an unqualified assumption and the permanent seat on the Delaware."[30]

Even Madison, though wary of being accused by suspicious constituents of further laxity on their interests, half assented to the bargain. The initial defeat of assumption, he told Monroe, "has benumbed the whole revenue business. I suspect that it will yet be unavoidable to admit the evil in some qualified shape."[31]

And later, after it had passed, he philosophically explained that "in a pecuniary light, the assumption is no longer of much consequence to Virginia," since amendments had eradicated former injustices; though he still believed that in a larger sense it ran counter to the "true interests" of the people.[32]

Yet there was a sufficient number of irreconcilable congressmen to make the issue hang momentarily in the balance. Jackson of Georgia "bellowed" so loudly against it, so Ames satirically reported, that the noise disturbed the Senate and forced them to close their windows "to keep out the din."[33]

Jackson, indeed, grimly continued his opposition to the very end. When assumption passed the Senate and came to the House, he rose bitterly to inquire why a measure which had convulsed the nation and been voted down repeatedly, nevertheless reappeared again and again in new and Proteus-like forms. "The Senate of the United States," he thundered, "a power not known to, nor chosen by the people, have undertaken to load the citizens of the United States with an enormous debt." He called on the House to resist this encroachment on its own constitutional right to initiate money bills.[34]

He found allies among members from those states which had held private hopes of their own for the seat of government. But all attempts to shift the capital met with defeat. Wilmington, Baltimore, Germantown and the banks of the Delaware were each taken up in turn and discarded. The bargain was rigorously adhered to. By a vote of 32 to 29 the banks of the Potomac were chosen. An attempt by New York to hold on to the temporary capital went down to defeat by 32 to 28; and it passed to Philadelphia for ten years.

The Virginians thereupon fulfilled their part of the agreement. Assumption came up finally for a vote on July 26, 1790, and was passed by a vote of 34 to 28. Victory had perched on the Hamiltonian banners.[35]

The funding act, embracing both the national and state debts, became law on August 4th. But the scars remained. The defeated party licked its wounds and meditated eventual revenge; and the day came when Jefferson bitterly regretted the role he had acted in the proceedings. Parties were born, irreconcilable and opposed at every point; a denouement never contemplated by the framers of the Constitution, and fraught with portentous consequences for the future of America.

The state of Virginia refused to follow its ostensible leaders. Resentment ran high and passions mounted. James Monroe, who accurately took the public pulse, warned Jefferson that, sweetener or not, the local politicians were up in arms.[36]

Jefferson tried to allay the storm. He hoped, he wrote, that such a controversial measure would never come up again and that, in spite of inherent evils in the funding bills, everything would work out in the end.[37]

Monroe proved the better prophet. Virginia was not to be placated. When her legislature convened in the fall it sent Monroe—who had been vehement against funding—to the United States Senate. Patrick Henry, confirmed by recent events in his inveterate opposition to the Constitution, introduced a resolution denouncing assumption as "repugnant" even to that Constitution.[38]

The resolution passed by a large majority and was elaborated into a fiery Protest and Remonstrance which plainly asserted that the general government had encroached on the prerogatives of the states; that assumption constituted an attempt to create a moneyed interest which would conflict with the interests of the owners of land and would eventually "prostrate agriculture at the feet of commerce." [39]

The Protest and Remonstrance was the first open and avowed defiance of the central government by a state, and foreshadowed the future Kentucky and Virginia Resolutions of 1798 and 1799. It was an ominous beginning; though the key word "nullification" had not yet been employed, it was implied both by tone and general tenor.

Hamilton was quick to visualize the potentialities of the Protest. He wrote grimly to John Jay: "This is the first symptom of a spirit which must either be killed, or it will kill the Constitution of the United States. I send the resolutions to you, that it may be considered what ought to be done." Jay advised his hotheaded friend to do nothing; that it would be better to keep silence and let Virginia's wrath die for lack of fuel on which to feed. [40]

Reluctantly Hamilton followed the advice; but he determined to await a better opportunity to prove to the people and the states that the general government possessed powers which it knew how to use. That opportunity came several years later with the so-called Whiskey Rebellion.

Even the concurrence of the New York legislature in the Virginia resolutions failed to stir the now cautious Hamiltonians to overt action. They had won the victory; why endanger it by needless squabbles?

Governor Clinton of New York exulted that his legislature had approved Virginia's stand in spite of "the Aristocratic Faction among us, supported by a host of Stock Jobbers and Speculators who have suddenly amassed great Wealth, and consequently possess a considerable degree of Influence." [41] The alliance between the agrarians of New York and Virginia was in the making.

The moneyed classes of the North, however, paid little heed to these signs and portents; and hastened to avail themselves of the fruits of their labors. The tremendous upsurge in the value of the debt certificates over the next nine months is eloquent testimony to the fortunes that were being garnered by forehanded speculators.

In May 1790, when Hamilton's entire program hung doubtfully in the balance, the national certificates stood at nine shillings sixpence to the pound—a little under half the face value. The state certificates varied widely, depending on the financial condition of the state of issue. But even the best of the lot, Pennsylvania, rated no more than four shillings sixpence to the pound, or less than a fourth of face value. The other states fell considerably under. North Carolina's certificates could get only a shilling sixpence; South Carolina a bare sixpence more; while there seemed to be no market at all for the debt evidences of Georgia and Rhode Island.[42]

By February 1791, however, after Hamilton had completed his funding operations and fused the national and state debts into a single system, his funded certificates, bearing six per cent, found a ready market at seventeen shillings sixpence and eventually rose to within a few pence of face value.[43]

Whatever the inequities initially involved, whatever chicanery concurred in the making, it appears plain from the long view of history that Hamilton's operations were an essential preliminary to a stable government and a united America. In spite of the impetus it gave to the rise of parties, in spite of the rancors and discontents that accompanied it, any other plan would have led to insuperable financial difficulties, smashed the credit of the United States, and made of the Union a loose aggregation of states without any binding cement or common goal.

Even Jefferson noted that Hamilton's measures tended to "secure to us the credit we now hold at Amsterdam, where our European paper is above par, which is the case of no other nation. Our business is to have great credit and to use it little." Then, with an eye to the war clouds hovering over Europe, he added: "Whatever enables us to go to war, secures our peace. At present it is essential to let both Spain and England see that we are in a condition for war."

That Jefferson was as practical in his own way as Hamilton in his is obvious from his concluding remarks: "Our object is to feed, and theirs to fight. If we are not forced by England, we shall have a gainful time of it." [44]

In one sense, however, Hamilton allowed his passion for ingeniously contrived and intricate solutions to run away with him. Instead of a simple and uniform series of bonds redeemable at set times and bearing a similar rate of interest, he reared a complex structure so delicately balanced that it threatened at times to topple of its own weight and gave rise to the accusation that it had been deliberately so erected as to permit a juggling of accounts to suit the purposes of the Treasury; not to speak of the saddling of the country with an "immortal" debt.

No creditor was compelled to turn in his old certificates for the new; but it was obvious that few would hold on to the old, unsecured by any guarantee, when they could be exchanged at par for government bonds in which the interest was guaranteed by the national revenues and the principal by eventual sale of the Western lands.

What Hamilton did was to float two loans, one to cover the national and the other the state debt. Subscriptions to the national loan were payable in the old Continental certificates with one exception, the so-called "bills of credit" which had lost all market value and could be converted only at a token rate of a hundred to one.

In return the subscribers received two bonds; one for two-thirds of the amount, with interest at six per cent; and one for the remaining one-third, non-interest-bearing until the year 1800, when six per cent would accrue. Indents, or evidences of previously unpaid interest, were replaced by three per cent bonds.

Subscriptions to the state loan were payable in the certificates of any state. For every one turned in, three new bonds were issued—one for four-ninths of the total sum, carrying a flat six per cent interest; one for two-ninths, non-interest-bearing until 1800, when the yield would also be six per cent; and one for three-ninths, with a straight three per cent interest.

Commissioners were appointed to adjust the accounts between the states and the federal government on the old war debts. Those states which were found to have balances to their credit were entitled to receive government bonds in exchange.

No definite dates were set for the extinguishment of the mass of these new government bonds; though the government was given the option of retiring certain proportions on an annual basis. A sinking fund was provided out of revenues to take care of such retirements, when and if exercised.

These final arrangements were complicated enough; but Hamilton's original scheme had been even more intricate, with a bewildering array of insurance tontines, annuities and survivorships, which Congress had mercifully eliminated.

CHAPTER 8

Growing Pains

THE BITTER DISPUTES over Hamilton's funding operations and the site for the national capital, the growing realization of a radical divergence in social, political and economic interests between the North and the South, the fear of an increased power to the national government, the sudden emergence of the slavery issue—all these led to a pessimistic view of the nation's future.

The Virginians particularly were filled with forebodings. One of them complained angrily to Washington that "the Northern phalanx is so firmly united, as to bear down all opposition, while Virginia is unsupported, even by those whose interests are similar to hers." Even Madison, it was felt, had let his native state down by his allegedly lukewarm attitude on funding, and there was considerable talk that Virginia would have to separate from the rest of the Union and go her way alone.[1]

Washington sternly reproved the complainant. Was it not human nature, he asked, for interests to clash? Who was to blame if the North stood solid in the pursuit of their interests and the South was divided? Let Virginia and her sister states heed the lesson and present a similar front. Separation would not solve the problem; a divided America would be even more dangerous. No, concluded Washington, a "common danger brought the States into confederacy, and on their union our safety and importance depend."[2]

From a different standpoint the British consul in Philadelphia was also noting evidences of disunity. He found the existence of an "extreme jealousy" between the two sections of the country. "The people of Maryland and Virginia," he reported, "avow their preference to Great Britain, and do not hesitate to declare they had rather old England should enjoy the advantages of their trade than New England."[3]

One ray of light penetrated the general gloom. On May 29, 1790, the state of Rhode Island, after an extended struggle and by a close Convention vote of 34 to 32, finally decided to enter the Union.[4] She might have remained out longer had not the Senate of the United States, only eleven days before, approved a bill to prohibit all commercial intercourse with the stubborn little state and to make immediate demand for the sums she owed to the national government.[5]

No matter what the reason, the original thirteen states were now safely reunited, and at least one danger point had been eliminated.

Political excitement, however, did not seem to disturb the even tenor of New York society. The social whirl continued unabated during the most acrimonious debates in Congress. Assemblies were held once a fortnight, lavish balls every month. In addition, reported Alexander White of Virginia, "Mrs. Washington has her drawing room every Friday Evening; Mrs. Adams every Monday, Lady Temple [wife of the resident British consul] on Tuesday, Mrs. Knox on Wednesday, Madam de la Forrest [wife of the French minister] and Mrs. Jay on Thursday." [6] This left only the week end free for assemblies, balls and private social events.

The intense social climate, the cares of office and a lingering weakness from his earlier operation laid the President low again in May. Pneumonia set in, and so grave was his condition that two of three attending physicians gave him up for dead. He rallied in spite of them and slowly recovered. The general alarm had been so great that it proved, Jefferson commented, "how much depends on his life." [7]

By the middle of August he was sufficiently well to make a courtesy visit to Rhode Island to welcome her into the Union. Accompanied by Jefferson, Governor Clinton of New York, several congressmen and his private aides and secretaries, Washington sailed up Long Island Sound to land at Newport and Providence, there to be greeted with parades, dinners and congratulatory addresses from patriotic and religious bodies.

The ceremonial visit was rendered noteworthy by the famous reply which the President penned to the address of the Jewish congregation of Newport, in which he echoed approvingly some of their phrases. "It is now no more that toleration is spoken of," he wrote, "as if it was by the indulgence of one class of people, that another enjoyed the exercise of their inherent natural rights. For happily the government of the United States, which gives to bigotry no sanction, to persecution no assistance, requires only that they who live under its protection should demean themselves as good citizens, in giving it on all occasions their effectual support." [8]

While the President was busy taking the pulse of the country with journeys through New England, Rhode Island, Long Island and at a later date through the Southern states, the Vice-President was busy in another fashion. With his usual talent for doing the wrong thing at the wrong time, he gave the *Gazette of the United States* for publication a series of philosophical and analytical discourses on statecraft and government which had employed his leisure time during the preceding year.

In form these were a commentary on his readings in the political work of an Italian historian, Henrico Caterino Davila, published abroad in 1757 under the title of *The History of the Civil War in France*.

It is doubtful whether anyone else in America had taken the trouble to peruse the three ponderous volumes which were more a disquisition on politics than a history; but John Adams, passionate student of everything pertaining to political theory, read them from cover to cover, and was moved to jot down his comments and personal observations on Davila's argument.

Mingled in the utmost confusion in these "Discourses on Davila" were long extracts or digests from the original books and Adams's own personal convictions. Since the extracts were copied without benefit of quotation marks, it is difficult for even the modern student to dissociate what Davila himself said and what Adams said on his own; small wonder then that the Vice-President's contemporaries took the entire work as a true and fundamental statement of his private beliefs.

Even when thus dissociated, there was sufficient to excite the alarm of the radical and the egalitarian. One of the most powerful drives in man, declared Adams, was the passion for distinction and power, with its handmaidens of envy, jealousy and vanity. To regulate this drive was the chief end of government; but at the same time a wise government employs it as a means toward its own end by creating a system of order and subordination which provides the necessary nexus for obedience to its own laws.[9]

Adams deplored distinctions among mankind based on birth, wealth or other adventitious possessions, and thought that men ought

to be valued solely for "their talents, virtues, and services." But he
noted realistically that even the mass of the people who had most to
lose from such distinctions unhesitatingly chose (when they had the
choice) their rulers for their elevated birth, families, landed estates,
offices and other external trappings. Furthermore, a single-chambered
popular assembly, no matter how chosen, could not be depended on
to act differently or less tyrannically than any king or set of nobles on
earth. Were not its members, Adams queried, actuated by the same
motives, rivalries, ambitions and vanities?

The only solution, so Adams thought, was to establish a government which could control or set off one set of ambitions and rivalries
against the others. This called for a system of checks and balances,
of *independent* branches in the legislature itself, and an independent
executive and judiciary. But even this was not enough. It was essential both to attract able and ambitious men to office, and to gain
for them the respect of the governed, by such a use of the gauds of
office, titles, robes, chairs and honors as the Romans in their wisdom
liberally bestowed.[10]

A balanced government was his constant theme. Yet he had no
illusions about its ease of operation. "It has been said," he remarked
in a postscript, "that it is extremely difficult to preserve a balance.
This is no more than to say that it is extremely difficult to preserve
liberty. . . . It is so difficult, that the very appearance of it is lost over
the whole earth, excepting one island [England] and North America. . . . If the people have not understanding and public virtue
enough, and will not be persuaded of the necessity of supporting an
independent executive authority, an independent senate, and an independent judiciary power, as well as an independent house of representatives, all pretensions to a balance are lost, and with them all hopes
of security to our dearest interests, all hopes of liberty." [11]

On this note he was forced abruptly to conclude. As the essays ran
their course in Fenno's paper, the outcry against them in the opposition press swelled to a damning chorus. They proved, it was said,
what had already been suspected, that Adams was a monarchist and
an aristocrat, and hated the plain people.

In vain the Vice-President denied the imputation; in vain he told
Dr. Rush that he upheld neither monarchy nor aristocracy, and asked
that he be not misrepresented to posterity. In vain he protested to
that fount of radicalism, Sam Adams, that all good government *must*
be republican in nature, though he believed "there is not in lexi-

cography, a more fraudulent word." *He* meant by it "a government, in which the people have, collectively, or by representation, an essential share in the sovereignty," which meant in turn a balance of three powers, with checks upon the multitude as well as the nobles.[12]

Neither protests nor explanations were of any avail. Phrases were taken out of context, qualifications ignored, and for years to come the monarchical and aristocratical leanings of John Adams became a favorite and repetitious accusation.

He was compelled, so he put it, by "the rage and fury of the Jacobinical Journals" to leave his Discourses unfinished. In old age he added the rueful comment that his ill-advised publication had "powerfully operated to destroy his popularity"; that for all his disavowals of the sentiments imputed to him, "not one man in America then believed him. He knew not one and has not heard of one since who then believed him." [13]

The Act providing a judicial system of the United States became law on September 24, 1789. It established a Supreme Court consisting of the Chief Justice and five Associate Justices, added thirteen district courts roughly coterminous with the several states, and three circuit courts, each of which was presided over by two Justices of the Supreme Court in association with a district judge.

There had been considerable opposition to the establishment of district and circuit courts from those who saw in them another attempt by the federal government to override the sovereignty of the states. The declaration was made that "it wears so monstrous an appearance that I think it will be *felo-de-se* in the execution" and must eventually be destroyed.[14]

John Jay of New York was duly appointed Chief Justice. His Associates were William Cushing, chief justice of the Massachusetts Supreme Court; James Wilson, prominent Pennsylvania lawyer, politician and legal theoretician; James Iredell, attorney general of North Carolina; John Rutledge, governor and judge in chancery of South Carolina; and John Blair, chief justice of the Virginia Court of Appeals.

It was a learned bench and geographically well distributed; yet it had been assembled with much difficulty and after a number of refusals by others to whom the seats had been first offered. The Supreme Court, as an untried body, with powers as yet vague and undefined, and the object of distrust, did not appear attractive to men already well and comfortably placed in their respective states. For years the court was held in little esteem; men like Rutledge, Jay and later Ellsworth did not hesitate to resign to accept positions in the state courts or return to private practice and political office. It was not until John Marshall raised the Supreme Court to a position of commanding importance that a place on its bench became a thing to be sought and aspired for.

The Court first met in session on February 1, 1790, in the Royal Exchange on Broad Street in New York. Ten days later it adjourned, having no business before it. The same empty procedure occurred in the fall. Indeed, for almost three years the Supreme Court was a sinecure. Practically no cases came before it, either of original jurisdiction or on appeal from the lower courts.

The chief work of the individual Justices was done on the circuits, where they sat in pairs in conjunction with a district judge. But there the work was hard and tedious, and the Justices complained bitterly about the long trips over roads dusty in summer and frozen in winter, exposed to the elements and away from home for unconscionable periods of time. "It is more than the strength of any man can bear," complained Nathaniel Pendleton, the district judge for Georgia, whose peregrinations at least were limited to the boundaries of his own state.[15]

The discontent focused eventually in a memorial addressed to Congress by the entire bench in which they spoke at length of the rigors of the road, the poor accommodations at the inns they were obliged to frequent, the perils to their health and other forms of suffering they endured. They raised also a pertinent point: that in the current system the same district judge who had heard a case in the trial court also sat on the circuit bench to which an appeal was taken from his alleged errors in the court of first instance. This, rightly complained the members of the Supreme Court, is "unfriendly to impartial justice."[16]

It took Congress a long time, however, to correct the manifest inequities of the system; and the paradox continued of justices sitting in judgment on their own acts.

In view of the later agitation over the right and competence of the federal courts to override state laws and state decisions, and the acts of Congress itself, as unconstitutional or in contravention of existing treaties, it is worthy of note that no such question was raised in the beginning. Both Hamilton and Madison had agreed in the *Federalist* papers that the Court had such powers; and Jefferson had indicated as much. Not until many years later, when their exercise impinged on vital interests, was the matter reconsidered and the claim then made that the Court itself was acting beyond its capacity and without constitutional warrant.

The first instances in which the federal courts assumed jurisdiction over the states involved one of the most politically explosive issues of the day. Under the treaty of peace with England, the nation had agreed that no impediment should be offered by the several states to the collection of prewar debts owed by Americans to British merchants. Nevertheless certain states defiantly kept on their books stay legislation which forbade the use of their courts for the collection of the debts or denied the claim of interest on the unpaid sums during the war years.

In May 1791, a circuit court declared a Connecticut law invalid which prohibited the collection of the additional interest; in the following year the circuit court for Georgia adjudged that the treaty overrode an earlier state law impeding the recovery of the original debt.[17] In decision after decision, the federal courts held consistently to this position, and thereby armed the national government with plausible arguments when the entire question became a matter of bitter dispute on an international scale.

These rulings set forth and established the Court's power over treaty obligations. The next group took a similar position on state laws which it was contended were contrary to the Constitution.

A Rhode Island statute was examined and held in violation of the federal Constitution as impairing the obligations of private contracts.[18] No voice was raised at the time in outcry of usurpation; yet when John Marshall ruled in approximately the same fashion in the famous Dartmouth College case (differentiated, however, because a state legislature was one of the parties to the contract), the resultant clamor and denial of the court's jurisdiction rocked the nation.

The next decision was of even more far-reaching importance. On April 5, 1792, John Jay and William Cushing declared an act of *Congress* unconstitutional. The ruling was made on a curious set of facts. About two weeks before, Congress had enacted a law granting the federal courts jurisdiction over all pension claims against the government. But the courts refused to accept this increase in their powers—and in their labors—as not expressed in the Constitution.

Ironically, it was the old antifederalists and new-fledged Republicans who applauded the decision. Freneau, the most ardent republican of them all, expressed editorial satisfaction and called the ruling a palladium of the people against "Legislative or Executive oppression." [19] Bache agreed with equal vehemence, and derided the demand of offended congressmen for the impeachment of the justices. "As if, forsooth," he jeered, "Congress were wrapped up in the cloak of infallibility which has been torn from the shoulders of the Pope; or that it was damnable heresy and sacrilege to doubt the constitutional orthodoxy of any decision of theirs, once written on calfskin." [20]

Obviously, the applause emanated from the fact that the decision of the Court accorded with their own conception of the merits of the instant case; it was felt that veterans could gain more from a politically pliable Congress than from a sternly legalistic bench. Later, however, when the Court presumed to question the constitutionality of congressional enactments which were more to republican taste, then a deeper search into the Constitution disclosed the patent fact that the Supreme Court had no power to nullify a law of Congress.

Even in Congress itself, during this early period, good republicans and true declared unequivocally that "we are not the expositors of the Constitution. The judges are the expositors of the Constitution and Acts of Congress." [21]

When the Supreme Court finally went the whole way and asserted that the citizen of another state had the right to sue a state itself in the federal courts,[22] the roar of protest that arose was not so much over the *power* of the Court to render the decision as over its *error* in the interpretation of the Constitution. There were even Federalists who disagreed with the decision, and helped support a constitutional amendment banning such suits in the future. The Eleventh Amendment went into effect on January 8, 1798; the first amendment to be added to the Constitution after the so-called Bill of Rights.

In spite of the decision, however, the state of Georgia, the defendant in the action, steadfastly refused to submit to the jurisdiction of the federal court; and the lower House of her legislature passed a measure purporting to inflict the death penalty on any federal marshal who would seek to enforce the decision within the state. The eventual passage of the Eleventh Amendment quietly pushed the entire matter into the discard; not to be renewed until, in a somewhat similar instance, Andrew Jackson made his famous remark: "The Supreme Court has made its decision; now let it enforce it!"

For all these trail-blazing decisions, the work of the Court was scanty, its judgments few, and the attention of the country was directed to it only at scattered intervals. The turnover among the Justices was heavy, its prestige was limited, and it was only with the reign of Marshall that a weapon was forged powerful enough to influence the political and economic course of the nation in innumerable ways.

Thomas Jefferson took office as Secretary of State at the end of March 1790. The government was already well under way and the foreign relations which he was supposed to handle had been tentatively set in a train not of his making. Yet it did not take him long to become acquainted with his job. His long years of service as the American minister to France had given him the requisite background for surveying the international scene. At Paris he had witnessed the beginnings and early progress of the French Revolution. He had even offered surreptitious advice to the participants. He had collaborated with John Adams in dealing with England, Holland and Prussia; he had conferred with William Carmichael on Spanish relations, and with a variety of diplomats and agents in seeking a solution of the perennial problem of the Barbary Powers. No one in all America, with the exception of Adams and the dying Franklin, was as well equipped to take charge of the Department of State.

Yet he entered his duties with definite preconceptions and a precise philosophy of government. He hated and feared England; he admired France, particularly in its new incarnation; and he despised Spain. But above all he loved America and would have preferred, in his own phrase, to have erected a Chinese wall of exclusion about her to keep her independent and self-contained, completely aloof from the quarrels and diplomacy of Old World powers and happily engaged on her own destiny.

That this was not possible had, however reluctantly, to be acknowledged. At every point the Old World impinged on the New. European colonies lay next door on the same continent, the fortified posts that strung formidably along the northern frontier were still in British possession, boundary disputes and Indian troubles kept all frontiers in a state of turbulence, commerce on the high seas met with a maze of bewildering restrictions, crippling regulations and outright piracy —in short, it sometimes seemed as if the infant nation would be strangled almost at birth by the giants who menaced its existence on every side.

To cope with this complex of forces, to handle them with delicacy and dispatch, to assert American rights against the entire world, Jefferson had at his disposal a departmental staff of five clerks, two messengers and a French translator—and a load of firewood. The total expense of the Department for the year, including his own salary, came to the staggering sum of $7961.[23]

The American diplomatic establishment abroad consisted of Carmichael remaining as chargé d'affaires in Madrid; young William Short, with a similar title in Paris; and a vacuum in London. The last existed in retaliation for British refusal to accredit a minister to New York. Washington, however, took advantage of the presence in London on private business of the aristocratically cynical, one-legged *bon vivant* Gouverneur Morris to constitute him an informal representative to conduct informal negotiations.

Even this scanty establishment evoked congressional suspicion. It was sought by law to restrain the President from disbursing more than a miniscule fixed sum for their respective upkeeps; a procedure which elicited a vehement protest from the representatives abroad and from Jefferson at home, who had bitter firsthand knowledge of the cost of living in Europe.[24]

But Congress could not be altogether blamed for its parsimony. Its members were subject to harassing outcries from their constituents over the high cost of government in general and the fabulous salaries (five to six dollars a day for actual attendance) in particular which they had appropriated for themselves.

The newspapers teemed with letters from "True Republicans," "Observers" and other variants of the inevitable "Pro Bono Publico" who demanded substantial cuts in the federal establishment, the pruning of "unnecessary" public expense, and a sharp reduction in the "enormous salaries" of Congress which enabled the spendthrift recipients to be "dressed in purple and fine linen and faring sumptuously." Why also, it was loudly inquired, send ambassadors and other parasites to Europe? They "would only reside at foreign Courts, to mimic their manners; and dissipate the public revenue."

The vigilant guardians of the public morals and revenues saw only absurdity in a proposal to institute a library for the benefit of Congress. "What connection has a Library with the Public?" they indignantly demanded. "With our Commerce; or with any other national concern? How absurd to squander away money for a parcel of Books, when every shilling of the revenue is wanted for supporting our government and paying our debts?" Either elect members to Congress who already have read a book, or let them go to the circulating library for their information! [25]

As America looked across the seas, she saw a Europe in the grip of strange new forces and on the verge of tremendous convulsions. The French had taken a leaf from the book of America and staged their own revolution. But the pattern and outcome bore little resemblance to the prototype. Moving with an irresistible logic of its own, the French Revolution imparted alien meanings to the great phrases of the Declaration of Independence, and the translated slogans of *Liberté, Egalité* and *Fraternité* rapidly took on a sinister cast.

In its early stages, however, the revolutionary winds of doctrine shook the rest of the world. Liberals everywhere rejoiced at the portent of the coming utopia and the brotherhood of man. Ancient monarchies rocked on their foundations, and even England for all her stability shook with fear.

Americans of course were overjoyed at the imitation of their own revolution by their former allies. "Liberty will have another feather in her cap," they exulted. "The seraphic contagion was caught from Britain, it crossed the Atlantic to North America, from whence the flame has been communicated to France." [26]

But, as the French counterpart accelerated its pace and grew in bloody excess, as the king became a virtual prisoner and the whole fabric of orderly society seemed about to crumble, the more conservative Americans drew back, at first in perplexity and then with mounting horror. The more radical, however, continued to view the revolution with rose-tinted glasses and either denied the reported atrocities as enemy fabrications or considered them inevitable in the fashioning of a brave new world. [27]

By the time Jefferson came to New York he found to his amazement and disgust that the company he would ordinarily frequent was vehement against the French, and eventually he had to seek a more congenial viewpoint in the humbler strata of society or among the intellectuals. [28] Within an all too short period the division between Francophobes and Francophiles, corresponding almost exactly with the split between Federalists and Republicans, grew so wide, deep and passionate that for the remainder of the era the more extreme of the participants on both sides were darkly certain that a similar revolution impended here.

In Europe, the opposing forces were already girding their loins and gathering their forces for the inevitable conflict; a conflict which Jefferson viewed with a singular complacency. From the larger viewpoint he foresaw that the revolutionary torrent, liberated by the French, would sweep the world into the haven of republican principles. From the narrower but more practical view of American self-interest he welcomed a total European conflagration. With unwearied insistence he hammered the theme: It is the business of Europe to fight and ours to remain at peace, feed the contestants and make a goodly profit in the process. In this laudable spirit he was even willing to take advantage of the hard necessities of his good friends, the French. "Their West India islands," he noted, "are all in combustion. There is no government in them. Consequently their trade [is] entirely open to us." [29]

He hoped and expected that the French would understand the situation and grant us official leave to do what we would do in any event. Such a precedent, he wrote, "must have consequences. It is impossible the world should continue long insensible to so evident a truth as that the right to have commerce and intercourse with our neighbors is a natural right. To suppress this neighborly intercourse is an exercise of force, which we shall have a just right to remove when we are the superior force." [30]

By July 1790, war in Europe seemed imminent. But not, as had been expected, between England and France; instead, the war clouds gathered suddenly over England and Spain. Nor did the inciting cause stem from the ferment in Europe; it came rather over a territorial squabble involving the inhospitable shores of the Pacific Northwest.

Spain laid claim to all the coastal lands north from California; a pretension which the British refused to accept. The latter established a trading post on Nootka Sound in what is now British Columbia to command the seal, otter and other fisheries of the northern waters. Spain dispatched a warship to seize the intruding post, but succeeded only in capturing a British trading vessel. The aroused British delivered an ultimatum for immediate apologies and reparations, and breathing war. Spain retorted defiance.

The American government watched the acceleration of events with the utmost alarm. Distant though the Pacific coast may have seemed at the time, Washington apprehended a clash of arms much closer to home. If war broke out, it was most probable that England would invade the more easterly possessions of Spain by land and sea; and this meant the Floridas and Louisiana. It was bad enough to have these in the hands of Spain; the imagination shuddered at the consequences if they fell to England. Spain held no present danger to the United States, and every good American was certain that eventually these plums must drop into our laps either through diplomacy or the use of force. England was another matter. Rich, powerful, mistress of the seas and, augmented and swollen with these new territories, in full strangling circle about her former rebel colonies, the future might well be disastrous. But what could be done about it?

In reality, nothing. As Jefferson observed, the United States was in no position to go to war with England. Lack of manpower, money, resources of taxation and credit, the new funding of the debt, all forbade it. Caution was indicated, and delay. Perhaps England might not attack; or, attacking, fail. Of course, Jefferson acknowledged, should she seize Louisiana and the Floridas, eventually "we should have to re-take them."

In the meantime, Jefferson offered two alternative courses of action, both to be employed simultaneously. Let us propose to Spain that since she must lose the colonies in any event, it would be preferable for her to proclaim their immediate independence. In that case the United States would join with France and Spain in guaranteeing their integrity. On the other hand, we would require from England as the price of our neutrality in the impending conflict a commercial treaty based on "perfect reciprocity" and the neutralization of the American possessions of both England and Spain.[31]

Both suggestions were naïve. Spain had no intention of supinely yielding her colonies or granting them an independence which would furnish a too obvious example to Mexico, sole source of her wealth and power. England saw nothing in our proffered neutrality to justify the surrender of the immense economic advantages derived from her commercial policies, particularly when she would also be debarred from seizing the Spanish colonies.

As a matter of fact, England's attitude toward the United States at this time was one of casual contempt. The gigantic chessboard of Europe absorbed all her energies and it did not matter much whether the youthful nation across the seas was enemy or friend. There were already issues in abundance between the two countries, but the issues were all on the American side. The English positions were well taken and strongly intrenched; the assaults and the requests for changes came wholly from the American government without making any perceptible impact.

The first and most irritating issue was the British retention of the border posts. Seven in number, and stretching from Lake Champlain across the Great Lakes, the forts commanded the northern waterways, gave their possessors access to the Indian tribes on the American frontier and control of the valuable fur trade (worth about £200,000 annually), and constituted so many invasion points in the event of future war. Because of the posts, Great Britain was in a position to seduce the inhabitants of Vermont, who were seething with discontent over their subsidiary status to New Hampshire and New York.

The Vermonters indeed were already considering themselves as an independent nation and casting about for alliances to protect them against the wrath of the states and the country they intended deserting. Levi Allen, brother of the redoubtable Ethan, sent a secret memorial under the seal of Vermont to the British which in effect proclaimed her independence and separate sovereignty and proposed "a *Commercial* and *Friendly* Intercourse between the said State and His Majesty's Dominions."

Confronted with this startling evidence that the Union was already breaking up, the British Privy Council for Trade reported to its government that such an arrangement might prove advantageous both commercially and politically. "It will be for the Benefit of this Country," they advised, "to prevent Vermont and Kentucky and all the other Settlements now forming in the Interior parts of the great Continent of North America, from becoming dependent on the Government of the United States, or on that of any other Foreign Country, and to preserve them on the contrary in a State of Independence, and to induce them to form Treaties of Commercial Friendship with Great Britain." [32] They might have added that eventually such splinter nations must fall within the English orbit and become mere dependencies in fact if not in name.

With so many advantages, therefore, arising out of her continued command of the posts, it is no wonder that England sought every excuse for their temporary or even permanent retention. It was true that the peace treaty had called for their delivery; but the breach of

other provisions of the same treaty by certain of the states with regard
to confiscated loyalist property and the payment of the debts furnished the British with a ready-made retort which they were quick to
employ.

Gouverneur Morris, in his informal negotiations with the British
Foreign Office, speedily discovered that he could make no headway
on either of the points which Washington had wished him to discuss:
the fulfillment of the terms of the peace treaty, and the adoption of
a commercial arrangement. The Duke of Leeds told him plainly that
"we have no scruple in declaring our object is to retard the fulfilling
such subsequent parts of the Treaty as depend entirely upon Great
Britain" until redress was obtained for the American violations. On
the question of a commercial treaty he was less frank and sought
refuge in vagueness.[33]

Disgustedly Morris reported his failure to the President. He was
convinced that the British intended both to keep the posts and to
refuse any compensation for the Negroes they had taken away during
the Revolution. And, he added sourly, they consider a commercial
agreement "absolutely unnecessary" since they already "derive all
benefit from our trade without Treaty." [34]

Indeed, he saw no point into our entering into any further treaty
with England because it would have to be entirely one-sided; or,
as he colorfully characterized it, "of a young Heir with an old
Usurer." [35]

Similarly, on the two other items which Washington had placed
on his agenda, he got nowhere. One related to the ever-increasing
impressment of American seamen into the British Navy. The other
was the appointment of a British envoy to the United States, with
powers to treat.[36] The English ministry stubbornly refused to entertain any protests on the first, and saw no advantage to be derived
from the second.

English security, commerce and far-flung power depended on the
maintenance of a navy superior to all others. But the brutal discipline,
the floggings and hangings for venial offenses, the bad food and pittance pay deterred voluntary enlistments. To man their ships, therefore, impressment was resorted to. Press gangs roamed the British
ports to seize at random likely-looking sailors; while British warships
on the high seas stopped vessels of British, American and neutral
registry to take off, by force if necessary, complements of men to fill

their vacant ranks. In time of actual or impending war, impressments rose to mass proportions.

Technically, only British subjects were impressed; actually, the needs or whim of the pressing officer tended to determine nationality. In the case of American sailors, differentiation was always difficult; and it was true that British tars, wherever possible, loudly asserted their American citizenship.

Further to complicate the situation, American merchant ships held a goodly number of British seamen in their crews, who preferred the comparatively easy life and high pay of the American service, where they were accepted with no questions asked, even though there might be reason to believe them deserters from the British Navy. And still further to compound the problem, England steadfastly insisted that an Englishman born remained always an Englishman and could never change his citizenship.[37]

There had been a trickle of complaints by the United States prior to 1790, but the Nootka Sound war scare brought them to sizable volume, as the British sought hastily to place their fleet on a full war footing. Morris was swamped with pleas from American sailors caught in the toils; and succeeded after infinite pains in obtaining the release of those whose claims to American birth were incontestable.

He suggested that perhaps bona fide American seamen could be furnished with certificates of citizenship by the American government; an idea that met with the qualified approval of the British ministry.[38] But Jefferson declared it an unwarranted limitation on the rights of American citizens and pointed out that sailors who had mislaid or lost the precious document would then be left without recourse.[39]

As a result of Morris's pessimistic reports and the worsening situation in Europe, Washington sent Colonel David Humphreys, his former aide, on a highly confidential and secret tour of the American missions abroad to confer with our emissaries, impart to them the views of the government and obtain first-hand information on the status of the various negotiations they were conducting.[40]

Meanwhile Hamilton, who had received confidential information of his own that Morris was *persona non grata* with the British because of his alleged peremptory ways, requested Humphreys to conduct a quiet investigation in London of the truth of the report and write the result either to the President or to himself. Humphreys properly refused; though basing his refusal on a more palatable ground than the obvious one: that Hamilton had no right either to make such a request or to receive the information.[41]

The report on Morris had come to Hamilton from a British agent in this country, whose mission was vague and status nebulous. He was Major George Beckwith, aide-de-camp to Lord Dorchester, the Governor of Canada. He came unostentatiously to New York in October 1789, without credentials and without any official standing other than his own whispered statements that he was Dorchester's emissary. His shadowy mission was in keeping with the British desire to keep all negotiations in a twilight zone of unofficial *pourparlers,* which made it easy to evade troublesome demands and permitted hints, half answers and even downright offers which could readily be disavowed whenever the need arose.

This agent who was not an agent never visited Washington, officially or unofficially. Instead, he made it his business to become' friendly with key figures in Congress and with Alexander Hamilton, Secretary of the Treasury. He succeeded so well that he was able to obtain information of the utmost value for his employer, Lord Dorchester, who in turn passed it along to the ministry in England. Members of both Houses of Congress were amazingly expansive with the pleasant-mannered Englishman, obligingly furnishing him with full details of what occurred in closed sessions and committees, and airing their personal views on the fate of pending measures.

One such measure in particular—perhaps the only one which caused the British some moments of anxiety—was an attempt by Madison to revive those retaliatory proposals against England which had formerly been defeated, but which he presented now with certain modifications.

On June 30, 1790, Madison spoke in the House—embodied as a committee of the whole and therefore under supposed rules of secrecy. He favored, he said, reciprocal trade relations with Great Britain. But none such now existed. American shipping was either totally excluded from British ports or suffered under such restrictions as to be tantamount to exclusion. On the other hand, British ships entered American ports freely and without hindrance. He therefore offered two resolutions: 1. Wherever American ships were prohibited by a foreign power from bringing goods from any of its ports to the United States, a like prohibition would be placed on the same goods brought by ships of that nation. 2. Wherever American ships were prohibited from carrying to a foreign port articles not of American growth or manufacture, ships hailing from that port could not bring the articles of that country into the United States.[42]

The resolutions were obviously directed against Great Britain and in particular against her West Indies possessions, where the most onerous restrictions had been imposed on the American carrying trade. American ships, faster, cheaper and more convenient than the ships of British make and registry, had prior to the Revolution practically monopolized that lucrative trade. Indeed one British publicist, a former American loyalist, had flatly declared that the British ought to be thankful for American independence, since it "happily freed the empire from the evil, for which the ministers of George the First could find no remedy." [43]

This explains the otherwise surprising *volte-face* in the House. Now it was Wadsworth, Sherman and Goodhue, all of New England, who upheld Madison's proposals; while Jackson of Georgia denounced them as "very extraordinary indeed," and, if adopted, certain to annihilate the trade of Georgia and North Carolina with the West Indies.[44] These states, not having ships of their own, did not care who carried their produce to the islands.

As a result of such Southern opposition, the committee rose without taking any action.

Information like this was definite grist for Beckwith's mill. One of his most fruitful informants—at least until Hamilton came within his ken—was Senator Samuel Johnson of Connecticut. He assured the British agent that he was personally opposed not only to retaliations in commerce but to any hostile measures for seizing the posts; and that the Senate would veto any "such wild ideas" in the event they should pass the House.[45]

But Hamilton proved a gold mine which Beckwith proceeded diligently to work. He first met the Secretary of the Treasury through the good offices of General Schuyler, Hamilton's father-in-law, and thereupon entered into a series of informal, confidential discussions which influenced British decisions on American policy perhaps as much as the formal negotiations through open and accredited representatives.

By July 1790, during the Nootka Sound war scare, they became pregnant with consequences. On July 8th Beckwith told Hamilton that England "entertained a disposition not only toward a friendly intercourse, but toward an alliance with the United States." Indeed, in the event of a rupture between England and Spain, the United States "would find it to be their interest to take part with Great Britain rather than with Spain." However, he cannily left the door for retreat wide open by declaring that these were merely Dorchester's personal views and were being given "without a previous knowledge of the intentions of the [British] cabinet." [46]

Washington, to whom Hamilton reported the conversation, analyzed it as follows: What the British are really saying is that "we did not incline to give any satisfactory answer to Mr. Morris, who was *officially* commissioned to ascertain our intentions with respect to the evacuation of the Western Posts within the territory of the United States and other matters into which he was empowered to enquire until by this unauthenticated mode we can discover whether you will enter into an alliance with us and make common cause against Spain. In that case we will enter into a Commercial Treaty with you and *promise perhaps* to fulfil what they already stand engaged to perform." [47]

The President's analysis was brilliantly accurate; yet there was one specific point which troubled him. Suppose, when war broke out, Lord Dorchester should seek to attack the Spanish possessions by land and, with or without American permission, march his troops from Canada through the intervening territory of the United States. In that event, what course should the American government adopt?

Accordingly, he framed a series of questions for Hamilton, Jefferson, Adams, Jay and Knox to answer. Suppose Dorchester should first ask our permission; what should we reply? Suppose, as was more likely, he marched without request, what notice should we take? Suppose he asked and we refused, and *then* marched, what then? [48]

In all these backstairs negotiations, which involved the primary business of the Department of State, not one of the three men involved—Beckwith, Hamilton and Washington—thought fit to inform Jefferson of what was being done. Beckwith's course is understandable. Hamilton's is less so, though he was ready and willing to assume the work of every branch of government if need be. Besides, he jotted a note on the back of his second report to Washington of his conversations with Beckwith—when, is not clear—that "Mr. Jefferson was privy to this transaction"; a statement which Jefferson later vehemently denied. But Washington's silence is difficult to understand. He owed it to his Cabinet officer who was responsible for the conduct of foreign relations to advise him of what was going on, or, better still, insist that Hamilton make his reports direct. He adopted neither course; and even later, when the private discussions were disclosed to the Cabinet at large, they were not divulged in their entirety.

As a matter of fact Hamilton preferred these clandestine conversations with an informal agent to the appearance of an official British envoy who, as he candidly explained to Beckwith, would perforce have to negotiate directly with the Secretary of State.

"The President's mind," he said startlingly, "I can declare to be perfectly dispassionate on this subject. Mr. Jefferson . . . is a gentleman of honor and zealously desirous of promoting . . . the interests of his country . . . but from some opinions which he has given respecting your Government, and possible predilections elsewhere [France], there may be difficulties which may possibly frustrate the whole, and which might be readily explained away." In any event, he added complacently, Beckwith could be assured that he, Hamilton, had constant access to the President.[49]

Unaware of this curious background of the President's official queries, Jefferson hastened to answer them. It was the unquestionable *right* of the United States, he wrote, either to grant or deny permission to Dorchester. But permission should, if at all possible, be avoided. A British seizure of the Mississippi River and its terminus at New Orleans must inevitably at some future date bring us to war with them. To deny such permission, however, and have the denial ignored, would place us in an unenviable predicament. We must then either fight the British immediately or pocket the insult in the face of the world. It was better therefore to return no answer at all. In that case we could demand apologies later, or "make it a handle of quarrel hereafter, if we should have use for it as such." In the event however that an answer *must* be given, let it be in the affirmative, since we were in no position to embark on a war.[50]

War for Jefferson never constituted an instrument of national policy, even though on occasion he thought it politic to assume a bellicose tone. Wars among the nations of Europe, however, he viewed benevolently, as long as we could stay out of them and wax rich on the proceeds. If war came now, he was ready to welcome it. "In that case," he wrote privately, "I hope the new world will fatten on the follies of the old. If we can but establish the principles of the armed neutrality for ourselves, we must become the carriers for all parties as far as we can raise vessels."[51] It was a dream which Jefferson was never able to realize, though he pursued it persistently all through his career.

Hamilton was far more forthright than Jefferson and employed no subtle or tortuous reasoning in his reply to Washington's questions. Like his colleague, he wished for no war with England. War would mean the collapse of his financial system before it solidified into a permanent structure. He also hated what he called "evasions," which, he declared, were "never dignified and seldom politic." Therefore he bluntly stated that if the British asked permission to cross our territory, it should be granted. If they should march without asking, we must content ourselves with a remonstrance after the fact. If, however, Washington decided to *refuse* permission, then we must interpose armed resistance to any violation of our frontiers, even to the extent of a full-scale war.[52]

John Adams, whose advice was called for only occasionally, submitted a brief memorandum. Refuse the request if made, he advised; but under no circumstances go to war.[53]

Fortunately, by the time the several opinions had been gathered, Spain backed down and the clouds of war rolled by. It is most unlikely that Dorchester had intended to invade overland in any event; the distances were vast and the lines of communication tenuous. It would have been much simpler for a British fleet to attack through the Gulf of Mexico. But it was just as well that the matter never came to a test. As everyone agreed, the United States was in no position to meet it at the moment.[54]

CHAPTER 9

A Bank Is Born

As the war clouds lifted from Europe, England's attitude toward the United States stiffened. All talk of possible commercial arrangements abruptly ceased, former evasions were dropped, and Morris was told plainly that he could expect no concessions. As the envoy's bitter reports reached home, Washington decided that all further efforts be dropped. We must bide our time until England herself, through force of outside circumstances, is compelled to change her tune, he told the fretting Morris. Meanwhile, he added rather optimistically, "the wheels of government move without interruption, and gather strength as they move." [1]

Time, and more time, was the constant cry. Time to gain strength, population and resources until that not too distant day arrived—so it was believed—when demands could be made and enforced, if necessary.

But there still was Spain, with whom a belligerent attitude could safely be adopted without any fear of consequences. While that nation was still embroiled at Nootka Sound, Jefferson pressed for a settlement of the vital Mississippi navigation. Humphreys carried a sheaf of instructions for Carmichael at Madrid. These were peremptory in tone and bellicose in manner. Spain *must* yield the navigation of the Mississippi; she *must* provide a port at its mouth for unloading and transshipment overseas. On these demands there could be no compromise.

In addition, Spain *ought* to cede us the two Floridas in exchange for the guarantee of her possessions west of the Mississippi.

If Spain should prove stubborn, Jefferson instructed Carmichael, then warn her that our Western citizens can no longer be held in check; that, should our efforts fail, they no doubt will take by force what has not been granted in peace. In that event, "neither themselves nor their rights will ever be abandoned by us." [2]

Unfortunately, just as Carmichael unfolded these menaces to the Spaniards, the ending of the dispute with England emptied them of content, and the ministry at Madrid shrugged them off with a maddening indifference. As a result, Jefferson was compelled to sheath his bluster and to await that future on which all American foreign relations seemed to depend.

The one bright spot in the European picture was France. Though the momentum of her revolution was already beginning to chill the enthusiasm of many Americans, officially we were still connected with her by favorable ties of commerce and the memory of past comradeship. Yet France could never replace England in the American markets, either as seller or purchaser. English goods were superior in quality and in price; and English merchants sold on liberal credit and purchased for immediate cash. France could do neither. So that, aside from his personal distaste for the French system, Hamilton disagreed heartily with Jefferson's thesis that we ought to cultivate France instead of England. To him, for good or ill, it was with England that we would have to deal.[3]

There were troubles closer at home, moreover, which could not be avoided. All along the western frontier white settlers and Indian tribes were locked in inevitable conflict. As fast as one area of disturbance was pacified, another one opened.

It is true that the most important threat was at least temporarily settled by treaty with the Creeks. A delegation of this powerful nation, headed by the half-breed McGillivray, came to New York, where they were feted and flattered. John and Abigail Adams entertained them daily and when, on August 7, 1790, the treaty was signed with all solemnity, the Indians built a huge bonfire and danced around it, so Abigail reported, "like so many spirits whooping, singing, yelling, and expressing their pleasure and satisfaction in the true savage style."[4]

The national government was doing its best to deal fairly with the Indians and remove all points of friction. Congress enacted laws for the strict licensing of all American traders on Indian soil, forbade Indian sales of land to individuals or states unless authorized by specific treaty, and made crimes against peaceable Indians committed within their territories a federal offense.[5]

Yet even such stringent laws were of no avail. The mutual outrages of Indians and whites were so interrelated and confusing that only a recording angel could attempt to assess particular responsibility; and they continued on such a scale that the federal government, in the face of Kentucky's threat to quit the Union, was compelled finally if reluctantly to intervene with force.[6]

It was with many misgivings that Washington and Knox ordered a punitive expedition against the tribe most flagrantly involved in border massacres—the Wabash Indians.[7] But this was easier to command than to put in effect. A parsimonious Congress, fearful of a standing army as a standing threat to the liberties of the people, had cut the regular establishment to the bone. In spite of Knox's vehement protests, it legalized an army whose total personnel consisted of 840 men![8] Of these, only 672 were in service; and they were spaced in tiny corporal's guards along a thousand-mile frontier. Too many Americans, despite all previous experience, had a touching faith that an armed and equipped militia could be made to spring up overnight in defense of the country against foreign invasion.

After the most strenuous exertions, Brigadier-General Josiah Harmar finally marched from Fort Washington on September 30, 1790, with a force of 320 regulars and 1,133 militia. James O'Fallon, private agent of the Yazoo Company, watched them depart with considerable forebodings. The expedition, he hastened to inform Washington, was certain to fail. It had been hastily and badly planned; the militia, unaccustomed to discipline and mutinous for want of meat, had already "lost" a hundred men in the first few days.[9]

At first, however, in spite of mutiny and desertions, everything seemed to go well. The little army triumphantly burned abandoned Indian villages and pressed on to new and similar victories. Then, while tangled in the dense forests and straggling in broken formation, the dreaded war whoop sounded, guns blazed from every tree and painted savages swarmed to the attack.

At the very first fire the militia threw down their arms, so reported the indignant general, "without scarcely firing a gun" and fled each man for himself. The regulars, caught unawares, nevertheless showed their discipline by keeping together, firing at every flash and puff of smoke, and retreating slowly and in good order. The fuming commander regathered those of the militia who were not already halfway home or dead, and threatened them with artillery if they ever straggled or quit the ranks again. Under these gentle admonitions, the militia's backbone stiffened and they redeemed themselves somewhat in a second encounter with the Wabash on October 22nd, though suffering heavy losses in the process.

In a gloomy summary of the net result of his inglorious expedition Harmar placed the Indian losses at 100 to 120 warriors; the American at 180 men.[10]

When the news traveled East, a great outcry was raised and a clamor for the immediate termination of the war. Washington flew into a passion, chiefly directed against the unfortunate Harmar. He had anticipated just such a "disgraceful termination," he told Knox furiously. "I expected *little* from the moment I heard he was a drunkard. I expected *less* as soon as I heard that on this *account* no confidence was reposed in him by the people of the Western Country. And I gave up *all hope* of success, as soon as I heard that there were disputes with *him* about command." [11]

It was impossible, however, for the government to stay its hand now. Emboldened by their victory, the Indians initiated a series of raids, murders and atrocities that would have compelled the abandonment of the entire line of frontier settlements had they not been summarily stopped.[12]

Harmar was in disgrace; and the command was transferred to Brigadier-General Charles Scott. He proved to be more able—or more fortunate. He started from the Ohio on May 23, 1791, and raided deep into Indian territory. He returned with a net of 32 Indian dead, 58 prisoners and several villages destroyed. The total American casualties consisted only of 5 men wounded.[13]

But this was a mere interlude. Later in the same year General Arthur St. Clair, governor of the territory, undertook a more formidable invasion and suffered one of the most disastrous defeats in early American history. Of this more in a later chapter.

Further to bedevil the frontier situation were the activities of the private speculative land companies. If the aggressions of the Ohio, Scioto and other companies had helped bring about the Indian troubles in the West and Northwest, the new Yazoo companies embroiled the entire Southwest in a series of notorious scandals which almost brought the United States into open war with a great Indian confederacy as well as the sovereign state of Georgia.

Actually there were three Yazoo companies to which Georgia, under unbelievable conditions of bribery and corruption, had issued grants totaling 15,500,000 acres of land, which stretched all the way to the

Mississippi. Political personages from many states had their fingers in the pie and participated in the devious transaction. Included in their ranks were Patrick Henry, Alexander Moultrie, David Ross, Abraham B. Venable, Zachariah Cox, Isaac Huger, John B. Scott and others of similar weight and influence. For this princely domain, whose extent was greater than that of many European countries, the total purchase price—most of which was to be paid in the distant future—came to $207,580.[14]

The claims of Georgia to this immense domain, which comprised almost all the lands of the Choctaw, Chickasaw and Cherokee nations, were shadowy and dubious at best. But the tenuousness of their title did not deter the companies from promptly opening offices in New England and Pennsylvania for the sale of small parcels of the grants to individual purchasers. This was smart procedure, as the event was to show.

The companies also raised contingents of armed men for forcible entry and settlement of their claims in the territory of the Indian nations. Alarmed at the proposed invasion, which would bring the Americans down upon their own borders, the Spaniards gathered their own forces to prevent the incursion.

Secretary of War Knox, greatly indignant over the fast developing situation, queried the President about it. Inasmuch as any attempt by private individuals or by a state to extinguish Indian claims without federal authority contravened the Constitution and former treaties, ought he not to interpose immediately to forbid invasion or settlement? [15]

Even the people of Georgia were outraged, but for a different reason. Their indignation was directed not against the validity of the state title, but against a corrupt legislature which had disposed of a fabulous domain for a pittance. Proof was soon forthcoming that practically every member had received either shares in the companies themselves or more direct bribes in the form of cash.

The erring members were turned out of office at the next election, and the new legislature zealously nullified the entire transaction. But this downright procedure ran into a thorny thicket of legal and constitutional questions which agitated the courts, the state and the general government for many years to come. It was argued on behalf of the purchasers from the Yazoo companies that they were third-party holders in good faith and that therefore their contractual possession could not be annulled because of any taint in the original transaction. After numerous vicissitudes this contention was upheld by the courts insofar as Georgia was concerned. But the federal government had a deep interest in the proceedings, because of their effect on Indian and Spanish relations. Eventually it paid off the claimants from its own pocket, during Jefferson's administration; thereby arousing the wrath of the simon-pure John Randolph of Roanoke, who seceded from his party and its President to form his own group of Tertium Quids.

At the end of 1790 the capital of the United States was moved from New York to Philadelphia, to remain there for ten years while a permanent seat of government was being laid out in swamp and woodland on the banks of the Potomac.

The transfer was a comparatively simple one. Congress shifted its meetings to a new brick building on the corner of Sixth and Chestnut Streets, in the neighborhood of Independence Hall. The officers of government rented houses where they could and took offices in the vicinity of Market and Chestnut Streets. Archives were few and easily transported.

The most difficult problem was to find private quarters. The influx of congressmen, government officials, servants, entourage and the inevitable hangers-on proved a harvest which the enlightened Philadelphians were only too happy to reap. Rents doubled over the previous year, and living costs soared.[16] Rooms, even not of the best, were at a premium. The unconscionable gouging, the drab Quaker atmosphere, the flat terrain, evoked nostalgic memories of New York. But forthright Abigail Adams, sighing for the pristine innocence of her native Massachusetts, lumped both cities in a sweeping condemnation. They were equal sinks of iniquity, she snorted, and their wickedness was due in large part to their extensive foreign populations. Nor did it improve her temper or modify her prejudice to discover that every woman cook she employed was a drunkard.[17] She did admit, however, that Philadelphia was a "General Resort during winter, and one continual scene of Parties upon Parties, Balls and entertainments equal to any European city." [18]

Under the impetus of the government transfer, Philadelphia became a fashionable town and the seat of a glittering society. Its undisputed social leader was Mrs. Anne Bingham, daughter of the wealthy merchant banker Thomas Willing, and wife to the even more wealthy William Bingham, who was later to enter the United States Senate in acknowledgment of his gift for making money.

Anne Bingham, stately and beautiful as a regnant queen should be, had married at the tender age of sixteen, then departed for Europe to receive social polish and the ultimate gloss of manners. For five years she was a London sensation; perhaps because London society, when it thought of American women at all, envisaged them as half Indian squaw and half horny-handed, hatchet-featured pioneer.

On her return, she set herself up as the social arbiter of Philadelphia society and built for herself a gargantuan copy of the Duke of Manchester's London house. "The Mansion House," as everyone called it, on Third Street near Spruce, was the most elaborate and costly private residence Americans had yet seen. Visitors came to gape and admire; and rival ladies swooned with envy. Everything about it was lavish and opulent; its grand interior ornament was a great self-supporting stairway of the finest white marble, the first of its kind in the country. Three acres of formal gardens, shady walks and imposing statuary completed the magnificent picture. An invitation to one of Mrs. Bingham's balls or assemblies was a passport to distinction; a nod or gracious word from the hostess proof positive that the lucky recipient was "in" society.[19]

It was this society which Jefferson was to find most uncongenial in its rampant federalism, antirevolutionary feeling and general aristocratic airs, until finally he fled from it to seek comfort in the society of less wealthy radicals, scientists and scholars.

Hamilton, on the other hand, was in his element. His slight, erect figure, his vigorous, positive speech, his views on finance, domestic and world politics proved *en rapport* with the Willings, the Binghams, their satellites and cronies. They had made money in the past from his financial system and expected to make much more in the future. These were ties stronger than steel bands.

That system, however, was not yet complete. Hamilton had in mind two other pillars to make of it a stately and enduring edifice. One was the establishment of a national bank.

The plan had been maturing ever since, as Washington's aide-de-camp, he had proposed the chartering of a bank with government participation as a means of financing the Revolution. It had then met with respectful attention but no action. Now he was in a position to bring it to fruition. Only such a bank, he was convinced, by tapping the financial resources of the rich, could stabilize the money economy of the country and render it invulnerable to ordinary shocks and disasters. That the rich would in turn profit by it merely brought his favorite thesis into play: the support of the moneyed men was essential to the government, and it could be had only by purchase.

Hamilton had mentioned the bank in his first report on public credit, but had left its creation until after the debt had been safely funded. Now, on December 13, 1790, he submitted two additional reports to the House of Representatives which in their essence neatly dovetailed.

The first was a supplemental report on the public credit. The annual debt service, he said, amounted to $826,624.73; a sum which the current revenues were inadequate to meet. He therefore proposed further duties on distilled spirits, imported and domestic.[20]

But the new duties, insofar as they were laid on spirits of domestic manufacture, ran into trouble in the House. They were, declared Jackson of Georgia, in form an excise tax. And excise taxes, with the memory still green of British searches and seizures, fell with an ominous ring on many ears. Raising his voice angrily, Jackson denounced the tax as "odious, unpopular and oppressive," and falling with particular hardship on the South, where distilled liquors were "not only necessary but salutary." [21]

Much to Jackson's surprise, however, members from that very South whose interests he so solicitously protected rose to confute him. Madison thought that of all types of excise taxes that on liquor was the "least exceptionable." William Branch Giles, a recently elected member from Virginia and destined to assume the leadership of the Republican group, objected to Jackson's cool assumption that he spoke for the South. If proper safeguards were placed on the manner of collection, he asserted, the people would "cheerfully acquiesce." [22] Even Jefferson, an interested observer, considered the tax on whiskey a proper source of revenue, both on fiscal and on moral grounds.[23]

The moral element, indeed, was a powerful one. There was a strong and steadily growing body of citizens who looked on spirituous liquors however derived as an evil and a poison which swallowed up the earnings of the poor and ruined their health. Their point of view had already been aired in the earlier debate on the revenue system and elicited angry sarcasm from Fisher Ames. Now they were fortified with a solemn memorial from the College of Physicians of Philadelphia. That learned group called on the Senate to impose sufficiently heavy taxes on distilled liquors to discourage their use. These were, the memorial asserted, "not only destructive to health and life, but . . . they impair the faculties of the mind, and thereby tend equally to dishonor our character as a nation, and to degrade our species as intelligent beings." [24]

But Jackson was not to be deterred. He quoted at length from a volume by the Reverend Mr. Morse in which that obvious expert exalted the beneficial effects of alcohol, and then persisted in his own oratorical flights until his wearied colleagues were reduced to silence; upon which Jackson taunted them with an inability to answer his arguments. This roused Lawrence of New York sufficiently to retort that his arguments were not impressive enough to justify any reply. The excise passed the House eventually by a vote of 35 to 21. In the Senate there was little opposition to it, and it became law on March 3, 1791. [25]

The denouement, however, proved Jackson a better prophet than his Southern colleagues. The western sections of Pennsylvania, Virginia, the Carolinas and Georgia rose in violent protest against the tax. It deeply affected their pockets, their economy and their way of life.

They would have agreed, had they only known of it, with Dr. Samuel Johnson's famous definition of "excise" as "a hateful tax levied upon commodities, and adjudged not by the common judges of property, but wretches hired by those to whom excise is paid."

The Appalachian range interposed a prohibitive barrier to the transport of Western grain to the Eastern markets for sale. By potstilling the bulky grain into the small and manageable compass of whiskey, the "Monongahela" rye could be shipped over the mountains and converted into desperately scarce hard cash. The additional tax, however, either raised the price beyond the reach of the poorer class (the wealthy drank imported wines) or ensured that it could not meet the competition of the local product.

In western Pennsylvania particularly, the opposition flared into violence. When it was discovered that protest meetings and demands for repeal were unavailing, one of the "wretches" who had been appointed collector was treated to a coat of tar and feathers; a simple old man whom the marshal had prudently deputized to serve his processes was first whipped, then given the same sticky coat; still another, mentally unbalanced, whose delusion took the peculiar form of believing himself to be a collector, was not only tarred and feathered but branded with hot irons. Witnesses to these outrages were threatened or abducted, and the chief inspector of the excise for the area, General John Neville, discreetly fled his own home. He departed hardly a moment too soon, for a band of armed men riddled his house with bullets in a vain attempt to rid themselves both of the law and of the inspector.[26]

Even worse was to come later, as the movement swelled to what seemed to the alarmed government revolutionary proportions. But enough was already disclosed to convince Jefferson, Madison and the leaders of the Republican party that they would lose their most valuable allies if they did not now discover a fact to which they had been singularly blind before—the complete odiousness of the tax on whiskey.

All this was still in the future as Congress, with the excise enacted into law, next turned its attention to Hamilton's bill for chartering a national bank. Once again Congress and the country divided into mutually antagonistic camps, the lines of which were daily becoming more and more sharp and clearcut.

Hamilton had written a powerful report. He hailed his proposed bank as "an institution of primary importance to the prosperous administration of the finances" and "of the greatest utility in the operations connected with the support of the public credit." He marshaled arguments to prove that it would increase the active or productive capital of the country, that it would provide the government with a ready means for borrowing money, and would facilitate the collection of taxes. None of these functions, he pointed out, could be performed by the state banks then in existence.

His bank was to be a mixed governmental and private institution, in which, however, the private interest would predominate. The capital stock would consist of 25,000 shares, of the par value of $400 each. Of these the government was authorized to subscribe to 5000 shares; the balance was open to private purchase. The shares were payable one-fourth in coin and three-fourths in the six-per-cent government funded debt. Hamilton explained this peculiar arrangement with the statement that there was not enough gold and silver in the country to pay the full price in cash. Besides, he added candidly, such an arrangement would enhance the value of the funded debt.

The management of the bank was in the hands of a board of twenty-five directors, of whom the government could appoint no more than five. This insured complete control by the private stockholders, which was exactly what Hamilton intended, and so openly declared. The bank, he wrote, "shall be under a *private* not a *public* direction— under the guidance of *individual interest,* not of *public policy.*"

The bank was given the power to issue bills and notes to an amount of $10,000,000 in excess of its deposits; and the notes so issued would be legal tender for all debts and taxes due the United States. The charter life of the bank was to be twenty years; during which period the government was prohibited from chartering a rival institution.[27]

The publication of the report aroused the country as not even assumption had done. The moneyed men, as Hamilton had anticipated, hastened to prepare themselves for the feast which was shortly to be spread before them. The first rush was for the six-per-cent funds— the essential requirement for the purchase of the bank shares when, as no moneyed man doubted, they would be authorized by Congress. Within a few days the public debt rose on the market with a speed that surprised even such an insider as Fisher Ames, while Dutch agents, vigilant to every breath of change in the American financial system, invested heavily in anticipation of a further rise.[28]

Nor were they disappointed in their expectations. The six-per-cents jumped to seventeen shillings on the pound, teetered around that figure during the doubtful days ahead; then, after the bill had finally passed Congress and was signed by the President, commenced a steady upward climb that lifted them to twenty-three shillings, well above par. Even the despised three-per-cents and the deferred sixes benefited from the buying wave, rising from a general level of nine shillings to thirteen six and thirteen eight respectively.[29]

But if the moneyed men hastened joyously to the fleshpots, the people who had no ready cash for investment now discovered in Hamilton and his schemes the obvious image of the Devil himself. The farmers of the North and West, who hated and feared even local state banks as engines specially designed for their destruction; the Southern planters, forever without hard money and convinced that a national bank would prove a new and more formidable drain on their scanty resources; the state-sovereignty men, who foresaw the doom of local prerogatives in this strategically centered money power—all joined in a huge clamor of wrath and terror.

Patrick Henry found in the report a complete justification of his original opposition to the Constitution. It was, he gloomily asserted, "a consistent part of a system which I ever dreaded. Subserviency of southern to northern interests are written in capitals on its very front; whilst government influence, deeply planted and widely scattered by preceding measures, is to receive a formidable addition by this plan." [30]

In Congress, each branch acted in accordance with the special interests of its members and their constituencies. The Senate passed the bill with extreme rapidity, riding roughshod over a rather weak opposition. Maclay of Pennsylvania, almost at the end of his short term of office, tried vainly to amend the bill so as to make the government an equal partner with private stockholders. But his colleague Robert Morris refused to join in the amendment. He had heard from General Schuyler, he explained, that Hamilton would not brook the slightest alteration in the bill. To which Maclay retorted—in his diary—that "Schuyler is the supple-jack of his son-in-law Hamilton."

Curiously enough, though Maclay thought any bank "an aristocratic engine," he voted in the end for the unamended bill, refusing to ally himself with those who would have destroyed the bank altogether.[31]

By this time, it seems, the backwoods senator was tired of politics and disgusted with his country. On January 20, 1791, he dined with the President for the last time and found him wasted, his movements slow and his complexion almost cadaverous. Even his voice, commented Maclay, was "hollow and indistinct, owing as I believe, to artificial teeth before his upper jaw." [32] On March 4th he shook the dust of Philadelphia from his feet and went home gladly to private life and obscurity. Perhaps the most egalitarian and homespun democrat of them all, in the end Maclay found even Jefferson and Madison insufficiently of the people for his taste.

In the House, however, the bill ran into the whirlwind. It was not taken up for debate until after the Senate had given its approval. As usual, the stormy petrel of the opposition, Jackson of Georgia, opened the proceedings. The bank, he cried, "is calculated to benefit a small part of the United States, the mercantile interest only; the farmers, the yeomanry, will derive no advantage from it."

But this had been the argument interposed to every Hamiltonian measure and had always failed to shake the solid mass of his supporters. In the realization that it must fail again, Jackson tried a new and more formidable attack. A national bank, he said, was unconstitutional. Nothing in the Constitution gave Congress the power to erect and charter corporations. From his desk he picked up a bound volume of the *Federalist* papers—coauthored by Hamilton! Opening it with a flourish, he read at length from the several papers to prove his point. Then, with a triumphant air, he sat down.[33]

But Lawrence of New York was instantly on his feet to meet the threat. The power to borrow money, he declared, *was* in the Constitution; and such a power implied and presupposed a right to create a capital from which borrowing might be done.[34] Thus early Lawrence adumbrated the classic and eventually victorious doctrine which Hamilton took up and polished, and which John Marshall finally erected into an unshakable pillar of the nation.

The next day Madison took the floor. Here was one of the fathers of the Constitution, an equal sharer in the *Federalist* papers, and certainly one whose opinions on the constitutionality of the measure merited the greatest attention and respect.

After a few brief remarks on the merits of the bank per se, he plunged directly into the heart of the matter. In low, even tones he developed to its full extent the theory which Jackson had previously bellowed. The Constitution, he said, was a limited document and had been intended as such. Indeed, the very matter before the House had been discussed at length in the Constitutional Convention; and had been there rejected. Madison raised his voice a trifle. Once powers not specifically given were read into the Constitution, he warned, the floodgates would be opened; and the sharply defined clauses and the enumeration of specific powers might just as well not have been written.[35]

Logical, legalistic, unemotional, Madison's argument was the ablest and most powerful that could be put forward for a strict construction of the Constitution; and it became the basis for Jefferson's later opinion to Washington and the future opposition to Marshall's exposition.

Only one man in the House could be relied on to combat Madison's careful discussion. This was Ames of Massachusetts, ready and resourceful in debate and a far more dazzling orator. Yet he prudently refused to meet Madison on the legalistic ground which the latter had prepared. Instead, he directed his whole attention to the theory of government itself and to an elaboration of the doctrine of implied powers.

Of what use was a government, he inquired, if it could not act for its own benefit? How could it continue to exist under such strict limitations as the opposition proposed? Of what value was the admitted right to borrow if a bank, its best possible source, were prohibited? In that event Congress might just as well go home, for it had been enacting unconstitutional measures ever since it came into existence. Have we not already laid taxes on ships, erected lighthouses and passed laws to govern sailors on the high seas—none of which was expressly stated in the Constitution—as incidents of the power to regulate trade? [36]

With the conflicting positions thus clearly stated by the respective champions, the debate continued until nearly every member of the House had had his say. By February 8th the arguments were worn threadbare with endless repetition and no man's opinion had been changed in the slightest. In common exhaustion the House took a vote; and the bank bill passed by a majority of almost two to one.

Hamilton and his friends exulted; but shortly thereafter their rejoicing turned to alarm. There had been one man who had followed the debate with the closest attention, and Madison's arguments had troubled his mind and engendered doubt. This was the President of the United States. As the bill came to his desk for signature, he hesitated. Was it in truth an unconstitutional arrogation of powers?

He called on the Attorney General, Edmund Randolph, for his opinion. Randolph, a Virginian and friend to Jefferson and Madison, declared it unconstitutional. Still undecided, Washington turned to Jefferson.

The Secretary of State had been watching Hamilton's flowering program with the greatest unease. Though he had gone along with him on assumption and the excise, he had already repented of his assent. More and more, as he saw it, the country was falling into the control of the moneyed and merchant classes; more and more the interests of the farmer and the plantation owner were being ignored. The bank was the last straw. Himself a plantation owner and a farmer, Jefferson was deeply suspicious of those who trafficked in paper evidences of money, who sought from gold and silver an artificial increase which did not come naturally from the fruits of the earth. Even state banks battened on the farmer's toil and took from him his sweaty gains; a national bank would extend its tentacles into every corner of the land and drain all money into the hands of a few northern financiers.

He could no longer look to the House of Representatives, popularly elected though it was, as a bulwark against the machinations of the money men. Events of recent months had proved the contrary. The only remedy, he thought, was to enlarge its membership, "so as to get a more agricultural representation, which may put that interest above that of the stockjobbers." [37] Just how a mere increase in members would increase the farmer interest without proportionately increasing the representatives of the "stockjobbers" he did not say. There is no evidence that he meant a broadening of the base of the electorate, which might have effected the compositional change he desired.

With Washington's request before him, Jefferson sat down to write his opinion that the bank was unconstitutional. The gist of his argument was based on the Tenth Amendment: that "all powers not delegated to the United States, by the Constitution, nor prohibited by it to the States, are reserved to the States and the people."

Had the power to erect a bank been delegated to the United States? No such clause existed in the Constitution. The proponents of the bank had read strange meanings into the "general welfare" clause and the further one which granted Congress the right "to make all laws necessary and proper for carrying into execution the enumerated powers." To these Jefferson retorted that the words "general welfare" possessed no such magical qualities as they pretended; while the words "necessary and proper" meant "indispensable" and not merely "convenient." Unless we adhered, he concluded, to the strict wording of the Constitution and ordinary dictionary meanings, there could be no system of laws or jurisprudence.[38]

Henry Knox, the next Cabinet member to whom Washington turned in his perplexity, delivered a terse statement that the bank was constitutional. Finally the President called on Hamilton, sending him the opinions of Jefferson and Randolph for consideration.

Working at his usual breakneck speed, in a single night Hamilton drafted his reply—a reply which has become the classic fount for all future discussions on constitutional powers.

As Ames had previously done, Hamilton first veered away from the Constitution itself to examine the nature of government. Emphasizing almost every other noun with italics (which can safely be removed) he hammered his thesis: "This general principle is inherent in the very definition of government, and essential to every step of the progress to be made by that of the United States, namely: That every power vested in a government is in its nature sovereign, and includes, by force of the term, a right to employ all the means requisite and fairly applicable to the attainment of the ends of such power, and which are not precluded by restrictions and exceptions specified in the Constitution, or not immoral, or not contrary to the essential ends of political society."

With this generalization as a tool, he now turned to the Constitution. Here, he asserted, was no case of any express restriction. On the contrary, Congress had been given the power to raise money, and the further power to enact such measures as were "necessary and proper" for that and other purposes. He took sharp issue with Jefferson on the meaning of "necessary." "It often means," he said, "no more than *needful, requisite, incidental, useful,* or *conductive to.*" What could be more applicable than these definitions to the function of a bank in providing a repository of money from which the government could borrow? [39]

With the opinions of the four members of the Cabinet now before him, Washington studied them with extreme care. Since a tie existed, he felt himself free to come to an independent decision. It was Hamilton's argument that turned the scale and convinced him that the bank was constitutionally proper. He therefore signed the bill on February 25, 1791.

Now that the bank was a *fait accompli,* Jefferson knew that he had come to the final parting of the ways. Hereafter between Hamilton and himself there must be war eternal. Nor did he feel the old friendship or trust for Washington. Only two weeks prior he had expressed faith in the "prudence" of the President as "an anchor of safety to us." [40] He no longer considered it as such; Washington to him had been definitely taken into the camp of the enemy.

The only satisfaction that Jefferson could derive at the moment came from the admission of Vermont on March 4th into the Union. That turbulent nest of highly individualistic men, who had resented equally the claims of New Hampshire and New York to domination over them, and had been willing not long before to secede altogether and adhere to Great Britain or proclaim themselves an independent republic, had finally been granted sovereignty on an equal footing with the older states. With a population of farmers and frontiersmen as granitic as their fields, and radical in their politics, Vermont could safely be counted in the growing fold of Republican states. So could Kentucky and Tennessee, already slated for entrance into the Union; so could other states to be carved out of the vast Northwest in the more distant future.

In the long view, thought Jefferson, the current rule of the moneyed men must pass and the bright sun of republicanism rise, never to set.

CHAPTER 10

The "Rights of Man"
Versus the "China Trade"

IN SPITE OF revolutions abroad, onerous restrictions and closed economies throughout the world, impressments, seizures and outright
piracies, wars actual and threatened, the foreign trade of the United
States flourished mightily and American ships sailed the seven seas,
making the stars and stripes a familiar sight in every port and every
clime.

Great Britain was still America's best customer and her chief source
for manufactured goods—a fact which accounted for the reluctance of
the merchants to adopt measures which might lead to a complete
stoppage of trade, and for Hamilton's determination to hold fast to
amicable relations, no matter how difficult, as the sheet anchor of his
financial system.

For the year ending September 1790, the United States exported
products, almost wholly agricultural in nature, amounting to over
$20,000,000; and imported goods, chiefly manufactured, valued at
more than $15,000,000. Slightly less than half of the exports went
to England, less than a fourth to France, with the remainder scattered
among Spain, the Netherlands and Portugal. Of the imports, about
$13,300,000 came from England and her colonies—almost ninety per
cent of the total—eloquent testimony to the havoc which would have
been created by Madison's semiembargo.[1] Neither France nor the
Netherlands nor Spain, nor all of them combined, could have filled
the breach. They did not have the manufactured goods, the quality
or the long-term credit terms required for the American market.

The one fly in the ointment was the fact that American ships
carried only fifty per cent of the total stream of goods because of the
restrictions imposed by the British, who sought thus to favor their own
merchant marine. But the merchants and mariners of America refused

to repine unduly. Barred from many markets, they looked for compensation elsewhere. The Mediterranean beckoned, and the Far East.

On August 9, 1790, a storm-battered ship, her paint blistered and peeled, her rigging tattered, her sails bearing great patches and her bottom dragging with strange encrustations, moved slowly into Boston harbor. But her first glimpse in the vigilant spyglasses and telescopes on shore set the waterfront into commotion and the great church bells of the town to furious ringing. For the limping ship was the *Columbia,* Robert Gray captain, home after years of voyaging, the first American vessel to circumnavigate the globe.

The treasures in her hold, the tales of fabulous Cathay, of strange, spice-odorous islands, of nankeens, tin, spices, teas and sugars, touched off a wave of outfitting for the distant East; though American ships had already found their way to Canton and Bombay.

Fortunately, the story may be read intact with all its perils, tribulations and rewards, in the business correspondence of one of the great trading firms of New York, William Constable and Company.

Explicit, detailed instructions went with every captain and supercargo of their little fleet. Not the meanest trifle was overlooked. Captain Peter Hodgkinson and supercargo William Bell, sailing out of New York at the turn of 1790-1, were instructed to carry full sail all the way around the Cape of Good Hope in order to reach India and China before rival ships from European ports, leaving early in the spring, could make the run. Those first on the ground could dispose of their cargoes and pick up return merchandise at the most advantageous prices.

Speed, and more speed, was the constant theme. "Use every method to get to market before your Competitors," exhorted the merchant, and get back to port "earlier than the other vessels out of China." Economy was another favorite watchword, and many a captain was roundly abused for "the system of extravagance which has been introduced into our Ships in the trade" and which, "unless corrected, must put a total stop to our carrying on that commerce."

The trade was a complicated affair, involving barters, sales, purchases and transshipments all along the way. The eastbound vessels would start from port—New York, Boston or Philadelphia—laden with ginseng (an aromatic root found in New England which was in huge demand in China for its alleged medicinal and magical virtues), lumber, spars, cables and cordage, muskets and other firearms, sometimes grain, and always a large chest in which was securely locked gold and silver coins from every nation.

The first landfall was either London or a Spanish port. There the grain would be disposed of, and in its place Holland gin, cherry brandy, madeira, sherry, pig iron, steel bars, sealskins and other furs were stowed on board.

Then, coasting down Africa and rounding the Cape of Good Hope into the Indian Ocean, the ship put in at Bombay. The supercargo bore letters of introduction to the English factor in residence, but he was advised if possible to employ "a black broker" in order to save double payments of commissions. In case American ships proved to be subject to undue restrictions in Bombay, he carried additional letters of a confidential nature to show to the "right" people in the British East India Company.

In Bombay the entire cargo was to be disposed of with the exception of the ginseng and the furs. Since this was also the time of the Nootka Sound incident, Constable took all eventualities into consideration. If war between England and Spain had in the meantime broken out, then, he suggested, there might be a possibility of selling everything, including the ship itself, in India to the British at a price that would cover the anticipated profits of proceeding to China. In that case, or in the further event that East India personnel returning to England chartered the ship for their private use, do not, warned the merchant, say anything to the officers and crew about it, since they would be certain to demand higher wages. This was a bit of sharp practice on the part of the owners, for such a sale or charter in mid-voyage would deprive the crew and ship officers of their proportionate share, usually a small graded percentage, of the profits of the cargoes later to be picked up in China and the Spice Islands.

Normally, however, after picking up a cargo of replacement goods in India, the vessel's next ports of call were in the Malay Peninsula and the Spice Islands. At "Pulo Pinang" tin and pepper were taken on board. In going through the Malacca Straits, Constable instructed, inquire of Mynheer Ingleheard Shabandar of Batavia (evidently a half-breed of Dutch and native parentage) whether Dutch East Indies sugar and pepper could be picked up in exchange for American dollars. "This Gentleman, we are informed," wrote the merchant, "will be willing to deal with you altho the trade is prohibited, but he is the Governor's son in Law, and at the Head of the Department of Trade."

With the ship now fully loaded—in part because of the financially profitable complaisance of the "Governor's son in Law"—it proceeded next through the China Sea to Canton. There the ginseng, furs, sealskins, elkhorns and teeth, tin and India cotton, were sold; and tea and additional "nankings" ("always a good article as they do not spoil with age") were purchased for the cargo home.

Tea, of course, was the most desirable import to America. Buy Bohea tea only, urged Constable. It is "an unfailing article, about 4000 Chests are annually consumed on this Continent." But, he warned the supercargo, make certain that the rival *President*, already en route, did not clear from China before you with a cargo of that popular brew. Because if it did, by the time you return they will have glutted the market and depressed the price; in which case "the less you have of it the better." Load up then with Hyson tea; but neither Souchong nor the common green varieties. The American people do not like them.

Pepper was also a good staple, while the American consumption of sugar was immense. The French West Indies, the usual source of the latter, had already decreased its output because of revolutionary distractions; the early prospect of an Anglo-French war would cut it off altogether. In that case, calculated Constable, the price of sugar at home would go to eight dollars a barrel; and it would be exceedingly profitable to buy up as much as possible in the East Indies.

The pay of the ship's officers and crew next engaged the close attention of the merchant. The supercargo—perhaps the most important man on the voyage, for he was entrusted with the buying and selling—received five per cent on the entire cargo price both ways; with the added inducement of free shipment of any goods he picked up for his own account. The sailing captain received a flat sum of five hundred pounds sterling for the voyage. As for the crew, wrote the parsimonious merchant, the strictest economy was to be observed in supplying them with provisions. He had stocked the ship with plenty, he said, and "although we are willing to allow the Crew some fresh provisions [obtained at the several ports of call], we do not think it at all requisite to have them maintained at so enormous expence as has heretofore been practiced by the American ships." [2]

In such meticulous detail, with every possible contingency provided for, did the shrewd American merchants plot the voyages of their ships and send them, every sail set for utmost speed, careering over the seven seas.

That the voyages proved most profitable is evidenced by the figures.

Captain Hodgkinson's cargo, including freight picked up in Europe, cost £37,015. It sold in Bombay for a gross of £101,157; handling charges and import duties brought down the net to £90,375. On the Bombay-China run, Hodgkinson's ship, the *Washington*, carried for the account of Indian owners goods worth £30,820, and on their own, worth $16,096. The cargo back to the United States—teas, sugar, silks and cotton—cost $138,950. On each ton of Bohea tea, the owners figured a clear profit of $28.65; on the more expensive Hyson tea, selling for three times as much, a net profit of $285 a ton.[3] No wonder the trading dynasties of Boston, Salem and New York waxed mighty and prevailed![4]

If the Far East proved a bonanza for American enterprise, the Mediterranean did not. The Mohammedan states on the north coast of Africa—Morocco, Algiers, Tunis and Tripoli; more generally lumped together as the Barbary Powers—had been a scourge to the maritime Christian countries for many decades. Their swift piratical cruisers darted out of fortified ports, swooped down on helpless merchantmen and sold into slavery passengers and crew.

Yet the great powers of Europe—England, France, Spain and Portugal—for all their navies and armed might, suffered the depredations with supine fortitude, preferring, as Jefferson bitterly remarked, to count "their interest rather than their honor" and pay annual tributes for exemption from molestation instead of punishing the aggressors.

The Americans, as comparative newcomers to the Mediterranean trade, suffered severely from the piratical forays. Their ships were taken and their crews enslaved; a development viewed with a certain benevolence by England and the others as helping to eliminate an upstart intruder in their maritime preserves.

While minister to France, Jefferson had strenuously sought concerted action by the European powers against the Barbary pirates. When that failed, he called on the United States to proceed alone. But he met with as little success at home as abroad.

Now, as Secretary of State, the matter came up again. In two official reports Jefferson recapitulated the long, sad history of the depredations and captivities. The ships and cargoes were hopelessly lost, but there were unfortunate Americans languishing in slavery from as early as 1785. The Dey of Algiers demanded $59,496 for their release —an exorbitant sum which, while still minister, Jefferson had vainly tried to reduce.

Now as then he was resolved to pay neither ransoms nor tribute. He wished, he declared, to consider the plight of the captives and the havoc to our Mediterranean commerce as a single issue, requiring a single set of measures. These were to meet force with force, to build a fleet for pounding the pirates into submission. Nevertheless, since only Congress could decide for war or peace, he left the choice to them between "war, tribute and ransom." [5]

Washington laid the two reports before Congress and adverted to them in his opening address. But the lawmakers, though agreeing that our commerce in the Mediterranean could be protected only by a naval force and that one ought to be built "as soon as the state of the public finances will admit," preferred for the moment the more immediate if ignominious method of paying ransom.[6] In fact, Jefferson had to wait for his own presidency before he could put his ideas into action and whip the Barbary States into a wholesome respect for American rights.

Since the Department of State served as a catchall for every government activity not specifically included in any one of the other three departments, it had jurisdiction over a host of diverse matters. Such were the establishment of a patent and copyright system, the direction of the Mint—though Hamilton insisted it properly came within the domain of the Treasury—the standardization of weights and measures, and the state of the whale and cod fisheries.

At least this last had international implications, and Jefferson deftly joined a report on the fisheries to a full-dress review of "the nature and extent of the privileges and restrictions of the commercial intercourse of the United States with foreign nations." [7]

In this report Jefferson for the first time threw the weight of his influence and office behind the proposals in Congress for retaliations against England.

Relations had steadily worsened since Madison's unsuccessful attempts to discriminate against British shipping in the tonnage and tariff bills. Even Gouverneur Morris, who had previously favored England, was now compelled to admit his inability to arrive at any satisfactory settlement of grievances with her. His reports home to that effect caused the President to submit the entire correspondence to Congress with the comment that England "without scruple" did not intend to fulfill the terms of the peace treaty or enter into any commercial arrangement with the United States. "Their views being thus sufficiently ascertained," he concluded grimly, "I have directed Mr. Morris to discontinue his communications with them." [8]

In reply a House committee brought in a bill which practically reintroduced Madison's original retaliatory measures.[9]

Even relations with France had taken a turn for the worse; though this time it was the French who did the complaining. On December 13, 1790, M. Otto, the chargé d'affaires, sent a formal protest to Jefferson against the discriminatory provisions against her ships under the tonnage act as contravening the treaties between the two countries. Though Jefferson formally denied the fact, he advised Congress, in view of the possibility that France might institute reprisals against American whale oil, to grant her a special dispensation on the tonnage tax.[10]

"A nation," he also wrote to Hamilton, "which takes one third of our tobacco, more than half our fish oil and two thirds of our fish, say one half of the amount of these great staples and a great deal of rice, and from whom we take nothing in return but hard money to carry directly over and pour into the coffers of their enemies, such a customer, I say deserves some menagemens [sic]." [11]

Surprisingly enough, Hamilton was tempted to agree, though he would have preferred to use the concession as a lever to win a new commercial treaty from France which would provide permanent reciprocal advantages. Yet he could not refrain from adding a note of warning concerning Jefferson's attitude toward England, in the course of which he disclosed the basis for his own commercial philosophy.

"My commercial system," he avowed, "turns very much on giving a free course to trade, and cultivating good humor with all the world. And I feel a particular reluctance to hazard anything, in the present state of our affairs, which may lead to a commercial warfare with any Power; which, as far as my knowledge of examples extends, is commonly productive of mutual inconvenience and injury, and of dispositions tending to a worse kind of warfare. Exemptions and preferences which are not the effect of treaty, are apt to be regarded by those who do not partake in them as proofs of an unfriendly temper towards them." [12]

At the same time Hamilton was privately informing Beckwith that "I think I can assure you that nothing will take place during the present session to the injury of your trade." [13]

He was as good as his word. When the House prepared to act on the committee bill for excluding British ships from the general carrying trade to the United States, it was Hamilton's influence on his friends in Congress that postponed consideration until the following session.

But he failed to convince Jefferson. In the case of France, while denying Otto's claim of right under the old treaty, the latter hinted that the new session of Congress might act to their mutual advantage.[14]

In the case of England, he clung to his convictions. He saw no reason for placating her. She had snubbed, insulted and humiliated us; she had consistently barred us from the West Indies trade and manipulated her navigation system in such fashion as to deprive us of a good percentage of the general carrying trade to our own ports. What worse could she do?

Acting under considerations such as these, Jefferson told New England fishermen who demanded government subsidies to meet foreign competition that the proper answer was free markets for their fish. These, he declared, could be obtained "by friendly arrangements towards those nations whose arrangements are friendly to us."[15] Since this could mean only France, Jefferson by this indirect means thought to gain New England support for that "mutual advantage" he had hinted to M. Otto.

The British consul in Philadelphia was also alert to the implications of Jefferson's indirect approach. "The very strong desire of the Officer from whom the Report on the Fisheries springs," he reported to his home government, "to favor the intercourse with France at the expense of the commerce of Great Britain, is manifest from the scope and terms of his Report; couched in a language of severity not practiced between nations at peace with each other."[16]

Had he waited only one more day before penning his complaint, the consul would have had even more positive proof for his assertions. On March 15, 1791, Jefferson sent to Congress his Report on the commercial intercourse of the United States.[17]

Just as Hamilton had laid bare the springs which motivated his policy in his private letter of January 13th, so Jefferson now did the same publicly in his communication to the House.

He had worked hard on the Report. He listed American exports in detail—breadstuffs, tobacco, rice, fish, salt meats, whale oil—and pointed out on each the hindrances, heavy duties and downright prohibitions we suffered at the hands of England, Spain and Portugal, and to a less degree from France. He animadverted also on the deplorable state of our carrying trade. England, Spain and Portugal prohibited *all* carriage by our ships to their West Indies colonies; and England further forbade the entry of American ships into her home ports with goods not of American growth or production.

What could we do to remove these onerous restrictions on our goods and trade? Jefferson approached the problem in circuitous fashion. Of course, he began, the best possible plan would be a friendly arrangement. Could all commerce "be relieved of all its shackles in all parts of the world, could every country be employed in producing that which nature has best fitted it to produce, and each be free to exchange with others mutual surpluses for mutual wants, the greatest mass possible would then be produced of those things which contribute to human life and human happiness; the numbers of mankind could be increased, and their condition bettered."

Jefferson realized full well that there was no possibility of realizing these propositions in a nonutopian world. But he thus eloquently discoursed for a specific purpose which became apparent in the ensuing section.

Should even *one* nation, he proceeded, act in this wise with us, we could reciprocate. Even if this hypothetical nation met us only halfway, we could meet her on the other half. He had, of course, France in view.

Should any nation, however, he continued sternly, suppose it were more to her advantage to maintain her present system of prohibitions, duties and regulations, then it behooved us to protect ourselves by counterprohibitions, duties and regulations.

Thus, by gentle gradations, he led up to his main point of retaliations on England, which he compressed into two proposals. The first called for warning duties on the products of any nation that heavily taxed or prohibited American goods. If the warning failed of its effect, then we must interpose a total prohibition.

This was sound Madisonian doctrine, with one important modification. In order not to disrupt entirely the American economy, Jefferson would select for retaliation only those products which we could either obtain elsewhere or manufacture here with the aid of artisans from the offending country whom we could induce to migrate to these shores.

On the carrying trade itself, Jefferson was even harsher than Madison in his system of retaliations. He would not only introduce prohibitions in kind, but would carry them over from prohibitions of our ships in foreign colonies to a total prohibition in our ports of the ships of that nation, no matter whence they came.

Jefferson's report proved strong meat indeed. Though some of his recommendations could have been applied equally to Spain and Portugal, neither he nor his party in Congress wished to do so. England was their single target and it was England against whom their bill had been aimed. Jefferson was quick to point this up. The bill, he wrote, "is perfectly innocent as to other nations, is strictly just as to the English, cannot be parried by them, and if adopted by other nations would inevitably defeat their navigation act and reduce their power on the sea within safer limits." He therefore exhorted the American representatives in France, Spain and Portugal to suggest to those countries that they adopt similar measures. If they did, thought Jefferson, "it would soon be fatally felt by the navy of England." [18]

It is difficult to believe that Jefferson took seriously the possibility of such an alliance by mutually suspicious powers against England, nor that he could not envisage the end result if the impossible did happen—total war with England.

Yet he acted as if he thought his plan quite feasible; though perhaps his primary intention was to use it as a means for augmenting the fortunes of the Republicans at home. Everywhere he probed hopefully for signs of discontent with and resistance to the Federalist program, particularly assumption and the excise taxes; and everywhere he urged the election of pure and zealous Republicans to Congress. He even told his friends, though privately he no longer believed it, that Washington was such a Republican. But, he warned, "we cannot expect all his successors to be so, and therefore should avail ourselves the present day to establish principles and examples which may fence us against future heresies preached now, to be practiced hereafter." [19]

Jefferson had chosen a singularly unpropitious moment to approach Spain on joint action against England. Only a few days before, he had instructed Carmichael to demand damages for the unwarranted seizure of an American citizen and his possessions on the *eastern* bank of the Mississippi. It was incidents like this, the Spanish court must be told, that imperiously pointed up the necessity for a complete acknowledgment of our right to navigate the river. To which Jefferson added his usual threat. "Should any spark kindle [the impatience] of our borderers into a flame, we are involved beyond recall by the eternal principles of justice to our citizens, which we will never abandon." [20]

But Spain shrugged off both demand and threat. Now that she was settling with England, she did not fear the bellicose attitude of the American government, already staled by too much repetition.

Nor was Carmichael the best possible diplomat for handling the subtle court of Madrid. He was well-meaning, but dilatory and infuriatingly lax in his dealings. A thick blanket of silence covered his operations, if any; and Washington was later to explode into one of his infrequent but all the more terrible rages. "I believe we are never to hear *from* Mr. Carmichael; nor *of him* but through the medium of a third person. His—I really do not know with what epithet to fill the blank, is, to me, the most unaccountable of all the unaccountable things!" [21]

Nor were the eternal border incidents confined to the Southwest. The geographically opposite Northeast now began to stir uneasily. There had never been an adequate definition of the boundary which separated British Canada from Maine and New York. The Maine boundary had been drawn from an inaccurate map which gave the St. Croix River as fixing the line of demarcation. Unfortunately that river had three branches, and no one knew which one could be called the true St. Croix. As a result a substantial area, called the Passamaquoddy, which lay between the two outside arms, was claimed by both sides. The Americans diligently gathered affidavits to the effect that the extreme eastern branch was the St. Croix; the British with equal testimony asserted the honor for the western arm. [22]

In northern New York, where the St. Lawrence swung to the north and thereby left no natural boundary, there was a similar dispute. The British summarily moved into the no man's land and established settlements; a procedure which evoked indignant outcries coupled with local threats to evict the intruders by force. An international incident impended.

Jefferson approached this new trouble spot with the utmost caution. The bellicose attitude he had used with Spain could not safely be employed with Great Britain.

The situation was most perplexing, he confessed to the President. Perhaps it were best to tell the aggrieved states that they neither move into the disputed territory themselves nor suffer the British to do so. Force might indeed be used to keep the British out; but only the militia was to handle the situation and even then with extreme restraint. [23]

Washington approved the suggestions; but did not stay in Philadelphia to witness their effect.[24] He was already on his way south to survey that section of the country at first hand and thus complete his travels. On the way he stopped at the site of the new national capital, still mired in swamps and bogged down even worse by the mutual jealousies of the neighboring towns of Carrollsburgh and Georgetown, which refused to cede the requisite public lands. He succeeded in inducing the wrangling rivals to make the proper patriotic gesture, then rode deeper south all the way to Georgia before returning by slow stages to Mount Vernon. What caught his professional eye most on the journey were the old battlefields of the Revolution on which Greene and Gates had tried in vain to stem the British invasion.[25]

During his absence, fortunately, the northern borders had been comparatively quiet, and the entire dispute simmered on until it was finally settled under the terms of the Jay Treaty by a mixed commission. They chose the middle branch of the St. Croix as the boundary line—a sensible compromise in an explosive situation.

As it was, there were sufficient headaches over British policies. Parliament was considering a bill to grant free storage to wheat imported in British bottoms. Since American ships, the prime movers of grain from their own country, would not be entitled to the same privilege, the cost differential would practically drive the Americans from the sea. In addition, the British refused to consider any ship American unless it had actually been built in this country. This meant, said Jefferson indignantly, that in the event England became engaged in a war (a development he hopefully anticipated) "they put it out of our power to benefit ourselves of our neutrality, by increasing suddenly by purchase and naturalization our means of carriage. If we are permitted to do this by building only, the war will be over before we can be prepared to take advantage of it." [26]

France too was acting badly. The previous favorable treatment of American whale oil and tobacco was replaced by stringent regulations; a not too gentle hint to the United States to reconsider its own discriminatory tonnage tax. Even Jefferson, disposed to think the best of France's "so beautiful revolution" and hoping "for the good of suffering humanity" that it would spread over the entire world, was taken aback.[27]

Since Virginia tobacco was involved as well as Northern whale oil, for the first time Jefferson became sharply critical of the French. In a note bristling with wrath he called on Short to interpose a strong protest in Paris. It was "such an act of hostility against our navigation," he exclaimed, "as was not to be expected from the friendship of that Nation. It is as new in its nature as extravagant in its degree, since it is unexampled that any nation has endeavoured to wrest from another the carriage of its own produce, except in the case of their Colonies." Even the British Navigation Act, he asserted, "so much and so justly complained of, leaves to all nations the carriage of their own commodities free." [28]

What the French had done was to decree that American tobacco and oil, when imported in American ships, were to carry a much higher duty than when imported in French vessels.

With France now taking its stand along with England and Spain in attempts to cripple American commerce, the outlook was dark indeed. In this moment of gloom Jefferson even toyed with the idea of America's turning seriously to manufactures. "If Europe will not let us carry our provisions to their manufactures," he wrote, "we must endeavor to bring their manufactures to our provisions." [29]

But this genuflection in the direction of a Hamiltonian thesis was short-lived. Almost immediately he returned to his pristine belief in the agricultural future of America. The shift in his attitude was occasioned by two sudden and unexpected rays of light in the darkling impasse. France declared her intention of replacing Otto by a full minister in the person of Jean-Baptiste Ternant; and simultaneously came the cheering news that the British ministry had finally decided to dispatch a minister to the United States with powers to settle all issues in dispute and to arrange a satisfactory commercial settlement.

If Jefferson for the moment had turned on France, his Republican followers had remained steadfast to the faith. Neither the restrictions on American goods and ships, nor the dramatic flight of the French king with his subsequent recapture, nor the growing excesses and totalitarianism of the French Revolution, shook their convictions in the slightest. They continued to cling to the bright and glittering slogans with which the revolution had been invested, and shut their eyes determinedly to the disparities between profession and act; or, if these became too patently visible, ascribed them to the wickedness of the aristocrats and the hostility of the monarchs.

Certainly they would have been shocked by the cynical description by Gouverneur Morris of the first French revolutionary assembly. It was composed, he said, of the aristocrats, the *enragés* or madmen, and a middle party who, meaning well, "have unfortunately acquired their ideas of Government from Books and are admirable fellows upon Paper; but as it happens somewhat unfortunately that the men who live in the World are very different from those who dwell in the heads of Philosophers, it is not to be wondered at if the Systems taken out of Books are fit for nothing but to be put into Books again." [30]

Such an opinion, echoed somewhat in the devastating if rather jaundiced *Reflections on the Revolution in France* by Edmund Burke in England, roused the Republicans to fury. Thomas Paine was more than merely furious; he sat down to compose a reply to Burke.

Paine had become the stormy petrel of two continents. Brilliant, restless, passionate in his convictions and devoting every feverish energy to the causes in which he believed, his writings had once been a trumpet blast in the American Revolution. Now he was back in England, the country of his birth, with plans teeming in his fertile mind for building iron bridges and for bigger and better revolutions. Such a one he saw in the French convulsion. He rushed to its defense with even more ardor than he had displayed in the espousal of the American prototype; particularly since the accomplishment of the latter had brought in its train conservatism and a dimming of the vision.

Paine wrote his reply to Burke at top speed and published it in London in March 1791 under the title of *The Rights of Man,* with a dedication to George Washington. The volume created an immense sensation. It sold so enormously that the British government, alarmed at the spread of French ideas, took steps to suppress the book and eventually to prosecute its author for treason. Neither step was successful. The attempted ban only furthered the book's circulation through underground channels; while the indicted author fled to Paris, became a citizen of France and endured fantastic vicissitudes.

The Rights of Man made a similar sensation in the United States and was immediately adopted by the Republicans as their bible. Yet the very statements which had enraged the British were American commonplaces: that aristocracies and hereditary monarchies were tyrannical institutions; that every civil right grew out of a natural right; that no man or government had the right to bind succeeding generations (a thesis which Jefferson ardently promulgated); and that if laws do continue in effect "they derive their force from the consent of the living."

An American edition was published in Philadelphia. Prominently displayed as a masthead was a letter to the printer from Jefferson that he was "extremely pleased to find it will be re-printed here; and that something is at length to be publicly said against the political heresies which have sprung up among us." [31]

The publication might have passed without too much notice, had it not been for the Jeffersonian masthead. For everyone knew, or thought he knew, on whose "political heresies" the Secretary of State thus publicly animadverted. They were those of no less a personage than John Adams, Vice-President of the United States, whose "Discourses on Davila" had been running serially in Fenno's paper for more than a year. The coincidence was most marked. The "Discourses" were widely believed to advocate the rule of aristocracies and hereditary monarchies, and to display a profound contempt for the "mob," and Paine's volume was one long violent attack on just these concepts.

The Republicans were delighted at the juxtaposition; the Federalists went into a rage. Jefferson, greatly embarrassed at the unauthorized publication of what he had written as a private communication, hastened to explain the contretemps to the President.

While he admitted that Adams and his "Discourses" had been intended by the reference, he denied any hand in the publication. He sincerely esteemed Adams, he protested, though he lamented "his apostacy to the hereditary monarchy and nobility," as well as the fact that his writings were "the bell-weather [sic]" of the "Anglo-man." [32]

Washington seems to have passed over the explanation, if it can be considered one, in silence; though there is evidence that Paine's dedication of *The Rights of Man* to him, and Jefferson's endorsement, had led to diplomatic repercussions. Beckwith protested against both to Tobias Lear, the President's private secretary, as indicating that the administration approved the contents of a book which attacked the British government. But, Beckwith added hastily, he spoke only as a private person. To which Lear retorted that he knew him in no other capacity. [33]

For the moment Jefferson prudently said nothing to the person most aggrieved, John Adams. Events, however, soon forced him to break his silence. On June 8, 1791, the Boston *Columbian Centinel* began a series of anonymous "Letters of Publicola," which Federalist papers all over the country immediately reprinted.

Publicola minced no words in denouncing both Burke and Paine, the original antagonists; Burke for having passed "a severe and indiscriminating censure" on every act of the French National Assembly;

and Paine for "approving every thing they have done, with applause as undistinguishing as is the censure of Mr. Burke."

Having thus passed judgment on the merits of the dispute itself, the anonymous writer next turned his attention to Jefferson's unfortunate letter. What did Jefferson mean, he demanded, by "political heresies"? Was Paine's volume "the canonical book of political scripture"? Was it supposed to contain "the true doctrine of popular infallibility, from which it would be heretical to depart in one single point"?

On the contrary, this "Papal Bull of infallible virtue" by a new "holy father of our political faith" was full of misstatements and errors. Paine said that what "a whole nation chooses to do, it has a right to do." Nonsense! retorted Publicola. "The eternal and immutable laws of justice and morality are paramount to all human legislation." Paine's generalization would set up a tyranny of the majority under the euphemism of "a whole nation." There must be, the writer asserted, a balance of powers to avoid *all* tyranny, from whatever source derived. Because the American Constitution provided such a balance, it was superior to both the British and French systems; and by the same yardstick the British surpassed the French.[34]

With the publication of Publicola, the champions of the Republicans and the Federalists sprang full-throated to the fray. A host of classical and mythological characters thundered and denounced, defended and attacked in the public prints. The rumor spread that John Adams himself had written Publicola; and there were those who believed, or pretended to believe, that he had done so at Burke's express request.[35]

The attribution to Adams was promptly denied. Actually, Publicola was John Quincy Adams, his young and brilliant, if sharp-tongued, son, who had come forward in his father's defense. But it was long before Jefferson and his friends credited the son rather than the father with the devastating "Letters."

Jefferson was in a quandary. Ought he to break his silence and seek to placate the aggrieved Vice-President? Madison, to whom he turned for counsel, saw no reason for it. "Mr. Adams," he felt, "can least of all complain." Had he not himself sought to destroy the state and confederated constitutions under the guise of a pretended defense? "Surely," Madison was convinced, "if it be innocent and decent in one servant of the public to write attacks against its Government, it cannot be very criminal or indecent in another to patronize a written defence of the principles on which that Government is founded."[36]

In the end, however, Jefferson wrote to Adams to explain his connection with Paine's book. "That you and I differ in our ideas of the best form of government," he soothed, "is well known to us both: but we have differed as friends should, respecting the purity of each other's motives, and confining our differences to private conversation." [37]

He was not being quite frank with his old friend. Almost simultaneously he was engaged in the writing of other letters. One to Monroe expressed skepticism of the claim that Adams was not Publicola. "To produce any effect," he declared, Adams "must disavow Davila and the Defence of the American Constitutions. A host of writers have risen in favor of Paine and prove that in this quarter at least the spirit of republicanism is sound. The contrary spirit of high officers of the government is more understood than I expected." [38]

Another went in cipher to his protégé William Short in Paris. Under the secrecy of the code Jefferson felt safe in accusing Adams, Jay, Hamilton, Knox and the entire Society of the Cincinnati (of which Washington was a member) of seeking to set up a monarchy in the country. "They pant after union with England," he charged, "as the power which is to support their projects, and are most determined Anti-Gallicans. It is prognosticated that our republic is to end with the President's life. But I believe they will find themselves all head and no body." [39]

These were serious charges to promulgate against practically every high officer of the government with the exception of himself and Edmund Randolph, as well as against the main body of the military men who had fought the Revolution. At this time Washington had again taken painfully to his bed with that "blind tumor" of which he had once before almost died; [40] and Jefferson may have felt that the denouement was close at hand.

In the evaluation of causes and consequences it does not matter whether the beliefs which motivate men have any basis in fact; the consequences may flow as inexorably from false as from true convictions. Jefferson and his party sincerely believed that their opponents were sedulously aiming at the establishment in this country of an aristocratical monarchy on British lines. If they as yet exempted the President from complicity in the conspiracy, they nevertheless considered him as a tool in the hands of the plotters. There were some, like Jefferson, who believed him an unwitting tool; others, more extreme, credited him with an open-eyed benevolent neutrality.

Hamilton, of course, was supposed to be the head and front of the alleged conspiracy. Adams was a close second. Jefferson carefully jotted down on scraps of paper (later to be known as his *Anas*) almost daily reports, first, second or even third-hand, of conversations in which these two had privately aired their monarchical views.[41]

Since he was thus convinced that the fate of the republic depended on the instant and united exertions of the Republicans, Jefferson cast about for some means by which he could communicate his knowledge to the great body of the American people and rouse them to repel the conspiracy.

The press of the country, he complained, was wholly in the hands of the Federalists. If this was not entirely consonant with the facts —Bache's *General Advertiser* in Philadelphia, the *Daily Advertiser* in New York, the *Independent Chronicle* in Boston, and other papers scattered from Vermont to the Carolinas vehemently presented the Republican viewpoint—it was true that the Federalist press was more numerous and financially better off. Fenno's *Gazette of the United States,* published in Philadelphia, received semiofficial support through the largesse of government advertising and in turn supported every administration measure.

Madison and Henry Lee of Virginia, in conjunction with Jefferson, thereupon tried to remedy the defect by setting up another Republican newspaper in Philadelphia. They chose Philip Freneau, ertswhile fiery poet and present radical, for editor and publisher. But Freneau, presently employed by the New York *Daily Advertiser*, at first turned the proposition down as financially unattractive. Whereupon Jefferson sent him a formal and cautiously worded offer of the clerkship for foreign languages in his department. "The salary, indeed, is very low," he acknowledged, "being but two hundred and fifty dollars a year; but also, it gives so little to do, as not to interfere with any other calling the person may choose." [42]

Both Jefferson and Freneau knew of course that the "other calling" would be the establishment of a newspaper under Republican auspices and for the purpose of disseminating Republican doctrine. But Freneau again refused, having other projects in mind. Thus rebuffed, Jefferson turned to Bache with the suggestion that his *General Advertiser* broaden its national circulation by dropping or condensing its local advertisements from a "country" edition in order to avoid heavy mailing costs.[43] Bache dismissed the idea as impracticable.

In despair, Jefferson returned to Freneau. He now put his proposition in unmistakable language. If Freneau came to Philadelphia and published a paper which enunciated sound Republican principles, he would furnish him with all the foreign intelligence that came into his office, and place in its columns such official advertising and legal publications as the State Department had at its disposal.[44]

This second offer, coupled with the previous one of the clerkship, finally persuaded Freneau to accept. He came on to Philadelphia and initiated the *National Gazette,* which speedily justified the fondest expectations of the Republican leaders. Freneau had a caustic pen, a biting wit and a gift for diatribe that only the English Richard Cobbett could later match. Certainly Fenno, on whom Freneau concentrated his fire, could not meet him on equal terms.

But Fenno was, after all, small game. Freneau was out after much more important targets. He first went after Hamilton, whose person and policies were criticized, assaulted and ridiculed. Nor was the President himself immune. On the other hand, Jefferson, Madison and the other Republicans in Congress and out were consistently held up as noble and virtuous patriots. The cause of the French Revolution became the ideal of the world, while the British were never spoken of except in the most sneering and derogatory fashion.

The administration, with the exception of a pleased and satisfied Jefferson, winced and writhed under the incessant bombardment. Washington went into a rage, and Hamilton exploded with a counterattack that threatened to split the government in two. But of this more will be said in a later chapter.

CHAPTER 11

Frenzied Finance

THE REPUBLICAN PRESS found ample material for their blasts against Hamilton in the wild outburst of speculation which greeted the opening of the books to take subscriptions for the bank stock. Nothing like it had ever been seen before in the country's history.

On July 4, 1791, at eleven in the morning, the eagerly awaited moment arrived. In Philadelphia, New York, Boston, Baltimore and Charleston, the moneyed men gathered at the offices where the books were held, long before the magic hour. As the clock struck and the books were opened, they rushed forward in a solid mass, clamoring their offers and demanding instant attention. Within half an hour all books were closed. Frantic late-comers protested indignantly that they had been abused and overreached. The stock was subscribed and over-subscribed, and double the amount would have been immediately snatched up had it been available.

The investors of Boston, determined that the Philadelphia financiers should not monopolize the bank, clubbed together to send an emissary laden with cash to subscribe for them to the limit.[1] In New York, William Seton, cashier of the Bank of New York, announced exultantly that the full allotment had been taken, with double offered if Hamilton would permit it.[2] In Philadelphia, the rush was so great that influential men like Senator Robert Morris and Congressman Thomas Fitzsimons found themselves without a single share. In hot anger they accused the directors of the subscriptions of having deliberately given the preference to their own friends. Morris threatened legal proceedings, and Fitzsimons stormed that he would haul them up before Congress.[3]

Baltimore also promptly filled its quota; but the South lagged strangely behind. In Charleston, headquarters for Southern subscriptions, only seven hundred offers were made, considerably less than

179

the quota. Virginia took practically no stock. The reasons for such disinterest were twofold. There were few in the South with sufficient fluid capital, and they feared and hated a national bank which they beheld as another noose for Northern capitalism to encircle their agrarian necks.

Hamilton expressed uneasiness over the Southern lag. He had hoped that a sufficient number of influential and wealthy men in that stronghold of Republicanism would be attracted to his banner by the chance for easy profits. He even proposed that the government offer some of its own allotted shares to Virginia and North Carolina as a special inducement. But Jefferson coldly remarked that such open partiality would not please the favored states while offending the others. "For I presume," he added sardonically, "they would rather the capitals of their citizens should be employed in commerce than be locked up in a strong box here: nor can sober thinkers prefer a paper medium at 13 per cent interest to gold and silver for nothing." [4]

The idea was therefore dropped. Jefferson never did have an adequate understanding of the functions performed by banks. Madison, though more realistic in his appraisal, was equally indignant. The plan of the bank, he wrote, "gives a moral certainty of gain to the subscribers with scarce a physical possibility of loss. The subscriptions are consequently a mere scramble for so much public plunder which will be engrossed by those already loaded with the spoils of individuals. . . . It pretty clearly appears in what proportions the public debt lies in the country, what sort of hands hold it, and by whom the people of the United States are to be governed. Of all the shameful circumstances of this business, it is among the greatest to see the members of the Legislature who were most active in pushing this job openly grasping its emoluments." [5]

But a shrewd English observer viewed the situation from a different angle. He thought the energy of speculation made the Americans feel "free and happy," and no longer willing to enter into a commercial treaty with Great Britain. "I much fear Mr. Hammond [the newly appointed minister to the United States]," he mourned, "will come out too late." [6]

The procedure for subscribing to the bank stock opened up another field for indulging in a speculative orgy. On each share subscribed, the purchaser put down a deposit of $25 in cash, for which he received a receipt known as "script" or "scrip." The full price of $400 was to be met in four semiannual installments, of which $100 (including the deposit) was in cash, and the balance by the transfer at par of certificates of the public debt.

Since the largest part of the payment could therefore be made only in the certificates, a wild scramble followed for their possession; and, as Hamilton had expected, their price began to soar. But most of the public debt had already fallen into the hands of far-sighted moneyed men. It was therefore necessary to unearth those old certificates of state and national origin which had not yet been converted into the new funds. Once again swift packet boats and expresses raced south to the hinterlands to ferret out the holdings still to be found in isolated communities where their true value was not known. "The stock-jobbers," Madison commented indignantly, "will become the pretorian band of the Government, at once its tool and its tyrant; bribed by its largesses, and overawing it by clamors and combinations." [7]

Neither indignation nor jeremiads stopped the avid speculators in their appointed courses. Besides the profits to be gained on the old debt certificates and the new, a tremendous trade sprang up in the scrip itself. Since it was anticipated that the bank stock when issued would pay dividends of eight to ten per cent per annum, the fortunate possessors of the scrip discovered that the token itself could be sold at an enhanced price.

Within a month the scrip (representing a cash down payment of $25) stood at $45 to $50; in August, a month later, the market boiled over as eager investors who had been unable to obtain an original subscription bid one another up for the precious documents.

The whole country went mad. Henry Lee, traveling from Philadelphia to Virginia, saw "one continued scene of stock gambling; agriculture, commerce and even the fair sex relinquished, to make way for unremitted exertion in this favorite pursuit." [8]

Even the common man—the farmer, the mechanic, the artisan—was bitten by the mania, and forsook his accustomed toil to plunge into the golden stream.

"The SPECULATION MANIA, which now rages in the United States, for Bank Stock," reported a Boston paper, "is unequalled by any thing ancient or modern, except the *South Sea* or *Mississippi* schemes." Since pedestrian prose could not hope to deal with this "scrip-mania," the paper burst into verse:

Mechanicks, running from their shops
Come here, and burn their fingers—
The Farmer reaps no more his crops—
No occupation lingers.[9]

By August 11th the craze had reached its peak. In New York the
scrip sold for $280; in Philadelphia it soared to $320. Even the ordinarily prudent president of Yale, Dr. Ezra Stiles, believed the scrip
to be actually worth $200. Nevertheless, he hastened to sell the Col-
lege's rights to seven shares and thereby netted a profit of $1050.[10]

Jefferson observed the progress of the speculation with bitter eyes.
"Ships are lying idle at the wharfs," he cried resentfully, "buildings
are stopped, capitals withdrawn from commerce, manufactures, arts
and agriculture, to be employed in gambling, and the tide of public
prosperity, almost unparalleled in any country, is arrested in its
course, and suppressed by the rage of getting rich in a day. No mortal
can tell where this will stop, for the spirit of gaming when once it
has seized a subject, is incurable." [11]

Fisher Ames, viewing exactly the same situation, saw it with different glasses. "The eagerness to subscribe," he advised Hamilton,
"is a proof of the wealth and resources of the country, and of the
perfect confidence reposed by our opulent men in the government.
People here [in Boston] are full of exultation and gratitude. They
know who merits the praise of it, and they are not loth to bestow it."
The only fly in the ointment was the "partiality" of the commissioners
in giving Philadelphia more than her fair share of the stock.[12]

But Hamilton, though flattered by the "exultation and gratitude"
of the Boston rich, was becoming deeply disturbed by the skyrocket-
ing prices. The memory of the South Sea and Mississippi bubbles
was only too vivid. "A bubble connected with any operation," he
warned, "is of all the enemies I have to fear, in my judgment the
most formidable." [13]

His judgment was accurate. By August 12th the bubble had burst.
The scrip, selling only the day before at prices ranging from $280
to $320, fell to $150. On the same toboggan slid the government
debt.

Immediately the press teemed with exhortations. "It has risen like
a rocket," exclaimed the Republican *Daily Advertiser* of New York.
"Like a rocket it will burst with a crack and down drops the rocket

stick. What goes up must come down—so take care of your pate, brother Jonathan." [14]

Even the organ of the Federalists, the *Gazette of the United States,* had broken into Cassandra verses a few days before:

> Touch'd by the wand of speculation,
> A frenzy runs thro all the nation,
> For soon or late, so truth advises,
> Things must assume their proper sizes—
> And sure as death all mortals trips,
> Thousands will rue their faith in SCRIPS. [15]

The warnings and the exhortations, however, came too late. Consternation and a sense of disaster clutched the cities of Philadelphia and New York, scenes of the worst excesses. In New York, at least one young man who had lost his all took rope and hanged himself. "It may all be charged to the funding system," cried the pugnacious Dr. Rush. "It has introduced into our country half the miseries and vices of hell itself." [16]

While the vast frenzy of speculation cannot properly be charged to any single individual, certainly William Duer, Hamilton's friend and former aide, had done more to initiate it and keep it rolling than any other man alive. Forced to resign from his Treasury post, he nevertheless continued to use his connections and sources of confidential information to help his private manipulations and to attract the cash of the unwary. He dealt in huge quantities of the funds and scrip, employing the technique of "wash sales" to bring about a rise, then causing a sudden drop by quoting Hamilton as authority for the opinion that stocks were too high, and even specifying the exact price which, so he diligently disseminated, Hamilton had set as the true value. [17]

But he too eventually got caught in the mesh of his own chicaneries, was clapped into jail and ended his days in prison, execrated by his victims and his former friends.

When the crash came, Hamilton threw the weight of the government into the breach. On the black days of August 15th and 16th he drew $150,000 from the Sinking Fund and authorized the Bank of New York to buy public stocks to that amount in order to bolster the market. On September 7th he added another $50,000 for the same purpose. Privately he wrote William Seton, the bank's cashier: "If there are any gentlemen who support the *funds* and others who *depress* them, I shall be pleased that your purchases may aid the *former*. This in great confidence." [18]

Seton, friendly to Duer, took this as a tip to relieve that slippery gentleman from the load of stock with which he had been caught. He used $52,695 of the initial government fund—more than a third of the total—to purchase Duer's top-heavy holdings, and thereby saved him temporarily from his final fate.[19] Hamilton obviously knew of the transaction; yet there is no evidence anywhere that he ever condemned it.

Then, as now, governmental confidences had a habit of leaking out. When Hamilton sent Seton the order for additional purchases the news, so the cashier ruefully reported, "flew over the town like wildfire." On his arrival at the Tontine Coffee House, the Stock Exchange of the day, he found the speculative gentry prepared for his coming and, broadly smiling, refusing to sell at his stipulated price. In spite of this firming of the market, Seton managed to purchase some widely scattered lots. The situation, he reported, was thereby markedly relieved; and even the bank scrip, which he was not authorized to buy, moved up from a low of $110 to $140. The latter, he added, was "now getting into the proper hands." [20] By this cryptic phrase no doubt he meant that the interlopers—the petty shopkeepers, the bakers, the apprentices and the widows—had been squeezed out and the moneyed men were coming in.

By processes such as these the market finally revived and reassumed its advance. The funds reached an all-time high by the beginning of the following year; while the more speculative scrip, which had fallen as low as $67, climbed to $140.[21] There they remained until, a year later, Duer pulled the house down about his ears and touched off a financial panic and train of bankruptcies that rocked the country.

The cause of all this furious activity and financial legerdemain, the Bank of the United States, chose its twenty-five directors in October 1791, and opened its doors for business in Philadelphia. Among the directors were such solid men and financial stalwarts— including members of Congress—as George Cabot and Fisher Ames of Massachusetts, Jeremiah Wadsworth of Connecticut, Philip Livingston and Rufus King of New York, William Bingham and Thomas Willing of Pennsylvania, Charles Carroll of Maryland,

Samuel Johnston of North Carolina and William S. Smith of South Carolina.[22]

Under their prudent management, and with the aid and blessing of the government, the bank flourished and planted its roots firmly into the commercial and financial life of the nation. In spite of deep Republican suspicion and the occasional carping of the unreconstructed, it became such an integral part of the national structure that Jefferson, when he became President, found it impossible or even desirable to destroy it. Only at the expiration of its second charter did Andrew Jackson, by refusing to permit a third extension, bring the bank finally to an end.

The speculative frenzy and the dramatic rise and fall of the bank shares and the public funds had unexpected repercussions on another one of Hamilton's fertile schemes.

While building the financial foundation of the nation he clearly realized that it must always be insecure unless a state of national self-sufficiency was attained. But this could come about only through industrialization. Agriculture was well enough and even indispensable; Hamilton's readings in history, however, and the example of England, proved conclusively to him that no nation ever waxed strong on agriculture alone. Even trade and shipping could not long exist without a steady supply of manufactured goods.

Jefferson believed that if America continued as a primary source of raw materials, the rest of the world would be only too happy to exchange its manufactures for them on a fair and profitable basis. To this Hamilton opposed the cynical lesson of the times. That country which controlled the supply of fabricated goods—and the gold and silver which were attracted thereto—controlled the world.

Early in 1790 Hamilton instigated a request from the House of Representatives that he submit a plan for the encouragement of manufactures in the United States. For almost a year he gathered facts and figures on which to build his argument. Letters of inquiry went all over the earth; and from every land the replies poured in. From distant China, from England and the Continent, from domestic North and South came statistics, opinions, discussions of sources of supply and markets, labor conditions and special skills.[23]

By and large the information he received was disheartening. The letters disclosed a country still in the preindustrial era, fumbling pathetically and against almost insuperable odds to achieve some measure of self-sufficiency. The industrial nations of Europe kept a jealous hold on trade secrets and processes as well as skilled man-power; and made it a penal offense to export any of them or to induce their export. Technical knowledge was therefore sadly lacking in the United States, labor costs were high, the capital for investment scanty or nonexistent, and attempts to smuggle machinery, processes and workers to this country in the main unsuccessful.

The only hope, insisted Hamilton's informants, lay in govern-mental aid through bounties, prohibitive tariffs on competitive goods, and special inducements and privileges to entice skilled labor from abroad.

On December 5, 1791, Hamilton submitted his famous Report on Manufactures. It is perhaps the most eloquent argument ever made to prove the necessity for industrializing a nation.[24]

The preamble sought to placate the suspicious agrarians. Agricul-ture, he agreed with them, was fundamental and primary; yet it neither should nor could, he qualified, be all-exclusive. Flourishing manufactures not only did no harm to the farmer, but helped him in innumerable ways. The wealth manufacturing provided was of equal importance with that derived from the fruits of the earth; it made for a balanced and prosperous economy; it employed fully all the diversified resources of the country; and it offered new outlets for the employment of labor.

Experience has conclusively shown, he asserted, that the dream of certain agrarians (he did not mention them by name, but he meant Jefferson and John Taylor of Caroline in America, and the physiocrats in France) of a free and ideal exchange of raw materials, farm products and manufactured goods among nations was a mirage and never existed in fact; that the only weapon for prying open the trade barriers of other countries interposed against *our* products was to become independent of *their* goods, and thereby force them to a mutual accommodation.

The introduction of machinery into our economy, he proceeded, made jobs easy and pleasant. Machines could be tended by women, children and the aged, whereby our gainfully employed population would be increased and the family income augmented. He pointed admiringly to the example of England, where four-sevenths of the workers in the cotton manufactories were women and children. Such a vast extension in the number of wage earners, he argued, would

have the most beneficial repercussions on agriculture; for there would
be more mouths to feed and more money for the farmer's pocket.

Nowhere in this glowing description is any mention of the evils
inherent in factory child labor; but then, those evils were as yet
implicit, not apparent. The English system had not fully disclosed
its darker side—the long, stupefying hours, the stunted growth and
physical decay, the exploitation and the starvation wages. The labor
of women and children was taken for granted in the prevalent home
industries of the United States and on the land. Indeed, the poets
waxed lyrical over the vistas disclosed by the introduction of the
factory. David Humphreys wrote "A Poem on Industry" in its
praise:

> Teach little hands to ply mechanic toil,
> Cause failing age o'er easy tasks to smile!
> With gladness kindle rescued beauty's eye,
> And cheek with health's inimitable dye;
> So shall the young, the feeble find employ,
> And hearts, late nigh to perish, leap for joy!

Thomas Hood's eloquent "Song of the Shirt" was still half a century away.

The situation was not altogether dark, continued Hamilton. Already certain industries existed in the United States on a factory
basis. But they required encouragement, and others had to be called
into being. A rounded and complete program was essential, based on
the cornerstone of government aid.

Such aid must consist of protective duties against competitive foreign manufactures, bounties for the establishment of new industries,
premiums for excellence and quality of manufactured articles, exemption of essential raw materials from abroad from import duties (or, if
not feasible, a system of drawbacks), the encouragement of inven-
tions, improvements in machinery and processes by substantial grants,
the increase in number and geographical distribution of banks to
facilitate an even flow of money and credit, and, finally, the construction of roads and canals for a similar flow of physical goods and
materials.

All in all, Hamilton's Report brilliantly expounded the doctrine of
a powerful, prosperous and self-contained nation and blueprinted
the exposition with a program well calculated to achieve it. But he
had failed to reckon adequately with the deep-rooted forces in oppo-

sition. The premises from which he worked and the end results he envisioned roused only fear and horror among thoroughgoing agrarians.

To Jefferson and others the vision of a land crowded with populous cities, swarming with workers huddled in rabbit warrens and confined to narrow streets, pestilent with fevers and outlandish foreign diseases, belching soot and grime into the air and befouling a fair landscape that might otherwise be used by a sturdy, wise and independent yeomanry, evoked only the profoundest of shudders. "The mobs of great cities," wrote Jefferson in disgust, "add just so much to the support of pure government as sores do to the strength of the human body." [25] Nothing he had witnessed in Europe altered his conviction that the artisans of great cities were mere slaves and tools of absolutism and misgovernment.

In detail, too, Hamilton's plan frightened and offended large and important groups. To the farmer, prohibitive duties on foreign manufactures meant that he would have to pay more for the domestic products. The haters of banks and the money power foresaw a wider extension of and increased influence for the Bank of the United States. The upholders of state sovereignty noted particularly the recommendation for roads and canals. Even though Hamilton had not mentioned them specifically as national projects, no one doubted that such was his intention. The question of federal intervention in so-called "internal improvements" was always to arouse the bitterest passions.

So that it is not surprising that the Report, though based on a congressional request, was maneuvered into a pigeonhole from which it never emerged. The times were not yet ripe.

Hamilton was disappointed, but did not repine. Even while he was busy with the composition of the Report, he had started a grandiose scheme for furthering manufactures through private initiative and with private capital.

Acting on the assumption that the lack of sufficient capital was the chief impediment, and that no one man or limited partnership of men could adequately finance the expensive machinery and importation of skilled workmen necessary for success, he proposed a mammoth joint-stock company which he called the Society for Establishing Useful Manufactures. Such a venture, he believed, would attract by the prospect of dazzling profits a large group of moneyed men to join their individual capitals in a common fund.

In the beginning the scheme rolled with well-oiled smoothness. Hamilton's eloquence, leadership and official position were sufficiently effective to interest such men as Elias and Elisha Boudinot, William Duer, Robert Troup, Jonathan Dayton, Henry Knox, Nicholas Low and Philip Livingston as investors and promoters.

Prospectuses, newspaper advertisements and private blandishments sought out additional investors. Government aid was hinted at, and subscription books were opened. The company, so it was announced, intended to engage in a bewildering variety of industries—paper, blankets, stockings, sailcloth, carpets, shoes, cotton and linen goods, beer and ale. The capitalization was set at $500,000.

So attractive were the prospectuses and so galvanic Hamilton's enthusiasm that by October 1791 over $250,000 was already underwritten. The site chosen for the establishment of the factories was at the falls of the Passaic River in New Jersey, where the town of Paterson now exists. The state legislature granted the proposed company a charter of the most amazing liberality (influenced no doubt by the fact that Hamilton himself had carefully written its provisions and that influential New Jersey politicians were numbered among the promoters).

With every prospect bright, the company commenced operations. Unfortunately it had barely got under way when it ran headlong into the financial panic of 1792, the collapse of the speculative mania and the bankruptcy of Duer and his associated enterprises. Duer, whose mere presence seemed sufficient to blight any enterprise, had been selected as governor of the Society. When he departed for debtor's prison, his accounts were examined and it was soon discovered that the funds of the Society and his private moneys were indistinguishably mingled. Subscribers to the company shares whose purchase price had not yet been paid in full found themselves unable or unwilling to fulfill their commitments. Attempts by agents in England to entice workmen and their know-how to America ended in lamentable failure.

It is true that 4000 Irish emigrants embarked at Londonderry during the summer of 1791,[26] but they were either agricultural laborers or unskilled diggers of ditches, and unfit for the purposes of the Society.

In spite of Hamilton's herculean efforts, the company gradually lost its initial momentum; and the scheme, so ambitiously commenced and with such fanfare, eventually lapsed. Only the land holdings—and the charter—remained. But these were sufficiently valuable to net a substantial income from leaseholds until modern times, when the state of New Jersey finally entered into an accommodation arrangement with the heirs for the surrender of the lands and charter.[27]

Another activity, seeming far removed from speculative concerns, was heavily affected by the craze for getting rich quick. This was the establishment of the national capital on the banks of the Potomac.

Congress had enacted a bill specifying the area and authorizing the acquisition of the necessary land. At once a new field was opened for roving capital eager for large returns. Philadelphia became the center for those who hastened to partake in the purchase, sight unseen, of tracts within or near the proposed establishment. The communities abutting the site strove in rivalry for special advantages, and refused to cede the territory required for public purposes unless they could gain thereby.

Slowly and painfully, however, the land was gathered and staked out. Both Washington and Jefferson displayed the keenest interest in the proceedings, envisioning a noble city that would rival, if not surpass, the finest that Europe had to offer.

Jefferson in particular, himself an architect and builder of extraordinary attainments, followed every step of the construction, offering for the benefit of the actual builders suggestions involving the minutest details, the width of streets, the style of architecture, the distances between and setbacks of houses, the kind of material to be used; and even submitted anonymously a design for the Capitol building which failed to meet with the approval of the unwitting authorities.

Three commissioners were appointed to supervise operations. Major Andrew Ellicott was chosen to lay out and survey the city. Assisting him was Major Pierre Charles L'Enfant, the famous city engineer and planner from France.

Unfortunately the two engineers were soon at loggerheads, and joined only in a common contempt for the commissioners in authority over them. L'Enfant in particular, irascible, headstrong and convinced of his own and sole genius in a barbarous America, disregarded all orders from the commissioners. The situation finally exploded when he committed the unforgivable sin of ripping down a house which belonged to Charles Carroll because it protruded into a street he was planning. Unfortunately, Carroll was the nephew of Daniel Carroll, one of the commissioners, and the mails between Virginia and the seat of government at Philadelphia bulged with the outraged protests of the commissioners.

Time and again Washington and Jefferson sent stern warnings to L'Enfant about his insubordination, without affecting his course in the slightest. Since the enraged commissioners threatened to resign in a body if he were not curbed, in the end L'Enfant was dismissed; but not before he had set his mark on the city with his conception of broad avenues radiating like the spokes of a wheel from the Capitol and intersected at frequent intervals by open circles, which gives the city of Washington today its sweeping vistas and noble approaches.

As though these difficulties were not enough, subterranean and mysterious obstacles were interposed from Philadelphia, so Washington complained, to the completion of the work.[28] The reason for the sabotage should have been plain: the longer the work was delayed, the longer the government would be compelled to remain in the City of Brotherly Love.

The net result of jealousies, rivalries, land speculation and internecine quarrels was that the building of the new city—named in honor of the first President—went on at a snail's pace. The quarrels continued even after L'Enfant's dismissal. Ellicott, no longer able to clash with L'Enfant, concentrated his attention on the commissioners. Accordingly, he too followed his insubordinate subordinate into retirement; and the triumphant commissioners, their dignity vindicated, nevertheless were hard put to it to find adequate—and less temperamental—replacements.

By 1799, the year set for the transfer of the government, there was only the merest sketch of a city, with a few half-finished buildings dotting the discouraged landscape and streets laid out in mud and ending abruptly in swamps. But the administration determinedly followed the ukase of the original act and moved quarters to the "city of magnificent distances," which as yet was only a quagmire of magnificent intentions; there to languish in untold discomforts for many years to come while the sound of hammering construction bedeviled their ears and their carriages bogged down in fathomless mud.[29]

Speculation in lands, or "land-jobbing" as Washington termed it, was also one of the fundamental causes for the continuing troubles with the Indians. In a bitter complaint Washington listed a second cause: the incessant interference of the states in what should be and constitutionally was the sole affair of the federal government. "To sum the whole up in a few words," he wrote, "the interference of the States, and the speculation of Individuals will be the bane of all our public measures." [30]

The British industriously aided and abetted these domestic banes by stirring up the discontented tribes and supplying them with guns and munitions of war. On the same day that the President denounced domestic meddlers, he sent an equally angry note to Jefferson for the latter to convey to Colonel Beckwith (now militarily, if not diplomatically elevated) a plain intimation that such aid must stop. "The notoriety of such assistance," he wrote, "has already been such as renders inquiry into particulars unnecessary." [31]

Jefferson had his own plan for ending the Indian troubles. "I hope," he avowed, "we shall drub the Indians well this summer [1791] and then change our plan from war to bribery. We must do as the Spaniards and English do, keep them in peace by liberal and constant presents." This, he explained, was much cheaper than waging war; besides which—and here was his true reason—it left "no pretext for raising or continuing an army. Every rag of an Indian depredation will otherwise serve as a ground to raise troops with those who think a standing army and a public debt necessary for the happiness of the United States, and we shall never be permitted to get rid of either." Yet our Treasury, continued Jefferson in the same breath, still believes that the encroachments of Great Britain on our carrying trade "must be met by passive obedience and non-resistance, lest any misunderstanding with them should *affect our credit, or the prices of our public paper.*" [32]

Every officer of the national government wanted to treat the Indians fairly and honestly, and fumed over their abuse by the states and their inhabitants. Knox, as always, was their most valiant defender. Washington was equally concerned. He commented harshly on the belief of the frontiersmen "that there is not the same crime (or indeed no crime at all) in killing an Indian as in killing a white man," and somewhat hopelessly informed Congress that strict measures must be evolved to govern the alienation of Indian lands and to punish infringements. [33]

Timothy Pickering, acting as plenipotentiary to the Iroquois, thought the Indians generally easy to please, and that a man must want humanity, honesty or common sense not to be able to deal with them or sympathize with their plight.[34] Hamilton joined the common chorus with a demand for direct federal action to punish whites who slew friendly Indians, instead of allowing state governments jurisdiction over such crimes.[35] Only too often local juries acquitted the killer, no matter how unprovoked or barbarous the offense.

It was all to no avail. The general attitude of the frontier is best exemplified by the public avowal of Hugh H. Brackenridge of Pennsylvania, an otherwise just and kindly man. He did not hold, he wrote, with those who spoke of the *right* of the Indians to their lands. "I consider the earth as given to man in common, and each should use his share so as not to exclude others and should be restricted to that mode of using it which is most favorable to the support of the greatest numbers, and consequently productive of the greatest sum of happiness, that is, the cultivation of the soil. I pay little regard, therefore, to any right which is not founded in *agricultural occupancy*." [36]

In other words, since the Indians were hunters and not agriculturalists, the white men had the right and the duty to drive them off their immemorial lands.

Inevitably the Indians struck back at the aggressors, and sent the punitive expedition of General Harmar reeling in defeat. It was necessary therefore—such is the logic of events—for the national government, no matter how reluctantly, to avenge the disaster to its arms. Arthur St. Clair, governor of the Northwest Territory, dispatched a new expedition under the command of Major General Richard Butler, amply manned and equipped with artillery, to invade the Indian country.

On October 4, 1791, the Army moved out of Fort Hamilton and wound slowly through the wilderness. As usual, the militia adjuncts melted away the farther they penetrated. On November 3rd the troops encamped on a creek about fifteen miles from the main village of the Miamis, the goal of the invasion.

The following morning, at sunrise, Butler lined up his troops for inspection in accordance with the best European military traditions. Satisfied with their appearance and the spotless condition of their accouterments, he dismissed them. As they broke ranks the surrounding woods, hitherto silent, burst into a hell of eerie screeches and a storm of arrows and gunfire. Swarms of hideously painted savages, tomahawks uplifted and guns still flaming, bounded into the clearing. At the first assault, those of the militia who still remained, broke and fled through the press of Regulars behind, throwing them also into disorganized confusion. The artillery, hastily manned, threw aimless shot into the woods, harming nothing but the branches of the trees.

Yelling, firing and wielding their tomahawks with deadly effect, the Indians slaughtered almost at will. Every horse was slain, the artillery was abandoned, and both regulars and militia reeled back in a wild rout for the safety of the nearby posts.[37]

It was one of the bloodiest defeats in the history of early Indian warfare. When the news filtered East, consternation reigned. A wave of fear swept the entire frontier. The powerful Iroquois confederation, already restless, gave every indication that they would go into action on their own. Every Indian tribe, nursing ancient grievances, took heart and meditated revenge.

The self-seeking policy of the states, the greed and callousness of the settlers, and the open hostility of the Republicans to any increase in the tiny federal Army, as well as their stubborn reliance on the militia, had come home to roost.

In Massachusetts, remote from all Indian troubles, instead of a cry for revenge at the disaster, a clamor rose for the end of the war itself as unjust.[38] A belated Congress stirred to request the President to institute an inquiry into the causes of the defeat. The first attempt to do so met with failure on the argument that such a request was an encroachment on the executive; a second motion succeeded by the ingenious subterfuge of calling for the information from the Secretary of War.[39]

But this evasion did not satisfy Jefferson, who insisted that all requests on heads of departments should first be directed to the President. He feared that under the urgency of the moment a precedent might be established for a direct line of communication between Congress and Hamilton. Naturally, Hamilton took an opposing point of view.[40]

Lord Grenville of the British ministry, watching from afar, seized upon the occasion of the disaster to reap an English harvest. Smoothly he offered to interpose his good offices in the war between his good friends the Indians and his good friends the Americans. Peace could be restored, he suggested, by setting up a buffer state of independent Indians between the United States and Canada. Within this territory neither America nor Great Britain would have any claims.[41]

Since this area would include most of the posts which England was obligated to turn over to the United States, and would act as a bar to any American advance on Canada in the event of future hostilities, the offer was coldly rejected.

A curious situation arose over both offer and rejection. It was not made directly to the American government or its proper officer, the Secretary of State. Instead, the new British minister, George Hammond, took it unofficially to Hamilton. For once that usually amenable individual showed intense irritation. No such "external intervention" could be allowed, he told Hammond tartly. It would only degrade the United States in the eyes of the Indians and lead to future troubles. No, he exclaimed, the only way to end the war would be by the "terror and success of the American arms."

Thus rebuffed, Hammond went next to the proper authorities, Jefferson and Knox. Both turned his proposition down with speed and dispatch. Nor would they hear of his further proposal: that the United States, Great Britain and the Six Indian Nations meet in joint conference for the purpose of establishing boundaries among them.[42]

It was one thing, however, to talk of the "terror and success of the American arms"; it was another to make the boast good. That had to wait for the appointment of General Wayne, the "Mad Anthony" of Revolutionary days, to the command of the army of the frontier.

CHAPTER 12

The Foreign Pot Keeps Boiling

THE SECOND CONGRESS opened its doors on October 24, 1791; or rather, the House did. The Senate, in spite of Republican attempts, steadfastly refused to permit the public to witness its proceedings.

The membership of the two Houses had not radically changed in the recent election. The Federalists were still safely in control, particularly in the Senate; though the Republicans had made gains in the lower House. Party lines were still fairly fluid. No party leader cracked the whip; no caucuses existed to compel discipline; and on most occasions congressmen voted either from conviction or in accordance with commands emanating from their home states. The actual leaders of the two parties were not members of Congress at all. The Federalists generally looked to Hamilton for guidance; while the Republicans more and more turned to Jefferson rather than to Madison. Since these two usually saw eye to eye on most issues and regularly conferred on congressional measures, the shift made little appreciable difference in Republican strategy.

The President made his customary speech to the assembled lawmakers. It was couched in general terms and recapitulated rapidly the state of the nation, with only two specific recommendations for congressional consideration. First, that a Mint be established for the coinage of money, particularly of small denominations, since their scarcity was "so peculiarly distressing to the poorer classes." Second, that provision be made for the sale of the public lands, the proceeds of which were to be applied to the extinguishment of the public debt. Some mention was made of the discontent over the whiskey tax; but Washington dismissed it lightly with the remark that it was no doubt due to the novelty of the excise and a misconception of its purport.[1]

Congress dutifully established a Mint and officially introduced a decimal system of coinage to replace the former chaotic use of the

English pound with its confusing subdivisions, as well as the coins of Spain and Portugal. The ratio of silver and gold was established at fifteen to one. A general Post Office was set up with local branches and post roads. And, under the spur of the Indian debacle, Congress enacted a general militia system and even made some tentative, if vague, gestures toward increasing the Regular Army for the duration of the emergency.

What most vitally interested the lawmakers, however, were the disclosures of the returns on the first census ever taken in the United States. The count of heads as of 1790 showed a population of approximately 4,000,000 in the country, including slaves. Washington was disappointed; he believed the real population was substantially greater. He attributed the discrepancy to religious scruples on the part of some against answering the census-taker's questions, fear on the part of more that it was a mere blind for gathering data on which to base capitation and other taxes, and the indolence, negligence and ignorance of the census-takers themselves. Even so, he was certain that the rapid population increase evidenced in the actual figures would astonish and impress the nations of Europe.[2]

Congress scanned the figures carefully from a different point of view. While the composition of the Senate was fixed under the Constitution, with two senators from every state, large or small, the House membership was apportioned among the states according to their respective populations. A slave, though without a vote or any of the other indicia of citizenship, counted for congressional purposes as three-fifths of a freeman.

The original representation in the House had been arbitrarily fixed. It had been declared at the time, however, that after the 1790 census the membership would be readjusted to conform to the returns. The membership, so ran the Constitution, "shall not exceed one for every thirty Thousand, but each State shall have at least one Representative."

It might appear that reapportionment according to the census should be a routine matter, swiftly computed. Actually, it blossomed into another one of those political tempests which seemed regularly to rock Congress and the nation.

Lawrence of New York started off innocently enough with a proposal that the House should consist of one representative for every thirty thousand inhabitants of a state, the minimum requirement under the Constitution. Livermore of New Hampshire, Sedgwick of

Massachusetts and Dayton of New Jersey promptly disagreed. They thought a ratio of one to forty thousand was more equitable and would keep the size of the House down to its earlier proportions; though Dayton was willing to compromise at one to thirty-five thousand.[3]

Instantly Alexander White, John Page and William Branch Giles, all of Virginia, were on their feet protesting vehemently. Giles, a newcomer in the House and destined to replace Madison as leader of the Republican group of Southerners, this early displayed his peculiar forensic abilities. "The revolutions in property in this country," he cried, "have created a prodigious inequality of circumstances. Government has contributed to this inequality; the Bank of the United States is a most important machine in promoting the objects of this moneyed interest. This Bank will be the most powerful engine to corrupt this House. Some of the members are directors of this institution; and it will only be by increasing the representation that an adequate barrier can be opposed to this moneyed interest."

To this curious chain of reasoning Page added another argument; how could a representative, he inquired, "be sufficiently informed of the opinions, wishes, and real interests of thirty-five thousand of his fellow-citizens?"[4]

Abraham Clark of New Jersey ridiculed the arguments of both Giles and Page. What pertinent relation was there, he demanded, between a numerous representation in the House and liberty; or, for that matter, between the Bank and liberty? "If the liberties of the people are endangered," he lectured the Southern members, "it will not be by the smallness of the representation, but by the corruption of electors and elections." And let Congress look to *that*, he added meaningly.[5]

Actually, neither side was quite frank in the discussion. The small states were confronted with a dilemma. At the lower ratio they might gain a representative; at the higher they would not. Yet a more numerous representation would benefit the large states unduly by a substantial increase in their contingents.

By the same token, the large states should have been unanimously for the smaller ratio. But here again there was a dichotomy. The large states of the North would then be at a disadvantage with such Southern states as Virginia and South Carolina, where the heavy slave population added importantly to the number of their representatives. As Fisher Ames was to put it ironically: the Southern members "pretend that the new House will be more equally representative. The negroes will then be represented; our oxen not." [6]

But the South, with their usual allies in New York, overrode the arguments, the ridicule and the irony of the Northern members, and forced through a ratio of one to thirty thousand.

The bill then went to the Senate, where the Northerners rallied to amend the ratio to one to thirty-three thousand. This was supposed to be a compromise; actually, as Hugh Williamson of North Carolina was quick to point out, when the amended bill came back to the lower House, it now favored the North. Under the new ratio only two members would be dropped from the roster of Northern representatives, while four less would appear from the South, because of unrepresented fractions of population. Sedgwick, however, countered with the claim that the original House plan would have given Virginia twenty-one representatives, even though she was entitled only to nineteen by population proportion to the rest of the country. [7]

The House refused to recede and returned its original bill to the Senate. There, after a bitter debate and only with the casting vote of John Adams to break a tie, that body similarly stood firm. Once again the bill went back to the House. Ames made a powerful speech for concurrence with the Senate; again the House refused.

Since the reapportionment bill was no ordinary measure which could be tabled, the two warring Houses went into conference by committees. Eventually, on March 23rd, the House yielded by the close vote of 31 to 29.

The struggle, however, was by no means over. The bill now went to the President for signature. For once Washington was moved by sectional considerations. He viewed the solid vote of the North on the measure as a possible omen of future separation; he failed to note the similar solidity of the South. Jefferson and Madison, fellow Virginians, urged on him the alleged unconstitutionality of the law. It did not apportion the population (including the slaves) of the several states properly, they said. Eight states to the north, by virtue of a clever juggle with fractions, were given more than one representative for every 30,000 of population, the constitutional limitation.

For the first time also, Washington refrained from polling his Cabinet on such a grave issue. He did not call for the opinions of Hamilton and Knox, both Northerners. He *did* accept the opinions of Jefferson and Edmund Randolph, both Virginians, as well as that of Madison (also a Virginian), who was not in the Cabinet at all.

Fortified with their arguments, he vetoed the apportionment bill; the first such veto of an enactment of Congress on the ground of unconstitutionality.[8]

The country took the veto measure calmly. Only Ames countered the incessant cry (as he put it) of the old foes of the Constitution that "this is unconstitutional, and that is," with his own sardonic remark: "I scarce know a point which has not produced this cry, not excepting a motion for adjourning." [9]

Both Jefferson and Madison hailed the veto as evidence of remarkable firmness in the President. Madison took a further significant position. He similarly approved at about the same time a Supreme Court decision holding an act of Congress unconstitutional and void. They might perhaps have been wrong in the particular exercise of their power, he wrote, "but such an evidence of its existence gives inquietude [only] to those who do not wish Congress to be controlled or doubted whilst its proceedings correspond with their views." [10] The later outcry against the veto power of the court would have met with no sympathy from Madison.

Ames's remark had really been directed against members of Congress like Giles and Page. The Senate had granted a bounty to ships engaged in the cod fisheries as constituting "a copious nursery of hardy seamen" for naval protection. When the bill came to the House, Giles declared it of doubtful constitutionality and added disparagingly that the real defense of the nation came "from the land, and not from the sea."

Page was more brutal in his comments. "It is not clear to me," he said acidly, "that those fishermen would not be more profitable to the United States, if they were cultivating the lands which now lie waste, and raising families, which would be of ten times more value than their fisheries. A nursery of virtuous families, which will produce soldiers, sailors, husbandmen, and statesmen, must be preferable to a mere nursery of sailors, who generally live single, and often perish at sea." [11]

This narrow agrarian view met with Southern approval, only Madison standing to the contrary. Nevertheless a combination of New England and the Middle States, for once united, was able to push through the bounty and make it law.

The same cry of unconstitutionality was raised—again by the irrepressible Page—on a resolution directing the Secretary of the Treasury to report his opinion of the best mode for raising additional revenues during the next fiscal year.

Page cried out that he would always vote against any resolution such as this. It was, he insisted, "the peculiar duty of this House to originate money bills and to devise ways and means," and it was a dangerously subtle and unconstitutional attempt to subvert the government and introduce an absolute monarchy to delegate that duty to the Secretary of the Treasury.[12]

Once more the Federalists were unimpressed, and the resolution passed by a vote of 31 to 27.

In October 1791 the newly appointed minister to the United States from Great Britain landed in Philadelphia and paid his respects to the American government. George Hammond, whose providential arrival extricated Hamilton and the Federalists from a most embarrassing position, was amazingly young for such an assignment. Only twenty-eight years of age, his previous diplomatic experience consisted merely of a term as chargé d'affaires at Vienna and a few months in Madrid. Nevertheless, considering the difficulties of his new assignment and the inflexible nature of his instructions, Hammond proved an able and sufficiently tactful diplomat.

The instructions he brought with him were meticulously detailed, and permitted him neither latitude nor authority to do more than to convey the points they contained to the American government. He was to yield nothing and demand everything.

In his hands was placed a copy of the confidential "Report of the Committee of Lords of the Privy Council on the Trade of Great Britain with the United States." This was to constitute his arsenal of facts and arguments in defense of England's commercial policy; but he was warned to keep the document itself out of American hands. (Nevertheless Jefferson managed by some unknown means to obtain a copy.)

Hammond was to impress the United States, so ran his instructions, with the "honorable conduct" of Great Britain in all commercial and property matters; and he was to "occasionally allude, in proper terms, to the very different line of conduct which many of the said States have pursued towards the subjects and merchants of Great Britain." He was also to convince the American government that they were still receiving many of the advantages in British trade "which they enjoyed before the late War, as British Colonies, and which no other independent State at present enjoys."

They must be made to understand, however, that they could not expect the same full privileges which they had enjoyed as colonies, especially in the West Indies. England was willing to continue that trade on its present limited footing, but intended to close it altogether and adopt other retaliatory measures if Congress enacted any further discriminations against British ships and imports.

This warning was particularly to be conveyed to members of the Senate, to the Southern representatives (whose states depended almost wholly on an uninterrupted commerce with England and her colonies) and to "all moderate men who wish for a connection with Great Britain."

On the controversial matter of the retention of the posts, Hammond was to inform the government that they would not be given up until the United States fully complied on its part with the treaty provisions governing the payment of British private debts.

That England was only too happy to have this pretext for continued possession of the posts is evidenced in a confidential footnote to Hammond's instructions. "I have only to observe," wrote Lord Hawkesbury, "that as these posts are of great service in securing the fidelity and attachment of the Indians, and as they afford Great Britain the means of commanding the navigation of the Great Lakes, and the communication of the said Lakes with the River St. Lawrence, they are certainly of great importance to the security of Canada, and to the interests of this Country, both in a commercial and political view. It is to be wished therefore that they should remain in His Majesty's possession, if the conduct of the United States should continue to justify this measure on the part of Great Britain."

As for the perennial claim of the United States that free ships made free goods, Hawkesbury peremptorily commanded Hammond not to admit it for a moment. "It would be more dangerous," he pointed out, "to concede this privilege to the ships of the United States than to those of any other foreign country."

In fact, England was willing to compromise on only one of the innumerable issues in dispute: to offer a vague and indefinite promise of a commercial treaty which would grant Americans most favored nation treatment in her ports provided the United States reciprocated.

This proposal sounded better on paper than it was in fact. Actually the United States already was enjoying such treatment in England. What she really wanted were the rights she had previously held as a part of the British empire—complete equality everywhere with British ships and British goods. On this the British were adamant. They declared with thinly veiled sarcasm that "the United States at present enjoy all the rights and privileges of an independent Nation, and as such they now have no pretence to claim the privileges which they once enjoyed as British Colonies." [13] In plain language, they could not expect to eat their cake and have it.

With instructions as inflexible and unyielding as these, it would appear that an impossible task confronted Hammond. Yet both Hawkesbury and Grenville were well aware that they had powerful allies in the United States, and had cannily instructed Hammond to take advantage of them.

The first and foremost was Hamilton, with whom Colonel Beckwith had established most satisfactory relations. The Senate, as Hammond was complacently to report, held other well-wishers to England; so much so that they kept him informed of the most secret proceedings of that most secret body. For example, during the heated debate over the appointment of Gouverneur Morris as minister to France, Hammond was able to write home that "in the whole course of this discussion, I have been regularly informed of the proceedings of the Senate, and have received every mark of personal and unreserved confidence."

Nor were members lacking in the House to provide him with tidings of their closed debates in committee of the whole, or to present him with details of the President's confidential communications.[14]

No one seemed to consider such conveyance of confidential information to the representative of a foreign power as at all reprehensible. Yet when a Republican paper later printed a report of a senatorial debate, the editor was promptly threatened with contempt proceedings.

Jefferson, whose first personal contact with the former, unofficial British agent had been when Beckwith came to say good-by, was happy enough to have a properly accredited minister with whom to deal.[15] Yet he expected no immediate results from direct negotiations, unless and until Congress passed the retaliatory measures then pending. But of this he had no great expectations either.

"I have little hope," he had written, "that the result will be any thing more than to turn the left cheek to him who has smitten the right. We have to encounter not only the prejudices in favor of England, but those against the Eastern states whose ships in the opinion of some will overrun our land." [16] Despite the confusion of language, this was perhaps the only time that Jefferson stood up for the East as against the South.

He was also well aware that Hamilton would not hesitate to interfere in the work of his Department, and continue his private and irresponsible conversations with accredited ministers as with unofficial agents. Even with the recently appointed French minister, Jean-Baptiste Ternant, the irrepressible Secretary of the Treasury had conferred without Jefferson's knowledge or consent.

Relations with France had deteriorated since the Revolutionary days of allied cordiality. The French National Assembly, engrossed in its own revolution and determined to bring France rapidly to a commercial par with the great enemy, England, had adopted discriminatory measures in favor of French ships which closely resembled the Navigation Act of that enemy.

The chief victim, as always, was the United States. Tobacco, it had been decreed, was to pay a lesser duty when carried to France in French bottoms than when conveyed in American vessels. A similar differential was laid on whale oil.

Jefferson protested the decree vigorously and, though politely laying the discrimination to mere hurried consideration on the part of the National Assembly, nevertheless hinted at retaliation in kind if the decree were not rescinded.[17]

He still believed in France and in her revolution, and was convinced that the fates of the two countries were interdependent. "I feel that the permanence of our own [revolution]," he avowed, "leans in some degree on that; and that a failure there would be a powerful argument to prove that there must be a failure here." [18]

Impressed with this belief, he was therefore certain that when Ternant arrived all difficulties would be ironed out and the discriminations lifted. He was soon disabused.

Ternant had no powers to treat on the matter or to discuss a new commercial treaty. He was more interested in obtaining arms in the United States for the suppression of the bloody Negro insurrection in Santo Domingo. In this he was partially successful; the government furnished him with a thousand stand of arms and a credit of $40,000 for provisions, all to be applied against the old American debt to

France.[19] As for any discussion of commercial arrangements, however, he informed Jefferson that it must be taken up in Paris.

Hamilton, who had readily provided the credits, suggested to him that he might perhaps discuss the matter as a "volunteer" and then ask his home government for confirmation. Washington thought it an excellent solution; but Jefferson objected strenuously. When the President pressed the point, however, Jefferson reluctantly drafted terms for a proposed treaty. He asked for complete reciprocity with but one exception—that the current schedule of import duties remain in force, provided the charges did not exceed a specified sum. If either nation, however, later reduced its duties, the other must reduce also by a similar amount.[20]

To this Hamilton objected. Such an arrangement would severely damage the structure of his financial system—the revenues on which he counted for the debt service would be diminished and Great Britain, confronted with heavier duties than those imposed on France, would be certain to retaliate. He insisted, therefore, on the insertion of a clause which would protect American specific duties at a higher level regardless of any action which the French might take.[21]

With the interests of his own country in mind, Ternant agreed with Hamilton and not with Jefferson. He too refused to freeze French duties at the current level, and demanded the right to increase them in the future as much as fifty per cent. On this note of futility the discussions ended, and the idea of any new commercial arrangement was momentarily dropped.

Now that both France and England had sent accredited ministers to the United States, it was necessary to appoint ministers of equal standing to Paris and London.

Thomas Pinckney of South Carolina was nominated for the post in England, and his appointment was promptly confirmed by the Senate. William Short, the chargé d'affaires in France, was shifted to the Netherlands with the full title of minister.

Then Washington sent the name of Gouverneur Morris to the Senate as minister to France. There was immediate and intense opposition to his appointment. Morris's views on the country were well known. He had been in Paris during the early stages of the revolution and, in the intervals of his *amours* with titled French ladies, had spoken frankly and cynically of the revolution and its leaders.

The Republicans in and out of Congress demanded that the nomination be rejected. Morris was a known monarchist, declared George Mason of Virginia, and his nomination constituted a direct insult to France.[22] Tom Paine, from England, called it *"a most unfortunate one,"* underscoring the phrase heavily to show the depth of his feeling.[23]

A strenuous struggle to defeat confirmation commenced in the Senate. That such men as Aaron Burr of New York and James Monroe of Virginia, both newly appointed and both Republicans, were in the opposition was to be expected. Burr objected on the ground that Morris's negotiations in England had been so offensively conducted as to preclude success; Monroe more forthrightly called him "a monarchy man" who had gone to Europe to "sell land and certificates."

But opposition came also from such a staunch Federalist as Roger Sherman of Connecticut, and on a ground which disclosed the power of Calvinist morality in his native state. "I consider him," Sherman avowed, "as an irreligious and profane man. He is no hypocrite, and never pretended to have any religion—he makes religion the subject of ridicule and is profane in his conversation. I do not think the public have as much security from such men as from godly and honest men—it is a bad example to promote such characters." [24]

In spite of assaults from the left and from the religious right, Morris was confirmed by a vote of 16 to 11. John Jay, Chief Justice of the United States, angered at the senatorial opposition to a presidential nomination, thought it time to call a halt to such encroachments on the prerogatives of the Executive (perhaps forgetting in his wrath that the Constitution had specifically placed the power to confirm or reject in the hands of the Senate).[25]

But Washington conveyed to Morris with a certain brutal candor the sentiments expressed by Sherman, Burr, Monroe and others in the Senate, and coupled them with a hint that perhaps he ought to profit from them.[26]

There was another ground on which objection was taken, not only to Morris's appointment, but to the appointment of *any* minister to a European post. Both George Mason and Tom Paine had already stated the general Republican conviction that the United States required *no* envoys abroad, nor, indeed, treaties of any kind with foreign countries.[27] It was better, so ran the argument, to have nothing to do with Europe, to keep within our own Chinese Wall of exclusion and remain independent of European political squabbles and corruption, to cultivate our own garden and neither seek nor grant favors. In that way not only would we avoid being drawn into European wars, but we would save the expense of maintaining vain and ostentatious establishments.

Shortly after he landed in Philadelphia, George Hammond, the British envoy, punctiliously submitted his credentials to Jefferson. By this time, however, the harassed Secretary of State was fed up with ministers who had no plenipotentiary powers and who engaged in backstairs diplomacy. In a sharply pointed letter he called for plain answers to plain questions. The treaty of peace, he said, had been breached by the British in two vital articles: Negro slaves had been carried away; and the posts had not been delivered. Had Hammond any explanations? [28]

The youthful British envoy retorted with a *tu quoque*. We had suspended those articles, he replied tersely, because the Americans had breached equally vital articles of the treaty: the American loyalists had been badly mistreated and their confiscated possessions never returned; and the private debts to British merchants had not been paid. However, he added slyly, he was willing to discuss *all* these questions as a single whole. [29]

But this was exactly what Jefferson did not want. He knew well enough, and had often deplored, the fact that the Americans had not been innocent on their own part; though the fault lay with the states and not with the national government. Once embarked in that morass, the negotiations could be depended on to flounder in endless futility.

He therefore shifted his tactics. On the pretense that it would take some time to copy out all the pertinent documents for Hammond's perusal, he asked him whether in the meantime he had power to discuss a commercial treaty. Hammond admitted that he had; adding hastily that he could not *"conclude* any *definitive* arrangement." [30]

Since this meant that the chances of negotiating any such treaty were remote, Jefferson reluctantly turned his attention to the complaints under the peace treaty. But he refused to be put on the defensive. To him the "indispensable" items were the border posts and the Negroes. These violations he was able to document easily enough. Let Hammond, if he wished, list his own complaints. [31]

Hammond took his good time in doing so. Not for him the short and succinct documentation which Jefferson had employed in presenting his own charges. Armed with the ample and detailed Report of the Lords of the Privy Council, and with additional data furnished

by the resident British consuls, he finally submitted a mass of official
and unofficial acts, either by the states themselves or with their acquiescence, which in his estimation had fractured the treaty of peace
in every possible way.[32]

Before he finished drafting his voluminous complaint, Hammond
received some vital information from Hamilton. That gentleman told
him confidentially that the question of the Negroes "did not strike
him as an object of such importance as it had appeared to other members of this government"; that the single substantive complaint in
Jefferson's list related to the posts; and that even on that it might be
possible to grant British subjects "such privileges and immunities in
the respective posts as would protect and secure them in the undis-
turbed possession of the Fur trade." He also readily admitted the
"magnitude" of the American infractions, though blaming them on
the inefficiency of the Continental Congress, and expressed the hope
that the federal courts, which were uniformly deciding in favor of
British creditors, would shortly remove altogether that ground for
complaint.[33]

Completely unaware of the fact that his Cabinet colleague had
thus cut the ground from under his feet, Jefferson studied with considerable perplexity the lengthy and minutely documented bill of
particulars which Hammond had submitted. The facts were accurate
and the documentation exact. Washington, to whom he showed the
indictment, could come up only with an offset. "May not our loss of
the Indian trade," he inquired of Jefferson, ". . . and the expences
and losses sustained by the Indian War, be set against Mr. Hammond's list of grievances?" [34]

Jefferson thought not. He had already officially accepted Hammond's denial that the Canadian government supported or encouraged
the Indians in their conflict with the Americans; though privately he
remained unconvinced.[35]

Instead, he determined to match Hammond point for point; and
then go on to overwhelm him with arguments and statistics. If
Hammond had been lengthy in his exposition, he, Jefferson, would
expand to book-length proportions. While Hamilton would have admitted the technical validity of the British position and interposed
merely an extenuation that the impediments to the debt collection
were the fault of the states, over whom the federal government had
no control, Jefferson realized that such a procedure would place the
United States wholly on the defensive. He preferred to attack.

Accordingly he called Hammond's attention to the exact wording of the articles in the peace treaty: that Congress would *recommend* to the states that confiscated property be restored to the loyalists. Congress had so recommended. If the states failed to comply, it was no fault of Congress; the article had been precisely complied with. Furthermore, he asserted, the British had known all along what the situation was.

So far, his argument was legally unimpeachable. But he ran into difficulties on the next item of complaint—that the stay laws enacted by the states had made it difficult if not impossible for British merchants to sue and collect on prewar debts. For the treaty article said nothing of mere recommendations; it was unequivocal and mandatory. "It is agreed," declared Article IV, "that the creditors on either side shall meet with no lawful impediment to the recovery of the full value in sterling money, of all bona fide debts heretofore contracted."

Yet Jefferson's own state of Virginia, as well as other Southern states, in complete disregard of the treaty article and the pleas of the national government, had enacted stay laws forbidding the courts to entertain such suits against their citizens. It was true that under the Constitution the general government was helpless to intervene; though wherever a case could be brought before the federal courts, those tribunals almost uniformly upheld the treaty in favor of the British plaintiffs.

Therefore Jefferson neatly avoided meeting the issue squarely. He took the position that the stay laws had actually been the *result* of prior British infractions, and not the cause. Had you not first confiscated Southern property—the Negro slaves—and refused to yield possession of the posts, he argued, these stay laws would never have been passed. The fault was primarily yours, and you must bear the consequences.

Having thus turned the enemy's flank, Jefferson next devoted the major portion of his reply to a detailed and damning account of British infractions and the incalculable damage which had flowed therefrom. Until you rectify these ancient wrongs, he concluded, you cannot expect the Americans to consider your own complaints as justified or even remediable.[36]

The voluminous response, the imposing parade of legal citations, the clever shifting of ground, caught Hammond completely off balance. He confessed to Jefferson that he was overwhelmed by the sheer size and volume of the rejoinder and declared he would send it to

England for responsible consideration. He merely observed in passing that "some of the principles, which you have advanced, do not appear to me . . . to be actually relevant to the subjects under discussion between our respective countries," while some of Jefferson's alleged "positive facts" clashed irreconcilably with those in his own possession.[37]

To Hamilton, however, Hammond was considerably more frank. Into that sympathetic ear he poured his indignation at the mass of irrelevancies, denials and "the general acrimonious stile and manner of this letter" handed him by the Secretary of State. It was, he avowed, an "extraordinary performance."

The Secretary of the Treasury, however, so Hammond reported, "treated me (as he has done upon every occasion) with the strictest confidence and candour. After lamenting the intemperate violence of his colleague, Mr. Hamilton assured me that this letter was very far from meeting his approbation, or from containing a faithful exposition of the sentiments of this Government. He added that at the time of our conversation the President had not had an opportunity of perusing this representation. For, having returned from Virginia on that morning only on which it had been delivered to me, he had relied upon Mr. Jefferson's assurance that it was conformable to the opinion of the other members of the executive government." [38]

Hamilton may thereby have smoothed over the ruffled feelings of the British minister, but at the same time he played hob with the management of American foreign relations and ruined the efficacy of Jefferson's presentment. Nor was he honest in his implication that Washington had not known in advance just what line Jefferson was going to take, or that he would disapprove of it when he did know. As a matter of fact, Jefferson had submitted his draft to Washington, with Hamilton's criticisms attached to it; and Washington had clearly approved the draft as it stood.[39]

The role of Hamilton in this business is indeed extraordinary, and can be accounted for, if not justified, only by his passionate conviction that good relations must be maintained at any cost with England. How effectively he had spiked Jefferson's diplomacy may be seen from the aftermath. The British government, thus forewarned of the dissension in the American government, pigeonholed Jefferson's rejoinder without reply. A year and a half later, to Jefferson's insistent queries, Hammond was still returning the uniform answer that he had received no further instructions from his home government, and that therefore the negotiations must be considered suspended.[40] An additional year and a half was to elapse before the matter was finally settled, not by Jefferson but by virtue of Jay's treaty.

On one point only was Jefferson able to obtain satisfaction. Great Britain had announced her intention of enforcing strictly the provisions of the Navigation Act enacted in the reign of Charles II against the importation of foreign goods, alleging as the reason the innumerable frauds she had discovered in the importation of American tobacco.

The announcement threw American merchants into a "universal alarm and commotion"; and Jefferson protested formally to Hammond. The clause of the Act which England intended to invoke, he declared, was so broad that America might not be able to export *any* commodities to that nation. If this were so, he threatened, the United States must retaliate.

Hammond knew this to be no empty threat. Even his best friends in Congress, the Federalists of New England, were now as angry as any Republican. Faced with the probability of a complete cessation of trade between the two countries and the certain enactment of retaliatory measures at the next session of Congress, he acted on his own and without waiting for instructions from home. The clause, he assured Jefferson, would not be taken broadly, and no additional restrictions would be placed on American goods. With these private assurances the Secretary of State was content, and Hammond thankfully reported that this once "Mr. Jefferson has manifested the utmost liberality, confidence and candour." [41]

At the moment, indeed, the United States was fighting a losing battle on every foreign front. France was similarly proving intransigent, particularly on the importation of tobacco; while Jefferson, for all his friendly dispositions, was compelled to acknowledge that "our commerce with their West Indies had never admitted amelioration during my stay in France" or at any time thereafter. He instructed Gouverneur Morris, on the eve of his departure to assume his new post, to inform that government that "we cannot consent to the late innovations without taking measures to do justice to our own navigation." [42]

This was an idle threat which Jefferson himself had no intention of enforcing, and the French paid no heed. The radical Jacobins, then engaged in a furious struggle for the control of France, were not disposed to placate the Americans, whom they contemptuously dismissed as futile, and backsliders from the true revolutionary cause. Jefferson, however, returned good for evil. He spoke kindly of the Jacobins as "representing the true revolution-spirit of the whole nation, and as carrying the nation with them." And he philosophically attributed their arrogance toward America to a lack of experience in business and an impatience with the "established style of communication with foreign powers." [43]

He displayed no such generous understanding when it came to Spain. He sent William Short to join the dilatory Carmichael in Madrid as an interim commissioner. The disputes between the two nations were ever-recurring and much worn in the retelling. They included the problem of the southern boundary, where Spain laid claim to a sizable part of the state of Georgia; the Spanish instigation of the Creeks, the restrictions on American commerce in Spain's colonial possessions, and, of course, the navigation of the Mississippi.[44]

The former Spanish envoy to the United States, Don Diego de Gardoqui, had returned to Madrid full of ominous warnings. His stay had convinced him that in the case of Spain the energetic young nation of the New World distinctly meant business. He eloquently advised the Spanish Court to settle all disputes as speedily as possible. Let the United States have the navigation of the Mississippi, he urged; and safeguard Louisiana, "that invaluable bulwark," by placing a wedge between England and America. This could be done, he proposed, by offering England the Floridas in exchange for Gibraltar. But speed was of the essence, he exhorted. "The first rifle shot I would regard as the beginning of our disasters in America." Even now, perhaps it was too late. "Cursed be the day," he prophesied, "when any hostility is committed in that part of the globe, for those seas will be inundated with privateers fitted out by all nations, which will end by introducing revolution into the possessions of the King." [45]

The Spanish Court was not impressed by Gardoqui's Cassandra-like croakings. As usual, they paltered and delayed. Instead of dispatching a minister with powers to Philadelphia, they contemptuously entrusted their diplomacy to two young businessmen, Joseph Jaudenes and Joseph Viar, to act as agents without the slightest authority to make commitments.

It took Jefferson some time to discover the true situation, for the two agents adopted an arrogant and vehement tone which further roiled the already troubled waters. But when he did, he sent Short to Madrid, with the private admonition that this was the most important mission of his career and to "meditate the matter day and night." [46]

Short had no more success than Carmichael alone. Manuel de Godoy, later to become known as the "Prince of the Peace" and acknowledged lover of the unattractive queen of Spain, paid no attention to the insistence of the American envoys. He evaded and delayed, he uttered polite nothings, and so infuriated Jefferson that by October the latter was ready to lay the entire matter before Congress and let them decide on the issue of peace or war.

Here, however, he ran into the unfaltering opposition of Hamilton, who objected to war with any nation at this stage of American existence. "War," he argued, "would derange our affairs greatly, and throw us back many years in the march towards prosperity. . . . A year, even, was a great gain to a nation strengthening as we were." Since war with Spain was nevertheless inevitable at some future date we ought, Hamilton added, to prepare for it by an alliance with Great Britain. To this idea Washington remarked, much to Jefferson's satisfaction, that the "remedy would be worse than the disease." [47]

CHAPTER 13

The Domestic Kettle Explodes

IF FOREIGN RELATIONS were in a parlous state during 1792, domestic affairs were perhaps even worse. Various pots and kettles boiled over and threatened the very existence of the nation.

By March the speculative mania had finally borne its evil fruit. The earlier collapse late in 1791 should have been taken as a warning; but as the public stocks and bank shares recovered and once more began to climb, all forebodings were forgotten and the speculators, the dupers and the duped, the butcher, the baker and the candlestick maker pressed forward eagerly again to partake of the glittering feast.

William Duer, to whom Madison sarcastically referred as the "Prince of the tribe of Speculators," resumed his feats of legerdemain. He had previously established a corner in the stock of the Bank of New York and forced the price up as much as forty per cent. The successful operation gave him the idea of doing the same with the new shares of the Bank of the United States. Since the operation called for considerably more funds, he brought into partnership in what came derisively to be known as the "six per cent company" such other seasoned speculators as William Livingston of the powerful Livingston clan; Alexander Macomb, whose vast land grab in northern New York had evoked violent political repercussions; John Pintard, the translator in the Department of State before the green fields of easy money beckoned; and other gentry of similar stripe.

Duer, however, held the strings firmly in his own hands. His mode of operation was deceptively simple. He offered his dupes as much as six per cent a month (hence the name) for the use of their life savings. Even bawdyhouse madams, so it was alleged, rushed to present him with the proceeds from the trade; while reverend ministers of the gospel did not disdain this unholy addition to their income. With the funds thus eagerly entrusted to his receptive hands he sought to corner the market in the Bank stock, though not averse to some side speculations in the government funds, forcing the price up with each manipulation.[1]

The first depositors with him duly received their six per cent a month, and the word spread, bringing in a flock of new dupes. Then of course the inevitable happened. As he pyramided his operations, the market stiffened. Holders of securities held out for higher and higher prices, with few takers other than Duer himself; while the ever-widening circle of his "investors" clamored for their monthly usury.

Duer saw the handwriting on the wall, and appealed frantically to his friends in office for aid and a shield against proceedings. For Oliver Wolcott, who had taken his place as Assistant Secretary of the Treasury, had in the meantime discovered that Duer still owed the United States a substantial sum from the days when he had been a member of the Board of Treasury under the Confederation, and was now pressing for a settlement. He had even taken the decisive step of placing the claim in the hands of the United States Attorney for New York for legal action.[2]

But Duer's friends failed him, though there is evidence that some of them brought pressure to bear on Wolcott to stave off proceedings. Wolcott, however, righteously declared that "under the special circumstances which attend this business, of which the gentlemen could not be acquainted, I consider his obligation to fulfill his engagements to the United States as superior to all others."[3]

Hamilton, though rigidly refraining from any attempt to influence his Assistant, and similarly bombarded with pleas from Duer, could not refrain from compassion for his old friend. Unfortunately, he replied to one particularly anguished plea, it was too late to do anything now. Meet your trials with fortitude and honor, he exhorted, and "God bless you, and take care of you and your family. I have experienced all the bitterness of soul on your account which a warm attachment can inspire."[4]

Duer must have smiled a bitter smile on receipt of these brave words. Within a few days thereafter he crashed. Petitions in bankruptcy were filed against him, and by March 23rd he was ensconced in jail. With his fall the entire structure of speculation and usury collapsed. Others fell with him, and respectable business firms suspended payments, going down one after another like a house of cards. The dupes set up a huge wail and turned their fury against the authors of their misfortunes. Crowds gathered outside the jail and

shouted threats of storming the barred doors to drag the chief malefactor out and hang him from the nearest tree. Stones were hurled
against the sturdy walls and clubs were brandished. Macomb followed
his partner to the temporary safety of the prison; Pintard went into
hiding and Livingston prudently retired to his country seat "amidst
his tenants." [5]

From his jail precincts Duer continued to call on Hamilton for
help. But the latter, aware that his own political fortunes were involved and that his enemies were already making capital of the
association, exercised what was for him unusual caution. He wrote
vaguely of government business which detained him in Philadelphia
and ended with the lame remark that "I can hardly flatter myself that
my advice could be of any real importance to you." [6]

Trapped, Duer spoke wildly of exposing men in high places if they
did not come to his rescue. But no one did, and Duer eventually died
within the stone walls, having brought ruin and desolation to
thousands as well as to himself.

All in all, it was reported that $5,000,000 was lost in New York
City alone, and about $1,000,000 each in Boston and Philadelphia;
to mention only the 3 major towns. New building was suspended,
workmen roamed the streets in idleness, and farm produce went
begging at any price. [7]

Only Jefferson, who termed "that stuff called scrip . . . folly or
roguery," managed to extract a moral lesson from the proceedings.
Any man of sense, he observed, who had learned from the experience
of previous famous bubbles would have understood exactly what was
going to happen in this one. Yet, he admitted, "such is the public
gullibility in the hands of cunning and unprincipled men, that it is
doomed by nature to receive these lessons once in an age at least." [8]

He also found a grain of comfort. With a glance toward Hamilton
and his friends in Congress, he now expected "public detestation . . .
to tumble its authors headlong from their heights," [9]

He was disappointed. Hamilton rocked and wobbled; but he
survived. The decisive measures he took were responsible for his
ability to ride out the storm. Once again he threw the weight of the
Treasury in support of the government funds and the money market
in general.

On March 25, 1792, he sent William Seton, of the Bank of New
York, $50,000 with which to purchase the six per cent bonds if they

dropped below par. Later, he threw an additional $100,000 into the market, which, declared Seton unhappily, found so many takers he was compelled to allocate his purchases among a horde of sellers.[10]

By June the pump-priming and the general resiliency of the country steadied the situation, and Fisher Ames was able to report that in Massachusetts at least everything was well, the people prospering and attributing their excellent condition to the general government. Only one thing disturbed him. "The high sense of honor in the paying duties is cooling. When money is in the case," said Ames solemnly, "merchants need watching." [11]

While the financial pot thus boiled over, the political kettle exploded with a roar. Ever since the famous trade of assumption for the national capital, relations between Hamilton and Jefferson had steadily gone downhill. Hardly an issue arose on which they were not immediately at loggerheads: Hamilton's financial schemes; relations with England and France; division of powers between their respective Departments; division of powers between the national and state governments; manufactures *versus* agriculture; banking, excise taxes, and so on down the line.

Thus far Hamilton had generally been the aggressor, with Jefferson fighting what seemed to him a hopeless rearguard action. In Congress the Hamiltonian forces usually emerged victorious; chiefly by virtue of their impregnable position in the Senate from which they could block any radical action by the House. In the Cabinet the same situation usually held true. Knox voted always with Hamilton; while Jefferson could not always rely on Edmund Randolph for support. Even the semiofficial *Gazette of the United States* upheld Hamilton's policies *à outrance* and abused the opposition; though never mentioning Jefferson by name.

It was with these cumulative grievances in mind that Jefferson finally struck back by calling in Freneau to found the *National Gazette*. The first issue appeared on October 31, 1791, and the newspaper became almost at once a tower of strength to the Republicans. The French Revolution was extolled, and England decried. Every Federalist move was savagely attacked, and every Republican measure lauded.

This was permissible enough. On January 12, 1792, however, Freneau turned his attention to Hamilton personally; and from then on not an issue appeared without caustic and bitter castigation of the

Secretary of the Treasury. He was denounced as a "bold adventurer" whose systems "have already produced consequences most pernicious to the interests, honor and happiness of our country; systems which, like seas of corruption, will, if pursued, overwhelm and destroy in their poisonous current, every free and valuable principle of our government." Hamilton was compared to Machiavelli and his followers sneered at as "ministerial sycophants." The funding system was calculated to aggrandize the few and oppress the many. "The fate of the excise tax [currently proposed by Hamilton] will determine whether the powers of the government of the United States are held by an aristocratic junto or by the *people*." The income derived from it would not be sufficient to "pay the salaries of its pimping officers." In spite of this, "a prepared majority in the legislature are about implicitly to adopt the opinion of this infallible secretary" whose reports are replete with "cunning and sophistry." [12]

Nor was the President of the United States immune; though Freneau deftly employed insinuations and innuendoes instead of a direct assault. But Washington penetrated the thin disguise. He complained angrily to Jefferson that Freneau, as well as other Republican editors, were "attacking him directly, for he must be a fool indeed to swallow the little sugar plumbs [sic] here and there thrown out to him. That in condemning the administration of the government they condemned him, for if they thought there were measures pursued contrary to his sentiment, they must conceive him too careless to attend to them or too stupid to understand them."

Jefferson kept a discreet silence during the long tirade, particularly when he found Washington justifying all Hamilton's measures—the Bank, assumption and the excise.[13]

If the President had been thrown into a rage over Freneau's indirect attacks, Hamilton, the prime and personal target, reacted with even greater violence. He knew Freneau to be a translator in Jefferson's office; and he knew something and suspected more of the method by which the *National Gazette* had been established.

On July 25, 1792, a squib appeared in the columns of Fenno's *Gazette of the United States*:

> Mr. Fenno: The editor of the *National Gazette* receives a salary from government.
> *Quere.*—Whether this salary is paid him for *translations*, or for publications, the design of which is to vilify those to whom the voice of the

people has committed the administration of our public affairs—to oppose the measures of government, and, by false insinuations, to disturb the public peace?

In common life it is thought ungrateful for a man to bite the hand that puts bread in his mouth; but if the man is hired to do it, the case is altered.—T. L.[14]

The satirical query created a furore. Everyone knew that "T. L." was Hamilton himself; especially when "An American" (again Hamilton) followed it up in succeeding issues with chapter and verse, and involved Jefferson by name. If the Secretary of State, thundered Hamilton, disapproved of the government "and thinks it deserving of his opposition, can he reconcile it to his own personal dignity, and the principles of probity, to hold an office under it, and employ the means of official influence in that opposition?" [15]

The entire country buzzed with excitement. The long-concealed hostility had burst into the open, and the nation was treated to the unedifying spectacle of the two chief members of the Cabinet belaboring each other in public. Hamilton had been ill-advised to write these attacks himself; but he knew that the revelations would not have had the same impact if written by an outsider.

Jefferson knew better than to take up the pen in his own defense. But others sprang to his aid, while he kept a public silence. Dr. George Logan of Pennsylvania, under the pseudonym of "Aristides," defended him vigorously; whereupon Hamilton, now "Catullus," believing that "Aristides" was in fact Jefferson, retorted in kind and widened the range of the controversy by accusing Jefferson of having been originally opposed to the Constitution.

Nor had Hamilton come to the end of his pamphleteering. Under half a dozen other classical concealments the sharp-penned Secretary of the Treasury returned to the assault, growing more and more specific—and more violent—in the process.[16]

Yet he failed to stop Freneau, who boldly denied everything, stepped up his own furious assaults and searched out new invectives with which to characterize the Secretary of the Treasury.

Washington watched the lid blow off with somber eyes. Though he himself had personally raged at Freneau's diatribes, and probably knew that Jefferson approved of them, he had not by word or gesture disclosed his knowledge. To him the welfare of the country was the sole consideration; and Jefferson, he believed, was almost as essential

to his Cabinet as Hamilton. The two, though in nowise a harmoni-
ous team, balanced each other. Hamilton spoke for the North, the
wealthy and the merchant class. Jefferson was the idol of the South,
the farmer and the artisan. Each represented definite segments of the
nation—geographic, political, social and economic. If either one departed from the Cabinet, and the administration shifted partisanly
to the side of the other, the balance of forces would be destroyed
with ruinous consequences.

At no time did Washington better display that innate wisdom and
sense of statesmanship than he did now. Without doubt he sympathized with Hamilton's personal resentment, as with his financial
policies; yet he kept his private views carefully concealed and sought
to reconcile the irreconcilable.

He wrote soothing letters to both parties to the dispute, asking
them in the name of patriotism and the welfare of their country to
exercise mutual forbearance and charity.[17]

But neither man was in any mood to shake hands and forgive.
Aside from bitter personalities, the matters in issue were too deep-
seated and fundamental. Both replied at length and with vehemence.

Jefferson denied all charges and accused Hamilton of duping him
on assumption and making him an unwitting tool in forwarding his
schemes. "Of all the errors of my political life," he declared angrily,
"this has occasioned me the deepest regret." But this was only the
beginning. Hamilton had time and again interfered in the administration of his Department and forced a reversal of Jefferson's policies
toward France and England by "his cabals with members of the legislature, and by high-toned declarations on other occasions." Hamilton's system "flowed from principles adverse to liberty, and was
calculated to undermine and demolish the republic." Hamilton
sought "to draw all the powers of government into the hands of the
general legislature," which he could readily corrupt; and to have a
corps therein "under the command of the Secretary of the Treasury
for the purpose of subverting step by step the principles of the constitution, which he has so often declared to be a thing of nothing
which must be changed."

Jefferson closed on a bitter and unnecessarily personal note. He
himself had longed to resign from public life (which was true); but,
he said, "I will not suffer my retirement to be clouded by the slanders
of a man whose history, from the moment at which history can stoop
to notice him, is a tissue of machinations against the liberty of the

country which has not only received and given him bread, but heaped its honors on his head." [18]

Hamilton was briefer in his response and less personal. He admitted he had attacked Jefferson in print; but justified his squibs with the charge that Jefferson had uniformly opposed him ever since coming into office, and that he had formed a party in Congress "bent upon my subversion." Nevertheless, though considering himself "the deeply injured party," he was willing to heed Washington's plea for peace. If the President could "form a plan to reunite the members of your administration upon some steady principle of cooperation, I will faithfully concur in executing it during my continuance in office." Otherwise, he suggested, *both* contestants should resign and proper and more amenable substitutes be found.[19]

Neither man resigned, and the Cabinet continued outwardly intact, though inwardly shaky, for a year or so longer. But the rift was never healed, and steadily widened and deepened. The controversy continued in the newspapers, though at a diminishing intensity, until other and newer issues brought it to full blaze again.

What had done more than anything else to touch off the entire bitter exchange was the excise tax. The funding of the public debt and the assumption of the burden of the state debts had created the necessity of discovering other sources of income than those specified in the Tariff Act of 1789. Hamilton recommended an internal tax or excise to be placed on the distillation of whiskey. Congress enacted the measure, albeit reluctantly; but the flood of protests from state-sovereignty men who claimed that internal taxes were peculiarly state reservations, and from farmers and backwoodsmen who did the actual distilling, caused the lawmakers hurriedly to reduce the amount of the tax. Since this sop did not allay the storm, the harried legislators asked Hamilton to find another means of income.

But the Secretary of the Treasury did not intend to bow either to the states or to the embattled distillers. Indeed, he rather welcomed the opportunity for a showdown of strength between the national government and the states. On March 5, 1792, he reported to the House with a vigorous defense of the tax and its underlying principle. Why should not the consumer of domestic goods, he argued, share in the burden of supporting the government equally with the consumer of foreign wares? Or the farmer and backwoodsman be taxed as well as the merchant and manufacturer? The government required an adequate income, and this was the best means for supplementing the existing import duties. He dismissed as nonsense the cry that thereby the liberties of the people were jeopardized, and calculated the extra cost of a year's consumption of liquors by a family of six at the insignificant sum of less than a dollar and a half.[20]

On the basis of this report, Congress refused to repeal the controversial tax; whereupon the clamor rose to furious heights. The Republican press attacked Hamilton as the sole author of the tax; in the affected areas, notably western Pennsylvania, the riots of an earlier year were renewed. Once again protest meetings were held, revenue officers were chased into hiding, and defiant liberty poles erected. At Pittsburgh, the heart and center of the disaffection, a great meeting was held—with the liberty poles, reminiscent of Revolutionary times —which passed by acclamation a remonstrance to Congress, appointed committees of correspondence and resolved to cut off all intercourse with the federal excise officers and "treat them with the contempt they deserve."

This was the last straw. Goaded by Hamilton, Washington decided to take action.[21]

Hamilton kept urging haste, and even drafted a copy of a Proclamation to the offenders for the President to sign. Knox and Randolph assented to the draft, but Jefferson was then at Monticello. Uneasy over former accusations that he had not consulted Jefferson on important measures, Washington determined to forward the Proclamation to the absent Secretary of State for his perusal and signature. Hamilton fumed and fretted. "Every day's delay," he insisted, "will render the act less impressive, and defeat part of its object." But Washington was not to be swerved. He would rather, he told the impatient Secretary of the Treasury, let the local militia deal with the rioters. To send regular troops, he said, would raise the sudden cry: "The Cat is out; we now see for what purpose an Army was raised."[22]

Jefferson countersigned the Proclamation with the mild statement that he hoped it "'will lead the persons concerned into a regular line of application which may end either in an amendment of the law, if it needs it, or in their conviction that it is right." [23]

The Proclamation was thereupon issued, calling on all disaffected persons to cease and desist. As a result the revolt hurriedly collapsed, much to Hamilton's disgust. He had to wait almost two years more before he could unsheath the sword of the government and display its majestic might.

Even the leaders of the movement in western Pennsylvania privately acknowledged that they had committed that most devastating of errors—a political blunder. One of them, the Swiss emigré Albert Gallatin, destined for national prominence and office, admitted that "our resolutions [at the Pittsburgh meeting] were perhaps too violent, and undoubtedly highly unpolitic"; and that the meeting had "hurt our general interest throughout the State and has rather defeated the object we had in view, to wit, to obtain a repeal of the Excise law, as that law is now more popular than it was before our proceedings were known." [24]

The summer of 1792 marked the emergence of definite party lines in the United States. Parties in fact had existed before, but there had been a reluctance to call them by their proper names. The Constitution had not envisaged the growth of a two-party system, complete with candidates and platforms; and the word "party" or "faction" when applied to either side was angrily resented as a term of opprobrium.

Even now definite labels were sedulously avoided; though the names Federalists and Republicans were gradually coming into general use. The Federalists were usually alluded to by their opponents as monarchists, aristocrats and Anglomen. In turn the Republicans were assailed as democratical schismatics, demagogic appealers to the mob, French-lovers. More and more, as the revolution continued its headlong course in France and threatened to extend its sway over all Europe, the attitude toward her and her great opponent, England, became one of the two touchstones of American politics. The other was Hamilton's fiscal policies. The lines of demarcation grew sharply marked; and it was rare indeed for a Hamiltonian to favor France, or for an admirer of England to denounce his system.

These two criteria generally coincided with geographical areas, which in turn were coterminous with specific economic interests. Trading and seafaring New England favored the Federalists; the agricultural South adhered to the Republicans; while the large Middle States of Pennsylvania and New York, with their mixed economy, became the battleground of the contending parties.

Because the party labels were essentially economic in character, it followed that geography was not the primary determinant, except insofar as it conditioned the economic interests and way of life of the inhabitants. By the same token the attitude toward slavery, more and more coming to the fore as a dividing line and fissionable factor, depended on the general economic milieu. Religious beliefs, however, tended to complicate the simplicity of this analysis. By and large the Calvinists in their various manifestations were Federalists; the revivalist groups of Methodists, Baptists and to a lesser extent Presbyterians were Republicans; while the more easygoing Anglicans divided politically on other grounds.

The year 1792 was a general election year. Every elective office was in contest. In the states, governors and legislatures were being chosen; in the general government, the President, Vice-President, the entire lower House and one-third of the Senate. Since this was the first full test for the nation as a whole since the formation of the Union, and since the divisive issues were now clearly developed, it was obvious that a stirring and acrimonious election impended.

On one elective office only was there virtual unanimity. That was the presidency. The name of George Washington still retained its magic, in spite of miscellaneous sniping. To the vast majority of the people he continued to be the symbol of their travail and of their unity. He stood above the battle, unobscured by the smoke and sweat of the contending forces. If there were grumblings from the initiate, if certain Republican leaders and publicists believed he was already halfway into the camp of the enemy, even they considered him as the only possible brake on an extreme Federalist policy, that he still represented a moderating influence to which they could appeal, and that without him all was lost.

The Federalists certainly required the majesty of his name and the prestige of his office as an invulnerable cloak in which to wrap themselves against the slings and arrows of their enemies.

Washington, however, was determined to retire. He had entered upon the presidency with reluctance and a sense of personal unfitness. He had held before him steadily the goal of a united nation, in which sectional interests should be subordinated to the common good. He had conceived of his office as a symbol of the nation and one not to be used for partisan purposes on the one hand, or attacked for partisan purposes on the other. He neither wished to encroach on the prerogatives of the legislative branch nor permit it to poach on the executive domain. He very rarely recommended specific measures to Congress, nor did he seek to influence its decisions by those methods which later Presidents came to employ: direct argument and suasion, political pressures and the sweet uses of patronage.

He had formed a Cabinet of those whom he believed to be the best men available; and once chosen, he generally gave them ample liberty of action. He presided at Cabinet meetings or took their opinions in writing as a chairman rather than a chief. The discussion of policies came from below rather than from above. He proposed the questions and then listened attentively to the opinions of his officers. Hardly ever did he inject an opinion of his own into the course of the debate. Not once did he assemble the department heads to lay down a rule for them to follow. As already pointed out, he always accepted the unanimous opinion of the Cabinet, and usually followed the majority. Only in the case of a tie did he render his own decision. The Cabinet of Washington had greater powers than any since.

Several reasons might be adduced for this. First, it followed the English idea of the Cabinet; second, there were in the Cabinet at least two men of outstanding ability and positive, if conflicting, ideas; third, the members were political leaders in their own right with large and enthusiastic followings in Congress and in the nation; and fourth, Washington was diffident concerning his own qualifications for civil administration.

The diffidence was now gone, but the storms of partisanship and calumny had astonished and angered the President. He would rather, he told Madison, "go to his farm, take his spade in his hand, and work for his bread, than remain in his present situation." He abhorred "the spirit of party" which had become evident both in the government and among the people, and he was going to retire at the end of his term. Would Madison therefore draft a valedictory address for him?

Madison sought to dissuade him with the argument that the emerging party spirit was the best reason for his assuming a second term. Of the eligible candidates for the office, Jefferson was anxious for private life, and both Adams and Jay were too "monarchical." But Washington persisted, and Madison drafted a tentative farewell address.[25]

When the President's decision was announced to Hamilton and Jefferson, they were aghast. Both pleaded with him to reconsider. "The affairs of the national government are not yet firmly established," Hamilton said frankly, and "its enemies, generally speaking, are as inveterate as ever. . . . If you continue in office nothing materially mischievous is to be apprehended; if you quit, much is to be dreaded." [26]

Jefferson, who was one of the "enemies" to whom Hamilton alluded, had his own reasons for wishing Washington to remain. He dreaded far worse from Adams, Jay or any other candidate whom the Federalists might offer. Only Washington, he told the President, could hold the country together. If he left, the "corrupt squadron" in Congress and the machinations of others (he meant Hamilton without specifying any name) might lead to the overthrow of the republican form of government in favor of an English-type monarchy.[27]

Confronted with a unanimity of pleas not merely from his closest advisers but from leaders everywhere, Washington at length yielded, the valedictory was put aside, and both parties heaved huge sighs of relief. Neither one was as yet anxious for a trial at arms. The Federalists had nothing to gain and much to lose; the Republicans were not yet prepared for a decisive test.

With the presidential post thus unanimously offered again to Washington, political attention centered on the vice-presidency and the new Congress. Adams had by no means been a unanimous choice in the first election, and since then the doubts of the Republicans and agrarians had sharpened into open hostility. Whether deserved or not, the sturdy old patriot of Revolutionary days had achieved an unenviable reputation as an English monarchist, vain, tactless, in love with the trappings of royalty and a believer in a hereditary aristocracy.

Worse still, he had written a book—or rather, two; for the earlier *Defence of the American Constitutions* also rose to haunt him. Of no one was the ancient biblical exclamation more apropos: "Oh, that mine enemy would write a book!"

The real struggle for electors centered in the spring elections for the several state legislatures; since in many states the presidential electors were chosen by the legislatures and not by general vote. It was conceded that all New England would tender their ballots to Adams; and that most of the Southern states would seek another candidate. New York, precariously balanced, might well prove pivotal. Therefore all political eyes converged on that key state.

George Clinton, perennial governor, was running again. His cross-grained antifederalism, his vehement championship of agrarianism, his opposition to every Hamiltonian measure, endeared him to the Southern Republicans. In order to capture the state and its legislature, the Federalists looked about for a strong candidate to oppose him for the governorship. They finally chose John Jay, the Chief Justice of the United States, to enter the lists against the powerful Clinton.

The resulting election was hotly contested and the results close.

When the smoke cleared, it at first appeared that Jay had been victorious. But Clinton, desperate in defeat, found technical grounds on which to dispute the validity of the ballots cast in three upstate counties for Jay. The Board of Canvassers, composed of Clinton's appointees, decided in favor of Clinton and threw the ballots out. With the returns from these three counties voided, they declared Clinton elected.

The Federalists, and many of a nonpartisan cast, raised such an outcry that it was finally agreed to place the decision for arbitration in the hands of the two United States senators from New York— Rufus King and Aaron Burr. The arbitrators split, as might have been expected, on strictly political lines; and again the matter went back to the Board. They reiterated their former decision, and the legislature, with a majority of seated Clinton followers, backed them up.

The Federalists uttered wild threats of an appeal to the people of the state and even of the employment of force. But Rufus King and Hamilton sternly deprecated such measures and the crisis passed, with Clinton once more ensconced in the gubernatorial chair.[28]

But even the Republicans of other states felt ashamed over the cavalier tactics of their New York associate. Jefferson thought Clinton should have declined the office and called for a new election. "To retain the office," he said, "when it is probable the majority was against him is dishonorable." [29] Clinton was troubled with no such qualms and eventually rode out the storm. In fact, he became one of the avowed Republican candidates for the vice-presidency.

Another candidate was Senator Aaron Burr. That subtle, complex and brilliant individual of distinguished ancestry (his father had been president of Princeton College and his maternal grandfather was the great theologian Jonathan Edwards) had gradually come to national prominence. In New York he had snatched the senatorship from General Philip Schuyler, Hamilton's father-in-law, and built an efficient political machine out of the Society of Tammany. In many respects he resembled his greatest opponent, Hamilton. Slight of stature, soldierly in bearing, handsome, with a splendid reputation from the Revolution and irresistible with the ladies, rivaling Hamilton for leadership of the New York bar, literate, politically astute, he had gone with the Republicans while Hamilton went with the Federalists. Liberal but not extreme in his politics, speaking ill of no man, he counted many friends among the Federalists themselves, much to

Hamilton's dismay and furious reaction. The seeds of future tragedy had thus early been dropped in fallow soil.

When Hamilton heard the initial rumors of Burr's candidacy, his alarm and wrath rose to the point where he talked with unrestrained violence of his personal and political rival. Burr, he warned his Federalist friends, was "unprincipled, both as a public and a private man. . . . He is determined, as I conceive, to make his way to be the head of the popular party, and to climb *per fas aut nefas* [by hook or crook] to the highest honors of the State, and as much higher as circumstances may permit." It was, he solemnly averred, "a religious duty to oppose his career." [30]

As if this were not enough, he adverted to Burr as a man whose "integrity as an individual is not unimpeached. As a public man, he is one of the worst sort—a friend to nothing but as it suits his interests and ambition." He was "secretly turning liberty into ridicule. He knows as well as most men how to make use of the name. In a word, if we have an embryo-Caesar in the United States, 'tis Burr." [31] Which was exactly what the Republicans were saying of Hamilton himself.

Hamilton would have been wiser to have held his thoughts to himself, for Burr's alleged candidacy did not survive the decision of the New York Republicans to support Clinton for the office.

Before the electors were finally chosen, however, the congressional elections were held. The Republicans attacked fiercely all along the line, encouraged by the addition of Kentucky to the Union on May 1, 1792.

The frontiersmen in that turbulent territory were chiefly Virginia-born, which was logical since it had originally been a part of that state. Many Virginians, tired of the exhausted soil at home, had taken up land in the lush new country. Some, like John Breckinridge of Albemarle, took their Negro slaves along to the "almost paradise." Breckinridge sent his slaves ahead, even before he wound up his affairs in Virginia, fearing that the "Kentucky politicians," many of whom hailed from western Pennsylvania where the sentiment was decidedly antislavery, might interpose barriers against further importations. But as the influx of Virginians increased, that fear was quieted; and the Negroes were reported to be well pleased with their new surroundings. Besides the standard rations of bacon, bread and molasses, wrote Breckinridge, his slaves must have whiskey, "or they are unable to work." [32]

Kentucky, peopled from Virginia and western Pennsylvania, soon became one of the strongholds of Republicanism, extremist in its views, restless in its temperament, and ready at the drop of a hat to enunciate the fiercest defiance of conservatives back East.

The results of the congressional elections were highly satisfactory to the Republicans. For the first time they found themselves in the majority in the lower House; though their joy was somewhat dampened by the unchanged complexion of the Senate, where only one-third had been up for re-election.

But they knew now that the country had swung over to their tenets and that Hamiltonian principles were on the wane. "I think we may consider," remarked Jefferson with considerable satisfaction, "the tide of this government as now at the fullest, and that it will, from the commencement of the next session of Congress, retire and subside into the true principles of the Constitution." [33]

Slowly the several states nominated and selected their presidential electors. This time each elector was committed in advance to the two candidates for whom he was to vote. For the presidency, all would vote for George Washington. For the vice-presidency—or rather, for their second and constitutionally equal choice—the contest had finally narrowed down to the incumbent, John Adams, and Governor Clinton of New York.

The Republicans hammered away at Adams's supposedly monarchical leanings. Freneau's *National Gazette* published a list of items which were asserted to be indicia of eventual monarchy. Such were the use of titles like Excellency, Honorable and Esquire; the custom of "Levees!" . . . keeping the birth days of "the servants of the public" . . . ceremonial isolation of officials from the people . . . the ostentatious display of carriages . . . feasts . . . "tawdry" gowns . . . high salaries . . . etc., etc.[34] Many of these usages might equally be attributed to Washington—and Freneau no doubt so intended—but everyone knew that Adams had advocated these aristocratic rituals.

The newspaper campaign started too late, or so the Republicans declared,[35] and Adams was re-elected. But there had been a battle. Whereas Washington was given every one of the 132 electoral votes, of the second ballots Adams received 77, Clinton obtained 50, Jefferson was tendered Kentucky's four as a testimonial, and Burr viewed sadly a single salute from South Carolina.

Once again the touchy Adams brooded not too silently over his substantial unpopularity in the country.

CHAPTER 14

Neutrality by Any Other Name

THE SECOND ADMINISTRATION of George Washington did not commence under the most benign auspices. Both at home and abroad the portents were ominous. Clouds of war were massing thickly on the European horizon; at home, in spite of the unanimity of the vote of confidence in the President, the sniping against him continued and the rift in the Cabinet was as wide as ever. Money was again tight, with the public funds trembling on the brink of another slide. The opposition to the excise tax merely went underground on the issuance of the President's Proclamation, and was shortly to erupt with even greater violence than before. The Congress which began its sessions on November 5, 1792, was still the old one, but the knowledge that within several months the new one would take over, with the Republicans booted and saddled in the House, imbued them with arrogant confidence.

Washington's first act was to hold his Cabinet intact. Jefferson however, who had spoken several times before of resigning, now declared his firm resolve of giving up the bootless battle and leaving Hamilton in possession of the field.

On his way north from Monticello, Jefferson stopped at Mount Vernon to announce his intention. Washington urged him to reconsider. The interview ended inconclusively. But when he reached Philadelphia, the aggrieved Secretary of State found Hamilton's attacks on him in the columns of the *Gazette of the United States*. These, coupled with the admonitions of friends that he would be accused of retiring under fire, decided Jefferson to remain and he so notified the President. Delighted, Washington poured oil on the troubled waters. Hamilton, he wrote, was ready to "coalesce" with Jefferson in the affairs of government. Would the latter undertake a similar agreement? That, retorted Jefferson, was impossible. It would require one of them to yield his principles.[1] He refrained from the obvious addition that he would be the one.

With that the President had to be content. It might be inquired why he was so anxious to keep Jefferson in the administration. The split had become a public scandal, with both men employing the press to air their quarrels. He himself approved of Hamilton's fiscal policies and disapproved of Jefferson's. In foreign affairs, however, he preferred to act as a balance wheel between their respective leanings toward Great Britain and France.

The answer is that Washington still could not conceive that two separate and irreconcilable parties had emerged in the nation, each full-panoplied with a philosophy and a program. He still believed that the disputes represented mere sectional jealousies; and that the retention of the supposed leaders of the North and South in the Cabinet would prevent them from going to extremes.

The House of Representatives was shortly to disabuse him. On January 23, 1793, William Giles of Virginia rose on the floor to move a resolution calling on Hamilton for an account of all foreign loans negotiated by him, a statement of the balances existing between the Bank of the United States and the government, a report on the operations of the sinking fund, and the current unapplied revenues and where they were on deposit. In short, Hamilton was to inform the outgoing Congress of practically everything he had done since he took office, with complete financial details and supporting schedules.

It was a most unusual request, particularly since Hamilton had already filed his annual report on January 3rd. To complete an answer before Congress passed out of existence was almost impossible; or at least so it was thought. Yet the House adopted the resolution and duly sent it to the Secretary of the Treasury.

Behind the sudden demand lay a complicated series of maneuvers. Fisher Ames had already noted a curious tightening of the ranks in the Virginia delegation. "Virginia," he remarked, "moves in a solid column, and the discipline of the party is as severe as the Prussian. Deserters are not spared. Madison is become a desperate party leader, and I am not sure of his stopping at any ordinary point of extremity."[2]

The discipline had a goal of which Ames was as yet only vaguely aware. Madison and Jefferson had determined that the time had come to make a supreme effort to get rid of Hamilton; and the results of the recent election encouraged them in the belief that the country would back them in the attempt. But before the assault could be made, there must be a sufficiency of ammunition.

With this in mind, Madison studied the regular annual report of the Treasury with a vigilant eye; and pounced on one item in the maze of figures as the handle for dislodging the Secretary.

On August 4 and 12, 1790, Congress had authorized the Treasury to borrow $14,000,000 in Europe for the purpose of paying part of the old foreign debt as it accrued. Specific sums from these new loans, Congress decreed further, might be transferred to the United States on the authorization of the President.

Pursuant to these acts of Congress, Hamilton had, among other loans, negotiated one of 3,000,000 florins through the great Dutch banking house of Willinks, Van Staphorsts and Hubbard. This particular sum he transferred to America, deposited in the Bank of the United States and employed in part to purchase the government funds during the time of financial crisis.

Madison considered this a distinct dereliction of duty under the terms of the acts of Congress. The loan, he noted, ought to have been applied in Europe on the old foreign debt to stop further interest payments. Instead, it had been brought here "to extend the speculations and increase the profits" of the Bank.[3]

This and other alleged discrepancies he placed in Giles's hands for action. Giles was young, hot-tempered, able and effectively sharp-tongued in debate. He had studied law under Jefferson's old master, George Wythe, and came to Congress to take his seat as a representative with a letter of introduction to Madison from—of all men—John Marshall. He promptly entered the orbit of the two great Virginians and diligently followed their lead; though on occasion displaying a marked independence of mind.

If the Republicans thought it was humanly impossible for Hamilton to prepare the necessary reply to Giles's resolution before Congress rose, so as to enable them to make political capital of the failure during the interval between sessions, they were sadly mistaken.

Hamilton detected at once the animus and the strategy, and determined to confound his enemies. Working at top speed both day and night he drafted a complete report of all his transactions and submitted it to the House on February 4th, less than two weeks after the passage of the resolution. Being Hamilton, however, he could not refrain from adding to the dry facts and figures some highly undiplomatic references to the congressional move. In a supplementary report he animadverted bitingly on the reasons which lay behind the extraordinary request. Those reasons, he declared, had already been rushed by the Republicans to the press; and they were "of a nature to excite attention; to beget alarm; to inspire doubts."

Why, he demanded hotly, was not an explanation of the transferred loan requested of him privately instead of first blazoning it to the public? "Was it seriously supposable," he wrote, "that there could be any real difficulty in explaining that appearance [of misappropriation], when the very disclosure of it proceeded from a voluntary act of the head of this department?" [4]

It must be confessed that much of Hamilton's many difficulties arose from his own nature. Secure in the knowledge of his own abilities and the integrity of his motives he wrote, spoke and acted with an impetuousness and reckless disregard of consequences which a more prudent man might easily have avoided.

The Republican leaders, though taken aback at the speed with which the report was rendered, studied it closely for discrepancies and evidence of possible illegalities. The results were transmitted to Jefferson, who, with the utmost secrecy, drafted a series of ten resolutions for Giles to submit to Congress as his own. On February 27th the youthful Virginian once more rose in the House and moved nine of the ten resolutions. They named specific charges against Hamilton and they were intended, as everyone realized, to overwhelm and drive him irrevocably out of office and public life.

The first two resolutions asserted as preamble that "laws making specific appropriations of money should be strictly observed by the administrator thereof" and that any violation was a constitutional offense. The others were specific accusations: that Hamilton had applied part of the loans to interest payments instead of the principal of the foreign debts as the Act of Congress had ordered; that he had drawn other parts to the United States without instructions or authority from the President; that he had failed to inform Congress of what he had done; that he had deviated from the President's instructions in making new loans; that he had acted contrary to the public interest in borrowing $400,000 from the Bank of the United States at five per cent interest at a time when large sums of public money were available on deposit; and that he was "guilty of indecorum to this House, in undertaking to judge of its motives in calling for information which was demandable of him." Finally, Giles moved that the foregoing resolutions be transmitted to the President of the United States.[5]

The tenth resolution which Jefferson had drafted was prudently omitted by Giles. This was a forthright statement that the Secretary of the Treasury "has been guilty of maladministration" and should be removed from office.[6]

The next day Giles moved to refer the resolutions to the Committee of the Whole. William Smith of South Carolina, a staunch Federalist who represented the seaboard commercial interests and large land-holders of that Southern state, was promptly on his feet. Why the delay? he demanded in a voice dripping with sarcasm. Was it perhaps because the session was due to end in a few days, so that there would be no time left for a public consideration of the resolutions? The Secretary of the Treasury had been accused of certain malfeasances of office. He was either guilty or he was not; let the members have a chance to decide, and terminate the issue.[7]

Though he was unable to prevent the reference, the sting of Smith's sarcasm forced the resolutions out into the open a day later. On March 1st, with the hands of the clock moving inexorably toward the session's adjournment on March 2nd, the debate began.

Giles took the tack that Congress was actually helping the President get rid of a guilty Cabinet member without embarrassment; but this line of argument was immediately punctured by Barnwell. Had the President ever complained to Congress of Hamilton? he inquired. Why not wait until he did before offering unsolicited help?

Smith next rose for the defense. In a long, closely argued speech, he took up each resolution in turn and tore it to shreds with facts and figures taken not only from Hamilton's own report but from sources and documents not mentioned therein.[8] The exposition was brilliant, powerful and devastating, displaying an easy familiarity with every intricacy of finance of which only Hamilton could have been capable. Everyone was convinced, in fact, that the speech had been prepared for Smith by the Secretary of the Treasury.

Though Giles, Madison and others sought to eradicate the profound impression made by Smith, it was obvious to the impartial that the resolutions no longer had any chance of success. Nevertheless the debate dragged on into the night, and candles were brought to illuminate the scene. The Republicans called for adjournment, but the determined Federalists blocked every move. At length voices tired and the weary members proceeded to vote.

The first two resolutions, as merely declaratory, were not even taken up. The other seven, each voted on in turn, went down to decisive defeat. The largest number of votes that could be mustered in favor of any resolution was on the fifth—that Hamilton had failed to notify Congress officially of the withdrawal of funds from Europe to the United States. Fifteen members voted aye; while thirty-three voted nay. By the time the final specific resolution came on for a vote —that Hamilton had been guilty of an "indecorum" against the House —only seven diehards voted in favor. These were Giles, Madison, Ashe, Baldwin, Grove, Richard Bland Lee and Nathaniel Macon, all from the South and most of them from Virginia.[9]

Hamilton had triumphed again. Viewing the rout from the outside, Jefferson sourly attributed it to a House composed of stockjobbers, bank directors, ignoramuses and lazy or good-natured members.[10]

The next day Congress disbanded; two days later, on March 4, 1793, Washington and Adams once more took their oaths of office, and the second administration of the United States began.

During the acrimonious debate over Giles's resolutions news came from Europe which brought fresh complications to the United States and the lengthening shadow of years of trouble. On January 21st, France had guillotined her king; on February 1st she declared war against England and Holland.

There had been war in Europe the preceding year; but it had been landbound, with France arrayed against Austria and Prussia. Now, with England's entrance into the conflict, the oceans became belligerent ground and the bloody tide rolled closer to American shores. From this time on, the United States was in a sense a participant, and her destiny or even ultimate survival depended in large part on the outcome of the gigantic struggle overseas.

There never had been any question where the sympathy of the great majority of Americans had lain. They still remembered their own Revolution and their gratitude for French aid. The French Revolution, studded with phrases and catchwords taken almost verbatim from American slogans, seemed but an extension of the earlier Revolution and a further step forward in the indefinite progress of mankind.

Only a few cynics like Gouverneur Morris surveyed the scene and declared it odious; only those deep-read in history and immune to idealistic fervors like John Adams could doggedly consider the unfolding of events as "a complication of Tragedy, Comedy and Farce" which all sensible men should have foreseen.[11]

It is true that the number of doubters was increasing as the spectacle unfolded and the guillotine took the center of the stage, with group after group of old revolutionaries becoming suddenly "counter-revolutionaries" and their heads rolling in consequence. But the doubters were still in the minority. Most Americans agreed with the dictum of a Boston paper that, in spite of excesses, "the cause of the French is still that of humanity—is still the cause of freedom." [12]

The above was the pronouncement of a Federalist newspaper. As for the Republicans, no doubts, no qualms were permitted to mar the bright texture of their fervor for France. The news of an encounter between the French and allied troops and the rout of the latter reached America late in 1792 and touched off immense celebrations. Not a Republican but failed to feel a vicarious thrill or to echo Freneau's ecstatic apostrophe to the victors:

> O France! the world to thee must owe
> A debt they ne'er can pay:
> The Rights of Man you bid them know,
> And kindle Reason's day! [13]

In Baltimore, New York, Philadelphia and Boston, as well as in smaller towns and villages, the friends of France gathered to celebrate the glorious triumph with dinners, an endless array of toasts, the ringing of bells and liberty poles surmounted by red Phrygian caps. Boston in particular went wild. There the populace, benignly presided over by "Citizen" Sam Adams, participated in the greatest outpouring ever witnessed in America. On January 24th they woke to the thunder of guns from the harbor fort. At eleven o'clock a huge procession escorted a sacrificial ox, its horns gilded, its roasted flanks garlanded with ribbons and surmounted by the flags of France and the United States in loving embrace. Numerous carts, piled high with loaves of bread and hogsheads of punch, followed the gilded carcase. The parade wound its way to State Street, where a liberty pole soared majestically over long tables set up in the middle of the street. There the ox and his accouterments were deposited, and the marchers partook of meat, bread and drink without further ado.

When the last crumb and the last draught of heady punch had disappeared with remarkable rapidity, the partially sated procession moved on to Faneuil Hall, where they partook of even more substantial fare. Within the Hall symbolic figures reared aloft: The Spirit of Liberty, the Rights of Man with the fetters of despotism shattered at his feet; communal flags were everywhere. Someone suddenly remembered, possibly with the aid of the flowing punch, that there were unfortunate criminals in the town jail. A purse was promptly subscribed to pay their fines so that they too could "join their festive brethren and again breathe the air of Liberty." After this second feast of reason and flow of soul, interlarded with speeches, meat and drink, they staggered out for an evening of bonfires, illuminations, dancing— and further drinking.[14]

Jefferson rejoiced with his fellow Republicans. The "glorious news" of the French victory was celebrated in Philadelphia with a clamor of bells and an eruption of fireworks. Only "our monocrats here," he added sarcastically, have "wry faces." The Republicans, on the other hand, were proudly accepting the "name of Jacobins which two months before had been affixed on them by way of stigma."[15]

When his own protégé William Short wrote disparagingly of the Jacobins from his vantage point abroad, Jefferson replied with some heat that they were patriots of purest ray serene; that while some innocent blood had perhaps been shed, rather than that the revolution should fail "I would have seen half the earth desolated. Were there but an Adam and an Eve left in every country, and left free, it would be better than as it now is."[16]

Imbued with sentiments such as these, it is no wonder that Jefferson received with silent contempt the steady stream of reports which the irrepressible Morris persisted in sending to the State Department from France. Nevertheless they add up to a vivid and firsthand account of the rise of the Jacobins, their violent overthrow and barbaric treatment of their more moderate opponents, and all the bloody excesses of a revolution within the revolution.

Lafayette, idol of the Americans, had become so unpopular with the Parisian mob because he opposed the Jacobins that he dared not appear in the streets without his army for fear of being torn to pieces. "Thank God," commented Morris, "we have no populace in America, and I hope their education and manners will long prevent the evil."[17]

After a vain attempt to stem the rise of the Jacobins, Lafayette was finally compelled to seek refuge elsewhere. As the enragés grew more enraged, even the foreign envoys packed up and fled the scene. Only Morris remained, alone and solitary, to survey the carnage and continue his acid reporting. No one could deny his personal courage; for

the Jacobins knew only too well that he detested them and the entire
revolution.[18]

Back home, Jefferson understood the danger to which Morris was
exposed, and wrote a warning note that he ought to leave as soon as
"the scene becomes personally dangerous to you." While unsympa-
thetic to the minister as a man, he wanted no incident which might
blow Franco-American relations sky-high. He had already ordered
Morris to suspend payments on our debt to France during the internecine struggle for power; but now, on Morris's request for further
instructions, he laid down the principle that business could be trans-
acted even with a *de facto* government. Such, for example, was the
necessity for obtaining a change in the French restrictions on American commerce. Unless these are modified, said Jefferson, speaking now
as a responsible government official, "we must lay additional and
equivalent burthens on *French* ships, by name." [19]

The news of the trial and execution of the king of France reached
America by the middle of March. But even this violence, and the
strange circumstances that attended it, did little to shake the faith
of the Republicans; though Federalists, who recollected that Louis
XVI had befriended America in her darkest hour, expressed horror
and pity. They even suggested that the ladies show their respect for
the decapitated monarch by wearing a black rose on the bosom for a
month.[20]

Jefferson considered the act an excellent warning to the other
crowned heads of Europe that their persons were no longer inviola-
ble.[21] The Republican press extolled the guillotining and poured abuse
on those who disagreed. Hugh Brackenridge, frontier lawyer and
novelist, fashioned a coarse squib which won wide popular approval.
"Louis Capet," he exulted, "has lost his caput. From my use of a pun,
it may seem that I think lightly of his fate. I certainly do. It affects
me no more than the execution of another malefactor." [22]

The French declaration of war on England brought a renewed
wave of partisan rejoicing from the Republicans; but this time the
Federalists closed their ranks and henceforth moved in a solid column
against what they termed the anarchic beast abroad and its sympathizers at home. The former they abused with mounting fury; while
they jeered and mocked at the more hysterical manifestations of the
latter.

There was indeed much to ridicule in the more violent Republicans.

Such courtesy titles as Mister, Sir, Esquire, Reverend, Honorable and Excellency were decried as aristocratic, servile and "diabolical." Instead, exhorted the Republicans, let us follow "glorious France" and use only "the social and soul-warming term Citizen."[23] Even the marriage ceremony had to conform to revolutionary usage; and the public announcements of it followed a set pattern: "Married. By Citizen Thatcher, Citizen Frederick W. Geyer, Jr., to Cit[izen]ess Rebecca, daughter to Citizen Nathan Frazer."[24]

To which the Federalists retorted in jeering rhymes:

> No citess to my name I'll have, says Kate,
> Tho' Boston lads about it so much prate;
> I've asked its meaning and our Tom, the clown,
> Says, *darn it*, 't means "a Woman of the Town."[25]

The extension of the war in Europe, however, was no matter for rejoicing or mockery to the President of the United States. Washington was sojourning at Mount Vernon when he received the news. He returned in haste to Philadelphia and addressed thirteen questions to the members of his Cabinet for answer and guidance in the grave days that lay ahead. Even earlier, the President had foreseen the coming of a general war and had determined at all costs to keep out of it; though there was always the danger of being forced in by the provocations of others.[26]

Just how that danger might be avoided and how the government could be kept off the rocks and reefs of war was the substance of his questions. Every eventuality was considered, every hidden shoal marked and identified.

Ought a proclamation be issued, he queried, to prevent American citizens from participating in the war? If issued, should it contain a declaration of our neutrality? The French minister Ternant had been recalled by the new Jacobin masters of France, and a replacement was on the way. Should he be received; and if so, ought there be any qualifications to his reception? Was the United States obligated to uphold the old treaties with France (which guaranteed our aid in the event of an assault on the French West Indies)? Or should they be declared suspended for the duration, or altogether renounced? Were those treaties applicable only to defensive wars; and if this interpretation was correct, what actually was the status of the French declaration of war? Did the treaties prohibit the entry of British

warships into American ports? And finally, should Congress be convened as an emergency measure? [27]

These were pertinent questions, with a single exception—whether
the new French envoy ought to be received. Certainly it would have
been a breach of neutrality not to have accepted his credentials. Jefferson was properly indignant over the inclusion of this query; but he
considered the others as equally illegitimate. He detected in them the
Machiavellian hand of Hamilton. "It was palpable from the style," he
noted, "their ingenious tissue and suite that they were not the President's, that they were raised upon a prepared chain of argument, in
short that the language was Hamilton's and the doubts his alone." [28]
In which surmise he was no doubt correct.

It was not that Jefferson wished the United States to deviate from
neutrality, or enter the war on the side of France. On this point the
entire Cabinet was agreed, whichever party they favored in private.
Washington had not waited for his return to Philadelphia to query
his two major officers on that. He had asked both Hamilton and
Jefferson to propose measures which would prevent the activities of
American citizens from embroiling us with the warring powers. Hamilton was one step ahead of him, however. He had already anticipated
the request by calling on John Jay to draft a proposed Proclamation
of Neutrality.[29]

It was one thing to agree on the general principle of neutrality;
it was another to agree on the specific details. Hamilton was certain
that France intended to involve us in the war; and had confidentially
assured Hammond, the British envoy, that he would oppose any such
attempt. This in itself was perhaps not improper; but his further disclosure that we would not permit our treaties with France to involve
us "in any difficulties or disputes with other powers" literally ham-
strung future American diplomacy. In effect he offered Great Britain
carte blanche to seize the French West Indies without fear of repercussions in America. No wonder that Hammond reported to his government that he would continue to cultivate Mr. Hamilton and bypass
Mr. Jefferson, since the latter was "blinded by his attachment to
France and his hatred of Great Britain." [30]

The Cabinet convened on April 19th to consider the President's
questions. Hamilton urged the issuance of a Proclamation of Neutrality; either in the form of Jay's draft or something similar. Jefferson
objected to any public declaration by the executive branch without the
consent of Congress as unconstitutional. To which he added a more

NEUTRALITY BY ANY OTHER NAME

formidable objection: that it first ought to be dangled before England as a *quid pro quo* "for the *broadest privileges* of neutral nations." [31]

These last, to Jefferson, consisted in the right of neutrals to sail the seven seas unmolested by search and visitation, and to traffic with all belligerents. But such a definition had never really been accepted by any nation and certainly not by Great Britain, mistress of the seas. Even in time of peace Great Britain made and enforced her own rules, which had greatly hampered the trade of the United States. In time of war, obviously, they would become much more stringent.

Why not, argued Jefferson, keep England guessing as to our future course, and obtain valuable concessions as the price of our neutrality? How was he to know that England already knew—through the accommodating Mr. Hamilton—that we were committed to neutrality?

Jefferson was outvoted on the Proclamation. Even Edmund Randolph, Republican though he was, joined with Hamilton and Knox in favor of its issuance; whereupon Jefferson added his reluctant consent. He did, however, manage to salvage a point of phraseology. The key word "neutrality" must be omitted. The victory, if it was such, proved of no avail. In spite of the fact that Randolph, who drafted the Proclamation, dutifully omitted the suspect word, everyone referred to it immediately on issuance as the Proclamation of Neutrality; and as such it has been known ever since.

When the second question came up for Cabinet consideration—should the new French minister be received?—Jefferson was adamant. A negative answer, he insisted, would constitute a denial of recognition to the French National Assembly, already officially recognized by us, and go counter to the principles of neutrality about to be set forth in all public solemnity. [32]

Hamilton, who had probably inserted the query, retreated under his colleague's vehement denunciation and consented to the reception of the envoy. On the all-important question of the treaties, however, it became his turn to be adamant. He deftly hooked up the reception of the minister with this far weightier matter. When the new envoy arrived, he insisted, he must be informed that the United States reserved "to future consideration and discussion the question—whether the operation of the treaties . . . ought not to be deemed temporarily and provisionally suspended." [33]

This was a sensible move. France would be put on notice that she might not be able to count on American military aid in the defense of her island possessions. Any such forcible intervention would necessarily precipitate this country into a full-scale war with England; an eventuality which even the Republicans (except for their extreme wing) would have considered a national disaster.

Unfortunately Hamilton, instead of stating the plain fact that a temporary suspension of the guarantee was a legitimate measure for self-preservation, wandered far afield with ingenuous and tortured arguments to prove the treaties altogether invalid. They had been made with the *king* of France, he reasoned. That king was dead, and had left no successor. The French National Assembly was a new and revolutionary government, with whom we had made no compact. Therefore the treaties had lapsed.

To this specious chain of reasoning Jefferson retorted that no treaty became void merely because of a change of government. The obligation existed between nations as such, and not between individuals or groups of individuals.

The argument raged long and furiously, ar ended in an impasse. As usual, that "fool" Knox—the adjective is Jefferson's—supported Hamilton; while Randolph took his stand with Jefferson. Washington, who had listened patiently to the wrangling, eventually decided in favor of the continuing validity of the treaties.[34]

This did not mean that either Washington or Jefferson was willing to go to war with England over the islands. Should the question ever arise in fact—and Jefferson did not believe it would—the entire matter would then be surveyed afresh.

The final query—should Congress be convened?—was unanimously answered in the negative. Neither party wished for public debate on issues as delicate as these, or hotheaded and precipitate action which might subvert the uses of diplomacy.

Randolph's draft of the "Neutrality" Proclamation was submitted to the Cabinet and approved with minor changes. On April 22, 1793, Washington issued it over his signature; perhaps the first proclamation of its kind ever promulgated by a nation.

It called attention to the existing war and declared that "the duty and interest of the United States require, that they should with sincerity and good faith adopt and pursue a conduct friendly and impartial towards the belligerent powers." In pursuance of this aim, it became the President's duty "to exhort and warn the citizens of the United States carefully to avoid all acts and proceedings whatever, which may in any manner tend to contravene such disposition."

Any American citizen who committed acts punishable under the law of nations, or aided and abetted the warring nations with force of arms or with contraband, would receive no protection from this country if captured and punished by the aggrieved power. In fact, if the offenses were committed within the jurisdiction of the United States, the perpetrators would be subject to prosecution in the American courts.[35]

The significant phrase in the proclamation was that which defined *contraband*. It consisted, declared Washington, of such articles as were deemed such by "the modern usage of nations." Actually, no particular usage, whether modern or ancient, was universally recognized. That was contraband which a belligerent nation with the power to enforce its fiat considered as such.

From the very beginning of its existence as an independent nation, the United States had diligently sought to narrow the definition to arms, ammunition and military accouterments. Pledged by conviction and convenience to an indefinite neutrality in all European conflicts, she anticipated considerable profit from the carriage of foodstuffs and other goods not manifestly arms to all the belligerent powers. It was with this in mind that the famous slogan was coined: "Free ships make free goods." In other words, goods belonging to an enemy power which were not contraband in the restricted sense, when carried in a neutral ship were not subject to seizure by its opponents.

Wherever possible, the United States incorporated these provisions in the treaties she negotiated with European powers. Her treaty of amity and commerce with France, concluded in 1778 when both countries were allied against England, restricted contraband to armaments alone, gave both parties the right to trade freely with the enemies of the other and stipulated that "free ships shall also give a freedom to goods" other than contraband.[36] Somewhat similar provisions were later incorporated in a treaty with Prussia.

But such definitions, slogans and provisions were largely ineffectual unless Great Britain, mistress of the seas, could be brought to assent to them. To this end the efforts, energy and diplomacy of the United States were to be directed for many years to come; and always in vain. England did not intend to have her sea power nullified by a definition or a slogan; or to stand idly by while her enemies were being supplied with goods by means of neutral carriers. Even France, in spite of former agreement, later found it to her advantage to adopt the British view.

Only the United States steadfastly adhered to her position and continued to allude to a nonexistent "modern usage." Jefferson was willing even to consider the prohibition by Great Britain and her allies of the carriage of foodstuffs to France as a justifiable cause of war. But, being adverse to war as an implement of national policy and considering other less openly belligerent methods far more effective, he advocated that Congress "instantly exclude from our ports all the manufactures, produce, vessels, and subjects of the nations committing this aggression." Such action, he believed, would "work well in many ways, safely in all, and introduce between nations another umpire than arms." [37]

CHAPTER 15

Citizen Genêt

THE FRENCH NATIONAL ASSEMBLY, now that it had declared war on England and was already at war with most of Europe, displayed a sudden interest in American affairs. Hitherto indifferent to American protests over the discriminatory duties on tobacco and the closure of the French West Indies to American ships, the Jacobins thought it time to institute a new policy.

Ten days after the declaration of war, the Assembly opened the West Indies to United States vessels on an equal basis with the French; and immediately the treaty definitions of free ships, free goods and contraband took on a new meaning. For the English fleet would shortly make it difficult, if not impossible, for ships flying the French flag to maintain communications with the islands. It was no generous gesture, therefore, on the part of the Assembly; it was a scheme to use American neutrality as a means of breaking an English blockade. If, in the process, England and the United States became embroiled, so much the better.

Another evidence of the new orientation was the dismissal of Ternant from his post as minister to the United States and the appointment of Edmond Charles Genêt in his stead. There were indeed good grounds for Ternant's summary removal. He was out of sympathy with the regnant Jacobins, and had ostentatiously gone into mourning on the news of the execution of the king.[1] To Genêt was intrusted the task of exploiting to the fullest American good will for the French, and of obtaining from their government, if not a direct commitment to arms, all other aid short of war which a stretched interpretation of the old treaties would permit.

The instructions to Genêt, both public and secret, were detailed, explicit—and astounding. Publicly, he was to see to it that the treaty provisions were fully enforced; that no privateers were to be outfitted in American ports "except on behalf of the French nation," and no prizes permitted entry "except those captured by the Republic." These were legitimate instructions under the treaty, with one vital exception. While the pertinent treaty article specifically prohibited the outfitting and arming of privateers in American ports for use against the French, it said nothing at all of a positive grant of such a privilege to French privateers.

Genêt was also empowered to negotiate a new treaty—"a national pact in which the two nations should amalgamate their commercial and political interests, and establish an intimate cooperation in order to assist in every way the extension of the Kingdom of Liberty, guarantee the sovereignty of nations, and punish the Powers that still cling to an exclusive colonial system." [2]

This was a tall order, vaguely and grandiloquently expressed, and would, if consummated, inevitably lead to American participation in the war. Yet, from the point of view of French interests it was a legitimate aim for their diplomacy, no matter how injurious it might have been for American interests.

Genêt was further to incorporate in the new treaty a clarification and extension of Article XI of the old treaty, which dealt with the American guarantee of the French possessions on this continent. Most significantly, in view of the current dispute over its interpretation in the Cabinet, the French considered the guarantee as "imperfectly stipulated" and demanded that it be "established on general principles." So vital indeed did the Assembly consider this point that it commanded Genêt to sound out the American government immediately on it "and make it a condition *sine qua non*" for the free entry of American ships into the French West Indies. [3]

These instructions bore out Hamilton's contention that the United States was not obligated under the old treaty to defend the French islands by force of arms against a British attack. And, by the time Genêt actually landed, the dangled bait of the West Indies trade had lost its value; for the Assembly, in anticipation of a British blockade, had already hastened to throw them open unilaterally and without any conditions.

Also included in the bulky packet of Genêt's instructions was a secret plan for the seizure of Louisiana from Britain's ally Spain. This was similarly justifiable to a nation at war, except that the plan called for the employment of a private army of Americans to do the job. George Rogers Clark of Revolutionary fame had already hearkened to the siren voice and proposed, if supplied by the French with "some *small* resources by letters of credit or cash" to raise a force of fifteen hundred adventurous Americans which, in conjuction with French and American inhabitants of the coveted province, could easily overcome the small Spanish military establishment. In return for his services, Clark expected for himself and his men both pay and lands, for which they were ready to expatriate themselves and become French citizens. "My country," Clark wrote bitterly, "has proved notoriously ungrateful." [4]

What he meant was that his native state of Virginia had turned down his numerous claims for compensation for alleged services during and after the Revolution. Nor was this the first occasion on which he offered his sword and citizenship to a foreign power. In 1788 he had made a similar proposition to Spain, the very nation against which he was now willing to fight. [5]

Such a recruitment of Americans on American soil for service against a country with whom we were at peace was an unneutral act which could serve only to embroil the United States with Spain and her allies. The subsequent course of the conspiracy gave the American government many an anxious moment. But Jefferson viewed the proceedings with an equanimity perilously close to official approval. In the rapidly changing situation, he even withdrew his first instructions to the American mission in Madrid proposing an American guarantee of Spanish possessions across the Mississippi in exchange for the cession of those on the east bank. For then, he explained, we had feared that England might seize the latter and thereby encircle us. That danger had been removed by the recent alliance between Great Britain and Spain. [6]

Evidently Jefferson had no such fears concerning the proposed French conquest. For when André Michaux, ostensibly on a botanical tour, went to Kentucky to meet Clark with instructions from Genêt, he also took with him warm letters of introduction from Jefferson, in spite of the latter's awareness of the true purpose of the journey.

Fortunately Clark's expedition never got under way. Washington was warned of the plan by the Spanish agents in Philadelphia; and Senator William Blount of Kentucky, whose own private scheme to sell his services to England was thus unduly interfered with, intervened to reduce it to impotence. [7]

It was, however, in the final secret instruction to Genêt that the French Assembly betrayed its utter misconception of American politics and its complete misunderstanding of the American people. Convinced by the clamor of the Republican press, and seduced by the furious public speeches of the Republican leaders to the belief that only the President and the Senate stood in the way of a war alliance with France, the Assembly ordered Genêt "to make your representations more effective to direct opinion by means of anonymous publications. The Boston and Baltimore gazettes [Republican of course] will be the best ones to use for distributing such publications in order to turn aside suspicion of authorship from you; but the more you contrive to influence public opinion indirectly, the more your official discussions with the President and with the Senate must be kept secret so as not to arouse alarm and give them time to cabal against you." [8] In other words, speak cautiously to these two agencies responsible for the execution of treaties while whipping up public opinion to force them eventually to your bidding.

It is with these extravagantly conceived and worded instructions in mind that Genêt's mission and performance must be evaluated.

Yet for all the handicaps thus gratuitously loaded on the shoulders of their minister, the French Assembly could not have sent a worse representative to the United States than this same Edmond Charles Genêt. Young in years though already old in the diplomatic service of France, he was flighty, vain, voluble, opinionated, impatient of advice, obsessed with the notion of the superiority of his country to all others, and constitutionally unable to judge the temper and character of those with whom he dealt.

Had he possessed even a modicum of tact, intelligence and prudence, he might have succeeded in at least part of his instructions and considerably altered the future course of events; for England was shortly to adopt policies which exacerbated Anglo-American relations to the breaking point.

On April 8, 1793, Genêt debarked from the French frigate *Embuscade* in Charleston, South Carolina, hundreds of miles south of Philadelphia, the seat of the American government. Why he sailed to such a distant point is still a matter of conjecture. It was claimed that he had intended to land in Philadelphia, but that the presence of British warships in that vicinity forced a change of course. It has also been said that he deliberately chose the Southern destination so as to give him an opportunity to set certain plans in motion without embarrassing governmental scrutiny. Whether this was his original intention or not, he did not fail to avail himself of the opportunities thus providentially provided.

The welcome accorded him in Charleston served only to solidify the preconceptions with which he had arrived. It was as enthusiastic and fervid as he could possibly have wished. He was feted and banqueted; there were speeches, processions, artillery salvos and a profusion of spirituous toasts. William Moultrie, the governor of the state, was amenable in every way to the desires, expressed and unexpressed, of the new French envoy. In Genêt's own words, Governor Moultrie "allowed me immediately to arm some privateers, while taking certain precautions in order still for a while to safeguard the [temporary] neutrality of the United States."

One wonders what these precautions were, for Moultrie placed the harbor forts in a state of defense against any possible incursion by the British on the French vessels in their comings and goings; "seconded with zeal the operations entrusted to me for provisioning the navy, the armies and colonies of the [French] Republic"; and "concerning other sections of my instructions, he furnished me with useful information." [9]

As a result of Moultrie's most useful aid, even before Genêt had presented his credentials to the United States and been properly accredited, four French privateers were armed and outfitted at Charleston to prey on British commerce: the *Republican, Sans-Culotte, Anti-George* (a fling at the English king) and the *Patriot*. As though this were not a sufficient breach of American neutrality, Genêt recruited American citizens for service on the privateers and gave them commissions as officers, of which he had brought over a supply signed and sealed in blank.

Gouverneur Morris, still maintaining his solitary watch at Paris, had already warned Jefferson that Genêt had taken with him three hundred blank commissions for this purpose. But he trusted, rather optimistically, that "few of my countrymen will be so lost to all moral sense as to embark in a game so abominable." [10]

At about the same time, Morris entered a vigorous protest with the French over the capture of four American merchantmen by French warships, and particularly over the brutality with which their crews had been treated. The French officials promised an investigation of the charges, politely explaining the brutalities by "the difficulty of distinguishing an American from an English vessel, and from the

probable connivance between several individuals of the two nations
to make masked expeditions." [11]

But French aggressions on American commerce did not interfere
in the slightest with the ardor of Genêt's reception nor prevent Americans from entering the service of France. It is true that the Proclamation of Neutrality, specifically prohibiting American enlistments, was
not yet signed; but it is to be doubted, in view of what occurred
after its issuance, whether it would have made much difference.

Henry Lee, the Federalist governor of Virginia, on the other hand,
heard of the proceedings in South Carolina with considerable alarm
and, not knowing that his suggestion had already been anticipated,
dashed off a letter to the President proposing a proclamation which
would define our neutral status.[12]

The four armed privateers, accompanied by the frigate *Embuscade,*
and employing Charleston as a regular base of operation, played havoc
with British ships in Southern waters. A considerable number were
captured and sent as prizes to Charleston and Philadelphia for condemnation and sale.

Having thus accomplished his purpose—and incidentally stirred
up a hornet's nest of international complications to plague the government to which he was accredited—Genêt started out overland for
a leisurely journey to Philadelphia.

All along his road the people flocked to cheer and serenade this
mobile symbol of the French Revolution; so that perhaps Genêt cannot be unduly blamed for becoming confirmed in his belief that only
the President and a handful of reactionary and monarchical senators
stood in the way of an immediate declaration of war on England.

To the Federalists, however, and to Washington and Hamilton, the
slow triumphal progress of the envoy brought other feelings—of
alarm, apprehension and mounting anger. A Virginia Federalist was
certain that the world was coming to an end and called hysterically
on Hamilton to save the country from being dashed on the rocks of
bloody revolution.[13] Even Boston, remote in space from the kindling
effects of the fiery apostle, was declared by the merchant Stephen
Higginson to be a hotbed of sedition and Francophiles.[14]

It became increasingly obvious that the President's Proclamation
was going to be put to a severe test. Opinions as to feasibility or expediency of the doctrine of neutrality were sharply divided. The
Federalists, understanding that any deviation must favor the French,

were naturally for it. Young John Quincy Adams, writing as "Marcellus," vigorously upheld the Proclamation and demanded a rigid impartiality in word and deed, if not in thought, between the British and the French.[15]

The great majority of the Republicans considered the pronouncement as a betrayal of the cause of liberty as exemplified by the French. A few, however—at least in the beginning—evinced a cautious approval. James Monroe was one of these, on the curious ground that neutrality would actually favor the French. If the United States entered the war against England, he reasoned, the latter would be freed "from any embarrassing questions respecting the rights of neutrality" and could then employ her fleet to prevent us from furnishing France with safe ports, ships and vital materials.[16]

A little later, when the American government proved that it meant to enforce what it had proclaimed, Monroe shifted his ground. He now decided that the proclamation was "unconstitutional and impolitick," since it sought to restrain states as well as individuals.[17]

The Republican press was more consistent. It attacked the Proclamation at once and without hunting for fine distinctions. For months and years it kept up a constant chorus of denunciation against both the document itself and its promulgator. As usual, Freneau's *National Gazette* led the pack.

An unsigned squib, attributed to Hugh Brackenridge, called neutrality a "desertion" of the cause of mankind, and demanded war on England and the seizure of Canada. "Veritas" took Washington to task for his "double dealing . . . court intrigue . . . and monarchical mystery." He was sharply informed that he was only a "temporary magistrate" and "amenable to your fellow citizens for your official conduct." [18]

Even Jefferson spoke of the Proclamation as "pusillanimous" and disclosing a fear of displaying any affection toward France. "This base fear," he added, "will produce the very evil they wish to avoid." [19]

In any event, the efficacy of the Proclamation in changing the emotional "set" of the American people must be considered as extremely slight. The frigate *Embuscade,* cruising for prizes, pursued the British merchant ship *Grange* into the territorial waters of Delaware Bay and there captured it.

Indifferent to the consequences of this invasion of American sovereignty, the *Embuscade* sent the *Grange* and other captured British ships under French prize crews to Philadelphia.

As the ships came up the river the well-wishers of France ran in great crowds—"thousands and thousands of the *yeomanry*," as Jefferson called them, carefully underlining the word—to the wharves. When they saw the British flags reversed and the French colors triumphantly flaunted above, they rent the air with cries of exultation.[20]

Privately, Jefferson exulted with the "yeomanry" of Philadelphia. Officially, he was compelled to view it in a different light. Hammond protested sharply against the capture of the *Grange* in American waters. Jefferson assured him that if the fact were proved, satisfaction would be rendered. The fact was clear, and eventually, after many vicissitudes, the French reluctantly gave up the ship.[21]

But incident followed incident with accelerating pace. From his home government Hammond received instructions to defeat Genêt's avowed intention to outfit privateers in American ports. But a codicil was added which did much to hamper his efforts. The American position that "free ships make free goods," declared His Majesty's ministers, "is one which never has been recognized by this Country," and never would be.[22]

It was hardly to be expected that, confronted with such an unyielding attitude, the Americans would be disposed to return anything but the exact letter of the law. The French, however, came to Hammond's rescue by displaying a complete disregard of the most elementary rules governing neutrality; so much so, that in most instances where Hammond lodged a protest, Jefferson upheld his contentions.

The examples were numerous. A British vessel, captured on the high seas, was brought in as a prize to Charleston. The French consul in that port assumed the jurisdiction of an admiralty court, condemned the ship and officially offered it for sale. Hammond protested the proceedings as an arrogation of French sovereignty on American soil.

Jefferson assented. If the facts were true, he replied, everything which the consul had done was a nullity and he had been guilty of "an act of disrespect towards the United States." [23]

As more and more reports of French illegalities reached Hammond, his complaints to Jefferson redoubled. He protested against the purchase by French agents of arms and military equipment destined for France. He complained in the strongest terms of Genêt's action in outfitting French privateers in Charleston and recruiting Americans for their service. For their acknowledgedly heavy depredations he demanded either restitution or reparations.

On the first point, Jefferson refused to concede that American neutrality had been violated. Our citizens, he argued, had the right to manufacture and sell military goods which anyone, including the French and the English, were at liberty to buy. What the purchasers did with them afterward was no concern of this government.

On the second point, however, he conceded the justice of Hammond's initial position. The commissioning, equipping and manning of privateers in American ports to cruise against a belligerent, he admitted, merited censure and must be disapproved of. Measures would be taken, he assured Hammond, to prevent any repetition of the offense.[24]

He turned over the complaint, coupled with his own denunciation, to Ternant (still minister pending Genêt's much-delayed appearance). The United States, Jefferson informed Ternant, felt highly indignant over the recruitment of Americans for French privateers and would search them out for "condign punishment." As for the outfitting of the ships themselves, this was an act so contrary to international law that Jefferson could not bring himself to believe, so he pretended, that it had been done with the official approval of the French government, and would therefore suspend judgment while awaiting further advices.[25]

Hammond's final demand, however, met with Jefferson's stubborn opposition and required a full-dress Cabinet meeting to resolve. This was his claim for either the restitution of all British ships taken by the Charleston privateers, or adequate indemnities from the United States. To which he added another demand: that the American government refuse sanctuary in American harbors to the illegal privateers and their prizes.

Jefferson had already expressed the belief that "we shall be a little embarrassed occasionally till we feel ourselves firmly seated in the saddle of neutrality" and that "a fair neutrality will prove a disagreeable pill to our friends, tho' necessary to keep out the calamities of war." [26] But now that the pill was being presented to him, he himself considered it much too disagreeable to swallow.

He was willing to prevent American citizens from being recruited on American soil, and even to forbid the future outfitting of privateers in American ports; but there he stopped. When Hamilton issued instructions to the officers of the Customs to watch for and report any violations of the principles of the Neutrality Proclamation, Jefferson was vehemently opposed. Such an order, he asserted, made them "an established corps of spies or informers against their fellow citizens." [27] He considered it enough to observe the letter of the law; he saw no reason for displaying any undue enthusiasm for the sake of England.

Before any of these issues could finally be resolved, Genêt arrived in Philadelphia. The reception tendered him by the city Republicans was sufficient to turn his head further askew, had such an anatomical distortion been possible.

A committee of the most prominent members of the party was formed to welcome the French envoy. Unfortunately there was a miscue in timing, and Genêt came to Gray's Ferry some hours in advance of the scheduled outpouring of the "yeomanry." The mortified Republicans hastily revised their plans and plunged into even more lavish arrangements.

A tumultuous concourse escorted the committee to Gray's Tavern, where Genêt was lodged. There an address was formally tendered the minister, in which the cause of France was proclaimed "important to every republic and dear to all the human race." This was followed by a round of banquets calculated to test the endurance of "the human race." At each, endless toasts were imbibed, the "Marseillaise" shook the rafters, while the inevitable Phrygian cap—symbol of liberty—was clapped in turn on the head of each orator as he rose to laud France and her envoy.[28]

Genêt complacently accepted every flattering attention as his due. His entry into Philadelphia, he reported, had been "a triumph for liberty. The real Americans were wild with joy." [29]

He was shortly, however, to meet with Americans who obviously were not authentic. George Washington, President of the United States, had been observing the antics and the actions of Genêt in Charleston and since, on his dilatory way to Philadelphia, with ill-repressed anger. Nor did the incessant adulations of Genêt by the Republican press, alternating with savage criticism of himself, help to assuage his wrath.

Genêt's first official contact, after his arrival, was with the Secretary of State. On May 18, 1793, Jefferson welcomed him with the utmost cordiality; then took him in to see the President. A chill pervaded the room. Washington greeted him with icy formality and

expressed only those sentiments which protocol prescribed. The ebul-
lient minister was taken aback; but later solaced himself with the reflection that "le vieux Washington" was jealous of his triumph with
the American people, and that the voice of the latter would continue
to "neutralize" the President's declaration of neutrality.[30]

Several days later, Genêt presented to Jefferson a written proposal
for a political and commercial alliance between the two nations. If
his instructions on that point were extravagant enough, Genêt managed to achieve the impossible by embellishing them to the limits of
absurdity.

"Single, against innumerable hordes of tyrants and slaves, who
menace her rising liberty," he proclaimed, "the French nation would
have a right to reclaim the obligations imposed on the United States,
by the treaties she has contracted with them, and which she has
cemented with her blood; but strong in the greatness of her means,
and of the power of her principles, not less redoubtable to her enemies than the victorious arm which she opposes to their rage, she
comes, in the very time when the emissaries of our common enemies
are making useless efforts to neutralize the gratitude—to damp the
zeal—to weaken or cloud the view of your fellow-citizens; she comes,
I say—that generous nation—that faithful friend—to labor still to increase the prosperity, and add to the happiness she is pleased to see
them enjoy."

After which mighty discharge of preamble, Genêt took a deep
breath and proceeded. "The obstacles raised with intentions hostile
to liberty, by the perfidious ministers of despotism; the obstacles whose
object was to stop the rapid progress of the commerce of the Americans, and the extension of their principles, exist no more. The French
republic, seeing in them but brothers, has opened to them, by the
decrees now enclosed, all her ports in the two worlds; has granted
them all the favors which her own citizens enjoy in her vast possessions; has invited them to participate in the benefits of her navigation . . . and has charged me to propose to your government to
establish, in a true family compact, that is, in a national compact,
the liberal and fraternal basis, on which she wishes to see raised the
commercial and political system of two People, all whose interests are
confounded [sic].

"I am invested, sir," continued Genêt, "with the powers necessary
to undertake this important negotiation, of which the sad annals of

humanity offer no example before the brilliant era at length opening on it." [31]

The decrees which he enclosed were those dated February 19, 1793, which had opened the West Indies to American trade. Unfortunately, even as Genêt was handing over the decrees with a flourish, French policy at home was performing a double somersault. Angered by the continued British seizures of American ships for carrying alleged contraband—under the English definition—the French government on May 9th hastily drafted a decree providing for the similar seizure of American ships carrying provisions to England.

Gouverneur Morris protested swiftly and sharply before the ink had even dried on the fatal document. His arguments were so much to the point that the officials paused to reflect. They had sense enough to perceive on second thought that they had played directly into the hands of the British by cutting away their own most powerful argument for gaining the support of the United States. On May 26th, only seventeen days later, Le Brun, Minister of Foreign Affairs, furnished Morris with a copy of a new decree rescinding the order.[32]

The rescission initiated a new policy of conciliation. The old complaint by Morris concerning the capture of the American ship *Little Cherub,* and the shooting of her mate in cold blood *after* the seizure, was now suddenly held to be justified, and assurances given him that those responsible for the outrage would be rigorously punished. As Le Brun told Morris in a moment of candor, the motivations for his change of policy were not merely those of justice. "The United States," he said, "become more and more the granary of France and her colonies; they manifest the most favorable dispositions of succoring us; and the courage they have discovered in acknowledging formally the French republic, in spite of the menaces and intrigues of England, prove that their friendship for us is above all political or interested considerations." [33]

The French rescinded their retaliatory decree just in time; for the British, on hearing of it, had hastened to make official what had been merely unofficial before and therefore subject to negotiation. They now declared formally that foodstuffs destined for France constituted contraband and were subject to seizure; though they ameliorated the hardship of the rule by avowing a willingness to pay for the confiscated foodstuffs. The official imprimatur by the British on earlier practices which could be blamed on the excessive zeal of naval captains and port officials raised a new storm in the United States, of which the French were now in a position to avail themselves.

Unaware as yet of the double shift in French and British policies, Jefferson read Genêt's memorial with an interest which left no room for amusement at the verbiage. He no doubt would have been willing to enter into an alliance with France, provided the United States was not thereby committed to a war with England. But the continuing spate of French violations of American neutrality gave him no opportunity to pursue the subject. He was in sufficient difficulties at the moment with the indefatigable Hammond and with his own colleagues in the Cabinet.

Hamilton was opposing his diplomacy at every point, and Knox silently and phlegmatically supported the Secretary of the Treasury. This was bad enough; but when Edmund Randolph, supposedly Republican, began on occasion to vote with Hamilton, Jefferson's exasperation knew no bounds.

Of Hamilton himself Jefferson spoke with concentrated venom. That worthy, he declared, "is panic-struck if we refuse our breach to every kick which Great Britain may choose to give it. He is for proclaiming at once the most abject principles, such as would invite and merit habitual insults. And indeed every inch of ground must be fought in our councils to desperation in order to hold up the face of even a sneaking neutrality, for our votes are generally 2½ against 1½. . . . If we preserve even a sneaking neutrality, we shall be indebted for it to the President, and not to his counsellors." [34]

What Jefferson meant by his curious fractional division of votes in the Cabinet was that Randolph would vote sometimes with Hamilton, sometimes with Jefferson in the numerous considerations of the problems arising out of neutrality. This the latter considered a betrayal and a desertion of Republican principles, and meriting the utmost contempt. Randolph, he sneered, "always contrives to agree in principle with one [Jefferson] but in conclusion with the other [Hamilton]." [35]

And later, the rising tide of his wrath exploded altogether. Randolph, he now wrote, "is the poorest chameleon I ever saw, having no color of his own, and reflecting that nearest him. When he is with me he is a whig, when with Hamilton he is a tory, when with the President he is that [which] he thinks will please him." What made this alleged "chameleon" all the more unendurable was the fact that his "opinion always makes the majority, and . . . the President acquiesces *always* in the majority; consequently . . . the government is now solely directed by him." [36]

These animadversions on Randolph's character and conduct were unfair, to say the least. A careful analysis of the Attorney General's Cabinet votes discloses a consistent firmness in upholding the principles enunciated in the Proclamation of Neutrality. Similarly, as the legal officer of the United States, it was his duty to discover and prosecute infractions of neutrality by whomever committed, and there is no evidence that he did not perform it with rigid impartiality. Certainly independence of judgment, untainted by party politics or national prejudices, deserves commendation rather than stricture.

On May 20, 1793, Washington called his Cabinet together to discuss a long list of complaints presented to him by the indignant British minister against alleged violations of American neutrality by the French. Chief and foremost on the list was the matter of the privateers put in commission by Genêt at Charleston and their subsequent depredations.

The President used the case of one of these as a touchstone. He presented a written question to this Cabinet: "Shall the Privateer fitted out at Charleston and her prizes be ordered out of the ports of the U.S.?"

Hamilton and Knox took the position that since the original outfitting had been illegal, all prizes taken by the privateers that were still in American ports ought to be restored to their British owners. If this were not agreed to, then both the prizes and their captors should be ordered immediately out to sea and their further re-entry forbidden.[37]

Jefferson opposed any such decision. Though he had earlier rated Ternant severely on the Charleston privateers as an infringement of international law, he now veered to a different position. Since the treaty with France, he argued, had been silent with respect to that nation while prohibiting to her enemies the equipment of privateers in American ports, the existence of such a right must be implied. Under the prodding of the other Cabinet members, however, he admitted that we might by positive proclamation forbid it even to France. But then, he added, the Proclamation had not yet been published at the time of the Charleston incidents; hence they constituted only a "slight offence" and could not be made retroactive. He grew more heated as he involved himself in contradictions. Are we going to play the same part that England played, he cried, and force France to attack us?

Randolph came up with a compromise. It was obvious that to adopt Hamilton's severe logic would embroil us with France. At the same time Jefferson's complete denial would have similarly involved us with England. He cut the Gordian knot by proposing that the illegal privateer be forbidden further shelter, but that her prizes be granted the usual haven permitted under international law. With this view Washington agreed, and it was so decided.[38]

Three days after this acrimonious session, Jefferson was called in privately by the President. He found Washington with a copy of Freneau's *National Gazette* in his hand, and "evidently sore and warm." Jefferson did not have to be told what was amiss; he too had read the sharply personal attack by his translator-clerk and protégé on the President of the United States.

In a voice trembling with rage, Washington burst out that while he despised these assaults on himself as an individual, this man Freneau was attacking *every* act of the government. Then he paused and stared significantly at his Secretary of State. But Jefferson said nothing, and bowed himself out. It seemed to him that Washington had expected him to put a stop to Freneau's diatribes or dismiss him from the Department. "I will not do it," vowed Jefferson in the privacy of his diary. "His paper has saved our constitution which was galloping fast into monarchy." [39]

It was becoming increasingly obvious that the Cabinet could not be held together much longer. It had never really functioned as a smooth-working unit, and only the personality and pleadings of the President had kept it this long intact. Now the situation had become impossible and within a few months it was to explode.

Before it did, Jefferson enunciated a body of doctrine which was to become the secure foundation of American foreign policy for generations to come. It is a matter of irony that the man responsible for these doctrines disliked their application in numerous instances and considered himself "only as a passive instrument of the President" in their making.[40]

The question which Washington had put to the Cabinet on the Charleston privateers had been theoretical. It was now to be put to the test. One of them captured an English merchant vessel, the *Little*

Sarah, and sent it into Philadelphia. Hammond promptly demanded that the American government compel its return to its owners.

Once again the Cabinet divided, as though no decision had previously been reached. Hamilton as usual said we should. Jefferson declared that under the rules of war legal title was now in the captors; and an attempt by us to seize the ship by force would be "a very serious proposition" that could well lead to war. And war, he insisted, was a prerogative of Congress and not of the Executive.[41]

This time Randolph sided with him, and so did the President. Hammond was informed that his demand could not be acceded to; though the blow was softened by the assurance that no further French privateers would be armed or outfitted in American waters.[42]

If Hammond was winning as many of his demands as he lost, his home government displayed not the slightest disposition to accede to *any* American complaint. Thomas Pinckney reported from London that the British were forcibly impressing American sailors wherever they could find them, and that all his protests had proved unavailing. To which Jefferson bitterly reported that their conduct "contrasts remarkably with the multiplied applications we are receiving from the British minister here for protection to their seamen, vessels and property within our ports and bays, which we are complying with, with the most exact justice." [43]

Similarly, the new entente between England and Spain put an end to any hope of success in the current negotiations at Madrid over the navigation of the Mississippi and the Spanish-instigated raids of the Creek Indians into Georgia. These are "delicate times," wrote Jefferson to the American envoys, and they would have to soften or even suppress any further protests to the Spaniards.[44]

When Genêt officially replaced Ternant, the latter handed him Jefferson's sharp note of May 15th. Genêt took umbrage over its contents, as he naturally would, since it related to his own personal acts during his stay in Charleston. On May 27th he replied to the note with equal sharpness. Under the treaty, he declared, France had the right to arm ships in American ports, bring prizes in and sell them. Perhaps, he did admit, the French consul in Charleston had been a trifle overzealous in setting himself up as a court of admiralty on American soil; but such an error, if error it was, was purely "formal."

As for his own actions in arming and commissioning privateers, and in enlisting Americans in the service of France, what was wrong with that? he demanded. Had not the governor of South Carolina been an assenting party? Did not the treaty apply? And his American volunteers, "at the moment they entered the service of France, in order to defend their brothers and their friends, knew only the treaties and the laws of the United States, no article of which imposes on them the painful injunction of abandoning us in the midst of the dangers which surround us."

In the case of the British vessel the *Grange,* which the *Embuscade* had taken in American territorial waters, he sarcastically acceded to the "learned conclusions of the Attorney General of the United States" and agreed to restore the ship and its crew.[45]

Jefferson could not afford to allow Genêt's contentions on the arming of the privateers and the enlistment of Americans to pass unnoticed. In spite of his personally friendly relations with the French minister, he insisted that both practices cease at once.[46]

Genêt again expressed "pain" at these demands. However, while continuing to stand by his guns, out of "deference" to the American government he would instruct his consuls in the future to give commissions only to American "captains" and to respect the territory of the United States "and the political opinions of their President, until the representatives of the sovereign [i.e., Congress] shall have confirmed or rejected them."

As if this were not insulting enough, Genêt proceeded to compound the injury. The people of the country, he asserted boldly, "whose fraternal voice has resounded from every quarter around me," do not agree with the President. Let the government heed that "fraternal voice" and honor their engagements with France! [47]

Such language from the envoy of one nation to the President and government of another was unprecedented as well as insolent, and was good cause for a demand for his immediate recall.

Unfortunately, the Philadelphia Republicans were justifying Genêt's belief with the strength and clamor of their "resounding" voices. The feastings, addresses, poems and adulation which were constantly showered on him would perhaps have turned the head of a wiser man. How was he to know that the voice of these adulators was not the voice of all America?

On June 1st, for example, they tendered him a Civic Feast at which a song written for the occasion by Freneau was sung to immense applause:

God save the Rights of Man!
Give us a heart to scan
Blessings so dear:
Let them be spread around
Wherever man is found,
And with the welcome sound
Ravish his ear.
Let us with France agree,
And bid the world be free,
While tyrants fall!

Having thus implied that he intended to appeal to the Congress and the people of the United States against their government, Genêt next brazenly demanded the release of two "French" officers of the privateer *Citizen Genêt* who had been taken into custody in Philadelphia by the federal authorities.

The crime imputed to these two men (who bore the "French" names of Gideon Henfield and John Singletary) cried Genêt, "the crime which my mind cannot conceive, and which my pen almost refuses to state, is the serving of France, and defending with her children the common and glorious cause of liberty." These men, he blustered, must be set free at once, if not as Americans then as citizens of France.[48]

To this furious note Jefferson merely replied that the accused were in the custody of the civil authorities, over whom the Executive had no power, and that their rights without doubt would be properly safeguarded.[49]

The trial, when it occurred, raised fundamental issues. The defendants were American citizens who had been enlisted by Genêt during his short but busy stay in Charleston. Did the presidential Proclamation of Neutrality, with its penalties for disobedience, have the force of law without any authorization from Congress? It was a ticklish point, and the prosecution neatly avoided it by taking the position that the crime actually charged was a breach of the peace and a contravention of treaties made with nations now at war with France.

But the jury, drawn from overwhelmingly Republican panels, disregarded the argument and acquitted the defendants, to Genêt's grim satisfaction, the delight of the Republicans and the dismay of the administration. Even the unanimous charge of the federal bench of three judges that the facts were admitted and the law plain went for naught; while the distinguished group of lawyers for the defense, all prominent Republican politicians, made the political implications of the case sufficiently clear to the most innocent observer.[50]

The administration was now belabored from both sides; both the British and the French ministers kept up a constant stream of protests and peremptory demands. The ever-recurring theme of the outfitting of privateers came up with a sharp protest by Hammond over the *Polly*, a sloop which the French were openly converting into an armed privateer in New York under the name of the *Republican*. Notice of it was sent to Governor Clinton, who, though a radical Republican and sympathizer with the French, promptly seized the vessel and also a British brigantine which had been brought into port as a prize.

Jefferson ordered the prosecution of the offenders in both cases; a course that elicited an outraged cry from Genêt. The *Republican*, he protested, was being armed only for defense.[51]

By this time Jefferson was losing patience with the voluble envoy. He retorted snappishly that the French consul in New York himself had admitted that the armament was an offensive, not a defensive one; and he repeated his—or rather the official—contention that neither the treaty, the law of nations, the law of nature nor the legists permitted the arming and commissioning of privateers in our waters.[52]

Genêt was also getting fed up with the increasingly chilly attitude of his erstwhile friend; and the unctuous resort to laws of nature, laws of nations and Dutch writers on international law like Vattel and Puffendorf infuriated him. He overlooked his own regular appeals to such abstractions as liberty, fraternity, etc., etc.

For once he dropped his usual turgid, high-flown style and resorted to a short, plain, sarcastic and most undiplomatic retort. "Discussions are short," he wrote, "when matters are taken upon their true principles. Let us explain ourselves as republicans. Let us not lower ourselves to the level of ancient politics by diplomatic subtleties. Let us be as frank in our overtures, in our declarations, as our two nations are in their affections; and, by this plain and sincere conduct arrive at the object in the shortest way. All the reasonings, sir, contained in the letter which you did me the honor to write to me the 17th of this month, are extremely ingenious; but I do not hesitate to tell you, that they rest on a basis which I cannot admit." Why, for instance, did Jefferson interpose to his just complaints the "aphorisms" of Vattel?[53]

The bitter pill was only a little sweetened when Jefferson informed him that a *British* privateer which was being outfitted in Georgia had also been seized.[54] Genêt expressed his approbation, but could not refrain from a dig: "It is to be wished, sir, that the same watchfulness and firmness may be employed in all the States of the Union"; and specified Charleston, Baltimore, Philadelphia and New York as places where they were not.[55]

The French envoy found it difficult to believe that Jefferson was turning against him, and attributed his official letters to the malignity of that "old man" Washington. Since this was so, he wrote his government, he was being compelled "to press secretly for a convocation of Congress of whom a majority, led by the first men of the American Union, will be decidedly in our favor." [56]

Washington was indeed becoming an old man. He looked ill and ran low-grade fevers. The incessant attacks, both public and personal, were taking their toll. Though he pretended invulnerability to "the arrows of malevolence . . . however barbed and well pointed" which were aimed at him by Freneau and Bache among others, he nevertheless cried out on them as "outrages on common decency." [57] Jefferson thought him too "extremely affected by the attacks," forgetting his own almost morbid sensitivity in a similar case.[58]

Indeed, practically the entire executive arm of the government was by now anxious to retire from public life. Washington bitterly regretted that he had ever been induced to take a second term; and Jefferson and Hamilton were forever offering their resignations.

Freneau was perhaps the worst of Washington's tormentors. "I am aware, sir," he lectured the President in his paper, "that some court satellites may have deceived you with respect to the sentiment of your fellow citizens. The first magistrate of a country, whether he be called king or president, seldom knows the real state of a nation, particularly if he be so buoyed up by official importance to think it beneath his dignity to mix occasionally with the people. . . . Let not the little buzz of the aristocratic few and their contemptible minions of speculators, tories and British emissaries be mistaken for the exalted and generous voice of the American people." [59]

Even such an ordinarily prudent Republican as Madison thought that Washington had been taken into the camp of "Anglomany." To him the Proclamation had been "a most unfortunate error." It wounded the national honor, disregarded our obligations to France, and displayed a seeming indifference to the cause of liberty. Above all, it violated the Constitution by assuming the powers of war and peace; powers expressly delegated to Congress.[60]

The more radical Monroe, who had believed the Proclamation at first to be a "mere harmless pronunciamento," now that it had been proved to have teeth, called it "both unconstitutional and impolitick." [61]

Yet it was not true, as Freneau charged, that the President was not attentive to the voice of the people. Though he did not and could not mingle indiscriminately with the mythical "man in the street," he sought information whenever and wherever he could.

At his behest the moderately republican Edmund Randolph journeyed through Maryland and Virginia to discover the public sentiment on recent government measures. He found Maryland overwhelmingly proadministration; Virginia was a different story. Her citizens clamored against the Proclamation and the prosecutions under it; but they were particularly incensed against Hamilton's financial reports, even though, as Randolph caustically observed, very few had ever read a line of them.

He attributed the general unrest chiefly to the efforts of two men. One was Senator John Taylor, and the other was Patrick Henry. In Richmond, a hotbed of discontent, the real grievance related to the British debts, whose attempted collection in the federal courts was driving every debtor into the arms of Patrick Henry and the anti-federalists. However, commented Randolph with considerable acuteness, Patrick Henry "grows rich every hour, and thus his motives to tranquillity must be multiplying every day." [62]

No special trips of investigation were necessary in the New England states. With the exception of a few cities like Boston—and even there the Republican admirers of France, for all their vociferousness, were in the minority—approval of the Proclamation and hatred for France were overwhelming.

Randolph had imputed much of the Virginia discontent to the powerful propaganda of John Taylor of Caroline. Taylor was indeed a trumpet voice; at least in his writings if not on the Senate floor. This strange figure, who in recent days has been acclaimed as the true begetter of Jacksonian democracy, poses something of a riddle. If ever there was a "pure" republican, almost even an anarchist, in American history, it is John Taylor. According to his rigid standards even such men as Jefferson, Madison and Gallatin were not simon-pure.

Born in Caroline County, Virginia (hence the attribution usually affixed to his name), Taylor had studied law, been elected to the legislature and there strongly opposed ratification of the federal Constitution unless it was amended to safeguard individual and states' rights. Since he did not believe that the so-called Bill of Rights had done the job adequately, he continued to call for further and stronger amendments.

His first and supreme love was farming, which he considered the only proper occupation for mankind. Government in any form was to him a necessary evil, the antithesis of "a state of nature," and to be subjected at every point to the immediate will of the people.

Any officeholder, he asserted, no matter who, "will act politically unnaturally" and must be curbed. A government should be founded on moral principles only, and these must control its course at all times.[63]

Unfortunately, he said, "the executive power of the United States is infected . . . with a degree of accumulation and permanence of power, sufficient to excite evil moral qualities." These resulted in banks, paper credit and standing armies. Banks and armies, he was convinced, were "the only two modes extant of enslaving nations." Taxes should be abolished, because they transfer wealth from the many to the few and destroy political liberty and equality. "As the miasma of marshes contaminate the human body," he wrote, "those of taxes corrupt and putrify the body politic." [64]

With these esoteric doctrines in mind, it is not strange that Taylor concentrated all his bitterness on Hamilton's bank as the enemy in chief and declared that it must be destroyed like another Carthage. Since he considered newspapers as "a species of ephemera," he preferred to embody his attack in a printed pamphlet which called for the repeal of the Bank Act and a constitutional prohibition of any future charter.[65]

Though the pamphlet was not publicly distributed until the following year, sufficient copies passed from hand to hand in 1793 to color the thinking of Virginia's leaders and to awaken anew the old suspicions of Hamilton, his funding system, his excise and his bank. Like all Taylor's works, the pamphlet was written in a prolix, wandering and confused style that caused John Randolph of Roanoke to cry out: "For heaven's sake, get some worthy person to do the second edition into English." [66] Nevertheless it impressed and influenced by its very crabbedness and fanatical absorption in its theme.

What helped was the fact of a financial depression at the time of its appearance. This was not due, as Taylor singlemindedly attributed it, to the machinations of Hamilton and the Bank. The involvement of England in an all-out war with France had touched off a sharp break in the money markets of London. Credit became almost non-existent. There was talk that the largest and oldest mercantile houses in England would have to close their doors and stop payment on their accounts.

The shock was felt at once in the United States. As credit tightened in England, American importers, perpetually without ready cash, found themselves without goods. On the other hand, the fear of failures abroad and the withholding of their grain by American farmers in the hope of a rise, brought exports almost to a standstill. The funded debt, that delicate barometer of every vagrant breeze, promptly fell from above par to a substantial discount. [67]

The times were therefore ripe for an earnest consideration of the doctrines purveyed by Taylor. Since Congress was not in session, however, action on them, if any, had to await its convening in November.

CHAPTER 16

Privateers and Plagues

IT MAY SOMETIMES have appeared to the harassed American government that matters could not possibly get worse, and that the great experiment was doomed to destruction before it was well under way. Beleaguered on every side, their rights trampled on and their protests disregarded by the warring powers of Europe, beset with internal schisms and dissensions, how could they hope to survive?

Even Spain, now safely allied with mighty England, not only treated their demands with cavalier contempt but seemed bent on deliberately picking a quarrel. Her governors of Louisiana and the Floridas were inciting the powerful Creeks to new raids and outrages, her agents in Philadelphia were adopting an increasingly insulting tone, and Jefferson was convinced that war with both Spain and the Indians was inevitable.[1]

Nor did Hammond, as England's representative, give the government any rest. As each alleged breach of neutrality which he pressed on the attention of the administration was remedied or promised immediate investigation, his peremptory demands redoubled. The slightest delay in action brought from him an avalanche of letters. Washington and Jefferson grew restless and exasperated under the torrent. Jefferson angrily told Pinckney in London—whose own protests obtained no hearing from the British—that unless *they* did not hasten their pace, he would give Hammond a dose of the same medicine on this side of the ocean.[2]

After a particularly sharp demand for haste from Hammond, the President himself exploded. Already galled by the impudence of Jaudenes and Viar, he lashed out impartially at Hammond and the Spaniards. "It would seem," he stormed to Jefferson, "as if neither [Hammond], nor the Spanish Commissioners were to be satisfied with any thing this Government can do; but, on the contrary, are resolved to drive matters to extremity."[3]

It therefore gave Jefferson a peculiar satisfaction to turn the tables for once on the insistent British minister. News came that an American ship, the *Snow Suckey,* bound from Philadelphia to Port-au-Prince with a cargo that under no stretch of the term could be called contraband, had been captured by a British privateer and sent to Jamaica for condemnation. He immediately sent a note of protest to Hammond demanding the release of the ship and punishment of the offenders.[4]

Meanwhile Jefferson had soured completely on Genêt. His conduct, his bluster, his sullen mien even when he yielded, his rejection of the American's well-meant advice, brought to an end the old warmth and cordiality. "I fear," Jefferson lamented to Monroe, "he will enlarge the circle of those disaffected to his country. I am doing everything in my power to moderate the impetuosity of his movements, and to destroy the dangerous opinion which has been excited in him, that the people of the United States will disavow the acts of their government, and that he has an appeal from the Executive to Congress, and from both to the people."[5]

But now Hamilton moved boldly into the situation. He had been watching Genêt's conduct with an exasperation that far exceeded Jefferson's. He had also observed the violent partisanship of the Republicans for all things French with an equal exasperation. It was high time, he thought grimly, to awaken the country to the perils that threatened its existence from without and within.

Whenever Hamilton felt deeply he took to the pen. On June 29th he sounded the alarm in Fenno's *Gazette of the United States,* and in subsequent issues marched headlong to the attack.[6] The signature was "Pacificus"; but no one was fooled by the transparent disguise. Only Hamilton was capable of the trenchant style, the copious outpouring of words, the powerful argument and the slashing attack of these articles as they came, one after the other, at white heat from the press.

"Pacificus" was the first reasoned if impassioned defense of American neutrality and of the Proclamation which had given it form and substance. He took up every Republican charge in detail and ripped it to pieces. The President had invaded the domain of Congress, which alone had the right to declare war and peace? —Not at all. While only Congress could decide for war, it was the President's duty to preserve peace until such a decision was made. The Proclamation violated our treaty engagements with France? —In what way? he retorted. The single pertinent clause related to the American guarantee of the West Indies if France were attacked. But France had *not* been

attacked; she herself had declared war on England. The Proclamation
publicly evinced ingratitude for French aid during the Revolution?
—Gratitude? Hamilton sneered at the concept and ridiculed the word.
Must we sacrifice the true interests of our country in behalf of a
shibboleth? he cried. Was it not true that France had helped us solely
for her own self-interest and advantage? And even so, *who* had furnished us with aid? That king whom the French themselves and our
Republicans had labeled "tyrant" and who had gone to the guillotine
execrated by the very men who now talked of "gratitude." It was dangerous, he warned, to overrate foreign friendships or attachments. The
influence of foreign nations, he concluded, "is truly the Grecian horse
to a republic. We cannot be too careful to exclude its entrance."

As Jefferson perused "Pacificus" from week to week, his alarm
over its tenor and probable effects steadily mounted. For all his personal disgust with Genêt, his own attachment to France remained
unshaken. To him that nation, in spite of any excesses, was still the
solitary hope of the world which the monarchs of Europe were seeking
to crush. He had consented to the Proclamation to avoid worse—
Hamilton's proposal to abrogate the French treaties altogether. It was
true that he favored neutrality, but not the brand which the Proclamation proposed or Hamilton advocated. And certainly the arguments
which "Pacificus" set forth were to his mind fallacious and dangerous.
They must be answered at once, before they had a chance to make
an ineradicable impression on the people.

But how and by whom? There was only one man able to meet the
redoubtable Federalist champion on anything like even terms; and
that was Madison, then taking his ease in Virginia. "For God's sake,
my dear Sir," Jefferson wrote to him frantically, "take up your pen,
select the most striking heresies and cut him [Hamilton] to pieces in
the face of the public. There is nobody else who can and will enter
the lists with him."

Genêt, however, continued the agitated Jefferson, was not to be
defended. His appointment had been a "calamitous" blunder. He was
"hot headed, all imagination, no judgment, passionate, disrespectful
and even indecent towards the President in his written as well as
verbal communications, talking of appeals from him to Congress, from
them to the people, urging the most unreasonable propositions, and
in the most dictatorial style." To this scorching characterization, the
aggrieved Secretary of State added a plaintive note: "He renders my
position immensely difficult." [7]

It was only with the greatest reluctance that Madison finally consented to enter the lists with Hamilton. As he composed the first paper in reply he found it "the most grating [task] I have ever experienced. . . . One thing particularly vexes me is that I foreknow from the prolixity and pertinacity of the writer, that the business will not be terminated by a single fire, and of course that I must return to the charge in order to prevent a triumph without a victory." [8]

In spite of these only too well-founded fears, Madison forced himself to the task, and the "Letters of Helvidius" made their appearance in August and September 1793. [9]

Madison's distaste for his chore is evident in almost every paragraph; and after five "Letters," devoted entirely to the constitutional argument that the Proclamation violated the congressional power over war and peace, he let the whole business drop and Hamilton's animadversions on the treaties and gratitude go unanswered.

Certainly the conduct of the French was not calculated to aid their champion. Aside from the antics of Genêt, not yet known to the general public, the French sailors from the various warships coming into Philadelphia were conducting themselves in a manner that excited universal indignation and disgust. They swaggered through the streets in bands, armed with cutlasses, and attacked on sight lone British seamen, or even Americans whom they mistook for Englishmen. In New York also, a pitched battle took place between French and British sailors, complete with cutlasses, clubs and knives. It did not end until the authorities called out the watch, and carted the wounded and the dying either to hospitals or to jail. [10]

But the decisive blow, more damaging to the French cause in America than wounds and deaths, came from Genêt himself.

The inciting incident came from the captive *Little Sarah,* already the source of sufficient headaches to the administration. Since May she had rested quietly on the placid bosom of the Delaware River, just below Philadelphia, while British, French and American officials wrangled over her eventual disposition. Hammond demanded her restitution, by force if necessary; a demand which Jefferson, backed by Washington, had refused to grant. Now she figuratively exploded, brought Genêt to his ultimate destruction and almost tumbled Jefferson with him.

On July 6, 1793, Hamilton hastily informed Jefferson and Knox

that the *Little Sarah,* which the French had renamed the *Little Democrat,* was being secretly armed to put out to sea as a privateer.

The news shocked his auditors. It was midsummer, and both the
President and Attorney General Randolph were vacationing in Virginia. Congress was not in session. If Hamilton's report proved correct,
a first-class international incident was in the making. For Genêt had
previously agreed, though not without protest, that no further privateers would be outfitted in American waters. The full responsibility
for action, therefore, lay upon the three members of the Cabinet on
the scene; and Jefferson saw himself a helpless minority of one against
Hamilton and Knox.

For once, however, Hamilton was moderate. He suggested only
that Governor Thomas Mifflin of Pennsylvania be notified and asked
to conduct an immediate inquiry on the truth or falsity of the report.
Mifflin was accordingly put in possession of the alleged fact—which
Hamilton had probably received from Hammond. A preliminary investigation by Mifflin, himself a radical Republican, proved so alarming
that he sent the state attorney, Alexander J. Dallas, also a Republican,
posthaste through the midnight streets to Genêt.

That worthy, awakened from his slumbers, heard a grim Dallas
declare that there was evidence that the *Little Sarah,* already fully
armed and equipped, was scheduled to depart at dawn. She must not
sail, said Dallas flatly. You will be good enough to countermand any
such orders and hold the ship in port until the national government
decides what should be done.

Genêt, now wide awake, flew into a rage and refused the request
outright. As the astonished Dallas stared, the French envoy ranted and
screamed. He was tired of the execrable treatment, he shouted, he had
received from certain officers of the American government (Hamilton
and Washington); it contrasted markedly with the cordial attachment
to himself of the people at large. The President, he cried with many
an interspersed epithet, was not the country's sovereign; only Congress
had the right to interpret the treaties, and it was the President's duty
to convene that body and let them decide. If Congress decided against
him—and he doubted if they would—then and then only he would
withdraw and let the two nations settle their disputes in some other
fashion.

By this time Genêt had worked himself into such a passion that he
lost all sense of caution. He intended, he thundered, to publish his
entire correspondence with the American government, so that the

people would know exactly what had taken place and how he had been abused by their executive officers. Yes, he cried—or so it was afterward told—he was going to appeal from the President direct to the people.[11]

Dallas, shaken by what he had heard and witnessed, hastened back to report to Mifflin. It was still some hours to dawn, and Mifflin rushed the story to Jefferson, complete with its tale of Genêt's alleged threat to appeal to the people. Without question Mifflin was merely repeating what Dallas had told him. Furthermore, as we have seen, Jefferson had already heard the same threat uttered by Genêt himself. Nevertheless, when the whole business finally came out into the open and became a party matter between the Federalists and the Republicans, Dallas denied that Genêt had said anything of the sort, and Jefferson was discreetly silent, even when called on for confirmation.

At the moment, however, the alleged "appeal" was not in issue. The sailing of the *Little Sarah* was.

As soon as Jefferson heard the story, he quickly dressed and hurried over to Genêt's quarters. Do not permit the ship to sail, he begged, until it is first determined whether she has been armed in violation of the Proclamation or not. Besides, the President is due in Philadelphia on July 10th, only three days off; and out of courtesy, if nothing else, Genêt ought to wait for his arrival.

But the French minister was in no state to listen to Jefferson's pleadings, any more than to Dallas and Mifflin. He burst out on the Secretary of State with the same torrent of abuse, complaints and epithets with which he had previously belabored Dallas. He would do nothing, he screamed, to appease a nation which violated its treaties and supinely permitted the British to insult its flag, confiscate French goods from its ships and ride roughshod over its neutrality. If the Americans would not or could not defend themselves, he yelled, then the French would do it for them.

His fury next vented itself on the "old" and doddering President of the United States. He had come, he shouted, with the friendliest of intentions, but how had he been received? With frigid mien and cold aloofness. Why, Washington had even refused to convene Congress when he, Genêt, had modestly requested it. But now, he cried, he would *demand* that Congress be called into session.

Throughout the whole fantastic scene Jefferson had listened in thunderstruck amazement, seeking vainly to halt the headlong flight and get a word in edgewise. It was impossible. But now, as Genêt paused for breath, he seized the opportunity to inform the raging minister that under the Constitution it was the President, and *not* Congress, who was final court of appeal on the terms and validity of a treaty. Coming from Jefferson, this astonished Genêt somewhat and he quieted down.

Nevertheless, to all Jefferson's questions on the sailing of the *Little Sarah,* he refused to make any commitments. All that the too eager Secretary of State could manage to extract was a statement that the ship was not yet actually ready to put to sea, and a certain "look and gesture" which he clairvoyantly construed as an agreement that in fact the *Little Sarah* would not.[12]

Hugging this tenuous wisp of comfort to his bosom, Jefferson met with Hamilton and Knox on the following day in rump Cabinet. He reported the net result of his own endeavors with a fair degree of accuracy, admitting that Genêt had refused to give an "explicit assurance" that the ship would not sail. But, at the same time, he deftly stressed the "look and gesture" which he took for positive proof that Genêt had agreed to hold the vessel until Washington arrived.

Hamilton and Knox were singularly unimpressed. The *Little Sarah* lay at anchor in midstream of the Delaware, some distance below the city and above the euphoniously denominated Mud Island, a small flat in the river. They advocated the immediate placement of a battery of artillery on the strategic mud flat to prevent, by force if necessary, any sailing before a final decision had been made.

Jefferson objected violently, and set forth his views in a formal memorandum on the following day, July 9th. Genêt's implied word, he argued, was sufficient. The erection of a battery would merely hasten the departure; if the guns actually fired on the ship, "bloody consequences would follow." Furthermore, the entire French fleet was momentarily expected to move up the Delaware; and what would happen then was "unfathomable."

Not content with reasoned arguments like these, Jefferson took a leaf from Genêt's book. What right had Great Britain, he asked indignantly, to complain even should the *Little Sarah* go out as a privateer? In conscious or subconscious recapitulation of Genêt's tirade to himself, he insisted that the United States had been "patiently bearing for ten years the grossest insults and injuries from their late enemies [the British]," and it was "inconsistent" now for her "to rise at a feather against their friends and benefactors [the French]. . . . I would not gratify," he ended passionately, "the combination of kings with the spectacle of the two only republics on earth destroying each other for two cannon; nor would I, for infinitely greater cause, add this country to that combination, turn the scale of contest, and let it be from our hands that the hopes of man receive their last stab." [13]

From any point of view this was a most unusual document for an American Secretary of State to place on record. By the afternoon of the same day, indeed, Jefferson most likely wished that he had never written it. For, in reply to a formal Cabinet inquiry as to his intentions, Genêt declared with equal formality that the *Little Sarah* was now ready to sail. [14]

Even with this startling piece of information at hand, Jefferson was able to block decisive Cabinet action. For all their wrath and awareness of the consequences, Hamilton and Knox could do nothing on their own under the peculiar circumstances. Fuming but helpless, they were compelled to await the coming of the President, expected on the following day.

While Jefferson thus fiddled, blinded by his pathetic belief in Genêt's nods and becks and meaning smiles, and resolved above all to do nothing that might offend France, an unknowing Washington continued his leisurely journey to Philadelphia. He rode into town late in the afternoon of July 10th, on schedule, and was immediately met by the three members of his Cabinet. He listened in silence to a résumé of the situation, colored by the divergent views of the narrators.

It is most probable that he took Jefferson's assurances that there was no need for immediate measures at face value; for he waited until the next day to submit a written question to his officers. That question seems to have been motivated more by anger at Genêt's threat to appeal from him to the people than by the issue of the *Little Sarah*.

"What is to be done in the case of the Little Sarah, now at Chester?" he inquired indignantly. "Is the Minister of the French Republic to set the Acts of this Government at defiance, *with impunity?* and then threaten the Executive with an appeal to the People. What must the World think of such conduct, and of the Government of the United States in submitting to it?" [15]

Pertinent, if somewhat rhetorical questions, no doubt; but hardly the ones which the urgency of the situation required. Another day interposed before the Cabinet met, and it was gravely decided, this time unanimously, that the entire question of the arming of French and British ships in American ports, as well as the disposition of their prizes, be referred "to persons learned in the law"; that is, to the Justices of the Supreme Court. It was also decreed, with equal solemnity, that the *Little Sarah* and other ships in similar case, "do not depart till further order of the President." [16]

But by this time, indeed, the Cabinet could do nothing more than utter words; for the *Little Sarah* had quietly slipped down the Delaware past Mud Island, the only point at which it could have been stopped, and anchored farther down the river.

Confronted with this stolen march, Jefferson hopefully sent a note to Genêt in which he tried to take it for granted that there had been an understanding that the ship was not to sail. [17]

Genêt left the note unanswered; but his actions spoke with exceeding eloquence. While the Cabinet debated and drafted legal questions for the Supreme Court to ponder, the *Little Sarah* weighed anchor and went out to sea to commence her career as raider on English commerce.

The Cabinet was in an uproar. Washington was grim-lipped and silent; it was obvious he was sorry there had been no battery in position to stop, and, if need be, sink, the defiant privateer. Hamilton made no pretense at hiding his fury. Genêt's recall must be demanded immediately, he raged. In the meantime, suspend his functions as minister. Jefferson was mightily embarrassed, knowing that he had been chiefly responsible for the unfortunate situation. Yet at Hamilton's proposal he interposed objections. Let us rather, he said, send all the correspondence with Genêt to France, with some "friendly observations" thereon. And, until we hear from Paris, we must continue to recognize the minister. The stormy session ended inconclusively; the President giving no sign of what he intended to do. [18]

Strangely enough, Hammond did not seek to capitalize on this heaven-sent opportunity. Perhaps it was Hamilton who explained to him that the government did not have on hand the artillery and troops required to prevent the privateer's escape. At least that was the explanation Hammond forwarded to his own government as the reason why the American administration had suffered this "indignity." [19]

If Jefferson had been placating in public, he was sufficiently exasperated in private. Genêt's conduct, he raged to Monroe, "is indefensible by the most furious Jacobin. I only wish our countrymen may distinguish between him and his nation." But there was the rub. For Hamilton was quick to seize on the advantage he had gained, and was insisting that the administration publish the entire story of Genêt's machinations, including his threat to go over the heads of the government to the people.[20]

The proposal deeply alarmed Jefferson. It must, he feared, lead almost inevitably to a rupture with France and a concomitant alliance with England. This must at all costs be avoided, and he wrote urgently to Madison to meet with him prior to the opening of Congress to discuss ways and means of counteracting the Federalist strategy. "Those are pressing for an appeal to the people," he bitterly commented, "who never looked towards that tribunal before." [21]

But the Federalists beat the gun. Judicious leaks broke the story to the press, and a wave of indignation swept the country. To the great body of the people, whatever their politics, Washington was still an idol and above criticism or reproach. The idea that their President had been insulted and treated with contempt by the representative of a foreign nation evoked a fury of execration. Indignation meetings mushroomed all over the country, resolutions were passed and memorials transmitted to Washington inveighing against Genêt and testifying their approbation of the President's acts, including his controversial Proclamation of Neutrality.

Even the Republican stronghold of Virginia sent word that "any attempt of any Foreign Minister to excite the people of the United States, against the Establish'd Government . . . is a violation of his Mission and a daring insult to the people of America," and all Americans who dared support him were "lawless advocates for plunder, and disturbers of the peace of the Nation." [22]

Since he could not stem the tide, Madison cannily rode with the current to keep it from overwhelming the Republican party. In John Taylor's own county of Caroline, Madison composed the resolutions for the indignant citizens to adopt. Genêt, he admitted, "ought to be treated with contempt by the people, yet it should not affect his Nation, unless it shall avow and justify his conduct therein." [23]

Hamilton, however, was determined to press his advantage to the utmost. He rushed into the papers a series of articles signed "No Jacobin" in which he belabored Genêt's former defenders and present apologists, with ungracious insinuations that their language and idiom betrayed their own foreign origin. More legitimately, he defended the entire administration policy and castigated Genêt's resort to popular intrigue, his breaches of decorum, his arrogance and sneering contempt for the President, the forms of our government and our sovereignty as a nation.[24]

Watching the whirlwind, Jefferson decided that the only way in which the party could survive was to cast Genêt adrift. Unfortunately some of "the more furious Jacobins" refused to follow his prudent advice. In their eyes neither France nor her representatives could do any wrong. Even Monroe, his personal friend and lieutenant, balked a bit. "There is no sacrifice," he cried, "I would not be willing to make for the sake of France and her cause." Nevertheless he reluctantly agreed that Jefferson's suggestions were sound. He only hoped, he added, that the French would understand the tongue-in-cheek policy of the Republicans in now publicly standing by the President.[25]

The Philadelphia Jacobins, however, were bitter-enders. They and their party press boldly continued to extol Genêt and blame Washington and Hamilton for their most "unneutral" neutrality. But, as Jefferson commented, the *people* of Philadelphia were deserting Genêt. If the politicians did not have sense enough to go along with them, they would soon find themselves leaders without a following.[26]

He was having troubles of his own in the Cabinet, where a triumphant Hamilton kept insisting on Genêt's immediate recall and the official publication of all the correspondence. To avoid the latter, which he knew would mean a break with France and the destruction of the Republican party, Jefferson consented reluctantly to the former.

On August 1st, therefore, it was unanimously decided to send the damning correspondence to the French government with a demand for Genêt's recall. When Hamilton, refusing any compromise, pressed for the publication here, Edmund Randolph joined Jefferson in vehement objection. Washington, who as usual took little part in the debate, seemed to be inclined to adopt Hamilton's position when Knox suddenly created a diversion in an attempt to clinch the point.

He pulled out from a portfolio a printed broadside and held it up for all to see. On it was a crude drawing of Washington, a crown upon his head, kneeling under the suspended blade of an ominous guillotine. The text was equally crude and inflammatory.

As the sheet passed from hand to hand, Jefferson reddened and Washington burst into such a temper as the assembled men, accustomed to his iron repressions, had never seen him exhibit before. All restraints gone, he stormed up and down the room. He was tired, he shouted, of being constantly abused; he repented every moment of the day and night that he had not resigned when he had wished to do so. By God! he'd rather be in his grave than President of the United States. He defied any man to produce a single act of his which had not been animated by the purest motives. He'd rather be on his farm than emperor of the world; yet every impudent rascal accused him of seeking a throne.

The author and printer of the libelous pasquinade had naturally not put their names to the sheet; but Washington guessed at the instigator. "That rascal Freneau!" he burst out afresh. How dared he send three copies of his calumnious rag to him every day? Did he think that he, Washington, was going to distribute it for him? No; it was a manifest and malicious design to insult him!

When Washington finally flung himself back into his chair, exhausted and silent, pregnant minutes passed without a word from any member of the Cabinet. Jefferson turned red and white in alternation —not at the vicious libel on the President, but at the sudden assault on his protégé Freneau. He raged inwardly at the corpulent Knox as "a fool" for having exhibited the pasquinade and thus aroused the President to his outburst of wrath.

At long last Hamilton spoke up. He made no mention of the intervening episode, but reverted to the question of the publication of the correspondence. But Washington, exhausted and perhaps ashamed of his own unwonted display of his private emotions, seemed indifferent and listless; and the meeting adjourned without a decision.[27] Knox's diversion, though Jefferson did not realize it at the time, had saved the day.

Sick of the whole mess and fully aware that he had no further influence over the foreign or domestic policies of the government, Jefferson once more sent in his resignation; this time determined to make it stick. He had been placed in the thankless and embarrassing position of having publicly to execute measures of which he personally and politically disapproved. He was certain that the President was now definitely in the Federalist camp, and that he himself was being kept merely as a blind to hide the true situation from the nation.

In spite of all that had passed, however, Washington pleaded with him at least to delay the date of his going, if he could not be induced to remain. After the interview, in which he had made no commitment, Jefferson went home to write a long and most illuminating letter to his friend and political coworker, James Madison. In it he outlined the strategy and tactics which the Republicans must employ if they were not to be overwhelmed in a common disaster with Genêt.

First, public attention must be distracted from the unfortunate

recent events and brought back to first principles. This meant a recon-
centration on what Jefferson considered the Achilles heel of the
government and of the Federalist party—Hamilton's financial policies.
To combat these, the Republicans must propose a positive program,
and Jefferson outlined what form it should take. The Treasury must be
shorn of its overgrown and bloated powers by dividing it into two
departments, each with its own Secretary: one devoted to the collection of import duties; the other to internal taxes.

Second, the House of Representatives, where the Republicans held
a majority, must declare the true intent of the Constitution on the
Bank of the United States, and see to it that it was wholly divorced
from the government in policies and in management.

Third, a careful and cautious course must be taken on the Proclamation of Neutrality. "The desire of neutrality is universal," Jefferson
warned, and "it would place the republicans in a very unfavorable
point of view with the people to be cavilling about small points of
propriety; and would betray a wish to find fault with the President
in an instance where he will be approved by the great body of the
people."

Fourth, it would be the part of wisdom for the Republicans to
abandon Genêt entirely, "with expressions of strong friendship and
adherence to his nation and confidence that he has acted against their
sense. In this way we shall keep the people on our side by keeping
ourselves in the right."

He himself, Jefferson avowed, had been "under a cruel dilemma
with him." He had adhered to him as long as possible; but finding
him "absolutely incorrigible, I saw the necessity of quitting a wreck
which could not but sink all who should cling to it." [28]

In these succinct phrases Jefferson charted the road for the Republican party to follow and disclosed himself as a master politician.

Madison, himself no mean politician, promptly conferred with
Monroe, the third member of the Virginia triumvirate. They jointly
decided that Jefferson's advice should in the main be followed, though
the radical and impetuous Monroe believed it a tactical error to desert
Genêt altogether. Let us keep silence as much as possible, he advised.
Where not possible, let us palliate his conduct by pointing up the
errors in our own government which might have exasperated and
inflamed him.

But both men agreed that Jefferson must not resign. His continued
presence in the government was essential for several reasons: it dulled

the edge of Federalist attacks on the Republicans as obstructionists and traitors; and it served as a moderating influence in an administration which would otherwise be under Hamilton's sole domination. They also believed that Washington wanted Jefferson to remain in order to keep him as a shield against Republican attacks on himself. In that case, he ought to be able to extort substantial concessions from the President in return for the favor.[29]

Convinced by the counsels of his associates, Jefferson informed Washington that he would stay at his post until the beginning of the year.

While the Republican leaders were thus planning their strategy, vital aid came from a most unexpected quarter—France herself. Unknown as yet in America, the party of the Gironde, to which Genêt was attached, had fallen from power and the Mountain, the party of Robespierre, had seized the reins.

Robespierre promptly repudiated the American policy of his predecessors as certain to drive a hitherto friendly country into the arms of the enemy, England. At the very zenith of the American turmoil over Genêt, a letter was already on its way across the Atlantic, addressed by Deforgues, the new Minister of Foreign Affairs, to the minister in the United States.

In terms at once violent and reproachful, the missive excoriated Genêt and his conduct in America. Everything he had ever done was taken severely to task, even though much of it accorded with his secret instructions: the arming of privateers, the enlistment of American citizens, which, so he was now told, had been done "before even having been recognized by the American Government, and before having received its assent to a measure of such importance."

"You are ordered," continued the dispatch peremptorily, "to treat with the Government and not with a portion of the people, to be the mouthpiece of the French Republic before Congress, and not the leader of an American party." It belabored Genêt for consorting with "ignorant or very evil intentioned people" and of "being dazzled by a false popularity"; so that "you have alienated the one man [Washington] who must be for us the mouthpiece of the American people."[30]

It was one of the worst tongue lashings any envoy had ever received; not even the Federalists could have added a jot to it. But it arrived too late to save Genêt from the consequences of his folly. Before it reached the United States, Jefferson's instructions to Gouverneur Morris to demand the repudiated minister's recall were already crossing the ocean.[31]

Meanwhile, the fantastic affair was rapidly coming to a climax. Jefferson called on Genêt either to restore the prizes taken by the illegal privateers or pay in damages for them. He also admitted to Hammond, American responsibility for restoration or payment in all cases of prizes taken by these vessels prior to August 7, 1793. After that date, the government would restore only if it lay within its power. An order was issued to all French consuls stationed in American ports warning them that any attempt by them to exercise admiralty jurisdiction within the country would result in the revocation of their exequaturs and summary prosecution.[32]

Washington had hoped to obtain rulings from the Supreme Court on the legal questions involved; and to that end a series of questions was sent to the justices.[33] But the Court, under Jay's direction, refused to be brought into the matter. It took the position that it was not proper for them to be called on for extrajudicial opinions when no actual case lay before them.[34]

The Court's decision to confine itself strictly to judicial matters and not to render advisory opinions was perhaps the most important of its early career. Had it acceded to Washington's request, it could then have been asked to perform a similar function in legislation pending before Congress. Inevitably the Court would have been drawn into the maelstrom of political controversy and lost that judicial and dignified poise which has generally operated as an effective shield against political pressures and popular clamor. On the other hand, many a legislative or administrative act which was later nullified when in due course it came before the Court, could have been prevented *ab initio* and irretrievable damage and disruption avoided.

On receipt of this judicial rebuff, the Cabinet drafted its own rules to govern neutrality. It was decided that no further outfitting of privateers be permitted, and that asylum be refused to them if they managed to evade the order. All prizes taken by such privateers and coming within American waters were to be seized and restored to their rightful owners.[35] All these vital decisions were reached by a unanimous vote.

In this wise, and under stress of circumstances, a definite law of neutrality was shaped and forged, precise in its terms and capable of even-handed enforcement. It was the first rounded and compact body of regulations to be issued on the subject by any nation in the world.

Still ignorant of the bludgeon blows which fate had in store for him, Genêt continued on his reckless course. He journeyed to New York, where he was tumultuously welcomed by unreconstructed Republicans. A committee of forty met him at the ferry dock and escorted him in style to the Tontine Coffee House "amidst the acclamations of a vast concourse of citizens." He harkened to flowery speeches of praise and responded in kind.[36]

As if by predetermined cue both he and the New York populace were treated to the spectacle of the French frigate *Embuscade*, every flag aflutter, sailing triumphantly up the harbor after a victorious encounter with the British warship *Boston* just off Sandy Hook. The New Yorkers, roused to a pitch of enthusiasm (several degrees higher than in Philadelphia, so an eyewitness reported), cheered the French to the echo, the harbor battery boomed fifteen guns, and a liberty cap was carried ceremoniously through the streets.[37]

Even the consuls treated the decrees of the American government with contempt. In Philadelphia the French representative inserted a bilingual advertisement in the Republican press inviting enlistments on the French frigates then at anchor both from French sailors and from "Friends to Liberty." [38]

Freneau too was intransigent. "Why all this outcry against the Minister of France," he queried, "for saying he would appeal to the people? Is the President a *consecrated* character, that an appeal from his decisions must be considered criminal?" [39]

It was no wonder that Genêt, puffed up with this "false popularity," continued to ride the road to destruction.

Writing to a home government he did not yet know was overthrown and proscribed, he spoke with much self-satisfaction of his reception in New York and of the readiness of the Kentucky conspirators under George Rogers Clark to descend the Mississippi on his signal to conquer New Orleans and Louisiana. Unfortunately, he complained, that "Fayettist Washington has annulled my efforts by his system of neutrality," while Hammond, Hamilton and Knox, "alarmed by the extreme popularity which I enjoy," were acting in concert against him. Even Jefferson, whom he patronizingly admitted was endowed with good qualities, had proved a broken reed.[40]

Even when the stunning news came of the internal revolution in

France and his personal repudiation, Genêt remained obstinate. With an impudence worthy of a better cause he insisted that Washington's demand for his recall be laid before Congress. "It is in the name of the French people," he declaimed, "that I am sent to their brethren—to free and sovereign men: it is then for the representatives of the American People, and not for a single man to exhibit against me an act of accusation, if I have merited it. A despot may singly permit himself to demand from another despot the recall of his representative, and to order his expulsion in case of refusal. . . . But in a free State it cannot be so, unless order be entirely subverted."[41] Insult could go no further.

It was most fortunate for him that this extravagant communication did not find Jefferson, to whom it was addressed, in Philadelphia. The yellow fever was raging and Jefferson, in company with most members of government, had fled the pestilent town. Not until December 2nd, when the Secretary of State ventured to return, did he find the explosive letter on his desk. By that time, however, it no longer mattered. Genêt's power to annoy and badger the administration had already come to an end.

In the interim, Gouverneur Morris had presented the demand for Genêt's recall and Robespierre readily acceded. He dispatched Jean Antoine Fauchet to replace him, with instructions for Genêt's arrest and shipment to France to stand trial.

Luckily Washington proved magnanimous. He had no wish for the blood of the rash young diplomat, and refused to honor the request for his deportation. Granted permission to remain in personal safety by the man whom he had so bitterly maligned, Genêt married the daughter of Governor Clinton of New York and retired to a welcome obscurity on a Hudson Valley farm. In 1797, however, he emerged inexplicably to denounce *Jefferson* as "the real author of all my ills" and as one who under the mask of friendship had secretly thwarted the success of his righteous mission.[42]

The French government had an excellent reason for acceding so readily to Genêt's recall. Just as the latter had been a thorn in the side of the Americans, so Gouverneur Morris had enraged the French with his unconcealed disdain for their revolution, his aristocratic airs, and his caustic proddings on American rights.

They demanded now his recall as a *quid pro quo*. Washington regretted it, though Jefferson did not; but he had no other choice than to agree. The one-legged diplomat took his orders with his accustomed cynical insouciance. He quit France promptly and gladly, but remained for four years in Europe, pursuing both business and women. With the latter at least, for all his wooden peg, he was irresistible. On his return to the United States he re-entered political life, was sent by a Federalist legislature of New York to the Senate, and became one of the pillars of the party. Only recently, the unexpurgated diary of his racy adventures in France has been presented for the delectation of a modern public.

Jefferson was relieved to see Genêt retire. He had almost wrecked the Republicans; and his agents, the consuls, were attempting to finish the job. In Boston the consul personally led a force of French sailors and marines to board and recapture a prize ship which the United States marshal had seized in conformity with the Proclamation. Jefferson retorted on the highhanded action with an order for the consul's immediate arrest and prosecution.[43]

Exasperated beyond endurance by these agents of a foreign power who, in his words, were "conducting themselves as if their object was to disgust and alienate all the friends of their nation," Jefferson nevertheless tried hard to persuade the American people to differentiate between them and the nation they purported to represent.[44]

It was a difficult if not impossible task. The plain citizen was unable to perceive the distinction, and as a result republicanism plummeted to its lowest strength. The *National Gazette*, Freneau's paper, was compelled to suspend after a short but stormy career; and, in spite of Jefferson's efforts to get him both money and subscribers for a resumption of publication, the sheet which had goaded Washington to more than one outburst of wrath and pain, quietly folded.[45]

From his bitter contemplation of the French debacle, Jefferson turned to more congenial tasks. With a full heart he penned a protest to Hammond over the British decree declaring provisions destined for France and her allies to be contraband. The order, asserted the Secretary of State, struck at the roots of American agriculture. Only by the free exchange of our agricultural products with Europe could our citizens obtain those "numerous articles of necessity and comfort which they do not make for themselves." [46]

He also enunciated another rule which has since become standard in international relations. What constituted the offshore limits of a nation bordering on the ocean? Genêt had refused to restore British prizes captured within sight of the American coast, on the ground that no such limits had ever been defined. Jefferson was quick to perceive the importance of placing the limits of sovereignty as far out to sea as possible, and declared we should not hesitate to sacrifice present damages to Great Britain in any amount whatever for captured vessels provided she agreed to those limits. He was even willing to waive any claim on France for the restoration of such prizes if the latter would consent to a claim of American sovereignty to a distance of three leagues (about nine statute miles) from shore.[47]

Neither nation consented; and finally, after considerable negotiation, offshore limits were placed at one sea league, or three statute miles—the putative range of a cannon shot.

The dreaded yellow fever which had sent the officers of government fleeing to their respective homes struck Philadelphia in August 1793. For years the fever had been endemic in the seaport towns, and every so often it reached epidemic proportions. In the then state of medical knowledge neither its cause nor its treatment was known; nor was the mosquito identified as the carrier.

The "malignant fever" first appeared on Water Street in a small area between Arch and Race Streets, close to the wharves and the incoming ships from the West Indies. By August 21, 1793, twelve persons had died; not enough as yet to cause any great alarm. The best medical opinion in Philadelphia attributed the local outbreak to some putrefying coffee lying in an abandoned heap on one of the wharves.[48]

A few days later, however, the plague had spread far beyond its original precincts. Water Street itself was desolate; and the inhabitants who had fled in terror spread the contagion all over the city. The College of Physicians met in learned consultation and Dr. Benjamin Rush was appointed a committee of one to discover a method for combating the disease.[49]

Dr. Rush was perhaps one of the most vigorous and colorful personalities in an era that teemed with vigor and color. Considered the most eminent physician in America, he refused to be restricted to specialist pursuits. His talents and restless energies spilled over into domains far removed from the practice of medicine; and invariably he became a storm center in any field he was pleased to enter.

An active participant in the Revolution, he had suggested both the writing and the title of *Common Sense* to Tom Paine. He was a member of the Continental Congress in 1776; his signature sprawls lustily across the Declaration of Independence. He was a prolific writer and humanitarian; there was hardly a social or moral cause which did not attract his support and pen. He wrote passionately eloquent essays against capital punishment, on the curse of drink, against slavery, in behalf of free and universal education. He was one of the most active members of the American Philosophical Society and its tower of strength.

Nor did he neglect his own profession. He was the first professor of chemistry at the Medical College of Philadelphia, and he published an important treatise on the *Diseases of the Mind*. Opinionative, combative, he lashed out recklessly at persons and ideas which met with his disfavor; and with equal stoutness and passion defended his own positions to the final ditch.

The enemies he raised were legion; yet he managed the agile feat of keeping both John Adams and Thomas Jefferson as personal friends; and eventually negotiated their reconciliation. And now Rush threw every energy, every dogmatic conviction, into the fight against this impersonal enemy which threatened to depopulate the city.

The symptoms of yellow fever were horrible enough practically to frighten the victim to death. The disease began with headaches, lassitude and a queasy stomach. From then on it ran a rapid and violent course which lasted from twelve hours to four days. The sufferer went into a stupor, then delirium and the vomiting of thick black matter. His eyes turned yellow and were suffused with blood. Thereafter the fatal yellow tint spread over the entire body. He bled copiously from every orifice—the nose, the mouth and the bowels. Most patients died on the second or third day; those who survived the fourth could be counted on to live. These, alas, were lamentably few.

The physicians worked valiantly but without effect. The time-honored treatment consisted of infusions of bark, port wines and baths of hot vinegar. Dr. Rush, however, proposed a new remedy. He dosed his patients with liberal amounts of calomel to purge the bowels, and bled them copiously to purge the general system.[50]

With his usual pugnacity he trumpeted the merits of his own treatment and denounced in unmeasured terms the remedies of his rivals. The result was obvious—every doctor in town turned against him. To their protests Rush only retorted with further denunciations.

He worked like a madman, sleeping barely at all and then with his clothes on, tending every patient he could reach and refusing his services to none. Whether they could afford a fee or not was a matter of complete indifference to him. More efficacious than his heroic purgings, no doubt, was his accessory advice of rest, cleanliness, a temperate vegetable diet, and "a very small portion of porter."

In the beginning his regimen actually seemed to work. He triumphantly claimed that out of a hundred patients who followed his treatment on the very first day of their symptoms, not one had died.[51] As a result of his trumpet assertions and claimed record of cures, all over the city sufferers deserted their regular physicians and flocked to Rush. The temper of the abandoned medical men grew hot, and they banded together to denounce their colleague as a charlatan and his remedies as worse than useless.

Within a short period, however, the efficacy of Rush's treatment seemed to wane. His patients added their corpses to the dread carts that went from house to house, intoning the frightful monody: "Bring out your dead! Bring out your dead!"

Rush himself came down with the fever, purged and bled himself, and went on treating others. He succumbed a second time, and now despaired. "O! that God would rend the heavens and come down," he cried in anguish, "and save our guilty city from utter desolation! for vain—vain now is the help of man." [52] Eventually he recovered.

The daily total of deaths mounted to almost a hundred. Business shops pulled down their shutters, residences were abandoned, and the stricken people fled into the surrounding country. Government was at a standstill. Washington had left early for his accustomed vacation in Mount Vernon; Knox was gone; Jefferson remained a while for fear it might be said he had run away, then he too departed for Monticello.

Hamilton took the fever and his life was despaired of for days. Only the strange and violent remedies prescribed by Dr. Edward Stevens, his boyhood friend from the West Indies, saved his life. Each day, no matter how violently he shook with fever, Hamilton was immersed in a bath of ice-cold water. Miraculously the fever broke and he mended gradually. Then, in a carriage, he was taken to Albany to convalesce in the home of the Schuylers.

The epidemic ran its full course, in spite of the devoted if ignorant ministrations of Rush, of Stevens and of unsung heroes, among whom must be mentioned the Negroes of the town. Possessed of some degree of immunity to the plague, they remained behind when the white people fled, and faithfully ministered to the sick and the dying.[53]

With the coming in October of cold weather (and the disappearance of the mosquito carriers) the plague gradually subsided. By November it was over. In the short two-month period more than 3500 had died: a substantial percentage of Philadelphia's population. Other towns along the coast had similarly been visited by the yellow fever; though not at this time in as deadly or widespread a form.

But for years the fever continued endemic, with further outbreaks in Philadelphia, New York, Baltimore, Boston and Charleston. New York was especially hard hit toward the end of the decade. Fumbling in the dark, the health officers finally managed to adopt a means of prevention—the quarantining of incoming ships from foreign ports at the first sign of an epidemic.

As the disease subsided and the frightened inhabitants returned, they vented their anger and fear upon Dr. Rush and his remedies. The clamor was instigated and maintained by the doctors he had previously maligned. Rush compounded his offenses by declaring the disease was not imported (in which he was wrong) but that it was generated within the city itself. Such a position, it was furiously countered, would "destroy the character of Philadelphia for healthiness, and drive Congress from it"; not to speak of the decline in trade and real estate values.[54]

Rush was ostracized. He answered abuse with abuse, and the controversy raged on for years in learned articles and the newspapers; to be given a new lease of life in the later New York epidemic when Noah Webster poured ridicule on Rush and his theories in the columns of his paper.

CHAPTER 17

Retaliations and Retorts

THE PEOPLE OF Philadelphia had good reason to fear the loss of Congress and of the business which it brought to their town. During the actual epidemic, the legislative branch of the government had not been in session; but the report of the plague spread rapidly and alarmed the more timid of the members. Nor were the neighboring towns and villages less alarmed. At Trenton, Hamilton's carriage was stopped and forced to take a wide detour through country lanes. At New York, the ferry from the Jersey shore was met by a mob and ordered to turn back. A New Yorker who had inadvertently stepped on board during the altercation was compelled, in spite of his anguished wails, to make the journey with the rest.[1]

With members of Congress refusing flatly to come to the beleaguered capital, Washington wrote to his scattered Cabinet to inquire whether he had the right to convene the lawmakers in some safer spot.[2] Hamilton, Knox and Randolph replied that he had; Jefferson thought he had not. Only Congress itself, he argued, was authorized under the Constitution to change its meeting place. The President adopted the majority opinion and set Germantown, on the outskirts of Philadelphia and unvisited by the fever, as the place of convocation.

As the government somewhat reluctantly assembled at Germantown, with many a fearful glance in the direction of near-by Philadelphia, it found itself immersed in a mass of troublesome affairs.

Not the least of these, to the jaundiced eyes of the members, was the crowded condition of the little town. It possessed no accommodations to take care of the unexpected influx. There was only one public house of any size, the King of Prussia tavern, which was already packed with prior refugees from Philadelphia. A cot stuck into a corner of the public dining room commanded the exorbitant price of four to eight dollars a week. Important personages were pushed in groups of four into a narrow cubicle bare even of bed, table or chair. Jefferson was more fortunate. After angrily turning down such Spartan accommodations, he managed to obtain in a private dwelling a room which not only possessed a fireplace, but two full-size beds into which he invited Madison and Monroe with himself.[3]

These were personal and temporary inconveniences. Foreign relations, as always, loomed ominously on the official horizon. Though the French sky had somewhat lightened with the recall of Genêt and the dispatch of Fauchet, other sections of the firmament presaged new and more violent storms.

Spain had turned bellicose and redoubled her incitements of the border Indians. From the Ohio to Georgia the tribes were raiding, burning and slaughtering. It was small comfort to the President to know that in many instances the whites had given ample justification for retaliations.[4] The invaded states clamored for protection and threatened the direst consequences if it were not immediately received.

Accordingly, the mightiest effort of the interminable war was made. General Anthony Wayne was given the task at which so many other generals had failed—to whip the Indians once and for all, and compel them to sue for peace. Practically the entire Regular Army was mobilized for the job. Of an establishment of 3,861 men, Wayne took 3,229. Of these, however, he found only 2,600 fit for duty. On October 7, 1793, Wayne commenced his expedition into the Ohio wilderness, where already the bones of many men lay scattered. The influenza struck before the first lurking savage was seen; and the strength of the little army dwindled with the sick and dying. It was "not a pleasant picture," Wayne reported in considerable understatement; but he refused to lose heart. Something *had* to be done "to save the frontiers from impending savage fury."[5] It was a full year, however, before Wayne was able to do that something, and finally break the power of the Ohio tribes.

The West had other grievances against the federal government, the chief of which was the perennial question of the navigation of the Mississippi. An angry remonstrance, more bitter in tone than any previous one, was dispatched to the President and Congress. The Western people were tired of the delays and indolence of the government, it flatly declared. Every other part of the Union was getting service except themselves. They were patriotically attached to the Union but, they added defiantly, "attachment to government cease [sic] to be natural, when they cease to be mutual." They had no intention of sacrificing themselves to the prosperity of the East. Either the government obtained for them their just rights on the Mississippi, or they would get it for themselves; in which case, it was most unsubtly indicated, they would have no further need for the Union.[6]

Spurred by the open threat, Jefferson again sought to compel Spain to yield. Again and again letters went to the American envoys concerning the Mississippi and the Indian incitements. On the Mississippi, Spain remained adamant. On the Indian question the envoys finally succeeded in obtaining an order addressed to the colonial governors to render no further assistance to the Creeks.[7] It was one thing to get the order; it was another to have it enforced thousands of miles away from the not too vigilant eye of Madrid.

But Great Britain still remained the primary and most ominous source of danger. Impressments, restrictions on commerce, seizures and highhanded confiscations increased in volume. Ten years after the peace treaty, the posts were still in English hands. All negotiations directed to the settlement of the numerous grievances, both in London and in Philadelphia, had met with delays, equivocations and ultimate failure.

For a year and a half Jefferson's laborious argument for the return of the posts had moldered in British files in spite of repeated proddings. Now, on November 22, 1793, Hammond reported that inasmuch as he also had received no word from his government, he must suspend all further negotiations on the controversial theme.[8]

Even the posts, however, paled into insignificance compared with the threatened destruction of all American foreign trade by a series of British Orders in Council. Fighting for her own life, England employed every weapon, permissible or not, to bring her great antagonist to her knees. If the United States and other neutral nations suffered in the process, she was sorry but could not help it.

On June 8, 1793, the first of the Orders went into effect, authorizing the detention of neutral ships carrying provisions to France, and their enforced "purchase" by Great Britain for her own use.

Jefferson protested that the order was contrary to the law of nations. Agricultural products were not contraband; and neither England nor any other country, he wrote Pinckney, had any right to a practice which struck at "the roots of our agriculture." Nor was he mollified by the provision to buy the confiscated grain. We have the right to decide for ourselves, he insisted, to what market we wish to send our goods. It was an essential of true neutrality to sell indiscriminately to all belligerents, and not to one alone.[9]

Even Hamilton, ordinarily willing to take the British side of the argument, in this instance thought that they were going too far.[10]

A much heavier blow was still to come. On November 6, 1793, England decreed the seizure of all vessels which attempted to trade with the French West Indies. By slamming the door shut on one of the most lucrative carrying trades, and a door which the French had only recently opened, the destruction of American commerce seemed practically sealed.

Hundreds of American ships that defied the decree were seized and taken into English ports for condemnation. Numerous instances of brutality, which lost nothing in the telling, filled the American press. Ship captains and crews were placed in irons; there were floggings and even maimings.

The United States seethed with indignation. The Republicans, gratified at the shift in the international current which made England now the enemy instead of France, filled the air with bellicose cries for retaliation. The Federalists, the chief sufferers from the obnoxious Orders and decrees, sought in vain for a peaceful method for bringing England to an accommodation.

In such an atmosphere of storm and clamor Congress began its sessions at Germantown. Washington in his opening address on December 3rd touched these explosive matters only lightly, preferring to make them the burden of special messages. He adverted rather to the less recent past: the Proclamation of Neutrality and its consequences. He did end, however, on a significant note. "The United States," he warned, "ought not to indulge in a persuasion, that, contrary to the order of human events, they will forever keep at a distance those painful appeals to arms with which the history of every other nation abounds." [11]

Two days later he wrote a special message concerning relations with France and England. But even now he passed quickly over the crippling Orders of Great Britain and concentrated chiefly on the Genêt incident.[12]

On December 16th he discussed Spain. As always when it came to Spanish relations, no words were minced. He assailed the Spaniards as the chief inciters of the Indian troubles and repudiated with indignation their countercharge that it was the Americans who had been the aggressors. Carefully concealing his own private agreement with the Spanish claim, he publicly professed his shock. "It could not be conceived," he declared with honest heat, "we would submit to the scalping knife and tomahawk of the savage, without any resistance." [13]

Jefferson's resignation took effect on the last day of the year 1793; and he departed for Monticello vowing that never again would he partake of political life. No matter how sincerely this was meant at the time, he was soon enough participating by letter and by personal contact in the deliberations and strategy of the Republican leaders.

Washington had accepted his resignation with regret. It was the first break in his Cabinet of "able men," and it meant that whatever faint restraint Jefferson's presence might have exercised on Republican assaults was now gone. In another sense, the balance wheel had been taken away; and administration and Federalist party had practically become one.

Hamilton and Knox were also ready to resign, but the President managed to hold on to them for another year. Only Edmund Randolph evinced no desire for the blessings of private life.

Before Jefferson left office, he put the finishing touches on a report which the House of Representatives had called for a full year earlier, relating to the state of American commercial relations with all foreign lands.

It is difficult to understand the reasons for Jefferson's long delay in responding to the call; he was ordinarily quite prompt. It is probable, however, that the delay was purposeful. From the Republican point of view, an earlier publication would have been most unfortunate. During the first half of 1793, France had been the chief offender against American commerce. Now, the timing was perfect. The accounts with France were in a measure closed, and England again took the spotlight with her confiscatory decrees. The country was aroused, and Congress would be in a mood to hearken to the cry for retaliation.

Whatever Jefferson's political motive might have been, he was meticulously accurate in his report. Great Britain, as always, proved to be the chief customer of and largest seller to the United States. She took almost half of American exports and furnished about eighty per cent of all imports. In view of the perennial protests over the restrictions on our goods this may sound surprising; but Jefferson himself freely admitted that the restrictions related rather to the colonial possessions than to the mother country herself.

In fact, the main American complaint was directed against the obstacles imposed to our ships as the carrier of goods for others. Here the restrictions were both onerous and numerous and, on occasion, downright prohibitive. In the profitable carrying trade we were England's most formidable rival; and our swifter sailing vessels, lesser rates and, above all, our favorable neutral position in time of war, threatened the very existence of the British merchant fleet.

To redress the balance, or even to drive us altogether out of competition, was the single intent of the British system. They did not permit our ships to carry the goods of other nations into English ports; and refused even the carriage of our own into her West Indies islands. Most European nations operated on the same mercantilist theory. Neither Spain nor Portugal allowed any carriage at all to their possessions; and France pursued the same course until the exigencies of war forced her to grant temporary intercourse with her West Indies colonies.

Jefferson would have preferred a policy of free trade throughout the world, but he knew that this was not yet possible. He therefore proposed that the United States adopt a system of reciprocities. Whenever a foreign power lifted a restriction on our commerce, we would in turn lift one on theirs. On the other hand, wherever restrictions were continued or augmented, we ought to reciprocate in kind.[14]

As a practical matter, the proposal constituted a provision for retaliation on England, and the Republicans in Congress promptly seized upon it for that purpose.

The report was followed by an opinion which dealt with the laws of neutrality, the historical basis for the slogan that "free ships make free goods" and our efforts to compel England's acquiescence to that doctrine.[15]

With this swan song, Jefferson took the road to Monticello and private life. Washington offered the management of the State Department to Edmund Randolph, who accepted the post. William Bradford of Pennsylvania was appointed to the office of Attorney General in his stead. Bradford was an average lawyer and political nonentity; though his early death did not afford an opportunity for the display of any talents he may have possessed.

The interlocking relations between Jefferson's final report and Republican strategy were soon revealed. On January 3, 1794, Madison took the floor in the House to announce a series of resolutions. He frankly declared that they were based on the report of the Secretary of State.

In a low, calm voice Madison called for retaliatory measures on Great Britain reminiscent of those he had sought to enact in the first days of the nation.

Let us, he demanded, place additional duties on the goods and ships of those countries which have no commercial treaties with us. Let us reduce the tonnage duties on those which have. Let us match restrictions on our goods and ships abroad, point for point; and place extraordinary penalties on the offender in our ports where such reciprocity is impossible. These penalties, he added, could be used as recompense for the damages sustained by us in the past.[16]

Madison did not have to specify which particular offender he had in mind. Each resolution was aimed directly at a single nation—Great Britain.

The timing of the resolutions was perfect, and the current situation made their passage practically self-evident. Almost daily reports from the Caribbean painted harrowing pictures of seizures, confiscations and brutality. The most rigorous Federalist was almost as wrathful as any Republican. Hamilton denounced the proceedings as the veriest outrages, and for once Hammond found no sympathetic ear for his own complaints.

Yet, as Madison ticked off his resolutions, the Federalists paused and reflected. They spelled, if enacted, a revival of the waning Republican fortunes and a possible war with England. The Federalists wished for neither. They therefore abruptly ceased their own clamors and closed their ranks to oppose the resolutions.

That it would be a difficult battle they knew. Both Congress and the country were in a belligerent mood. New England trade was practically at a standstill. The merchants thought seriously of laying up their ships rather than run the risk of almost certain seizure and loss. From the West Indies to the shores of Europe and the interior waters of the Mediterranean, the American flag seemed an invitation to search and capture.[17]

Meanwhile the confident Republicans pressed to the attack, aided and abetted in their cries against England by a swarm of so-called Democratic Societies which proliferated over the land.

The parent Society had been organized in Philadelphia, and the model was the Jacobin Society of Paris. The Federalists accused Genêt of having officiated as midwife, though the Republicans denied it. In any event, there were a sufficient number of native Americans to lend their names as sponsors. In Philadelphia they included such prominent political figures as Alexander J. Dallas, the state attorney; Charles Biddle, Peter S. Duponceau, Michael Leib and Israel Israels. The philosopher-scientist David Rittenhouse, whom Jefferson somewhat extravagantly declared to be "second to no astronomer living," became its president.

The Society's initial pronunciamento, issued on July 17, 1793, declared its intention "to cultivate a just knowledge of rational liberty, to facilitate the enjoyments and exercise of our civil rights, and to transmit, unimpaired, to posterity, the glorious inheritance of a free Republican Government." [18]

If these aims sounded praiseworthy and innocent enough, the Federalists charged that they concealed more sinister purposes—to subvert the government and Constitution of the United States, to foment a French-type revolution, and to drag us into the war on the side of France.

The violent and immoderate propaganda of the Societies did much to bolster the accusations. In the wake of Philadelphia's, other Democratic Societies sprang up like mushrooms after a spring rain. Kentucky organized a vociferous group whose avowed purpose was to watch "over the conduct of the servants of the people." [19] The western counties of Pennsylvania, Charleston, Boston, New York and other vicinities, set up their own clubs. An interrelated network of committees of correspondence followed the old Revolutionary pattern. What one club agitated or resolved was taken up by all the others in a consistent chorus. Their general procedure was to elect Republicans to office, cry down the Federalists, support France and abuse England. And more and more, the President became a target of attack.

Perhaps the most vehement and outrageous of the Societies was the one of Charleston. It openly requested the Jacobin Society of Paris to adopt it as their child. The Jacobins solemnly debated the petition in full meeting. A member rose to protest that the Americans ought first to spill their blood for France before they could be considered for adoption; but Collot d'Herbois remarked significantly that the necessary bloodletting might come *after* the adoption. On this assumption the petition was granted.[20]

Thus bound in symbolic ties of blood, the Jacobins of Charleston proved their mettle by denouncing "the daring outrages and diabolical machinations of the British Court" and their own Federalist congressmen as "possessed of the basest and most dangerous principles." In fact, the British insults to America were "but trifles, when compared to the prosperity of the funds in which, by their infamous speculations, they are become deeply interested." However, since war with Great Britain was inevitable, it was necessary for all "good republican citizens" to obtain arms speedily for their own defense.

The mere mention of Washington's Proclamation of Neutrality threw the members into an apoplectic rage. It was "unconstitutional, tyrannical, arbitrary, and in the highest degree dangerous, an usurpation of authority of the most despotic nature, and a direct attack upon the liberties of the people."

It might be thought that invective could go no further, but the "good republican citizens" of Charleston managed to surpass even these efforts. "The cause of France is our own," they proclaimed; and for any man or set of men "to advocate doctrines and principles derogatory to the cause of France, or her commerce with America, or in support of the base measures of the combined despots of Europe, particularly Great Britain, is a convincing manifestation of sentiments treacherous and hostile to the interests of the United States, and well deserves the severest censure from all true republican citizens of America." [21]

If resolutions such as these represent perhaps the high water mark of abusive and threatening language, the other societies did not lag far behind. The reported resolutions of any one group was usually adopted verbatim by a baker's dozen of other groups; for, as the Washington County (Pa.) Society resolved, it is necessary to convince our brethren "that we feel ourselves the same people with them in many of the most important political considerations." [22]

The violence of the resolutions, comparable in tone and language with those which the French revolutionary clubs had issued in the past, gave the Federalists the uncomfortable feeling that the guillotine was being sharpened for their collective necks. It was difficult for them to believe that such a mighty discharge of menaces could come from meetings in which the average attendance was less than twenty.[23]

Hamilton and Knox were quick to take advantage of the personal attacks on the President. They had seen to it that the infamous cartoon displaying Washington's head under the guillotine was brought to his attention; and Hamilton later embarked on an hour-long harangue to prove the close connection between Genêt and the Societies.[24]

Jefferson defended the clubs vigorously at the Cabinet sessions, but was unable to convince the President. The latter was certain that they were seeking to overthrow the government and bring us into the war. "It is not the cause of France (nor, I believe, of liberty)," he exclaimed, "which they regard; for could they involve this country in war (no matter with whom) and disgrace, they would be among the first and loudest of the clamourers against the expense and impolity of the measure." Washington was waiting for the states themselves to take action against the allegedly conspiratorial clubs. If they did not, he proposed that the federal government intervene.[25]

The states took no measures to repress the Societies, and in the end it was Washington who took the field against them, as we shall see.

Against this ominous and sometimes riotous background—for the playing of the revolutionary "Ça Ira" in the theaters often ended in fisticuffs and the hurling of missiles—the debate on Madison's resolutions commenced in the House of Representatives.[26]

William Smith of South Carolina, second only to Fisher Ames as the leading Federalist in the House, opposed the resolutions in a long and brilliant speech. He charged that Jefferson's commercial report, on which they were based, was false and misleading. No account had been taken, he said, of the condition of our trade with France and England *since* the French Revolution. The picture which Jefferson had painted in such fiery colors was deliberately drawn from a bygone era. In turn, Smith analyzed on his own the state of our present commerce and made it appear that the regulations imposed by England were actually more favorable than the French.[27]

His speech created something of a sensation. It was charged by the Republicans that Hamilton himself had written it; that Smith was not capable of such an effort. "The sophistry is too fine, too ingenious," wrote Jefferson, "even to have been comprehended by Smith, much less devised by him." [28] Jefferson was correct in his surmise; the proof of Hamilton's hand in the composition is now available in his papers.[29]

Madison retorted with a speech of equal force and length. He examined Smith's statistics and found in them material for the assertion that, insofar as the South was concerned, Great Britain was the chief offender. Himself an advocate of the mercantilist theory of trade, Madison pointed out that the value of our imports was double that of our exports, and hence the balance was unfavorable to us. "We send necessaries to her," he declared. "She sends superfluities to us. We admit everything she pleases to send us, whether of her own or alien production. She refuses not only our manufactures, but the articles we wish most to send her—our wheat and flour, our fish, and our salted provisions." A retaliation would soon bring her to terms; for we could ruin her merchants, her revenues, her navigation and her West Indies possessions.[30]

And so the debate went on, with champions entering the lists on both sides and tempers growing ever more heated. The usual courtesies went by the board. In a temporary absence of Madison and other Republicans from their seats, a Federalist moved suddenly for a vote on the first resolution. Messengers were dispatched posthaste for the missing members, while Republican orators took the floor in filibustering harangues on the subject of congressional "courtesy."

As the absentees came hurrying in, Abraham Clark of New Jersey glanced meaningly at Smith with the assertion that "if a stranger were to come into this House, he would think that Britain had an agent here." To which Ames lashed back that the whole business was a Southern plot; that no commercial state would be found to favor the resolutions.[31]

The House was rapidly approaching a state of exhaustion, and finally adjourned further consideration until the first Monday in March so that pressing business could be attended to.

One such item was a consideration of the ravages of Algerian pirates, which had practically put a stop to American ventures in the Mediterranean. A proposition was made to build four frigates of forty-four guns each, and two lighter ones of twenty, to harry the corsairs. But Madison thought it would be quicker and simpler to buy them off; a curious argument for one who advocated measures that might well lead to war with England. He also managed to drag that country even into this debate with the charge that it was Great Britain which was surreptitiously instigating the Algerines against us.

Ames took up the challenge to inquire sarcastically why Madison did not display with the Algerines "some part of the spirit which he had exerted on the other occasion." Unruffled, Madison moved an appropriation for the purpose of bribing the piratical state. It was defeated, and the original measure for building ships of war was passed on March 10th by a vote of 50 to 39.[32] The Senate concurred and it became law on March 27th.

On March 14th, the House reverted to Madison's resolutions against England. Jonathan Dayton of New Jersey, a Federalist who on unpredictable occasions would defy his own party, made a surprise move to sequester British debts in America as a pledge for the indemnification of losses by reason of British violations of neutrality. The Republicans gleefully supported him while members of his own party rose in denunciation.

But the first test on Madison's resolutions came in somewhat different form. A motion was made to lay an embargo on all shipping leaving American harbors for a period of one month. Though at first defeated by a close vote of 48 to 46, it was later renewed and passed by a large majority. Madison attributed the change of heart of the Eastern members to the growing wrath of their constituents over their losses in the West Indies.[33]

Madison was right. Even Ames was expressing his private indignation over the continued seizures of American ships attempting to trade with the French islands, and declared that, if they were not stopped, we must be driven to the wall. Nevertheless, he insisted that "the line of duty is plain. Peace, peace, to the last day that it can be maintained; and war, when it must come," must be made to appear "the act and deed of the Republicans." [34]

Nor was General Schuyler, whose opinions could generally be taken as those of his son-in-law Hamilton, far behind in his excoriations of the folly of the British. War, he felt, was inevitable in the present temper of Congress; but he foresaw in its coming the ruin of Hamilton's financial system and the prostration of American credit.[35]

For all their outcry against English folly and ruthlessness, however, hardly a New England merchant wanted war. A recourse to arms could only increase, not diminish, their losses; and there was always the possibility that a course of negotiation would eventually bring them an adequate indemnity. The merchants of Salem were the solitary exceptions to the general view. They looked forward to a profitable career of privateering in case of war.[36]

On the other hand, the South would have welcomed a war on England; but not against France. There were even those who declared that if France were made the enemy, they would refuse outright to bear arms.[37]

Against the background of rising anger, the Federalist-controlled Senate deemed it prudent to pass the embargo resolution within a day after its receipt from the House, and it became law on March 26, 1794. In accordance with its terms, Washington issued a proclamation forbidding all ships to clear American harbors for any foreign port for a period of a month. The cut-off date was appended to give Great Britain a chance to reconsider its policy.

Indeed, unknown as yet in the United States, England had already yielded in part. On January 8, 1794, the ministry modified the objectionable Order of November 6, 1793, so as to permit American ships to carry noncontraband cargoes directly between the United States and the French Indies; though still keeping in force the prohibition of any carriage between the islands and France herself.

Both the original Order and its modification were sent hastily to Hammond, with supporting arguments for him to employ in defense of the temporary necessity of the first and the ameliorating effect of the second.[38]

Immediately on their receipt, Hammond hastened to his good friend Hamilton to explain the first document and exhibit the precious second. Hamilton was properly impressed and thought that a compromise might be reached whereby the American government would accept the principle of the still earlier Order of June 8, 1793 (declaring foodstuffs to be contraband), in return for indemnities on those cargoes already seized in the West Indies where French ownership had not legally been proved. On this compensation Hamilton was prepared to insist, and grew excited as he told Hammond that the staggering total of 250 ships had been taken without warrant or justification. All of which proved, Hammond mournfully reported to his government, the extent of the popular ferment, when even Hamilton, "uniformly the most moderate of the American Ministers," could grow so heated.[39]

But Hammond did not receive the modification until April; and by that time the "popular ferment" had hastened Congress into the passage of the temporary embargo and the apparently certain future passage of Madison's retaliatory measures.

On April 7th, Clark took up Dayton's proposal and greatly enlarged it. He demanded that until restitution for all losses *and* for the illegal retention of the posts had been received, "all commercial intercourse between the citizens of the United States and the subjects of the King of Great Britain, so far as same respects articles of the growth or manufacture of Great Britain or Ireland, shall be prohibited." [40]

Sedgwick objected that this would certainly mean war. Though neither he nor any other Federalist, he said, attempted to defend the "unprovoked and inexcusable" injuries inflicted by Great Britain, we ought first to seek reparation "in the way dictated by prudence and humanity." [41]

This was cryptic; but the Federalists were already feverishly engaged on a plan which they intended to spring on the country within the next few days.

Clark's resolution, however, with minor amendments by Madison, passed the House on April 25th by a vote of 58 to 34. The Federalists rallied in the Senate to cause a tie vote on the second reading, and John Adams from the chair killed the measure.[42]

It was the first victory for the embattled Federalists in the long and angry debate. Nevertheless they bowed sufficiently to the storm to continue the temporary embargo for another month.

What had impeded the Federalists and added fuel to the fires of hatred against England was the report of a speech made by Lord Dorchester, the governor general of Canada, to a meeting of Indian tribes. He was alleged to have said: "I should not be surprised if we are at war with the United States in the course of the present year; and if we are, a line must then be drawn by the warriors." The line he referred to was the disputed boundary between the Indians and the United States; and the invitation to the Indians to draw it in their own behalf with tomahawk and scalping knife was sufficiently clear.

This alarming invitation was further highlighted by the receipt of intelligence that three companies of British soldiers had been dispatched to the foot of the Miami rapids (well within the territory of the United States) to build a fort. Such an act, promptly warned the new American Secretary of State Edmund Randolph, if true, was "hostility itself." And, he wrote Hammond, what explanation could he give for Dorchester's speech? [43]

Hammond's explanation was lame enough. He replied that the governor general had been quoted out of context. He had merely referred to the aggressions of the Vermonters against Canadian soil; that if these invasions did not cease, *then* war might come and a boundary would have to be drawn. Knowing that this would not satisfy, Hammond resorted to the time-honored trick of taking the offensive. He expatiated at length on British wrongs: those very aggressions by Vermont men, the ancient grievance of the Charleston privateers (long settled) and their outrages on British shipping.[44]

The Federalists, realizing the explosive nature of Dorchester's Indian address, professed to believe that the speech itself was a "fabrication by some landjobbers" for purposes of their own.[45] Washington, however, was convinced of its authenticity, in spite of the denials of those whom he irascibly termed "Anglophiles."[46] He took immediate steps to counteract its impact on the Indians by instructions that no stone must be left unturned to keep the powerful Six Nations well disposed and to buy off their most influential chief, Joseph Brant, "at almost any price."[47] The Secretary of War thereupon offered an annuity of $1000 to $1500 to Brant, who had already evinced his hostility toward the United States.

The embargo which Congress had enacted, and now extended for an additional thirty days, had disastrous effects which Madison and Clark had not contemplated. All business in the seaport towns ceased, large quantities of wheat assembled in the warehouse for foreign disposal was offered at panic prices without a taker, and some of it was returned to the original sellers for storage pending the end of the crisis.[48]

It also proved singularly ineffective in its avowed purpose of bringing England to her knees. That nation pursued its former tactics as if the embargo never existed. Therefore, though the Republicans protested that the measure be given a longer trial, it was not renewed after its cut-off date, nor did Washington exercise the discretionary powers vested in him to keep it alive during the adjournment of Congress.

Indeed, in spite of the British Order of November 6th relaxing the rigidities of the previous Order, the British officials in Bermuda paid little or no attention to it. They continued their previous cavalier condemnations of American ships and even initiated new seizures. Nor was there the slightest hint of eventual compensation for earlier and manifestly illegal condemnations. Unless something was done immediately, avowed a disgruntled New York merchant, "the Sword will be unsheathed and the Consequences to both Countries ruinous."[49]

Randolph, however, was not willing to concentrate all blame on the British. He cited chapter and verse for his contention that *every* belligerent country, including the French, Spanish and Dutch, made a habitual practice of taking American ships bound from the West

Indies to the United States. Even though some of them were eventually released, he reported to Congress, "yet the loss by plunder, detention and expense, is so great as to render it ruinous to the American owner"; not to speak of the shocking insults and outrages committed on the crews during their capture and detention.[50]

Meanwhile, the old plan of Genêt for the employment of American volunteers to seize Spanish Louisiana and the Floridas similarly came to a head. George Rogers Clark, according to reports, was diligently recruiting restless and dissatisfied Americans in Kentucky.

This was obviously a bad moment to become embroiled with both Spain and her ally England over a clear-cut violation of neutrality. The administration therefore called on the governors of the affected areas to arrest and prosecute Clark and his associates. The Kentucky governor, Isaac Shelby, refused to do so. No overt act, he claimed, had been committed; and he did not intend, he added violently, to assume any doubtful power "against men who I consider as friends and brethren, in favor of a man [the king of Spain] whom I view as an enemy and a tyrant." [51]

Faced with this open defiance, the Cabinet decided that the President issue a proclamation against the expedition; that Shelby be sternly reprimanded for his contumacious conduct, and that General Wayne be ordered to dispatch troops to Fort Massac on the Mississippi to intercept any force that attempted to descend the river.[52]

The only Cabinet dissent from these sweeping measures came from Randolph, who thought that the Army should not be employed; since the crime if any was solely within the jurisdiction of the civil authorities. But he was overruled.[53]

It was with the greatest reluctance that Randolph complied with the decision and sent a formal reprimand to Governor Shelby. He was in a most uncomfortable position: a Republican reprimanding a Republican for a crime he did not consider a crime. He managed to soften the reproof, however, with a lengthy explanation that the delicate negotiations at Madrid might be jeopardized by the over-enthusiastic conduct of otherwise well-meaning individuals.[54]

A combination of forces and events put a peaceable end to the proposed expedition of Clark—the governmental action, an authority from Congress to employ militia rather than the Regular Army, Deforgue's disavowal of Genêt, the hasty suspension by Spain of a fifteen per cent duty on Kentucky goods going down to New Orleans,

and certain countermeasures by Spanish secret agents operating on
Kentucky soil.

One of these secret agents was General James Wilkinson, whose
fantastic career is one of the enigmas of early American history. During the Revolution he was involved in the Conway Cabal; at this time
he was a spy in the service of Spain; later, he commanded the American forces in the West; still later, he was a copartner with Aaron
Burr in the so-called Burr Conspiracy and eventually betrayed him;
and finally, he led the American Army to disaster in the War of 1812.
For his present services in stopping Clark a grateful Spain paid him
$12,000.[55]

The coming of Fauchet to replace Genêt did much to improve
relations with France; at least for a while. Unfortunately he was not
a free agent. The new regime in France, headed by Robespierre,
trusted no one. Every minister, every general in the field, every important official everywhere, was vigilantly checked and counter-
checked.

Three men accompanied Fauchet to the United States—La Forêt,
Petry and Le Blanc. Their public functions were vague; actually they
constituted a committee of supervision and vigilance over Fauchet.
He could take no step without their consent and sometimes without
their presence.

Even when the unfortunate minister paid his first formal call on
Washington and Randolph, Petry was at his side. The American
President and Secretary of State stared at the intruder in surprise;
and Randolph, noting how the unauthorized visitor took the lead in
the conversation with Fauchet somewhat uncomfortably assenting,
soon surmised the true state of affairs.[56]

The new minister brought with him a demand from his government
for the recall of Gouverneur Morris. However reluctantly, Washington could do no other than comply. And Randolph, though a Republican and with the knowledge that his party considered Morris
the primary cause of French antagonism, after examining all the recalled minister's official correspondence, was astonished to find "so
little of what is exceptionable, and so much of what the most violent
would call patriotic." [57]

Washington dispatched the requested recall to Morris, making it
clear to the deposed minister that it was being done only because
France had demanded it. In the private accompanying letter, the

President allowed himself one of the few ironic comments on record from his pen. "The affairs of this country," he underscored, "*cannot go amiss.* There are *so many watchful guardians of them,* and such *infallible guides,* that one is at no loss for a director at every turn." [58]

Meanwhile Gouverneur Morris, still unaware that he was being recalled, continued his duties with proper diligence. In the course of them he fell in with Tom Paine.

That stormy petrel of revolution, fleeing England to avoid prosecution, came to France to find utopia. But even in utopia he ran into his usual ill-starred luck. When the Brissotins, with whom he had ardently identified himself, fell, and the Jacobins rose to power, he was promptly clapped into jail. In fact, as Morris sarcastically remarked, Paine would have shared the scaffold with the others of his party had not the Jacobins viewed him with contempt.

Languishing in jail, Paine bethought himself of his former American citizenship—he had since become a citizen of France—and peremptorily demanded of Morris that he effect his release.

The single sentiment which Morris could be said to share with the Jacobins was a contempt for the passionate Paine, who, so he affirmed, was amusing himself in jail with the composition of a pamphlet attacking Jesus and simultaneously consoling himself with strong drink. And, aside from any question of personal distaste, Morris did not believe that he could properly claim American citizenship for a man who had assumed another. Furthermore, argued Morris, since the Jacobins had overlooked Paine in their first employment of the guillotine, why remind them of his presence? [59]

These arguments, as was to be expected, found little favor with their unfortunate recipient. Paine continued to languish in prison and—again according to Morris—drowning his sorrows in drink, until the arrival of James Monroe in Morris's stead. Monroe, who considered Paine as one of the great men of his time and agreed thoroughly with his political beliefs, interposed a formal demand for his release as an American citizen. Within two days, Paine was a free man. [60] It must be added, in all fairness to Morris, that by this time Robespierre had fallen victim to his own guillotine, the Jacobins were in flight and a new party was in power.

In the days to come, however, Monroe may perhaps have regretted his intervention. He took the ailing and penniless Paine into his house, where the irrepressible apostle of liberty immediately sat down to write pamphlets which violently assailed the American administration. Monroe remonstrated with his guest on the just ground that their publication would place himself in a highly awkward position. Paine pretended to yield to his expostulations, but shortly thereafter sent a sealed envelope to Thomas Pinckney, the American minister to England, with a request that it be transmitted to the United States.

Monroe, suspecting the contents, wrote a hasty warning to Pinckney, who thereupon turned the letter back. It was fortunate he did so, for the package contained an excoriating attack on both England and the United States which Paine intended to have published in Philadelphia.

Unable to rid himself of his unpleasant house guest, the embarrassed Monroe sought to protect himself against other and more successful attempts by Paine to slip material through by sending a full account of the situation to Madison for use "as occasion may require to guard me against unmerited slander." [61]

CHAPTER 18

Jay Mission and Whiskey Rebels

THE SLIM Federalist majority in the Senate, shaky in its grip and faced with a Republican House of Representatives, saw itself reduced to the margin of a single vote by the surprise election of Albert Gallatin of Pennsylvania. What made the blow even more mortifying was the fact that it had been a Federalist legislature which sent him to the Senate.

Albert Gallatin was something of a phenomenon in American life. Born in Geneva, Switzerland, of a noble family, he left his native country because his grandmother had boxed his ears for the expression of some radical sentiments. Coming to America in 1780, after much wandering he settled in western Pennsylvania, where he soon became immersed in the turbulent border politics of the day. He entered the state legislature, opposed the ratification of the Constitution, and wrote a report on the chaotic finances of the state which disclosed a grasp of financial problems second only to that of Alexander Hamilton.

He stood with his home counties in their opposition to the excise tax, drafted a resolution which declared it "subversive of the peace, liberty, and rights of the citizen," and that it "exhibited the singular spectacle of a nation resolutely opposing the oppression of others in order to enslave itself." [1] When the excise nevertheless passed, he joined his neighbors in their riotous proceedings and officiated as clerk to the notorious meeting at Pittsburgh on August 21, 1792.

It was this strange foreign-born radical of an ancient house, whose heavy accent never left him, whose placidity never deserted him even when uttering the most violent sentiments, able, tenacious, always thoroughly prepared and with a profound knowledge of fiscal matters, who came to the Senate at the end of 1793.

His very first action in the Senate gladdened the hearts of his Republican colleagues and alarmed the Federalists. Up to this time the attacks on Hamilton's financial system and mode of operation had been of the order of the Jefferson-Giles resolutions, which displayed a baffled ignorance of financial intricacies and therefore could readily be repulsed. But with the advent of Gallatin, the Republicans for the first time had a champion able to tilt on equal terms with the hitherto invincible Secretary of the Treasury.

Within a month after taking his seat, Gallatin called for a full report from Hamilton on all his measures while in office—a statement of the domestic debt, the amount already redeemed, the foreign debt, the loans made abroad, and a summary of the annual receipts and expenditures since 1789, according to the source of revenue and specific appropriations, and a statement of the unexpended balances now in the Treasury or in the hands of its agents.

The final demands were the most significant; for they called for a breakdown, item by item, of those appropriations which Congress had allotted for specific purposes. The Republicans had always felt that Hamilton was in the habit of disregarding both congressional and presidential directions for the disbursement of funds, and commingled all appropriations as a general fund in order to keep his financial books in balance. The Giles resolutions had tried to drive him out of office on this particular charge, but failed because there was no one then in public life with sufficient financial knowledge to disentangle the twisted skein of Hamilton's figures.

Since Gallatin's new resolutions were proper in form, the Senate was compelled to adopt them on January 20, 1794. But the beleaguered Secretary of the Treasury realized he was confronted with a new and more formidable antagonist in the Senate, while the House simultaneously revived its own dormant inquiry. There was one item in particular which was causing Hamilton considerable uneasiness. This related to his disposition of the proceeds of a foreign loan obtained under specific acts of Congress in 1790. The enabling laws had provided that the money be used abroad for the payment of old loans or employed otherwise on the authorization of the President. Actually a good part of the sums realized had been transferred to America and placed on deposit in the Bank of the United States.

Hamilton's problem, then, was to prove that Washington had authorized the change of destination. But frantically as he searched his papers, he found no scrip of writing from the President to that effect. He therefore wrote to Washington asking him to confirm an alleged oral authorization for the transfer. The President cautiously replied that he *thought* he had been told of the matter and given his approval; and then qualified the recollection with the damning addition that such approval, if given, had been predicated on the condition that "what was to be done by you should be agreeable to the laws."[2] Unfortunately, the law had plainly said the moneys were to be expended in Europe.

Under these alarming circumstances, the Hamiltonian adherents in the Senate determined to rid themselves of the formidable newcomer who might succeed where Giles had failed. A diligent search produced a technicality on which to contest Gallatin's seat. The Constitution provided that a senator to be eligible for office must have been a citizen of the United States for at least nine years. Since Gallatin had actually been a resident in America for thirteen years, it was necessary to prove by complicated testimony and even more complicated state regulations that he had not technically fulfilled the requirements by his final residence in Pennsylvania.

The argument was somewhat tenuous, but the Federalists rode roughshod over all protests to unseat Gallatin on February 28, 1794, by a strict party vote of 14 to 12.

Some good, however, emerged from the sorry proceedings. To avoid the charge of Star Chamber action, the Federalists agreed to hold these hearings, and all future business where secrecy was not involved, open to the public.[3] The innovation, however, evoked a growl from John Adams that public attendance at debates might tempt the younger members "to court popularity at the expense of justice, truth and wisdom, by flattering the prejudices of the audience."[4]

If the triumphant Federalists thought they had finished with Gallatin, they were soon disabused. At the congressional elections the next fall he was returned to the lower House by his constituents. That Republican-dominated body raised no embarrassing issue of citizenship, and Gallatin forged rapidly to the leadership of his party in Congress.

In one vital respect, however, the Federalists had accomplished their purpose. The original unseating had brought to a pause the persistent inquiries into Hamilton's methods; and his resignation at the beginning of the following year brought them altogether to an end.

The turn of the year found Anglo-American relations at the breaking point. The temporary embargo, instead of bringing England to terms, had found its deadliest target in American trade. The Federalists were confronted with a painful alternative—financial panic or war. They wanted neither. After all, in spite of their exasperation with England, France was still the true enemy. Most of them hoped for the complete destruction of the French and their revolution; though one of their sanest leaders, George Cabot, looked to an end of war in mutual exhaustion and a peace without victory. An English victory, he said, meant the end of our commerce; a French success "would destroy us as a society." [5] To Fisher Ames, however, while the English might be "madmen . . . this French mania is the bane of our politics, the mortal poison that makes our peace so sickly." [6]

On March 10, 1794, a small group of Federalist leaders met in strict secrecy in the quarters of Senator Rufus King to determine on a plan of action for ending the intolerable situation. The assembled men represented some of the best brains in the party. Ames was not present; nor was Hamilton; but King, George Cabot, Oliver Ellsworth and Caleb Strong—all members of Congress—met in the conclave.

The plan they finally agreed upon was to send Ellsworth to the President with the following proposals: first, that the country be put in a state of defense; second, that someone be dispatched to the West Indies to report on the seizures of American ships and to defend their rights; third, and this was the heart of the proposals, that an envoy extraordinary be sent to England to seek an adjustment of all pending issues.

It was also agreed that Ellsworth was to insinuate to the President that the mission could not succeed unless the envoy possessed the highest talents, enjoyed the "confidence of the friends of peace [meaning the Federalists]," and would be agreeable to the English. The only man whom these qualifications fitted, Ellsworth was further to intimate, was Alexander Hamilton.[7]

Ellsworth went off to see Washington, who listened to his exposition at first with some reserve, but finally with the most serious attention. On one point, however, he balked. Hamilton could not go as envoy, he said shortly, because he "did not possess the confidence of the country."

On this note the interview ended, and the matter rested for almost a month, during which time the embargo was renewed and Congress boiled with demands for sterner action against England. On April 7th, King spoke confidentially to Hammond, who seemed pleased with the idea of an envoy. Hammond did not see fit to inform his informant that he had already received word through his own personal channels of the Federalist secret move and that his letter was on the seas to his government advising them that the choice of the proposed envoy lay among Jay, Hamilton and Knox.

But Washington confounded his self-constituted advisers. On April 8th he asked Robert Morris to accept the mission. Morris refused and, as once before in connection with the Treasury, suggested Hamilton for the post. It must have seemed to the President that there was a conspiracy on foot to force Hamilton on him. His own list included the names of Jay, Adams and Jefferson.

King was now certain that Secretary of State Randolph, at Fauchet's instigation, was employing every means to defeat Hamilton's nomination. Perhaps he thought that the sudden emergence of Jefferson's name as a possibility stemmed from the same source. When John Jay arrived in Philadelphia on April 12th to hold circuit court, King closeted himself with him and laid all his cards on the table. Though the Federalists would be satisfied with Jay, he told the Chief Justice frankly, they preferred Hamilton. Whatever his private thoughts might have been, Jay seemed to agree.

Meanwhile the devious maneuvers had leaked to the Republicans, probably through Randolph. At once a storm of protests descended on the President. From Monroe, senator from Virginia, came a hectoring letter that Hamilton's appointment would be "not only injurious to the publick interest, but also especially so to your own." He was willing, Monroe added, to furnish the proof of his charges in a private interview.[8]

From Virginia came a similar protest from John Nicholas, who went further to declare his opposition to the whole idea of a mission.[9] Madison, more intimately acquainted with Washington's character, did not attempt a frontal assault; but worked circuitously to circumvent Hamilton's appointment.[10]

As Madison doubtless surmised, Monroe's communication—and, to a lesser degree, Nicholas's—enraged the President. He stormed into Randolph's office with both letters in his hand, and flatly accused his Secretary of State of having been their secret instigator. Randolph denied the allegation and managed finally to calm the angry President down. What should be done about Monroe's request for an interview? Randolph replied that he did not think it "decorous" for a senator to seek to influence nominations in advance unless he were possessed of irrefutable *facts*. Randolph said he would personally tell Monroe so; but he also advised that the President write him granting the interview, on the condition that only facts, and not political arguments, were to be adduced.[11]

Washington disregarded the advice. He dispatched a cold note to Monroe that "if you are possessed of any facts or information, which would disqualify Colonel Hamilton for the mission to which you refer, that you would be so obliging as to communicate them to me in writing."[12]

Thus put on the spot, Monroe could reply only with political arguments: that Hamilton was head of the British party in the United States and an enemy of France; that his mission would be responsible for further intrigues at home against republicanism and France; and that the French would certainly be displeased with his appointment.[13]

Had Monroe deliberately intended Hamilton's nomination, he could not have pursued better tactics. Fortunately for the tactless Virginian, the President had already made up his mind to send John Jay to London. In this he was abetted by Hamilton himself.

There is no doubt that Hamilton was eager to go himself; and it is most probable that he would have done far better than Jay. He had the resourcefulness, the talents, the ability to drive straight through to a given point, and he also possessed the confidence of the English. Yet, convinced by now that Washington did not intend to appoint him, he preferred to yield gracefully and thereby be in a better position to influence the course of the negotiations.

He therefore asked the President to drop his name from further consideration and to nominate Jay for the mission.[14] Whereupon Washington sent Jay's name to the Senate on April 16th.

The Republicans were not appeased. To them Jay was almost as narrow a Federalist as Hamilton and equally suspect to their beloved France. Though Madison exulted over Hamilton's mortification in being set aside,[15] Monroe could remember only how Jay had once almost "bartered away" the Mississippi River to Spain, and wondered audibly what he would give to England, particularly since the fortunes of the Federalists were wrapped up in his mission.[16]

Nor was the generality of Republicans in a more amenable mood to welcome a mission to England, regardless of the envoy. Glorious news had come to them from abroad—news of a great French victory at Toulon, in which the British had been sent reeling back to their ships. New York celebrated the triumph with a monster parade whose terminus was the home of the French consul. It was complete with the military in gaudy uniforms, a salute of cannon, the playing of the

"*Ça Ira*" and the "*Carmagnole*," a banquet, cheers, toasts to France, the Democratic Societies of the world, Tom Paine (even then, ironically, languishing in a French prison), and confusion to the Federalists and their "British" measures.[17]

Hammond himself was disturbed over the increasing bitterness of the anti-British tone. Particularly did he stress to his government the exacerbation of it as a result of the case of Captain Joshua Barney. That stout American seaman had forcibly recaptured his ship after its seizure by the British, and in the process two British tars had received dangerous wounds. On a later voyage, Barney was retaken by a British warship and sent to Jamaica to stand trial for "piracy."

This in itself, Hammond complained, was sufficient to inflame American public opinion. But coupled with this provocation was the status of Barney himself as a naval hero from the days of the Revolution. As a result, the public temper had risen to such a fever pitch that in Barney's native town of Baltimore there were threats of immediate retaliation on the resident British consul should Barney be convicted and hanged. So dangerous did the situation become that Hammond thought it prudent to order the consul to Philadelphia for safety.[18]

Nor was Congress in a more amenable mood. Even while the mission to England was under consideration, the Clark resolution for a suspension of all commercial intercourse was on the House floor. So was Dayton's motion to sequester British debts in this country. Fearing their passage and the probable failure of the mission as a result, the members of the Federalist cabal, reinforced by Hamilton, jointly visited Jay to impress on him the need to inform the President that he would refuse to go if these "menaces and complaints" were put into effect.[19]

If Jay did so, it was without result. For Clark's resolution passed in the House; and in spite of it, Jay accepted the nomination. The Republicans in the Senate sought to block his appointment. Monroe denounced the entire venture as supine surrender to the British; John Taylor argued that the employment of the Chief Justice tended to destroy the independence of the judiciary; while Aaron Burr employed his talents to defeat the nomination. All efforts were in vain, and Jay was confirmed on April 20th by a vote of 18 to 8.[20]

With their plan thus far crowned with success, the Federalist cabal proceeded further. In effect they were assuming the functions of the

Executive, with or without the President's knowledge or consent. Hamilton, Jay, Ellsworth, Cabot and King met on the day after the senatorial confirmation to discuss the instructions to be furnished Jay on his mission. It was agreed that they must include satisfaction for the spoliations, freedom of the seas, the full execution of the peace treaty by England, and the settlement of such vital issues as a commercial treaty, the delivery of the posts, the Indian trade and navigation of the Great Lakes, and the opening of the British West Indies to American ships. In exchange for these concessions, the United States would settle the unpaid prewar debts in a sum up to £500,000 sterling.[21]

The group also probably decided that Hamilton was to draft the official instructions. This was unprecedented; since the drafting of instructions for envoys was an integral function of the State Department. But Washintgon saw nothing wrong in letting Hamilton make the preliminary draft.

In the main it followed the suggestions made at the Federalist conference. Jay was to demand compensation for the losses suffered by our commerce; a declaration that foodstuffs were not contraband; prompt restoration of the posts and indemnification for the slaves carried away after the war; and the opening of the West Indies to trade. In return, the United States would pay an indemnity for the still existent debts, and grant most favored nation privileges in the ports of this country. Hamilton added a significant proviso to any negotiation of a commercial treaty—that it must not violate the terms of our previous treaties with France.[22]

Hamilton's preliminary draft was then turned over to Randolph to put into formal guise. What the latter's emotions were at thus being made into a mere copyist for the Secretary of the Treasury is unknown. He had already been compelled to deny responsibility for the leak on Hamilton's putative appointment, and to defend himself against insinuations that he had unduly favored Southern interests in office. To the latter charge he replied with dignity that he belonged to no party and that his independence had actually brought on him the hostility of the Republicans.[23]

Randolph did not favor the idea of the mission insofar as it contemplated the negotiation of a commercial treaty. Such a power given to Jay, he urged, infringed on the rights of the Senate; since it would be difficult to refuse to ratify any arrangement to which the envoy had already affixed his signature.[24]

Washington overruled his objections and Randolph thereupon obediently set to work to copy out Hamilton's proposals. He did manage to add some points of his own: the Jeffersonian slogan that "free ships make free goods"; fishing rights in the Newfoundland and other banks "now engrossed by the British"; and, perhaps most important of all, the suggestion that Jay sound out the ministers of Russia, Denmark and Sweden resident in England on a possible alliance to uphold the principles of an armed neutrality.[25]

When the Chief Justice took his departure for London, he left behind him a maelstrom of political emotions. The administration and the Federalists hoped for the best and prepared for the worst. The Republicans feared a surrender of American rights to the British and preferred that the mission fail. In the meantime they employed it as a political weapon. "If the animadversions are undertaken by skilful hands," declared Madison, "there is no measure of the Executive administration perhaps that will be found more severely vulnerable." [26]

Evidences of such "animadversions," skillful or not, were immediately visible. All of Jay's ancient sins were raked up anew. The West remembered his "former iniquitous attempt" during the period of the Confederation "to barter away their most valuable right" of the Mississippi navigation. In Kentucky, the effigy of "this Evil Genius of Western America," clad in what passed as court dress, was put in a pillory. From its neck dangled a copy of John Adams's *Defence of the American Constitutions* (another bête noire of the Republicans). On the book a tag from Ovid (in translation) was prominently displayed: GOLD BADE ME WRITE!

The effigy with its burden was first pelted and mocked; then placed on an improvised guillotine and the head struck off. A match was put to the headless corpse, previously stuffed with gunpowder. The resulting explosion was most satisfactory. As one observer complacently noted, "there was scarcely to be found a particle of the *disjecti membra* Plenipo." [27]

On the other side of the ledger, party lines were crossed in Congress when the embargo came up for renewal on May 12th. The proposed extension was overwhelmingly defeated in the House by a vote of 73 to 13. By less considerable majorities the attempts to sequestrate British debts and to prohibit the entry of British ships into American ports were turned back. Instead, Congress voted supplies and fortifications for the seaport towns and gave legislative sanction to the tenets of the controversial Proclamation of Neutrality.

Even Hammond was surprised at "this sudden alteration of sentiment" in Congress, particularly on the part of the Southern representatives. He attributed the change of heart to the remonstrances of their own constituents, who found that the embargo had choked their warehouses with unsold crops. It was not, he informed his government, that hostility to England had subsided. That was never at a higher pitch, due largely to Dorchester's notorious speech to the Indians and the report of Simcoe's descent on the Miami to erect a British fort.[28]

Hammond had taken a violent dislike to Edmund Randolph, the new Secretary of State. The unfortunate Randolph seemed fated, for all his efforts to steer a course independent of party—or perhaps because of them—to please no one and to arouse enmity and contempt on every side. Yet he pursued the same policy as his predecessor, Thomas Jefferson, whom Hammond had respected as a man. He did not respect Randolph.

When Randolph pressed the British minister closely on the placement of foodstuffs on the list of contraband and on the Dorchester-Simcoe incidents, Hammond retorted angrily. Randolph replied in kind, and a most undiplomatic and acrimonious correspondence resulted.

The bitterness was accentuated by the report of an alleged outrage against the armed British ship *Nautilus* at Newport. The warship arrived in harbor on May 8, 1794. Word immediately spread that thirteen impressed American seamen were on board and held against their will. The Rhode Island general assembly summoned the ship's officers before it for interrogation. They denied the charge. The assembly proposed that a representative go on board to investigate. The captain of the ship at first agreed, and then changed his mind. On quitting the legislative chamber—so the British asserted—the captain and his lieutenant were set upon by an angry mob and "kicked."

Meanwhile the assembly had voted to take the officers into custody pending a judicial hearing; whereupon the "kicked'" captain decided to yield. A committee boarded the ship and found six American sailors, who were only too happy to depart from the ship. The captain, expressing deep "surprise" at the unaccountable presence of Americans on his vessel, agreed to discharge them; and the incident seemed closed.

But barely had the committee and the seamen quit the *Nautilus* when the captain dashed off a furious complaint to Hammond, who in turn protested to Randolph. The Secretary of State blandly retorted with a statement of the facts as *he* had received them.[29]

Relations for the moment seemed better with Fauchet, the French minister. Washington cautiously accepted him as thus far temperate, placid and friendly—the very reverse of Genêt; nevertheless he adopted a wait-and-see attitude.[30]

The President had aged in the past two years; he had grown thin, and a seated anxiety was visible always on his haggard countenance. An English traveler attributed the change to the troubled times; though noting with surprise that no one else in Philadelphia appeared to take the state of the nation or of the world very seriously. The Philadelphia theater, he thought, was as commodious and elegant as Covent Garden. The rich attire of the audience, the skill of the acting and the splendid scenic effects transported the observer momentarily to his native England. At the ultrafashionable Oeller's Hotel, lavish in its appointments, he found all the amenities of civilization. Lumps of ice from the hotel's private icehouse cooled his punch; the strictest rules of etiquette prevailed in the great assembly room with its handsome music gallery.

Mrs. Bingham's mansion astonished even a visitor accustomed to Belgrave Square and ducal appointments. Its magnificent fittings, its gardens, its superb furniture, vied with anything he had seen at home. The lyre-backed chairs were festooned with yellow and crimson silks; the carpeting was imported and expensive; the drawing room was as gilt and showily decorated as the Vatican in Rome. The garden bloomed with lemon, orange and citron trees, with aloes and rare tropical exotics.

All this luxury and splendor, reflected the traveler, came from the land speculations of the fortunate lady's husband and her father, Thomas Willing. Indeed, the husband told him proudly of one nice little investment he had made: in 1783 he purchased some land on the outskirts of Philadelphia for 850 pounds; today the same parcel brought in that sum annually as rent.[31]

Elsewhere too, the traveler found, if not the same elegance, an abundance unknown to Europe. A Boston inn served him endless courses of salmon, veal, beef, mutton, fowl, ham, puddings and all the trimmings, together with a pint of Madeira. On the post road to New York, his breakfast consisted of beefsteaks and coffee, bacon and eggs, veal cutlets, toast and butter. But the bill he received for this light snack was excessive—it came to two shillings. The overcharge, he felt, was doubtless due to the fact that General Washington had once slept there (obviously the beginning of a mighty legend).

His chief complaint, however, was the prevalence of bedbugs wherever he went, so that he found himself unable to sleep. Americans to whom he voiced his complaint merely stared. The bugs never bit *them,* they said.[32] Unspoken doubtless was the thought that the insects smelled an Englishman.

A considerable addition to the tone and elegance of the larger American towns was furnished by the influx of French emigrés. The first group to take the sea voyage was made up of noble families fleeing the revolution. Many of the greatest houses of France partook in the migration: the Duc de la Rochefoucauld-Liancourt, the Vicomte de Noailles, the three sons of the royal Duc d'Orléans (better known to history as Philippe Égalité), M. and Mme. de la Tour du Pin, the latter of whom was genially adopted by General Schuyler as his "sixth daughter," the redoubtable Talleyrand, readying himself for eventual return and placement in the seats of the mighty; and such poets, philosophers, scientists and artists as Chateaubriand, Volney and Saint-Memin, the last of whom was to sketch and engrave the lineaments of the most important Americans of the day.

The second migration came from the tortured island of Santo Domingo, where the Negro slaves had taken too literally the shibboleths of the revolution and risen to exterminate the French white population. Those who could escaped in crowded ships to Charleston, Philadelphia and other seaport towns. Their vast influx posed a considerable problem. They came with no possessions but what was on their backs; and the French government at home, immersed in war, had no funds for their relief. Fauchet requested from the American government an advance payment of $1,000,000 on its debt; to his chagrin he received only half that sum.[33]

Eventually all the refugees set up enclaves of their own in the various towns, duplicating Paris as nearly as they could from nostalgic memory. They opened French-type shops and *pensions;* they published French newspapers and organized French schools. They hired their services to Americans eager for veneer as language teachers, dancing and music masters, watchmakers, dressmakers and shoemakers, and purveyors of wines, rouges and perfumes. Their number, augmented by successive waves of migrations as the revolution at home moved to further and further extremes, has been variously estimated from ten to twenty-five thousand.

Moreau de St. Méry, a liberal noble, remained in France until he incurred the enmity of Robespierre; then he too fled to America. Eventually he settled in Philadelphia, where he opened a bookshop and set up a printing press. His shop became the center of the intellectual life of the refugees, while Americans flocked to purchase his French and English editions. One of his most profitable items, however, proved to be a prophylactic syringe, a device which he and his French friends were amazed to hear had hitherto been unknown in America.

Eventually these enclaves, quickening to America in many respects though they were, became a source of embarrassment and a focal point for anti-French and antiforeign feeling. By 1798, when relations with France reached the status of an undeclared war, and the Alien and Sedition Acts were passed, the colonies broke up and the tide reversed itself. Now the French fled from America to seek a second safety abroad.[34]

With the enforced recall of Gouverneur Morris it became necessary to send another minister to France. Washington first proposed to shift his ministers around; to appoint Jay to the permanent post in England and transfer Thomas Pinckney to Paris. But Jay declined a permanent establishment; whereupon Washington offered the French post to Robert R. Livingston, chancellor of New York and a Republican in politics. When he turned it down, it was given to James Monroe, senator from Virginia. The President thought it best to send a Republican and known friend to France. Monroe accepted the appointment.[35]

This time the task of writing the instructions was left entirely to Randolph. The new minister was to assure the French that the American President had been "an early and decided friend of the French Revolution" and still wished it every success; that both nations understand it would be most unwise for the United States to depart from its neutrality; and that Jay had been "positively forbidden to weaken the engagements" between America and France.

He was also to disabuse the French of the idea that there existed two irreconcilable parties in this country; and to counter any complaints on the recent embargo (which seemed to have hit France as much as England) with a well-chosen reference to their own earlier embargo against American ships. He was not to discuss the delicate

question of the status of the old treaties or the guarantees, but to refer
any inquiries to Philadelphia.

In case the United States *did* get into the war, Monroe was to inform the French, we would look to them as "our first and natural ally"
and seek their aid in obtaining from Spain the navigation of the
Mississippi. This was obviously a tentative feeler for the use of the
French fleet in reducing New Orleans. And finally, Monroe was instructed to conduct all his negotiations in writing and in *English*.
Randolph wanted no disputes or "misinterpretations" of ministerial
stumblings in the alien French.[36]

With these eminently sound instructions Monroe departed; unfortunately he failed to follow them with diplomatic rectitude. At home,
Fauchet got on a confidential basis with Randolph. The new Secretary
of State seemed not to have learned a lesson from Jefferson's unhappy
dealings with Genêt.

He unbosomed himself at length to the attentive French minister,
and complained bitterly of the machinations of Hamilton and Knox in
the Cabinet and the Federalist leaders in Congress. He hoped, he said,
to prove to the President the "perfidy" of those who calumniated the
great principles of the French Revolution. Indeed, though Washington
was personally friendly to France and the "mortal enemy" of England,
he had been "often duped by the dark maneuvers of Mr. Hamilton,"
so that Randolph's countermeasures required "great secrecy and prudence."

All this was most gratifying to Fauchet; yet it did not prevent him
from summing up his confidant as no doubt an excellent gentleman
and partisan to France, but of a weak character and one whose secrets
it was only too easy to penetrate.[37] In the end, Randolph's expansive-
ness was to prove his own undoing.

The long-simmering cauldron of the frontier boiled over in July
1794 with a violence almost as catastrophic as the explosion which
had dismembered the gunpowder-stuffed effigy of poor John Jay.
From the western counties of Pennsylvania, south to the border regions
of Georgia, and west into Kentucky and Tennessee, the strange brew
spattered and scalded.

For years the frontiers had seethed with intense agitation against
the national government and its administration. Each section had its
particular grievance. The western counties of Pennsylvania, Virginia
and the Carolinas hated the excise tax on the distillation of their

grain into the more potable and portable whiskey with a surpassing hatred. The Georgia border folk had been frustrated time and again in their amiable efforts to exterminate their Indian neighbors. Kentucky and Tennessee, devout believers in the thesis that the only good Indian is a dead Indian, found the government similarly obstructive. Even worse, the administration paid no heed to their just demands for an immediate war on Spain to open the Mississippi and a free entry into New Orleans.

Disparate as these incitations to unrest might appear, all sections found a common ground in the ardor of their republicanism, their unremitting hate of England and their almost convulsive love for France. The cult of the Democratic Societies swept all the frontiers; their resolutions vociferated on all issues, domestic and foreign—invariably in opposition to the measures of the government—and they swooped on Jay's mission as the ultimate evidence of Anglo-monarchical-aristocratical intent.

The western counties of Pennsylvania, which included Washington County, Mingo Creek and Pittsburgh (a town of barely a thousand population), took the lead. In Pittsburgh, an excited meeting avowed that "we are almost ready to wish for a state of revolution and the guillotine of France for a short space in order to inflict punishment on the miscreants that enervate and disgrace our government." [38] In Washington County, the Democratic Society denounced neutrality and Jay's appointment with equal fervor. "Is our president," it inquired, "like the grand sultan of Constantinople, shut up in his apartment," that he dared to give two offices to one man? Only he, in fact, could have "insulted the majesty of the people by such a departure from any principle of republican equality." [39] At Mingo Creek, the local Society assumed governmental powers and openly threatened violence on any citizen benighted enough to bring suits at law in the regularly constituted courts instead of applying to the club for redress. [40]

In Wythe County, Virginia, the indigenous Society asserted that Washington had verged on despotism in appointing Jay; that the government had "uniformly *crouched* to Britain" while treating the French, "to whom we owe our political existence," with contumely and abuse. "Blush Americans," it cried, "for the conduct of your government!!!" [41]

To such unmeasured abuse the Federalists retorted in kind. "The Democratic Societies in *America*," shouted a Boston paper, "are the spurious, unnatural offspring of the Jacobin Societies in France." Their leaders were "factious incendiaries, who lust after domination, who will and do violate every right principle, to gain the power of tyrannizing at pleasure." Genêt had founded and directed them; and his hellish offspring conspired by night behind close doors, abused the President as an aristocrat and, in desperate conclave, attacked every aspect of his character, acts and principles.[42]

In such a superheated atmosphere, the transition from vehement words to action required only an inciting spark. That came from the excise taxes and the attempt in Congress to increase the amount and widen their scope.

The old liberty poles were taken out and once more flaunted their ancient defiance. Slogans plastered poles and barns: "An equal tax and no excise," "United we stand, divided we fall," and crudely painted snakes writhed in axed dismemberment. Great mass meetings of angry farmers and backwoodsmen hearkened to the denunciations of inflammatory orators. Collectors of the hated tax were first warned, then tarred and feathered and pursued with menaces from the insurrectionary counties. Those who obeyed the law and paid the tax found their stills riddled with bullets. Witnesses who dared testify against the rioters returned to the smoking ashes of their barns and dwellings; and were themselves tarred and feathered and left roped to trees. The so-called Whiskey Rebellion was in full swing.

On July 15th, United States Marshal David Lenox, accompanied by General Neville, revenue collector for Pittsburgh, rode out to serve writs on those who refused to pay the tax. Armed bands who called themselves "Tom the Tinker's Men" waylaid them and pursued them back to Neville's home at Bower Hill. A set siege followed, in which Neville shot an assailant dead and wounded four others before the attacking party withdrew. Regular soldiers from Pittsburgh hurried to his rescue; the militia of Mingo Creek mobilized to oppose them. While Neville fled for safety, a pitched battle took place between eleven soldiers and an overwhelming force of five hundred militia. The little troop of Regulars was forced to surrender; the triumphant militia fired Neville's buildings and caroused on his liquor. Neville and Lenox both now fled the country; another collector, Robert Johnson, prudently resigned his commission by public notice.[43]

The Mingo Creek militia, emboldened by their success and swelled by new recruits to several thousand, now marched on Pittsburgh with the avowed intention of driving all tax-lovers out of the country. Led by David Bradford, their most inflammatory orator, member of the Pennsylvania legislature and self-styled major-general, they camped outside the town on historic Braddock's Field. The townsfolk sought to surrender, but the tiny company of Regulars garrisoning the fort refused to yield. There was much talk of storming the fort, but cooler heads prevailed and, after setting fire to some dwellings of "disloyal" folk, the militia disbanded.

As the excitement grew, some of the more hotheaded spoke seriously of severing themselves from the Union. One day two mysterious strangers appeared in Philadelphia and went directly to the house of the British minister. They claimed to represent the Whiskey Rebels of Pittsburgh, said that their purpose was secession and that they wished to place themselves under the protection of Great Britain. Hammond declined to hear them any further or to become in any way a party to their scheme. Whereupon one of them inquired for the address of the Spanish commissioners.[44]

Whether they next saw the representatives of Spain is not known; but the French minister, Fauchet, reported a conversation held at about this time with Edmund Randolph which, vague and mysteriously worded though it was, seemed to hint in curious directions. But more must later be said of this strange conference and its consequences.

As the reports of the many outrages poured by post, messenger and rumor into Philadelphia, the government was thrown into a mingled panic and fury.

The entire gross revenue from the excise taxes, collected from all over the country, had amounted for the preceding year to $422,026.86; and against this sum the expenses of collection were close to $70,000.[45] Certainly such minor avails were not sufficient to justify the political and revolutionary implications of their continuance; but Hamilton had intended the excise as a mere steppingstone to further internal taxes, and both he and the President were determined not to back down in the face of insurrection and violence. The matter became a test of the strength of the national government.

Hamilton in particular, outraged at this subversion of his policies, eagerly welcomed the opportunity to prove once for all that the general government was greater than the sum of its component parts. He had been balked of his prey once before when the rebels hastily yielded; this time he vowed that retribution must be exacted with celerity and with the full weight and majesty of the United States.

He also realized what most commentators since have overlooked— that the insurrection was not simple in its origins. Though the excise was the immediate inciting cause, other strands were inextricably interwoven: opposition to a national government per se, disgust with its foreign and domestic policies, hatred of the Eastern trading and commercial folk, saturation in French egalitarian and revolutionary principles, the agitation of the proliferating Democratic Societies, and a profound belief that any state, or even a section of a state, could annul national legislation at will.

When the first reports reached Philadelphia, Washington convened his Cabinet to discuss the situation. Hamilton submitted a written opinion that the proceedings constituted an act of treason and demanded that the militia be called out to suppress them. He estimated the number required to put down the rebellion at 9000 foot and 3000 horse.[46]

Three days later, already impatient at any delay, he sent the President an even more urgent note and, in collaboration with Knox, drafted a Proclamation for Washington to issue.[47]

Though the President had been galled almost beyond endurance by the personal assaults on himself from the Republicans, the Democratic Societies and the insurrectionists, he nevertheless shrank from open bloodshed until all other remedies had been exhausted.

He therefore asked Governor Mifflin of Pennsylvania for a meeting at which the cooperation of state and federal authorities might be discussed. Mifflin and his state attorney Dallas thought that the state alone could handle the situation, but were evasive on the action they would take. Hamilton promptly drafted a sharp reply to which Randolph, albeit reluctantly, affixed his signature.[48]

When Mifflin failed to act, Washington issued his Proclamation on August 7th commanding the rioters to cease and disperse. Even then, he sought for peaceful means before putting an army in motion. A mixed commission of state and federal nominees, including the Attorney General of the United States, William Bradford, and the chief justice of Pennsylvania, Thomas McKean, journeyed to Pittsburgh to meet with the leaders of the rebellion. The commission was empowered to offer a general amnesty, provided the excise taxes were thereafter obeyed. At first the rebels refused the terms, then decided to submit them to a popular referendum. This strange procedure was accordingly followed and ultimately, after some additional outbreaks in which the commissioners themselves were threatened, most of the townships signed a test oath of loyalty and obedience to the United States; and the rebellion was over.

But these developments were still unknown in Philadelphia as the militia, authorized on a national scale and under national supervision by prior acts of Congress, gathered and commenced their march. They came chiefly from Pennsylvania and Virginia, the two affected states; and the wellborn and the rich young men turned out en masse as for a holiday, vowing vengeance on the rioters and the Democratic Societies alike, those "sons of darkness . . . born in sin" as "the impure offspring of Genêt," in the language of Fisher Ames.[49]

What made these youthful scions of Anglican stock all the more eager to chastise the insurgents was the belief that "nine out of ten . . . are Irish and Scotch newcomers; scarce one in twenty of which have resided long enough in the country to become citizens!!"[50] This was a canard, though it was true that the Irish and the Scotch were numerous on the frontier. Many of the inhabitants, including the rebels themselves, came of as native stock as their opponents.

In the meantime Knox was resigning his post as Secretary of War, a step he had long contemplated. Though the resignation did not take official effect until the end of the year, the indefatigable Hamilton was only too happy to take over the duties of the War Office at an earlier date and combine them with his own. It gave him the opportunity for which he had long panted—the achievement of military glory. He begged permission of the President to accompany the expedition, and Washington acceded.[51]

On September 25, 1794, in spite of the fact that the commissioners at Pittsburgh had already brought the rebellion to a peaceful end, a mighty array of 9000 foot and 3000 horse marched out of Philadelphia, flags flying, drums beating, accompanied by a long train of wagons and supplies, including delicacies and appurtenances to ease the horrors of a wilderness trek. It was the greatest assemblage of armed men since the Revolution; and even then, most campaigns had been fought with a lesser force.

Dismayed at the decisive action of the government and fearful of the consequences of their former reckless attacks, the Democratic Societies hastened to take cover. The parent group in Philadelphia publicly resolved that though they "conceive excise systems to be oppressive, hostile to the liberties of this country, and a nursery of vice and sycophancy, we, notwithstanding, highly disapprove of every opposition to them, not warranted by that frame of government, which has received the sanction of the people of the United States." The "German Republicans" of the same town followed suit; and so did the "Republican Society" of Newark, with an additional denunciation of any attempt to connect the Societies with the riots.[52]

The disclaimers and the disavowals came too late. Thoroughly aroused and smarting under the epithets previously applied to him by the Societies, Washington was determined to break their power once for all. "I consider this insurrection," he asserted, "as the first *formidable* fruit of the Democratic Societies; brought forth I believe too prematurely for their own views, which may contribute to the annihilation of them." He had, he continued, watched their growth very attentively and he saw "under a display of popular and fascinating guises, the most diabolical attempts to destroy the best fabric of human government and happiness, that has ever been presented for the acceptance of mankind." [53]

Nor was he at a loss to attribute the shrill demands from Kentucky for an immediate war with Spain over the Mississippi to the same source.[54] "Can any thing be more absurd, more arrogant, or more pernicious to the peace of Society," he exclaimed in a final outburst of wrath, "than for self created bodies, forming themselves into *permanent* Censors, and under the shade of Night in a conclave, resolving that acts of Congress which have undergone the most deliberate, and solemn discussion by the Representatives of the people . . . to declare that *this act* is unconstitutional, and that *act* is pregnant of mischief . . . is such a stretch of arrogant presumption as is not to be reconciled with laudable motives." [55]

In his exasperation Washington had gone beyond the limits of just criticism. He was in effect declaring that acts of Congress were not subject to critical scrutiny; that "self-created" organizations (meaning thereby groups not formed with government approval) were *ipso facto* suspect; and that meetings held after dark were conspiratorially tinged with the shades in which they were enveloped.

Governor Mifflin and Dallas, hoping perhaps to exercise a moderating influence, accompanied the troops. Five days later, Washington and Hamilton set out to join the slow-moving array. As the reports of the army, multiplied and given wings by rumor, came to the western counties, the ringleaders of the rebellion, with some two thousand lesser adherents, incontinently fled. They scattered in all directions to escape the wrath to come. Some even took boat down the Ohio and into the Mississippi, striking into uncharted wilderness to seek new fortunes and never to return.

Albert Gallatin, home again after his expulsion from the Senate, hastily gathered the committees of Fayette County together and had them pass resolutions exhorting the people not to resist the approaching military and to employ peaceful methods alone for the repeal of the tax.[56]

But neither flights nor resolutions served to stop the inexorable if somewhat tortuous approach of the army. Washington and Hamilton caught up with the troops at Carlisle, where the President reviewed the serried ranks with pride in his heart and a reliving of his military past. He exulted at this outpouring of young men "possessing the first fortunes in the country, standing in the ranks as private men." [57]

Unfortunately some of these same young men—rich or not—had already acted in a manner singularly reminiscent of mercenaries on the loose. The officers of an entire corps, wearying thus early of a campaign in which not a single enemy had been met, deserted their troops and departed for home. The leaderless soldiers thereupon ran riot in indiscriminate pillage of the peaceful countryside. "In some places," Washington himself was forced to admit, "they did not leave a plate, a spoon, a glass or a knife." In others they tore down the fences and used them for firewood.[58]

There were worse incidents. Two civilians had been slain by quick-triggered militiamen for the erection of a liberty pole. Dallas prudently avowed that the slayings had been "for cause"; nevertheless he felt much relieved when the President expressed regret when he heard of it. Dallas was not at his ease with the army. He himself lay under suspicion as a confessed Republican who had not hesitated to state in the presence of the elite Philadelphia youth "that the army were going only in order to support the civil authority and not to do any military execution." This had aroused one fire-eater to draw his dagger halfway from its sheath and swear "that any man who uttered such sentiments ought to be dagged." In such surroundings, the state attorney was happy to find Washington and Hamilton, on their arrival in camp, supporting his sentiments and insisting on the strictest discipline among the marching men.[59]

After reviewing the troops, Washington returned from Carlisle to

Philadelphia. The Army continued over the Allegheny mountains under the command of Major-General Henry Lee of Virginia, with Hamilton riding at his side in an anomalous ex officio position. The rains set in, the mountain roads turned to bottomless mud, and the young men who had started out with such insouciance now sweated and toiled to drag artillery, baggage and themselves up the steep and slippery paths. The festive element was gone, and the picnic jaunt was over.

Yet still no "enemy" appeared on the scene. Everywhere they came, "peaceful" citizens readily swore allegiance and took the test oath, much to the private regret of the fire-eaters. If only "the Courage of the Insurgents had been equal to their Insolence," lamented one; then took comfort in the thought that some of the rebel leaders had personal enemies whose equally personal motives for vengeance would doubtless serve the cause of public justice.[60]

Hamilton too was furious at the supine surrenders which prevented him from furnishing those examples which he believed the country required. He sought to remedy the matter by demanding the enactment of a peacetime bill of outlawry which would permit the permanent banishment of those who had fled and the confiscation of all their possessions. "This business must not be skimmed over," he said grimly, or "the next storm will be infinitely worse than the present one."[61]

Even Dallas, for all his former sympathy with the rebels, was beginning to veer around to the idea of punitive measures. He now admitted that no trust could be placed in the professions of loyalty and the smiling faces of the erstwhile rioters. He had in fact heard some of them assert that once the army was gone they would renew their violence. "Nothing but fear and coercion," wrote Dallas, "will insure their submission."[62]

By this time, moreover, the Republicans had recovered from their initial panic. As the punitive force slogged its way through mud and over mountain roads, to meet up only with welcoming committees, the Republican press regained its former boldness. It sneered and chuckled over the futile show and heaped the fires of ridicule on its author, Hamilton. Even some of the Federalists began to feel a trifle foolish.

The swelling chorus in his rear served only to exasperate Hamilton the more. When finally the great army marched into Pittsburgh, he held a conference with General Lee and Federal Judge Richard

Peters. It was decided to arrest all known agitators and deal with them summarily. "All possible means are using [*sic*]," reported Hamilton to the President, "to obtain evidence, and accomplices will be turned against the others. I hope good objects will be found notwithstanding many have gone off." [63]

Hundreds of men were arrested. The chief offenders were sent under strong guard to Philadelphia to stand trial. The lesser fry were either handed over to the state courts or severely lectured and dismissed. Twenty who were transported to the capital found themselves jeered by hostile crowds that lined the streets.

By the time they were brought up for trial, however, the first wave of vindictiveness had ebbed. All were acquitted except two. Of this unfortunate pair, one conviction at least was caused by the overcleverness of counsel for the defense. He deliberately picked a jury composed entirely of Quakers, and was much chagrined when they promptly convicted his client of treason. Another defendant, tried almost simultaneously by a jury of Presbyterians and equally guilty, was acquitted.

As one law-trained defendant who witnessed the double proceedings remarked: "He would always choose a jury of Quakers or at least Episcopalians in all common cases such as murder, rape, & so forth—but in every possible case of insurrection, a rebellion and treason, give him Presbyterians on the jury, by all means." [64] There was merit in this contention—descendants of the old Scotch Covenanters could be depended on to sympathize with rebellion against civil authorities.

The Whiskey Rebellion thus came to an inglorious end. Even the unfortunate pair who had been convicted were later pardoned by the President. Most of those who had fled now sheepishly returned; though there were some who found permanent havens with the Spaniards and the British. Yet for all the *opéra bouffe* trimmings of the great expedition and the ensuing measures of the administration, one important matter had been pointed up for the consideration of the country—that the central government possessed the power and the determination to enforce its edicts.

Hamilton returned to Philadelphia to the accompaniment of jeers and laughter from the opposition; a chorus which he affected to treat with contempt. A short while later, he put into effect his long-expressed desire to retire to private life. On January 31, 1795, he quit his office and resumed the practice of law.

Of the four original members of the Cabinet, only Randolph remained. An era had come to an end. Knox might readily be replaced; but Hamilton and Jefferson could never be. Opposed though they were on every political measure and fundamentally divergent in concepts of government and the relation of man to man, in their respective ways they had towered above the surrounding scene. Through their very divergences and quarrels they had managed to create a nation where none had existed before. Driven first one way and then another by their almost equal and opposite pressures, the United States appeared to obey the vectorial laws of physics and steady itself on a compromise course between the two extremes.

CHAPTER 19

Jay Makes a Treaty

W HILE THE Whiskey Rebellion was engaging the attention of the nation, a different and bloodier war raged in the Northwest; this one with an alien enemy.

For several years intermittent expeditions had gone forth against the hostile Indian tribes, and each had ended in disaster or inglorious stalemate. Now, for the first time, a capable general was placed in command of the frontier—Anthony Wayne. His daring exploits during the Revolution, and seeming recklessness, had earned him the admiring if equivocal soubriquet of "mad." Actually, Wayne was neither reckless nor mad; and his most foolhardy assaults usually ended in victory.

Before Wayne had quite established himself, the Indians took the offensive and attempted a surprise attack on Fort Recovery in July 1794. They were beaten back with heavy losses; but Wayne reported some disturbing information to the administration. Sharp questioning of captured Indians indicated that the British had actively instigated the attack and were promising the tribes that they would join them in an all-out war on the United States.[1]

At the same time Governor Simcoe of Upper Canada was brazenly demanding that the Americans withdraw from their own lands near the Canadian border. The juxtaposition of the two reports roused Washington. "This may be considered as the most open and daring act of the British Agents in America," he exploded. It was not sufficient, he instructed Jay, who had already arrived in England, that the agents be disavowed. They must be punished. Unless British intrigues with the Indians ceased, and the posts—from which the intrigues emanated—were promptly given up, war was inevitable.[2]

While Washington was fulminating war on this side of the ocean, the injury was being compounded with subtle insult on the other. Lord Grenville graciously tendered to Jay the disinterested services

333

of Great Britain as a mediator between the United States and the tribes. The unwitting Jay might have accepted the offer had his instructions in any way covered the point; but he had sense enough to realize that his volunteer acceptance would stir up a storm against him at home. Thereupon Grenville wrote to Hammond to discuss the business confidentially with Hamilton without the knowledge of the Secretary of State. If Hamilton also were disinclined for fear of the public wrath, then he could be told that the arrangement might be made in secret and its terms communicated only to Simcoe for action. What Grenville was particularly anxious to effectuate was a buffer Indian state between the Americans and Canada prior to the time when the British would be compelled to evacuate the posts.[3]

Nothing could have been more certain than that Hamilton—or, for that matter, anyone in the American government—would have indignantly repudiated any such arrangement. But an event intervened which dissuaded Hammond from even making the attempt.

With the knowledge of British intrigue gained from his captives, Wayne decided on a bold move which would destroy the Indian power, though at the risk of finding himself at war with the British. His entire force, partly Regular soldiers and partly mounted Kentucky volunteers, consisted of only nine hundred men. Nevertheless he plunged with them into the wilderness and headed by forced marches directly for the log walls and shotted cannon of the fort which Simcoe, in defiance of American protests, had erected on the Miami River in the vicinity of Detroit.

He came suddenly upon the clearing about the intruding fortifications and found strong bands of Indian warriors encamped in the field, seemingly secure in the protection of the British and the intervening wilderness. The alarm was sounded, militia and volunteers rushed down from Detroit to join the surprised Indians, while the British guns of the fort trained threateningly on the invading Americans.

Wayne did not hesitate. On August 20, 1794, he hurled his little army against the combined enemy, who outnumbered him more than two to one, with the added threat of the garrisoned fort in the rear. The headlong charge of the Americans drove the allies with heavy slaughter right up to the walls and guns of the fort. Broken and beaten, the Indians fled in every direction. Their power was smashed, and the prestige of both Indians and the protecting British, fled with them and vanished.

The American losses were heavy; 166 men were dead and 84 were wounded. The enemy losses could obviously not be accurately assayed; but Wayne estimated that they doubled those of the victors.

The Battle of Fallen Timbers can be counted as one of the decisive battles of American history. It marked a turning point in American-Indian relations and opened up a vast new country into which settlers could thereafter venture in comparative safety.

Wayne had counted the costs of his daring blow. He had been prepared, if need be, at the first sign of direct intervention in the fighting by the British garrison to storm the fort itself. For three days after the rout of the Indians he camped outside the walls, while his men sedulously destroyed every Indian village and cornfield in the neighborhood. As a final disdainful gesture, fire was set to the buildings owned by Colonel McKee, "the British Indian agent, and principal stimulator," in Wayne's own language, "of the war now existing between the United States and the savages." Behind their walls and within a bare pistol shot, the British "were compelled to remain tacit spectators to this general devastation and conflagration." [4]

Major Campbell, the British commander of the post, dispatched an angry note to Wayne demanding to know the purpose of his presence and behavior. Wayne retorted that the answer ought to have been plainly read in the thunder of his guns and his victory over the Indians. Then he turned the tables with a demand of his own that the British remove from American soil. Campbell not only refused but threatened to fire on the Americans. Wayne contemptuously disregarded the warning, and kept his men ostentatiously in open view and range of the fuming British. Had the English fired, he afterward said, he would have ordered an immediate assault.[5]

Eventually and with considerable reluctance, Wayne fell back to his original base, particularly since the period of enlistment of the Kentucky volunteers had expired. Even though he praised their conduct as excellent, Wayne believed it a mistaken policy to employ volunteers instead of Regular troops. Without an adequate establishment of Regulars, he declared, "we have fought, bled, and conquered, in vain." [6]

Knox, with his resignation as Secretary of War already in the President's hands, tried to survey the Indian situation from a more statesmanlike standpoint. For years he had fought in vain against the suspicions of Congress and the country in the matter of increasing the Regular Army, and he knew only too well that further efforts for the present would be futile.

But he also objected strenuously to the usual outcries against the Indians. In his final report as Secretary, Knox asserted again, as he had so many times in the past, that the blame for the troubles lay in the constant encroachments, "by force or fraud," of the frontier whites on the Indian lands. If any of these whites happened to be slain by the resentful tribes, revenge followed fast, and the customary war of extermination. Rarely, if ever, he remarked, was a white man punished for murdering an Indian.

"It is a melancholy reflection," he submitted, "that our modes of population have been more destructive to the Indian natives than the conduct of the conquerors of Mexico and Peru."

He could only suggest as remedial measures the erection of a string of forts along the border which should constitute federal jurisdiction; and the making of mutual treaties with the Indians for the prompt and effectual punishment of any outrages or invasions on either side.[7]

Knox was a lone voice crying in the wilderness. The irresistible movements of the people, the gathering population pressure in the East, the ineradicable desire for more and more lands, could not be stayed by any one man or group of men. The Indians were doomed.

But at least there was temporary peace as a result of Wayne's victory. He forced a treaty on his beaten foes which established an advanced boundary in their territory and obtained the cession of border lands sufficient for a chain of American posts. At the same time, farther to the east and under more peaceful auspices, Timothy Pickering as Indian agent arranged a treaty with the powerful Six Nations and their allies.

With quiet restored in the Northwest and Northeast, only the Southwest remained as a source of irritation and danger.

John Jay arrived in London on June 15, 1794, to begin his delicate negotiation. That there was little chance of succeeding fully in carrying out his instructions, no one realized better than he. Nor did the outbursts of hatred for England and denunciations of himself and his mission which filled the Republican press and were brought by every ship from the United States, do anything to improve his chances.

One reported incident particularly incensed the British; even though Jay himself might have considered there was ample provocation for the deed. A schooner sailed into Boston harbor from the Barbados. At her masthead floated the British ensign and in her hold was a cargo of sugar for the account of Stephen Higginson, Boston merchant and sound Federalist.

But the loungers on the wharves recognized the schooner as the property of a Mr. Brown of Newburyport which, on a former voyage, had been captured by the British, condemned and sold to a Barbadian. Promptly the cry was raised and "the Jacobins" of Boston, as Higginson termed them, gathered a mob which boarded the vessel, drove the British crew overboard, cut the rigging and tore down the sails. They would have gone much further had not a magistrate and some hastily assembled Federalists come up in time to halt the proceedings.

Higginson, whose cargo was thus threatened with destruction, spluttered angrily that the mob action was intended as a deliberate "insult to the British, to serve as an engine to counteract the arrangements of the President" and to defeat the mission on which Jay had gone.[8]

There were other incidents as well. In New York, for example, attempts were made by those who had suffered losses on the high seas from British seizures to hold the naval officers who had made the captures personally responsible whenever they ventured to land in the city.

In spite of these irritants, however, had Jay but known it, he had come to London at a peculiarly propitious time. The British had suffered a bad defeat at Toulon and the war in general was not going well for them. In addition, a new power rose to dispute their hitherto unchallenged dominion of the seas.

The Scandinavian countries, Denmark and Sweden, both neutrals and both naval powers, whose trade had suffered heavily from the British Orders in Council, joined in a convention to assert by "armed neutrality" the doctrine of the freedom of the seas. To strengthen their position they invited other aggrieved neutrals to join with them in alliance.

On April 26, 1794, before Jay arrived on the scene, the Swedish minister in London handed Pinckney a copy of the convention and inquired whether the United States would be willing to join in it. Pinckney thought favorably of the idea and wrote home for official instructions.

Aware of what was taking place under their very noses, the British government was alarmed. A solid front of all neutral powers, including the United States, represented a formidable threat. A letter was immediately dispatched to Hammond ordering him to prevent at any cost the accession of the United States to the convention of the Baltic powers. Even those three countries, without any further additions, would mean the entry of a third force in an already complicated picture. They represented the chief sources for England's desperately needed lumber and naval stores, and they were also her best customers for her manufactures.

In the nick of time, from the British point of view, Jay arrived to supersede Pinckney. They knew the veteran Pinckney distrusted them; Jay might prove more amenable.

Meanwhile, Pinckney's note and the accompanying convention arrived in Philadelphia to receive the earnest attention of the Cabinet. The thought of such an alliance of "armed neutrality" had already crossed the minds of the administration. Indeed, Jay's instructions, drafted by Hamilton and fathered by Randolph, had specifically directed him to sound Sweden and Denmark out on just such a plan. But now that it was discovered that the Scandinavian powers had taken the initiative, the Cabinet retreated in some confusion.

Hamilton, Knox and Bradford joined in denouncing the idea. Bradford thought that, since the Baltic nations were already committed, there was no need for the United States to bind herself. Hamilton believed that the two nations were too weak to be of any strength to us, and that the Americans "had better stand on their own ground." Knox for his part dreaded "being linked in with the follies or vices of European powers," and said that we ought to travel alone. In any event, he added, let us wait to see what Jay can accomplish before unduly irritating England.[9]

Only Randolph dissented. He pointed out that Jay had already been authorized to discuss this very item with the Baltic nations, and he should be permitted in his discretion to do so. The convention, he argued, could be kept dangling against the day that England proved hostile, and would provide us with allies. As for Knox's fear of English reprisals, Randolph was certain that only the French successes had kept her from warring on us long ago.[10]

Both his protests and his arguments proved vain. Washington followed the advice of the majority and it was decided to turn the proposal down. For the final decision there were perhaps excellent grounds. It enunciated for the first time the principle which Washington was later to make famous in his Farewell Address—that the United States must stand alone and avoid entangling alliances with European powers.

But Hamilton eliminated any possibility that the "Armed Neutrality Pact," whether America entered it or not, could be employed as a bargaining point with England. Pursuant to his instructions, Hammond had sought out the Secretary of the Treasury as his first and best approach to the administration, and was immediately rewarded with a piece of the most amazing and gratuitous information. Responding to tactful prodding and an atmosphere of warm good-fellowship, Hamilton promptly gave away the whole show. "With great seriousness and with every demonstration of sincerity," he informed Hammond that "it was the settled policy of this Government in every contingency, even in that of an open contest with Great Britain, to avoid entangling itself with European connexions, which could only tend to involve this country in disputes wherein it might have no possible interest, and commit it in a common cause with allies, from whom, in the moment of danger, it could derive no succour." Then, to make certain that Hammond could not possibly misunderstand what he was referring to, Hamilton mentioned by name Sweden and Denmark.[11]

The delighted minister immediately sent off the vital information by fast packet to Grenville. That noble and subtle lord, after he perused the dispatch, smiled in profound satisfaction.[12] Now he knew exactly how to handle the unwitting emissary of the United States, John Jay.

Already Grenville had carefully planned his course of action. He had welcomed the envoy with every show of cordiality and showered every conceivable attention and flattery upon him. Jay was dazzled. His first reports home glowed and coruscated: everyone spoke of the United States in terms of the highest respect; everyone treated him with the greatest friendliness. Then a small disturbing note began to appear in his dispatches. Though Grenville was the soul of courtesy, and the conferences between them were conducted in a spirit of good feeling, the noble lord managed to say nothing decisive and did not commit himself on any point.[13]

A month later the two representatives of their respective countries were still talking. The tiny doubt in Jay's mind grew somewhat larger. "I know the impatience that must prevail in our country," he acknowledged. "At times, I find it difficult to repress my own impatience."

Actually, the only issue on which they had come to an agreement—if it might be called one—was Governor Simcoe's incursion into American territory. Pending further discussions, so ran the agreement, both sides would maintain the status quo in the wilderness.[14] But this in fact was a British victory; for Simcoe was in possession and the Americans wanted him out.

Grenville had reason to be satisfied with the negotiation. He was achieving his main purpose—to mark time and hold off the Americans from taking any drastic action until the world situation clarified itself. The British were gradually recovering from the blow they had suffered at Toulon, their government ministry was being reshuffled for greater strength and unity at home, and Jay showed no signs of doing the one thing Grenville feared—conferring with the Baltic powers. Jay, indeed, though still uninformed of the change of heart on "armed neutrality" in the American Cabinet, had no intention of following his original instructions on that point.[15]

Nor did Jay press unduly on the British certain other articles of his instructions. He privately believed that the British were justified in retaining the posts as long as the Americans failed to pay the prewar debts. He also felt that the so-called abduction of the Negro slaves at the end of the war was a humanitarian act which, though technically in violation of the treaty, ought not to be held strongly against them. He had maintained these positions in a report to the Continental Congress when he had been Secretary of Foreign Affairs. Though the report was supposedly confidential and not to be published, Jay had then graciously disclosed its contents to Sir John Temple, the British consul; with the natural result that Grenville now knew just where Jay stood on these two vital issues.[16]

It is obvious therefore that Grenville, possessed of this knowledge, would not be disposed to yield a jot or tittle in the current negotiation, and could safely count on a powerful ally in the inner recesses of Jay's own mind. What constantly amazes in any examination of early American diplomacy is the complete freedom with which responsible members of the American government laid bare the innermost secrets of American intentions to the representatives of foreign powers. Nor was it confined to the Federalists alone. If Hamilton, Jay, Wolcott and Federalists in Congress gave out confidential information to British agents, Jefferson, Randolph, Monroe and other Republicans were equally obliging with the French.

By August 8th, however, both parties began to see a glimmer of light ahead. Jay reported that he expected something definite within a fortnight. On the same day Grenville wrote Hammond that the conversations pointed to an early solution. He was ready to yield, he said, on the issue of the condemnations of American ships at Martinique. Since the British had no vice-admiralty court on that island, whatever proceedings had been taken there must be void. He expressed satisfaction with Jay as an amenable sort of man. Since Edmund Randolph had proved himself most "unfriendly," Grenville instructed Hammond to reply no more to any of his complaints, but to refer all matters to the negotiation in London with Jay.[17]

Grenville was as good as his word on the matter of the illegal condemnations. He caused instructions to be sent to all British naval officers abrogating the Order of June 8, 1793, which declared provisions to be contraband. He even sent a reprimand to Dorchester for his speech to the Indians prophesying war.

But at this point all concessions ended; or rather, Jay was only too ready to yield his positions before they were even attacked. A preliminary draft of a treaty which Jay drew up to serve as a basis for discussion ignored the matter of compensation for the Negro slaves entirely. As for the posts, though these were to be evacuated some time after the signing of a treaty, Jay made no demand for damages for the long detention.[18]

On August 6th Grenville received the draft. He surveyed the specifications which Jay had included—boundaries, a hands-off policy with the Indians, and neutral rights. Calmly the British minister wrote across them a proposal of his own—a demand that the United States cede to England a large stretch of territory in the Northwest which would in effect validate all previous British aggressions in that area and place the valuable fur trade entirely in their hands.

On receipt of this exorbitant demand Jay lost his head. His alarm and anxiety were so great that he did exactly what Grenville had expected him to do. He concentrated his protests so vehemently on this point alone that he dropped consideration of all others. Grenville thereupon played him skillfully along on this single issue, yielding a trifle, then stiffening and finally becoming adamant when Hammond's illuminating information that the United States would not become a party to the Armed Neutrality Pact reached him on September 20th.

Almost frantic with fear that the whole negotiation would fail on the rock of this demand—which he realized was wholly impossible from any American standpoint—Jay was by this time ready to accept practically every other British demand if they receded on this one. He made one last attempt, however, to adhere to his instructions. On September 30th he submitted another treaty draft, which covered every point of the American position *except* the abducted slaves and damages for the retention of the posts.[19]

When Grenville coldly refused to consider it, Jay immediately backed down. He was determined at all hazards to bring home a treaty of sorts. For the failure of his mission would spell disaster to the administration and the Federalist party.[20] He therefore indicated that he would settle for much less; and on November 17th the terms of a treaty were finally agreed on.

This treaty was certainly not what Jay had been instructed to obtain. Compensation for the Negroes and damages for the posts were conspicuous by their absence. There was no mention of the British incitement of the Indians or of the threat to use them in time of war. The long-fought-for contention that free ships made free goods was dismissed without a word. The complaints over British impressment of American seamen and British right of search were similarly overlooked. And the all-important question of the West Indies trade, which Hamilton himself had insisted was a *sine qua non* of the entire negotiation, was mentioned only to be subjected to such restrictions that it could be considered only, and was so considered, as an insult.

What was actually present in the final treaty was a mixture of the weakly good and the definitely bad.

The chief good lay almost wholly in Article 2, which provided for the evacuation of the posts by Great Britain. Yet even this was qualified by provisions which gave England until June 1, 1796, to comply, and granted British settlers and traders already within the precincts permission to remain.

Article 3 could be counted on to evoke a storm of resentment from the West. It gave the citizens and Indians of both nations the right of free passage in the territories of each other, free navigation of all waters in both areas and full privileges of trade and commerce except in seaports and river mouths. Especially bad from the American viewpoint, the Mississippi was "to be entirely open to both parties" in its full length.

Articles 4 and 5 called for the determination of northern boundary lines through further negotiation or by means of a joint commission.

Article 6 was written wholly for England's benefit. It declared that all debts to the British which had depreciated or become uncollectable because of legal impediments interposed by the states were to be lumped in full and paid by the United States, without offsets of any kind.

Article 7 provided for an eventual determination of losses sustained by American ships, cargoes and persons as the result of irregular or illegal British acts; but this was offset by a provision giving damages to the British for their losses from French activities within the jurisdiction and coastal waters of the United States.

Article 12, however, eventually overshadowed all others in the public eye. This related to the West Indies trade. It granted American ships the right to carry American goods to the British West Indies, *provided* the tonnage of the carrying ship did not exceed seventy tons; a capacity which barely fitted the smaller descriptions of fishing smacks. Ships of this minute tonnage could also carry goods out of the islands, *provided* they were destined only for the United States.

In exchange for these munificent privileges, this country agreed to prohibit its own ships of all sizes from the carriage to the rest of the world from both the West Indies and the United States of molasses, sugar, coffee, cocoa and cotton. Meanwhile, *British* ships were to be permitted to trade between the islands and the United States on an equality with American ships, and without any restrictions on size.

Other articles provided a limited trade by the United States with the British East Indies, and reciprocal trade between the United States and the British dominions in Europe. There was also a provision for most favored nation rights; in exchange for which this country agreed not to increase the existing tonnage taxes on British ships.

Article 18 raised a storm equal to that of the notorious Article 12. For it gave the British the right to declare foodstuffs and provisions a contraband of war, and to seize them on payment of the purchase price to the original owners.[21] The ground was thereby cut completely away from the innumerable previous protests of the American government, and gave France, the chief victim, an immediate cause for bitter recriminations over the surrender.

In general the treaty as Jay finally signed it must be considered

a very bad one. It brought to the United States nothing except an
agreement to surrender the posts at a distant date. It yielded everything else for which the American government had fought since its
inception to the British. About all that could be said in its favor was
that, no matter how bad in particulars, it brought temporary peace
to the country and saved it from the disasters of an immediate war
with England.

Jay was not wholly blinded to the deficiencies of his treaty nor
to the fact that there would be trouble at home when its contents
became known. He wrote cautiously to Randolph that "I have no
reason to believe or conjecture that one more favorable to us is at-
tainable." [22]

To Hamilton he was much more frank. His task was done, he
said. But "whether finis *coronat* opus, the President, Senate, and public, will decide." Let the treaty be ratified and published as quickly
as possible, he warned, lest troublemakers have a chance to mislead
the public. "If this treaty fails," he concluded uneasily, "I despair of
another." [23]

The mails across the Atlantic sometimes took months; so that often
people wrote at cross-purposes and in reply to points that had already
vanished. While the treaty was making its slow passage to America,
Randolph was dispatching a series of sharp rejoinders to Jay's previous
intimations on the Negroes and the posts, and insisting that he stand
by his instructions.[24] How was he to know that both matters had
already been settled beyond recall?

Jay retorted from London with some vehemence that it took two
to make a bargain; that the British were adamant on the Negroes,
and that the admission to the West Indies trade was compensation
enough both for the slaves and the detention of the posts.[25]

By this time, however, the entire question of the treaty had moved
into the realm of American politics, where it stirred up passions and
strife of an appalling magnitude.

The report that Jay had signed a treaty with England reached the
shores of France much before it traveled to the United States. James
Monroe had assumed his post as minister with eager anticipations.
To him, as to most radical Republicans, France was the lodestar of
the world, the fount of true democracy and equality, the sole make-
weight against the kings and tyrants of Europe. Convinced that the
revolution had taken the wrong turn in the United States through

the machinations of Anglophile Federalists, he looked to France to assist the "people" of America to counteract and eventually overthrow them.

Monroe landed in France early in August 1794, and hastened immediately to Paris. He arrived at an inopportune time. Robespierre had fallen and had been hurried to that guillotine to which he had sent so many others. The "incorruptible" hope of the world was now denounced as a monster and his fellow Jacobins accused as traitors.

For once the impetuous Monroe hesitated. He did not know on what ground Americans stood at this decisive moment. Though he despised Gouverneur Morris, whom he was replacing, protocol nevertheless compelled him to wait for Morris's formal presentation of him to the Committee of Public Safety.

Ten days passed without a word from the Committee; whereupon Monroe decided on an audacious move. On August 14th he appeared suddenly and dramatically before the general Convention, mounted the rostrum and delivered a speech of the most impassioned fervor to the startled assemblage.

France and America, he cried, are allies; twin republics who have met dangers together and surmounted them together. "America had her day of oppression, difficulty, and war," he declared; "but her sons were virtuous and brave," and they triumphed. Monroe flung out his arms to the Convention. "France, our ally and our friend, and who aided in the contest," he exclaimed, "has now embarked in the same noble career; and, I am happy to add, that whilst the fortitude, magnanimity and heroic valor of her troops command the admiration and applause of the astonished world, the wisdom and firmness of her councils unite equally in securing the happiest result."

The result indeed was all that Monroe could have wished. The Convention rose as one man; cries of *"Vive la République!"* thundered on every side; the President of the assembly rushed over to the American to embrace and kiss him on both cheeks amid "universal acclamations of joy, delight and admiration."

At one stroke Monroe had made himself *persona grata* and the idol of France. Within two hours the hitherto dilatory Committee of Public Safety hastened to receive this oratorical representative from the sister republic across the seas.[26]

Elsewhere, however, Monroe's effusions were received in a different vein. He had expected that his speech would be "scanned with unfriendly eyes by many in America." He was prepared for Federalist outcries as a small price for his success in overcoming French distrust. He was *not* prepared for the stinging rebuke administered by the Secretary of State. After all, Randolph was still supposed to be a Republican, even though something of a "trimmer."

The text of Monroe's speech came to the United States in the form of reports in the French newspapers. Randolph read it with anger and dismay, particularly after repercussions followed immediately from England. In strong language Randolph told Monroe that the nations at war with France had viewed in a most unkindly light the laudation by Monroe of French might and triumphs. It would have been much better, said Randolph, for Mr. Monroe, the public representative of the United States, to have been more restrained. There was nothing in his instructions, the Secretary of State concluded sarcastically, to impose on him "the extreme glow of some parts of your address." [27]

But, again, it was six months before the rebuke reached Monroe; and by that time events in France had proceeded at a gallop; so that, even if the minister had wished it, it was too late to correct the initial error.

Even so, Monroe himself discovered shortly that some of the effervescent glow had already departed. Within a few weeks after the acclamations, the *vives* and the embracements, he was in duty compelled to enter a formal protest with the Committee of Public Safety against the French seizures of American vessels carrying mixed cargoes of American and British goods. Such seizures, Monroe asserted, violated the provisions of the treaty between France and the United States. The French retorted that they were retaliating against American supineness in the face of similar seizures by the British in which French goods were involved. The case was *not* similar, insisted Monroe. We have a treaty with you covering the point; we have no such treaty with England.[28]

Monroe carried his point. By the beginning of 1795 the Convention unanimously decided to forbid further seizures and to adhere strictly to the treaty. But by this time another cloud had already appeared on the horizon, soon to reach enormous proportions. The first reports of Jay's treaty filtered across the Channel, distorted in the telling to an outright alliance of offense and defense between America and Great Britain.[29]

For the exaggerated rumors the extreme secrecy in which the treaty contents were wrapped was largely responsible. Randolph had con-

sidered the whole mission "illusory" and had previously written to
Monroe that it was therefore indispensable to "keep the French republic in good humor" against the day when America might need
her for an ally against England.[30]

Monroe required no such advice; in fact, he had already too diligently won France over. But now, with a treaty actually in being,
developments came thick and fast. Monroe found himself mightily
embarrassed with his new French friends, who suspected that there
was more to the treaty than a mere settlement of disputes.[31]

It was five days after the actual signing that Jay dilatorily announced it to Monroe, together with an assurance that it "expressly
declares that nothing contained in it shall be construed or operate
contrary to existing treaties between the United States and other
Powers." [32] And it was three days later that he promised Monroe a
confidential summary of the terms of the treaty.[33]

Monroe, however, wanted more than a mere confidential summary.
He wished to see the treaty entire, and to be able to show it to the
French as evidence that there was nothing in it that might prove
harmful to their interests. Jay refused either to send the full treaty
or permit any disclosure of its terms to the French, on the ground that
until it was ratified "it would be improper to publish it." [34]

Monroe stormed and pleaded; but Jay was adamant and, not trust-
ing his colleague in Paris, finally failed to send even the summary he
had promised. Monroe's position became more embarrassing than
ever. The French openly insinuated that the reason he did not show
them a copy of the treaty was because it was actually a treaty of
alliance. In a rage the harassed minister dispatched a bitter complaint to Randolph against Jay's ungracious tactics.[35]

He was not to see the treaty for seven long months—and then
only when the text appeared in the newspapers. Mortified and smarting under the insult, Monroe nevertheless managed to hold the
French in line and prevent them from taking the retaliatory action
they threatened. When he finally succeeded in allaying their resentment and brought Franco-American relations back to an amicable
footing, he was recalled—so he insisted—in order to give the glory
to another and to lay the blame on him for the previous failure.[36]

Monroe was not alone in his difficulties over the singular secrecy
that cloaked the treaty. Because of it, Edmund Randolph at home was
overwhelmed with tirades and belligerent declamations by Fauchet.
Gone was the French minister's former placid and friendly disposition.

His complaints and insults now vied with the best—or worst—that Genêt had ever offered.

The French, he complained, were being persecuted by America because of "the servile submission" of American agents to the demands of the King of England; while British warships were bringing French prizes into American ports on specious claims of emergencies with American connivance.[37] So thoroughly obnoxious did he become that even Randolph, with whom he had been on the most confidential terms, finally declared his communications to be "indecent" and proposed to lay down "new rules with respect to foreign ministers in general, and prevent them from meddling, as they do, in our internal affairs." [38]

Fauchet was finally recalled in 1795, after having done almost as much harm to French interests in the United States as his predecessor. The disgusted Secretary of State realized he had been made a tool of, and that Fauchet had been secretly plotting all during his stay with the enemies of the administration.[39] In his revulsion he turned even against his former friends, the American Francophiles, who were forever crying from the housetops how badly glorious France was being treated by the United States.[40]

The unfortunate Secretary did not realize that a much worse blow was to befall him; that prior to his departure Fauchet had laid a train which was to explode him higher than any petard.

The second session of the Third Congress convened in November 1794, and was addressed by the President on November 19th. This time Washington abandoned his usual recital of platitudes and generalizations to deal specifically with recent events. Still smarting under the personal attacks of the Democratic Societies and the outbreak of the Whiskey Rebellion, he now minced no words.

The rebellion had been crushed, he reported; due largely to the efforts of "the most and the least wealthy of our citizens standing in the same ranks, as private soldiers." That spectacle, it would seem, impressed him mightily, for he was to return to the congenial theme again and again. Then he turned to a sharp and bitter attack on the Democratic Societies themselves. In unprecedented language he castigated them as "self-created societies" which had sedulously fostered the rebellion and given it aid and comfort.[41]

The speech, its tone and undisguised hostility, its contemptuous references to the Societies and his curious characterization of them, first dismayed and alarmed and then infuriated the Republicans. Now thoroughly convinced that the President was altogether in the camp of their enemies, and fearful of his vast popularity with the people, the Republicans reacted with extreme violence. Whatever inhibitions had previously restrained them vanished, and the personal abuse they poured on him rose to new heights.

Their press retorted that "presuming guilt by construction and implication is as dangerous a principle as can be introduced into society." As for "self-created societies," were not others which Washington had not attacked, like the Scottish groups, Tammany, the Masons, and even the Society of the Cincinnati, equally "self-created?" [42]

From his mountain retreat at Monticello, Jefferson termed the speech "one of the most extraordinary acts of boldness of which we have seen so many from the fraction of monocrats. It is wonderful indeed, that the President should have permitted himself to be the organ of such an attack on the freedom of discussion, the freedom of writing, printing and publishing." [43]

Jefferson would have been even more vehement had he known that the instigator had been the erstwhile Republican Edmund Randolph. "I never did see an opportunity of destroying these self-constituted bodies," the Secretary of State had written to Washington a month earlier, "until the fruit of their operations was disclosed in the insurrection of Pittsburg. . . . They may now, I believe, be crushed. The prospect ought not to be lost." [44]

Congress heard the speech with emotions regulated strictly by partisan politics; the Federalists with approbation and delight, the Republicans with alarm and wrath.

The Senate, Federalist by a slim margin, responded first. Their reply to the address echoed almost verbatim its phraseology. Burr, seconded by Jackson of Georgia (whom a grateful state had rewarded for his services in the lower House with an appointment to the Senate) sought in vain to expunge the obnoxious phrases from the reply, but failed on a strictly party vote.[45]

In the House, where the Republicans held the edge, the fireworks started first on the reference to Jay's mission. The proposed reply contained an approval of the administration's foreign policy. Dayton, the *soi-disant* Federalist, again deserted his party with the remark that he "knew not why the envoy had been sent to Europe. He did not know what were his instructions, and he never would approve, or say that he approved, of what he did not know." [46]

The more cautious Madison called for an amendment which would express a generalized approval of "a policy in our foreign transactions" which would never lose sight of the blessings of peace. Hillhouse of Connecticut and Jeremiah Smith of New Hampshire promptly proposed to substitute *your* in place of the evasive *a* as the modifier of the word "policy" so that it would apply specifically to Washington. Dayton objected violently to the change, evoking in turn some bitter comments from Ames on his "habits of jealousy." The discussion thus taking on a personal flavor, Madison was prevailed on to withdraw his amendment. [47]

With one controversial issue temporarily tabled, Fitzsimons of Pennsylvania brought up the even more controversial issue of the Democratic Societies. He called on the House to insert a denunciation of the Societies in the reply. Giles was immediately on his feet with the by now classic retort. What individual in America, he inquired, is *not* a member of some "self-created" society? There were Baptists, Methodists, Quakers; there were dozens of political and philosophical organizations. Why, he added with a meaning look, "if the House were to censure the Democratic societies, they might do the same by the Cincinnati Society." [48]

William Smith of South Carolina ridiculed these analogies. No other society, he declared, held "nocturnal meetings of individuals, after they had dined, where they shut their doors, pass votes in secret, and admit no members into their societies but those of their own choosing." Has the House, he asked in a lumbering attempt at humor, ever "done much business after dinner"? [49]

Fitzsimons finally softened his resolution to a mere echoing of the presidential phrases; but this did not satisfy the aroused Republicans. Giles proposed that instead of the obnoxious generalization concerning "self-created societies" a specific reference be made to the "Democratic societies of Philadelphia, New York and Pittsburg." But Nicholas, also of Virginia, took issue with his colleague. Those Societies, he asserted, had never been given an opportunity to defend themselves. It was no crime, he said, to criticize the government. It was the *nature* of these societies "to watch the errors of the Legislative and Executive, and point out to the public what they considered to be mistakes." [50]

Giles's amendment was adopted by a close vote of 47 to 45. Encouraged by this narrowing of the issue, he next offered another amendment to narrow it still further to "the four Western counties of Pennsylvania." But his strategy temporarily backfired. Instead of agreeing to it, the Federalists tried rather to add them to the original list. Even the obnoxious term "self-created" was restored to the resolution; and it was only after much further maneuvering, aided by the casting vote of the Speaker, that the Republicans were able to confine the entire censure to the four western counties.[51]

With this limited victory the Republicans perforce had to be content. Madison himself acknowledged that it was the best they could hope for in a most critical situation. To him the whole business was a deep-laid Federalist plot to maneuver the Republicans into "an ostensible opposition to the President" and "an *ostensible* patronage" of the Societies and the Whiskey Rebellion. Thereby the Federalists hoped to gain the forthcoming spring elections. Time alone will tell, added Madison gloomily, if they have succeeded.[52]

Washington and the Federalists gained a strange if unwitting ally in Monroe. He had come to France immediately following the collapse of the Jacobin party. Both Monroe and his fellow Republicans back home thereupon changed to the new party line which the French had established for them. The Jacobins, formerly hailed as patriots of purest ray serene, were now denounced in every Republican paper as enemies of their country. The once mighty Robespierre, hitherto the patron saint of revolution, was now an unmitigated monster. Their joint downfall and subsequent executions were hailed as the just reward for their enormous excesses—excesses, by the by, which the Republicans had previously defended passionately against Federalist attack.

In pursuance of this new tactic, Monroe wrote home to Randolph a long excoriation of the Jacobins and flatly stated that their club had worked incessantly to undermine the constituted government. "Moderate measures to check its enormities," he averred, "were found only a stimulus to greater excesses." It was with complete justification, therefore, that the Club had been ruthlessly suppressed.[53]

No more powerful ammunition could have been providentially placed in the hands of the administration. Were not the Democratic Societies of America self-avowedly modeled on the Jacobin Society of France? Had not some of them become the adopted children of the parent organization? Had they not also sought to undermine the constituted authorities and fostered armed rebellion against them?

Randolph caused selected extracts from these damning communications to be published in the Philadelphia papers as coming from "a gentleman in Paris to his friend in this city." No one was deceived. Both Republicans and Federalists attributed them to Monroe; and Madison besought him in rather cryptic language—in case of miscarriage of the letter—to be more discreet in the future.[54]

Bache's paper, now in the process of transformation from the *General Advertiser* to the *Aurora,* nevertheless continued to defend the Societies at home while applauding the extermination of the Jacobins in France. The latter, Bache reasoned tortuously, was actually an attempt by the government to "perpetuate the popular societies, by purging them of the abuses which have crept into these salutory institutions."[55] Contemporary analogies to events of the past are usually dangerous, but the modern observer cannot fail to be struck by the startling resemblance at times of incidents such as this to those with which he is currently familiar.

The main body of the American people was unconvinced by the apologetics of Bache and his fellow extremists. The weight of Washington's displeasure, the denunciations by Congress, the general aversion to the rebellion, and the turn of recent events in France, placed the Societies under a cloud. Their own intemperate language and agile following of every twist of the French party line brought their own reaction. The more moderate and prudent of the members resigned. The radical enthusiasts clung to the vine for some time longer; but eventually the Societies withered and died.

No doubt with them died a measure of free speech and the right of public criticism. Certainly Washington's denunciations of them had been expressed in improper language; but the Societies had forfeited the sympathy of the American people by their own immoderateness, their gross libels and their slavish adherence to a foreign power.

They served ill the cause of democracy and liberty they pretended to defend, and paved the way for the very reaction they sought to combat. Their suppression by mere denunciation and the force of public opinion proved the initial step for a later and more outrageous suppression by force of law in the Alien and Sedition Acts. Excess of any kind—if history can be held to teach any lesson—seems invariably to carry within it the seeds of its own destruction through an even more violent and opposite excess.

As a matter of fact the Federalists almost immediately moved into the opposite excess. They introduced resolutions in Congress to lengthen the period of naturalization and make its provisions more rigid. The ensuing debate disclosed some ugly prejudices in both camps. The Republican Giles attacked the French *émigrés* of noble birth in unmeasured terms. Samuel Dexter, a Federalist, countered with an equally violent diatribe against the Roman Catholics, whose "priestcraft," he asserted, "had done more damage than aristocracy." Baiting the Southern Republicans, he slyly proposed that aliens be not permitted to own slaves, and that they must also publicly declare that they hold "all men free and equal."

Madison sought to stem the tide of intolerance with the remark that there was nothing in the Catholic faith "inconsistent with the purest Republicanism"; while his Southern colleagues reacted wildly, if with less purity of motive, to the abolition proposal. In the end, as the debate took an ugly turn, Sedgwick rose to denounce roundly Dexter's amendment. "Here the slaves are," he cried, "and here they must remain."[56]

After this outburst by a conservative Massachusetts Federalist, the debate subsided into more decorous channels, and eventually a Naturalization Act was passed which provided for a residence of five years in the country and one year in the state as a requirement for citizenship. In addition, the applicant must take an oath of allegiance to the United States, renounce his former citizenship and titles, if any; and present evidence to the naturalizing court of his good moral character.[57] In its essentials, the Act is still operative today.

CHAPTER 20

"Tenor Indecent"

G ENERAL KNOX RESIGNED as Secretary of War at the end of 1794;
Hamilton quit the Treasury on January 31, 1795. With their
passing, and the earlier resignation of Jefferson, the Cabinet took on
a new and less vibrant complexion. Even Randolph, in the State Department, departed before the year came to a close.

Perplexed at the going of these great if controversial figures, Washington was hard put to it to find adequate substitutes; and in the end
was compelled to accept men of more pedestrian talents.

He elevated Oliver Wolcott, Jr., of Connecticut, who had served
acceptably as comptroller, to the head of the Treasury. Wolcott was
an industrious and conscientious official, and remained at the helm
throughout the Federalist period. He faithfully followed Hamilton's
basic policies and sought his advice whenever there was the slightest
doubt.

As his parting legacy before retiring, Hamilton submitted to the
Senate a blueprint for the ultimate extinction of the debt. He pointed
proudly to the surplus for the preceding year in the sum of $870,000,
which was available for debt redemption. This highly satisfactory
amount, he declared, was due to the additional duties which Congress
had levied on imports and tonnage; taxes on liquor sales, and excise
taxes; taxes on carriages and auctions; patent fees; and the profits
derived from the post office and from government stock in the Bank
of the United States.

A concluding paragraph of the report has a highly contemporary
ring. "To extinguish a debt which exists," wrote Hamilton, "and to
avoid the contracting more, are ideas always favored by public feeling
and opinion; but to pay taxes for the one or the other purpose, which
are the only means of avoiding the evil, is always, more or less, unpopular. These contradictions are in human nature. . . . Hence it is
no uncommon spectacle to see the same men clamoring for occasions

of expense . . . declaiming against a public debt, and for the reduction of it as an abstract thesis; yet vehement against every plan of taxation which is proposed to discharge old debts, or to avoid new, by the defraying expenses of exigencies as they emerge." [1]

For the War Department the President chose Timothy Pickering of Massachusetts, a former Army colonel, whose convictions were fixed, obstinate and deep-seated. The opposite of the easygoing Knox in almost every respect, he nevertheless agreed with him on the vital problem of the Indians. He had been sent on numerous occasions as commissioner to treat with suspicious or hostile tribes, and almost invariably his fair dealing had met with conspicuous success.

Himself poor, though hopeful of eventual riches through incessant land speculations, Pickering possessed every Federalist contempt for the common people and carried this attitude to extremes. Yet he proudly refused to accept a dinner invitation from Mrs. Bingham, the regnant social queen, because he could not afford to return the favor. [2]

Washington had earlier given him the office of Postmaster General, and he had done a good job in an arduous and thankless post. The heavy postal charges, the effective opposition of the states to every federal attempt to gain additional revenues by carrying passengers on the mail coaches, made it almost impossible to expand the service and create a better communications system.

When Randolph finally resigned from the State Department, Pickering was shifted to the more important post; there to remain almost to the end of the administration of John Adams, when he was incontinently dismissed for secretly subverting the policies of his superior.

William Bradford remained as Attorney General, a plodding, second-rate man whose death later in the year caused the appointment of Charles Lee, equally lacking in distinction. John Adams, surveying the scene from the doubtful elevation of the vice-presidency, mourned the passing of the gods. "The offices are once more full," he exclaimed. "But how differently filled than when Jefferson, Hamilton, Jay, &c. were here!" [3]

Hamilton's resignation was lamented in other quarters, though for different reasons. Hammond, the British minister, sincerely bewailed his going as depriving him of his best source of confidential information. Pickering he thought to be violently anti-British; wrongly so, as the sequel was to show. [4]

For all the furious party politics and the constant agitation of foreign and domestic issues, the country was in a remarkably healthy condition. The people addressed themselves to an almost immoderate extent to the making of money. Land values had more than doubled in the preceding three or four years; speculation was rampant (always a sign of easy money); and the merchants prospered in spite of the war abroad and the seizure and condemnation of so many of their ships and cargoes.

J. C. Constable, the great trading merchant of New York, was able to order an expensive pair of carriage horses from England, as well as a "Fashionable Chariot" of the most lavish design. It flaunted "patent wheels, handsome hammer cloth, lamps and spiral springs" shiny with brass. It sported conspicuously a coat of arms with three white roses reposing on a double shield. Beneath the window glass rode a painted ship in full sail, bearing the motto *fiat tot naufragia portus,* to commemorate the sources of his wealth.[5]

More significantly, the export figures disclose the prosperity of these years. In 1791, the country as a whole exported goods valued at $19,000,000 in round figures. By 1795 they had risen to almost $48,000,000; an increase of over 250 per cent.[6]

Since most of the exports were taken by Great Britain, it was no wonder that those who profited from the trade were adamant against any step that might tend to lessen or eliminate it entirely; while those who did not share in the profits—the inhabitants of Virginia, North Carolina and Georgia—were eager to seek customers other than England who might offer more lucrative markets for their agricultural produce.

A democratic leveling persisted throughout the land in spite of the alleged aristocratical leanings of the Federalists. European travelers were forever exclaiming with astonishment over the lack of classes in America. The stagecoachman sat down at the same inn table with his passengers. Conversation was free, frank and without servility. Americans were wont to stare at fastidious strangers who refused to sleep in the same bed with them or drink out of the same dirty glass.[7]

Americans displayed a healthy disrespect for their law courts and their judges. "They appear at the bar," asserted a perplexed European, "with their hats on their heads, talk, make a noise, smoke their pipes, and cry out at the sentences pronounced." Nor did they treat the Chief Justice of the United States with any greater deference. When he happened to walk into a tavern parlor while on circuit, the company paid no more attention to him than to "one of their negroes." [8]

Politics was the universal preoccupation of the day. At any public meeting place, in any private gathering, the talk was always of politics, and invariably ended in a quarrel. They continued their debates even when they crawled into the beds in the common room of an inn until, declared an amazed traveler, "at last sleep closed their eyes, and happily their mouths at the same time; for could they have talked in their sleep, I verily believe they would have prated on until morning." [9]

If such endless political discussion was perhaps a method of education, Americans did not omit more formal instruction. The system of free schools expanded rapidly, particularly in the New England states; and Washington proposed the establishment of a national university in the new capital, endowed in part with the gift of his own shares in the Potomac River Company. He believed that such an institution of higher learning would obviate the necessity for sending the youth of America abroad, where they imbibed principles "unfriendly to republican government." Also, by rubbing shoulders with other young men from every part of the country, they would tend to lose their local prejudices and imbibe a more national spirit.[10]

Jefferson was already beginning to plan his own university for Virginia. In one respect at least he was more parochial in his vision than Washington—he wanted to keep the youth of Virginia secluded from the prejudices which he claimed existed in the *Northern* colleges. Washington's plan never materialized; Jefferson's did.

The American press, however, which ought to have contributed to the political and intellectual education of the country, failed to fulfill any such essential function. Almost without exception, the newspapers were virulently partisan, prejudiced, localized in domestic news and filled with the most personal libels and inflammatory recriminations. To the ranks of these now came perhaps the most partisan and violent of them all. This was the notorious *Porcupine's Gazette*, edited and published by William Cobbett under the pseudonym of "Peter Porcupine." The appellation was exceedingly apt; for Cobbett's quill, like the porcupine's barbs, stuck in the flesh of the anguished victim and envenomed it with its poison.

Cobbett was an Englishman who remained an Englishman through all his years and activities in the United States. He left his native country under a cloud, but panted always for the day of his return.[11]

He landed in the United States in October 1792, possessed only of his scathing tongue and more virulent pen. Ironically, he first offered his talents to Jefferson, who, unfortunately for his party, failed to avail himself of the offer.[12]

Settling in Philadelphia, and struggling for a bare subsistence, Cobbett caught the public eye in 1794 with a polemic attack on Dr. Joseph Priestley, just arrived from England.

Priestley was a famous scientist whose discovery of oxygen as an element helped revolutionize chemistry; but in his day he was far better known for his unorthodox religious and political beliefs. In religion he was a freethinker; in politics an extreme radical who had openly supported France even at a time when his native England was at war with that country. As a result of his unpopular opinions, a mob burned his library and laboratory in Birmingham and compelled him to flee to London for safety. Here he continued his heterodox activities until the political and religious climate grew too warm for him. Thereupon he embarked for America in the company of another English radical, Dr. Thomas Cooper, with whom he hoped to establish "a large settlement for the friends of liberty" on the banks of the Susquehanna in Pennsylvania.[13]

The utopian plan did not materialize, though his arrival evoked a tremendous welcome from the Republicans and the enthusiastic regard of all liberal spirits. He became the close friend of Jefferson, of radical and Unitarian leaders; and he continued to write and preach the political and religious doctrines which had made him anathema in England.

Cobbett, however, hailed his arrival in a different vein. A transplanted champion of his native country, a hater of democracy and of what he was pleased to call "atheism," Cobbett's welcome to his fellow Englishman was embodied in a series of viciously excoriating pamphlets.[14]

With his porcupine's quill thus properly fleshed, Cobbett decided on the publication of a newspaper. The *Porcupine's Gazette* achieved notoriety almost over night. The Federalists adopted it as their own because of its barbed assaults on the Republicans and France. They failed to note the undercurrent of contempt for all things American and the laudation of all things British. Even the Federalists, in spite of their support, were not immune from his squibs; the one man whom he handled tenderly was Alexander Hamilton.

Eventually his libelous attacks on all and sundry rebounded on his head. Dr. Benjamin Rush sued and obtained a substantial judgment and, to avoid a debtor's prison, Cobbett fled first to New York and then back to England. Safe in his native country, he cast off all disguise and poured the vials of his contempt and fury on all America. Those who made the Revolution, he then wrote, were craftier than the Roundheads and more persevering than the Jacobins; their motives were venal and their Constitution abominable. Jefferson, he declared, hated the English because he owed them money; and both he and Washington had conspired to turn over England's trade to France.[15]

But all this was in the future. What pleased the Federalists at the moment was his pamphlet, "A Bone to Gnaw for the Democrats," published in January 1795, which attacked the Democratic Societies, the friends of France, and Republicans generally. They chuckled with delight when he characterized the American Philosophical Society as "a nest of such wretches as hardly ever met together before," or called Benjamin Franklin Bache, editor of the violently Republican *Aurora*, "the son of one of Doctor Franklin's bastards" and "an *avowed* atheist." Even the astronomer David Rittenhouse, who headed the Democratic Society in Philadelphia, was accused of having received French gold for his base betrayal of his country.[16]

A strange secrecy wrapped the treaty which Jay had signed in a blanket of confusion and fog. It came in silence and many sealings to the President and the Secretary of State, and was read by them behind closed doors and divulged only to a few chosen persons. From Paris, Monroe bombarded Randolph with angry protests that he had been denied access to the sacrosanct document, in spite of previous promises. How then, he demanded, could he quiet the suspicions of the French; or was there matter in it to justify them?[17]

Madison, the Republican leader of the House, complained that though three months had elapsed since it became known that a treaty had been made, Congress had received no official account of its contents. Only through fragmentary private advices and leakages came rumors that the treaty had sold American rights down the river. "I suspect," he wrote, "that Jay has been betrayed by his anxiety to couple us with England, and to avoid returning with his finger in his mouth. It is apparent that those most likely to be in the secret of the affair do not assume an air of triumph."[18]

Even when Jay himself returned in April, ailing and rather distraught, he promptly made himself incommunicado.

There was good reason for the unprecedented secrecy in which everything connected with the treaty was enfolded. Both Washington and Randolph had been startled, to say the least, when they read its provisions. It failed to conform in almost every respect with the instructions handed Jay before he left. There were many things in it that were positively obnoxious, and certain to create a furore in the country if prematurely disclosed.

The question therefore was—what should be done with the unsatisfactory treaty? It could of course be disavowed by the President, and either all negotiations dropped or new ones undertaken. But this would mean in effect a public confession of the bankruptcy of the administration's policy and a vindication of the Republicans. It might even lead to war with England. The few Federalist leaders who were given a glimpse of the document, particularly Senator King, thought there were sufficient good points in it to overcome the lukewarm and the bad; and that in any event it was wiser to ratify.

Though Hamilton was now a private citizen, he also had been apprised of the treaty's contents. After the first shock, he too believed it expedient to ratify, with the single exception of the twelfth article, which related to the West Indies trade. To send the treaty back for renegotiation, he advised, would entail unconscionable delay and public turmoil.[19]

In the end the perplexed President decided to call the Senate into special session on June 8th and place the responsibility of a final decision on the shoulders of that constitutionally coordinate branch of the government.

Unhappy over the entire treaty, Randolph obeyed the edict of the President and tried to put the best face on the business. He called on Jay for supporting material to send to the Senate, and obligingly assured the envoy that he would not furnish the lawmakers with his own critical communications.[20]

At the same time Randolph was compelled to defend the treaty to the French without furnishing any specification of its actual contents. Fauchet sent him an acid note that France "sees her enemies admitted to an intimacy with you at the moment in which your commerce and your sovereignty are alike insulted by them." What sort of neutrality is that, he snapped, in which you can no longer maintain your treaties inviolate with us and you abandon your foreign relations exclusively to the direction of England?[21]

Randolph could only respond with an *ad hominem* counterattack. Though he first assured Fauchet that the "treaties with France shall be sacred" and had been expressly saved in the instructions to Jay, he added coldly that the French envoys (lumping Fauchet and Genêt together) had themselves intrigued mightily to disturb relations between their two countries.[22]

Further to complicate an already complicated situation, the British chose this inopportune moment to issue secret instructions to their ships of war to seize all vessels laden with corn for France or ports under her control.[23] This was a reinstatement of the notorious Order of June 8, 1793; and almost wrecked the ratification of the treaty when American ships were again seized without a word of explanation.

In spite of the rigid secrecy, however, reports of the actual clauses of the treaty gradually leaked out to leading Republicans. Distorted and magnified in the telling, the reports ran like wildfire over the country and fanned a gale of indignation to which all previous winds had been the merest zephyrs.

Chancellor Robert R. Livingston of New York was among the first to obtain an inkling of the treaty's contents; particularly that section which permitted British traders free passage through American territory. He disclosed the objectionable provision to Madison and suggested that the House make an issue of it at once. Madison agreed with him that the grant constituted a clear infringement of American sovereignty; but refused to bring it up in the House before the entire treaty was delivered to it. He feared, he replied, that a premature discussion might harm the Republicans.[24]

At the moment Madison was deeply engrossed in checking political fences. Washington, he knew, was firm in his resolve not to stand for the presidency again. Madison hoped that Jefferson would be a candidate; but the latter refused and in turn suggested that Madison himself take the Republican nomination.[25]

In an atmosphere of excitement, uneasiness and alarm the Senate gathered in special session on June 8th to consider the treaty. The doors were locked and bolted, and the senators were put on their honor to disclose neither the contents of the treaty nor the course of debate.

By this time the Federalists had made up their minds to ratify, in spite of private qualms and objections. The Republicans were fully resolved to reject it if that were possible; if not, to delay any action until the rising sentiment of the country could be brought to bear on individual senators.

The more Hamilton studied the treaty in the privacy of his New York law office and pondered on alternatives, the more he became convinced that it must be ratified, but without the twelfth article. He informed Rufus King that the best way to handle the delicate business was to ratify with a "collateral instruction" which would declare that the United States would forbear to exercise the privileges or accept the conditions of the West Indies article. After ratification, a modification of the offending article could be drafted and sent to Pinckney in England for submission. If it was agreed on, it could then be annexed to and made a part of the original treaty.[26]

That the ensuing debate in the Senate was bitter in the extreme may be taken for granted; but nothing of it leaked out. Only the bare bones of motions and votes can be gleaned from the scant wording of the Executive Journal.

On June 17th a motion was made to ratify, with a suspension of the twelfth article. On June 22nd Burr moved to postpone consideration, and to substitute a resolution calling on the President to enter into further negotiations in order to obtain drastic alterations in the terms of the treaty. He proposed the following: 1. That the ninth, tenth, twenty-fourth and twenty-fifth articles, which related to the management of imports, be wholly expunged; 2. That the second article, concerning the delivery of the posts, be modified to ensure a speedy and unconditional surrender; 3. That the third article, which gave the British permission to traverse American territory, be expunged; 4. That the sixth article, which tendered compensation to the British for the uncollected debts, be amended to include payment of damages by the British for the detention of the posts; 5. That the twelfth article be expunged or made much more favorable to American ships; and 6. That the fifteenth and twenty-first articles, granting most favored nation treatment, be modified.[27]

Burr's amendments, which would in essence have effectuated Jay's original instructions, were defeated by the Senate by a vote of 20 to 10. Other Republicans rose to offer somewhat similar amendments, in toto or in part, and were overruled by approximately the same majority. The Federalist lines were holding firm. On June 25th the final vote was taken—on the original motion—and the treaty was declared ratified, with the exception of the twelfth clause, which even the Federalists were unable to stomach.

As the Senate debated behind closed doors, alarming rumors kept the nation on tenterhooks. New York heard that the treaty had been rejected, and the "solid" businessmen cried out in horror that trade and finance would go into a state of "shock." [28]

They were already in a state of nerves over the temerity of the city's radicals in unfurling a French flag on the roof of the Tontine Coffee House, sacred precincts of the Stock Exchange and gathering place of all good Federalist merchants, traders and speculators. The following night the Federalists tore down the hated symbol and made away with it. Now it was the Republicans' turn to express outrage, and they advertised a reward of $150 for the apprehension of the thief.[29] Needless to say, the reward was never collected.

One of the first to obtain knowledge of the Senate's ratification was Hammond, who received the news confidentially from no less a personage than Oliver Wolcott, Secretary of the Treasury.[30] Wolcott, in this as in other things, was following faithfully in the footsteps of his predecessor, Alexander Hamilton.

The treaty now went to Washington for signature. He hesitated. Should he sign an obviously defective compact or not? He sought advice from those whose opinions he respected and trusted. Among others he turned to Hamilton. He wished to learn "from dispassionate men," the President wrote his former Secretary of the Treasury, "who have a knowledge of the subject, and abilities to judge of it, the genuine opinion they entertain of *each* article of the instrument; and the *result* of it in the aggregate." [31]

In a measure the President's hand was forced by the action of a Republican senator, Stevens Thomson Mason of Virginia, who defied the Senate rules to furnish the text of the treaty to Benjamin Franklin Bache, the Republican editor. Bache rushed the treaty to press as a pamphlet and traveled personally over the Eastern states, scattering copies around like a veritable Johnny Appleseed.[32]

The crop he sowed sprang full-grown almost overnight. In Boston a town meeting petitioned Washington not to sign; and Bache urged other towns to follow suit so that "the people might express their disapprobation in the strongest manner of an instrument which reflects dishonour on America, and barters away her best interests and her dearest rights." [33]

Chancellor Livingston joined the hue and cry. All his previous fears were confirmed when he read the complete text. He even fumed against his fellow Republican, Thomas Jefferson, as actually responsible for the worst clauses of the treaty. While in office, Jefferson had maintained the "modern law" of nations; by his admission that there was such a "law" he had justified the British violations of neutrality. Livingston insisted that any so-called "law of nations" arose neither from past experience nor precedents (otherwise, he said, cannibalism and the enslavement of captives would be legal), but was merely "a rule of justice which reason prescribes as arising out of the *existing* state of civilized nations."

"It is yet possible," he wrote Madison, "to convince the president of the danger of a ratification. Write to him, write to the public, shew the dangers, the unconstitutionality of many parts of the treaty." [34]

Livingston followed his own advice. He dispatched a letter to Washington urging him not to sign; and under the guise of "Cato" denounced the treaty in the public press. [35]

In almost the same mail Washington received Hamilton's reply to his request for enlightenment. It proved to be a book-length analysis of the treaty and a defense of most of its provisions. Only the twelfth article evoked his entire censure; but that had already been excised by the Senate. [36]

Washington was still not convinced. He had qualms over some of the other articles; notably those which gave the British the right to trade on American soil and access to the Mississippi, and the right of ship entry into our ports, while our ships were excluded from theirs. [37]

Nevertheless, while thus confessing his doubts to Hamilton, the President assumed a wholly different tone with Livingston. He waited a month and a half before replying, and then only after he had affixed his signature to the treaty. "You deem the treaty palpably defective," he wrote coldly to the man who had administered the oath of office to him in New York, "and pregnant with evils: others think it contains substantial good. For myself, I freely own that I cannot discern in it the mischiefs you anticipate: on the contrary, altho' it does not rise to all our wishes, yet it appears to me calculated to procure to the United States such advantages as entitle it to our acceptance." [38]

What had stiffened Washington's attitude in the interim was the opposition of the Republicans, which transcended the bounds of argument and appealed primarily to the passions and hatreds of the country. In every section of the nation, no matter how remote, great mass meetings were organized, at which orators made inflammatory

speeches and presented imflammatory resolutions. Violent handbills
were circulated everywhere, and the newspapers teemed with incendiary articles.

In Portsmouth, New Hampshire, notices appeared on the walls
overnight. *"ÇA IRA!!"* it screamed in boldest type. Shut your shops
and warehouses! it thundered. Assemble at the state capitol to remon-
strate with the President against signing the treaty! "Your all is at
stake," it cried. "The Senate have bargained away your blood-bought
privileges, for less than a mess of pottage. That perfidious, corrupting,
and corrupted nation whom you vanquished with your sword, are
endeavouring to vanquish you, with their usual, but alas! too successful weapon, *British* gold!!" [39]

In Richmond, Virginia, a handbill strewed the streets: "Notice is
hereby given, that *in case the treaty entered into by that d——'d Arch
Traitor J——n J——y with the British tyrant should be ratified*—a petition will be presented to the next General Assembly of Virginia at
their next session, praying that the said state *may recede from the
Union.*" [40]

In Boston, "Atticus" denounced the treaty as "the illegitimate imp,
the abortion of Liberty," which has made us "a party to the confederacy of despots" against France, and has surrendered our independence to England.[41]

In Charleston, South Carolina, the treaty was burned by the public
executioner as a cry of "utter abhorrence" rose from the attending
multitude against it, coupled with threats of retribution against their
Federalist senators "as apostates to liberty, and connivers at a creeping
aristocracy." [42]

It was Boston that acted as the bellwether for the Eastern towns.
There a tumultuous meeting denounced the treaty and its makers
in the most unmeasured language; nor was its effect destroyed by a
later countermeeting sponsored by the Chamber of Commerce, which
solemnly decried popular assemblages in a system of representative
government.[43]

From Boston the conflagration spread to New York. A huge mass
meeting was called for July 20th in front of the City Hall. Hamilton
sought to address the turbulent throng, but they refused to hear him.
As he strove to speak above the clamor, stones volleyed about him.
He was struck on the forehead, and the blood poured down his face.
He bowed ironically: "If you use such knock-down arguments I must
retire." Nevertheless he stood his ground to offer a resolution express-

ing confidence "in the wisdom and virtue of the President to whom with the Senate the discussion of the question constitutionally belonged."

His motion never came to a vote. A storm of hissings and booings greeted him, and the mob became so threatening that Hamilton and his friends finally deemed it prudent to retire. The triumphant crowd then passed denunciatory resolutions of its own and marched down to the Battery to burn the treaty with shouts and execrations.[44]

Here too the Chamber of Commerce, under Hamilton's leadership, voted in favor of the treaty; which led a Republican paper to warn its readers that they were but "a handful of men . . . hostile to our government and prosperity" and mere tools in Hamilton's hands.[45]

Philadelphia was next in line. On July 23rd a gathering variously estimated at from fifteen hundred to six thousand in number listened to harangues from a platform on which sat such eminent Republicans as Judge Thomas McKean, William Shippen, Jr., Thomas Lee Shippen, Charles Pettit, Stephen Girard, Alexander J. Dallas, Frederick A. Muhlenburg and Melancton, specially imported from New York as a rabble-rouser.

First a memorial was read denouncing the treaty. It passed by acclamation with a single dissenting vote. Then Melancton waved a paper in the air and cried: "Friends and fellow-citizens. Here is the treaty. Take it; and kick it to the devil." He flung the copy from the platform into the sea of upraised hands. The mob seized the fluttering sheet, impaled it on a pole, and paraded it through the streets to the house of the British minister, where they burned it with loud mockery.[46]

From every corner of the land resolutions of protest poured in on Washington; only a sparse few called for signature. Those which favored the treaty and those which, though opposed, were moderate and dignified in tone, the President answered. Those, however, whose denunciation was shrill and violent, he grimly put aside in a large packet, noting on the outside, "Tenor indecent. No answer returned," or "The ignorance and indecency of these proceedings forbade an answer." [47]

Nevertheless, both Washington and Randolph were much alarmed over the storm that swept the country. At one time the Secretary of State thought to hasten to Mount Vernon, where the President was spending the summer, to discuss the ominous situation; while Washington believed this to be the greatest crisis of his administration and dreaded that the French might seek to take advantage of it.[48]

The single ray of hope came from the "respectable" groups of merchants and businessmen in the great towns, who uniformly rallied to the treaty. From New York, Boston and Philadelphia these beneficiaries of the British trade, though few in numbers, spoke with an authority to the President which in his mind outweighed the clamor of the turbulent many.

The Federalist press reinforced the Chambers of Commerce in their own inimitable way. They came up with a theory of government which, while agreeable to Washington himself, could serve only to infuriate the Republicans all the more and even cause more moderate men to draw back. As one paper enunciated the thesis: "The constituted authorities of the country are the only organs of the national will. What is done by them is an act of the nation as a body politic. The citizens of New York, Boston, Philadelphia, &c., are not the nation. Their voice is the voice of individuals only. Every attempt of towns or small bodies of men to influence the representatives of the nation, is an attempt to make a part govern the whole."[49]

Neither the Federalists nor the President discerned any inconsistency in the approbation and respect with which they perused the resolutions which stemmed from the very much smaller bodies of Chambers of Commerce or a dozen merchants in meeting assembled.

But now a more redoubtable champion took up the cudgels for the treaty. Hamilton had his own private reservations about the compact which Jay had made, but he felt that even a poor treaty was better than none at all. It put an end to uncertainty and the continual incitation to war. In this he was at one with Washington, who likewise, for all his own dislike, thought it better than to "suffer matters to remain as they are, unsettled."[50]

The first of a powerful series of letters appeared in the New York *Argus* on July 22, 1795. The signature was "Camillus," but the style, the logical flow, the wealth of citations and the polemic fury, pointed unmistakably to Hamilton. Thirty numbers rolled inexhaustibly from his pen—and eight somewhat duller ones written by Rufus King—for the remainder of the year. No more sustained or brilliant papers have ever been composed by an American. Hamilton had gathered all his powers and resources of mind to stem the tide of public sentiment as it threatened to overwhelm the treaty.

His chief theme centered on the supposed secret purposes of the opposition. They represented, he asserted, an almost traitorous party in the United States which played France's game and sought to embroil us on her side in the European war. Their howls of anguish over the treaty, so he maintained, were solely due to the frustration of their secret plans by the establishment of an honorable peace between us and Great Britain.

He next turned to a defense of the treaty on its own merits. Clause by clause, paragraph by paragraph, line by line, he dissected the document, pointed up the advantages to ourselves and played down the faults. Like a master organist, he employed every stop and run to excite emotion where logic necessarily failed.

The Republicans, he averred, were seeking to destroy both Jay and Adams as possible successors to Washington, in order to install Jefferson in the coveted seat. He made his appeal to the moderate Republicans with gruesome pictures of the horrors which the treaty, and the treaty alone, could avert—a Spanish and Indian war to drench our frontiers in blood, a civil war on the Jacobin pattern complete with ax and guillotine, an end to exports, the death of agriculture, a vast increase in the public debt and an insupportable burden of taxes. If you wish for these, he cried, by all means reject the treaty; if you do not, then pray that the President will sign it.[51]

Curiously enough, it was a Republican paper which printed this tremendous Federalist polemic; though the Federalist press promptly reprinted it across the nation.

Even while the letters were running in its columns, the *Argus* blasted them with editorial counterattacks. "If this detestable instrument is enforced," roared the editor, then the Union will speedily be dissolved. When Washington finally placed his signature on the abhorred treaty, the newspaper published a savage doggerel to commemorate Hamilton's share in the transaction:

> Camillus writes—but writes in vain,
> The Treaty is concluded;
> By which the British *all* will gain,
> While *we* are still deluded.
>
> Sure George the Third will find employ
> For one so wise and wary,
> He'll call Camillus *home* with joy,
> And make him *Secretary*.[52]

But Jefferson, as he read "Camillus," was in no mood for light verse. He never underestimated the formidable strength of his old adversary. From his retreat in Monticello he called frantically on Madison. "Hamilton," he warned, "is really a colossus to the anti-republican party. Without numbers, he is a host within himself. They have got themselves into a defile, where they might be finished; but too much security on the republican part will give time to his talents and indefatigableness to extricate them. . . . For god's sake take up your pen, and give a fundamental reply to Curtius [Noah Webster] and Camillus." [53] Jefferson thought that "Curtius," another defense of the treaty, had also been written by Hamilton.

On the other hand, the President hailed "Camillus" with considerable relief. He hoped that its appearance would still the current "mad-dog" outcry against the treaty; and he urged Hamilton to disseminate the letters as widely as possible in order that they might serve as an antidote to the poison of the opposition press—influence public opinion, and through it the members of Congress. [54]

Nevertheless he himself still hesitated about putting his name to the document, while Hammond fretted and fumed. The British minister was alarmed and angered by the daily scenes of violence, the insults to the British flag, the threats against himself and his consuls. When the Philadelphia mob burned copies of the treaty in front of his house and the homes of other British officials, he sent a strong protest to Randolph. But the Secretary of State merely deplored the occurrence and expressed doubt that any law existed under which the participants could be punished or such acts forbidden.

Randolph was in no mood to placate Hammond. Even while the British representative was entering his protest, Randolph drafted a memorial for transmission to him which contained an explicit warning that "unless the order of council authorizing the seizure of neutral vessels bound to France with provisions be previously revoked," the treaty even if signed would be suspended or never put into effect. [55]

Even Washington was exercised by the "high-handed conduct" of Great Britain in choosing this moment of all moments to revive the Order. Should it not be immediately revoked, he avowed, "it would seem next to impossible to keep peace" between the two nations. [56]

In spite of the Order, in spite of the unabated clamor of the country, Washington finally if reluctantly signed the treaty on August 14th. Then, much to Randolph's mortification, he watered down the

memorial to Hammond by excising the threat to suspend the operation of the treaty. The Secretary of State did not attempt to conceal
his chagrin when he handed the weakened memorial to the British
minister and openly confessed that he had been overruled by the
other members of the Cabinet. These things, Hammond reported to
his government with justifiable satisfaction, "are clear indications of
the declining influence of that Gentleman in the Councils of this
country." [57]

Randolph in fact was definitely on his way out; and it was Hammond who furnished the material for removing from the scene a
Secretary of State whom he hated and despised. Hammond himself
was quitting the post which he had successfully held during these
turbulent years and returning to England. He departed with a sense
of a job well done. The treaty, so advantageous to his country, had
been signed; and Randolph, whom he erroneously believed to be
England's worst enemy, had been forced out of office under a heavy
cloud.

CHAPTER 21

Triumphant Federalism

RANDOLPH'S DOWNFALL and forced retirement was due to a chain of circumstances whose full meaning is still hidden in murk and confusion. The unwitting if not so innocent agent of his disaster was the French minister, Fauchet.

Sometime at the end of May, or the beginning of June, 1794, while Jay was en route to England on his mission, Randolph and Fauchet met to discuss the situation confidentially. Fauchet was understandably disturbed over the implications of the mission with respect to France, and Randolph sought to quiet his fears. In so doing, he overstepped the bounds of official discretion; neither more nor less than Hamilton and Jefferson had done in the past under rather similar circumstances.

As Fauchet promptly reported it to his government in a dispatch marked No. 3, Randolph "appeared to open himself without reserve. He imparted to me the intestine divisions which were rumbling in the United States. The idea of an approaching commotion affected him deeply. He hoped to prevent it by the ascendancy which he daily acquired over the mind of the President, who consulted him in all affairs, and to whom he told the truth, which his colleagues disguised from him."

The Secretary of State was pulling a long bow, and perhaps Fauchet knew it. At the very moment that he was making his brag to Fauchet, he was being consistently overruled both in the Cabinet and by the President on every vital foreign policy, including the Jay mission itself.

To prove that Jay had no authority to make any treaty which would nullify or contradict the American treaties with France, Randolph gave Fauchet a copy of the pertinent part of his instructions, and begged him to destroy it after he had made himself familiar with the contents. This was naïve. As any good diplomat would have done, Fauchet forwarded the copy to France.¹

This was the first link in the chain. The second came early in August of the same year, when the first reports of the Whiskey Insurrection reached Philadelphia and the administration was deciding whether to issue a proclamation against it or not. Randolph hastened to Fauchet's house and presented himself in a state of extreme agitation and with a sorrowful countenance. "It is all over," he cried. "A civil war is about to ravage our unhappy country. Four men by their talent, their influence and their energy can save it; but they are debtors of merchants and will be deprived of their liberty if they take the least step. Can you lend them immediately enough funds to shelter them from British persecution?"

Who these men were, what they could do to save the country from impending civil war, in what way the British were interested in raising the riots to the status of a civil war and in using the debts of these men to compel them to silence, is either unknown or unclear. Only one ray of light exists—the mysterious strangers claiming to represent the Whiskey Rebels who appeared at about this time in Philadelphia to seek either British or Spanish aid against the United States, as previously described in Chapter 18.

Randolph's cryptic speech, his obvious agitation and his open request for French funds astonished Fauchet. Perhaps he thought this was a disingenuous method for obtaining money for Randolph himself. In any event, as he promptly set down the incident for the benefit of his government in a dispatch marked No. 6, "it was impossible for me to give a satisfactory answer. You know my want of power and lack of pecuniary means. I shall withdraw from the affair by some commonplace remarks and by throwing myself on the pure and unalterable principles of the republic." ²

The incident was seemingly closed, but the more Fauchet thought about the peculiar business, the more he clothed it in other and more sinister meanings. On October 31, 1794, he wrote a final dispatch home—No. 10—whose contents were wholly explosive.

After some mention of the satisfaction he derived from "the valuable disclosures [*les précieuses confessions*]" with which Randolph alone of the American government honored him, Fauchet returned to a consideration of the scene with the Secretary of State described in the previous dispatch.

"Two or three days before the proclamation [against the Whiskey

Rebels] was published—and of course before the Cabinet had resolved on its measures—Mr. Randolph came to see me with an air of great eagerness, and made to me those overtures of which I have given you an account in my No. 6. Thus with some thousands of dollars the [French] Republic could have decided here on civil war or peace! Thus the consciences of the pretended patriots in America already have their price [*Tarif*]! . . . What will the old age of this government be if it is thus early decrepit! Such, citizen, is the evident consequence of the system of finances conceived by Mr. Hamilton. He has made of the whole nation a stock-jobbing, speculating, selfish people." [3]

There is a decided inconsistency between this final dispatch and No. 6, which was written immediately after the conversation. Whereas the earlier one gives the impression—from Randolph's own words—that the money was to be used to finance men who would *suppress* a civil war fomented by England, this dispatch declares that civil war would be instigated for the benefit of France, and that the men involved would be ready to betray the United States for a price. No such construction can be placed on the actual words used by Randolph, at least as Fauchet then reported them.

Dispatch No. 10 was the last link in the fatal chain of circumstances. In 1795 Fauchet was recalled by his government and Pierre Auguste Adet sent to replace him. By this time too he was at loggerheads with Randolph. On August 31, 1795, Fauchet was at Newport preparing to board the French frigate *Medusa* for passage home. Behind him, however, the explosion had already occurred.

The fatal final dispatch, with all its ominous implications, had been entrusted to the French warship *Jean Bart* at the end of 1794 for transmission to the Ministry of Foreign Affairs. The ship was intercepted by the heavier British *Cerberus* and captured after a short engagement. Seeing that surrender was unavoidable, the captain of the *Jean Bart* threw the packet of diplomatic documents overboard. Unfortunately it stayed afloat and a boat putting out from the *Cerberus* picked it up.

The packet went on to England, where Grenville was quick to note the possibilities of exploitation in the damning No. 10. On May 9, 1795, he forwarded a summary of its contents to Hammond (the original followed on June 5th) with the remark that its communication "to well disposed persons in America may possibly be useful to the King's service." [4]

This was an understatement, to say the least. On July 26, 1795,

immediately on receipt of the original itself, Hammond invited the
American Secretary of the Treasury, Oliver Wolcott, to dine with
him. Over a genial bottle of wine, he opened Fauchet's strange communication and read from it to Wolcott, translating into English as
he went along.

The Secretary of the Treasury was aghast. Here seemed proof
positive that the Secretary of State had been conspiring with the
French to betray his country and throw it into civil war. He was
particularly struck by the reference to the previous *"précieuses confessions"* which Fauchet claimed to have received from Randolph.
Both Hammond and Wolcott (as well as later American translators)
understood it as the ominous-sounding "precious confessions" instead
of the more innocuous "valuable disclosures."

Considerably agitated, Wolcott avowed "that something highly
improper had been proposed by Mr. Randolph," and asked for and
received the original. Washington was then at Mount Vernon; so that
Wolcott first took the incriminating dispatch to Timothy Pickering,
the Secretary of War. The latter agreed with him that the matter
required instant action; and both went in to see William Bradford, the
Attorney General, on the following day.

The trio of Cabinet members decided that Washington must be
asked to return at once to Philadelphia. With rather brutal irony they
got the unsuspecting Randolph to write the letter of which he was
the intended victim, on the plea that there was pressing business to
discuss.

On receipt of the request, the President packed and started out,
reaching the capital on August 11th. That evening Wolcott saw him
privately, placed Fauchet's dispatch in his hands and told him the
story of his session with Hammond.[5] Like the others, Washington was
horror-struck and like them believed the worst of his Secretary of
State. He formally asked his Cabinet—Randolph was naturally excluded—what steps should be taken and what measures should follow.[6]
The result of the deliberations was to lay a trap for the absent member.

On August 19th Randolph received a summons from the President
to see him. Entering the room he found Wolcott and Pickering already
there, grim and silent. Bradford had been taken ill and was not present. He was to die of his ailment four days thereafter.

Washington stared sternly at the surprised Secretary and, without
a word of salutation, dramatically handed him Fauchet's dispatch.

"Mr. Randolph!" he said coldly, "here is a letter I desire you to read, and make such explanations as you choose."

In much astonishment Randolph took the document and perused it in silence. He had not gone far when he realized that this was an inquisition and not a mere meeting. He also knew that he was in trouble. He read the dispatch to the end without saying a word; then commenced at the beginning again. The atmosphere grew more tense and electric with every passing minute. Finally Randolph looked up and said: "Yes, sir, I will explain what I know."

But, as he himself afterward admitted, it was difficult to explain, since supporting documents were not at hand and his recollection of the conversation with Fauchet (the exact statement of which was not contained in this particular dispatch) was already hazy. He rambled on and on, sometimes contradicting himself, and answering the various points raised in monosyllables. He did, however, deny with considerable vehemence that he had ever asked for or received any money, or made any improper communications on the measures of government. That damning phrase which everyone, including Randolph, translated literally as "precious confessions" stuck in all craws.

It was a most unsatisfactory performance. After it was over, the President icily requested Randolph to step into the other room while he consulted with Wolcott and Pickering. After forty-five minutes Randolph was recalled. But he had already thought matters over, and the more he thought, the more angry and resentful he became at the whole inquisitorial procedure. Immediately on entering he declared he was resigning, and flung out of the room again. He hastened to his own office, locked his desk and files, then went home. There, that same evening, he wrote out his resignation.[7]

The political kettle now boiled over. Smarting under what he conceived to be an adverse judgment in advance and resenting the dramatic confrontation which had given him no opportunity for preparation, Randolph took coach and raced to Newport to catch Fauchet before he sailed. He found the recalled minister in a boardinghouse on the very eve of departure. It is a pity that no account of the meeting exists, but in the end Fauchet promised to write out an explanation of the strange wording of dispatch No. 10 and an exculpation of Randolph.

Randolph hurried out to obtain witnesses to attest to Fauchet's signature. While engaged in rounding up his men, word came that Fauchet had already boarded the *Medusa* and that the ship was weighing anchor. Desperate at the thought that his last hope for vindication was slipping through his fingers, Randolph rushed down to the wharf, hired a swift boat and rowed out to the ship as it stood slowly out to sea.

Clambering on board, he demanded the vital certificates. Fauchet blandly explained that he had misunderstood, that they had been written and were already on their way to Adet, the new minister, in Philadelphia. Heartsick and fearing the worst, Randolph dropped down the rope ladder to his boat, rowed back to Newport and took coach to Philadelphia. Adet gave him the statements and with them Randolph set about preparing a vindication of his conduct for public distribution.[8]

Unfortunately Fauchet's attempted exculpation was too ingenious. Had he merely copied out his own dispatch No. 6, he would have done much better. The contents might have proved embarrassing to Randolph insofar as they did disclose a request for a loan (which he had denied to Washington), but, however indiscreet, they afforded no handle for an accusation of treason or bribery.

Instead, Fauchet now claimed that he had misinterpreted the fatal conversation with Randolph (which perhaps he had). Actually, he asserted, he (Fauchet) owed money for flour to certain merchants with whom he had dealt on Randolph's recommendation. The latter, convinced of England's part in fomenting the Whiskey Rebellion, was also convinced that some three or four among these flour contractors could prove the fact of England's participation. However, so Fauchet alleged, Randolph knew that these men were indebted to British merchants who might revenge themselves for the denunciation of their nation by clapping the informers in jail for debt. Therefore he had asked Fauchet to anticipate the payments on his own existing contracts so that they could pay off those debts and be free to testify.[9]

It is obvious from a comparison of dispatch No. 6 and this piece of special pleading that no credence can be placed in this late explanation. No mention then was made of flour contracts or of an advance payment. The dispatch specifically mentioned a *loan,* and Fauchet had declared he had no authority to grant it.

One possible solution of the whole perplexing affair presents itself. Randolph may have gotten wind of the visit of the mysterious emissaries of the Whiskey Rebels to Hammond and concluded hastily that the British were involved in the proceedings. To circumvent them, and not daring to apply for funds elsewhere in such a delicate matter, he turned to Fauchet for sufficient money to bribe certain leaders of the insurrection whom he believed open to such persuasion, to call off their followers. Insofar as Randolph was concerned, his purpose was in part patriotic and in part political—to save the Republican party from the onus which must inevitably be attached to it if the revolt continued. Fauchet himself seems to have had an inkling of it—otherwise, how explain his curious meditations in dispatch No. 10 on the intended use of French gold to bribe pretended American patriots on the issue of civil war or peace? Certainly the prepayment of lawful debts to flour merchants could not conceivably give rise to any such animadversions.

As for the *"précieuses confessions,"* which perhaps more even than the talk of bribery damned Randolph in the eyes of Washington and the Cabinet—the latter of whom were only too eager to believe the worst—Fauchet's dispatch No. 3 affords a proper explanation. The "disclosures" lay in Randolph's loose talk of his struggles with the Federalists for the domination of the President and in the presentation of a copy of Jay's instructions.

If this was improper in a responsible member of the administration —which it was—it was no more improper than the regular course which Hamilton had pursued and which Wolcott himself was even now pursuing in transmitting even more confidential information to the British envoys. Certainly it was less harmful than Hamilton's divulgence of a secret which sabotaged the ace card in the possession of the United States during the period of Jay's mission—whether she would join the Armed Neutrality Pact or not.

Randolph's own conduct after his resignation did nothing to clear up the situation; rather, it excited the more the wrath of the President. He kept demanding through the public prints confidential state documents from Washington which he claimed were required for his defense, and insinuated dark maneuvers by the administration he had just quit. Wolcott was sincerely convinced that Randolph was a traitor who intended to do every mischief he could to the government.[10] Washington, badgered by Randolph's incessant demands and angered by the trial of the case in the newspapers in which his own conduct was held suspect, hardened in his attitude.[11]

When the ex-Secretary of State finally published his Vindication, it proved to be a long, rambling and passionate account which devoted as much space to attacking Jay's treaty and the course of the administration with respect to France as to a vindication of himself.

It convinced no one but Republicans; and eventually Randolph retired to Virginia to meditate new vindications and new assaults on the President and the Federalists.

"The President and his party," he accused, "have in view . . . to destroy the republican force in the United States. . . . I feel happy at my emancipation from an attachment to a man, who has practiced upon me the profound hypocrisy of Tiberius, and the injustice of an assassin." [12]

Even the Republicans, who supported Randolph for party purposes, did so halfheartedly. They had not forgotten nor forgiven his independent course in the Cabinet at a time when, according to them, party lines should have been strictly drawn. Madison, for example, though disavowing any belief that Randolph had been corrupt, remarked that "his best friends can't save him from the self condemnation of his political career as explained by himself." [13]

The excitement engendered by the charges against the disgraced ex-Secretary of State and his countercharges against the administration served only to point up and exacerbate the tone of the main controversy—the signing of Jay's treaty.

That definitive action had rocked the country. A hotheaded Massachusetts radical—no less a person than Dr. Nathaniel Ames, brother to the arch-Federalist Fisher Ames—exclaimed to his diary on receipt of the news: "Better his [Washington's] hand had been cut off when his glory was at its height, before he blasted all his Laurels." [14]

John Beckley, erstwhile clerk of the House of Representatives and indefatigable purveyor of gossip to the Republican leaders, sent circular letters over the country with form petitions enclosed to be addressed to the House demanding that it take action against the treaty. He exulted at the secrecy with which he worked and at the rising public indignation against the President. Washington's signature, he cried, had marked him "in indelible character as the head of a British faction, and gratitude no longer blinds the public mind." [15]

Bache's assaults on Washington grew, if possible, even more virulent. "A malediction on departed virtue," he exclaimed. The President's conduct, he fumed, was worse than that which had sent the King of France to the guillotine. Deluded "by a false ambition," Washington had driven the country "to the precipice of destruction." He was lectured as a spoiled child, as neither priest, prophet nor demigod.

Indeed, he acted as though he were "the omnipotent director of a seraglio, instead of the first magistrate of a free people." [16]

So concerted and furious were the attacks, culminating in the charge that Washington had drawn on the Treasury for his personal secretarial expenses, that certain fainthearted Federalists foresaw the end of their world. "I often think," wrote Stephen Higginson despondently, "that the Jacobin faction will get the administration of our Government into their hands. . . . It is a kind of warfare to which we can see no end, as the source of it exists in the nature of our Government." [17]

Other Federalists, however, of a stouter breed, returned blow for blow. The Boston *Columbian Centinel* noted reports that the slaves in Georgia were getting restless. If the restlessness grew, it declared meaningly, "it will be a very bad time for ambitious intriguers there to threaten the union of the States. . . . The Northern states have carried through one revolution almost by their sole exertions. They have, by the late Treaty, assumed a share of the debts of the Southern states. They have borne much and borne long—and if the Southern States will not suffer them to enjoy *peace with a good government,* it is apparent that a separation must be the consequence; an event greatly to be feared and regretted, but one for which the minds of the people seem to be fast ripening." [18]

To such a pitch had the temper of the opposing parties finally risen.

In the midst of this clamor and passionate declamation Washington was confronted with the necessity of reshuffling his Cabinet and appointing a new Chief Justice.

Jay sent in his resignation with the intention of seeking anew the governorship of New York. Randolph was out, and William Bradford had died. Wolcott, struggling with the affairs of a Treasury almost beyond his powers, was constantly appealing to Hamilton for help and advice. "Our foreign resources are dried up," he lamented; "our domestic are deeply anticipated, at least as respects the bank. Banks are multiplying like mushrooms. . . . Our commerce is harassed by the war, and our internal revenue unproductive of the expected sums. . . . Usury absorbs much of that capital which might be calculated upon as a resource, if visionary speculations could be destroyed." [19] All in all, it was a dismal picture.

Washington's first and most important task was to find another Secretary of State. He was by now determined no longer to have a so-called nonpartisan Cabinet. "I shall not," he resolved, "whilst I have the honor to administer the government, bring a man into any office of consequence knowingly whose political tenets are adverse to the measures which the *general* government are pursuing; for this, in my opinion, would be a sort of political Suicide." [20]

But every "right-thinking" man to whom he offered the post shied away. In a manner foreshadowing modern times it had become a graveyard of reputations. Thomas Johnson of Maryland, Charles Cotesworth Pinckney of South Carolina, Rufus King and even Patrick Henry—to whom Washington offered it with some private doubts as to the sincerity of his conversion to federalism—all declined the hazardous honor.[21] Hamilton, to whom the President turned for assistance in his perplexity, lamented that there were no first-rate men willing to accept. It was a "sad omen for the government," he replied, that a second-rater must be chosen.[22]

In desperation the President proposed the unwanted post to Timothy Pickering, the Secretary of War, who had also been acting as interim Secretary of State. Pickering accepted at once. Now the War Department was vacant; and James McHenry of Maryland, Washington's aide during the Revolution and since a practitioner of medicine and politics, took the office. Bradford's place as Attorney General was filled by Charles Lee after John Marshall had refused it.

With his Cabinet repaired, Washington looked about him for a successor to Jay as Chief Justice. His first nomination was John Rutledge of South Carolina. But Rutledge was rejected by the Senate. The Republicans contended that the rejection was due to Rutledge's active opposition to Jay's Treaty; the Federalists declared he had been turned down because his mind had given way over the death of his wife; adding slyly that the derangement accounted also for his denunciation of the treaty.[23] In the end Washington sent in the name of Oliver Ellsworth of Connecticut, who, as a senator himself, had no difficulty in being confirmed.

While the attention of the nation was concentrated on Jay's Treaty and relations with England, the diplomacy of the administration scored a notable triumph in another area that passed almost wholly unnoticed.

From the very beginning of the Republic the Western people had considered Spain as the prime enemy. To them, all problems revolved around the blockage of the Mississippi as an outlet for their goods into the open sea. With the passage of the years the West vented its wrath on the Eastern states and the general government, which they controlled, as indifferent and selfish to its necessities. There were threats of taking to the sword on their own and mutterings of secession from a Union that paid no attention to their needs. Jay's appointment as envoy to England brought matters to a head. It was proclaimed in Kentucky that he had been their "Evil Genius" from the start; that he was going to seek the benefit of the Eastern trade and none of theirs.[24]

The signing of the treaty opened the gates for a new flood of vituperative resolutions which denounced the pact as "shameful to the American name" and base ingratitude to France. The British were pictured inconsistently as a race of plotters, robbers and "a corrupt, degenerate and sinking people." Nor did the West fail to pay its respects to "the present contemptible and pygmy Race, who were generated by, and buzz about the Treasury." [25] Actually, these rancorous outbursts were bottomed largely on the exasperation occasioned by their own special problem—for Spain at this moment was England's ally.

In point of fact the government had neither overlooked the West nor let it down. Right along, every resource of diplomacy—including the rattling of a peculiarly ineffective sword—had been employed to bring Spain to terms. Special commissioners had vainly mingled threats with pleas to obtain satisfaction from Madrid. Secure in their new alliance with England, the Spanish officials evaded, derided and delayed interminably until the American government, at its wits' end, finally dispatched Thomas Pinckney, the minister at London, as envoy extraordinary to seek a conclusion to the long controversy. He was picked for the mission only after Jefferson and the inevitable Patrick Henry had turned it down.[26]

Though appointed in November 1794, it was only after considerable delays that Pinckney arrived in Madrid on June 28, 1795, to join Short and Carmichael, already on the ground.

He came at an opportune time. The world situation had changed; France had recovered from earlier defeats and had inflicted serious losses on the allied powers. Alarmed for her own safety, Spain now sought to withdraw from the coalition; to which England countered with the threat of war upon her and her colonial possessions if she did. Manuel de Godoy, all-powerful in Madrid, and the acknowledged lover of the Spanish queen, foreseeing that New Orleans, Louisiana, and the Floridas would be helpless in the face of British sea power, bethought himself of a plan. He would, he determined, concede certain advantages to the United States in exchange for a guarantee against British aggression on the colonies.

However, instead of broaching the subject to the American commissioners in Madrid, he disclosed his purpose to Jaudenes and Viar, his agents in Philadelphia. He was ready, he avowed, to fix the disputed boundaries between the two nations on a reasonable basis and to grant the navigation of the Mississippi in return for "a solid alliance and reciprocal guaranty of our possessions and those of the States in America." Jaudenes was therefore to request the United States to send a plenipotentiary to Madrid to negotiate a treaty along these lines.[27]

The letter reached Jaudenes only after Pinckney had already been appointed. The Spanish agent, *persona non grata* with the administration, and busy with his own intrigues with Kentucky disunionists and Whiskey Rebels, failed to inform Randolph of this all-important communication. When Randolph indignantly taxed him with the oversight—on receipt of a tip from Short—Jaudenes grudgingly turned over, not the original but a modified and watered-down translation.

This was on March 25, 1795, when it was too late to do anything about it on this side of the Atlantic. Therefore, when Pinckney arrived in Madrid, it was without knowledge that victory lay within his grasp. Indeed, even more recent events had further strengthened his position. For the news of Jay's treaty confirmed Godoy in his fear that the United States and Great Britain had entered an alliance which might be employed against Spain with devastating effect.

There was one solitary card which Spain still possessed—the ability through Americans in the West either directly in Spanish pay or under Spanish influence to foment secession from the Union. The number of Americans so involved is amazing. They included some of the most prominent men in Kentucky and the adjoining territories. General James Wilkinson was unquestionably a Spanish agent paid with Spanish gold—though he played on his own a complex game in which he double-crossed his paymasters with the same aplomb that he betrayed his country. More doubtfully concerned, and imbued with motives perhaps more honorable, were such leaders and political figures as Judge Harry Innes, Senator John Brown of Kentucky, General John Adair, John Smith of Ohio (later also to become a senator),

Thomas Power and a host of lesser fry. The complicated skein of conspiracies and motivations, the complete roster of those actually involved or accused of participation, has still to be fully unraveled.

To safeguard himself therefore against excessive demands by the American government, Godoy dispatched a note to Jaudenes to negotiate immediately with his Western contacts, but "to hold them off until we can settle the question of the important points on which we are now treating with the States. This will serve to keep them devoted to us in case the States do not accept the just propositions which we are making them." [28]

Under such conditions Pinckney arrived. Godoy promptly offered him what he had already transmitted to Jaudenes. Pinckney with equal promptitude declined to enter into any commitments of guarantee.[29] Instead, he drafted what he considered to be a satisfactory treaty for Godoy to examine.

Godoy gave up the idea of the guarantee with surprising speed. By now, indeed, he was willing to accept almost any terms. War with England seemed hourly more imminent; in which case a hostile United States would be able to take with ease far more than he could ever voluntarily grant.

Had Pinckney but known it, he could have demanded even more than he actually did. At the very moment of his final negotiations in Madrid a worried British ministry was instructing their chargé d'affaires in Philadelphia to prevent at any cost the American government from joining a Spanish-French-Russian alliance that was in the making. Impress on influential Americans, he was advised, the "mischievous consequences" of such an alliance; and hold out to them, if they *do* wish to throw off neutrality, the advantages of making common cause with England. Particularly to be seen, so ran the urgent missive, was Oliver Wolcott, Secretary of the Treasury.[30]

As usual, Wolcott was only too happy to soothe British fears. He gave Phineas Bond, the chargé d'affaires, the proper assurances that the United States had no intention of entertaining an alliance with Spain or anyone else. That early treaty with France, he declared, had been a sufficient lesson.[31]

While Wolcott was giving these assurances to England in Philadelphia, Pinckney had already consummated a treaty in Spain. The final articles were formally signed at San Lorenzo on October 27, 1795.

The Treaty of San Lorenzo was as favorable to the United States as Jay's Treaty was not. Practically every point on which there had been long years of fruitless controversy was now resolved for American benefit.

The most vital and all-important clause granted to the citizens of the United States the free and unrestricted navigation of the Mississippi "in its whole breadth, from its source to the ocean." As an adjunct of such navigation, they were given the privilege of the free deposit of merchandise in New Orleans, and the right of export and transshipment therefrom free of all taxes and duties. This precious privilege was to run for three years; at the end of which period Spain agreed to extend the right or to grant an equivalent entrepôt or port of deposit elsewhere on the banks of the river.

A definitive boundary was drawn between Georgia and the Floridas, and all troops and settlements of either power within the territories of the other were to be withdrawn within six months. A western boundary was similarly fixed.

Each contracting power agreed to restrain, by force if necessary, any hostility by the Indians within its borders against the inhabitants and territory of the other.

Contraband was so defined as to exclude foodstuffs, metals, clothes, oils, tobacco, wine, sugar and even ship supplies—a far cry from the British definition.

Damages to American citizens arising out of Spanish seizures were to be fixed and determined by a panel of three commissioners sitting in Philadelphia.[32]

The treaty represented one of the greatest triumphs that American diplomacy had ever won. It stilled the clamor of the Westerners and brought to a halt the very real threat of secession. It ended the incessant boundary disputes and the dangerous prospect of an all-out war with the Creeks, backed openly or surreptitiously by Spain.

Yet strangely enough, hardly a ripple of applause for the administration which had consummated the pact came even from its most favored beneficiaries. The East was too much engrossed in its own affairs to pay much attention to the problems of distant frontiers; the Westerners looked upon the treaty as a tardy act of justice which only their own protests and threats had finally compelled an indifferent government to obtain.

The Fourth Congress, convened on December 7, 1795, did not as yet know of the treaty which Pinckney had consummated. But even if they had, it still would have been submerged in their thoughts to the perennial question of Jay's Treaty.

In his opening address the President spoke gently of other matters, while hurrying over the controversial pact with a few words. He told of better relations with the piratical Barbary powers—achieved by a humiliating payment of tribute and ransom in the sum of $763,000, besides additional presents and perquisites. He expatiated more warmly on Anthony Wayne's victories over the Indians in the Northwest and the provisional treaty he had imposed on them. But chiefly he concentrated on the blessings of peace which this nation enjoyed in contrast to foreign convulsions, and hailed the rapid increase in population as the surest prognosis for future American might and security.[33]

But the House of Representatives had gathered in no mood to be fobbed off with soft phrases or apostrophes addressed to the future. The Republican majority was in a fighting temper, feeling certain that their home states would back them to the hilt. Virginia had already proposed a series of constitutional amendments designed to clip the powers of the Senate. These would reduce senatorial terms to three years, join the lower House in the treaty making power, and take from the Senate its judicial function in impeachments. In South Carolina a group of resolutions denouncing the treaty as an unconstitutional arrogation of powers by the general government failed in the legislature by the slimmest of margins.

Even Washington himself was not happy over the general situation, in spite of his soothing speech. He listed angrily a whole series of continuing grievances against England which the treaty seemed not to have cured: the strutting arrogance, insults and menaces of her naval officers even in our own ports; the search of American ships and impressment of American sailors without our territorial waters; the extensive depredations by privateers out of Bermuda, whom the President bitterly termed "more correctly, Pirates"; the continued aggressions of the governor of Upper Canada; and the obnoxious and insulting agents England sent as her representatives to the United States.[34] An impressive list of grievances; and one which the Republicans had no hand in drawing.

But before the House could get to work on the Jay Treaty, its wrath was first diverted by an absurd incident which must be regarded as indicative of the hair-trigger temper of the times.

On the first day of 1796, Adet, the French minister, ceremoniously presented a French flag to the President as an official gift from France. The presentation was innocuous enough, but it placed the American government in an embarrassing position. Monroe had similarly proffered an American flag to France—though not in his official capacity —and the French Assembly had enthusiastically draped it in a place of honor in their legislative hall. Adet blandly suggested that the French flag be given an equal display in Congress.

Neither Washington nor the Federalists had any intention to make a public show of the French emblem. Hasty conferences were held and it was decided that good manners might best be subserved by placing the flag in the "archives," where it could molder in peaceful oblivion.[35]

But they reckoned without M. Adet. The touchy minister entered a formal protest that such a shutting up of the flag constituted "a mark of contempt or indifference." [36]

Timothy Pickering, lately elevated to the State Department, retorted with the utmost solemnity that in the archives the flag would rest in company with the memorials of our own freedom. In this country, he added slyly, we do not exhibit in our legislative assemblies "any public spectacles as the tokens of their victories, the symbols of their triumphs, or the monuments of their freedom." [37]

Adet refused to be consoled by such sophistry. He brooded over the incident, and then came up with another that stirred him equally to the depths. A private directory of information was being printed annually in Philadelphia. In previous years it had listed the street addresses of the foreign ministers in town with France first, Spain second and England last. *This* year it appeared for sale with England first, France second and Spain last. This, considered Adet, was not to be borne. He dispatched a formal note to Pickering. If the insulting directory was an official publication, it must be suppressed; if private, then the government must issue a public announcement of disavowal. To which Pickering was again compelled to reply with a refusal, and included in the answer some talk concerning the freedom of the press in the United States.[38]

The Republicans might understand the merits of Pickering's stand in the matter of the directory, though most likely they were certain that the publishers had deliberately intended a Federalist insult to France. But they went into a rage over the incident of the flag. The administration, they cried, is hiding the "superb French flag" for fear it "should rekindle the feeling of the American people for the French Republic, or that it would injure that abortion, the Treaty." [39]

Every grievance, no matter how remote, in the end came back to the treaty. In the House, both sides prepared for battle. The Republicans were now led by Albert Gallatin, whose refusal of a seat by the Senate the previous year had raised a storm. He was now safely seated in the House, triumphantly elected by the voters of western Pennsylvania. Though a newcomer, he was soon to displace even the veteran Madison in the public eye, and to evoke a Federalist sneer that Madison had fallen to the position of "file-coverer to an itinerant Genevan." [40]

Gallatin entered Congress with the firm determination to unravel the Hamiltonian skein of finances, to pare expenditures to the bone and create a surplus from which to retire the national debt at the earliest possible moment. Hamilton's system of deficit financing was anathema to him, and he decided to make Congress the watchdog of the Treasury. The only way to achieve economy and avoid executive prodigality, he declared, was for Congress to pass no general appropriations. Each grant of money must be limited to a specific purpose, and vigilance must then be exercised to see to it that it was not misapplied. To accomplish this end Gallatin created a standing committee of the House to check all appropriations and expenditures. This was the famous Ways and Means Committee, of which he became the first chairman. [41]

It was Samuel Smith of Maryland who led off with the first, if only an indirect, attack on the Jay Treaty. On January 15, 1796, he introduced a resolution to forbid the entry into the United States of any goods carried in a ship of foreign registry which were not the produce of that nation. The resolution, he remarked, "contained the only provision left us by that Treaty to save our commerce from prostration." [42] The real debate on the treaty, however, did not begin until March.

On their part, the British did their share to inflame public opinion and to embarrass their own friends in the United States. Their seizures of American ships in the West Indies continued at such a pace that the Republican press could regularly display under the ironic title "Evidences of British Amity" instance after instance of "the cruelty and insolence of the officers of the British government in the West

Indies." Other papers more plainly headed the news items with the caption "More British Insolence." [43]

Even on the posts, as the time specified in the treaty approached for their surrender, the British ministry sought every excuse for holding them still longer. Wayne's Treaty of Grenville with the Indians, they complained, violated Article 3 of Jay's Treaty by forbidding white men to enter Indian lands or trade with them except under a license of the American government. The United States, asserted the ministry, must publicly declare that the prohibition did not apply to British subjects.[44]

Even Hamilton became exasperated beyond measure. "The British ministry," he exploded, "are as great fools or as great rascals as our Jacobins, else our commerce would not continue to be distressed as it is by their cruisers; nor would the Executive be embarrassed as it now is by the new proposition. . . . It will be an error to be too tame with this overbearing Cabinet." [45] Yet his anger did not prevent Hamilton from arranging meetings and petitions in New York to protest against any attempt by the House of Representatives to render the treaty ineffective.

Actually, the British were legally correct in the position they took on Wayne's Indian treaty. Jay's Treaty expressly guaranteed the right of free entry and trade by British subjects in Indian lands within the United States. Therefore the Senate, on May 9, 1796, faced with the threat that the posts would not be otherwise delivered, was compelled to adopt the required explanatory article.

The French were also creating embarrassments over the treaty with England. There was considerable logic in their position that while Jay's Treaty might not constitute an outright alliance between the two countries, it did place France in an awkward position vis-à-vis England by granting the latter through omission the right to seize food destined for France, while France's own treaty forbade her to retaliate on provisions destined for England.

Monroe was claiming from Paris that only his most persuasive powers had prevented the French from dispatching an envoy extraordinary to America to interpose a formal complaint and to consider their own treaty as "annihilated." [46]

Even more alarming reports came from Gouverneur Morris, acting temporarily in London until an official replacement for Thomas Pinckney arrived. He not only confirmed Monroe's statement, but added a rumor to the effect that a French fleet was preparing to convoy the intended envoy to the United States with a demand that if Jay's Treaty were not "annihilated" within fifteen days, war would be declared. Though Washington did not believe the rumor, he wanted to be ready for any such demand with an answer which he regretted would have to be softened, because of internal dissensions, from the "short and decisive" note he would have preferred.[47]

Adet was a fit successor to Genêt and Fauchet. In their best tradition he kept up a continuous bombardment. A constant stream of protests came to Pickering's desk. He demanded that British purchases of flour, horses and merchant ships in this country cease. The Secretary of State neatly confounded this by quoting Jefferson's reply to Hammond when the British minister had similarly protested French purchases of arms and military equipment.[48] Adet next insisted that the United States compel the British to stop their impressments of American seamen—as if this were not a sore enough point with the government. He maintained that the entire British colonial fleet was recruited in this fashion, and that if the French islands were lost, he would hold the United States responsible.[49] Pickering did not deign to reply.

The great debate in the House on Jay's Treaty commenced on March 2nd, when Edward Livingston of New York moved that the President be requested to lay before them a copy of Jay's original instructions, together with all the documents and correspondence relating to the negotiation of the treaty.

Uriah Tracy of Connecticut inquired as to the point of the motion. Was it intended to use the papers as a basis for contesting the constitutionality of the Treaty, or was it the intention of the House to impeach Jay or Washington, or both? Tracy, of course, was being sarcastic; but Livingston retorted frankly that the requested information might determine those very points.[50]

This brought the Federalists clamoring to their feet with denunciations of any House intervention in a treaty concern. Madison countered that an important principle was at stake. "It was to be decided," he declared, "whether the general power of making treaties supersedes the powers of the House of Representatives, particularly specified in the Constitution, so as to take to the Executive all deliberative will, and leave the House only an executive and ministerial instrumental agency." He did, however, try to soften the full impact of Livingston's resolution by giving the President full discretion in deciding which papers were to the interest of the nation to disclose. His own Republicans defeated his amendment.[51]

William Smith of South Carolina called attention to a possible breakdown of the constitutional division of powers; but John Nicholas of Virginia and Gallatin rejoined that the power given to the House to appropriate the funds necessary to put any treaty into effect was a sufficient constitutional basis for its intervention.[52]

For days the debate ranged over the entire realm of constitutional theory. Sedgwick triumphantly read the speeches made by Madison, Edmund Randolph, George Mason, George Nicholas and other Republican stalwarts during the Virginia Ratifying Convention in which they had admitted the sole power of the President and the Senate over treaties.[53] But sheer argument or the resurrection of former stands proved of no avail. On March 24th Livingston's motion was passed by the overwhelming majority of 62 to 37.

From a distance Thomas Jefferson highly approved of the resolution. Though he rendered lip service to Washington as the only honest man who had assented to the treaty, he added: "I wish that his honesty and political errors may not furnish a second occasion to exclaim, 'curse on his virtues, they've undone his country.'" [54]

Washington surveyed the resolution, when the House presented it to him, with grim anger. He took counsel with his Cabinet whether the House had the power to request the papers. They unanimously declared that the House had no such power. The newly appointed Chief Justice, Oliver Ellsworth, privately told him that the claim of the House to "participate in or control the Treaty making power is as unwarranted as it is dangerous." Washington next inquired of private citizen Hamilton what *he* thought of the matter, and received the same reply.[55]

Thus fortified with the unanimous opinion of his advisers, official and otherwise, Washington sent a Message on March 30th to the House abruptly refusing to comply with their resolution, on the ground that it would constitute a dangerous precedent, inasmuch as the treaty-making power did not lie within their province.[56]

The issue was now bluntly joined. The House listened in silence to the Message; then Thomas Blount of North Carolina demanded that it be referred to the Committee of the Whole. When the Federalists objected, he retorted that "this was the first instance of any importance of a difference between the House of Representatives and the Executive respecting a great Constitutional point," and he wanted the House to state its own position for the information of the people.[57]

The reference was carried; and on April 6th, once more in open House, Blount returned to the assault with two resolutions. The more important one asserted that while the House laid no claim to an agency in the making of treaties, when the finished product stipulated matters over which the House *did* have control, it became both the constitutional right and duty of the House "to deliberate on the expediency or inexpediency of carrying such Treaty into effect, and to determine and act thereon, as, in their judgment, may be most conducive to the public good." [58]

Again the debate was hot and furious, and again the Republicans carried the day by a vote of 57 to 35.

As the resolutions and debate rolled endlessly on, tempers frayed and passions mounted. It was indeed claimed that party spirit had never run so high since the beginning of the nation.[59] The Federalist press openly avowed that before the Northern states would submit to a consequent war with England over the Treaty's rejection, they would call state conventions, divide the Union, and establish for themselves a government "which shall not admit of Negro representatives." [60]

Hamilton bestirred himself in New York to obtain counterresolutions from merchants whose wrath became almost apoplectic when insurance underwriters refused to issue insurance policies on ships and freight, and the price of provisions in their hands fell from fifteen to twenty per cent within a few hours after the news of the House action.[61]

Hamilton followed this with a proposal to Senator King for a Federalist plan of action, should the House refuse to make the necessary appropriation for the Treaty. The President must send them a solemn protest on constitutional grounds; the Senate must affirm the protest and remain in continuous session; and all over the country merchants must meet and forward resolutions and petitions.[62]

It is significant how Hamilton's mind worked—that "merchants" alone could influence Congress and that in fact they ought to be considered as the sole responsible organs of public opinion.

But the congressional Federalists had already devised a cleverer scheme to halt the rampaging Republican majority.

While the House had been engrossed in the debate on Jay's Treaty, the Senate had ratified unanimously the Algerine and Spanish treaties.

These were admittedly noncontroversial. The Spanish treaty benefited chiefly those sections of the country where the Republicans were
strongest; while the Algerine treaty, for all its humiliating terms,
meant the freeing of enslaved American captives.

In the latter case, indeed, the Dey of Algiers was fuming because
he had not as yet received the tribute specified in the treaty, and
threatened to expel the American commissioners, tear up the document and remain forever at war with the United States. In their
despair the commissioners employed the services of one "Bacri the
Jew, who has as much art in this sort of management as any man we
ever knew." Even the all-skillful Bacri, however, could not budge the
Dey until, as a final bribe, the commissioners agreed to furnish a new
and speedy American warship carrying an armament of thirty-six guns
as a present to the Dey's daughter! [63]

In the end, even this crowning humiliation was acceded to at home;
though the Secretary of the Treasury gloomily estimated the total cost
of placating Algiers at a million dollars, not to speak of an additional
annual charge of $72,000.[64]

But the Federalists took advantage of both these treaties, as well as
the Indian treaty, all of which required substantial House appropriations before they could be put into effect, to bring the Republicans
to terms on Jay's Treaty.

These, as King replied to Hamilton's suggestions, would be voted
on as separate bills in the House. After their expected approval in the
lower branch, they must be sent to the Senate for final action. The
Senate, with its Federalist majority, would thereupon attach to each
bill a rider appropriating money for Jay's Treaty. In other words, as
King frankly avowed, it would be made plain to the House that *no*
treaty would pass unless and until the treaty with Great Britain was
properly included. It was his belief, chuckled King, "that the Opposition will give way before we have gone through this course." [65]

As debate was resumed in the House on April 13th, part of this
strategy was put in action. Sedgwick proposed that *all* four treaties
be given the necessary funds. Immediate outcries rose from the Republicans against any such omnibus disposition, and Gallatin demanded separate consideration for each, with the Spanish treaty first
on the agenda. Sedgwick refused to recede, and Page of Virginia
suggested as a compromise that the Algerine treaty receive first consideration. But this too was rejected by the Federalists. They were

compelled, however, by weight of opposing numbers, to yield; and the Spanish treaty was first assented to, then the Indian, and after that the Algerine.[66]

At length Jay's Treaty came up. Madison opposed any appropriation for it in a long speech which minutely considered every article and attacked it from every angle. The Federalists contented themselves with the sketchiest defense of the Treaty itself, devoting all their energy to the constitutional issue of the right of the House to examine it at all. And, throughout the debate, petitions piled up on the Speaker's desk—from "merchants" for the Treaty, and from "the citizenry" in opposition.[67]

Day after day the debate dragged its weary course until Fisher Ames, who had long been ailing, arose. Feeble, scarce able to support himself erect, gasping for breath between sentences, Ames nevertheless made what was universally conceded to be the finest oration of his career. In expectation that he would speak, the House chamber was crowded as it had never been before; the Senate adjourned to give its members a chance to attend.

A hushed silence greeted his extended effort, in which he argued the constitutional question with legal clarity and brilliant logic. When he had ended, at least so John Adams reported, there was hardly a dry eye in the House. Supreme Court Justice James Iredell, sitting next to Adams as an auditor, turned to him with an exclamation: "My God! how great he is!" Adams nodded: "It is divine!" [68]

Ames's dramatic address, which almost cost him his life, proved to be the climax and turning point of the debate. On the following day the House in Committee of the Whole voted on a resolution to make the requisite appropriation and found itself tied at 49 to 49. The Speaker, while declaring that he personally was not satisfied with the treaty, cast his vote in favor so that the question might come properly before the House.

On April 30th the doors were thrown open. An amendment to declare the treaty "highly objectionable" was voted down by 50 to 49; and the original motion was passed by 51 to 48. With this breaking of the log jam, the House peaceably voted an appropriation of $80,-808, and the great debate was over.[69]

The violently controversial treaty with Great Britain was now the law of the land.

CHAPTER 22

Washington's Farewell and
Adams's Election

THE EXECUTIVE BRANCH of the government had emerged victorious in the bitter contest with the House of Representatives; but the scars remained. Jefferson attributed the victory to the fact that "one man [Washington] outweighs them all in influence over the people, who have supported his judgment against their own and that of their representatives. Republicanism," he sighed, "must lie on its oars, resign the vessel to its pilot, and themselves to the course he thinks best for them." [1]

In spite of this mournful threnody Jefferson had no intention of allowing "Republicanism" to lie on its oars. This was a presidential year, and with Washington scheduled to retire, Jefferson permitted his name to be mentioned as a candidate.

Nevertheless the Republicans were disheartened and dismayed over their failure to kill Jay's Treaty. Madison wrote gloomily that the "crisis which ought to have been so managed as to fortify the Republican cause, has left it in a very crippled condition." He agreed with Jefferson that they had been defeated by the prestige of the President and the threat of war if the treaty failed. Nor did the early local election returns from New York, Massachusetts and elsewhere, which disclosed sharp Federalist gains, do anything to lighten the pervading gloom. [2]

In his exasperation Jefferson sat down to write a letter to his old Virginia friend and neighbor, the Italian-born Phillip Mazzei. Since Mazzei had returned to Italy, Jefferson felt that he could safely vent his accumulated load of anger to his distant friend. In this surmise, as the event will show, he was egregiously mistaken.

"The aspect of our politics has wonderfully changed since you left us," Jefferson declared. "In place of that noble love of liberty and republican government which carried us triumphantly through the war, an Anglican monarchical and aristocratical party had sprung up, whose avowed object is to draw over us the substance, as they have already done the forms, of the British government. The main body of our citizens, however, remain true to their republican principles; the whole landed interest is republican, and so is a great mass of talents. Against us are the Executive, the Judiciary, two out of three branches of the legislature, all the officers of the government, all who want to be officers, all timid men who prefer the calm of despotism to the boisterous sea of liberty, British merchants and Americans trading on British capitals, speculators and holders in the banks and public funds, a contrivance invented for the purposes of corruption, and for assimilating us in all things to the rotten as well as the sound parts of the British model. It would give you a fever were I to name to you the apostates who have gone over to these heresies, men who were Samsons in the field and Solomons in the council, but who have had their heads shorn by the harlot England." [3]

There is no question whom Jefferson meant by the biblical references—he had Washington primarily in mind, and perhaps also John Adams. It was an indiscreet letter to write; the more so since Mazzei, volatile and voluble, could not be trusted to keep such a juicy morsel to himself. On its receipt, Mazzei translated it enthusiastically into his native tongue and caused it to be published in a Florentine newspaper. The Paris *Moniteur* picked it up, clad the damning epistle in French dress and published it with even greater enthusiasm. As though the original contents were not sufficiently explosive, the *Moniteur* thoughtfully added to them, as coming from Jefferson, an apostrophe to France.

From then on the future of the so-called "Mazzei Letter" was predestined. A Federalist sheet, the New York *Minerva,* received the incriminating issue of the *Moniteur* in its regular packet of foreign mail. The editor pounced with joy on the peripatetic letter, retranslated it into English; and thus, on May 14, 1797, it reappeared after many vicissitudes in America to plague its original author.

Fortunately, by then the presidential election was over; or the publication might have decisively changed the course of American history. For the wave of resentment and anger that swept the country over the aspersions on the now-retired President could easily have swamped the Republican party and defeated Jefferson for the vice-presidency.

The embarrassed author thought it best to keep a discreet silence in the face of all attacks; though privately he complained that the round of translations had distorted the sense (which they surprisingly had not, with the exception of the forged insertion by the *Moniteur*).

The publication of the "Mazzei Letter" conclusively ended the already uneasy relations between Jefferson and Washington. For some time the latter had chafed under what he considered to be ungenerous and underhanded assaults on himself by his former friends, Jefferson and Madison. He spoke of them both as the foremost opponents of the government and "consequently to the person administering it contrary to their views." [4]

Even prior to the final break, Washington had received reports that Jefferson was denouncing him "as a person under a dangerous influence; and that, if [Washington] would listen *more* to some *other* opinions, all would be well." The angered President sent the report along to Jefferson, adding bitterly that a year or so ago "I had no conception that Parties would, or even could go, the length I have been witness to," or that "every act of my administration would be tortured, and the grossest and most insidious misrepresentations of them be made . . . and that too in such exaggerated and indecent terms as could scarcely be applied to a Nero; a notorious defaulter; or even a common pickpocket." [5]

It is no wonder that Washington thought it time for him to quit political life and retire to the privacy of his plantations. The Founding Fathers of the Republic were remarkably thin-skinned. The slings and arrows of their political opponents inflicted festering wounds which made them seek the shelter of obscurity in which to lick their hurts. Washington, Adams, Jefferson and Hamilton—all reacted in the same way and with the same air of anguished surprise.

Once the several treaties had been ratified, Congress speedily dispatched the remaining business of the session. Some of the matters, however, aroused bitter if brief debate.

Tennessee, outpost of the Union, applied for admission as a sovereign state. Since the inhabitants of the territory were predominantly Republicans, and radical ones at that, the Federalists opposed the application and the Republicans demanded immediate and favorable action.

The House voted admission largely on party lines. In the Senate the debate was longer and more violent, exacerbated by the arrival in Philadelphia of the blatant William Blount, who proclaimed himself the senator-elect "from our new sister Tennessee" and the harbinger of "the rights of man." [6]

These antics goaded the Federalists to increased resistance; and the final vote was decided only by the casting ballot of Samuel Livermore of New Hampshire, acting president in the absence of John Adams. By such a narrow margin was Tennessee admitted into the Union on June 1, 1796, as the sixteenth state.

Of far-reaching importance for the future of the country was the Act for the Sale of Lands in the Northwest Territory which went into effect on May 8th. The Act provided for the survey of the vast territory in sections of 640 acres each. Four such sections were to be reserved in every township for the public benefit; the balance was offered for sale to the highest bidder at a knockdown price of two dollars an acre.[7] With the passage of the Act the process of settling legally the public lands was placed on a sound basis, and settlers hastened to purchase the offered sections and to migrate with their families to the hitherto limitless forests and prairies.

Since Hamilton's departure from the Treasury, his successor had been struggling in vain to cope with the annual deficits. Now Wolcott confessed his failure and implored the help of his predecessor.[8]

Hamilton came up with his usual remedy—increased taxation. Thereupon Congress, over the protests of the Republicans, enacted additional duties on imports and laid a tax upon the keeping of private carriages and coaches.

Six frigates had been authorized in March 1794; but they seemed destined never to advance beyond the planning stage. Nine months later Knox was sarcastically reporting that the timber for the ships was still "standing in the forests; the iron for the cannon lying in its natural bed; and the flax and hemp, perhaps, in their seed." [9]

A full year after that, there had been little change; though some timber had been cut in the piney woods of Georgia and placed on board ship for carriage to the scattered shipyards where the frigates were supposed to be constructed. A House investigating committee, seeking to discover the cause of the unaccountable delays, issued a curiously modern-type report. The trouble was, it said, that there had been such an "unexampled rise of labor, provisions, and all other articles necessary to the equipment of ships of war" since the appropriation had been made that the costs had almost doubled. It recommended therefore that at such "advanced prices" work proceed on two of the authorized frigates only.[10] Congress decided to go ahead on three. It was late in 1797 before two frigates were launched—the *Constellation* and the *Constitution*. The third—the *United States*—took still another year to complete.

Treaties had been signed with Great Britain, Spain and Algiers; but they did not bring an end to European troubles nor even to disputes with the signatory states.

Rufus King, at the expiration of his senatorial term, was sent as minister to England to replace Thomas Pinckney. King, a staunch Federalist, proved a cautious and levelheaded diplomat who performed his duties as well as could be expected in a most difficult post.

The irritating issue of impressments had been left untouched in Jay's Treaty, and King tried hard to get England to abandon them. But this was one point on which England proved consistently adamant. It took years of peace after the Napoleonic wars before she allowed the obnoxious practice to wither.

The most that King could accomplish was to negotiate the release of impressed seamen who could prove their American birth and citizenship.[11] Citizenship by naturalization in the case of the British-born was not enough; England took seriously the slogan "Once a British subject, *always* a British subject."

The situation, however, was complicated by the cavalier disregard of British naval officers for orders which they believed to be, and doubtless were, issued tongue in cheek. As one captain bluntly declared: "It is my duty to keep my Ship manned, and I will do so wherever I find men that speak the same language with me, and not a small part of them British Subjects, and that too producing Certificates as being American Citizens." [12]

When Hammond quit his post in the United States the British government sent Robert Liston to replace him; but the Americans soon discovered, as in the case of successive French ministers, the change was one of person and not of attitude or arrogance.

On one point, however, and that most vital, the British yielded with obvious reluctance. In accordance with the provisions of Jay's Treaty they commenced the long-delayed evacuation of the border forts which they had held since the Revolution. When the last one was surrendered—Michilimackinac on the Great Lakes—a sigh of relief rose from all Americans. The Federalists were especially exultant. *"What think ye of the Treaty now?"* they taunted the Republicans. "Had ten thousand men been employed in besieging the Western

Posts—had one half of them fallen by sickness and the sword . . . the acquisition would have excited universal joy and triumph throughout the United States. . . . Eternal praises to the God of Peace and Negotiation!" [13]

The wrath of the French mounted steadily over Jay's Treaty and the strict neutrality of the Americans. They threatened to consider their own treaties as "annihilated," and practically did so by seizing every American ship found laden with goods for England. The climax of a series of captures came with the taking of the *Mount Vernon*.

Anger bubbled over in America at the news, though the Republicans justified French behavior by putting all the blame on Jay's "traitorous" treaty. Washington wished to send a special envoy to France to demand an explanation of the seizures; but the Senate was in recess. Had he the power to dispatch a special envoy, he inquired of Hamilton and Jay, without waiting for confirmation? And what should be done about Monroe, the regular minister, with whom he was thoroughly disgusted? [14]

Hamilton had not waited for the query to demand that Monroe be dismissed. As for the French aggressions, if only the British "had been wise, they would neither have harassed our trade themselves, nor suffered their trade with us to be harassed." Perhaps, he suggested, we should hint to them to put "a clever little squadron in our ports and on our coast." [15]

In truth, Monroe was acting most unaccountably in France. When the American merchants then in Paris asked him to submit for them to the Minister of Finance a memorial "claiming payment of what is due them by the government," he added an astounding postscript of his own. This was an apology for submitting the memorial, "as I know the difficulty of your situation and should be happy to accommodate with it." However, as the official representative of the United States, it was his duty to transmit the American claims. They were bona fide and acknowledged, and the creditor merchants were threatened with ruin if the payments were not met. Perhaps, he told the French Minister, he could act as an honest broker between them in such wise as to aid them and yet "not embarrass your affairs." [16] Monroe could hardly have expected that such an apologetic attitude would help the cause of the American merchants; and in fact it did not. The unfortunate creditors had to cool their heels a long time before any settlement was made.

Tom Paine added to Monroe's many difficulties by choosing this time to discharge all the venom he had accumulated against Washington while languishing in a French prison. Monroe, it is true, had tried to halt Paine; but not in order to shield the President of the United States. He openly sympathized with his semipermanent guest; and agreed with his complaints and diatribes. He feared only that the publication Paine contemplated might compromise himself. If he were personally in the clear, or if Jefferson by that time had won the election and become President, then he would be prepared to view the assault on Washington with complete equanimity.[17]

A moment after Monroe thus disclosed the state of his own mind on the matter, the bag of venom burst. With his accustomed facility of phrase and genius for vituperation, Paine published the most unmitigated attack on Washington and his conduct that had ever been put into print. He accused the President in set phrases of having been guilty of "double politics" in the conduct of his administration, of having granted "monopolies of every kind," of having grossly favored the speculators and betrayed the poor soldiers; of being, in short, "the patron of the fraud."

This was mere preamble. Paine was manifestly warming up to the congenial task. He next accused the President of lapping up adulation and calling for more, of "a mean and servile submission to the insults" of Great Britain and "treachery and ingratitude" to France. Paine harked back to the days of the Revolution to assert that the French alone had been responsible for its success, not Washington's "cold and unmilitary conduct." He even charged that "you slept away your time in the field, till the finances of the country were completely exhausted."

He vowed that Washington had deliberately wished to see him, Paine, executed in a French prison and that only Monroe's intervention had saved him. He lashed out at John Jay, at Gouverneur Morris, at John Adams, and at "the disguised traitors that call themselves Federalists."

He ended his open letter to Washington with an apostrophe which even for that free-speaking age was unexampled in its virulence. "As to you, Sir," he thundered, "treacherous in private friendship . . . and a hypocrite in public life, the world will be puzzled to decide whether you are an apostate or an impostor; whether you have abandoned good principles, or whether you ever had any."[18]

No wonder that Monroe feared the worst. But his fate had already been decided even before the excoriating pamphlet reached America.

Almost from the moment that Pickering took over the State Department, he had determined that Monroe must go. One of his first acts was to send a sharp reproof to him for having permitted French policy, on the basis of false reports of the contents of Jay's Treaty, to develop against us as it did.[19]

This was decidedly unfair; if anywhere, the fault lay with Jay, who had refused to furnish Monroe with a copy of his treaty. But Pickering was not concerned with evenhanded justice. The unfortunate speech which Monroe had delivered on his first arrival in Paris had convinced everyone in the administration—the President as well as his Cabinet—that Monroe was not a proper representative in France.

On July 2, 1796, the Cabinet took up the presidential queries concerning his power to dispatch a special envoy without the approval of the Senate and whether he should recall Monroe. They decided that the President had no power to send a special envoy unless Monroe was first recalled; and they decided further that Monroe's actions in France had been such that he ought to be recalled.[20]

Washington took no immediate action on the advice. But each letter that arrived from Monroe only deepened his anger, and brought him closer to the deed.[21] Finally, on August 22nd, Pickering had the grim satisfaction of writing a curt notification to Monroe that he was being superseded by Charles Cotesworth Pinckney of South Carolina.[22]

Monroe was thunderstruck. He had already sent home a long defense of his conduct against the rebuke administered to him on June 13th, and he thought that the episode was closed. But he should not have been astonished. Even as the notice traversed the sea, Monroe was writing a confidential letter to Madison which, had it ever fallen into administration hands, would have convicted him out of his own mouth.

He notified Madison that France had ordered Adet, the French minister to the United States, to return home and that no successor was contemplated. The reason for this abrupt breaking off of diplomatic relations, said Monroe, was the ratification and consummation of Jay's Treaty. "I have detained them seven months from doing what they ought to have done at once," astonishingly avowed the American minister. "Poor Washington. Into what hands has he fallen!" [23]

Monroe returned to the United States furious and determined at all costs to vindicate himself. Like Edmund Randolph in a similar situation, he bombarded the administration with demands for statements, justifications and the use of confidential material. Then he devoted a full year to the writing of his apologia and defense, as well as a full assault on Washington and his advisers.

When the book finally appeared, Monroe joined the perennial tribe of authors in his disgruntlement over the poor sales and notices it received; but he consoled himself with the reflection—again quite common—that "the book will remain and will be read in the course of 50 years if not sooner, and I think the facts it contains, will settle or contribute to settle, the opinion of posterity in the character of the administration, however indifferent to it the present race may be." As for the men who made up that administration, "a gang of greater scoundrels never lived." [24]

With the third presidential election in the offing, Washington was adamant in his decision to retire. He had consented to a second term only on the insistent pleas of his colleagues, Federalist and Republican alike. Now no Republican urged him to remain.

The increasing tempo of abuse during the preceding months bewildered and angered him. He winced at every epithet and reacted to every tirade. He did not intend, he declared bitterly, "to be longer buffeted in the public prints by a set of infamous scribblers." He regretted only that he had not earlier announced his decision to withdraw.[25]

He had been thinking over the form of this announcement for a long time; as far back, indeed, as the end of his first administration. He wished to make it a valedictory, in which he could give the nation the benefit of such wisdom and experience as he had accumulated in its service.

At that time, when his relations with Madison were not yet strained, he had asked him to draft the valedictory. Madison had done so; then it had been put away when Washington assumed the presidency a second time. This time he called on Hamilton to act as his guide. The first draft of what he wished to say Washington wrote himself. Hamilton revised, polished and offered suggestions.

"My wish is," said the President, "that the whole may appear in a plain style; and be handed to the public in an honest, unaffected, simple garb." [26] He also wished, he said at another time, to address "the Yeomenry of this Country" and warn them of the "consequences which would naturally flow from such unceasing and virulent attempts to destroy all confidence in the Executive part of the Government" as evidenced by the recent invectives against himself.[27]

After considerable correspondence and constant revisions of the several drafts, Washington's Farewell Address finally emerged in a form which both men thought satisfactory. In September 1796, copies were distributed to the newspapers for publication.

The Farewell Address has become one of the classics of American political literature. Its grave, measured tones, its solemn exhortations and impressive warnings, the spirit of earnestness which pervades its entire structure, have left their deep impress on American thought and diplomacy.

In retiring from public office, Washington declared, "a solicitude for your welfare" and "the apprehension of danger" had impelled him to offer certain sentiments and reflections for the consideration of the American people.

"The Unity of Government which constitutes you one people," he wrote, ". . . is a main pillar in the edifice of your real independence; the support of your tranquillity at home; your peace abroad; of your safety; of your prosperity; of that very liberty which you so highly prize." But as it was this "point in your political fortress" which both internal and external enemies sought to breach and to weaken in your mind the conviction of its truth, it was essential that all Americans guard and cherish it to the utmost, and to resist "every attempt to alienate any portion of our Country from the rest, or to enfeeble the sacred ties which now link together the various parts."

This was the major and indeed the only theme of the valedictory —the true interrelation and interdependence of North, South and West. With all the earnestness at his command Washington warned against party passions and "designing men" who sought to create the impression that "there is a real difference of local interests and views" based on geographical dispersion.

Only a "Government for the whole," he added, can give power and permanency to the Union. The Constitution, our own choice, provides that; and until it is changed by lawful means, it must be considered as a sacred obligation. "All obstructions to the execution of the laws, all combinations and associations, under whatever plausible character, with the real design to direct, control, counteract, or awe the regular deliberation and action of the Constituted authorities are destructive of this fundamental principle and of fatal tendency. They serve to organize faction, to give it an artificial and extraordinary force; to put in the place of the delegated will of the Nation, the will of a party; often a small but artful and enterprizing minority of the Community."

This section was an obvious denunciation of the Whiskey Rebellion, the Democratic Societies and the Republican party itself. The idea of political parties had not yet become fixed and permanent in the minds of the Founding Fathers; even the Republicans themselves hated the designation, avowing that it was the Federalists who in fact represented the party or factional spirit.

Washington kindled to this theme. "The spirit of party," he continued, is baneful and leads inevitably to despotism. "It serves always to distract the public councils and enfeeble the public administration. It agitates the community with ill founded jealousies and false alarms; kindles the animosity of one part against another; foments occasionally riot and insurrection. It opens the door to foreign influence and corruption, which find a facilitated access to the government itself, through the channels of party passions."

Thus Washington led into his second major theme—the dangers arising from foreign entanglements. "Observe good faith and justice towards all nations," he exhorted; "cultivate peace and harmony with all." Let there be neither "permanent inveterate antipathies against particular nations" nor "passionate attachments for others."

"The great rule of conduct for us," he declared, "in regard to foreign nations, is in extending our commercial relations, to have with them as little political connection as possible. . . . Europe has a set of primary interests, which to us have none or a very remote relation. Hence she must be engaged in frequent controversies, the causes of which are essentially foreign to our concerns. . . . Our detached and distant situation invites, and enables us to pursue, a different course. . . . Why forego the advantages of so peculiar a situation? Why quit our own, to stand upon foreign ground? Why, by interweaving our destiny with that of any part of Europe, entangle our peace and prosperity in the toils of European ambition, rivalship, interest, humor, or caprice? 'Tis our true policy to steer clear of permanent alliances with any portion of the foreign world."

These, he concluded, were the "counsels of an old and affectionate friend." [28]

It has been this final section which has always drawn the attention of the isolationists. They fail, however, to note the peculiar context of the times in which Washington issued his solemn warning. America was torn by contending groups who, in some instances, gave their allegiance more passionately to the foreign nation of their choice than to the country of their citizenship. The distance between the two continents seemed enormous, and took many weeks or even months to span. A determined and united people at home could withstand engulfment from abroad, no matter how ruthless the power or efficient the dictator. But the times have changed; jet planes, long-range bombers, submarines, atom and hydrogen bombs, radio and ideologies can penetrate the most formidable frontier. The ocean is neither frontier nor barrier any more; the outposts of the nation have moved to far-flung places whose very names were unknown to Americans in Washington's day. Indeed, it is highly probable that he would have been the first to disavow the interpretations which have since been placed upon his doctrine of "entangling alliances."

In its own day the Farewell Address made but little stir. The Republicans resented the manifest allusions to themselves, and their press printed the Address without comment. Nor did it put an end to previous attachments to France and inveterate hatred of England, nor did they hesitate a moment in their assaults on the administration at home.

"Have a care," continued their passionate invective, ". . . ye corrupt rulers—ye abandoned tories—ye minions of Great Britain—ye enemies of republicanism, and advocates for monarchy—you stand on a precipice. A war with France would produce a civil one. . . . Your heads will offer but a poor atonement to your injured country for the miseries you have brought upon it. May heaven avert the just indignation of France." [29]

Washington to them was still "perfidious," an "old Automatous," and one whose refusal to be a candidate again came not from "a want of ambition or lust of power" but from a consciousness that he would not be re-elected. He was still an aristocrat, ostentatious as any Eastern bashaw, and a slaveholder. Even Adams, so they said, was the better man; though theoretically aristocratic, nevertheless he would never be "a puppet" nor "sacrifice his country's interests at the shrine of party." [30]

The Federalists, on the other hand, if less passionately attached to

Great Britain, hated France and belabored their Republican enemies at home with abuse as intense as they received. They did indeed praise the Farewell Address, and covered themselves with the somewhat tattered glory which still surrounded Washington; but, though they rendered lip service to his admonitions, they continued their old courses as if they had never been uttered.

With Washington publicly withdrawn from the forthcoming election, a novel situation arose in American politics. For the first time there was to be a real contest for the presidency, complete with rival candidates and party banners.

John Adams, twice Vice-President of the United States, was the logical Federalist candidate for the office. Yet his nomination, unanimous to all outward seeming, evoked rumblings of discontent within the party ranks. Hamilton did not like the stubborn old man, who certainly would be no "puppet" in his hands. He would have much preferred Thomas Pinckney, the former minister to England and author of the advantageous treaty with Spain. But the other Federalist leaders, particularly from New England, would have none other than Adams. They were willing enough to have Pinckney in the vice-presidency.

Hamilton sought nevertheless to achieve his secret wish. It was all-important, he told his Federalist friends, to keep Jefferson out of the presidency. He had heard that New England intended to throw some votes away from Pinckney to ensure Adams's election. This must not be done, he avowed, since it might be the cause of Jefferson's slipping into first place. Even if Pinckney should as a result gain the major office, he cunningly insinuated, there would be no real loss.[31]

The New England men refused to hearken to his siren blandishments. As the specter of Jefferson lengthened, and another—even more gruesome and frightening in Hamilton's eyes—appeared upon the horizon, he was compelled to acquiesce in the arrangement.

The second specter was Aaron Burr of New York, erstwhile senator, Republican politician, organizer of Tammany as an efficient political machine, brilliant lawyer, and rival to Hamilton in almost every field. If Hamilton despised and feared Jefferson, he hated and abhorred Burr. For Burr was not only being considered by the Republicans as Jefferson's running mate, there were certain Federalists who seriously estimated him as a possibility for themselves instead of the unamenable Adams.

Jonathan Dayton of New Jersey, former Speaker of the House and a Federalist of sorts, secretly proposed to Sedgwick of Massachusetts that their party back Burr for the presidency. Sedgwick did not take kindly to the suggestion, and sent copies of Dayton's letters to Hamilton.[32]

Nothing could have alarmed Hamilton more than this underground conspiracy. He knew that Burr, with his personal graces, undoubted talents and glamorous career, as well as his moderateness in an age of partisan politics, might be agile enough to straddle both parties and become a most formidable contender. Rather than Burr, Hamilton would have accepted Jefferson himself; and certainly Adams was by far preferable to both.

On the Republican side there was no such problem. Jefferson was universally conceded as the presidential candidate. There were a number of contenders for the vice-presidential nomination; but Burr was finally chosen.

The curious maneuvering for position, the propositions to "throw away" votes from a party candidate, are explainable by the peculiar constitutional provision that each presidential elector cast his ballot for two men, without discrimination or preference between them as to office. The candidate who received the greatest number of individual votes became President; the second highest became Vice-President.

The voting for electors was even more complicated. Each state wrote its own provisions. In some states they were chosen by a direct vote of the qualified voters; in others by a mixture of voting at large and legislative election; in still others, the legislatures had the sole power of choice. In the last two categories, the spring elections for the state legislatures usually determined the complexion of the electoral ballots to be cast in the fall presidential campaign.

It must also be remembered that the "people" who voted in the general elections did not constitute by any means the entire population. Aside from the fact that minors, women, slaves and Indians had no vote, the stringent property and other qualifications disfranchised approximately five-sixths of the free adult white males.

In spite of the preference expressed by Republicans for Adams as against Washington, any such idea was cast aside in the current contest between Adams and Jefferson. They now concentrated all their fire on Adams. His ancient writings, like the *Defence of the American Constitutions* and the "Discourses on Davila" were exhumed from a decent obscurity and subjected to a microscopic examination for evidences of monarchical and aristocratical leanings. The results were immediately evident.

"MONARCHY or REPUBLICANISM," thundered the party sheets, "is the order of the day. If you wish Monarchy support the man who will support Mr. John Adams. If you wish a WAR with France, advocate the man who is their enemy." [33] In return, the Federalists warned against the belief that the election of Adams and Jefferson as his Vice-President would mean the union of "the roses red and white. . . . Fire and frost are not more opposite in their natures than those characters are; and the prosperity, honor and dignity of the United States depend on an administration perfectly federal." [34]

The British minister, Robert Liston, reported that though America might still be an "infant" society, it had already made rapid strides on "the road towards corruption." In Philadelphia, Republican sailors, armed with clubs, paraded the streets to intimidate voters. False votes were accepted at the polls, good votes were cast out, and "a great number of peaceable voters were prevented by force from even approaching the place of election."

Jefferson was accused of atheism, of loving France and hating England; Adams was attacked for his addiction to monarchy and hereditary distinctions; while extracts from his books were printed in handbills and carried in the thousands by express riders to the remotest parts of the country.[35]

Just as the campaign against Adams developed around his alleged monarchism, so the assault on Jefferson centered on his deism, which to the Federalists was in fact atheism. "What would be the situation of society in a few years," demanded the Federalists, "were all our public officers Deists? Would not the people turn Deists also, and kick the Christian religion out of doors? In the name of that religion then, let all who regard it use their influence in promoting the choice of such Electors as will give us A CHRISTIAN PRESIDENT." [36]

With domestic issues thus befogged and foreign affairs revolving solely on a choice between France and England, this first contested election in the United States moved to an exciting close. The parties were fairly evenly aligned, with the main Republican strength as ever in the South, and the Federalists entrenched in New England. Therefore the battle was sharpest and closest in the doubtful Middle States of New York and Pennsylvania.

In Pennsylvania we have seen to what lengths the Republicans went. In New York City a series of suspicious fires broke out in widely scattered places which the Federalists promptly attributed to Republican incendiaries. Their leaders instituted a nightly watch to catch the offenders. Hamilton made one of them, and sprained his leg for his pains.[37] The incendiaries were never caught; but the Federalists managed to extract effective propaganda from the scare.

What further complicated the situation was the internecine if hidden struggle among the Federalists themselves. Should they deliberately throw away a few votes from Pinckney to make Adams's election secure; or might that place Jefferson in the vice-presidency? Hamilton's good friend Robert Troup doubtless echoed his mentor when he put it as his wish and the wish of "our friends" that Pinckney would displace Adams in the presidency.[38]

Massachusetts, however, was determined to ensure the election of her favorite son. It was feared that if both Federalist candidates were given equal votes in New England, Pinckney might pick up enough votes elsewhere to win the presidency. In spite of Hamilton's arguments for equality, therefore, three Massachusetts electors threw away their second ballots from Pinckney. They made no secret of their belief that Hamilton and Jay were seeking to defeat Adams, whom they could not control, in favor of their creature, Pinckney.[39]

Their fears were not ill-grounded. Madison noted signs that the Hamiltonian adherents were secretly pushing Pinckney over Adams; and attributed the treachery to "the enmity of Adams to banks and funding systems which is now become public, and by an apprehension that he is too headstrong to be a fit puppet for the intrigues behind the screen." [40]

The Connecticut Federalists also dropped five votes from Pinckney, giving them all to John Jay. Rhode Island disdained Pinckney altogether, giving her four votes to Adams and her favorite son, Oliver Ellsworth. So did New Hampshire with her six votes.

It was fortunate for Adams that New England acted as it did; for Pinckney's native state of South Carolina knifed Adams and voted her eight electoral ballots for Pinckney and Jefferson!

On the Republican side there was similar chicanery. Aaron Burr, the official candidate for the vice-presidency, was deliberately passed over in Jefferson's own state of Virginia. Jefferson received the full twenty ballots; Sam Adams, the aging Massachusetts radical, received nineteen; and Burr obtained a solitary salute. In other Republican strongholds Burr was treated in the same fashion. Both he and his friends were convinced that the Southern Republicans had broken faith. Even Hamilton, who had sought and failed to do the same for Adams, remarked gleefully on Burr's disaster. "The event will not a little mortify Burr," he exclaimed. "Virginia has given him only one vote." [41]

So close was the balloting between Adams and Jefferson, with Pinckney formidably on their heels, and so tardy were the means of communication, that it was late in December before any definite trend could be established. The electors of the several states met separately and at different times; messengers and letters hurried the news over frozen roads to the candidates and their political managers in their widely scattered homes.

With every fresh batch of news the result seemed to shift. New York and New Jersey, listed as doubtful, went solidly Federalist. Pennsylvania went overwhelmingly Republican through a combination of the "yeomanry" of Philadelphia and the farmers of the western counties, still licking their wounds from the suppression of the Whiskey Rebellion. But a curious situation arose. In western Greene County, two Republican electors had been returned as expected. They failed, however, to appear in time at the appointed meeting place of the state electors. Instead, two Federalists showed up, brazenly claimed that *they* were the electors of Greene County and cast their ballots.

After the event there was an outcry that these two illegal votes had actually elected Adams over Jefferson. In fact, the usurping Federalists further confused an already sufficiently confused situation by their strange antics. One of them orthodoxly cast his votes for Adams and Pinckney. The other, however, voted for Pinckney and Jefferson! So that, even had the regularly elected Republicans voted, Jefferson could not have overcome Adams. [42] As it stood, the final count in Pennsylvania gave Jefferson fourteen, Burr thirteen, Pinckney two and Adams one.

By the end of December the national results were known. Adams had been elected with 71 electoral votes; Jefferson was Vice-President with 68 votes; Pinckney trailed with 59; Burr was far in the rear with 30. The remainder of the ballots was distributed among nine others.

The election had been very close, with the opposing parties fairly balanced. Had not New England votes been thrown away from Pinckney, he would have been President. On the other hand, had

South Carolina voted for Adams instead of joining Pinckney and Jefferson in unnatural union, Adams would have been far out in front. Already the curious cross-currents and local politics which characterize the American scene were making their appearance.

The closeness of the vote impelled Madison to the belief that the Federalists, and especially the new President, would find food for thought in their less than clear-cut victory, and perhaps temper their policies. "Your acceptance of a share in the administration," he advised Jefferson, "will not fail to aid this tendency." [43]

Jefferson rather welcomed his defeat for the higher office. He preferred not to accept ultimate responsibility in the gloomy aspect of foreign affairs. Even before the result was known he had declared: "Let those come to the helm who think they can steer clear of the difficulties. I have no confidence in myself in the undertaking." Indeed, when for a while it seemed as if he and Adams were tied and the election would be thrown into the House of Representatives, he asked that Adams be preferred to himself as the senior. [44]

His friends feared he might also refuse the vice-presidency. Madison urged him to accept because "your neighborhood to Adams may have a valuable effect on his councils particularly in relation to our external system. You know that his feelings will not enslave him to the example of his predecessor." [45]

Still strangely at war with himself, Jefferson composed an effusive letter addressed to his old friend John Adams, in which he congratulated him on his election, disavowed any previous competition, and warned him to beware of the treachery of "your arch-friend of New York [Hamilton] who has been able to make of your real friends tools to defeat their and your just wishes." [46]

But second thoughts caused him to send the letter first to Madison for his perusal and discretion in forwarding it. Madison considered the epistle too eager and liable to misinterpretation. [47] The letter was never sent, but discreet leaks advised Adams of Jefferson's cordial feelings toward him.

Adams was duly flattered, and wrote to an informant that he had the highest regard for his new Vice-President. Nevertheless, he admitted, he did not like Jefferson's friends and political entanglements. "But I hope and believe," he added, "that his advancement and his situation in the Senate, an excellent School, will correct him. He will have too many French friends about him to flatter him; but I hope we can keep him steady." [48]

Both Adams and Jefferson were to be disappointed in their mutual hopes and flatteries.

It was the honeymoon period, with everyone offering a kindly word for everyone else. The sad realities were still to come. But of the departing President few Republicans had anything good to say. Even Jefferson spoke sarcastically of Washington's luck in getting out just as financial ruin stared the country in the face. When it comes, he said, the trouble will be ascribed to the new administration; and Washington "will have his usual good fortune of reaping credit from the good acts of others, and leaving to them that of his errors." [49]

The Republican editors were more unrestrained. Bache speeded the parting President with vituperation that exceeded even his own previously fertile imagination.

"The man who is the source of all the misfortunes of our country," he exulted, "is this day reduced to a level with his fellow citizens, and is no longer possessed of power to multiply evils upon the United States. . . . If ever a nation was debauched by a man, the American Nation has been debauched by Washington. If ever a nation has suffered from the improper influence of a man, the American Nation has suffered from the influence of Washington. If ever a nation was deceived by a man, the American Nation has been deceived by Washington. . . . This day ought to be a JUBILEE in the United States." [50]

Under such benign auspices did the Father of his Country retire to private life.

CHAPTER 23

President Adams

THE TIME FOR Washington's retirement was not due until March 4, 1797. In the interim he was still President of the United States and faced with grave problems that could not wait for the accession of his successor.

On October 27, 1796, the French minister Adet transmitted to the American government a resolution of the French Directory dated July 2nd announcing their intention to "treat neutral vessels, either as to confiscation, as to searches, or capture, in the same manner as they shall suffer the English to treat them."

To the decree Adet appended an insulting query of his own. Had the United States any right to complain of what France did when she herself, "through weakness, partiality, or other motives," suffered England to sport with her neutrality? To which rhetorical question he furnished his own answer: "No, certainly." [1] To compound the insult, Adet sent both the official decree and his own biting comment to the Republican press.

Pickering in his reply following the line which the United States had always taken: France was precluded by her treaty from seizing provision ships; England, unfortunately, was not in treaty relation with us, and applied the regular definition of contraband. [2]

Adet swiftly turned the tables. If the treaty really was still in effect, then its terms must be adhered to in every respect. Washington and Jefferson had imposed restrictions on the use of American ports by French privateers and their prizes, contrary to the articles of that treaty. Let those restrictions be lifted; and let all Americans, whose country still displayed marks of "British fury," join again with their old allies and denounce Jay's Treaty. [3]

This new demand, complete with the rodomontade which every French envoy seemed to affect, was similarly rushed to the public prints. It aroused a storm. Hamilton inveighed against it as an attempt to influence the pending election.[4] Though indignant at this Federalist construction, Madison nevertheless admitted that Adet's note was "working all the evil with which it is pregnant," and feared it would lead to a perpetual alienation from France.[5]

Indeed, events were now moving swiftly toward that conclusion. France decided to withdraw her minister from the United States; tantamount to a break in diplomatic relations. Charles Cotesworth Pinckney, arriving in Paris to supplant Monroe, found his reception most frigid. On December 7th Monroe introduced him as his successor. Four days later he received a note from the Minister of Foreign Affairs that the Directory had decided not to "acknowledge or receive another minister plenipotentiary from the United States, until after the redress of the grievances demanded of the American Government, and which the French republic has a right to expect from it." [6]

Pinckney, to whom Monroe passed on this cavalier announcement, promptly inquired of the Foreign Minister, M. De La Croix, if this was a final statement of the French position, and if he was therefore required to quit the country.[7]

Instead of an official reply, Pinckney received a visit from M. Giraudet, the secretary of the department. Since Pinckney's very existence as an envoy was not recognized, asserted the secretary, no direct communication would be made to him. It was indeed intended that he leave France, and the police would so notify him. Pinckney protested vigorously against any such procedure, asserting his protection under the law of nations. If he must go, he added, then let the French hand him his passports, together with a safe-conduct.

While he adopted a strong stand, Pinckney acknowledged that he was in a most unpleasant position. The ministers of thirteen other nations had already been summarily expelled by the arrogant Directory; and America, so Pinckney discovered, rated with them no higher than the tiny city-states of Geneva or Genoa.[8]

Nevertheless he was resolved not to go until he was literally shipped off by force. Eventually the Directory modified their initial harshness to send the American envoy his passports and an official order of departure. In February 1797, Pinckney and his family left the country to seek refuge in Amsterdam.[9]

This ultimate outrage was not yet known in the United States when Congress convened on December 5, 1796.

Washington's opening address was cautious yet firm. He called for a naval force adequate to protect our commerce, secure respect for our neutral flag and discourage violations of our rights by belligerent powers. He called for the public manufacture of weapons of war, though confessing that he did not ordinarily favor manufactures "on public account." He asked for the establishment of Boards to encourage scientific agriculture, a national university and a military academy.

As for the French, he told of their interference with our West Indies trade, though expressing the pious hope that we might yet be able to maintain cordial relations. He made no mention of any countermeasures.[10]

The Senate supplied the deficiency. In their reply to the presidential address, they warned that, should peaceful negotiations fail, this nation was not "unprepared to adopt that system of conduct which, compatible with the dignity of a respectable nation, necessity may compel us to pursue." The Republican-dominated House, however, stressed only the necessity for a mutual agreement based on "a mutual spirit of justice and moderation."[11]

In the House, indeed, there was much bitter criticism of the outgoing President. "I may be singular in my ideas," avowed Giles of Virginia, "but I believe our Administration has been neither wise nor firm." Nor, he added, did he think very much of Washington; the government of the United States could get along quite well without him.

The Federalists rose in outraged protest, but Giles stood his ground. He was aided by Blount, the member from the new state of Tennessee, who insisted on a roll-call vote on the reply to the address because he wanted "posterity" to know that he did not approve of it.[12]

Even Washington's suggestion of a national university ran into trouble. Though Madison tried to forward the idea, his Virginia colleague Nicholas objected to any national seat of learning. Small local colleges were much preferable, he declared, and expatiated on the dangers to the morals of young men so far away from their parental homes. Much to Washington's mortification, the plan was voted down.[13]

Since the Treasury reports disclosed an alarming deficit in government revenues, the old question of a direct tax was again raised; this time in the form of a general assessment on land holdings. To this the South raised its usual clamor, demanding instead additional duties on salt, wines, spirits, stamps and windows. Most of these, Robert

Goodloe Harper of South Carolina frankly stated, could be avoided by persons not having such "luxuries."

Findley of Pennsylvania rose to observe that this was again the old contest between the agricultural and the trading interests. Why should not agriculture pay its share of the public expense? "Was it not a little surprising," he pointedly asked, "to see members of that House, whose estates were mostly in land, so desirous of avoiding a land tax?" [14]

In spite of initial successes by the advocates of the tax, it was finally defeated. In its place duties were levied on stamped paper and on salt. Once more the Southern bloc, abetted by the large landowners of the Middle States, proved victorious.

Fisher Ames, still not recovered from his illness, viewed the state of the country with disgust and gloomy forebodings. In a remarkable letter to Hamilton he discoursed passionately on the present and the future.

"Our proceedings smell of anarchy," he wrote. "We rest our hopes on foolish and fanatical grounds—on the superior morals and self-supporting theories of our age and country; on human nature being different from what it is, and better here than any where else."

We fail to provide a means of revenue, or enforce collection of what has been provided. The Western country holds to the Union by a precarious thread; yet we disband regiments. Our foreign trade is systematically despoiled by France and England; yet we refuse to protect it with a navy.

"An European would be ready to believe we were in jest in our politics, or that newspaper declamation and the frothy nonsense of town-meeting speeches comprise the principle of our conduct. . . . What we call the *government* is a phantom." It was actually "a mere democracy, which has never been tolerable nor long tolerated." The heads of departments were in effect clerks who cannot, as in other countries, communicate with Congress. The executive branch had no power or momentum, and neither courts nor officers received the respect or acquiescence of the people.[15]

Ames lumped all these ills under the single heading of "democracy." To him Congress itself was a mere forum for town-meeting tactics, in which the members postured and ranted for the benefit of the groundlings instead of acting as responsible statesmen. There was unfortunately an element of truth in his caustic descriptions; yet he failed to realize that even the "statesmen," of whom he considered himself one, sought measures that would benefit the particular class from which they sprang or the constituency they represented. Nor was his example of the mythical European particularly happy. The rulers of England, which he specifically had in mind, had not displayed that wisdom, statesmanlike view and unselfish devotion to the entire nation which Ames considered to be desiderata.

Yet there was much to alarm in the state of the country during the interval before Adams took office. Diplomatic relations with France were at an end, and the report that Pinckney had been ordered out of that country caused a panic in the shipping trade. Marine insurance jumped ten per cent overnight.[16]

The British, observing the uproar from a distance with satisfaction, graciously offered the protection of their navy to American commerce, and proposed convoys under their escort.[17] On January 19th, Washington laid the rapidly worsening situation before Congress.

Hamilton, from his private observation post in New York, now rose to statesmanlike heights. He saw our relations with France in the same cul-de-sac as with England before Jay went on his mission. Why not, he argued, get out of it in the same way? He sent letters to Washington, Pickering and Wolcott urging on them the dispatch of an extraordinary mission to France composed of three envoys. He even offered names—James Madison, Charles Cotesworth Pinckney and George Cabot. Madison would represent the Republicans; Pinckney the same in an "inferior degree"; while Cabot would act as "a salutary check upon too much Gallicism, and his *real* commercial knowledge will supply their want of it." The fact that there was in the making a change of administration in the United States, he believed, would afford France an opportunity to save face.[18]

For once his ordinarily pliant Federalist friends dared dispute with him. Wolcott disagreed altogether with his proposition; though, as he put it, "I am accustomed to respect your opinions; and I am not so ignorant of the extent of your influence upon the friends of government, as not to be sensible that if you are known to favor the sending of a commission, so the thing must and will be." [19]

Wolcott overestimated Hamilton's influence. The Federalists had the bit in their mouths and were hot for war with France. This was the first time that the country at large was backing them up, and they were disposed to make the most of it. Pickering, Wolcott, William Smith, McHenry, Uriah Tracy—Hamilton's usually subservient followers—took issue with him and turned down the plan as mere truckling to the enemy. Only Rufus King, from his vantage point in London, urged that the United States keep out of war.[20]

The Republicans knew nothing of Hamilton's repeated if futile attempts to stave off war. Even if they had, they would have imputed pernicious motives to his proposal. They pinned their faith rather on John Adams, the incoming President. Jefferson, waiting to take his seat as Vice-President, did not believe Adams wanted war with France, or that he would "truckle to England as servilely as has been done." To Jefferson, England was still the true enemy. "I think," he wrote, "we should begin first with those who first begin with us, and, by an example on them, acquire a right to re-demand respect from which the other party [France] has departed." [21]

On March 4, 1797, the nation witnessed its first change of administration. The entire country united to welcome the new President. If some of the Federalists had reservations about their anointed leader, the opposition Republicans had none. They were as fulsome now in their praise of Adams as, during the election contest, they had been with their brickbats and filth. They hailed him as the hope of America and drew invidious comparisons between him and his predecessor. They exulted over the friendly relations existing between Adams and Jefferson, and found auguries that the lion and the lamb would now lie down together.

Even a Justice of the Supreme Court, William Patterson, took heart from the fact that Adams and Jefferson had taken quarters in the same house. "The thing looks well," he reported with much satisfaction; "it carries conciliation and healing with it, and may have a happy effect on parties. . . . I hope that, in a short time, we shall have no interest or views but what are purely American." [22]

Only Hamilton viewed the proceedings askance. "Skeptics like me," he wrote, "quietly look forward to the event, willing to hope, but not prepared to believe. If Mr. Adams has *vanity* 'tis plain a plot has been laid to take hold of it." [23]

Hamilton was right. The Republicans had in fact plotted to pilot Adams into proper Republican channels through his association with Jefferson. But Adams upset their plans. A few days prior to the inauguration he met Jefferson privately. Like Hamilton, Adams favored an immediate mission to resolve our difficulties with France. He would have preferred to send Jefferson, he told the latter; unfortunately there were constitutional difficulties in sending the Vice-President out of the country. He wished therefore to nominate Madison, Charles Cotesworth Pinckney, and Elbridge Gerry. The first two had already been suggested by Hamilton; Adams was replacing Cabot by his personal friend Gerry.

Would Jefferson, asked Adams, inquire of Madison if he would go? Jefferson did so, and reported that he had declined. It seemed to the Vice-President that Adams looked relieved, muttering that objections had in the meantime been raised to his name. Jefferson thought that the holdover Cabinet had spiked the whole idea of the mission and diverted Adams to "former party views." Jefferson was never consulted again on any governmental measure.[24]

The inaugural ceremonies were quiet yet impressive. Washington came to the Federal Hall unattended and afoot, his first appearance as a private citizen. The assembled populace greeted him with tremendous applause. Adams also met with a rousing reception and took the oath of office with dignity. Then he adjourned to the Senate to deliver his Inaugural Address.[25]

His speech was simple, short and avoided controversial issues. He traced the genesis of the Constitution and found it good. Like Washington in his Farewell Address, he called attention to the dangers of party government for party purposes and not for the national welfare.[26]

Everyone was happy, including the incoming and outgoing Presidents. Adams detected a smile of triumph on Washington's face over the fact that now his successor would have to bear the burdens. And, so Adams said, his own speech left not a dry eye in the house. When he ended, everyone came up to congratulate him and to declare that they had never listened to such a public speech in their lives; indeed, "it was the sublimest thing ever exhibited in America." [27]

Adams may be pardoned this small exhibition of vanity. He had tossed and trembled all the night before; while the cost of being President filled him with alarm. Though his salary was $25,000 a year, he noted apprehensively that his house rent came to $2700, his carriage cost $1500 and the horses to draw it put him out of pocket in the sum of $1000. What with glassware, ornaments, furniture, crockery, linens, secretaries, servants, swords, firewood, charities, "and the million dittoes," the prospect for breaking even looked very gloomy to him.[28]

In spite of these forebodings, he appeared at his first levee smiling and self-satisfied, clad in full formal dress complete with sword, wig and every appurtenance.[29]

Washington quietly packed his household goods and in a few days unostentatiously departed for his sanctuary of Mount Vernon, never to return.

But the abuse of the Republicans pursued him into retirement even as they continued to laud Adams. Who could read Adams's Inaugural Address, they exclaimed, without applauding it to the skies? "It is so long," they said, "since the citizens of America heard an acknowledgment on the part of their executive that all power was derived from the people."[30] Nor did they disguise their "sincere and undissembled satisfaction at the idea of their so soon getting rid of a President whose administration had brought his country to the brink of ruin."[31]

The honeymoon did not last long. In fact, it did not last out the month. By that time Adams was already asserting that to have seen "such a character as Jefferson, and much more such an unknown being as Pinckney, brought over my head" in the election would have demonstrated to him that "our Constitution could not have lasted four years."[32]

And, as Adams's policies unfolded, the Republicans changed their tune and turned to a hate equal to that which they had previously displayed toward Washington. On the other hand, Hamilton now approved of him as both prudent and firm; an estimate which was shortly to be reversed again.[33]

Hamilton, indeed, was almost at the breaking point with his former cronies and followers. He was taken aback at their summary dismissal of his proposal for a special mission to France. "A suspicion begins to *dawn* among the friends of the government," he declared angrily, "that the *actual* administration is not much averse to war with France."[34] He meant not Adams, but his Cabinet advisers—Wolcott, Pickering and McHenry.

The more prudent merchants who made up the strength of the Federalists upheld Hamilton. One of them sighed that while English depredations on their ships and goods would eventually be recompensed, French spoliations would never be. In spite of this, he would rather submit to loss than resort to war.[35]

Pickering, the Secretary of State, was eager for war. Liston, the British minister, was happy to report to his superiors "the complete conversion on Mr. Pickering" caused by his recent passages at arms with Adet. He had now "become one of the most violent Antigallicans I have ever met with. There seems to be no risk that either he or any of his Brother Ministers . . . will be inclined to allow to France the enjoyment of any advantages that may be denied to Great Britain." In fact, when Liston offered him the use of a British frigate for convoying American merchant vessels from Philadelphia to the West Indies, Pickering accepted with the greatest alacrity.[36]

Meanwhile Adams was submitting to his warlike Cabinet the question whether the refusal of France to receive Pinckney should be taken as "bars to all further measures of negotiations"; and if not, what problems ought a mission to discuss.[37]

McHenry, the most amenable of the Cabinet, turned to Hamilton for advice and replied almost verbatim in his mentor's language. Hamilton reiterated his former suggestion of a special mission. At the same time he called for measures of defense against further depredations: a naval force for convoy duty, permission to merchant ships to arm for their own defense, a temporary embargo, fortification of the seaports, a trained army and an increased revenue. He even drafted a set of instructions for the envoys to carry. While the conduct of France, he concluded, had been insulting in the extreme, the United States had the strongest motives for avoiding war, with nothing to gain and everything to lose by a resort to arms.[38]

As always, Hamilton considered peace absolutely essential to the country until its structure had been placed on solid and permanent foundations, and it had grown in power and resources.

He even prevailed on Uriah Tracy, the most fiery of the Federalist congressmen, to await the issue of a possible negotiation. But Tracy was ready, if the House Republicans attempted to force through a resolution laying the fault at the door of the administration, to break up the Union. The South, he exclaimed, was rapidly increasing its population "by frequent importations of foreign scoundrels as well as by those of home manufacture" and would eventually swallow up the Northern states, so that "the name and real character of an American" would soon be only a tradition. The Northern states, he avowed with passion, had been "carrying the Southern on their backs"; and if a choice had to be made, he would prefer to be once more under Great Britain than under France.[39]

If such extreme sentiments could ever be justified, they would have been by the evidence, complete with names and details, that American citizens were captaining French privateers and preying on the commerce of their fellow countrymen. The brutality of their conduct was such that it put the foreign privateersmen to shame.[40]

The receipt of Pinckney's dispatches from Paris and Amsterdam with their accounts of the treatment to which he had been subjected brought already superheated passions to the point of explosion. Next came a report that the French had decreed the hanging of any American seaman found on a captured British ship, whether his presence was voluntary or not.

This last report goaded the Federalists into a fierce outcry on those "patriots" in Congress who "will attempt to soften and palliate the bloody decree, and kneel to kiss the dagger that is to be plunged in the breasts of our seamen." [41]

On May 15, 1797, the Fifth Congress convened in special session in an atmosphere of turmoil and passion that had come to seem indigenous to the American scene. There were several new faces in the House. Of these perhaps the most notable were Harrison Gray Otis of Massachusetts and Matthew Lyon of Vermont.

No more contrasting pair could be imagined. Otis, a Federalist, was fastidious in dress and manners, a cultured and ready orator whose vocabulary was one of the phenomena of the day. When Noah Webster announced a dictionary which would contain three thousand new words, Chief Justice Shaw of Massachusetts humorously held up his hands in horror. "For heaven's sake," he cried, "don't let Otis get hold of it!" [42]

Lyon, on the other hand, Irish-born and still sporting a brogue, was vulgar in speech and manners, slipshod in dress, and accustomed to knockdown debates reminiscent of the kicking, gouging and maiming of frontier disputes. He soon rose to notoriety if not to fame as one of the loudest and fiercest Republican partisans in an already well-equipped House.

Peter Porcupine hailed the Vermonter's arrival with his accustomed satire: "To-morrow morning at eleven o'clock will be exposed to public view the *Lyon of Vermont*. This singular animal is said to have been caught on the bog of Hibernia, and, when a whelp, transported to America." [43]

Adams addressed Congress on the state of relations with France. He presented the fact of the Directory's refusal to receive Pinckney. He spoke of French efforts to alienate the American people from their government and declared that these "ought to be repelled with a decision which shall convince France, and the world, that we are not a degraded people . . . fitted to be the miserable instruments of a foreign influence." He advocated those measures of defense which had been embodied in Hamilton's memorandum, as transmitted by McHenry: an increased army and navy, convoys, and the arming of merchant ships.[44]

The reaction to his speech was what might have been expected. The Federalists loudly applauded and spoke of the President's firmness and dignity; the Republicans decried the address as an unnecessary irritant to France.

John Nicholas of Virginia somewhat cryptically asserted that Pinckney's rejection might have been due to the nature of his credentials; and then launched into a long and wordy defense of France. She was the only force in the world, he averred, which protected us from a direct assault by perfidious Britain. William Smith in turn wanted to know why Nicholas was so tender of French pride, yet thought nothing of American pride.[45]

For almost two weeks the House debated on the subject of French policy and Nicholas's amendment to the proposed reply to the President's speech. Nicholas sought to insert a statement that in dismissing Pinckney, France meant only to suspend "ordinary diplomatic intercourse" in order that "extraordinary agencies" might be employed for the composition of differences; and that the United States ought "to place France on the footing of other countries, by removing the inequalities which may have arisen in the operation of our respective treaties."

After lengthy and embittered debate the House voted to incorporate the second section of Nicholas's amendment into the reply. It was the custom of the House to attend on the President in a body while presenting their reply. Matthew Lyon of Vermont thereupon made his first bid for notoriety. He refused flatly to participate in what he asserted was a monarchical ceremony which was unworthy of a free American like himself.[46]

With the preliminary procedure out of the way, William Smith rose with a series of resolutions based on the suggestions made by Adams. He called for the speedy completion of the three frigates still on the stocks, the purchase of additional warships, an authorization to the President to employ the navy for convoy duty, the arming of merchant ships, an increase in the Regular Army and a discretionary authority in the President to raise a provisional army, temporary loans and additional revenues with which to meet them, and an embargo on the export of arms and military stores.[47]

Though Giles fought vigorously against the entire program on the ground that just as Europe was tiring of war we were getting ready to rush into it, the determined Federalists managed at first to push through the major provisions in the committee of the whole; and were even successful in enacting into law a bill already passed by the Senate which embargoed the export of arms and military stores.

Then the tide turned, with Gallatin actively leading the Republican forces. Abetted by Edward Livingston, Gallatin decried the resolution for arming merchant ships as opposed to the law of nations and as placing the peace of the country in the doubtful discretion of merchants who were in some cases not even American citizens. By a parliamentary maneuver he pushed through an amendment which limited such arming to ships engaged in the Mediterranean and East Indies trade and refused it to the much more important West Indies route. As a result, the disgusted Federalists joined in voting down the entire resolution.

The Senate had also passed a bill for an increased navy; but the House whittled down the provisions one after another until it was completely emasculated. Even in this innocuous state Gallatin vowed that he would not vote for it. He saw no reason for the United States to possess a navy, he said. Look at the figures! The initial cost and upkeep of a navy could not be met out of existing revenues; nor was it useful for protection. All that was necessary was a militia which would rush to arms on any invasion of our shores. As for our maritime trade, let it shift for itself.[48]

This line of reasoning enraged the Federalists of the maritime states. Samuel Sewall of Massachusetts shouted furiously: "Gentlemen who depended on agriculture for everything . . . need not put themselves to the expense of protecting the commerce of the country; commerce was able to protect itself, if they would only suffer it to do so. Let those States which live by commerce be separated by the Confederacy. . . . Let them," said he, "be abandoned, but let it be done before they are reduced to poverty and wretchedness. Their collected industry and property were equal to their own protection, and let other parts of the Confederacy take care of themselves."

After delivering himself of this open appeal to disunion, Sewall sat down trembling with rage. Macon declared that such language had never before been heard in the House—which was not true—and the Speaker ruled Sewall wholly out of order.[49]

Unimpressed by Sewall's tirade, the Republicans pushed through their emasculated bill, which prohibited the purchase of warships and restrained the navy, when and if put into commission, from being employed on convoy duty. The Senate refused to accede to these amendments; but the House stood firm. Conferences were held, and a compromise achieved. The Senate receded on the purchase of warships, and the House finally agreed by a vote of 51 to 47 to convoys.[50]

The angry and passion-charged sessions of both branches had debated nothing else but foreign relations from the middle of May into the month of July; and only shreds and tatters of Adams's program had been enacted into law.

Jefferson, presiding over the Senate in his capacity as Vice-President, attributed the Federalist setbacks to the general feeling that the great European struggle was soon terminating. France's victories in the field, the forced withdrawal of Austria from the coalition, the shattered finances of Great Britain, all seemed to point to an early French triumph. If only we could "rub through this summer without war," thought Jefferson, we ought to be able when peace came so to arrange our commerce and navigation "as to make them instruments of preserving peace and justice to us hereafter. Our people must consent to small occasional sacrifices to avoid the greater evil of war." [51]

What he really meant by these somewhat less than luminous comments was the establishment of a total embargo on American shipping and trade until Europe would be compelled to yield to our demands. This panacea for all our foreign ills was persistently advocated by Jefferson throughout his long career. Yet it seemed that it was never to be employed against France; it was only to be used against England. As for the President's speech, Jefferson considered it an incitement to war and an attempt to make the Executive "the sole power in the government." [52] From this point on, the two men drifted steadily further and further apart.

The news that the Bank of England had failed, coupled with the military debacle of the allied coalition, tempered the Federalist enthusiasm for war and warlike measures, and resigned them to their defeat in the special session.

The Republicans were now decisively set against Adams. They denounced his convocation of Congress, his speech as a "war whoop" and himself as "gasconading like a bully, swaggering the hero, and armed cap a pee [*sic*] throwing the gauntlet to the most formidable power on earth—again we behold him placing himself the file-leader of a British faction." [53]

Their press harped constantly on the fears of their readers. The theme most joyously proclaimed was that France was the mightiest nation in the world, her power was endless, and she could land 200,-000 men, "accustomed to conquest," on American shores to drench us in blood and horrors. To these appeals to fear was added the open threat that "a War with France would immediately involve us in a Civil War, or at least such commotions as would render its prosecution impracticable. It must also terminate by an ignominious Peace. It is wanton and unprovoked." [54]

On the Federalist side, the threat of secession; on the Republican, the warning of civil war!

But Adams had not waited for the end of the congressional debate to act. In spite of Republican accusations that he was a warmonger, he took a decisive step for peace by submitting on May 31st to the Senate the names of Charles Cotesworth Pinckney, Elbridge Gerry and John Marshall as envoys extraordinary and ministers plenipotentiary to France.

Enough of passion and even traitorous sentiments had been aroused in the United States by the dispute. "Men who have been intimate all their lives," complained Jefferson, "cross the streets to avoid meeting, and turn their heads another way, lest they should be obliged to touch their hats." [55]

Adams and Jefferson were now openly at loggerheads. A kind friend had communicated to the President the animadversions on him in a private letter written by the Vice-President. These furnished him, replied Adams, with an additional motive "to be upon my guard. It is evidence of a mind, soured, yet seeking for popularity, and eaten to a honeycomb with ambition, yet weak, confused, uninformed, and ignorant." [56]

Had he known the unflattering description of himself which even then Jefferson was conveying to the French consul general, he would have found even grosser epithets for his former friend. Adams, so Jefferson confided, was "distrustful, obstinate, excessively vain, and takes no counsel from anyone." From the very beginning he had resented the preference by the French for Benjamin Franklin when both men had been commissioners to France. [57]

When Jefferson heard of the nominations for the French mission he expressed a fear of Marshall, thought Pinckney a weakling, and fastened on Gerry as the one man to salvage peace. In a long, flattering letter he urged Gerry to accept the appointment, and go to any lengths to preserve peace; otherwise the Union would be destroyed. Only you, he ended, can moderate the extremism of the other two joined with you in the mission.[58]

There was indeed a great need for a speedy settlement, if not for moderation. The official report disclosed that since October 1, 1796, the French had taken 316 American ships with their cargoes; while English seizures had fallen to a low of two! [59]

The three envoys were quickly confirmed, and sailed for France bearing instructions from Adams which asked for harmony and unanimity among them, and an attention to "the great objects" rather than lesser matters. "It is my sincere desire," Adams privately told Gerry, "that an accommodation may take place; but our national faith, and the honor of our government, cannot be sacrificed. You have known enough of the unpleasant effects of disunion among ministers to convince you of the necessity of avoiding it, like a rock or a quicksand." [60] In the sequel Gerry paid no attention to this sound advice.

Yet, even as the envoys set sail, Adams expected little to come of their voyage. The French, he was convinced, would spin out the negotiations to interminable lengths—while continuing their depredations on American commerce—unless they were "quickened" by the clamping down of an embargo on their trade and the arming of our merchant ships.[61]

Inevitably, the fever over France cooled while the nation awaited advices from the envoys; but it seemed impossible for the country to forego even for a moment its daily crisis. Simultaneously with the departure of the mission, relations with England took a sudden turn for the worse.

England had been continuing her impressments of American seamen, and the American representatives in London for all their efforts could manage to obtain the release of a comparative few. Of a total of 401 applications submitted by Pinckney, King and their agents, only 86 had been discharged. Among those still in British service, while a handful might perhaps be British subjects, the vast majority were American citizens, and entitled to relief. But, no matter how complete the evidence which King submitted, the British invariably retorted that the men were in fact Englishmen and that American consuls were too prone to grant certificates of citizenship "on very slight and insufficient evidence." [62]

With the issue of impressments a continual sore in Anglo-American relations, evidence came to the House of Representatives that William Blount, senator from Tennessee, had been secretly seeking British aid for a private filibuster he meditated against the Spanish possessions of the Floridas and Louisiana, with confused overtones of a secession of the West to join with these provinces in a vast new empire.

Blount had gone to Liston, the British minister, with his plan, which would have necessitated a combined British and Indian force with Western volunteers, and given in exchange hegemony over the conquests to England. Liston disapproved of the idea, but he shifted responsibility to his home government. He gave Blount's emissary a covering note and paid his passage money to England.[63] There the ministry coldly rejected the proposition.

In the meantime, however, an incriminating letter written by Blount, in which he optimistically assumed that he already had British support, fell into the hands of the American government.[64]

The House brought impeachment proceedings against the Tennessee senator on July 7, 1797. The following day, without waiting for the receipt of the formal impeachment, the Senate acted on its own and expelled Blount as guilty of a high misdemeanor. Nevertheless the House persisted in its impeachment and the Senate, early in 1799, finally determined that it had no jurisdiction, on two grounds: first, that Blount was no longer in office; and second, that a member of Congress was not "a civil officer" of the United States within the meaning of the Constitution governing impeachments. Blount's expulsion and the disclosure of his conspiracy did not harm him in Tennessee. On the contrary, when he returned he was immediately elected to the state senate and became its presiding officer.

But the prompt senatorial action did not still the hubbub. The Republicans seized on Blount's malfeasance as another weapon for belaboring Great Britain. "In any other country but America," fulminated their press, "Liston would have been sent home, for listening to such a proposal as that of Blount's. . . . How long will Americans see themselves thus degraded and dishonored by a weak and wicked administration." [65]

Even the yellow fever, it was intimated, was somehow a British plot, since it was brought to American ports by ship "from the *English* West Indies." [66]

Madison too was convinced that both Liston and Pickering were involved with Blount, and hoped that none of "the large fish" would escape the net of the congressional investigation.[67] Just how Pickering came to be involved, he did not say.

Spain now injected herself into the proceedings. After the signing of Pinckney's treaty, Spain sent a regularly accredited minister, Don Carlos Martinez de Yrujo, to the United States. Yrujo was a young man of talent, but inclined to be flighty. Later on, he married the daughter of Judge Thomas McKean of Pennsylvania, an ardent Republican.

If Great Britain was alleged to be dealing with Blount at this time to separate the West from the United States, Spain was in fact, through the agency of another American, Thomas Power, seeking to induce certain influential Kentuckians to place the West under the protection of herself.[68] Spain also, in contravention of the treaty, continued to hold on to the posts at Natchez and Walnut Hills in lower Mississippi on the pretext that a British attack on their territories was momentarily expected. This, however, Liston vigorously denied to Pickering.[69]

When Pickering, therefore, peremptorily demanded the yielding of the posts, Yrujo retorted that the British expedition was actually in the making, that it was tied in with Blount's conspiracy, and that Andrew Ellicott, the American commissioner sent to Natchez to survey the boundaries, was plotting to seize Natchez in a surprise assault.[70]

Such accusations against American designs were bad enough, but Yrujo compounded the injury by giving his note to Bache for publication. Unfortunately for Yrujo, his agent blundered and sent a copy of it also to William Cobbett for publication in his Porcupine's Gazette. Porcupine did not print the note; instead he commented on the contretemps in his usual inimitable manner. He called Yrujo another Don Quixote and his blundering agent a Sancho Panza "trotting quietly at his heels." On second thought, he repudiated the comparison as doing "infinite injury to the hero of the romance." For weeks therafter he employed every epithet in his repertory—and he had many—to insult both Yrujo and that "tawny-pelted nation" which he represented, and which "Americans had ever been taught to despise!" [71]

Yrujo writhed under the blows and threatened suit. By this time Cobbett had bludgeoned so many heads that one suit more or less did not matter very much. He had already made one serious blunder of his own. He had taken on the doughty Dr. Rush, whose old exploits in the great yellow fever epidemic of 1793 now revived in men's memories through the recurrence of the plague in Philadelphia.

Cobbett outdid himself in ridiculing Rush's alleged cures; and when the outraged doctor similarly threatened court action, retorted that he would not, "were I even as poor as you are, endeavour to recover my broken fortunes by bleeding people to death by scores." He followed this with a straight-faced report of a partnership between a coffinmaker and Rush, whereby the doctor received twenty dollars "for every one of his patients for whom the former furnishes a coffin." [72]

But the toils were slowly enveloping Cobbett. Both Yrujo and Dr. Rush made good their threats to sue. Yrujo chose the way of criminal libel; while Rush preferred a civil suit for damages.

Judge McKean issued a warrant for Cobbett's arrest on Yrujo's complaint. When the case was presented to a Grand Jury, McKean (later to become Yrujo's father-in-law!) delivered himself of some amazing statements on the law of libel. "Where libels are printed against persons employed in a public capacity," he charged, "they receive an aggravation, as they tend to scandalize the Government, by reflecting on those who are intrusted with the administration of public affairs, and thereby not only endanger the public peace, as all others do, by stirring up the parties immediately concerned to acts of revenge, but have also a direct tendency to breed in the people a dislike of their governors, and incline them to faction and sedition." [73]

The charge, in an attempt to indict a Federalist editor for libel, is all the more astonishing because it was delivered by a radical Republican judge in favor of the emissary of the King of Spain. The sentiments are indistinguishable from those uttered by *Federalist* judges not much more than a year later against *Republican* editors under the Sedition Act, and had not even the excuse of a specifically written statute under which to utter them. Yet no Republican now raised his voice to repudiate this pillar of his party for these most unrepublican sentiments.

In spite of McKean's amazing version of the law of libel, the grand jury refused to indict Cobbett—though by a single vote—and he escaped for a while the consequences of his poisoned quill.

Dr. Rush's civil action came to trial considerably later. This time Cobbett did not escape. A judgment was rendered against him in the enormous sum of $5000. He was compelled to flee to New York to escape debtors' prison. There he fulminated a while longer, then went back to his native England to decry all things American and carve out a new and unexpected career for himself. It cannot be said that the United States suffered from his departure, except that there was a distinct falling off in the flavor of the billingsgate.

Though the flavor may have deteriorated, there was however a sufficient supply of that commodity left behind. At no time in the history of the country has there existed such a community of quarrelsome, brimstone-tongued, vile-epitheted journalists. They did not confine their efforts to political figures of the opposite party; they assaulted their own kind in most unfraternal fashion. When words gave out, fists and bludgeons took over.

Cobbett himself had paid his respects to Bache by referring to his grandfather, the revered Doctor Franklin, as "his crafty and lecherous old hypocrite of a grandfather, whose very statue seems to gloat on the wenches as they walk the State House yard." [74]

Fenno spoke of the editors of the *Independent Chronicle* as "those two-walking images of murder, treason, plots and dark conspiracies"; throwing in for good measure that they were "a dirty crew of groveling miscreants." [75]

William Duane, who became editor of the *Aurora* on Bache's death, published a notice in his paper: "To Mr. Fenno: This is to announce you to the world as a scoundrel and a liar!" [76]

Fisticuffs were not infrequent, and Fenno and Bache used cudgels on each other, then retired to their respective sanctums to breathe defiance at a safer distance.

Some of the more sober editors protested at the orgies of personal abuse and slander. They denounced those of their fellow editors who "have carried this business of *murdering characters* to its utmost pitch. No reputation, however virtuous and unsullied, no station, however exalted, has escaped the shafts of their envenomed malice. Men who have served their country with great ability and integrity, and whose names will descend to posterity as the fathers of the people and the benefactors of the human race, have been vilified and stigmatized as the scourges of society, nay as the most infamous traitors." [77]

CHAPTER 24

The XYZ Affair

AFTER THE FIREWORKS of the special session, it was a somewhat chastened and listless Congress that convened in Philadelphia on November 22, 1797. It was a period of waiting, of marking time until news came from Europe and from Paris in particular as to the success or failure of the extraordinary mission.

Meanwhile, the European scene had not been static. The amazing Italian campaign of Napoleon Bonaparte had forced practically all the powers of Europe to make peace with a triumphant France. Only England, secure behind the barrier of the Channel and the wooden walls of her fleet, remained at war. Within France herself, the triumvirs of the Directory had anticipated their enemies with a series of arrests and expulsions and seized all power for themselves. This boded no good for the American negotiation, inasmuch as those now in the saddle were inveterate enemies of the United States, while those who had previously advocated a more conciliatory policy were among the fallen and proscribed.[1]

John Adams warned Congress in his opening address that not too much must be expected from the mission. Whatever the issue of their negotiation, or even if peace should come to war-torn Europe, he declared, "I hold it most certain that permanent tranquillity and order will not soon be obtained." America must continue all its previous precautions; in the current state of society a commerce without protection is inevitably subject to plunder.[2]

For this sensible advice the President was belabored in a pamphlet by the poet, Connecticut Wit, land salesman and diplomat, Joel Barlow, from his propagandist seat in Europe. "The Second Warning, or Strictures on the Speech delivered by President Adams" did not reach the United States until January 1799. It then infuriated Adams into referring to Barlow as "a worthless fellow" on a par with Tom Paine himself.

At home, however, the speech aroused no particular repercussions. There was a calm of waiting for news out of Paris. Congress busied itself largely with the impeachment proceedings against William Blount, which ground slowly along. Jefferson, presiding over the Senate, complained that "we are here lounging our time away, doing nothing and having nothing to do." [3]

Gallatin surveyed his fellow members and thought that on the whole it was the most mediocre Congress yet assembled. The Federalists had regained control of the lower House, and the minority Republicans were neither diligent in attendance nor possessed of effective speakers. Gallatin believed, in spite of the Federalist resurgence, that no further action would be taken against France unless our mission was badly treated. He himself was biding his time to introduce a program for reducing expenses. Economy in government was his eternal watchword; nothing delighted him more than to pare appropriations to the bone. "We will attack the Mint and the whole establishment of foreign ministers," he declared.[4]

In the Senate, Humphrey Marshall of Kentucky proposed a constitutional amendment which would have provided separate electoral ballots for the presidency and vice-presidency.[5] Had the amendment been carried it would have prevented the disastrous situation which actually arose in the next election. Unfortunately the proposal died in its inception.

In the House a desultory debate began on the question of appropriating more money to complete the three frigates previously authorized. Two of them had already been launched—the *Constellation* at Baltimore and the *Constitution* at Boston. Both, however, were far from ready for service; and the *Constitution,* which had ingloriously stuck on the ways during the launching, evoked an ironic ode from Philip Freneau, *redivivus* in New York as a newspaper editor.

> Madam!—Stay where you are . . .
> O frigate Constitution! stay on shore . . .
> Was man design'd
> To be confin'd
> In those fire-spitting hells a navy nam'd?[6]

There were congressmen who agreed with Freneau. Livingston of New York openly wondered what had happened to the money already appropriated for the ships, and managed to obtain a committee to inquire into the excessive costs.

Gallatin applauded the move as tactically sound; and even more so the launching of a violent assault on the idea of any increase in the number of ministers to foreign governments. He admitted privately that these public assaults on navy costs and excessive expenditures for diplomatic establishments were grounded on the necessity "that we should begin to assume that high tone which we must necessarily support in case of worse news from France, and because there is no other way to make any important impression upon public opinion." [7]

But a more tittilating impression was shortly to be made on public opinion by Matthew Lyon, the transplanted Hibernian of Vermont. That gentleman on January 30, 1798, while the House was counting the ballots for the impeachment managers in the trial of Blount, spoke up loudly and at random to abuse the Connecticut representatives as pursuing their own private views, itching for office and blinding and deceiving the people they pretended to represent.

Whereupon Rufus Griswold, one of the abused Connecticut men, walked up to him and warned the Vermonter that if he ever came to Connecticut, he had better wear his "wooden sword." The allusion was well known to everyone present; for Lyon had been cashiered out of the Army during the Revolution. In a passion Lyon turned and spat squarely into Griswold's face.

As soon as the counting was ended, another Griswold (Roger) of the Connecticut delegation moved formally for the expulsion of the offensive member from Vermont. The motion was referred to a committee which, even though Lyon offered a qualified apology to the House, recommended his expulsion.[8]

The debate on the recommendation took on a bitter partisan tone. The Federalists pressed angrily for the extreme penalty; the Republicans palliated and sought Lyon's retention on the technical ground that the House had not been in actual session at the moment of the incident. When it came to a vote, while there was an actual majority for expulsion, it did not reach the requisite two-thirds.

Brooding over the unavenged insult, Rufus Griswold walked into the House on February 15th before it had been called to order, armed with a heavy hickory stick. He sat down quietly; but as Lyon entered and took his seat Griswold rose, made straight for him and beat him about the head with his cudgel.

Caught between desk and chairs, Lyon was soundly thrashed before he could extricate himself and flee toward the stove, where he seized a pair of fire tongs, with Griswold in hot pursuit.

Several Republicans had started up to go to Lyon's rescue, but old General Daniel Morgan stood threateningly in their path and allowed no rescue until he was satisfied that Lyon had been well flogged. The two men in their struggles fell to the floor and rolled over, kicking, clawing and punching until a number of members managed to part the combatants.[9]

Now it was the turn of the Republicans to demand punishment; while some North Carolina representatives, who had been balked by Morgan in their attempt at rescue, angrily threatened to go home. But this, reported a Federalist, "makes no impression on the northern gentlemen. They are tired of dragging on the Government against people whose existence depended on it. It is their common opinion that they can do much better without the Southern States than with them."[10]

The next day Davis of Kentucky moved to expel both parties to the undignified scuffle. Once again an investigation was ordered and testimony taken. In the end, after endless debate, all sides grew heartily tired of the proceedings and of the humiliating spectacle they made in the public eye. Not only was the motion for expulsion overwhelmingly defeated, but even a resolution of mere reprimand failed by a single vote.[11]

As though this were not enough scandal, another if more genteel uproar arose over the action of President Adams in refusing to attend the annual birthday ball for George Washington. The old Federalists thought this a direct insult; Adams's friends apologized for him that he held conscientious scruples against attending balls. But Adams's stouthearted and forthright wife Abigail minced no words in her rage and contempt against "these Proud Phylidelphians [sic]" who had the audacity to celebrate, not the birthday of the President, who was now John Adams, but the birthday of a private citizen, George Washington![12]

But these incidents, humiliating or diverting though they might be, were mere froth on the surface of a deep-seated uneasiness. It was known that the three envoys had arrived in Paris early in October; yet so far as further news of them was concerned they might well have been swallowed up in mid-ocean. Not a letter came through to an anxious government and citizenry at home; not even a scrap to prove that they were still alive.

As November changed to December, and then the new year commenced, Jefferson began to suspect that the envoys had actually written, but that the administration was hushing up their dispatches.[13] Even though he was Vice-President, Jefferson knew as little or as much of the executive doings as the meanest citizen. By February he was convinced that no news was good news. If, as he believed, Adams and his Cabinet had imposed a veil of secrecy, that meant that negotiations were in such a train that their publication would end the war scare and "check the disposition to arm." [14]

Jefferson himself expected that the entire situation would eventually be cleared up by a French invasion and conquest of England, which, by republicanizing that country, would bring peace to the world and safety to America.[15]

But March arrived, and Washington from his retirement in Mount Vernon demanded: "Are our Commissioners guillotined, or what else is the occasion of their silence?" [16] This was a question and a fear which more and more stirred the country as the months slipped by.

Actually Adams was as much in the dark as everyone else. As early as January 24, 1798, he uneasily queried his Cabinet what to do in certain eventualities. Suppose the envoys had been refused an audience or were later ordered away, should they be required to return at once to the United States? What should he as President then recommend to Congress—war or embargo? In that event, what policy ought to be adopted toward England? Should we ally ourselves with her, await her overtures, or would any alliance be imprudent? Suppose she then fell, would not we go down with her? Suppose her fall led to internal revolution, would not our connection with her increase the danger of a similar revolution here? [17]

Once again, with the President's queries before him, McHenry entreated Hamilton for aid in answering them.[18] Hamilton obliged with a detailed draft for the Secretary of War to follow. "There is a very general and strong aversion to War in the minds of the people of this Country," he declared, and particularly to a war with France. Since this was so, and since nothing could be gained by a formal declaration, it would be better in the event of a breakdown of current negotiations to adopt a vigorous defensive plan while continuing to evince a readiness to treat. His plan in the main was a repetition of earlier suggestions: arm the merchant ships, prepare twenty sloops of war, complete the three frigates, declare the old French treaties suspended, increase the Regular Army and raise a provisional one; enlarge revenues and float a loan. He advised however against an embargo or an alliance with England. "Mutual interest," he commented, "will command as much from her as Treaty." [19]

Armed with this draft, McHenry practically copied it word for word and sent it to the President as his own. Attorney General Lee, however, stood for more radical measures. He recommended the recall of the envoys, a declaration of war and the seizure of New Orleans if Spain, now under French domination, should attempt any hostile action. But he too was opposed to an embargo or a formal alliance with England.

The inability of McHenry to make a move without seeking outside advice, and the incompetent handling of his Department, were already well known to prominent Federalists, though not as yet to the person most interested—the President of the United States. John Jay had queried Hamilton on taking over the post; now Robert Goodloe Harper, congressman from South Carolina, proposed it again.[20] Hamilton refused to consider the suggestions, of which Adams knew nothing.

The English knew more of what was going on inside France than the Americans did. On January 18, 1798, the new French Directory issued a decree that all neutral vessels carrying cargo of any kind to Great Britain or her possessions were subject to capture. Lord Grenville unctuously pronounced this decree as "carrying the principles of maritime War to an extent to which no Country ever thought of carrying them" and as putting an end to American commerce. He saw, he said, no way out for the United States but war; and offered Rufus King, the American minister in London, the use of a swift packet to convey the information home.[21]

In great alarm King asked Pickering for instructions. The American shipmasters stranded in England because of the decree were demanding of him permission to arm their ships; a permission he had no authority to grant. There was a better alternative, thought King—to avail themselves of the British offer of convoy. But the shipmasters wanted official approval before they placed themselves in a British convoy. Also, King wrote, he had not heard a word from the mysteriously silent envoys in France since the beginning of the year.[22]

But by the time King's letter reached Philadelphia, far worse news had arrived. The log jam had burst, and the long-silent envoys dispatched a bundle of documents that was destined to rock the country from end to end.

Elbridge Gerry, the last of the commissioners to sail from America, arrived safely in Paris on October 4, 1797, to find Pinckney and Marshall already on the ground. On October 8th the three men presented their credentials to Talleyrand, recently appointed Minister for Foreign Affairs. That subtle and unscrupulous genius had risen to the heights again after a period of exile, which included a sojourn in America. Gerry was favorably impressed with the politeness of their reception and the manner of the minister. He thought Talleyrand had been misrepresented and abused at home. The somewhat naïve Gerry, who had once shifted from antifederalism to the Federalist party, and was now in the process of shifting over to the Republicans, had been feted and flattered ever since he arrived.

On his first morning in Paris, the official musicians of the Directory serenaded him. On his second morning a deputation of fishmongers male and female visited him and, according to custom, demanded presents in exchange for certain favors. Fortunately he had been warned in time of what had happened to his colleagues and he was able tactfully to avoid being smothered by the odorous embraces of the men and the no less flavorsome kisses of the ladies.[23]

Pinckney, with memories of an earlier and decidedly more frigid reception, and John Marshall, grim Federalist, were less favorably impressed than their colleague. Talleyrand, it was true, had greeted them politely; but he delayed an official reception until, so he explained, he had finished a report on the United States for the guidance of the Directory. But Major Mountflorence, attached to the American consulate, heard privately from Talleyrand's secretary that the real reason for the delay lay in the Directory's exasperation over Adams's speech to the special session of Congress.[24]

As the envoys cooled their heels waiting for Talleyrand to finish his alleged report—which was supposed to have taken only a few days—they grew more and more uneasy. They saw no one, they heard from no one; and in the meantime American ships were daily being seized and their condemnation "pressed with ardor." Marshall wanted to demand an immediate showdown, but Gerry protested that hasty action might "irritate" the French. Since Adams had stressed that all their moves be unanimous, Marshall and Pinckney reluctantly agreed to wait a little longer.[25]

William Vans Murray, the American minister at The Hague, wrote satirically of Gerry as an "innocent" who mistook "the lamps of Paris for an illumination on his arrival, and the salutations of fisherwomen for a procession of chaste matrons hailing the great Pacificator." He thought that of all Americans Gerry was "the least qualified to play a part in Paris, either among the men or the women—he is too virtuous for the last—too little acquainted with the world and himself for the first." [26]

On October 18th, however, the impasse was broken, and one of the most fantastic episodes in the history of diplomacy began.

As in any spy thriller, the stage was first set with a succession of mysterious callers. That morning a Parisian, name unknown, came to Pinckney and whispered that a Mr. Hottinguer, a Swiss financial agent of mysterious antecedents, would shortly visit him. That evening Mr. Hottinguer appeared, whispered that he had a private message from Talleyrand and adjourned with Pinckney to the next room, leaving his fellow commissioners somewhat bewildered behind.

With the door shut, Hottinguer most mysteriously unfolded his mission bit by bit. The members of the Directory, he said in a hushed voice, were most angry over Adams's address to Congress; but, he added with a knowing look, two of them might find their wrath considerably abated and mollified if certain appropriate means were employed. What were they? Well, for example, a *douceur* or softener of 1,200,000 livres (50,000 pounds sterling) to be paid over to Talleyrand for lining the pockets of the Directory and ministers, as well as a substantial public loan from the United States to France, amount as yet unspecified, might work wonders. Then too, pursued the emissary, America must pay to her own citizens the debts owed them by the French government for purchased supplies, and also for the damages sustained by them as a result of French seizures and condemnations. [27]

Pinckney listened in silence to the unfolding tale of bribery, corruption and impudent demands; then dismissed Talleyrand's agent with the remark that he would have to discuss the matter with his colleagues. He returned to the waiting pair and narrated the whole astounding story. Both Pinckney and Marshall were hotly indignant; they refused to take any notice of such an "absolute surrender of the independence of the United States"; but Gerry dissented on the ground that thereby the whole negotiation would be broken off and war would follow. On his representations it was finally agreed that Pinckney should try to get this amazing proposition put in writing.

The next morning Pinckney met with Hottinguer again and asked for a written proposal. Hottinguer now confessed that he was not in direct contact with Talleyrand; that a Mr. Bellamy was the real confidential agent and that he, Hottinguer, dealt only through him. Nevertheless he expressed his willingness to place the transaction on paper. He was as good as his word. He returned in the evening with everything written out except that the loan to France was masked— to avoid giving England cause for complaint—as an advance for the payments of the French debts to American citizens.[28]

On the following evening of October 20th the plot took on additional complications. Both Hottinguer and Bellamy appeared. (The names of the three successive agents from Talleyrand, two of whom have now come on the stage, were prudently put into cipher by the envoys in their reports. An equally prudent administration, when it submitted the whole affair to Congress, interposed arbitrary letters for the names: X for Hottinguer, Y for Bellamy and Z for Hauteval, as yet lurking in the wings. As a result the fantastic episode has since been denominated the XYZ Affair.)

The two agents now met for the first time with all three American commissioners. Marshall wished to break off the whole business, but again Gerry overruled him. Bellamy, for all his English name, turned out to be a Genevan like Hottinguer. He affected no mystery, but came straight to the point. While his friend Talleyrand, he said, was most amiably disposed to America, the hardhearted Directory would not permit him to receive or hold any communication with the envoys. However, while he, Bellamy, was not "authorized" to make any promises, he was certain that once Talleyrand's terms were met, that gentleman would be able to assuage their wrath.

But there was another condition that must be met, avowed Bellamy, besides the sordid financal ones outlined in Hottinguer's memorandum. The American envoys must formally disavow in writing all of the obnoxious statements contained in the speech of the President of the United States, and "reparations" must be offered for them. If all these conditions were properly attended to, then France was prepared to enter into a new treaty with the United States on the same terms as those provided in Jay's Treaty with England. There would also be a secret clause arranging for the "loan" previously mentioned.

Then, fearing that the Americans might forget the main point in this exuberance of new conditions, Bellamy concluded sternly: "I will not disguise from you, that this satisfaction being made, the essential part of the treaty remains to be adjusted . . . *you must pay money, you must pay a great deal of money.*"

The next morning Hottinguer and Bellamy, at Gerry's invitation, returned to partake of breakfast and resume the conference. By this time Marshall and Pinckney, in spite of Gerry's fears that any untoward act would mean immediate war, were determined to bring the whole malodorous business to a close. The envoys had wrangled through the greater part of the night; and Marshall finally declared that he would return to America at once to consult the government, but only on the express condition that France would suspend her depredations pending his journey.

Bellamy seemed depressed at breakfast. He had just come from Talleyrand, he said, and the Directory was most determined. But perhaps, he hinted, knowing the state of mind of the envoys, Adams's speech need not be disavowed. When pressed, he coyly allowed himself to be coaxed into the disclosure of another idea. France would sell to the United States 32,000,000 Dutch florins (which now had a market value of ten shillings to the pound) at *twenty* shillings to the pound. This meant of course a profit of one hundred per cent for the French; but, Bellamy asserted with the most engaging confidence, the Dutch would be only too happy at the end of the war to redeem their florins at par, *and,* Adams would not suffer any humiliation. But of course, he hastily added, the original *douceur* of 50,000 pounds sterling must still be paid.

The Americans were singularly unimpressed with this benevolent bit of legerdemain, and handed the emissary a note which embodied the conclusions to which they had come during the night. The note caused the hitherto suave Bellamy to lose his temper. He stormed and threatened; when that failed, he appealed to their worldly wisdom, which certainly required broadening. He shuddered at the consequences, should they refuse to change their minds.

A day elapsed before Hottinguer, this time alone, returned to the attack. From the American point of view matters were steadily growing worse. Bonaparte was knocking all the Italian states, including Venice, out of the war. On October 17th he forced the humiliating treaty of Campo Formio on the beaten Austrians; and exultant boasts were heard that England was his next objective.

The attitude of Talleyrand's agents stiffened. The Directory, declared Hottinguer, was ready to "take a decided course with America if we could not soften them." The Americans stood their ground with equal firmness. That meant war, exclaimed the agent; the Directory was determined "that all nations should aid them, or be considered and treated as enemies."

Marshall replied in that event America would protect herself. "Gentlemen," cried Hottinguer, "you do not speak to the point; it is money; it is expected that you will offer money. . . . What is your answer?"

Losing all patience, Pinckney shouted back: "It is no; no; not a sixpence!" 29

In after-legend, this cry was transmuted to the immortal "Millions for defense; not one cent for tribute!" Actually, this was the substance of a toast proposed at a banquet in Marshall's honor when he returned to the United States.

Now a new figure came on the scene in the unfolding drama. A Mr. Hauteval (Z) first called in private on Gerry alone, then on the three envoys together, with the same plea. Why did they not visit Talleyrand in his personal and not his official capacity?

Marshall and Pinckney asserted that it did not become their dignity to do so; however, added Marshall, since Gerry had known Talleyrand in Boston, *he* might go without impropriety.

Gerry went on October 23rd and found the minister "not at home." He persisted in his visits until, on October 28th, Talleyrand graciously decided to be "in." By a curious chance Hauteval happened to be with him at the time. Talleyrand reiterated the demands of his agents, and displayed the decree of the Directory, not yet made public, which, as previously mentioned, Rufus King had transmitted in all haste to America.

However, said Talleyrand, he would withhold promulgation of the decree for a week while the envoys considered the matter. He spoke only of the "loan"; he made no mention of the private bribe.

In great perplexity Gerry returned to his colleagues, who jointly reiterated their previous assertion that they had no powers to treat on the proposition.

Once again, the thoroughly frightened Gerry invited Hottinguer and Bellamy to breakfast, where they sought to improve on his fears. Let America beware, they warned, lest she suffer the fate of Venice! Nor could she expect any help from England, already scheduled for conquest. War! War! Utter destruction! The dreadful words dinned in Gerry's ears until he did not know which way to turn. After breakfast, the other envoys entered, and again the precious pair of agents croaked their ominous words. Almost as an afterthought they added: the French party in America will join us in throwing the blame for the consequences on the Federalists.

This final trump card shook Marshall and Pinckney momentarily; but they declined to budge. Only Gerry prevented them from sending a formal note at once to the Directory demanding an official reception of their credentials and proceeding with their official business as though no private and unauthorized conversations had ever taken place.

On November 11th, however, even Gerry yielded, and the note was dispatched.[30] Nothing came of it, and all inquiries proved futile. Gerry lost his original optimism and "innocence." He wrote despondently to Vans Murray at The Hague that they were "in a very unpleasant situation"; that informal propositions had been made to them which "the most extravagant imagination of any Citizen of the United States could never have suggested." As he saw it now, "a small cargo of Mexican Dollars would be more efficient in the negotiation at present than two cargoes of Ambassadors."[31]

In spite of the fact that all three men daily expected an order of expulsion, Gerry managed to entertain himself. Like any tourist he visited the monuments and curiosities of Paris, jaunted to Versailles, changed his quarters over a stable for more agreeable ones, and attended the theater and opera. Though he admitted that the French government had taken not the slightest notice of their presence, and that he had no expectation of the mission's success, an invitation from Talleyrand to dine made his spirits soar again.[32]

Talleyrand, the subtle fox, was carefully working on a preconceived plan. He sought to separate Gerry, the quasi-Republican, from his two Federalist colleagues; and in the end he succeeded. He flattered Gerry with assiduous attentions; invited him again to dinner, and sent him an invitation, so Gerry described it in pleased excitement, "to a superb supper made for General and Madame Buonaparte; at which will be the Directory, all the foreign ministers, except the American Envoys, and the finest collection of ladies in Paris." It was with the deepest regret that Gerry, because his colleagues were excluded, felt compelled to turn the invitation down.[33]

These attempts at seduction were noted with considerable suspicion by Marshall and Pinckney. The latter also viewed with disgust the flattering court paid Gerry by the group of "American Jacobins" resident in Paris.[34]

As the weeks passed, and the months, on several occasions the envoys thought of asking for their passports; but each time it was decided to wait a little longer. Their stay was enlivened by the injection of a new element into the situation—one without which, indeed, no tale of international intrigue would be complete: the beautiful female agent.

This was Madame de Villette, whom gossip whispered to have once been the mistress of Voltaire. Since Gerry was already succumbing to the blandishments of Talleyrand, and Marshall seemed sternly incorruptible, she chose the handsome Pinckney as the object of her attentions.

Why *not* make the loan? she asked him one day after first obtaining a measure of his confidence. After all, did we not lend you money during your Revolution? When Pinckney most ungallantly refused to hear of it, she bared her pretty claws. The French party in America, she told him plainly, was considerable and "strongly in our interest." [35]

By the end of January 1798, the patience of the envoys was exhausted. A lengthy communication to Talleyrand was drafted by Marshall which recapitulated the entire history of the disputes between the two nations and concluded with the flat statement that if adjustment was possible, they would remain; if not, they were going home.[36]

It was difficult to get Gerry to sign this ultimatum; but the others in effect laid down their private ultimatum to him, and he finally affixed his signature, though not without many an uttered foreboding of the consequences.[37]

Rufus King, whom Pinckney kept apprised of the proceedings, hoped Gerry would "overcome a miserable vanity and a few little defects of character," and urged Pinckney to use tact with him and thereby avoid a schism among the envoys.[38]

But Marshall's masterful effort was never read by the members of the Directory, while Talleyrand himself did not get around to it until March, when he replied with a sharp note full of recriminations on American conduct and ended with an insulting proposition. The Directory, he said, refused to treat with either Marshall or Pinckney. They were, however, "disposed to treat with that one of the three [Gerry], whose opinions, presumed to be more impartial, promise in the course of the explanations more of that reciprocal confidence which is indispensable." [39]

This cynical offer was of course indignantly repudiated, even Gerry concurring. No single one of them, they stiffly replied, had any authority to take upon himself the conduct of the negotiations. If that were insisted on, they were ready to get their passports.[40]

Talleyrand, for all his cunning, had blundered in making his offer thus bluntly to all three. Perceiving his error, he shifted his ground. He caused unofficial hints to be dropped to Marshall and Pinckney that they would be ordered out of France, but that Gerry might remain. To which the favored one dramatically exclaimed: "To prevent war I will stay!" Marshall stared at him coldly and made no response.[41]

In a private letter Gerry complained that his colleagues had not displayed toward him "that frank and friendly" conduct "which I expected," and defended his decision to stay on the ground that it would prevent a rupture. Should he decline, he said, he would be "responsible or at least chargeable for the consequences."[42]

On April 24, 1798, Marshall sailed for home. Pinckney, whose daughter was gravely ill, took her to the south of France for recuperation. Neither man bade Gerry adieu as he departed.

In vain did Rufus King from London plead with Gerry to go home with the others. He had authentic information, he wrote, that France intended to extend her conquests to North and South America; that the safety of the United States depended on swift preparations to meet the threat; and that "so long as she expects success in negotiation, she will neglect these preparations." In a second letter he implored Gerry not to be taken in by French machinations. "You must either all go, or all stay."[43]

Pleas and warnings fell on deaf ears. Gerry had convinced himself that he alone stood between peace and war, that Talleyrand's flattering attentions were sincere, and that eventually he would return home in triumph with a satisfactory treaty in his luggage which would prove to the warmongering Federalists that the French were excellent fellows and intended the utmost benevolence to America.[44]

Pinckney viewed his conduct in a somewhat different light. "I never met a man of less candor and so much duplicity as Mr. Gerry," he exploded. For Marshall, however, he had the greatest admiration. He is, Pinckney wrote, "a man of extensive ability, of manly candor and an honest heart."[45]

Gerry had done an unprecedented thing in remaining. His instructions did not envisage it; he stayed on without any official powers, and with the knowledge that if he failed, an official reprimand on his return would be the least of his troubles.

Yet, now that he was alone, he displayed a fortitude of character and a steadfast regard for American rights in the ensuing informal and unofficial negotiations which he had not hitherto evidenced.

Talleyrand now chose a different tack. Since his attempt at bribery had failed and it was obvious that Gerry was in no position to promise *douceurs*, he pretended to Gerry that the envoys had been made the dupes of impostors, and demanded their names.[46] This was particularly essential because the reports of the XYZ negotiations had already exploded in both the American and British press.

It is incredible that Gerry could have been taken in by this new development, since he had met all three gentlemen in Talleyrand's own house on several occasions. But Hauteval (Z) hastened to assure Gerry that he too had been the dupe of Hottinguer (X) and Bellamy (Y).[47]

Whether Gerry actually believed the preposterous story or not, he acted as if he did, and continued his negotiation. He made no headway, however, inasmuch as he refused to go outside of his original instructions. On July 26, 1798, he quit Paris for the United States, empty-handed except for a vague statement from the French that they wished for peace with his country and a conviction that somehow he had singlehandedly staved off a war.[48]

The mission was now wholly at an end.

CHAPTER 25

The Alien and Sedition Acts

THE DISPATCHES of the envoys to France took a long time to reach the United States. They had to travel by a circuitous route because of the exigencies of war and to ensure that they did not fall into unfriendly hands. The first had been written on October 22, 1797, and thereafter the others were regularly frequent; yet, while the country waited and wondered, the communications with their highly charged contents did not come into Pickering's hands until late in the evening of March 4, 1798. Then they came all together in a single packet.

Pickering read them with mounting anger and astonishment; then he hastened with them to the President. Adams, probably roused from sleep, read them with equal wrath. Only a few of the letters could be read *in toto*; the greater number hid their most alarming tales in a code which would take some days to decipher. But enough was immediately legible to convince the President and his Secretary of State that the nation had come to a supreme crisis.

That same night or early the next morning Adams wrote out a short message which was immediately delivered to Congress.

"The first dispatches from our envoys extraordinary since their arrival at Paris," wrote Adams, "were received at the Secretary of State's office at a late hour last evening. They are all in a character which will require some days to be deciphered, except the last, which is dated the 8th of January, 1798. The contents of this letter are of so much importance to be immediately made known to Congress and to the public, especially to the mercantile part of our fellow-citizens, that I have thought it my duty to communicate them to both Houses without loss of time." [1]

The dispatch of January 8th contained no references to the saga of Talleyrand's emissaries and their propositions of bribes and loans; it declared only that there was no hope that the envoys would be re-

ceived, and transmitted the provisions of the new French decree ordering the capture of all neutral ships bound with goods for England
and her colonies.

This in itself was enough to create a sensation; yet everyone realized
that if such alarming news could be put in plain English, much worse
must lie concealed in the crabbed intricacies of the code.

Yet, while both Congress and the nation waited in apprehension,
the days passed without any further report from the administration.
For Adams was in a dilemma. As the full picture emerged from the
slow decipherment of the dispatches, with their sordid story of bribery,
corruption, cynicism and threats, it became evident that their disclosure to the country might raise such an outcry as to hasten the United
States into immediate war.

Nine days after their arrival, Adams queried his Cabinet: should
all the letters, with only the names of Talleyrand's agents omitted,
be placed at once before Congress? Should the President recommend
an immediate declaration of war? [2]

McHenry advised a disclosure to Congress, but no open declaration
of war. Let us rather, he said, see to our defenses and prepare to repel
any aggression. Charles Lee opposed the disclosure until we knew that
the envoys were safely out of France; then, communicate the dispatches with a recommendation for war. Pickering's views were well
known; he was all for war, and had been so even before the mission
had departed.

Hamilton, who as yet knew only what everyone else knew, wrote to
Pickering that the President ought to send "a *temperate,* but *grave,*
solemn and *firm* communication" to Congress and institute those measures for defense which he had previously advocated.[3]

On March 19th, Adams took his decisive step. He delivered a Message to Congress whose contents and tone were peculiarly his own,
and reflected only in part the discordant views of his Cabinet.

He did not communicate the dispatches themselves, nor even a
summary of their contents. He stated merely that he was now satisfied
that the pacific efforts of the government of the United States as evidenced by the mission had failed; therefore he was repeating his previous recommendations for measures of defense. In addition, in view
of the French decree and other factors, he would permit those merchant ships that wished to arm for their own defense, to do so.[4]

Inasmuch as the delivery of the Message brought an immediate and extraordinarily vehement reaction from Republicans, it might be worth while to examine its contents in detail.

It is obvious that had Adams wished war at this time, he could have achieved his purpose simply by transmitting the full text of the dispatches. He contented himself instead with the mere statement that there seemed no hope of coming to honorable terms—a statement amply confirmed by the dispatch of January 8th already published, and which had been signed by all three envoys. As for the defense measures he advocated, they constituted nothing new; they had long been under discussion both in Congress and in the country at large.

The one point on which Adams now took action was the arming of the merchant ships. Yet, in view of the French decree to capture on sight, unless he took this step he had only two other alternatives. One was to embargo all ships from leaving port, which would have yielded to the French the full advantage of their decree. The other was to avail ourselves of the British offer of convoy. The merchants generally would have preferred this solution. With them it was a case of letting ships and goods rot here and in English ports, or risking capture on the high seas and paying in any event exorbitant insurance rates.[5]

But Adams did not wish to be placed in the humiliating position of officially requesting such aid from England. It might be all right if the British undertook the job without request and in her own interest; yet even then, as Pickering reported the President's sentiments, "how disgraceful to the United States if we continue to depend on the protection of the British Navy without any reasonable exertion on our part to protect ourselves." [6]

Yet the Republicans cried up and down the land that Adams was rattling the sword and had in effect declared war; that the arming of the ships was a direct incitement to its formal proclamation. Thomas Jefferson, Vice-President of the United States, called the President's Message "insane"; and demanded that Congress pass a legislative prohibition against arming. Once that was done, he continued, let the members go home and "consult their constituents on the great crisis of American affairs now existing." [7]

Bache shouted that the Message was a call on Americans "to draw the sword," and wanted to know if Adams intended to override Congress, which alone had the right to declare war. Shall the people of the United States, cried "Centinel" in the columns of his paper, "stand in hostile array against the French Republic" because of "the vain ambition of one man" and to further the intrigues of British agents in our midst?[8]

A Republican congressman from Virginia, John D. Dawson, got up a printed circular which he signed and sent to prominent people in his state.

"After fourteen days delay," it read, ". . . the President sent to us the inclosed important, intemperate, and unconstitutional Message, which is referred to a Committee of the whole on the State of the Union.

"Circumstances prove clearly to my mind, that the fixed policy of our Administration will involve us in the war on the part of Great-Britain—an event which I very much dread, but which I fear we shall not be able to avert.

"On a former occasion, the expression of their sentiments by the people produced a good effect, and I submit to your wisdom the propriety of obtaining them, in your county and district, on the present. War is a dreadful thing, and we ought to prevent it by every exertion in our power."[9]

All this, of course, was without any actual knowledge of the contents of the dispatches. Madison, similarly in the dark, agreed with both Jefferson and Dawson. The Executive, he underlined, was *always* "most prone" to war; which was the reason the Constitution "with studied care, vested the question of war in the Legislature." Adams's Message, he declared, was "only a further development to the public, of the violent passions and heretical politics which have been long privately known to govern him."[10]

Only one man outside the immediate circle of the President and his Cabinet knew what the dispatches contained. This was Hamilton, to whom Pickering without Adams's knowledge confidentially disclosed them.[11] By this time three of the four members of the Cabinet—Pickering, McHenry and Wolcott—were in the regular habit of seeking the advice of their leader in New York on all affairs of state, no matter how secret or confidential; and, in most instances, submitting Hamilton's ideas to the President as their own.

The Message threw Congress into a ferment. The House behind closed doors in Committee of the Whole discussed its purport. Abraham Baldwin offered a series of resolutions that war with France was not expedient, that the arming of merchant ships be restricted and, as a sop, that provision be made for coastal and internal defense.

When a Federalist slyly moved to strike out the specific reference to France from the first resolution, so as to generalize the inexpediency of war, loud protests came from the Republicans. Thereupon Robert Goodloe Harper of South Carolina, who had at first called for unanimous consent to the resolution, now declared that the scales were dropped from his eyes. "It is not peace with all the world which we want," he shouted furiously, "but peace with France—a servile and abject submission to one nation; a nation, in behalf of whom they have hitherto been eager of war." [12]

As the debate rolled on, the embattled Republicans, determined at all costs to prevent the arming of the ships and intent on embarrassing Adams, bethought themselves of a new tactic. Why were the dispatches of the envoys withheld from them? Could it be that they did not bear out the statements of the President? Would not their publication prove that France was actually ready to treat?

On March 30th John Allen moved a resolution calling on the President to submit the dispatches mentioned in the Message, or at least such portions as the public safety and interest would permit. The proviso did not suit the radical Samuel Smith of Maryland, who demanded that it be struck out; and Giles of Virginia stoutly supported him.

After a heated debate the Republicans forced through Smith's amendment; and on April 2nd, by a vote of 65 to 27, a bald demand was made on Adams for the dispatches without deletions and for the instructions with which the envoys had started on their mission.[13]

A somewhat similar debate took place in the Senate. But here Humphrey Marshall of Kentucky demanded that an embargo be placed on all American vessels to hold them in port. This was too much even for the Republicans, and his resolution went down to ignominious defeat by a vote of 22 to 5. The single positive measure on which both Houses agreed was to speed the completion and commissioning for service of the three authorized frigates.[14]

Adams promptly complied with the demand of the House of Representatives. He presented the dispatches the very next day, complete except for the deletion of a few personal epithets and the names of Talleyrand's agents, to whom he referred as X, Y and Z. He added, however, the admonition that Congress ought to reflect carefully on the consequences of publishing the documents.[15]

The President might well have chuckled over the trap into which the Republicans had fallen. Had he planned this very course from the beginning, it could not have turned out better. If, after his warning, the House published the dispatches, then the consequences would be on their heads and not his own. It would then be evident, at least so he thought, how moderate his own procedure and recommendations had been.

With the President's warning before them, the House shut its doors even tighter and went into a secret debate, the purport of which can only be surmised from subsequent actions and sentiments.

Something of what took place, however, seeped out in private and partisan letters. Theodore Sedgwick, seated in the Senate, thought that the lower House was almost evenly divided. Fifty-two of its members were "determined and rancorous Jacobins," and fifty-four were supposedly administration supporters, though he believed four of these were unpredictable. The "Jacobins," he declared, "under the control of the Genevese [Gallatin] are a well organized and disciplined Corps, never going astray, or doing right even by mistake." [16]

The House Republicans, whether disciplined or not, were aghast when they read the full correspondence of the envoys. Whereas previously they had been clamorous for a public disclosure, supposing that the contents would prove that Adams had exaggerated the gravity of the situation and French arrogance, they now discovered that he had in fact played down the true state of affairs. What they held in their hands was a primed and loaded shell that might detonate at any moment. In a panic they changed their tune and voted solidly *not* to publish.

The House action afforded an opportunity of which the majority Federalists in the Senate—which had also received copies of the dispatches—were quick to take advantage. They pressed through a resolution directing immediate publication—a procedure which one of Hamilton's friends, Robert Troup, admitted was without precedent "and a novel and extraordinary act in diplomatic concerns." Nevertheless he exulted over the ensuing magical effect. Not only was the country swept with a wave of resentment and anger directed against France, but in a trice Adams was elevated in the public estimation to a position which, so Troup asserted, had never been achieved "since man was created and government was formed." [17]

The Republicans were hoist by their own petard. They knew not which way to look or turn, or what to say. The evidence was overwhelming—and infinitely damning. Chapter, verse and day-by-day accounts gave the whole story of the gross humiliation suffered by the envoys; the sordid attempts of Talleyrand and his agents—rendered more sinister by their alphabetic designations—to line their own pockets; the cavalier refusal to receive the representatives of a hitherto friendly nation; the arrogant demand for a forced tribute under the guise of a loan; and, finally, the open allusions to a French party in America which the Directory could manipulate at will.

Jefferson tried desperately to wriggle out of a seemingly impossible situation. He insisted that the dispatches did not "offer a single motive the more for going to war." He referred to the £50,000 bribe as mere "swindling propositions" which were probably intended for the agents' pockets alone or even Talleyrand's, for whose character he had little regard. "But there is not the smallest ground," he vehemently asserted, "to believe the Directory knew anything of them." In fact, "it is evident on the whole that the President's speech [of May 1797] is the only obstacle to an amicable negotiation, that satisfaction being given them for this by disavowals, acknowledgement or money, they are willing to proceed to arrangements of our other differences and even to settle and acknowledge themselves debtors for spoliations."[18]

But the people of the country were in no mood to hearken to such refinements of probabilities and interpretations of self-evident facts. Even Jefferson was compelled to admit that public sentiment ran strongly the other way; and that the disclosures brought most of "the waverers" over to the "War Party" in the House, which, coupled with the prudent departure of four Southern members, gave the administration forces a good majority.[19]

While the Republicans were feverishly seeking for some ground on which to stand, the mass of the people rallied to their country's cause and fiercely denounced the French and all their works. Petitions, resolutions, protests and offers of support poured in an overwhelming flood upon the President.

Even Republicans joined the swelling chorus. From the heart of Republican Georgia came an address of young men who declared that though they had hitherto staunchly supported the French and the French Revolution, the XYZ revelations decided them to stand firmly with the President against "the ferocious frenzy of the 'Terrible Republic'" which "threatens the United States with bloodshed, massacres and desolations."[20]

The merchants naturally were everywhere active, and succeeded in obtaining an immense number of signatures to their resolutions and offers of support. From Philadelphia, Baltimore, Providence, Boston, Portsmouth, Hartford, Portland, Alexandria, from Georgia, Virginia and the Carolinas, the resolutions came in thundering flood.[21]

It was suggested and met with wide approval that every true American display the American cockade in his hat—a black ribbon rose, fastened with a white button. To the ladies was offered the more decorative white rose.[22]

The New Theater in Philadelphia, the town's most fashionable place of entertainment, was the scene of disorder and riot. Its managers were Republicans, and, as had been the custom for some time, during the entr'actes the actors would come out upon the stage and, to orchestral accompaniment, sing the French revolutionary airs—the *"Marseillaise," "Ça Ira"* and the *"Carmagnole."*

But now the audience no longer brooked such obeisances to a hated power. They hissed, booed and catcalled, and shouted for the "President's March" instead; or at least "Yankee Doodle." When actors and musicians refused, the audience rose and pelted them with ripe fruit, eggs and missiles of every description.

The dismayed management protested that it was impossible to give them the "President's March," since there were no words to sing with it. Thereupon a young man in his late twenties promptly scribbled some stanzas to the stirring music of the "March." On April 25th the theater management rather reluctantly agreed to have the new verses sung from the stage.

Abigail Adams, the President's strong-minded lady, veiled herself heavily and went to the theater that night with a party of friends. When the curtain-raiser, a one-act play, was ended, one of the singing actors, Gilbert Fox, came out upon the stage. The crowded house hushed to silence. The orchestra struck up the "March," and Fox swung into the words. They proved an instantaneous hit. At every chorus, the audience broke into wildest applause; and after the regular play had been performed, shouted for the song's repetition. This time they joined in the choruses and cheered so loudly that Abigail exclaimed, ". . . you might have heard a mile—my head aches in consequence of it." [23] This was sheer pretense, for Abigail was mightily tickled at the tribute to her husband.

The young lyricist's name was Joseph Hopkinson, and the verses he had written to the old tune began with "Hail, Columbia." Words and music swept the nation. Only Jefferson could discover no merit therein, sneering at it as "a poor song" and its author as a youth with no other qualification than "extreme toryism." [24]

Under the pressure of an aroused public opinion, with the Republicans thoroughly disorganized and fighting but a rearguard action, the so-called "war-whoop faction" proceeded full speed ahead. A flood of new bills was submitted in the House to put into effect the President's recommendations: for port and harbor defense, for organizing a national militia and augmenting the Regular Army, for empowering the President to use the Navy for convoy duty.

Nicholas objected violently to the last. We can defend ourselves against the whole world on land, he cried, but not on the sea. Gallatin admitted that the French were infringing the law of nations and oppressing our commerce, but he clung stubbornly to the thesis that convoys meant war, and there must be no war. To this, Jonathan Dayton, one of the "waverers" who had now jumped on the bandwagon, indignantly retorted that he had never expected a representative of the American people to employ "such tame and submissive language." [25]

Dayton's remarks paved the way for an outburst of xenophobia directed against the Swiss-born Gallatin. With a meaningful stare, Dana of Massachusetts commented that *Dayton* was "a native American, and had been an American soldier through the late Revolution"; while John Allen hotly resented "the insults to my country" from Gallatin.[26]

Actually Gallatin had said nothing to justify these outbursts; certainly Nicholas had been much more violent in his opposition. But Nicholas, a native Virginian, was not as vulnerable to sneers as Gallatin; and the ugly tide of antiforeignism was rising higher and higher.

Even as these retorts were befouling the air in the House, the Senate was engaged in the much more serious business of writing them into law. On April 25th James Hillhouse of Connecticut proposed the appointment of a committee to consider the deportation by law of such aliens from the United States "as may be dangerous to its peace and safety"; and on May 4th such a bill was regularly introduced, to be passed after considerable debate on June 8, 1798.[27]

The Senate, with a larger and more cohesive Federalist majority, was moving speedily to enact the entire program. The House, where

Gallatin battled every move and ingeniously interposed every possible delay and modification, was somewhat slower in final action. Nevertheless the juggernaut pushed forward and could not be denied.

The Senate had voted for the construction, purchase or hire of sixteen ships of war, carrying an armament of twenty-two guns or less apiece. The House reduced the number of ships to twelve, and in this form the bill became law. Gallatin tried in vain to attach a rider to forbid their use for convoy duty; it was defeated by a vote of 50 to 32.

An appropriation of $250,000 for port and harbor defense met with little difficulty in either House; but the Senate bill authorizing a provisionary army of twenty thousand men was scaled down in the House to ten thousand. A separate Navy Department was established, with a Secretary holding Cabinet rank; and a direct tax, to be apportioned among the states, was imposed on "dwelling houses, lands, and slaves."

One after another the "war" bills were pushed through by the administration supporters. The President was authorized to instruct the tiny Navy to seize the warships of any foreign nation "found hovering on the coasts of the United States for the purpose of committing depredations on the vessels belonging to the citizens thereof." Though the designation was general, only French warships were meant.

Acts were passed to suspend all commercial intercourse between France and the United States, to arm merchant ships and give them the right to defend themselves against search and seizure, to abrogate all existing treaties with France; and finally, on July 9th, a measure went on the books which created an actual if not a legal state of war. American naval vessels were authorized to seize French warships or privateers encountered *anywhere* on the high seas, and the Executive was empowered to issue letters of marque to *private* armed ships owned and manned by American citizens.[28]

Nothing that the dismayed and disorganized Republicans could do was able to halt the inexorable rush of enactments. The Senate, impatient even with the rapid passage of bill after bill, suspended the rule requiring the lapse of a day between the several readings. Rumors and anonymous accusations goaded the "war-whoop faction" to even greater efforts.

It was reported and widely believed that the sizable French colony in Philadelphia, in conjunction with native allies, was conspiring to fire the city and massacre the inhabitants. The Mayor promptly instituted an augmented watch; Governor Thomas Mifflin, a Republican who walked softly these days, put a troop of horse in readiness; and more than a thousand young Federalists, sporting the "American" black cockade, paraded the streets, vowed ardent support of the President and serenaded the Adamses by night with the "new" song "Hail, Columbia." The more panicky packed their valuables and prepared to flee.

Defiant bands of Republicans donned the French tricolor, and the opposing mobs clashed in riotous melee. The Republicans were put to rout, the loathed tricolor was torn from innumerable hats and trampled into the ground.[29]

Hamilton called on Washington to leave his private affairs and tour the South, the chief focus of opposition to the government and still inspired with an immoderate love for France. Pretend, suggested Hamilton, that you are traveling for your health. Your presence would give rise to addresses, public dinners and entertainments which in turn will give you an opportunity to express such sentiments as would "revive an enthusiasm for your person that may be turned into the right channel."[30] Already Hamilton was envisioning Washington as commander of the provisional army, with himself as second.

But the ex-President declined to make the journey, though avowing his anxiety over the current situation and declaring himself "not a little agitated by the outrageous conduct of France towards the United States."[31]

Meanwhile Jefferson, presiding over a Senate that heeded him not, was filled with gloom and forebodings. He and his fellow Republicans had finally agreed on a common line—that the tale told in the dispatches of the envoys was a mere "swindling experiment" attempted on them by private persons; that the reports themselves were tissues of libelous absurdities and improbabilities which would eventually "bring as much derision on the Envoys, as mischief the Country."[32]

Madison did however deliver himself of a pregnant thought. "Perhaps it is a universal truth," he wrote, "that the loss of liberty at home is to be charged to provisions against danger real or pretended from abroad."[33]

In the crisis, Gallatin found himself almost alone in the House. For one reason or another—mostly prudential—his active lieutenants found it necessary to go home, and left him to bear the brunt of debate and the obloquy of the Federalists. Yet he continued unswervingly on his course. He did not try to excuse France; but he believed we should wait patiently for the European conflict to end, when the seizures and confiscations must necessarily cease. If we go to war now, he averred, we must submit to even greater depredations and eventually be compelled to sue for peace on most disadvantageous terms. Worse even than war, the Executive party had seized the occasion to "increase their power and to bind us by the treble chain of fiscal, legal and military despotism." [34]

John Taylor of Caroline, to whom the Constitution of the United States was by its very nature an instrument of despotism, flirted with the idea that Virginia and North Carolina might secede from the Union. But Jefferson wisely discouraged the thought.

"In every free and deliberating society," he wrote, "there must, from the nature of man, be opposite parties, and violent dissensions and discords; and one of these, for the most part, must prevail over the other for a longer or shorter time. . . . But if on a temporary superiority of the one party, the other is to resort to a scission of the Union, no federal government can ever exist. . . . A little patience, and we shall see the reign of witches pass over, their spells dissolve, and the people, recovering their true sight, restore their government to its true principles." [35]

Liston, the British minister, watched the course of events with much satisfaction. He noted that Adams, who had hitherto suffered by comparison with his predecessor in office, was risen to the pinnacle of popularity. Whereas formerly he would enter and leave the theater without any mark of attention from the audience, *now* his appearance was a signal for the playgoers to rise and shake the house with their cheers.[36]

But Liston also noted, with a keen perception of American conditions and psychology, that England might easily lose her present advantage if the unjust seizures, confiscatory judgments and even bribery which was prevalent in some of the West Indies vice-admiralty courts were continued. He asked his home government to investigate the alleged conditions and to rectify them if possible.[37]

At the same time Hamilton was urging King to take the same matters up in London. "By what fatality," he exploded, "has the British Cabinet been led to spring any new mine, by new regulations, at such a crisis of affairs? . . . Why are weapons to be furnished to our Jacobins?"[38]

The surge which had carried Congress to the verge of an actual declaration of war on France now hurried it into even stormier waters. Rumors and the reports of rumors, anonymous denunciations and their own fevered spirits, convinced the Federalists that a vast conspiracy was brewing in the United States; that its head and front were the thousands of French aliens come originally as refugees; that these were instigating and spurring the native Francophiles to plots and deeds of darkness.

Under the impulse of this conviction a series of bills were introduced in both Houses which strained the Constitution to the breaking point, instituted a quasi reign of terror, brought the country to the brink of civil war and disunion, and created repercussions the echoes of which have not yet died away.

These bills were three in number—the Naturalization Act, the Alien Bill and the Sedition Law.

Of the three, the Naturalization Act was the least objectionable, though conceived in prejudice and midwifed by fear. As finally enacted, it extended the period of residence before naturalization from five to fourteen years. There could be no question that such a requirement was constitutionally within the powers of Congress to enact, however unwise it may have been. But the sentiments uttered in the course of debate in the halls of Congress throw a singular illumination on the motives which animated its proponents.

Robert Goodloe Harper asserted on the floor of the House that "it was high time we should recover from the mistake which this country fell into when it first began to form its constitutions, of admitting foreigners to citizenship." To which Otis chimed in that no alien-born should be entitled to hold a federal office; which Harper promptly capped with the remark that the alien-born should not even be permitted to vote for federal congressmen or state legislators.[39]

Gallatin, with the full realization that comments such as these had a personal relation to himself, sought hard to exclude from the provisions of the bill the recently arrived Irish who made up a considerable part of his constituency in western Pennsylvania by incorporating a cut-off date; but his amendment was defeated and the bill passed in its original form.

That it was the Irish immigrants at whom the bill was chiefly aimed—rather than the French refugees, most of whom intended to return home when conditions permitted—is similarly evidenced by the action of Rufus King, the American minister to England. There had been a rebellion in Ireland which was crushed in blood, with hundreds of insurgents clapped into British jails. Alarmed at reports that the British government contemplated offering them their freedom if they emigrated to America, King interposed an official protest. We do not want them, he wrote, and we shall not accept them. "Your timely interference," applauded Secretary of State Pickering, "to prevent the emigration of the Irish traitors to this Country is extremely acceptable to the President." He asked King to send him a list of the names and descriptions of the incarcerated rebels, so that in the event the British set them free and they managed to make their way to the United States they could be apprehended and shipped back.[40]

Harrison G. Otis, the silk-stocking congressman from Massachusetts, avowed that "if some means are not adopted to prevent the indiscriminate admission of wild Irishmen and others to the rights of suffrage, there will soon be an end to liberty and property." Uriah Tracy, the Connecticut congressman, was to prove even more violent at a later date. "In my lengthy journey through [Pennsylvania]," he then wrote, "I have seen many, very many, Irishmen, and with a very few exceptions, they are United Irishmen, Free Masons, and the most God-provoking Democrats this side of Hell." [41]

Tracy placed his finger squarely on the real reason, aside from a generalized xenophobia, for the profound Federalist distaste for the Irish. Next to the native-born Southerners of Anglo-Saxon stock, they represented the most substantial bulwark of the Republican party. Whether they were frontiersmen and whiskey-distillers in western Pennsylvania, or mechanics and laborers in the large Northern cities, they were animated by a common hatred for England and a common regard for anyone—France or any other country—who fought the British. And, as the hewers of wood and drawers of water, they fell into the neat classification which Freneau, returned to newspaper activity in New York, had drafted in anticipation of Karl Marx.

In all civilized countries, wrote Freneau, there exists two classes of men. "One are laborers, men who produce by their industry something to the common stock of commodity. This class is made up of farmers, mechanics, etc. The second class are such, as live on the stock of the community already produced, not by their *labor*, but obtained by their *art* and *cunning*, or that of their ancestors. These are for the most part merchants, speculators, priests, lawyers, and men employed in the various departments of government." [42]

The second of the three bills—the Alien Act—is usually lumped with the third under the common denomination of the Alien and Sedition Laws. But they must be separated. Here too, for all its lack of wisdom and display of fear, the Alien Act was constitutional. Nor was it general and indiscriminate in its terms. Apprehension and a determination to protect the country against possible subversive alien elements in their midst—particularly in the event of a full-scale war with France—was at the bottom of it.

The precedent of the Act has been followed in modern times, notably in connection with the internment of German and Japanese aliens during the Second World War; and was exceeded by far in the internment of the Nisei—American citizens of Japanese ancestry.

The Alien Act, as finally passed, empowered the President to order "such aliens as he shall judge dangerous to the peace and safety of the United States, or shall have reasonable grounds to suspect are concerned in any treasonable or secret machinations against the Government thereof," out of the country.

Gallatin argued that under its terms alien "friends" as well as alien "enemies" were subject to deportation, and that therefore the proposed law was unconstitutional. In its legal aspects this was an untenable argument. Livingston of New York—in whose bailiwick the Irish were particularly strong and marched under the banner of Tammany—delivered a passionate oration against the bill in its totality. It took the judicial power of review from the courts, he cried, abolished the right to a jury trial, and provided a secret inquisition where "all is darkness, silence, mystery, and suspicion." But John Wilkes Kittera of Pennsylvania retorted sarcastically that even France, "that land of liberty, removes both alien friends and enemies," and that the danger to liberty came not from too much power in the government, but from a want of it. [43]

The bill passed the House by a vote of 46 to 40, leading Jefferson to lament the absence, or "desertion," as he called it, of ten Republicans from the chamber. "Had every one been in his place," he said bitterly, "not a single one of the dangerous measures carried or to be carried would have prevailed. Even the provisional army would have been rejected." [44]

The French aliens, fearing the worst, commenced to quit the

country "by the shipload." One of the most prominent was Constantin
François Chasseboeuf, Comte de Volney, savant, philosopher, Egypt-
ologist and radical in political and economic theory. He had fled to
the United States in 1795 after narrowly escaping the guillotine at
the hands of the Jacobins. The Federalists believed him to be a spy,
and he was certain to be one of the first against whom the new law
would be enforced. "It suffices for a man to be a philosopher," exclaimed his friend Jefferson, "and to believe that human affairs are
susceptible of improvement, and to look forward, rather than back to
the Gothic ages, to mark him as an anarchist, disorganizer, atheist
and enemy of the government." [45] Without question Jefferson was
thinking also of himself when he penned these bitter words.

Moreau de St. Méry, the Philadelphia bookshop proprietor, was
another who conceived himself marked for deportation. Not only was
antagonism mounting daily against the French, but St. Méry's Republican friends also feared that they would be the victims of violence,
and met in secret to organize for defense. St. Méry asked Senator
Langdon of New Hampshire to inquire of the President what he was
charged with. "Nothing in particular," replied Adams, "but he's too
French." On hearing this, St. Méry thought it wise to depart, and
sailed for France in August 1798. [46]

The third of the triad of laws—the Sedition Act—though joined
with the others in passage and in popular estimation, must be set
apart. Of this law alone can grave constitutional questions be put.
On this, more than on any other, did the country come close to disruption, and civil war loom formidably in the offing. Not only were
constitutional problems evoked in its making, but newer ones resulted,
embodied in the claimed rights of nullification and secession, which
pointed directly toward the great Civil War of more than half a
century later.

The Sedition bill passed the Senate with celerity, and came to the
House on July 5, 1798. In its final form it contained three sections.
The first declared that any conspiracy to oppose or impede the proper
authority or the laws of the government of the United States, or
counseling insurrection or riot against it, subjected the offenders to
an imprisonment of six months to five years, and a fine of $5000.

The second and major section provided that "if any person shall
write, print, utter, or publish, or shall cause or procure to be written,
printed, uttered, or published . . . any false, scandalous, and malicious,

writing or writings against the Government of the United States, or either House of the Congress of the United States, or the President of the United States, with intent to defame the said Government, or either House of the said Congress, or the said President, or to bring them, or either of them, into contempt or disrepute; or to excite against them, or either or any of them, the hatred of the good people of the United States; or to excite any unlawful combinations therein, for opposing or resisting any law of the United States, or any act of the President of the United States, done in pursuance of any such law, or of the powers in him vested by the Constitution of the United States, or to resist, oppose or defeat any such law or act; or to aid, encourage, or abet, any hostile designs of any foreign nation against the United States, their people or Government," he shall be liable to imprisonment for two years and a fine of $2000.

The third section was really a subjunct of the second. It declared that the truth of the utterances or libels specified therein constituted a good defense; and that the defendant was entitled to a trial by a jury with power to determine both the law and the fact.[47]

The bill was comprehensive in its sweep and scope. The first section cannot be considered as unduly objectionable. It granted powers that are inherent in every government to protect itself against resistance to its laws, law enforcement officers, and riot and insurrection.

The second section, however, was the crux of the Sedition Act. In effect it made libelous or defamatory remarks or criticism of specific members of the government—senators, representatives and the President—a criminal offense triable in the federal courts. It also made utterances calculated to excite "unlawful combinations" to oppose or resist laws or acts of the President a federal offense. What constituted an "unlawful combination" was not defined, and therefore was left dangerously vague.

In the main the Act followed and was patterned on a set of recently enacted laws passed in England as a war measure. It was therefore legitimately subject to criticism on the ground that it did not take cognizance of the inherent differences between a monarchical and republican form of government.

But there was one significant variation from the British prototype, and indeed from the common law of libel as generally applied both in England and in the several American states. The common law had always held that the truth of a defamatory utterance did not constitute a defense in a prosecution for criminal libel; that it was the duty of the presiding judge to determine whether or not a particular utterance was legally liable, and for the jury to determine only whether the utterance had actually been made. The third section of the Act, however, introduced revolutionary changes in the old procedure—truth now could be interposed as a defense, and it was within the province of the jury to decide both the fact of utterance and its legal effect.

Besides, with the exception of the sweeping generalization that the "government of the United States" as an entity could be libeled, or that the Houses of Congress as similar entities could also be maligned, any libel against a specific individual, whether he was President of the United States, a particular member of Congress, or not, was already subject to criminal penalties under the common law and could have been prosecuted in the *state* courts on application of the aggrieved party.

It is too often forgotten that such prosecutions have been held in the United States on many occasions without more than passing comment. Even Thomas Jefferson, the stoutest opponent of the Sedition Act and the proponent of the doctrine of nullification because of it, on at least one occasion while President requested the criminal prosecution of certain Federalist editors in the state courts of Pennsylvania for their libelous attacks on him; while in New York another editor, Harry Croswell, was convicted and jailed for a similar offense against him without a word of protest from Jefferson or any other Republican. And, in this instance, the alleged truth of the libel could not be interposed as a defense, nor could the jury, as in the case of the federal statute, judge both the law and the fact.

In its narrowest essence, therefore, the Sedition Act added nothing to the old law of libel, enforcible in the state courts; and in fact liberalized it for the benefit of the defendant. What it did do was to grant jurisdiction to the federal courts in specific cases, and such a jurisdiction was constitutionally arguable as not within the powers granted to the United States.

While in actual practice the Sedition Act was enforced chiefly against libels directed against the President as a person, theoretically it enlarged the area to include corporate bodies (the government and the Houses of Congress) and added another area which did not involve people at all (acts and laws). *This* section must be carefully dissociated from the rest. Yet even here it may be asserted that Congress or any other lawmaking body has the right to declare that one can libel a body of men, a group, a corporation, a class, or even a whole nation, as well as a single individual; and in recent times there have been attempts to enact just such laws.

However, when we come to the second area—the attempt to punish opposition or resistance to *laws* and presidential *acts* under those laws, or the incitement of "unlawful" combinations against them, we are in a different category altogether. These are not libels by any stretch of the term, since they involve abstractions or things, and not persons. They constitute despotic acts of a government which intends to brook no opposition. *Forcible* resistance to laws duly enacted, or Executive acts performed under them, are proper subjects for punitive regulations, if any government is to continue to exist; but "opposition" to laws, or the promotion of "unlawful" combinations against them, brings us immediately into the realm of conjecture.

Opposition in its usual dictionary meaning includes active dissent from a law or act, and an attempt to bring about its repeal. The party out of power is universally called the "opposition." Yet by the terms of the Sedition Act, if narrowly construed—and, in the event, they were so construed—agitation for repeal or even published criticism could be considered as punishable. Furthermore, what constitutes an "unlawful combination"? Washington and the Federalists thought the Democratic Societies unlawful because they met behind closed doors at night, allowed no one but members to be present, and criticized the government. Could Congress merely by the passage of a law, or the Executive by direct fiat, make an organization unlawful without the establishment of general criteria? What happened then to the guarantees of free speech, press and assemblage embodied in the Bill of Rights? What happened to the general theory of what constitutes a republican form of government?

The real purport of the Sedition Act was immediately disclosed in the House debate. Allen of Connecticut sought to prove the necessity for the law by reading two items from the Republican press. "Let gentlemen look at certain papers printed in this city and elsewhere," he shouted, brandishing the offending issues, "and ask themselves whether an unwarrantable and dangerous combination does not exist to overturn and ruin the Government by publishing the most shameless falsehoods against the Representatives of the people of all denominations."

The first, which he forthwith read, was a squib from Bache's *Aurora* of June 28th: "It is a curious fact, America is making war with France for *not* treating, at the very moment the Minister for Foreign

Affairs fixes upon the very day for opening a negotiation with Mr. Gerry. What think you of this, Americans!"

It was an unfortunate illustrative choice. Compared to other items in the same paper, this was wholly temperate; true or false, it came within the realm of general criticism of a governmental course and certainly lay within the protection of the Tenth Amendment.

Allen's second choice, however, was of a different order. He read from the New York *Time-Piece*, edited by that infuriating gadfly Philip Freneau: "Where a person without patriotism, without philosophy, without a taste for the fine arts, building his pretensions on a gross and indigested compilation of statutes and precedents is jostled into the Chief Magistracy by the ominous combination of old Tories with old opinions, and old Whigs with new, 'tis fit this mock Monarch, with his Court, composed of Tories and speculators, should pass in review before the good sense of the world."

This was a personal attack on the character and opinions of John Adams, and as such, whether he was President or not, might well have been taken into the state courts under the common law of libel; though the actual allegations might not have passed muster as constituting legal libel. Certainly there was a sufficiency of truly libelous utterances which could have been culled from the Republican press.

But Allen, waving these two examples, exclaimed: "God deliver us from such liberty, the liberty of vomiting on the public floods of falsehood and hatred to everything sacred, human and divine!" [48]

Livingston rose to protest that the bill before them was not merely an abridgement under the Constitution but "a total annihilation of the press." McDowell, after defending Bache with fulsome praise, inquired as to Fenno and Cobbett, Federalist editors, "whose paper contains more libels and lies than any other in the United States?" [49]

This last was a *tu quoque* retort and not properly an argument against the bill itself. Gallatin took a more moderate and sounder position. He admitted the intemperateness of the article in the *Time-Piece*, but asserted that the question of truth and error could not and must not be determined by coercion. "Was the Administration afraid," he asked pointedly, "that in this instance error could not be sucessfully opposed by truth?" In the past it had, and the nation had flourished. Did they now fear the contest? Did the pending bill mean that anyone who disliked the measures of the present Administration or of "the temporary majority in Congress," and freely expressed his disapprobation, "is an enemy, not of the Administration, but of the Constitution, and is liable to punishment?" [50]

In spite of Republican arguments, however, and of lengthy and exacerbated debate, the Federalists grimly overrode all opposition and pushed the bill to passage by the ominously close vote of 44 to 41. Adams promptly signed it and it became the law of the land.

It must be confessed that the Federalists, and the President, had received ample provocation from the Republican press. The personal attacks, the innuendoes, the brutally plain statements, were in truth indecent, maddening and in many instances outright calls to armed insurrection and civil war. The invectives which had driven George Washington into retirement were exceeded by far by those which were now directed against John Adams. The upholding of everything French against everything American in a factual state of war verged perilously close to sedition and treason.

Being human, the Federalists were goaded to a literal frenzy by the incessant sniping and the thunderous salvoes. But their frenzy blinded them to the consequences of their Sedition Act with its shotgun provisions. The problem always arises, as it still does today, where to draw the line between, on the one hand, the constitutionally protected freedom of the press and the right freely to criticize public individuals and public measures, and, on the other, the legally punishable abuse of those privileges. A less broadly provisioned Act, or a recourse to the state courts in specific instances of true libel, might better have served even the Federalist cause than the passage of the Sedition Act.

Hamilton himself, archpriest of federalism though he was, thought that the bills went too far. He wished to draw a few "guarded exceptions" to the deportation of aliens; and he attacked the Sedition Act as containing provisions "which, according to a cursory view, appear to me highly exceptionable, and such as, more than any thing else, may endanger civil war. . . . I hope sincerely," he told Wolcott, "the thing may not be hurried through. Let us not establish a tyranny. Energy is a very different thing from violence." [51]

When Hamilton was personally libeled by a charge in the Philadelphia *Aurora* which was reprinted by the *Argus* in New York, he went to the New York courts for redress. The newspapers accused him of seeking to suppress the *Aurora* by making an offer of purchase at its full valuation, and that the offer had been refused. Whether true or not, the assertion did not constitute libel. But the *Aurora* went on editorially to insinuate that Hamilton had expected to consummate the deal with "British secret service money—a hint to Mr. Liston would do the business at once." [52]

Since it was easier for him to prosecute the *Argus* for reprinting the libel than to journey to Philadelphia to prefer charges against the *Aurora*—and since he had smarted long in silence under the grossest attacks of the *Argus* on both his private and public life—he pressed the case against the latter to the conviction and jailing of David Frothingham, claimed by the defense to be merely a foreman but actually the managing editor. [53]

Indeed Hamilton took a far more statesmanlike view of the current situation than many of his Federalist friends. He found almost as much to blame in British aggressions as in French, and advocated that they be treated with equal strictness; to the extent, if necessary, of going to war with both offenders simultaneously. "One of them," he then believed, "will quickly court us, and by this course of conduct our citizens will be enthusiastically united to the government." [54]

But it was John Taylor of Caroline, the irreconcilable opponent of governments and constitutions as they usually existed, who wrote the last word on the Sedition Act.

"The design of substituting political for religious heresy, is visible in the visage of sedition laws. A civil priesthood or government, hunting after political heresy, is an humble imitator of the inquisition, which fines, imprisons, tortures and murders, sometimes mind, at others, body. It affects the same piety, feigned by priestcraft at the burning of an heretick; and its party supplies such exultations, as those exhibited at an auto da fe, by a populace." [55]

CHAPTER 26

Military Intrigues and Sedition Trials

THE ARRIVAL OF John Marshall in the United States coincided opportunely—from the Federalist viewpoint—with the debate on the Alien and Sedition Acts, and did much to hasten their passage.

His entry into Philadelphia was a personal triumph. Immense throngs poured out of the city to meet him, together with Secretary of State Pickering, three corps of cavalry and innumerable carriages, and he was escorted into town to the clangor of bells and the thunder of cannon. A banquet was tendered him at O'Eller's Tavern, where an unknown phrasemaker delivered the immortal toast which was later mistakenly attributed to Pinckney in Paris: "Millions for defense, but not one cent for tribute!" [1]

Marshall was unquestionably the man of the hour; he had stood up to the French and supported American rights with dignity and firmness. If Pinckney was adulated to a less degree, it was because he did not happen to be on the spot. As for Elbridge Gerry, who had remained in Paris at the behest of the French ministry, the Federalists lavished on him their fiercest invectives, while the Republicans sought in his staying their last hope of averting war with France and their own destruction.

The most furious of all at Gerry's "folly, meanness and treachery" was the Secretary of State. If the French would only guillotine him, he exclaimed, "they would do a favor to this Country; but they will keep him alive to write, à la Monroe, a Book." [2]

Even as he dispatched a stern letter to the errant envoy, peremptorily ordering him to return, Gerry in fact was demanding his passports and getting ready to sail home. [3] King warned from London that Gerry was on his way, bearing "a soothing and treacherous message from the Directory. Be on your guard," he wrote Hamilton. "France will not declare war against us. No. Her policy will be to pursue with us the same course she already has done, and which has served her purpose in Italy, and among the honest, but devoted and ruined Swiss. I will say, if after all that has occurred among ourselves, and in other countries, we are content to be duped, and cajoled, we shall deserve the fate which they are preparing for us." [4]

Meanwhile King sought to purchase from the British government 25,000 muskets, and naval and land cannon to the value of £10,000 sterling. [5] The British were favorably disposed, and proposed an alliance with the United States in the war everyone expected to follow. They would view with satisfaction, so Liston was instructed, an American conquest of Louisiana and the Floridas, provided the United States agreed to their own seizure of the French island of Santo Domingo. [6]

When Liston broached the subject to Adams, the latter expressed a guarded interest, but preferred to obtain a formal proposition direct from London. [7] Nothing in fact came of it.

In the meantime, Adams proclaimed to Congress in ringing words that "I will never send another minister to France without assurances that he will be received, respected, and honored, as the representative of a great, free, powerful, and independent nation." [8]

Having completed its work for good or ill, Congress adjourned on July 19, 1798. The *Argus* saluted its passing with a mock obituary on the following day: "DIED, last evening of a two years consumption, and under all the horrors of a guilty conscience, the HOUSE OF REPRESENTATIVES of the United States."

But the measures which Congress had taken were rapidly put into action by the administration. The newly completed forty-four-gun frigate *Constellation*, commanded by Captain Thomas Truxtun, and the smaller *Delaware*, under Captain Stephen Decatur, slipped out to sea to seize French ships wherever they could be found. The cruise in West Indies waters was not particularly successful. The big *Constellation* returned empty-handed; the little *Delaware*, however, netted a French privateer off the New Jersey coast. Our war with France, altogether naval in operation and without a formal declaration, had begun.

On July 2, 1798, the *Constitution*, with Captain Samuel Nicholson on the bridge, sailed out of Boston on a similar quest. Later to become enshrined in song and legend as "Old Ironsides," the *Constitution's* first cruise ended most ingloriously. Her sole conquest turned out to be an *English* privateer, which the American government apologetically restored, together with damages in the sum of $11,000. To cap the climax, the frigate sprung her bowsprit and had to limp home for repairs.

Even the French privateer taken by the *Delaware,* when it was reoutfitted and renamed the *Retaliation,* and sought to cruise on its own under young Lieutenant William Bainbridge, managed only to fall in with two French frigates and surrender.

By the end of 1798, we had not only not harmed the French but we had suffered considerable humiliation in the process.

At the same time arduous preparations were made on land for defense against any possible invasion by the veteran French armies. Congress had authorized the raising of a provisional army. But the chief problem at the moment seemed to be who was going to officer and command it.

There was no problem about the top command. Everyone looked to Washington to emerge from retirement and once more take the field against a foreign foe.

When the matter was broached to him, while expressing a reluctance to leave "the calm retirement" of Mount Vernon he nevertheless agreed to reassume his ancient burden when the occasion arose. His bitterness against the French equaled that of the most extreme Federalist. He spoke of them as "intoxicated with blood," as lacking in "every principle of justice" and "capable of *anything* that is unjust or dishonorable." [9]

On July 2, 1798, Adams sent his name to the Senate as lieutenant-general and commander-in-chief of the American forces; on the following day he was unanimously confirmed. But there the unanimity stopped. It was known that Washington did not intend to assume active command unless and until actual land war impended. Therefore his second in command would be the *de facto* if not titular chief.

Already Hamilton had commenced his campaign to obtain the second position. He had never given up his romantic dreams of glory, of that military career for which he secretly considered himself best fitted and which was most congenial to his restless temperament.

On June 2nd—a month before Washington was nominated—Hamilton wrote to him that he was willing to enter "a station in which the service I may render may be proportionate to the sacrifice I am to make." In short, he wished to be inspector-general, with a command in the line. Such a station would place him second only to Washington. [10]

In this secret move he was aided and abetted by the members of the Cabinet and by influential Federalists in Massachusetts and New York. Pickering and McHenry, unknown to the President, urged on Washington that he make Hamilton's appointment a *sine qua non* for his own acceptance of the post. Impressed by their solicitations and estimating Hamilton's abilities highly on his own, Washington wrote formally to Adams and Secretary of War McHenry indicating he would like Hamilton under him, and at the same time demanding that he be given the right to choose his own general officers.[11]

Adams was taken considerably aback at this upsurge of a demand for Hamilton's appointment in what was tantamount to full command. To put it bluntly, he had long distrusted Hamilton and chafed under his arrogance. There were other officers, influential in their own right, and with experience and seniority during the Revolution, whose claims were superior to Hamilton's. Among them were General Henry Knox, former Secretary of War, and General Charles Cotesworth Pinckney, recently returned from France.

One of the most amazing episodes in American history now took shape and form. While President Adams sought to place Knox second, Pinckney third and Hamilton in the rear, indistinguishably mingled with the mass of other candidates, his own Cabinet was secretly determined to place Hamilton in the lead. Pickering and McHenry were the heads and fronts of the conspiracy.

They sent confidential letters to Washington urging him to stand firm on Hamilton; and McHenry hastened personally to Mount Vernon to hold him in line. Pickering pulled everyone to pieces whom the President suggested, reiterating monotonously the single name: Hamilton! Hamilton! Only when McHenry returned in triumph from Mount Vernon, bearing with him Washington's list, did it begin to dawn on Adams what was going on behind his back. For Washington had placed Hamilton first, Pinckney second, and Knox third.[12]

His eyes opened to the web of intrigue in which he had been enmeshed, and faced with General Knox's wrath at being cavalierly thrust aside in favor of Hamilton, the President wrote sharply to McHenry that Knox *must* rank next to Washington, and Pinckney take precedence of Hamilton. "You may depend upon it," he added angrily, "the five New England States will not patiently submit to the humiliation that has been meditated for them." [13]

If Adams thought he had ended the matter or that, as President, he had the final say on appointments, he was grossly mistaken. The wheels within wheels kept turning. When Hamilton in disgust finally declared his reluctant agreement to serve under Knox, Pickering deliberately "concealed it," as he frankly boasted, in order to force through Washington's list, with Hamilton at the top.[14]

Every member of the Cabinet—Pickering, McHenry, Wolcott, even Benjamin Stoddert, who had just been appointed to the newly established Department of the Navy—joined in the attempt to compel Adams to appoint Hamilton. Only Charles Lee, the Attorney General, stood discreetly aloof from the conspiracy. Letters went posthaste in all directions—to Hamilton exhorting him to stand by his guns; to Washington urging him to stand equally firm and intimating that the President was disregarding his advice; to Federalist leaders everywhere to bring pressure to bear.[15]

But before these could develop to their full flower, Adams had ordered McHenry to make out commissions in the order of Knox first, Pinckney second and Hamilton third. "There has been too much intrigue in this business with General Washington and me," he declared angrily; "if I shall ultimately be the dupe of it, I am much mistaken in myself." [16]

He was. Indignant at the accusation—all the more fiercely because it was true—McHenry complained to Washington: "I have endeavored all in my power to preserve your arrangement, without effect." [17]

Thus brought to the sticking point, Washington bluntly wrote Adams that he had accepted the chief command only on certain conditions, and that he and McHenry had placed the proposed major-generals in a certain order. "But you," said Washington sternly, "have been pleased to order the last to be first, and the first to be last." What did Adams intend to do about it? The intimation was plain; if he persisted, Washington would resign.[18]

When the President read this peremptory note, he realized he was beaten. The consequences of Washington's resignation, military and political, would be disastrous. In bitterness and humiliation, he backed down. He tried to save face by dating *all* three commissions the same day; with the understanding that if the appointees could not agree on the precedence among themselves, Washington would have the final word.[19]

It was a bitter pill for a proud and touchy man like Adams to swallow that, while he might be President of the United States, he was not even master in his own house. His earlier resentment at Washington for consistently overshadowing him became fixed; his dislike, hate even, for Hamilton grew apace; while his anger at the treachery of his Cabinet—all holdovers, except for Stoddert, from the previous regime—knew no bounds.

Lee was not implicated, and Wolcott's defection, very curiously, he never suspected. It was on Pickering and McHenry that all his wrath concentrated; and it was on them that the storm finally burst.

Poor McHenry was caught between two fires. While he braved Adams's wrath in behalf of his old friend Hamilton, the latter repaid him with contempt. He was disgusted with McHenry's ineptitude and inefficiency, Hamilton complained to everyone. Washington hearkened and let his own cold wrath descend on the luckless Secretary of War; while Wolcott and others proposed that McHenry resign and let Hamilton take his place.[20]

As for Knox, he was furious at his displacement by Hamilton, and refused the commission altogether. "Our friend Hamilton's abilities," the old general wrote bitterly, "by some have been considered so transcendent, as to be a sufficient cause in their opinion to degrade all his seniors in rank and years of the late American Army. I subscribe to his talents but I cannot serve under him."[21] Pinckney, however, assented to his own subordination with a good grace; a surrender which Hamilton was to remember with gratitude in the next election.

For all his yielding, Adams had not yet fully drunk of the cup of humiliation. When he proposed to appoint Aaron Burr, whose services in the Revolution had been at least as eminent as those of Hamilton, to a brigadier-generalship, on the secret instigation of Pickering, McHenry and Hamilton, Washington coldly turned him down. Once more Adams was compelled to recede; to recollect in after years the painful sensations of the moment. The "Triumvirate," as he called them, had been too much for him.[22]

As had been anticipated, Washington remained at Mount Vernon and took little part, except through correspondence, with the management and recruitment of the provisional army. Now that he had realized that dream which even as a small boy in the West Indies had been his life's goal, Hamilton set to work with his accustomed phenomenal energy. The office he had sought and attained was no sinecure. It was his job to raise, equip and train an army where none had existed before; and to counter the furious opposition and sabotaging tactics of the Republicans, who not only attacked the Army itself but the man who acted as its virtual chief.

The *Argus*, later to be prosecuted for criminal libel by Hamilton, opened the Republican assault. It cried out that Adams, like his predecessor, had been deluded by intriguing men. "There is one man [Hamilton]," it thundered, "whose wily intrigues, whose shocking depravity, are known from one end of the continent to the other. . . . War and military command would be the paths in which his desolating ambition would fain riot." To him and his friends "hell is not so terrible as the thought of peace"; and "we hear these minions of the arch-fiend bellowing forth even against the president whom they have professed so long and so much to adore." [23]

Indeed, the Republican opposition was such that Washington himself peremptorily refused to have them in the Army, even when some volunteered for commissions. "You could as soon scrub the blackamore white," he wrote vehemently, "as to change the principles of a professed Democrat; and that he will leave nothing unattempted to overturn the Government of this Country." [24]

Hamilton was more moderate—and more subtle—than his commander-in-chief. He opposed the total exclusion of Republicans from the service as too stringent; the rule might be relaxed in meritorious cases and to fill the inferior grades. "It does not seem advisable," he told McHenry, "to exclude all hope and to give the appointments too absolute a party feature. Military situations, on young minds particularly," he let the cat out of the bag, "are of all others calculated to insure a zeal for the service and the cause in which the incumbents are employed." [25]

The new major-general absorbed duties and responsibilities with an insatiable appetite. He not only undertook to act in Washington's stead, but he assumed the functions of the War Department as well without a word of protest from McHenry. He hectored and bullied the unresisting Secretary, and only on one occasion was the latter goaded to a flash of spirit.

The energetic Hamilton let his fancies roam far afield, even while busy night and day with the arduous details of bringing a huge provisional army into existence. He dreamed that Mexico and all South America beckoned him—and gave a cordial ear to the conspiratorial plans of General Sebastian Francisco de Miranda, a Venezuelan revolutionary and exile, who had already enlisted the aid of Rufus King in London.[26] Perhaps he even expected to employ the Army—as the

Republicans repeatedly charged—to destroy their party and their principles in the United States. But all his efforts and all his dreams were
shortly to be dissipated by the action of the man he condemned and
flouted: John Adams, President of the United States.

The Alien and Sedition Acts became law with Adams's signature
on June 25, 1798, and July 14, 1798, respectively. The Alien Act
was never actually put into effect; though a large number of French
refugees, fearing its application, hastily departed the country.[27] The
Sedition Act was another matter.

Smarting under the lash of Republican newspaper sarcasm, invective and outright libel, the administration proceeded vigorously against
the offending editors. Actually, proceedings were commenced even
before the passage of the Act under the common law governing libel.

On July 7th, Pickering called on the United States district attorney
for New York to institute a prosecution for libel against the editor of
the New York *Time-Piece*, if he was an American citizen; if an alien,
then to invoke the Alien Act, already effective, for his deportation.[28]

The editor was one John Daly Burk, who had fled his native Ireland
to avoid arrest for sedition and, coming to America, scribbled bad
plays, immersed himself in radical Republican politics and eventually
took over the management of the *Time-Piece*. Under his guiding hand
it became one of the most fiery sheets in a land well stocked with material for the kindling.

Burk had accused the President of deliberately falsifying parts of
Gerry's communications from France so as to distort for partisan purposes the true situation there; in effect, he was charging Adams with
forgery and corruption.

By the time the district attorney was able to act, the Sedition Act
had become law and Burk was arrested on a charge of seditious libel.
Aaron Burr came forward to provide bail for the incarcerated editor
and, after considerable negotiation, obtained an agreement for quash-
ing the prosecution if Burk would quit the country. Instead, the editor
fled to Virginia, where he hid under an assumed name. Jefferson and
other Republicans offered him their protection and friendship; and
Burk, after the storm had cleared, was later to write, with Jefferson's
assistance, the standard history of Virginia. Ironically, he was slain in
1808 in a duel to which he was challenged by a Frenchman for having
called the French "a pack of rascals." [29]

Even Gallatin felt constrained to disapprove of such tactics as the

Time-Piece and other Republican sheets regularly employed. "Cool discussion and fair statement of facts," he avowed, "are the only proper modes of conveying truth and disseminating sound principles. Let squibs and virulent paragraphs be the exclusive privilege of Fenno, Porcupine & Co." [30]

His admonitions fell on deaf ears; the squibs and virulence spewed forth on either side; and the prosecutions—against Republicans alone —continued briskly.

Even before Burk's arrest, Benjamin Franklin Bache, the editor of the Philadelphia *Aurora* and the greatest thorn in Federalist skins since Freneau's folding up, felt the weight of the lash. He was indicted in the state courts under common-law principles for libel against the President. He died, however, before his case came to trial.

The fact of indictments such as this under *common law* proved that the Sedition Act was unnecessary for the prosecution of true libels; and the Federalists might well have prevented their own downfall had they heeded the lesson. But those whom the gods wish to destroy they first make mad.

Even after his arrest and return to freedom on bail, Bache continued his assaults with unabated vigor. When he heard of toasts drunk in Baltimore by Federalists which called for "a halter of strong hemp in the place of a French pension to Bache, Printer of the Aurora," and for health to Hamilton, he retorted viciously that he welcomed abuse from those "who can make a *confessed adulterer* and an *avowed monarchist* the object of their adoration." [31]

As the Sedition Act went into effect, the prosecutions moved into a wider field. In turn the editors of the Boston *Independent Chronicle,* the Vermont *Gazette,* the New London *Bee,* and individuals like Matthew Lyon, congressman from Vermont, James Thompson Callender, hack writer, and Thomas Cooper, educator and scientist, were indicted. Even strays who merely shouted an epithet against Adams or the government were made to feel the heavy hand of prosecution.

The arrests and the trials continued well into 1799 and 1800; and did not cease until Jefferson came into the presidency. He then pardoned those already convicted and sent to jail, and quashed further proceedings against those still under indictment and awaiting trial.

In a sense it might be called—as the Republicans did call it—a reign of terror. All legal safeguards laboriously erected by the common law and the Constitution were disregarded by the Federalist judges; and packed juries, under their threats and brutal charges, almost invariably brought in verdicts of guilty. Yet the actual number of arrests for all offenses was comparatively small—about twenty-five; while fifteen or so more were indicted but never taken into custody. And of the total, only some ten were brought to trial and convicted.[32]

Matthew Lyon of Vermont, he who had spat in a fellow congressman's face and been soundly cudgeled for it, went back to his own state to take up the pen. With this sharper weapon than saliva, he wrote in the Vermont *Journal* that under Adams he had seen "every consideration of the public welfare swallowed up in a continual grasp for power, in an unbounded thirst for ridiculous pomp, foolish adulation, and selfish avarice."

He also caused to be printed a letter purporting to have been written by Joel Barlow, the expatriate poet who had taken up an honorary citizenship in France. The whole trouble between the two nations, so Barlow said, was due to "the bullying speech of your President, and stupid answer of your Senate"; that instead of committing the President "to a mad house," the Senate had "echoed the speech with more servility than ever George III experienced from either House of Parliament."

On these two publications Lyon was indicted and brought to trial. He conducted his own defense with great aplomb. He attacked the constitutionality of the Sedition Act, asserted that the libels were true, and actually subjected the presiding judge to a cross-examination to prove his assertions. "Judge Patterson," he demanded in open court, "have you not frequently dined with the President, and observed his ridiculous pomp and parade?" Patterson, one of the few federal judges to display moderation and sense in the conduct of a sedition trial, quietly replied for the record that he had in fact dined with Adams, but had witnessed at his table only "a great deal of plainness and simplicity." With this retort, Lyon abruptly rested his defense.

Patterson ruled that the Act was constitutional; that the quoted publications constituted libel in law; and turned the case over to the jury. They found Lyon guilty as charged, and he was sentenced to four months' imprisonment and a fine of $1000.[33]

Confined to jail, Lyon became a Republican martyr overnight. The spitting episode was forgotten; so were the coarseness and vulgarity of his speech. From his cell he campaigned for re-election to Congress, and was triumphantly returned. A popular subscription paid his fine; and he emerged a national figure and a hero.

Thomas Adams, one of the editors of the Boston *Independent Chronicle,* was indicted both by the federal government under the Sedition Act and by the state for common-law libel. He died before either case was reached for trial. His brother, Abijah, however, went to trial under the state indictment for having asserted in conjunction with Thomas that the state legislators had violated their oath of office because they refused their assent to the Kentucky and Virginia Resolves.

Francis Dana, chief justice of Massachusetts, made a political football of the trial with his excoriations of all "Jacobins" and his hostile charge to the jury. Adams was convicted, fined and sentenced to a month in jail. But this, it must be remembered, was a *state* proceeding and not a federal one.

Anthony Hasswell, editor of the Vermont *Gazette,* was accused of publishing an advertisement soliciting subscriptions to pay Lyon's fine, in the course of which he made the "seditious" statement that Lyon was "holden by the oppressive hand of usurped power, in a loathsome prison." For this he was tried, convicted, sentenced to two months in jail and fined $200.

Charles Holt, editor of the New London *Bee,* had engaged in a series of attacks on the administration, the provisional Army and Alexander Hamilton. The paragraph, however, which brought him into court asserted that our farmers "will never spend their best days in arms and vice, in order to glitter in regimentals, wear a sword and lounge in idleness as drones, unpitied and penniless. . . . Are our young officers and soldiers," he asked, "to learn virtue from General Hamilton? Or like their generals are they to be found in the bed of adultery?" [34]

Tried for sedition, defamation of the government and the discouragement of recruiting, he received the comparatively heavy jail sentence of six months and a fine of $200. It must be noted that the discouragement of recruiting—for which purpose the paragraph certainly was intended—has been made in recent times the target of congressional enactments and penalties.

When Bache died during the yellow fever epidemic in Philadelphia at the end of 1798, James Duane married his widow and took over the *Aurora.* Duane, though born in America, had been taken by his parents to Ireland at the age of five. While still a youth he went to India, set up a newspaper, and ran into trouble with his denunciations of the East India Company. That semisovereign entity caused his arrest and deportation. Eventually he drifted to Philadelphia, joined forces with Bache, and after the latter's death forged the *Aurora* into an even more powerful Republican organ than before.

Once again he fell into difficulties. With a parade of alleged documentary proof, he accused the British minister of employing a slush fund of $800,000 to bribe members of Congress; as a result of which a secret alliance was being entered into by the United States and Great Britain for the purpose of dismembering France.[35]

Such statements, unless proven, definitely constituted a common-law libel. He was arrested under the Sedition Act; but never brought to trial. The same thing happened on another indictment against him for a supposed libel on the Senate when he published a purported secret debate in that House. This case was still pending when Jefferson became President and ordered its dismissal.

Thomas Cooper, editor of the Northumberland (Pa.) *Gazette,* educator, scientist, English radical, friend of Jefferson, attacked Adams in an "Address to the People of Northampton County." He called the President a despot who sought to rivet his despotism on the nation through the Sedition Act and the creation of a standing army. Adams ordered his indictment for the libel, without success.[36]

But Cooper, English-born and only recently an American citizen, got into trouble in the famous case of Jonathan Robbins, of which mention will be made later. Cooper charged Adams with interfering "to influence the decisions of a court of justice—a stretch of authority which the monarch of Great Britain would have shrunk from—an interference without precedent, against law and against mercy."

He was tried for this before Supreme Court Justice Samuel Chase. Chase was one of the most amazing figures ever to sit on an American bench. For his like one must go to England to seek out "Bloody" Francis Jeffreys, the notorious "hanging judge" of an earlier era. A member of the Continental Congress and of the legislature of his native Maryland, a signer of the Declaration of Independence, he had been publicly accused by Alexander Hamilton during the Revolution of cornering the market in grain and raising the price unconscionably to the government and the Army. Though whitewashed by a partisan state legislature, the taint remained with him. Washington appointed him to the Supreme Court in 1796; but his claims to "fame" date from the trials over which he presided under the Sedition Act. Gross of feature, heavy-jowled, a furious Federalist who conceived all Republicans to be the spawn of hell, his bullying tactics, his violent and partisan charges, his intimidation of defendants, witnesses, lawyers and jurymen, made him the most hated judge of the time. The Republicans, after their triumph, brought impeachment proceedings against him for his antics during these trials; but the Senate, though mustering an actual majority on some of the articles of impeachment, could not summon the requisite two-thirds to sustain any one of them.

When, in the instant case, Cooper claimed truth as a defense, Chase blocked every defense effort with his insistence that he must prove *every* part of his publication, no matter how insignificant—a manifest impossibility. His final charge to the jury was a personal attack on Cooper, a prosecution harangue rather than a judicial summing up. He termed Cooper's article "the boldest attempt I have known to poison the minds of the people," and Cooper's assertion that there was a standing army in the United States as betraying "the most egregious ignorance, or the most wilful intention to deceive the public."

Obviously, after being subjected to such a harangue from the bench, the jury brought in a verdict of guilty; and Cooper was sentenced to six months in jail and fined $400.[37]

In later years the convicted Cooper himself became a judge in the state courts of Pennsylvania and, in 1811, was accused of employing exactly those bullying tactics which he had suffered from Chase. Cooper, however, was removed from the bench as a result.

Even more notorious than Cooper's trial was that of James Thompson Callender in Richmond. Here Judge Chase sat again. No sympathy need be wasted on Callender. He was perhaps the worst party hack and mercenary in an age not noted for a scarcity of them. Like most of his fellow scribblers and character assassinators, he was an alien—this time a Scot who had been expelled from England. His poisoned pen was at the service of anyone who paid him—at the moment it was the Republicans. Even Jefferson steadily supported him with funds and the cloak of his own respectability until Callender, failing in an attempt at blackmail on his former protector, turned on Jefferson and subjected him during his presidency to innuendoes as libelous and as vicious as any with which he had formerly abused the Federalists.

The particular libel on Adams for which Callender was indicted appeared in a long pamphlet entitled "The Prospect Before Us," written in part with money raised by Jefferson and read by the latter in proof without a word of censure for its unmeasured diatribes and libelous statements.

Among other libels cited were the following: that Adams's "reign

. . . has been one continued tempest of malignant passions"; that Adams threatened, calumniated and destroyed all who dared differ with him; that Adams joined with Washington in making "paper jobbers into judges and ambassadors"; that Adams was seeking war with France "for the sake of yoking us into an alliance with the British tyrant"; that Adams's hands "are reeking with the blood of the poor, friendless Connecticut sailor [Jonathan Robbins]"; that "with all the cowardly insolence arising from his assurance of personal safety . . . this hoary headed incendiary . . . bawls out to arms! then to arms!"

Eminent Republican counsel appeared for Callender—George Hay, Nicholas and William Wirt. But Judge Chase converted a trial that very probably would have ended in a conviction in any event into a Donnybrook Fair in which he alone wielded flail and cudgel. He interfered with the attempts of counsel to examine prospective jurors; he demanded that questions to be put to witnesses be first presented to him in writing, and when counsel obeyed after protesting the procedure, ruled that most of them were inadmissible on the ground that they did not cover *all* points of the indictment. When Nicholas declared he would prove truth by several witnesses, Chase exclaimed in bullying tones that this was "irregular, and subversive of every principle of law; that it had no relation to the issue; that it was a popular argument, calculated to deceive the people, but very incorrect."

Wirt had entered the case late and asked for an adjournment so that he could prepare himself; Chase refused and compelled him to trial. In his address to the jury, Wirt told them that they had the right to decide both the law and the fact; and that included in the matters of law was the question of the constitutionality of the Sedition Act.

In a passion Chase ordered the lawyer to sit down. You have no right to inform the jury on the law, he thundered. That is my province. Whereupon he read to the jury an extended opinion in which he declared the Act to be constitutional. He did, however, express a willingness to listen to argument from counsel on the point. But when the lawyers began argument, he interrupted so much that Hay in anger refused to proceed. For once, Chase had the grace to apologize and promise not to interrupt again. But Hay, with the idea that he found a reversible error, persisted in his refusal. Thereupon Chase charged the jury that the law was constitutional and that the statements mentioned in the indictment were libelous in law. The jury brought in a verdict of guilty; and Chase sentenced Callender to nine months in jail and a fine of $200.[38]

Callender's conviction became a *cause célèbre,* cried up by the Republicans and agitated for years to come. What added to the flames was the boast attributed to Chase prior to the trial that "he would teach the lawyers in Virginia the difference between the liberty and the licentiousness of the press," and his instruction to the United States marshal in charge of the jury panel "not to put any of those creatures called democrats on the jury." [39]

There is no question that Chase's conduct in the trial was reprehensible and constituted reversible error. Yet it must be said in his defense that he was correct and Hay wrong when he asserted that only the court could rule on the constitutionality of a statute. Furthermore, Hay was seeking an unwarranted advantage in refusing to proceed *after* Chase had apologized for his actions. Also, Wirt's complaint that Chase did not permit an adjournment from May until November, in order that the defense might summon practically every congressman and every member of the Cabinet as witnesses to testify that Adams was indeed "a hoary incendiary," etc., etc., must similarly fall to the ground.

Most of the other cases involved, not published writings, but individual utterances and acts. Such was the farcical incident of Luther Baldwin, town drunkard and tavern lounger in a New Jersey village. It seemed that Adams had driven through the community, and the cannon on the green had been discharged in his honor. Baldwin and several boon companions were in the tavern, imbibing deeply. One of them exclaimed on hearing the report of the gun: "There goes the President, and they are firing at his arse." To which Baldwin, equally drunk, retorted: "I do not care if they fired *through* his arse." Whereupon the tavern keeper cried out in horror: "That is sedition!" and reported him to the authorities.[40]

For this alleged "sedition" Baldwin was indicted, not under the Sedition Act, but at common law by the state of New Jersey; and was fined $100.

In Dedham, Massachusetts, one David Brown had erected a liberty pole bearing the slogan: "No stamp act, no sedition and no alien acts, no land tax. Downfall to the tyrants of America: peace and retirement to the President: long live the Vice President [Jefferson] and the minority."

It would have been difficult to spell out sedition from this; but a riot followed as indignant Federalists sought to cut down the pole and Republicans battled to prevent them. Brown was arrested and pleaded guilty in the belief that he would be let off easy; but Chase—once more presiding—sentenced him to eighteen months and fined him $450. This was the heaviest sentence meted out in any case; and Brown, for lack of money to pay the fine, languished in jail for two years until Jefferson pardoned him.

The final prosecution—that of the so-called Fries' Rebellion—does not properly come within the category of these other indictments. It is related in kind rather to the prosecutions of the Whiskey Rebellion, and will be considered later.

In summation of these indictments, prosecutions and trials which are usually claimed to have been held under the Sedition Act, it must first be noted that a good number of them were not so held at all, but were common-law prosecutions for libel, disorderly conduct and breaches of the peace in the state courts. Others, like the Callender trial, could have been brought to a conviction in the state courts without the Sedition Act; provided, of course, that political and partisan emotions did not becloud the issues involved. In most of the cases where the indictments were based on newspaper squibs and printed pamphlets, the matter was libelous under common law and would normally be held libelous even today, when the law of libel has been much liberalized. Whether prosecution in such instances is politically or personally wise, is another matter. Today, utterances of a similar nature, though perhaps not as gross, are usually ignored by political figures.

Nevertheless, when all is said and done, the Sedition Act constituted a dangerous precedent. Its terms were too broad and vague, and therefore it was subject to abuse; it unjustifiably chose specific public officers for its protection and not others; it furnished a handle for political rather than legal prosecutions. Nor can libel, per se, by any stretch of the term, be converted into a sedition against the United States.

Thomas Jefferson, Vice-President of the United States, was attacked as viciously by the Federalist press as Adams by the Republican; yet he had no recourse under the Sedition Act. Nor was it invoked as a mantle to cover the *Republican* members of Congress. When Fenno's *Gazette of the United States* spoke of "the hordes of ruffians yearly disgorging on us" to convert America "into one vast store house of assassins" and pretended that, if the Republicans had their way, revolutionary tribunals would be set up and "the heads of rich men would roll down the kennels, while scoundrel convicts would be revelling in their chariots, or rioting in their palaces," this might be dismissed as sheer rodomontade. But when Fenno linked with these gory proceedings those whom he called "Jeffersons in cowardice," he was guilty of libel.[41]

Yet neither John Adams nor Timothy Pickering ordered Fenno's arrest and prosecution. Nor was Cobbett touched, except on a personal and civil suit by Dr. Rush for a nonpolitical libel; though, from a medical viewpoint, his charge that Rush had been the cause of his patients' deaths with his bleedings and violent purgings had the merit of truth.

In the midst of this political turmoil the yellow fever returned to the seaports with a virulence equal to the great epidemic of 1793; and was the inciting cause of Cobbett's animadversions. There had been other outbreaks of the dread disease during the years between, but this one outdid all the others.

New York and Philadelphia were the hardest hit. The first cases were reported in August 1798; by October, fourteen hundred persons had died in New York, and seventy were daily carted away in Philadelphia. It cut down the newspaper editors without regard to politics. Bache and Fenno succumbed in Philadelphia; Greenleaf and McLean in New York. The inhabitants fled the stricken cities, business ceased, and the bottom dropped out of real estate values. The gloomy prediction was made that unless some means could be found to prevent these recurring epidemics, all the seaboard towns would become depopulated.[42]

The physicians disputed and quarreled even more vigorously than before—and their patients continued to die. It was evident that not enough of them thought to prescribe the "Poudre Unique" which was advertised in the newspapers as a "certain" and "infallible" cure for "yellow fever, putrid fever, pleurisy, bloody flux, inveterate rheumatisms, sciatica, apoplexy, ringworm, worms in children and in grown persons, whites, chronical head and stomach aches, hepatick and nephretical or stone colic, the king's evil, scurvy and the most inveterate and complicated venereal disease." And, for good measure, the "Poudre" also cured measles and smallpox, and was "of the greatest utility for young as well as for elder ladies at the critical epoch of their life."[43]

CHAPTER 27

Kentucky and Virginia Resolutions

At the end of June 1798, Thomas Jefferson, Vice-President of the United States, yielded his gavel in the Senate chamber and departed for Monticello. His defection was all the more surprising because the Senate was then engaged in the debate over the Alien and Sedition Acts: bills which Jefferson was convinced were calculated to destroy the liberty of the country, institute a reign of terror and bring on a shooting war with France. Nevertheless he went home.

Since he knew that he could do nothing to stem the tide in Philadelphia, a bold plan was maturing in his mind to bring the country back to first principles and a clear-cut definition of the limited powers of the general government. But this required the intervention of the states.

Ensconced in the utmost secrecy on the mountaintop of Monticello, the draftsman of the Declaration of Independence wrote a series of resolutions which he intended as another declaration, of equal importance with the first, and designed to arouse the American people to a second revolution against all forms of tyranny.

He hoped to clarify for all time the exact relationship between the states and the federal government; to distinguish the limits of the latter and to promulgate the thesis that the states had the power, once those limits were transcended, to declare the arrogated authority null and void.

The pending Alien and Sedition Acts provided the initial impulse, but Jefferson had in mind to utilize them as means to a more far-reaching end—to halt now and forever the encroachments of the general government on the powers of the states, to destroy the system of finance, the mercantile and banking economy which Hamilton had fastened on the country, and to restore that agricultural base which he believed essential for liberty and freedom.

Jefferson penned nine Resolves. The first was preamble, setting forth the general principles of what was to follow. It asserted that since the several states were not united "on the principle of unlimited submission to their general government," but only by virtue of a limited Constitution, it followed that "whensoever the general government assumes undelegated powers, its acts are unauthorative, void, and of no force." Nor could the general government be the sole or final judge of the extent of its powers; the states had an equal right to judge for themselves whether such powers had been exceeded.

The next five resolves examined in detail the provisions of the Alien and Sedition Acts, and declared them not within the constitutional powers of the general government to enact or enforce, and hence "altogether void, and of no force."

The seventh resolution returned from the specific to the general, and boldly asserted that the entire course of the federal government since its inception, insofar as it had enacted and enforced Hamiltonian measures, had been unconstitutional and therefore illegal. It singled out for specific attack the doctrine of the so-called "broad construction" of the Constitution which had been invoked in behalf of those measures.

The eighth resolve brought back memories of the Revolution. It called for the appointment of committees of correspondence by the respective states for mutual consultation. It openly proposed the "nullification" by a state within its borders of any federal law which that state considered unconstitutional. Congress itself, declared Jefferson, was "subject as to its assumptions of power to the final judgment of those by whom, and for whose use itself and its powers were all created and modified."

This was extreme doctrine. If put into effect, the federal union would have been unable to take any step or enforce any measure which a single state, in its sole judgment, decided to be unconstitutional. No union could possibly exist under such circumstances.

In fact, this key resolve went even beyond that. It declared that unless the general government stopped immediately its assumption of arrogated powers, it would "necessarily drive these States into revolution and bloodshed." And, in conclusion, it issued a call to all the states to adopt similar expressions of sentiment, and to take concurrent steps to declare the Alien and Sedition Acts null and void.

The final resolve provided for the appointment of a committee of correspondence.[1]

The next step was to ensure the enactment of these resolves by one of the states. For prudential reasons, Jefferson did not wish his name or authorship to be known. He therefore asked Wilson Cary Nicholas, a neighbor, friend and political follower, to act as the intermediary in the negotiations.

It had been Jefferson's intention to use North Carolina as the initiating and promulgating state; but Nicholas feared this might disclose Jefferson's hand in the matter, and suggested Kentucky instead. It happened that John Breckinridge, now of Kentucky and Speaker of its Assembly, was visiting Nicholas at the time. On being shown the resolves under the strictest confidence, Breckinridge readily agreed to introduce them in the Kentucky legislature.[2]

In fact, Breckinridge was the more amenable because he had already taken his own steps in the same direction. A mass meeting in Woodford County, Kentucky, which he initiated, had drafted resolutions similar in many respects to those now offered by Jefferson. They declared the Alien and Sedition Acts to be "direct violations of the Constitution, and outrages against our most valuable rights. . . . That for the servants of the people to tell those who created them, that they shall not at their peril examine into the conduct of, nor censure those servants, for the abuse of powers committed to them, is tyranny more insufferable that [the] Asiatic." [3]

Breckinridge returned to Kentucky with Jefferson's manuscript resolutions. At first he asked Caleb Wallace, a member of the legislature, to redraft them and introduce them as his own. But Wallace professed himself ill and incapable of such an important task.[4] Thereupon Breckinridge did the job himself.

As finally redrafted and introduced in the Kentucky Assembly, Breckinridge's version of the first seven resolves followed Jefferson's word for word. But he radically modified the eighth, which was the keystone of the entire structure. He realized that Jefferson had in this resolve enunciated certain revolutionary doctrines which might evoke incalculable consequences. He therefore carefully toned it down to a mere provision that copies of the Resolves be sent to the Kentucky delegation in Congress with instructions to seek a repeal of the "aforesaid unconstitutional and obnoxious acts."

Breckinridge did however transfer much of Jefferson's lengthy discussion of general principles to the ninth resolve, together with the important declaration that any acts of the general government which the Constitution did not authorize were void and of no effect. But the vital pronunciamento that a state could within its own borders *nullify* any congressional statute as unconstitutional quietly disappeared from the resolves; and so did the threat of forcible resistance and bloodshed. Thereby the teeth of Jefferson's resolutions were drawn, and they became a mere matter of eloquent protest rather than an invitation to nullification, revolution and disunion.[5]

Nevertheless, when the resolves were under debate in the legislature, Breckinridge made his position clear. He wanted first, he said, to give Congress an opportunity to reconsider its position. If, after receipt of the resolves, Congress persisted in enforcing the Acts, then it would be "the right and duty of the several States to nullify those acts, and to protect their citizens from their operation." [6]

It is evident therefore that Breckinridge was in complete agreement with the principles enunciated by Jefferson; but he was politically more cautious.

The Resolves, in Breckinridge's draft, passed both Houses of the Kentucky legislature with but a single dissenting vote; on November 16, 1798, the governor affixed his signature and ordered a thousand copies to be printed for distribution to the members of Congress and the governors of all the other states.

In the meantime Jefferson had been working actively to enlist a much more important state in the cause—his own state of Virginia. Some time in October he met with Madison, with whom he had already been in touch through Wilson Cary Nicholas. The meeting was most secret, and the two friends and political allies formulated a plan for Virginia to follow Kentucky's example and issue a set of resolves on her own.

But here the two men parted company. Madison, always the more legalistic and cautious of the pair, disapproved, just as Breckinridge had done, of the more violent sections of Jefferson's draft resolutions. When Madison came to redraft them before they were to be introduced into the Virginia Assembly, he proved even more careful in his choice of language than Breckinridge. The Resolves as they issued from his hand were more moderate and conciliatory, and less specific, than the Kentucky Resolutions.

They set forth the nature of the federal compact and asserted the right and duty of the states to maintain "within their respective limits the authorities, rights and liberties appertaining to them." They spoke of the various abuses of which the general government had been guilty, climaxed in the Alien and Sedition Acts. But when it came to taking positive measures, Madison proposed only that the states cooperate in declaring that the Acts complained of were unconstitutional, and that they take all measures necessary for "maintaining unimpaired the authorities, rights, and liberties reserved to the States respectively, or to the people." [7]

This was moderation indeed. Not a word was breathed of nullification or committees of correspondence, and certainly nothing of forcible resistance or bloody revolution. There was not even a mention of the fact that the statutes in question were void and of no effect, or that any one state, on its own initiative, could declare an act unconstitutional.

Madison was obviously doubtful of the legality of nullification of federal laws by the states; and he was certainly convinced that the *legislature* of a state did not constitute, or was invested with, the full powers of that state.

"Have you ever considered thoroughly," he asked Jefferson significantly, "the distinction between the power of the *State* and that of the *Legislature*, on questions relating to the federal pact. On the supposition that the former is clearly the ultimate Judge of infractions, it does not follow that the latter is the legitimate organ, especially as a Convention was the organ by which the compact was made." [8]

Jefferson was not at all happy over Madison's draft when it was submitted to him. He wished it at least to be strengthened by the additional declaration "that the said acts are, and were *ab initio*, null, void and of no force, or effect." [9] But Madison firmly refused to change his original text.

As Jefferson had hidden his authorship of the Kentucky Resolutions, so Madison concealed his hand in the Virginia set. John Taylor of Caroline, who had no national ambitions and did not care what people thought of him, was chosen to introduce them in the Virginia Assembly. The basic ideas had already passed through his mind. Without knowing that Jefferson had fathered the Kentucky Resolves, he had written him that it was his "project, by law to declare the unconstitutional laws of Congress void, and as that would have placed the State and general government at issue, to have submitted the point to the people in convention, as the only referee." [10]

Taylor was adopting a position midway between Jefferson and Madison. While in agreement with Madison that it was the people in convention who ultimately held the power, he had no hesitation in taking it upon himself to insert in Madison's draft the two key words of Jefferson: that the Acts were "null" and "void."

In this form he introduced the resolutions on December 13th. But strong opposition, led by the Federalists in the legislature, developed on the floor of the lower House; and the insertions were stricken out. Even in this emasculated guise they passed the House by a vote of only 100 to 63, compared to the practically unanimous vote on much stronger resolutions in Kentucky. Surprisingly, the Virginia Senate passed them by a considerably larger majority. On December 24th the governor signed them, and copies were printed and distributed.

The famous Kentucky and Virginia Resolutions had now entered history. But it took some time for the repercussions and reverberations to develop.

A strange combination of forces was working to keep the United States out of war with France. One was official, or rather semiofficial, since Gerry had been peremptorily ordered home. The other was wholly unofficial; no less than a one-man peace mission undertaken by Dr. George Logan of Pennsylvania, who held no position of any kind in government.

When Gerry finally quit France in July 1798, there was good reason to assume that the French government had changed its tune and was now decided on a policy of peace with the United States. Whether the shift was due to the firm stand of Marshall and Pinckney, or the final stubbornness of Gerry, or alarm over the efforts of England to build up a second coalition of Continental powers, or the current French commitment in the Egyptian adventure, in any event Talleyrand decided to issue new feelers to the obstinate Americans. He set to work with his accustomed subtlety and indirection.

Talleyrand had intimated to Gerry before he sailed that an arrangement could be arrived at; and Gerry reported the hint to Pickering when he set foot in the United States again late in December 1798. He himself felt certain, he added, that the Directory was "very desirous of a reconciliation between the republics." [11]

Even before Gerry quit Paris, Talleyrand had taken the trouble to inquire of Victor-Marie Du Pont, just returned from a long stay as consul in the United States, "what are the acts of the French cruisers on their coasts and in the Antilles of which they complain?"

Du Pont obliged with a lengthy report. He pointed out that the conduct of the French warships and privateers had been one of the

principal causes for the rapid deterioration of American friendship
for France, and that matters were tending toward a "long and cruel
war between the two Republics." Even though Adams had refused him
an exequatur as consul general in Philadelphia, Du Pont spoke up
strongly for the Americans. One could write volumes, he exclaimed,
on the piracies committed by the French cruisers; and he documented
his contention in great detail. Even Jefferson, he declared, had
warned him that should France continue her present course, the
United States must unite with England in the war.[12]

Impressed by the report—and by other considerations—Talleyrand
told Gerry in the presence of Richard Codman, a Boston Federalist
then in Paris on business, that he would drop his demands for money,
issue an *arrêt* withdrawing the commissions of French privateers
hitherto issued in blank, and receive a new American minister whenever he was sent. To prove his good faith, Talleyrand actually did
release the captured American seamen and lifted the embargo at
Bordeaux hitherto imposed on American ships.[13]

All this was reported by Codman to Harrison Gray Otis, who
showed the letter to Adams, who in turn showed it to Pickering. But
the Secretary of State was by now beyond all conviction when it
came to the French, and sputtered in reply that they were insincere
and he would never trust them again.

He shut his ears and his mind even to the letters from Rufus King
in London confirming Gerry's and Codman's stories and his exultant
"You will have no war! France will propose to renew the negotiation
upon the basis laid down in the President's instructions to the envoys"; a flat statement which King immediately qualified with an "at
least, so I conjecture."[14]

Pickering's smoldering rage against Gerry burst into the open on
the latter's return, in the form of public slurs on his conduct in
France. Gerry wrote an eloquent defense in his own behalf and sent
it to the President with a demand that it be published. Adams, who
had been friendly with Gerry and still retained some of his old affection, turned the defense over to Pickering for publication; but the
Secretary of State flatly refused. Adams, still not master in his own
house, returned the document to Gerry with a note advising that it
would be better to keep the controversy out of the public prints. As
for himself, he wrote, he was satisfied that Gerry's conduct had been
"upright and well intended."[15]

Talleyrand did not place all his new eggs in Gerry's basket, correctly surmising that the envoy would be *persona non grata* with the American government. His contemplative eye now turned to William Vans Murray, the American minister to The Hague. Murray was a native of Maryland, had studied law and been elected to Congress in 1791. He remained a comparatively obscure member until 1797, when Washington appointed him to the diplomatic post. Although he was a comparatively young man—he was now only thirty-seven years old —his mission abroad had modified his rather narrow federalism and opened his eyes to the nuances and subtleties of European politics.

On July 17, 1798, Murray received a visitor. This was Pichon, former secretary in America to Genêt and Fauchet, and now the French secretary of legation at The Hague. After considerable inconsequential talk—while Murray inwardly wondered at the object of the visit—Pichon finally showed his hand. He deposited a note from Talleyrand with the astonished American. The note, coupled with hints which Pichon had dropped in the course of the conversation, pointed to a desire to resume the negotiations which had been broken off in Paris.[16]

Other evidences were soon forthcoming. A month later a high Dutch official informed Murray that he would shortly receive proof "of an amicable disposition in France." Convinced that the Dutch government was being employed by the French as to act as mediator, Murray thought he might also be able to use them to get the French "to come down yet lower" and obtain a guarantee that a new American mission would be most favorably received.[17]

Two weeks after, Pichon returned; this time accompanied by La Forêt, who, it may be remembered, had acted as commissar to Fauchet when the latter first came to the United States. The two men now openly avowed themselves to Murray as Talleyrand's agents to seek "a friendly conclusion, if we will but enter upon negotiation." [18]

Matters were definitely in a train; and Adams, receiving Murray's report, began to see a strong gleam of light ahead.[19]

But now a new figure injected himself into the delicate situation. This was Dr. George Logan, private citizen. Logan was another of the unique characters who seem to have crowded the American scene at the time. Born in Pennsylvania, he studied medicine in the British Isles while the Revolution ran its course in his native land. Then he returned home and practiced his profession, though scattering his numerous enthusiasms over many other fields. He experimented with

new agricultural methods and organized the first Agricultural Society
in Pennsylvania. He dabbled in politics and entered the state legislature. He made friends with Jefferson and the intellectual elite generally. His political views were radically republican, his instincts
humanitarian and vaguely enthusiastic. The French Revolution be-
spoke his complete allegiance, and his house became a place of resort
for Genêt, the French *émigrés* and the local and national leaders of
the Republican party.

The rapidly worsening relations with France disturbed him, and
the XYZ Affair shook him to the depths. To him war with France
was inconceivable, and must be stopped at all costs. In this dejected
and brooding frame of mind, an idea burst on him. The diplomats
had failed. Why could not he, a private individual, imbued with a
love for both contending nations, succeed where they had failed with
their formalistic and suspicious approach? He took his idea to Jefferson and to Thomas McKean, chief justice of Pennsylvania. Doubtless they approved of the quixotic plan, for both men gave him
certificates attesting to his American citizenship, and Jefferson added
a private note of commendation. Le Tombe, the French consul general in Philadelphia, furnished him with a letter of introduction to
Talleyrand.

Thus armed and equipped, Dr. Logan sailed secretly for France
on June 12, 1798. The secret was ill kept; for the Federalists got
wind of the one-man peace mission and raised a furious outcry. They
accused Logan, not of seeking peace, but of acting as a spy to disclose
American secrets to the French and carrying with him the assurances
of American Jacobins that they would support France in case of war.
"Can any sensible man," cried Brown's *Philadelphia Gazette,* "hesitate to suspect that his infernal design can be anything less, than the
introduction of a French army to *teach us the genuine value of true
and essential liberty* by re-organizing our government, through the
brutal operation of the bayonet and guillotine. Let every American
now gird on his sword. The times are not only critical, but the secret
of the Junto *is out. Their* demagogue is gone to the directory, for purposes *destructive of your lives, property, liberty and holy religion."* [20]

In happy ignorance of the storm he left behind him, the bearer of
the dove of peace landed in Hamburg. There difficulties awaited him.
It was not easy to pierce the iron curtain of France. He sought
Lafayette's influence to gain him entry, and journeyed to Rotterdam
to await the result.

There another unforeseen obstacle loomed in his self-appointed path. Vans Murray heard of his mission, and furious at "this propagandist of sedition and philosophy [sic]," whom he was convinced was up to no good, hastened to his friends in the Dutch government to demand that the apostle of peace be arrested and detained. Even if the charges he laid could not be made to stick, so thought Vans Murray, he would at least have an opportunity, with Dutch connivance, to examine Logan's papers and find out "what he is after." [21]

Vans Murray never did find out, except by report. Though the order for Logan's arrest was actually issued, the bird had already flown. In receipt finally of the coveted French passport, the missionary was on his way to Paris, arriving on August 7th to find Gerry gone. A sizable colony of American semiexpatriates, however, headed by Joel Barlow, welcomed him with open arms.

Barlow was surprisingly pessimistic; but Logan refused to become discouraged. With his letters of introduction and the good offices of the Batavian minister, he managed to reach important personages in the French government—including Talleyrand himself; Merlin, chief of the Directory, as well as his associates; and Adet, the former minister to the United States.

Everyone proved most friendly and cordial. Though they had already tendered the olive branch to Gerry and Vans Murray, they were not averse to placing another one in the hands of the Republicans of America. In the belief that Logan was their authorized representative, they actually gave him a copy of an *arrêt* which liberated all captured American seamen and lifted the embargo on American ships.

The elated doctor, with this documentary proof in his baggage, hastened to Bordeaux to sail for home. He had received, he exulted, "the most positive assurances . . . that France is ready to enter on a treaty for the amicable accommodation of all matters in dispute." [22]

On his arrival in Philadelphia Logan went immediately to see President Adams, certain that he would be received as became the messenger of glad tidings. To his astonishment his reception was decidedly chilly. Adams was polite enough and heard him through. But when he excitedly declared that France was ready to accept a minister, Adams rose with the remark: "Yes, I suppose if I were to send Mr. Madison or Mr. Giles or Dr. Logan they would receive either of *them*. But I'll do no such thing; I'll send whom I please."

Pickering was not even polite. He cut Logan short in midspeech, railed at France and, as he showed the stunned doctor the door, stammered in his wrath: "Sir, it is my duty to inform you that the government does not thank you for what you have done." [23]

Pickering had his own reasons for his outburst. The cumulative evidence from Gerry, Codman, Murray and Logan indicated that a *modus vivendi* might at least temporarily be reached with France. But this did not fit in with Federalist plans. They sincerely suspected French motives, and just as sincerely believed that neither the United States nor the world would be safe until France was crushed.

French aggressions and the XYZ disclosures had brought the great mass of the American people to a unity never before achieved. They were largely united in favor of Federalist measures for an increased Army, Navy and taxes; and they even backed, though to a considerably less extent, the Alien and Sedition Acts.

From a more personal and selfish point of view, the Federalists expected the current wave of enthusiasm to last to the next presidential campaign. If the country was then at war with France, the result of the election was a foregone conclusion, and the Republican party would disintegrate. If, however, the United States came to terms with France, the future for the Federalists might well prove dark; for the Republicans would be quick to claim the *rapprochement* and the lifting of the war clouds as the result of the efforts of Gerry and Logan.

Robert Liston, the British minister, whose sentiments coincided with those of the Federalists, now shared their gloom. "There is no meanness," he wrote indignantly, "to which the Directory will not stoop, when an important object is in contemplation." Gerry and Logan, he exclaimed, had served to confuse not only the "ignorant and the profligate," but even some men of character and education "who, from timidity, or indolence, or avarice, are anxious to avert the immediate approach of war." [24]

With the impending collapse of all their issues, the Federalists concentrated their wrath on the unfortunate doctor. On December 24, 1798, Griswold of Connecticut moved in the House to extend the penalties of the Act covering crimes against the United States to "all persons, citizens of the United States, who shall usurp the Executive authority of this Government, by commencing or carrying on any correspondence with the Governments of any foreign Prince or State, relating to controversies or disputes which do or shall exist between such Prince or State and the United States."

Nicholas of Virginia wondered audibly if by any chance the motion related to Dr. Logan. "Oh, no," disclaimed Griswold, "it was general." But of course the entire debate ranged around the Logan mission. Gallatin vigorously defended the doctor's purity of motive and asserted that he deserved the country's admiration instead of punitive measures. Nevertheless the Federalists pushed the bill through, with minor amendments, by a vote of 58 to 36; while only two negative votes were cast against it in the Senate. Adams signed the bill, and the so-called "Logan Act" still stands unrepealed on the statute books of the United States.[25]

Since the law could not be made retroactive, no proceedings were taken against Logan. The Republicans acclaimed him as a hero. They put him up for a seat in the Pennsylvania legislature as the man "who risqued his all for his country" and singlehandedly averted "misery and blood." A vote for him, screamed the press, is a vote for "Peace! Peace! Peace!" [26]

Meanwhile Adams was groping his way for a solution of the impasse. With the various French feelers before him and Congress shortly to convene, Adams queried his Cabinet on October 20th as to possible courses of action for recommendation to the legislative branch of the government. He offered two alternatives for consideration—a declaration of war, or a notice of his intention to nominate a minister to France who would sail as soon as satisfactory assurances were received that he would be fully and properly accepted. In the latter case, whom should he nominate—someone who had hitherto shown public enmity toward France or one who had not? [27]

The Cabinet in the main followed Hamilton's advice of a middle course—no immediate war, but no further negotiations; and continuing preparations for war.

Adams adopted some of the propositions, but made significant additions when he addressed Congress on December 8, 1798.

He reported the failure of previous negotiations with France and asserted the necessity of proceeding at full speed with defense measures on the assumption that war was impending. However, he said, there had been recent overtures which indicated that France would receive a minister, *provided* his qualifications suited her. (This was not so.) He would neither submit to any such proviso, Adams declared strongly, nor would he send a minister "without more determinate assurances that he would be received." The next step, he concluded, must come from France.[28]

Congress was only too willing to increase the tempo of defense measures. The Federalists sought Hamilton's advice assiduously and followed it with zeal. Harrison Gray Otis, the chairman of the House Committee on Military Affairs, wrote to the distant leader that his suggestions would be treated with the utmost respect and their source disclosed to no one.[29]

For one thing, Hamilton opposed any move to decrease the size of the provisional army; war or no war. He was exceedingly anxious to have a full-scale army under his control; not only, as he frankly avowed, because its reduction might encourage the enemy, but because "with a view to the possibility of internal disorders alone, the force authorized is not too considerable. The efficacy of militia for suppressing such disorders is not too much to be relied upon." [30] This indeed was what the Republicans were forever saying—that Hamilton wished his army not for foreign war but to impose his system, by force if necessary, on a discontented America.

Recruiting, however, proceeded at a snail's pace. The Republicans openly boasted that Hamilton would be able to get none but officers in his army,[31] and the boast was not altogether untrue. Washington, the titular commander, complained that there had been too much delay in getting under way. Had recruiting started immediately while the XYZ Affair was at its peak, he told Hamilton, we might have had an army equal to any in the world. "*Now,* the measure is not only viewed with indifference, but deemed unnecessary by that class of people, whose attentions being turned to other matters, the officers who in August and September could with ease have enlisted whole companies of them, will find it difficult to recruit any; and if this idle and dissipated season is spent in inactivity, none but the riff-raff of the country, and the scape gallowses of the large cities will be to be had." [32]

Hardly had Congress opened its doors when the Federalists, alarmed over the Kentucky and Virginia Resolutions and a flood of petitions demanding the repeal of the Alien and Sedition Acts, rather naïvely proposed that 20,000 copies of the Acts be printed and disseminated to counteract the "misinformation" concerning their contents.

Gallatin retorted that even lawyers could not determine their true meaning; and Dawson of Virginia sarcastically suggested that the sections of the Constitution pertaining to free speech be also included. The motion was eventually defeated.[33]

The new Secretary of the Navy, Benjamin Stoddert, urged Congress to authorize the construction of twelve ships of the line carrying seventy-four guns each; twelve frigates, and twenty to thirty smaller vessels.[34] Such a formidable addition of heavily armed ships of the line—a class of warship not yet built in the United States—would have placed this country at one bound in the first rank of naval powers, ready to cope on equal terms with either France or England.

There had been a recent flurry with the British. One of their ships of the line had stopped an American sloop of war, the *Baltimore*, on the high seas and taken off a number of alleged British subjects. The news caused immense excitement; an order was issued to all commanders of American warships to resist by force any future stoppage and search; and the unfortunate captain of the *Baltimore*, which the British battlewagon could have blown out of the water with one broadside, was summarily dismissed from the service for his failure so to resist.[35]

The Republicans centered their attack on Stoddert's proposals on the cost involved. The Federalists argued that there had been a saving in insurance premiums of $8,500,000 as a result of the activities of the small navy then in existence. Certainly, with a larger and more effective force, the additional cost would be more than counterbalanced by the savings in premiums, ships and cargoes. After considerable debate a more modest bill became law, authorizing the construction of six ships of the line and six sloops of war.[36] Actually, not a single ship of the line was ever built.

In vain did the Republicans again and again gather their forces to seek the repeal of the controversial Alien and Sedition Acts; in vain did Gallatin unlimber his most powerful constitutional arguments against them. The Federalists merely sat tight, allowing the Republicans to talk and thunder as much as they wished, without offering a single reply. Then, when all oratory and the orators were exhausted, they called for a vote and defeated the repealer.[37] As one Republican member bitterly commented, the Federalists controlled the House because of the "criminal absence" of Republicans from the floor, while the former attended sessions to a man.[38]

With their silent, solid ranks the Federalists pushed through the remainder of their program—the renewal of the nonintercourse act with France; a measure authorizing retaliation on French prisoners in our hands if the French put into effect their threat to hang any Americans found on British ships; and an increase in the Army establishment in case of war or "imminent danger."

They were also able to stave off the assaults on the Alien and Sedition Acts as a result of the reaction of the other states to the Kentucky and Virginia Resolves. That reaction dashed all Republican hopes of frightening the general government into yielding.

John Marshall, immensely popular since the XYZ Affair, had courageously announced his opposition to the Acts; but no other Federalist had followed his example. Instead, he lost much of his original standing with them; Ames going so far as to lump him with "false federalists" and "moderates" as the "meanest of cowards, the falsest of hypocrites" and lamenting that "federalists are forever hazarding the cause by needless and rash concessions." [39]

The inestimable weight of Washington was on the Federalist side. Still smarting from the wounds suffered from the Republican press, Washington gave his entire approval to the laws, called the opposition to them partisan and intended "to torture and disturb the public mind," and berated Virginia's "mad" and "extravagant" folly in issuing her resolutions. [40]

Jefferson had hoped to get at least the influential Middle States of New York, Pennsylvania and New Jersey to endorse the resolutions; particularly if the general government should attempt, as had been threatened, to punish Virginia for her boldness. [41] But his hopes were doomed to speedy disappointment.

The first state to reply to the Kentucky and Virginia Resolutions was Delaware. Her legislature denounced them as "a very unjustifiable interference with the general government and constituted authorities of the United States, and of dangerous tendencies, and therefore not a fit subject for the further consideration of the General Assembly."

Delaware's reaction might have been expected from such a strongly Federalist state; and the same held good for similar responses from Rhode Island and Massachusetts. But when New York, on whom such hopes had been built, followed suit, with Connecticut, New Hampshire and Vermont trailing; when Maryland, New Jersey and Pennsylvania placed themselves on record as opposed to the principles embodied in the Resolutions, then the Republicans knew that they were completely routed. Even the Southern states kept a discreet silence. The backfire which Jefferson had intended to start and then fan into a furious flame fizzled and died for want of nourishment. It was not until the year was on the wane that he plucked up sufficient heart to attempt a regrouping of his shattered forces.

But even as the other states were denouncing Kentucky and Virginia, and Congress was enacting further war measures, Adams suddenly made up his mind. Long-delayed dispatches had been received from Vans Murray, for the first time giving him the proof he demanded that the French were in earnest.

Vans Murray reported that Pichon had showed him a note from Talleyrand expressing satisfaction over Pichon's conversations with Murray. "You were right," wrote Talleyrand, "to assert that, whatever plenipotentiary the Government of the United States might send to France, to put an end to the existing differences between the two nations, would be undoubtedly received with the respect due to the representative of a free, independent, and powerful nation." [42]

By repeating verbatim the language which Adams had used in his address to Congress as the *sine qua non* for a resumption of discussions, Talleyrand removed the last obstacle in the President's path.

Adams had never wished for war. He had never run with the hounds of Federalism or sought to gain a meretricious popularity by rattling the sword. He knew by this time that his Cabinet was not his own, that its members looked for direction to an outsider who held no present government office and of whose policies and ambitions he did not approve. Always solitary in his cross-grained but stubbornly honest thinking, Adams felt now more alone than ever, personally as well as politically. His beloved Abigail lay dangerously ill at their quiet home in Quincy, and he spent more time at her bedside than in Philadelphia.

He now took an unprecedented step. On February 18, 1799, he sent to the Senate the name of William Vans Murray as envoy extraordinary to France. He consulted neither his Cabinet nor any political figure; only his wife, recuperating slowly, knew of his move. He chose Vans Murray because he was on the spot, had already participated in the delicate preliminaries, and was experienced in the French and general European political climate.

The nomination, with all that it implied, burst on the country like a thunderbolt. Not a hint of the intended action had been permitted to seep out. The Federalists were filled with consternation and dismay. The Republicans, after a period of hesitation and suspicion over this strange gift horse, hastily revised their public estimates of the President.

Congress was thrown into complete confusion. There were scurryings and conferences. Jefferson noted with complacency the "graveled and divided" ranks of the Federalists. The Senate passed the day without action, while the party leaders sought desperately to make up their minds.[43]

With one bold stroke Adams had cut the Gordian knot; but he had also spiked the guns of triumphant Federalism. Their chief rallying cry to the country had vanished. The President's action gave seeming approval to the thesis of Republicans Gerry and Logan that France had never wanted war, had always been prepared to negotiate. That meant—at least so the Republicans promptly claimed—that the XYZ business had been a canard, a fabrication or at the best a misapprehension on the part of the Federalist envoys.

Under these circumstances, what would happen to the huge provisional army, the increased navy, the additional taxes? What, above all, would happen at the next presidential election?

The Federalists made up their minds. Adams had let them down; and he had done so without consulting a single one of them. The members of the Cabinet were furious; and not without reason. Supposedly the President's confidential advisers, they had neither been consulted nor been given the slightest inkling of a move which changed the entire complexion of foreign and domestic affairs. Only a few weeks earlier, Pickering had written sharply to Vans Murray to decline at once any offer by the Dutch government to mediate between the United States and France. He termed the offer farcical if not insulting; for in fact the Dutch were the creatures of France.[44]

Now Pickering had to eat his words. His humiliation and rage knew no bounds. His least opprobrious comment was that "we have all been shocked and grieved." [45] McHenry and Wolcott stood with him. Stoddert, still strange in his office, did not make any open comment. Only Charles Lee approved of the President's course. On the outside, John Marshall, already under attack, believed that Adams had done the proper thing; while Henry Knox, disgusted with the shabby treatment meted out to him by the Hamiltonians on the Army appointment, sent a message of support.[46]

But they were almost solitary among the mass of angered Federalists. Theodore Sedgwick, risen to leadership in the party and in the Senate, denounced the nomination as mischievous and "the result of

Presidential wisdom, without the knowledge of, or any intimation to any one of the administration. Had the foulest heart and the ablest head in the world," he wrote to Hamilton, "have been permitted to select the most embarrassing and ruinous measure, perhaps it would have been precisely the one which has been adopted." [47]

Two days later, Sedgwick's anger had become almost apoplectic. "It is one of the misfortunes," he asserted, "to which we are subjected by the wild and irregular starts of a vain, jealous and half frantic mind that we are obliged to practice an infraction of correct principles—a direct communication between the President and Senate. I am this morning to wait on him and solicit an interview between him and the committee upon his nomination." [48]

What had happened was that the Federalists had determined on a plan of action. Since constitutionally the President had the right to appoint envoys without consulting the Senate or anyone else—subject only to an inquiry into the personal fitness of the particular envoy—it had been decided to hamstring the mission by adding two envoys to Vans Murray. These, it was proposed, should be safe and sound Federalists who would either ensure the mission's failure; or, if that was not feasible, act as watchdogs for the Federalist interest in the negotiations. Vans Murray, they felt—and Hamilton agreed—was not "strong enough for so immensely important a mission." [49]

As a result of the meeting between the Senate committee and the President, in the course of which the covert threat was made that Vans Murray's nomination would not be confirmed if it stood alone, Adams was compelled to yield. He sent in the additional names of Oliver Ellsworth, Chief Justice of the United States, and Patrick Henry, *ci-devant* antifederalist and now equally vehement Federalist. At the same time Adams openly announced that he was appointing them as a concession to "public opinion"; with the proviso, however, that the mission would not sail until formal assurances had been received that they would be accepted fully and fairly by the French government. [50]

Even this yielding to their wishes did not appease the implacable Federalists. Ames asserted that it still "disgusts most men here. Peace with France they think an evil, and holding out the hope of it another, as it tends to chill the public fervor." [51] Frankness could go no further.

But the Republican press rushed to their erstwhile enemy's defense. "Whatever sentiments," they declared, "men may entertain of the President's attachments to English modes of government or to English connexions, every one must applaud his appointment of Mr. Murray to go to Paris." The line was now adopted that Adams, like Washington, had been "deluded and deceived, by men whose intrigues are too deeply laid to be easily exposed to view." As usual, Hamilton was considered to be the chief intriguer.[52]

Adams was well aware of the scurryings, the intrigues and the machinations behind his back. He attributed them to the fact that he had been elected President only by a slim margin and was therefore helplessly dependent on his own party for support. But, he cried out, the leaders were greatly mistaken if they thought they had him in their power. "If combinations of senators, generals and heads of departments [Sedgwick, Hamilton and Pickering]," he exclaimed, "shall be formed, such as I cannot resist, and measures are demanded of me that I cannot adopt, my remedy is plain and certain. I will try my own strength at resistance first, however." [53]

The clear implication was that as a last resort he would cut loose from the party and appeal to the country.

CHAPTER 28

The Second Mission to France

NEWS NOW CAME out of the Caribbean which, while it aroused the exultation of the Federalists, convinced them all the more that Adams had made an irretrievable blunder in reopening negotiations with France.

After the inglorious cruises of the previous year, Stoddert had worked hard to redeploy our pitifully small Navy. Practically the entire fleet was sent in four squadrons to the West Indies, to blockade the French privateers in their harbors. One squadron consisted of the frigates *United States* and *Constitution*, accompanied by four lighter vessels and four revenue cutters, under the command of John Barry, now raised to the rank of commodore. A second squadron was composed of the frigate *Constellation* and four light ships, under Thomas Truxtun, also promoted to commodore. The other two groups were miscellanies of the rest of the Navy, all light in character.

The squadrons did an effective job. They convoyed American merchantmen at sea, sometimes a hundred sail strong; they cruised the waters of the Caribbean, forcing the piratical craft to remain in port or capturing them if they ventured out. The American coasts were swept clear, captures of American ships fell to a new low, and the insurance rates (a most practical indication) dropped to one half of their former levels.[1]

On February 9, 1799, the *Constellation*, Commodore Truxtun's flagship, was cruising off the island of Nevis when it sighted the French frigate *L'Insurgente*. The *Constellation* carried 38 guns and a crew of 309; the Frenchman was armed with 40 guns and a complement of 409 men. Truxtun promptly gave battle. After a short but heavy action the *Insurgente* struck its flag and surrendered.

The news of the action gladdened most Americans as evidence of the seaworthiness of their ships and the gallantry of their men. Pickering boasted that "the only negotiation compatible with our honor or safety is that begun by Truxton in the capture of L'Insurgente." [2]

The extreme French partisans, who had always insisted on the vast superiority of the French, sought vain excuses. The defeat was due, they said somewhat cryptically, to the "effect of British intrigue." [3]

Just what constituted "intrigue" in a naval engagement they failed to make clear. But they soon discovered other evidences closer to home on which they raised a furious clamor.

One Jonathan Robbins had been taken by a British press gang and shipped on the British frigate *Hermione*. There, in company with other impressed sailors, some of them unmistakably American, Robbins mutinied, murdered the ship's officers, and sold the ship in a Spanish port. This was in 1797. Now, in 1799, he was discovered by the British consul on an American vessel in Charleston harbor. The consul demanded his arrest under the terms of the Jay Treaty, and transference to British hands to stand trial for piracy and murder.

Robbins swore he was an American citizen, born in Danbury, Connecticut. The British insisted he was a British subject whose real name was Thomas Nash. But aside from his own word, Robbins could offer no proof of his birth or dwelling in Danbury. On the contrary, affidavits were produced from the records and residents of that town that they knew of no such man. On this basis, Adams directed the judge of the United States District Court of South Carolina to hand Robbins (or Nash) over to the British. This was done, and the man was tried, convicted and executed.

Other members of the mutinous crew had also been arrested in the United States on the demand of the British consuls. One of them, William Brigstock, conclusively proved his American citizenship, and Pickering refused to deliver him, informing Liston that he would be tried for the alleged crime under the laws of the United States. Still others, against whom the evidence produced was insufficient, were set free. [4]

The Republicans, ignoring the cases of Brigstock and the others, fastened on Jonathan Robbins as an American martyr supinely yielded up to British vengeance and British barbarity. The case became a *cause célèbre* which was agitated in Congress and in the public prints. It was insisted in Congress that Robbins should have been tried by a jury in the American court and that the interference of the Executive in directing his delivery to the British was a dangerous meddling with the judiciary. The debate and the wrangling continued for months, developing into a full-scale personal and political attack on the President. It was only in March 1800 that the House finally defeated a resolution of censure by a vote of 61 to 35.[5]

But the press refused to let the agitation die. Philip Freneau concocted a satirical epitaph on Robbins:

TO THE MEMORY of a Citizen of the United States
JONATHAN ROBBINS, *Mariner;*
A native of Danbury, in the pious and industrious state
of Connecticut;
who,
Under the PRESIDENCY of JOHN ADAMS,
And by his advice,
Timothy Pickering being Secretary of State,
Was delivered up to the British government,
By whom he was ignominiously put to death . . .
Alas poor Robbins!
Alas poor Liberty!
Alas my country! [6]

Even more violent was the reaction to the so-called Fries' Rebellion in that mother of rebellions, Pennsylvania. This time, however, it was the eastern sections that were harassed by riot and insurrection.

Just as the Whiskey Rebellion had been touched off by the tax levied by the general government on the distillation of whiskey, so this one flared up as a result of the tax placed on lands and houses under the Act of July 9, 1798. A provision of the Act called for the inspection and registration of the number and dimensions of the windows in every house.

The appearance of the federal inspectors was the signal for riots and rough handling. When one of the obstructionists was arrested for resisting an inspection, John Fries, an obscure individual of Pennsylvania Dutch descent, organized and led an armed band to rescue him. The President issued a proclamation on March 12, 1799, terming the riots a levying of war on the United States and calling on them to cease. But the riots, resistance and gathering of armed bands continued, with Fries actively in the lead. The militia were called out and prepared to march; whereupon the insurrection ended. Fries and some of his associates were arrested and charged with treason.

Fries came up for trial in April 1799 before Judge James Iredell of the Supreme Court. In his charge to the jury, Iredell launched into an irrelevant harangue on the constitutionality of the Alien and Sedition Acts. Both the administration and the federal judiciary were exceedingly touchy and sensitive at this time; and it was firmly believed that the rioters were not merely protesting the particular tax but were motivated by general political reasons.

The jury brought in a verdict of guilty; but on appeal a new trial was ordered on the ground that one of the jurors, after being summoned for duty, had been heard to express a decided prejudice against the defendant.

The second trial opened on April 29, 1800. This time the redoubtable Chase presided. In his accustomed fashion he rode roughshod over counsel for the defense, minced no words in his remarks from the bench or in his legal opinions delivered before the jury. Again an eminent group of Republican lawyers had come to Fries' defense, including William Lewis and Alexander J. Dallas. They withdrew almost immediately from the case, charging prejudicial remarks to Chase, undue limitations on themselves in the citation of authorities and statutes, and a refusal to permit them to address the jury on the laws governing treason. Chase proceeded without them; the jury returned a verdict of guilty; and Chase promptly sentenced Fries to be hanged.[7]

Fries and his fellow conspirators, similarly tried, appealed to the President for mercy. From the beginning, however, both Pickering and Wolcott had urged that an example be made of the rebels and that Fries in particular should suffer the extreme penalty of the law.[8] Adams wavered, torn between his natural moderation and his rising anger at the incessant and to him traitorous resistance which was manifested to every administration act. In the end he pardoned all but Fries; but when that luckless individual sent a personal petition directly to him, humbly confessing his fault, the President weakened and issued a pardon to him also, much to the disgust of Pickering and likeminded Federalists.

In every way possible John Adams was losing the support, always reluctant, of the extreme Federalists. Even when he had consented to send three envoys to France instead of Vans Murray alone, they were not satisfied. George Cabot declared that the whole business of seeking another accommodation with France had occasioned Federalist "surprise, indignation, grief and disgust"; and that the origin of the move must be sought in "egotism, vanity, wounded pride and Gerryism," as well as in Adams's implacable hatred for certain "true men." By the latter, Cabot meant Hamilton, Pickering and their fellows.[9]

"Gerryism" now became a catchword and term of reproach to take its place with "Jacobin," "democrat" and "monster faction" in the lexicon of Federalist epithets. Laments were raised that Congress had been singularly remiss in not having declared war against France the previous summer, when the revelations of the XYZ Affair would have carried the country along. It was even asserted that Adams did not intend to enforce the Alien and Sedition Acts—though the Republicans would have been astonished at such a claim—or to raise the army which Hamilton was valiantly trying to organize and equip.[10] The only explanation the extremists could give was the charitable one that Adams had gone into his dotage. Liston, the British minister, declared however that he could see no evidences of this.[11]

Liston was certainly in a position to test the quality of the presidential intellect. For all his preoccupation with France, Adams had not overlooked American grievances against Great Britain. He continued vehemently to oppose the British claim to search and impress from American ships, even when the men taken were known British subjects or deserters. He complained incessantly of British depredations, abuses and the cruelty of their officers, until the embarrassed Liston did not know which way to turn.[12] He instructed Rufus King to press all complaints in London, and to give the British ministry no rest. King did so with dutiful diligence; but was compelled to report that there seemed "no prospect of a favorable change in the general system of England towards Neutral Nations."[13]

Yet, in spite of French seizures and British restrictions, in spite of a naval war with France, the commerce of the United States had never been in such a flourishing condition, prices so low or money in such great demand. An immense capital was invested in the carrying trade. Harassed and badgered though it was, the merchant fleet took profitable advantage of war conditions, carried goods to and for all the world, ran blockades and eluded frigates and privateers with aplomb. For every ship that was seized, dozens got through and made enormous profits. Voyages around the Cape of Good Hope in search of the treasures of India, China and the Spice Islands increased beyond all measure, and many a New England fortune was founded during this period. It was no wonder that a government loan offering eight per cent interest met with few takers; it was much more profitable to invest liquid capital in ships and cargoes.[14]

Nevertheless the very merchants who were most profitably engaged were among the worst denouncers of the President. They wondered audibly whether they ought to support him for a second term. A member of the powerful and feudally minded Van Rensselaer clan in New York thought that perhaps it was best to let the election go to the Republicans by default. A bill was pending in the New York legislature to change the method of choosing presidential electors, without which the Federalists might lose the state. Did Hamilton think, he inquired, it was worth while to bother about it? [15]

In spite of the Van Rensselaer pessimism, the New York Federalists believed it decidedly worth while to gain the local elections. Aaron Burr, now risen to a commanding position among the Republicans, was diligently welding them into an organized and disciplined party. One of his strategic moves was to obtain a charter for the establishment of a company to bring pure water to the city of New York—sorely needed—but with powers broad enough, as the Federalists later discovered with dismay, to establish a bank as well.

The existent Bank of New York had been a Federalist monopoly, from which few Republicans could hope to obtain either credit or favors. When the Bank of the Manhattan Company was formed under the charter, therefore, the angry Federalists cried out on such underhanded and unethical tactics. Actually, Burr adhered rigidly to the terms of the charter. A water company was also formed, and furnished good and abundant water to the city for decades.

But Hamilton and his followers seized on the charge of trickery to win the vital city election, which in turn brought the state under Federalist control. In the process, they were not averse to employing trickery and coercion of their own. They privately boasted that the merchants had warned their employees against voting the Republican ticket on pain of dismissal. To ensure compliance, the merchants stood all day in front of the polling places to watch how their underlings voted—the balloting being public and without benefit of secrecy. These tactics, Troup gleefully reported, "operated like a charm." [16]

The Republicans accused the victorious Federalists of even worse skullduggery. They asserted that armed groups of "Cockade Cubs" (their contemptuous epithet for the troops of the provisional army) tore Republican tickets from the hands of the voters, forced Federalist ballots in their grip and hovered threateningly near by to make certain the frightened men dropped them in the ballot box. They also, so the Republicans charged, bullied men from their homes, brought British officers up to vote, sent Negroes from the street to the polls, and released prisoners from Bridewell jail to cast their ballots.[17]

The campaign of 1800 was already under way.

With an eye to the next year's presidential election, the Federalists acted on another front. Though the Kentucky and Virginia Resolutions had been decisively repudiated by the other states, they were not disposed to let the matter drop. The Resolutions, and the opposition to the Alien and Sedition Acts, might well have an untoward effect on the coming election. Hamilton called the Virginia action in particular "a very serious business, which will call for all the wisdom and firmness of the government." At the same time he saw the possibility of turning the Resolutions to good Federalist account.[18] He issued a warning to Virginia that should she arm her militia to oppose the enforcement of the laws, as it was alleged she had threatened, she would find her sister states "as able in the field as in the cabinet." [19]

The whole weight of the Federalist press, and of the Federalist clergy, was employed in a concerted assault. The Resolutions, they cried, were "wicked and insolent declaration of war upon the United States," and "all Jacobins are irreclaimable and incurable. You can make no peace or truce with them." [20]

A Philadelphia divine imputed all the world's wickedness to the Republicans and their French friends. His catalogue of their sins left little to the imagination. They included "the profanation of the name of God . . . the dissoluteness of youth . . . the cherishing of seditious practices . . . the prevalence of duelling . . . the open practice of adultery and fornication . . . the covetous pursuit of wealth." All these, he thundered, were due to their attachment to the French; as a result of which the people have surrendered to "atheistic, infidel and immoral principles." [21]

Nor was "this infernal Aurora" or "those contemptible wretches, the United Irishmen" with their "assassinating cowardice" immune from the gentle attentions of the Federalist editors.[22]

The Republican press retorted in kind, and with an equal catalogue of sins to be imputed to the Federalists. But while the merry war raged in press and pulpit, the Republican leaders soberly planned strategic moves to overcome the disheartening effect of the adverse criticism of the Resolutions.

Taking a leaf from the Federalist book in New York, they sought changes in the election laws of the states under their control—notably Virginia, North Carolina and Georgia—so as to ensure a unanimous Republican electoral vote.

Let these states follow the procedure adopted in South Carolina, it was urged. In that state the choosing of the presidential electors had been taken from the people and placed in the hands of the legislature. That way the Republican majorities could make certain of a unanimous list. Under the old method of choice by the people in their respective districts, there were areas in all three states which regularly returned Federalist electors. "This is no time for qualms," exclaimed Charles Pinckney (not to be confused with Charles Cotesworth Pinckney, the envoy).[23]

It is a curious and enlightening commentary on the ways of politicians that the friends of the people, the Republicans, now sought to take the power of election away from them; while Hamilton, the friend of the rich and the wellborn, was seeking to change the New York laws so that the choice of electors would be thrown into a general election.

In the meantime, President Adams found himself subject to a withering cross fire. The Federalists abused him for sending the mission to France; the Republicans attacked him as the tool and lackey of the British, and a despot as well whose aim it was to overthrow freedom in America and set up a monarchy. In fact, the *Aurora* openly hinted that Adams had been bribed by British gold.[24]

Pickering was only too happy to bring the offending item to the President's notice;[25] and most understandably Adams flew into a rage. "Is there any thing evil in the regions of actuality or possibility," he stormed, "that the Aurora has not suggested of me? . . . If Mr. Rawle [the U. S. attorney for Pennsylvania] does not think this paper libellous, he is not fit for his office; and if he does not prosecute it, he will not do his duty. The matchless effrontery of this Duane merits the execution of the alien law. I am very willing to try its strength upon him."[26]

Lamenting that the Alien Act was in effect a dead letter, Pickering caused Duane's arrest under the Sedition Act; and continued to have the *Aurora* and other Republican papers read line by line for other prosecution possibilities. He came up gleefully with another item —this one the "Address to the Readers of the Sunbury and Northumberland Gazette," written by Thomas Cooper and distributed by Dr. Joseph Priestley in the form of leaflets.[27]

The "Address" was couched in the form of hypothetical possibilities. Suppose, said Cooper, I were in the President's chair and wanted to become a despot. How would I go about it? First, I would undermine the safeguards of the Constitution. Second, I would extend the powers of the federal courts and "throw obloquy" on the state governments. Third, I would restrict the liberty of the press and multiply laws against libel and sedition. Fourth, I would speak derisively of the rights of man and the sovereignty of the people, try to bring the French into contempt and favor the despots of Europe. Fifth, I would give no public office to anyone who did not wholly agree with me. Sixth, I would enlist the aid of the clergy by adhering to the strict forms of religion and declaim loudly against infidels and atheists. Seventh, I would show preference to moneyed merchants against the agriculturalists, and encourage banking and funding systems. Eighth, as the "grand engine, the most useful instrument of despotic ambition," I would create a standing army and a vast navy; for which, if no reasons existed, I would proceed to invent them.[28]

No one could mistake the target of these "if I were President" surmises. Once more Pickering acted. He demanded Priestley's deportation as an alien; unfortunately, as he put it, Cooper had taken care to become a citizen. But Adams, who had once attended a famous series of lectures by Priestley on the errors of revealed religion and the absurdities of the Trinity, dismissed him contemptuously as too insignificant for notice. Cooper's attack was another matter. Adams attributed the article to Cooper's revenge for not having received a public appointment, and gave orders that he be prosecuted under the Sedition Act.[29] Pickering hastened to comply.

Not only Adams, but Washington, was enraged at the taunts and libels which appeared unceasingly in the Republican press. He cried out against them for endeavoring "to prostrate discipline and to introduce anarchy in the military as they have attempted to do in the civil government of this Country," and for accusing the administration of having taken bribes from England. He called for Duane's arrest as the maker of innuendoes "no longer to be borne." This state of affairs, he concluded, "cannot progress much further without an explosion."[30]

Washington himself was veritably on the verge of explosion. To a

proposition that he stand again for President, he returned a flat negative. I no longer have any influence with the Republicans, he exclaimed bitterly. "Let that party set up a broomstick and call it a true
son of Liberty—a Democrat—or any other epithet that will suit their
purpose," and it will get "their votes in toto!" [31]

Gone was the judicial tone, the restrained utterance, the careful
balancing of parties, of earlier days!

But the Republicans did not depend on the guerrillas of the press
alone; they summoned up their heavy artillery. Wilson Cary Nicholas,
who had been the catalytic agent for the original Virginia and Kentucky Resolutions, was willing to repeat that function. If Jefferson
thought it "proper that the legislature of these two states should defend the ground they have taken," and if he would "put upon paper
what you think the Kentucky assembly ought to say," suggested Nicholas, "I will place it in safe hands." [32]

Jefferson jumped at the opportunity. He asked Madison to adopt
with him a common plan of action whereby the principles already
advanced by Virginia and Kentucky would not "be yielded in silence."
He proposed new sets of resolutions to serve definite purposes: first,
to reply to the states which had answered the first sets in the negative; second, to reiterate the earlier protests and to invite the states to
act in unison against any further infringements of states' rights; third,
to state plainly that while they desired to adhere to the Union, they
were prepared, "were we to be disappointed in this, to sever ourselves
from that union we so much value, rather than give up the rights
of self government which we have reserved, and in which alone we
see liberty, safety and happiness." [33]

At long last the ominous word "secession" had come into the open.
It bespeaks a turmoil and agitation in Jefferson's mind that he was
now willing to bring to an end that Union he had done so much to
originate and cement.

Madison, however, was still swayed by that strong sense of national-
ism with which he had commenced his public career. He refused to
follow his friend and mentor into courses which must inevitably lead
to secession. With a troubled and anxious spirit he hastened to Monticello to dissuade Jefferson from any such desperate avowal.

What arguments he used is not known, but he succeeded in part.
It was not only in deference to Madison's judgment, Jefferson wrote

to Nicholas, already in Kentucky, "but because as we should never think of separation but for repeated and enormous violations, so these, when they occur, will be cause enough of themselves." Therefore he was sending Nicholas nothing but a general idea of what the new resolutions ought to contain. Besides, he added, too many people had suspected his hand in the previous set.[34]

Jefferson's general instructions omitted the key paragraph on secession; and in this softened version Nicholas delivered them to John Breckinridge. Once again Breckinridge took the public role of author —this time in fact. The Resolutions which he introduced in the Kentucky legislature on November 14, 1799, while in the main following Jefferson's notes, were in his own language.

In them Breckinridge declared boldly that in the event the Alien and Sedition Acts were not repealed, "a nullification of those acts by the States [was] the rightful remedy." The significant phrase had a ring only slightly less ominous than the original demand for secession.

The House passed the Resolutions without a dissenting vote; but the more conservative Senate concentrated its fire on that single sentence and concurred only after a bitter debate and substantial opposition.[35]

In Virginia, where the opposition to the original set of Resolutions had been vehement, Jefferson turned to more statesmanlike and politically strategic maneuvers.

He drew up for Madison's consideration a plan for the Republicans to follow if they expected victory: peace with everyone, including England, a sincere cultivation of the Union, the disbanding of the provisional army, continued protests against violations of constitutional principles, but nothing more to be said about the use of force to keep them intact; and nothing at all about nullification or secession.[36]

He had hoped to sit down with Madison and jointly draft a second set of resolutions for Virginia, but Monroe advised against any meeting that might arouse the suspicions of their enemies; and Jefferson heeded the advice.[37] As a result Madison drew them up alone. They were not at all what Jefferson had first suggested, nor did they follow Kentucky in vehemence of tone or the use of the word "nullification." Conciliation was Madison's aim; if they failed of that purpose, no threats followed.

By the time the innocuous Resolutions passed the Virginia legislature, the campaign of 1800 was in full swing and the Resolutions dropped silently and almost unnoticed into the maelstrom of events.

Meanwhile the Federalist assault on Adams continued unabated. They thought at first that the distasteful French mission might never get under way. Murray had accepted a place on it; so had Ellsworth, though with some reluctance. Patrick Henry, as usual, turned down the offer of any national post; and Adams appointed William R. Davie, governor of North Carolina, in his place. The mission was now complete.

But the two envoys who were in the United States did not sail immediately; and if the Federalists had their way, they never would. Adams was waiting to hear from Murray that Talleyrand had formally agreed to the conditions precedent. Most of the President's waiting was done at his home in Quincy. It is true that Abigail had been seriously ill and was still not fully recovered; but the Cabinet and others complained not without reason that the lengthy absence of the President of the United States from Philadelphia left the government without a head.

"We have no President here," Wolcott remarked sourly, and complained also that McHenry, his colleague, was utterly unfit for his office.[38] Everyone seemed to be disgusted with poor McHenry, including his best friend, Hamilton, who took no pains to hide his displeasure and wrote hectoring and admonitory letters to his technical superior.

McHenry submitted to the browbeating with Christian meekness and remained loyal to Hamilton—if not to his own superior, the President. Only once did he utter a protest and then in the humblest of accents. "I think," he pleaded with Hamilton, "the head of the Department of war ought not to be held up in a general order as having been ignorant of, or having been inattentive to his duties."[39]

By this time, indeed, Hamilton was ready to assume the entire management of the government. Since the administration had no general plan, he informed the Cabinet, they ought to settle one themselves without delay and without the President. He expressed his willingness to come himself to Philadelphia and help them in the task. Among the various measures he had in mind was the conquest of the Floridas and Louisiana; and, he added, "we ought to squint at South America."[40] He did not intend his army to go to waste, nor his period of military command to end without some blaze of glory

Unaware of these plots and plans, Adams resisted every effort to get him back to Philadelphia. He informed protesters that he could administer the government quite as well from Quincy. The Cabinet, he said, sent him daily everything of consequence; and "nothing is done without my advice and direction." [41]

In view of what we now know, this last statement has an incredible air about it. Of the five Cabinet members, only Charles Lee and Benjamin Stoddert evinced any honesty or loyalty in their dealings with the absent chief of state. Pickering, Wolcott and McHenry were quite content that Adams remain away and give them a free hand; particularly in their efforts to keep the envoys from sailing. All three concurred in Pickering's private characterization of the President as "an opinionist of inordinate vanity" and hence most dangerous in public office.[42]

Vans Murray, close to events in Europe, had no illusions about the new French proposals. He considered they came from weakness and not from strength. "Had the gates of Vienna been sent to Paris," he pointed out, "ah! the clamour for moderation had never been heard!" Nevertheless he believed that Adams was right in exploring every road to conciliation and peace.[43]

On May 5, 1799, Vans Murray sent an official communication to Talleyrand announcing the appointment of the mission and demanding as a prerequisite for their appearance "explicit and unequivocal assurances of reception, rights of embassy, and negotiation." [44]

Talleyrand hastened to express effusive satisfaction over the news and declared his intention of receiving the envoys with every form of propriety and cordiality.[45]

This final note, with all preceding communications, was dispatched to the United States and came to Adams in Quincy. It is difficult to understand why Adams took offense at the tone of Talleyrand's reply and referred to it as "impertinent." Nevertheless he expressed his willingness to pursue the negotiations while continuing all defensive and offensive operations by land and sea.[46]

But the pursuit of the negotiations was exactly what the Cabinet trio did not wish. Aside from the selfish domestic reasons for not desiring a reconciliation with France, news came from England which convinced them that the United States was heading for trouble with England as a result.

Sir William Scott, presiding justice in the admiralty courts, had laid down what even Pickering angrily declared to be an "extraordinary doctrine"—that an entire seacoast could be legally blockaded by the mere assertion that it was. American ships were seized under this novel doctrine; and the Federalist merchant Stephen Higginson —tender for his cargoes—used it as evidence of the dire consequences that came from negotiating with France; since that had obviously aroused British resentment and led to Sir William's decision.[47]

He apparently saw no inconsistency in his readiness to submit to British aggressions as against his former fierce denunciations of the Republicans for wishing the same course with France. Even that rabid Federalist Robert Troup belabored the British for their conduct and spoke bitterly of a Bahama judge who "condemns with the rapacity of a shark every vessel that is brought in; a single contraband article, however trifling in value, is held by the Judge in all cases to be sufficient cause for condemning the whole vessel and cargo." [48]

Rufus King found that his every protest was greeted with a new coldness since the announcement of the American mission to France. He also found to his horror that Cobbett's *Porcupine Gazette* had been accepted by the British "as the most authentic source of information respecting the United States." [49]

In August 1799 the yellow fever struck Philadelphia again, and the government hastily decamped to Trenton. From there Pickering, with the concurrence of Wolcott and McHenry, again demanded that Adams postpone the mission, this time using as a reason the expectation that the present French government would shortly topple.[50]

There was no stratagem that Pickering disdained to gain his purpose. He tried to plant the seeds of doubt in the mind of Ellsworth, one of the envoys. It was remarkable, he wrote privately to the Chief Justice, that Vans Murray, who was on the ground, did not believe the mission to be expedient.[51] This was not so; Pickering was deliberately distorting Vans Murray's dispatches and paraphrasing or quoting out of context. So intent was he on ensuring failure that he penned instructions for the envoys which Ellsworth promptly protested as too spirited and lacking in conciliatory temper.[52]

On the other hand, Stoddert, though himself doubtful over the mission, felt that the final decision ought to rest, where it properly belonged, with the President. He implored Adams to come to Trenton. "All the solemnity possible," he wrote, "should perhaps be given to the decision. General Washington, one of the most attentive men in the world to the manner of doing things, owed a great proportion of his celebrity to this circumstance. It appears to me, that the decision in question would be better supported throughout the country, if it be taken when you are surrounded by the officers of government and the ministers, even if it should be against their unanimous advice." [53]

Adams was impressed by Stoddert's well-intentioned plea, though perhaps somewhat resentful of the allusion to Washington. He was tired of having his predecessor forever held up as a model for him to copy.

But when he wrote back to Stoddert that he would come to Trenton, and to Ellsworth that he would postpone the mission until the current convulsions in France subsided and a new government emerged, Pickering became alarmed.[54] It was no part of his plans to have the President on the spot to direct affairs. He therefore sent Adams a most respectful note. Of course, he submitted, Adams was "eligible" to come to Trenton if he wished. However, since the expected news from Europe would very likely strengthen the reasons for a suspension of the mission, "the trouble of your journey may be saved." [55]

It may have been the perusal of this too-subtle letter from Pickering that opened Adams's eyes. Or it might have been the forthright urgings of Charles Lee, outside the Cabinet cabal, that the mission proceed regardless of what took place in France, that made Adams suddenly change his mind again.[56]

He took coach to Trenton, where, without previous consultation with his Cabinet, he peremptorily ordered Pickering, on October 16, 1799, to deliver at once to the envoys their instructions, and for Ellsworth and Davie to prepare to sail on the frigate *United States* by November 1st or sooner, should the warship be ready earlier.[57]

Had a bombshell exploded directly over the Cabinet cabal and their confederates, there could not have been more consternation, indignation and scattering for new positions. Pickering was beside himself. Since he was compelled to repress his emotions with the President, he poured out his full wrath on the distant Vans Murray.

Only a constitutional monarchy could save France, he exclaimed. The present "execrable government of France" was doomed. There would most probably now be war between us and the allied powers; while at home "we shall be cursed with a revolutionary minister [from France] to intrigue with the numerous enemies of our government, until it be overturned." The Cabinet had unanimously asked

Adams while he still was at Quincy to suspend the mission; they had been flouted and ignored. Even at Trenton, Ellsworth was actually on his way to Adams's lodgings in a last attempt to dissuade him, when the orders came through.

As for Vans Murray himself, continued Pickering with rising intonation, he had been entirely too subservient and humiliating in tone in his letters to Talleyrand. His expressions of respect and esteem were disgracefully misplaced on a man like him; in fact, Pickering resented similar expressions in Murray's letters to himself when he saw them also bestowed on such an abandoned and hypocritical villain. And so on and on.[58]

If such ungoverned expressions emanated from a responsible Cabinet minister, it is no wonder that other Federalists discharged the most violent cannonades. George Cabot insisted that he could not sleep the night he heard of the President's move; and declared Adams must decline to stand for re-election.[59] Sedgwick was convinced that "the federal nerve" had become palsied, and that even "good men" in New England were wondering why the army was necessary, if peace was to be made.[60]

Uriah Tracy had already made up his mind that the campaign "to root out Democracy and French principles" in the United States was "lost and worse." In his despair, he almost determined to resign from public office.[61]

Even Washington, who heard in his retirement only what Hamilton, Pickering, Wolcott and other members of the coterie were willing to convey him, professed his surprise at Adams's "hasty" action. "This business," he said mournfully, "seems to have commenced in an evil hour, and under unfavorable auspices; and I wish mischief may not tread in all its steps, and be the final result of the measure." [62]

Nevertheless, Pickering was compelled to pen the necessary instructions to the envoys and they set sail, albeit reluctantly, on November 3, 1799. They arrived in Lisbon on November 27th, only to hear that a revolution had occurred in France—the coup d'état of the 18th Brumaire. The entire picture had changed. Napoleon Bonaparte, who for some time had been penned up in Egypt as a result of Nelson's naval victory at Aboukir, had finally destroyed a Turkish army; in Europe, the discouraged and defeated French armies had suddenly taken the offensive and overrun Holland and Switzerland; but above all, Napoleon had evaded the British blockading fleet and landed once again in France. His coming, which evoked the wildest enthusiasm from the populace, caused the tottering Directory to fall. By a series of bold strokes Napoleon seized power—in conjunction with the Abbé Sieyès and Roger Duclos; they proclaimed themselves Consuls, and issued a startling manifesto: "Citizens, the Revolution is established upon the principles which were its origin. It is at an end!"

In spite of this remarkable shift of power, the envoys continued on their way as if nothing had happened. From Lisbon and Corunna they went overland to Paris, and arrived in the tumultuous capital on March 2, 1800, to meet Vans Murray and enter upon their negotiation—confronted with the formidable figure of Napoleon himself.

CHAPTER 29

The Presidential Campaign Begins

THE SIXTH CONGRESS CONVENED in December 1799 and listened in silence to the President's noncommittal address of welcome. It had barely settled down to business, however, when news arrived which threw the entire country into sorrow and confusion.

On December 14th, George Washington, the man who had led the colonies to victory, who had been the first President of the United States, who had been brought out of retirement to head once more the forces of his country, died at Mount Vernon. His illness had been brief; unfortunately, the attending physicians could think of no other remedy than to bleed him copiously. He went into a coma from which he never emerged.

The nation plunged into deepest mourning. Whatever the more rabid Republicans may have thought, they discreetly kept it to themselves. As for the Federalists, their grief was sincere and open. They had lost their rock, their shelter, their strongest prop. The magic that still inhered in their great leader's name had kept them going in their darkest hours; now that magic was withdrawn.

Hamilton was perhaps the hardest hit, and could avow in all honesty that the departed Washington had been "an *Aegis very essential to me.*" [1] But his grief did not prevent him from assessing the effect on his own private fortunes. "Who is to be Commander-in-chief?" he wondered. "Not the next in command [Hamilton]. The appointment will probably be deferred." [2]

In this supposition he was correct. Adams had no intention of promoting a man whose first appointment had been forced on him. And besides, the reports that came out of Europe put an end simultaneously to Army, commands, and Hamilton's dreams of conquest and glory.

The mass of the nation mourned with more selfless sincerity. They knew they had lost a leader and that an era had come to an end. In the chamber of Congress, John Marshall drafted resolutions which contained an immortal phrase: he spoke of Washington as "first in war, first in peace, and first in the hearts of his countrymen." [3]

The newspapers teemed with eulogies and draped their pages in heavy black. He was buried with simple ceremonies at Georgetown, close to his beloved acres. But Philadelphia, New York and other towns and communities insisted on rites of their own.

As was fitting, the rites and ceremonial funeral in the capital city were the most impressive of all. All public and private business suspended. A coffin was placed in the House of Representatives directly in front of the Speaker's chair. A black pall was draped over it, surmounted by the old Revolutionary cockade hat and a sword. The chair and tables were shrouded in black, while the features of the dead leader gazed benignly on the scene from the wall in the rear.

On December 26th the cannon boomed every half-hour from dawn to sunset. At noon, the empty bier was placed in procession and escorted through the streets to the German Lutheran Church, where Henry Lee was to deliver the funeral oration. Immense crowds watched in silence and in tears. In the van paced the old general's favorite white horse, led by two sergeants. On his back rested the dead leader's saddle, pistols, holsters, and boots reversed in the stirrups. Behind marched the members of Congress with white scarves and black armbands, the inevitable military, societies, public officials and the general populace. [4]

But the period of mourning and stoppage of public and private concerns was necessarily brief. The country became again absorbed in its daily affairs, its politics and the approaching election. Within less than two months the *Virginia Federalist* was calling public attention again to Jefferson's "Mazzei" letter and vehemently inquiring, now that "the great and good WASHINGTON" was dead, whether the writer of that letter was worthy to succeed him in the presidency. [5]

Everything proceeded as usual; and the British minister sharply commented that "notwithstanding this ostentatious display of regret and veneration, I find a great proportion of his apparent friends and intimate acquaintances more inclined to depreciate his merits than to exalt his fame, and he seems already to be in a great measure forgotten by the multitude." [6]

Sic transit gloria!

As the year 1800 began, foreign affairs, which had held the center of the stage since 1793, now retired to the wings and domestic issues moved into the spotlight.

The chronic quarrels with Great Britain, like an aching tooth, had leveled to a dull plateau of pain. Relations with Spain were better than at any previous time—the Mississippi was open to Western traffic, the Indian troubles had subsided, and the one that ought to be fearful of the future was the aged empire rather than the youthful republic. With France the shadows of war seemed definitely dispersing and an accommodation appeared imminent.

France had been almost the single issue on which the Federalists had concentrated. They thought that the XYZ Affair could be waved forever, like the bloody shirt of a later generation. But that issue had been torn from their hands by their own party president, who, at the same time, conceived himself to be President of the United States.

The Federalists had no other issue to take its place. They had built the whole structure of their power on that single prop—the Alien and Sedition Acts, the provisional army, the increased navy, the internal taxes. When the prop was removed, the walls and superstructure came tumbling down.

The Republicans, on the other hand, had every reason to be grateful to Adams. He had done for them what they could never have done for themselves. At a moment when their entire party seemed indissolubly associated with the enemy France, and could be lumped together in a solid adjectival blast as un-American, traitorous, conspiratorial and the supporters of a foreign power and a foreign ideology as against their own, the President had washed them clean and raised them to their feet.

Once again they could cry up domestic—and American—issues. Once again they could deplore the undoubted inequities of the Federalist system, and could cry out without distractive counteraccusations against the perils to freedom inherent in that system. In the previous presidential campaign they had been close to victory; now, with foreign skies providentially cleared, they could reasonably hope to grasp the prize.

The Republican leaders noted the portents and worked diligently to achieve unity in their ranks. The Federalists, on the other hand, were now hopelessly divided. Even on the question of slavery—always an embarrassment to the South and the Republicans—the Federalists fumbled. First they exasperated the Southern states by ill-timed action; then they supinely withdrew.

A petition came to the House of Representatives from the free Negroes of Philadelphia praying for the revision of the laws governing the slave trade and fugitive slaves, and asking for the adoption of measures that would lead eventually to the emancipation of all slaves.

The Federalists supported the petition in the initial debate. Then John Rutledge of South Carolina rose to declare angrily that he thought it "a little extraordinary that when gentlemen from some parts of the Union were positively assured that very serious, nay, dreadful effects, must be the inevitable consequence of their discussions on this subject, they still would persist."

In the face of the plain threat the Federalists backed down and even concurred in a resolution—to which one lone member dissented—that those parts of the petition which invited Congress to legislate on subjects precluded by the Constitution "have a tendency to create disquiet and jealousy, and ought therefore to receive no encouragement or countenance from this House." [7]

Other matters, however, found the Federalists more ready to stick to their guns. When Nicholas called up a resolution to repeal the former legislation for the increase of the army, pleading economy and characterizing the threat of a French invasion as a "bugbear," John Marshall recovered some of his lost popularity by insisting that the threat was real and that we were in fact, if not in form, at war with France. The repealer was defeated; though the Republicans achieved a partial victory by suspending further enlistments until the next session or a formal declaration of war. [8]

The Senate concurred in the suspension, much to Hamilton's dismay. Yet his utterances went a good way to substantiate Republican fears that the Army was intended for use against them and not against a foreign foe. [9]

In the midst of serious business, the House became involved in another of those comic-opera incidents which seem regularly to plague American legislative bodies. John Randolph of Roanoke, brilliantly endowed but eccentric, not to say erratic, and eventually to become a thorn in the side of Federalists and Republicans alike, complained on the floor that he had been insulted at the theater by two officers in uniform because of his speech in the House favoring the reduction of the army. The insults consisted, it seems, in the officers' bringing their hips in contact with his in the theater box, tugging "violently" at his cape, and swaggering away.

On this basis the House took depositions, and debated the insult

gravely and at length. The Federalists managed, however, to reverse
the complainant into a defendant of sorts. John Randolph had appealed directly to the President to chastise and degrade the offenders;
and the House committee, to whom the entire matter had been
delegated, animadverted in strong terms on the impropriety of this
appeal. The committee report was defeated on the floor by a remarkably close vote of 51 to 49, which gave the insulted Randolph little
satisfaction. Then the Speaker of the House—the Federalist Theodore
Sedgwick—declared the motion to censure the two officers out of
order; and he was upheld when the Republicans appealed from his
ruling to the floor.[10]

With this grave question out of the way, the House could once
more attend to the matters before it. The most serious of these was a
concerted effort by the Republicans to repeal the Sedition Act. They
actually managed to pass a repealer, but the Federalists slyly attached
an amendment to recognize the common law as the law of the United
States. Thereupon the entire House united in voting the repealer
with its rider down. As a Republican senator remarked: "One party
from their attachment to the Sedition law, the other from the dangerous consequences apprehended from the admission of the common
law as applicable to the Government of the United States," had for
once joined hands.[11]

The common law had always been a bête noire with the Republicans, and particularly with Thomas Jefferson. They hated it as of
English origin and growth, and they believed that it was permeated
with aristocratic and monarchic implications that would stifle a free
America.

The Non-Intercourse Act against France, which had been placed
on an annual basis, next came up for renewal. On this the newly
appointed senator from South Carolina, Charles Pinckney (once
more to be distinguished from the other two members of the tribe,
Thomas and Charles Cotesworth, and politically at odds with them)
made his maiden speech. He declared the act an unconstitutional
delegation of power which evidenced the increasing influence of the
Executive, and he believed it was unfair to single France out for
retribution when other nations had been guilty of the same or worse
offenses.

The Senate nevertheless renewed the act by a vote of 19 to 10;
whereupon the angry freshman senator furnished the *Aurora* with
the details of *another* bill, still pending behind closed doors. This bill

related to the adjudication of disputed elections, whereby the Federalists hoped through their present control of Congress to favor themselves in the coming campaign. In addition, Pinckney stated for publication that though he was a member of the committee to which the bill had been referred, he had never been consulted on it by the other members. The *Aurora* published both the draft bill and Pinckney's comments, together with some inflammatory remarks of its own.

The Senate, sensitive of its dignity, declared the publication and accompanying comments "false, defamatory, scandalous and malicious"—the language of the Sedition Act—and also "a high breach of the privileges of this House."

William Duane, who had married Bache's widow and taken over the *Aurora*, was ordered before the Senate to defend himself; though Charles Pinckney, who had furnished him with the material, was left untouched. After an initial appearance and adjournment in order to obtain counsel, Duane declined further to appear. On March 27, 1800, he was declared guilty of a contempt, and a warrant was issued for his arrest. Duane evaded present arrest by going into hiding; but later the aggrieved lawmakers instigated the President to order his arrest and trial under the Sedition Act.[12]

The House also passed the Non-Intercourse Act, and it extended the breach of commercial relations with France for another year.

All in all, the Republicans found little comfort in the proceedings of Congress; and could only turn hopefully toward the local and national elections which would determine the composition of the next Executive and Congress.

It was universally conceded that Thomas Jefferson would be the Republican standard-bearer. No one among the Republicans approached him in stature, experience and achievements. He stood midway between the party radicals and conservatives, and was acceptable to both. His reputation was nationwide, and his organizational skill, deftly applied in a wide-ranging series of letters to key party figures, now bore fruit. His most serious error—the extremist tone of his draft of the Kentucky Resolutions—had not yet been traced to his hand. His other blunder, the "Mazzei" letter, had faded from the public consciousness in spite of Federalist attempts to revive it.

The second place on the Republican ticket, however, posed serious difficulties. Inasmuch as Jefferson was a Virginian and an agriculturalist, it was essential to pick a vice-presidential nominee from one of the

Middle States who could also attract the growing artisan and mechanic classes. The choice narrowed geographically to New York and Pennsylvania, where local conditions and local political interests—often clashing—required careful handling.

Aaron Burr, who was engaged in New York in his own intraparty war with the regnant Clinton clan, came down to Philadelphia to speak to Jefferson. He convinced the latter that Hamilton, the Federalist boss of New York, was the one man to fear in the forthcoming election; but that he, Burr, was well equipped to wrest the city, and therefore the state, from his control. He pointed to the disciplined ranks of Tammany, that took orders only from himself; and to former evidences of his organizing talents. So confident, indeed, were Burr and his friends of success that they proposed to change the election laws in New York and New Jersey so as to have the presidential electors chosen by the joint vote of the forthcoming legislature and not, as previously, by the ballots of the people. Jefferson gave his approval to the scheme, though confessing some qualms over its contradiction of "republican principles." [13]

In his own state of Virginia, Jefferson sealed with even more cordial approval the plan of his friends, Madison and John Taylor, to change the election law in his favor. Here at least he could maintain that "republican principles" were still being invoked. Heretofore, the people had voted for the presidential electors by districts; now the procedure called for statewide balloting on a general ticket. The change meant that there would be a unanimous Republican contingent; whereas in the past certain districts had invariably returned Federalists. [14]

Since the Republicans were also attempting the same tactics in Pennsylvania, the Federalists cried out at such "French" measures, and demanded retaliation in the states under their own control. New Hampshire followed the example of Virginia; while Massachusetts took a leaf out of Burr's book in New York, shifting from a vote by districts to a legislative choice. [15]

The wisdom of the Massachusetts countermeasure became immediately evident in the close and exciting election for governor. Caleb Strong, the Federalist candidate, barely nosed out Elbridge Gerry, the Republican idol since his return from France, by 19,630 to 17,019, with 2410 scattered ballots. [16] The closeness of the vote in this home of New England federalism was an ominous portent for the presidential campaign.

As a result of these maneuvers and countermaneuvers, most states were committed in the forthcoming national election to a general statewide choice of presidential electors, put up on party tickets and pledged in advance to the official party nominees. New York and Massachusetts were the most important exceptions; there the legislatures chose the electors.

Unfortunately, one serious flaw remained untouched. Each elector would still cast two ballots naming two men, without specifying which one he preferred for the presidency and which for the vice-presidency. There had been some talk the previous year of a constitutional amendment to correct the defect, but nothing had come of it. The result in this particular election was to be grave indeed.

It must also be remembered that barely one-sixth of the free adult white males in the country were eligible to exercise the franchise, and that these represented the owners of land or taxable personal property. All considerations of "election sweeps" and "uprisings of public opinion" must take this important factor into account.

Late in February 1800, advices were received from the Caribbean which brought the country once more to a realization that there was a *de facto* war with France still in progress. On February 1st, just a year after it had won the greatest naval victory of the undeclared war over the *Insurgente*, the frigate *Constellation* encountered the French frigate *La Vengeance* off the Guadeloupe station. The Frenchman was much heavier in tonnage and weight of metal. It was later claimed that she carried 54 guns against the *Constellation*'s 38; but the claim has been disputed, and it is probable that the disparity in armament was not as great as reported.

The *Vengeance*, disinclined for combat, took to its heels, and Truxtun, again in command of the *Constellation*, pursued. The chase lasted all that day and most of the next. At eight in the evening of February 2nd, Truxtun came within cannon range and commenced firing. By the light of battle lanterns, the conflict raged through the Caribbean night, the darkness illuminated by the flash of broadsides, and the silence shattered by the incessant cannonade.

The *Constellation*'s sails were shot away, the mainmast crashed to deck carrying all its topmen, the surgeon's quarters were filled with the dead and dying. But by one in the morning the guns of the *Vengeance* were completely silenced and she turned to flee. Truxtun sought to pursue, but could not. Fourteen men lay dead and twenty-five more were seriously wounded.[17]

In effect it was a drawn battle; yet Truxtun remained in possession of the field and he had driven off and heavily damaged a superior ship. In his dispatches he laid claim to a great victory; and both America and Europe agreed.

Slowly but surely the American fleet had been built up to serviceable proportions. By the end of 1800 ten frigates had been added to the original three—the *President, Chesapeake, Philadelphia, New York, Congress, Essex, Boston, John Adams, Adams* and *General Greene.* If none of them was a ship of the line or carried the heavy armament the Federalists had advocated, the fleet was nevertheless formidable, well-manned and highly maneuverable. It was capable of giving a good account of itself against all but the full-strength battle fleets of the British and the French.

The new revolution in France, in which Napoleon seized power and proclaimed the end of the original revolution, took the Francophiles in America by surprise. For this was tantamount to a one-man dictatorship, naked and unconcealed by the forms and verbiage in which former dictatorships had been swathed, and disclosed the classic example of the military man on horseback.

Jefferson, somewhat perturbed, tried to extract a lesson and a warning for America. Are we, he wondered, "to have over again the history of Robespierre, of Caesar, or the new phenomenon of an usurpation of the government for the purpose of making it free? Our citizens however should derive from this some useful lessons. They should see in it a necessity to rally firmly and in close bands round their constitution; never to suffer an iota of it to be infringed; to inculcate on minorities the duties of acquiescence in the will of the majority, and on majorities a respect for the rights of the minority; to beware of a military force even of citizens; and to beware of too much confidence in any man. . . . I have never seen so awful a moment as the present." [18]

Wise words and noble; yet there was nothing in them, except for the warning against an army, to which the Federalists could not subscribe. The difficulty lay in the matter of construction—what did the Constitution actually say or permit? who were the majority or minority? what constituted an infringement of rights? wherein lay too much or too little confidence? It had been on these matters of interpretation that the Federalists and the Republicans had come to the brink of civil war and secession.

All eyes were turned in the spring of 1800 to the local elections in New York. There the people—meaning those who legally qualified— were voting for members of the state legislature. Since, by the recent change, the legislature would ballot for the presidential electors, the political complexion of that body would be decisive.

It was conceded by all parties that New York was the pivotal state; that the votes of the New York electors would most probably decide the presidency; and it was also agreed that the city of New York held the balance of power within the state. As the city went, the state would go and therefore the nation.[19] It was no wonder then that all eyes were drawn to the crucial balloting in the city of New York, and that both parties strained every sinew to win the victory in that single city.

As yet, however, the national vice-presidential candidate of the Republicans was still in doubt. As previously pointed out, he would have to come from either Pennsylvania or New York. Pennsylvania put forward McKean and Dallas; while in New York, George Clinton and Aaron Burr held the edge. Since there was intense rivalry and animosity between the New York candidates, and since each commanded an important faction within the Republican party, it was decided to await the returns of the state election before making any choice.

The Federalists were divided and split even on their presidential nominee. John Adams was of course the logical man to succeed himself; but his enemies were both numerous and powerful, and they considered the mission to France as the final blow.

A frantic correspondence took place among the malcontents, spearheaded by Hamilton from the strategic state of New York. Even in the former election he had attempted to keep Adams from the first place; now, with both political and personal reasons greatly intensified, he was determined at all costs to substitute another—and sounder— Federalist in the presidency.

But this was not easy. Whatever the coterie of leaders thought, the plain Federalists were still loyal to their President, particularly in New England, and would resent *ad extremis* any attempt to displace him. The plan of substitution therefore could not be publicly disclosed; it had to descend to the dark and subterranean caves of conspiracy.

Like the Republicans, Hamilton decided to wait until the New York elections were over. Robert Troup, his man Friday, put the plan succinctly. There was, he asserted, "a decided and deep rooted disgust with Mr. Adams," and a general belief that "the preservation of the federal cause essentially depends on removing Mr. Adams and appointing a more discreet man to the Presidency." Hence the necessity in New York "of making every possible exertion to have a decided majority of sound electors." [20]

What Troup meant was that Hamilton would see to it that the members of the state legislature now up for election were men who would, when in office, vote obediently for that slate of presidential electors which Hamilton saw fit to hand them.

Under the spell of this deep-laid plan Hamilton went to work. New York City had been safely Federalist in the past, and he had every reason to believe it would continue so. He therefore chose as the Federalist candidates in the city men who would prove amenable to his every wish, but who were mediocrities in every other respect.

Hamilton reckoned without the resourceful Aaron Burr. The latter had purposely withheld picking a Republican slate until he saw whom the Federalists had nominated.[21] When the list was published—with every name on it that of a comparative unknown—Burr smiled and slapped his thigh. "Now," he cried gleefully, "I have him all hollow." [22]

Burr's tactics were completely the reverse of Hamilton's. He bestirred himself to obtain a slate composed of the best men in the party—men of national as well as local prominence. Such were his talents that he accomplished the seemingly impossible; he persuaded those who were his personal enemies as well as those who were his friends to stand for lowly legislative seats. Among them were the former governor George Clinton; General Horatio Gates, the hero of Saratoga; Brockholst Livingston, representative of the most powerful clan in New York; Samuel Osgood, former Postmaster General; and others of almost equal stature. He himself picked Orange County from which to run.

Burr's strategy was not yet exhausted. He card-indexed every voter in the city wards, drilled Tammany in the job of getting the vote out, and conceived the ingenious scheme of making a large number of new Republican voters by placing on record joint-tenancy deeds in their names to parcels of land of a size just sufficient to come within the franchise qualifications. Since in law each joint tenant owned the entire land, he could economically put ten to twenty names on a single deed.

Hamilton took alarm too late. On the day of the election he rode on a white horse from polling place to place, mustered his faithful merchants once more to exert pressure on their employees, and harangued the voters wherever he found them gathered. This time he failed, and Burr triumphed. When the votes were counted, it was found that the Republicans had swept their entire ticket into office; and the state of New York was assured of a solidly Republican slate of presidential electors.[23]

"Success!" exulted Burr's lieutenants. "To Col. Burr we are indebted for every thing." [24] They took advantage of the victory to push their leader's claim to the vice-presidential nomination; and they could not be denied.[25]

The city victory tipped the scales sufficiently in the lower House, even though the state Senate remained Federalist, to give the Republicans a *single* vote majority in the combined Houses. But that was enough to ensure a unanimous Republican slate of electors, casting twelve votes.[26]

Hamilton went into a veritable fury at this unforeseen culmination to his maneuverings. The man he most hated—Aaron Burr—had dashed all his expectations; and from now on he pursued the latter with a malignity surpassing every previous effort. In his excitement he lost his usual clearsightedness. He sent off a hurried letter to John Jay, the governor of New York. Let the present Assembly, he said, reverse the election laws. Let the presidential electors be chosen by popular vote in the several districts; thereby the Federalists would obtain a substantial number of New York's electoral votes. In effect, he wished to change the rules of the game after the game was over.

He justified himself with the accusation that Jefferson was an "atheist in religion, and a fanatic in politics." He argued that "in times like these in which we live, it will not do to be over-scrupulous. *It is easy to sacrifice the substantial interests of society by a strict adherence to ordinary rules.*" [27]

Whatever else might be said of Jay, he possessed an inflexible sense of rectitude. He stared at Hamilton's amazing letter, endorsed on its back: "Proposing a measure for party purposes, which I think it would not become me to adopt," and filed it in his private papers. He did not answer Hamilton.[28]

The more Hamilton thought over the situation, the more he was determined that Adams must not be the Federalist candidate. He was through as a political figure if either Adams or Jefferson gained the presidency. "My mind is made up," he wrote to Theodore Sedgwick. "I will never more be responsible for him [Adams] by my direct support, even though the consequence should be the election of *Jefferson*. If we must have an *enemy* at the head of the government, let it be one whom we can oppose, and for whom we are not responsible." [29]

He had a plan in mind, however, to avoid the election of either. This was to put up as the ostensible candidate for the vice-presidency Charles Cotesworth Pinckney of South Carolina, but secretly to manipulate the Federalist electoral ballots so as to elevate him above Adams. A confidential caucus of the Federalist leaders in Congress was held in Philadelphia, where the plan was expounded. They agreed to it with enthusiasm. Publicly it was to be insisted that all electors give their votes equally to Pinckney and Adams; and the New England conspirators were to see to it that no votes were dropped from Pinckney in their own states. But in South Carolina, Pinckney's native state, and in neighboring North Carolina, where he was popular, a quiet arrangement was to be made whereby, at the last moment, the electors would give all their first votes to Pinckney, and their second votes would be thrown away from Adams to someone manifestly not in the running.[30]

If Hamilton had any doubts about Adams's insufficiency in office, they were dissipated by the sudden news that came out of Philadelphia. The long-suffering President finally struck back at the men who were betraying and sabotaging his policies. Yet even now he left untouched Oliver Wolcott, Secretary of the Treasury, unaware that he was as deeply immersed in the cabal as the others.

But the ax swung hard and brutally on Pickering, Secretary of State, and McHenry, Secretary of War. Of Pickering in particular the strong-minded Abigail had exclaimed some five months before: "There is a man in the cabinet whose manners are forbidding, whose temper is sour and whose resentments are implacable, who nevertheless would like to dictate every measure. . . . But I am mistaken if this dictator does not get himself ensnared in his own toil." [31]

Adams first sent a peremptory demand to McHenry for his resignation. McHenry, whom even the Hamiltonian Federalists considered weak and incompetent, protested his dismissal but complied.[32]

Pickering was of hardier fiber. When he received a similar curt note from the President, he returned an offensive and insulting letter in which he not only refused to resign, but sneered that very shortly Adams himself would be out of office. The enraged President retorted with a short, sharp dismissal.[33]

In their places John Marshall was appointed Secretary of State and Samuel Dexter of Virginia became Secretary of War.

The news of the dismissals burst upon the already disorganized Federalists with terrific impact, and roused the extremists to a fury to which their previous ire had been the veriest milk of human kindness.

From Philadelphia, Sedgwick cried out to Hamilton: "Would to heaven you was here, but it is too late. There shall be a meeting of such men who remain here, and who can be perfectly confided in; I will inform you of the result. Every tormenting passion rankles in the bosom of that weak and frantic old man [Adams]." [34]

But if the Federalists were dismayed, the Republicans were jubilant. "If ever a man went out of a public station," exclaimed the *Aurora*, "loaded with the universal execration of a wounded country, it is Mr. Timothy Pickering." [35]

As for Hamilton, he now cast off all secrecy. He wrote to the dismissed Pickering to search through the confidential files of his department before he left and take copies of such documents "as will enable you to explain both *Jefferson* and *Adams*. . . . The time is coming," he added meaningly, "when men of real integrity and energy must write against all empirics." [36] Somewhat later he made a similar request on Wolcott, though the latter was remaining in office, and asked him to furnish whatever damning data he could find.[37]

Not one of the trio thought the request strange or its ethics doubtful. Both Pickering and Wolcott promptly advised Hamilton that they would furnish him with incriminating material. Pickering went so far as to copy out for him interesting tidbits from Adams's private journal from Revolutionary days, which was on deposit in the archives.[38] Wolcott, still in the Cabinet, self-righteously defended his treachery with the assertion "that the affairs of this government will not only be ruined, but that the disgrace will attach to the federal party, if they permit the re-election of Mr. Adams." [39]

With this material from the confidential files, and spurred on by his own passion, Hamilton composed one of his most fantastic productions—an inquiry into "The Public Conduct and Character of John Adams, Esq., President of the United States."

Smarting under a statement which Adams was alleged to have made concerning Hamilton—that he was the "head of a British faction" in America—that aggrieved individual left nothing unsaid of his detractor. In the pamphlet which he now dashed off at incredible speed, Hamilton poured out the vats of his wrath in a torrent of accusations: Adams was guilty of "disgusting egotism, distempered jealousy, and ungovernable indiscretion." Adams was wholly unfit for the high office he held, and which he wished again to hold. Adams had never done anything right, and if re-elected would ruin the country. On the other hand, Charles Cotesworth Pinckney was a man of the highest principles, of the purest character, and worthy in every respect of the presidency.

Hamilton continued in this vein page after page, subjecting every personal and political act of the President to the bludgeons of his anger, twisting, distorting, seeking mean and ignominious reasons wherever he could, or assuming them where he could not.

Yet, after thus damning Adams and exalting Pinckney, some measure of caution came to Hamilton at the end. He did not suggest, he concluded lamely, that a single vote be withheld from Adams, because the general mass of the Federalists in their ignorance were still attached to him.[40]

The puzzle is—why then did Hamilton compose this terrific blast? The answer is that he did not intend to publish the pamphlet; but to print and send it privately to his friends among the Federalist leaders for them to disclose to others under due precautions or to use as proof that Pinckney ought to be chosen among the so-called leaders of the "second-class."

But again Hamilton reckoned without the resourceful and talented Mr. Burr. That gentleman, through means known only to himself, was able to obtain a copy from the printer's shop where it had been set into type, read it with singular satisfaction, struck off his own copies and scattered them among Republican editors all over the country for immediate publication and quotation. William Duane of the *Aurora* went so far as to reprint the entire pamphlet at his own expense for wide distribution as a *Republican* campaign document.[41]

Waves of laughter and high glee rocked the Republicans, while the Federalists, already sufficiently bloodied, cried aloud their horror. Champions for Adams rushed into the breach with their own pamphlets of virulent attack on Hamilton; Hamiltonian defenders retorted with equal ferocity; while the Republicans impartially egged both sides on to the fratricidal fray. Whatever chance the Federalist ticket may have had was now shattered by the public revelation of the complete bankruptcy of the party.

Nevertheless the diehards, who included Hamilton, Pickering, Wolcott, McHenry, Fisher Ames, Theodore Sedgwick, George Cabot, Uriah Tracy and others, doggedly continued their conspiratorial efforts to replace Adams by Pinckney, in spite of the growing evidence that this would most probably mean the election of neither. What made the plot all the more fantastic was the fact that Pinckney, the intended beneficiary of their endeavors, not only did not know of the conspiracy, but repudiated it at the vital moment when his barest nod might have ensured its success.

Another curious element in the amazingly tangled situation was the additional fact that these men, the acknowledged leaders of Federalism, were leaders without a following in their frantic efforts to unseat Adams. They could depend only on word-of-mouth propaganda among a selected few, and that only on pledges of the utmost secrecy.

As one minor agent in New Jersey admitted: "A public avowal of a design to drop and oppose [Adams], would cause the loss of any ticket supposed to be actuated by those principles. . . . But if we use a prudent silence we shall get in our ticket of electors, and if I am not deceived, they will be men who will do right in their vote; they will go on the basis of securing a federal President. Mr. Pinckney will be the man of their choice." [42]

From Maryland came a similar word. "No direct attempt," it was there declared, "can safely be made to drop or supersede Mr. Adams. It would create uncertainty, division and defeat. Let both men be held up till the Electors come to vote; and then let those who think Mr. Adams unfit to be President drop him silently." [43]

It was a sore trial to these men that matters could not be cozily adjusted among themselves, and that there was a people to be considered. As Hamilton himself admitted, while the leaders of the *first* class were for Pinckney, the leaders of the *second* class, as well as the rank and file of the party, were for Adams. Hence skillful maneuvering and public deception were necessary to elect Pinckney.[44]

While the Federalist conspirators were burrowing like moles in the dark, the vital state of Pennsylvania was the scene of a tremendous struggle. Thomas McKean, chief justice of the state court and radical Republican, had swept the spring elections for the gubernatorial chair. The victory pointed obviously to a similar sweep of the Republican national ticket in the fall, since the presidential electors, by previous enactment, were to be chosen at a general statewide election. But the act was due to expire prior to the actual election, and the legislature was unable to agree on a new one. The Republicans were in the majority in the lower House, but the Senate was controlled by the Federalists. The Assembly called for a renewal of the old law; the Senate insisted that the electoral balloting be done by districts instead of a statewide ticket. Such a shift, the Federalists believed, would enable them to pick up either six or seven of the fifteen electors; if the law remained as it was, they would lose them all.

Unable to come to an agreement, the legislature adjourned without action. McKean thereupon declared he would issue a proclamation prescribing the old procedure.[45] It was because of the situation in Pennsylvania that Congress had sought secretly to push through a bill which would place the machinery of the national election and the resolution of disputes in its own hands. This was the bill whose premature disclosure to Duane had brought on contempt proceedings and a prosecution under the Sedition Act.

In a last desperate attempt to gain converts to his views, Hamilton took advantage of the mustering out of the provisional Army—enacted by Congress under Republican pressure—to make a swing of New England and New Jersey. The Federalists feted and honored their visitor, but the political results were disappointing. He had lost his grip. His auditors listened respectfully and remained unconvinced. One former admirer asserted that he did not even "appear to be the great general which his talents designate him"; while Robert Troup mournfully complained that his idol's "usefulness hereafter will be greatly lessened."[46]

Indeed, as his ill-advised pamphlet on Adams evoked increasingly bitter recriminations from the Federalists themselves, Hamilton was ready to retire altogether from the political scene and let the country go to perdition in its own willful way. How broken and scattered are the Federalists! exclaimed Troup. We have "no rallying point; and no mortal can divine where or when we shall again collect our strength!" [47]

It was the despised McHenry, returned to private life in Baltimore, who put his finger on some of the reasons for the Federalist debacle. "Have our party," he demanded, "shown that they possess the necessary skill and courage to deserve to be continued to govern? What have they done? . . . They write private letters. To whom? To each other, but they do nothing to give a proper direction to the public mind. . . . If the party recovers its pristine energy and splendour, shall I ascribe it to such cunning, paltry, indecisive, back-door conduct?" [48]

But McHenry was a lone voice crying in the wilderness. For even such an ordinarily cautious Federalist as George Cabot was shortly to declare that he was willing rather to see Jefferson the President, with Pinckney as his Vice-President, than to have Adams return to the helm of state. [49]

In the midst of their confusion, however, the Federalists found time to make merry over the proposals of Noah Webster to publish a dictionary of the *American* language, as opposed to the British, which would embody American words and expressions and use a simplified spelling.

This was sheer "Jacobinism," exclaimed the Federalists, and heaped ridicule on the idea that an American tongue and spelling existed. Communications in the "new style" were gravely published in the press.

One such purported to come from a Pennsylvania German: "As I find der ish no Donder and Bliksum in de English Dikshonere I hope youl put both in yours to oblige a Subscrybur—Hans Bubbleblower."

Another ridiculed the Irish: "I hereby certify that my wife Martha has the best knack at coining new words of any I ever knew—& with the aid of a comforting drop she'll fill you two dictionerys in an hour if you please—Dermot O, Gabble." [50]

Though Noah Webster was himself a Federalist, he had fallen in disgrace with the more rabid members of his party because he had written a counterblast to Hamilton's pamphlet and generally conducted his newspaper, the New York *Spectator,* with unbecoming moderation and fairness. Fortunately, he remained unperturbed under the ridicule and abuse he received from his former associates, and continued to work on his revolutionary plan of a *Dictionary.*

CHAPTER 30

Downfall of the Federalists

WHILE THE FEDERALISTS reeled bloodily in internecine strife and conspirators sought to displace Adams, the Republicans moved calmly and confidently to victory. Jefferson hailed the dissensions as "wonderful," and conferred with Madison as to the best methods for taking advantage of them.[1]

Jefferson was conducting an armchair campaign from the mountaintop of Monticello, surveying the scene and writing an occasional letter when the occasion seemed to warrant it. He adopted a philosophic tone and laid down the principles on which the nation ought to proceed if and when he was elected.

He thought for example that the country was too large to be under the direct supervision of a single national government. Since the servants of the public were too remote from the vigilant eye of their constituents, they were exposed to a constant temptation to "corruption, plunder and waste." Let the states, he argued, possess an independent sovereignty over domestic concerns within their borders, and reduce the federal jurisdiction to the field of foreign affairs. And even in that field, he wished the powers of the general government to be limited strictly to the domain of commercial relations. Therefore, he said, the federal establishment would require only "a very simple organization, and a very unexpensive one; a few plain duties to be performed by a few servants."[2]

Agriculture, Jefferson insistently declared, was the chief and most healthful occupation for the American people. He considered large cities, with their rabbit warrens of artisans, as a curse. He viewed the yellow fever as a providential device to discourage their growth and forcing the inhabitants back to the health, virtue and freedom of the country. He believed that religion was a private affair and the concern neither of the state nor of prying individuals. "I have sworn upon the altar of god," he vowed in an immortal sentence, "eternal hostility against every form of tyranny over the minds of men." [3]

When he penned this phrase he was thinking more of religious than of political tyranny. At the moment he was licking his wounds from the unremitting assaults on his own religious convictions. A Deist who believed that Jesus was a great ethical teacher, but not the Son of God or divinely inspired, he was compelled to endure the vicious attacks of the hell-fire-and-brimstone clergy of New England and the Middle States. It became in fact the chief campaign cry against him. No language was too violent, too obscene even, for their pens or denunciations from the pulpit. The cry of "atheism" and "infidelity" was among the mildest which these men of God applied to Jefferson.

"I do not believe that the Most High," piously ejaculated a Connecticut divine, "will permit a howling atheist to sit at the head of this nation." [4]

"Shall I continue in allegiance to GOD—AND A RELIGIOUS PRESIDENT," demanded another; "Or impiously declare for JEFFERSON—AND NO GOD!!!" [5]

"Christians!" thundered a third, as you value eternity, vote against this infidel who seeks to "destroy a regard for the gospel of Jesus," who attacks the scriptural account of the Deluge, who disbelieves in the common origin of mankind from Adam and Eve. [6]

Indeed, as the campaign progressed, it appeared as if this were the single issue on which the Federalists based their hopes for success. In some alarm, Republican pamphleteers rose to defend their candidate as in truth the finest Christian of them all. [7] But there is no question that considerable damage was done to Jefferson by the bigoted attacks.

Nor was the final result of the Pennsylvania imbroglio encouraging to the Republicans. Since the state Senate had refused to renew the law providing for a general election of the presidential electors, nor to accede to a further House proposal that they be appointed by the joint vote of the two Houses (which would similarly have given a unanimous Republican slate), a compromise had to be worked out if Pennsylvania were not to lose its ballots altogether. It was agreed finally that each House name eight electors; and that from the sixteen so named, the Houses in joint session would choose the requisite fifteen electors allotted to Pennsylvania. Since the combined Houses showed a Republican majority, the eight picked by the lower House led the ballot, and seven of the eight Federalists named by the Senate were perforce added to them. [8]

Aaron Burr, the Republican vice-presidential candidate, toured New England in an attempt to crack that Federalist stronghold. His first reports were optimistic: that Rhode Island would join Adams and Jefferson in strange coupling; and that inroads might be made in rock-ribbed Connecticut.[9] In both these predictions he was to be disappointed.

In the midst of the election excitement, the mission to France had been almost if not entirely overlooked. Yet this single act of Adams had been the catalytic agent which changed the hitherto reluctant support of him by Hamilton and his followers to unremitting hatred and active intrigue. One leader of the "first class," however, stood boldly in opposition to his fellows. This was John Jay, governor of New York. He asserted that the Federalists displayed "too much asperity" in their outcries against the mission; and he did not agree with them that it should have been detained.[10]

But other erstwhile administration supporters, like the journalists John Fenno and William Cobbett (Peter Porcupine), redoubled their assaults on both Adams and the mission. Fenno, saved from the loss of his paper by a loan from Hamilton, obediently followed his benefactor into the opposition. Cobbett's federalism was conditioned solely by the advantages which England could derive from it. The President angrily declared that the pair had "done more to shuffle the cards into the hands of the jacobin leaders, than all the acts of administration, and all the policy of opposition, from the commencement of the government."[11]

Yet, had the Americans but known it, the negotiations in Paris were proceeding fairly well. The three envoys had been received promptly, openly and with full ceremony. They set to work and slowly but surely a convention to settle the matters in dispute took form and substance.

But, as in the previous mission, news of what was taking place was inordinately long in reaching the United States. Confronted by empty pouches in arriving ships, Adams fumed that the French seemed to be stalling until Jefferson was elected. And he wondered if, as he expected, the envoys came home "loaded with professions and protestations of love" but no treaty, whether he would not be compelled to begin an all-out war against them.[12]

At about the same time Fisher Ames had convinced himself that Adams was seeking a war with *England* in order to win the election![13]

In Paris, the French offered at first to keep the old treaties in force, with a reciprocal promise of indemnities for any infraction of their terms.[14] The American envoys turned the proposition down; one of their fundamental instructions was to rid the United States of the incubus of the treaties altogether.

For almost six months the negotiations proceeded with proposals and counterproposals, but always within a framework of diplomatic correctness and mutual courtesy. Gone was the abruptness and arrogance of the previous missions; nor was there any talk of monetary bribery.

Finally, a compromise solution was worked out which the negotiators signed on September 13, 1800.

The convention (it was not put in the form of a treaty) made the following points: 1. The usual expressions of peace and friendship. 2. A declaration that inasmuch as no agreement could be reached on the old treaties or on indemnities for damages sustained by American commerce because of French seizures, these matters were to be laid aside for later negotiation. In the meantime, the treaties were to be suspended. 3. All public ships captured by either party were to be restored; and also all private property as yet not definitively condemned (except for actual contraband). 4. All ships of either nation, including privateers and prizes, together with its commerce, were to receive most favored nation treatment in the ports of the other. 5. There must be no interference with the trade of either nation with the enemies of the other, except in case of contraband or actual blockade. Contraband was defined as weapons of war only; and even then, while they were subject to confiscation, the carrier vessel and remainder of its cargo were not. 6. The American doctrine that free ships make free goods (with the exception of contraband or enemy soldiers) was accepted by both parties.[15]

Though the envoys doubted that their fellow citizens would be satisfied with a convention which left for the future the discussion of indemnities, it was, they reported apologetically, the best they could obtain.[16]

Actually, it was a good deal. It put an end to the war with France and cleared the international atmosphere. It protected American commerce and permitted a vast expansion of the carrying trade. As for the indemnities, the United States eventually paid them to claimants as part compensation for the purchase of Louisiana.

President Adams presented the convention to the Senate for ratification on December 15, 1800. It met with considerable opposition from the Federalists, who were averse to yielding on their favorite issue. But Hamilton thought it the wiser policy to ratify, and so informed his senatorial friends.[17] In the end, and with some minor amendments, the convention was adopted; and XYZ and its consequences went into history.

As the year of 1800 went into autumn, and more of the states proceeded to vote or their legislatures assembled for the final decision, the hitherto confident Republicans lost some of their original optimism. The Federalists were beginning to arouse themselves from the torpor and defeatism into which they had previously sunk. Hamilton's pamphlet on Adams had an effect exactly the reverse of that it had intended. The ranks of the President's supporters tightened, and the machinations of the conspirators rebounded only on themselves. Everywhere those who held faith with Adams bestirred themselves to see to it that no elector was placed on the Federalist ballot who did not solemnly pledge his vote to him.

The salvaging of seven of the fifteen electors in Pennsylvania encouraged them. Then New Jersey came through with a sweeping Federalist victory, the more heartening because it had been unexpected. In that state, so Liston reported, "every man of considerable property, made it a point to attend to give his vote, and to carry with him all those on whom he had any influence. The infirm and the aged, who had not been at any publick meeting for twenty or thirty years past, made an effort to reach the place of election; and an ancient law of the State having granted the privilege of voting to women as well as men, Gentlemen proceeded to the Hustings, followed by their daughters, their Housekeepers, their female relations and dependents." [18]

Liston, after serving his country well under difficult conditions, was about to return to England, and Edward Thornton took over his duties as minister on December 2, 1800. But before he left, Liston wrote with some bitterness to his government that if the Republicans (or Democrats, as he and the Federalists now termed them) should win the election, the result could be attributed to the continued British seizures of American merchantmen, and the decisions of the courts of vice-admiralty at Kingston in the West Indies and at Halifax in Nova Scotia, where the prizes were taken for adjudication and condemnation.[19] Time and again Liston had urged on the British government an amelioration of its policy, but without visible effect.

In the heat of the election excitement, a clerk in the War Department—a United Irishman, so it was said, and therefore a Republican —surreptitiously copied out a statement of account in Pickering's handwriting which seemed to indicate that when he quit office he owed the government the sum of $100,000. The clerk took the copied statement to the sanctum of the *Aurora* and Duane printed it with the opprobrious comment that it offered "incontrovertible proofs of infamous peculation." The charge was immediately denied, and the proper explanation given that the allegedly missing $100,000 represented a draft for "presents" to the Barbary Powers; and that it was regular practice to show it on the books as a debt of the Secretary until authenticated vouchers of payment were received from the consular disbursers in Africa.[20]

Inasmuch as neither the *Aurora* nor any other Republican paper saw fit to publish the explanation, the seemingly uncontroverted accusation did considerable damage to the Federalist cause. Still more was done by a mysterious fire which shortly thereafter broke out in the War Office and destroyed most of its records. The *Aurora* hailed the conflagration as additional proof, if proof were needed, of this and other probable defalcations. The paper proclaimed that it had predicted exactly such a fiery holocaust as the only method by which the Federalists could destroy the incriminating evidence. To which Fenno retorted that if the Republicans *had* such preknowledge, then they must have set the blaze themselves.[21]

The gutted War Office was in the new capital of Washington; to which, in June 1800, President Adams had already informally moved. Pending completion of as yet half-erected buildings, full government activities were not officially transferred from Philadelphia until November. Then the trek began of congressmen, government officers and departmental aids, and their camp followers; all of whom surveyed the muddied, pathless semiwilderness, its scattered unfinished structures and its general depressing air, with sinking hearts and a longing to return to the civilized amenities they had just quitted.

Abigail Adams, now recovered, departed from her comfortable home in Quincy to join her husband in the new capital. She arrived on November 16th after losing her way in the deceptive maze of trails that meandered toward the "city." She found her husband living a dreary existence as a bachelor in one of the boardinghouses; and with him went to view their new quarters.

The indomitable woman stared at the bleak, drafty, unfinished

President's House with a feeling of despair. How could they be expected to live in such quarters? It was like an immense and cavernous barn, in which not a single room was finished for proper occupancy. Thirteen fires, she exclaimed, had to be kept going in the empty quarters, or they would have to sleep in damp and cold. Her New England economy made her wonder how they would be able to bear the expense of such a place on John's "present sallery." [22]

Nevertheless John Adams valiantly opened the new session of Congress in the huddled and unfinished National Capitol building. Without irony he commemorated the removal of the government to Washington, and proposed for congressional consideration a thorough revision of the federal judiciary system. He also informed them that the envoys had been duly received in Paris and were already engaged in the negotiation. He hoped, he said, that the outcome would be happy; but warned at the same time against any slackening in the preparations for defense. [23]

But Congress was as yet in no mood for work. Its members were politicians as well as lawmakers, and the election absorbed their energies until the returns were all in and beyond dispute.

In these waning days, Adams was confronted with a series of resignations. One of these came from Oliver Wolcott, who announced his intention of retiring at the end of the year. The President, who still did not know that his Secretary of Treasury had been one of the prime plotters against himself, accepted the resignation with sincere regret. He placed Wolcott beyond the reach of political storms on the bench of the judiciary.

Chief Justice Oliver Ellsworth had already notified the President that he would not return to the Supreme Court on the expiration of his mission to France; and Adams offered the post to its former incumbent, John Jay. When he refused, it went to John Marshall, who had been Secretary of State in the brief interval since Pickering's summary dismissal. Here is another of the numerous "ifs" of history. Had Jay accepted the post, and Marshall never become Chief Justice, the course of constitutional theory and action might most probably have flown in different channels from what it did under Marshall's epoch-making sway.

As November waned and December moved up on the calendar, the interest of the country became more and more engrossed in the raging electoral battle. The result seemed more confused and more doubtful than ever. Each mail that arrived, each messenger that clattered over muddy or frozen roads, brought a new report that served only further to befuddle the recipients.

In the New England states, the votes were already fixed and determined. As expected, they went unanimously Federalist. But *one* vote of the thirty-nine electoral ballots allotted to New England had been cannily thrown away from Pinckney by the supporters of Adams to ensure that there would be no tie for the first place.

In New York, as a result of Burr's great victory, the full twelve ballots went equally to Jefferson and Burr. In Pennsylvania, in accordance with the legislative compromise, seven votes went to Adams and Pinckney, and eight to Jefferson and Burr. New Jersey's seven and little Delaware's three were solidly Federalist. Maryland split her ten electoral votes down the middle, presenting with a fine impartiality five to the Federalists and five to the Republicans. Virginia's twenty-one votes, the largest of any state, naturally went completely Republican. North Carolina split her twelve ballots: the majority of eight went to Jefferson and Burr, and four to Adams and Pinckney. Georgia's four were obviously Republican. Though the returns from the Western states of Kentucky and Tennessee, with four and three votes respectively, were late in coming in, it was assumed that they too would all be Republican.

Only South Carolina, where eight electoral votes were at issue, was still to be heard from and still doubtful. Thus far, without South Carolina, the election was a dead heat. Adams had 65 votes, Pinckney 64, Jay 1, Jefferson 65, and Burr 65.

Accordingly a fierce spotlight beat on the dilatory state of South Carolina. In her hands lay the event of the election. The choice of the presidential electors resided in the state legislature, and there the Federalists and Republicans were almost evenly divided.

Last-minute frantic efforts were made to influence the individual legislators. Pressures, threats and blandishments were exercised to the full; trades were consummated, broken and remade in an atmosphere of subterranean darkness. The full story of what actually took place in this tense and superheated atmosphere has never come to light, and probably never will. But certain patent facts have emerged.

This was Pinckney's home state, and his personal popularity was such that it rose above party passions. The Northern Federalists who wished to exalt Pinckney above Adams, and who had seen their intrigues fail in their own bailiwicks, now clamored for a Federalist vote in South Carolina to put Pinckney out in front. Their strategy might have succeeded had Pinckney been willing to cooperate. But his sense of justice and personal integrity did not permit him to be a party to an underhanded deal.

A committee of the state legislature, composed of Alexander Garden, Judge Johnson and Chancellor de Saussure, conferred with Pinckney to secure his consent to a tentative arrangement whereby the state's eight electoral votes would be cast for Pinckney and Jefferson. This would actually have given Jefferson the presidency and Pinckney the vice-presidency. At the time, however, it was not yet known that a New England vote had been withheld from Pinckney; and it was believed that the two men would therefore be tied. In that case the election would have gone to the House of Representatives, where the Federalist majority by *states* would have ensured Pinckney's choice as President.

Pinckney heard the delegation out; then in polite but steady tones declared that "in justice to Mr. Adams, with whom his name had been associated with his own consent," he "gratefully but firmly declined." [24]

The committee returned to the legislature to report his refusal; and the triumphant Republicans, their hitherto divided ranks now solidly closed again, overrode the Federalists by a vote of 18 to 13 and gave *all* eight votes to Jefferson and Burr. [25]

The bitterly contested election of 1800 was at an end. The final ballots, as officially declared in Congress, stood as follows: Jefferson 73, Burr 73, Adams 65, Pinckney 64 and Jay 1. The reign of the Federalists was over; a new party and a new philosophy had come into power.

John Adams was thunderstruck. Up to the very last he had been confident of his own election; and had stubbornly refused in the face of all evidence to believe that Jefferson intended anything else but to be Vice-President under him again. [26] Now that his eyes were opened, his rancor turned on his erstwhile friend, not to be assuaged until both men were aged and retired from the heat and conflicts of public office.

An analysis of the election returns discloses that the Republican victory and the Federalist defeat did not constitute a new revolution, as has often been claimed. Jefferson did not ride to power on the shoulders of an outraged populace who had decisively determined to repudiate Federalist policies and start afresh.

In the first place, the result was neither clear-cut nor decisive. Had

Pinckney accepted the bargain in South Carolina and the New England Federalists not thrown a vote away from him, without doubt he would have been President and not Jefferson. In the second place, the term "mass uprising" is a misnomer, since the ballot was limited to a small minority of the actual population. In the third place, even that limited use of the polling booth did not apply in states like Pennsylvania, Massachusetts, New York and South Carolina, where the legislatures chose the electors; and, as we have seen, in Pennsylvania and South Carolina the choice was the result of political maneuvering rather than an expression of the popular will. In the fourth place, the dissensions among the Federalist leaders themselves, together with Adams's own political ineptitude, prevented their party from exerting its full force and power.

Geographical divisions—the South against the North, with the Middle States wavering uneasily in between—were far more potent influences; and had not changed since the preceding election or even the beginning of the nation. These were the same divisions that were to culminate in the great Civil War, and were bottomed on the same essential conflicts. Nor did the Alien and Sedition Acts contribute appreciably to the result—another common claim that must be dismissed. There is no evidence that any votes were shifted from one party to another because of them. Those who opposed the Acts had been Republicans before, and continued to be so. Jefferson had failed of election four years before by a hairsbreadth without their aid and benefit.

Even in the pivotal city of New York, where a matter of four hundred votes decided the city, state and nation, there is no evidence of a reversal or particular trend. The result there was due to Hamilton's poor political judgment on the one hand and to Burr's superb quantity of the same invaluable article on the other.

But whatever the final judgment may be as to the root cause, there is no question that the Federalists, accustomed to long years of power, were bewildered, dismayed and alarmed. Befuddled by their own campaign oratory, they were convinced that the nation and the world were coming to an end, that anarchy and a French-type revolution impended, that they would be murdered in their beds, their wives ravished and their property distributed among the *sans-culottes*.

It is true that there were sensible men among them, like Joseph Hale of Boston, who "did not expect those evils to follow the administration of Jefferson or Burr which while they were candidates it was thought politic to predict. The experience of the past seven years has probably corrected the wild notions heretofore imputed to them." [27] But this cool, calmly appraising view was not general.

It took only a short time, however, for the Federalist leaders to discover that in the election figures which made them perk up and take comfort. Jefferson and Burr were tied for first place. The curious flaw in the constitutional electoral provisions was now visible in all its disastrous consequences. Yet many of the practical politicians had already foreseen the contingency, and warned against it. Theodore Sedgwick, more than a year before, had proposed a constitutional amendment; but nothing had been done.

As a matter of fact, the Hamiltonian Federalists had sought to take advantage of the flaw to get Pinckney in; while the Republicans similarly visualized the possibilities of a tie and tried, by a complicated series of maneuvers, to prevent what actually happened. Burr himself had made an arrangement with Governor Fenner of Rhode Island to drop a vote or two from him in favor of Jefferson. But the deal had been made on the supposition that Rhode Island would go Republican; and it did not.[28]

Meanwhile, a disturbing rumor had emanated from *Virginia* that Burr planned treachery in New York; but the informant later acknowledged that he had been mistaken.[29] Jefferson had made his own plans to have votes dropped from his running mate, *without* previous consultation with him. There had been an arrangement to drop one vote from Burr in South Carolina, and one or two in Georgia; but in the general confusion this had not been done.[30]

A vast scurry of personal conferences and endless letters back and forth ensued among the Federalist leaders. Here was a providential opportunity to recoup, in part at least, their shattered fortunes.

Under the Constitution, the election was thrown into the House of Representatives, where the membership, voting by unit states, would decide which of the tied candidates was to be President and which Vice-President. The House which made the decision, however, was not the newly elected one, in which the Republicans would have a clear majority, but the expiring lame-duck one, in which the Federalists controlled.

Two possibilities unfolded to the Federalist leaders in the House. One was to make their own choice between Jefferson and Burr; and obtain substantial favors as the price of their support. The other was to create an impasse, in which neither man would be elected. In that way the Federalists could hope for another year of power during the interregnum until a second general election could he held. In that case an acting President would be chosen by the Senate; and the Senate was also Federalist. The more moderate advocated the first alternative; the extremists the second.

As early as August, there had been talk among them that in the event it became apparent that no Federalist could be elected, it might be sound strategy to throw some of their electoral votes to Burr and thus place him in the presidency. "They conceive Burr," reported Cabot, "to be the less likely to look to France for support than Jefferson, provided he could be supported at home. They consider Burr as actuated by ordinary ambition, Jefferson by that and the pride of the Jacobinic philosophy. The former may be satisfied with power and property, the latter must see the roots of our society pulled up and a new course of cultivation substituted." [31]

Now, with the results of the election definitely known, this idea spread like wildfire. There were, of course, dissenters. Sedgwick and Gouverneur Morris took the honorable attitude that since it had been the manifest intention of the electorate to place Jefferson first and Burr second, their wishes should be complied with. [32] But both frankly admitted that they were unable to impose their point of view on their congressional colleagues. James A. Bayard of Delaware, though personally undecided, deemed it prudent to go along with the party majority if he wished to obtain and hold power among them. [33] Jonathan Dayton of New Jersey was all for Burr; he had in fact, during the previous election, secretly sought Federalist support for his candidacy.

The extremists, however, like Samuel Sewall of Massachusetts, demanded that neither candidate be chosen. They wished the Senate to appoint a President pro tempore to take over the government pending a new election, when the Federalists might have a second chance to win. [34]

But one Federalist stood rocklike against usurpation or an arrangement which would place Burr in the seat of power. This was Alexander Hamilton. All his previous distrust and hatred of his New York rival now flared into a veritable furnace blast. At the very first mention of Burr as a possibility he had erupted with invectives that surpassed all prior efforts. Burr, he raged, was "as unprincipled and dangerous a man as any country can boast—as true a Cataline as ever met in midnight conclave." [35]

Now, when the possibility had turned to high probability, he was beside himself with passion. His pen scorched the paper as he sent an unceasing stream of letters to the congressional Federalists, exhorting, commanding them to choose Jefferson; nay, to choose the devil himself rather than Burr.

Burr, he cried, was "without probity . . . a voluptuary by system"; a man who, habituated to excessive expense and heavily in debt, "cannot be satisfied with the regular emoluments of any office of our government. Corrupt expedients will be to him a *necessary* resource. Will any prudent man offer such a President to the temptations of foreign gold?" [36]

Inconsistencies crept into Hamilton's impassioned epistles. If on the one hand he declaimed against Burr's corruptness, on the other he warned the Federalists that should they put him in the presidency they would raise against themselves "a man who will possess the boldness and daring necessary to give success to the Jacobin system, instead of one [Jefferson] who, for want of that quality, will be less fitted to promote it." [37]

As for Jefferson himself, Hamilton did not hesitate to characterize him as "tinctured with fanaticism . . . crafty and persevering in his objects . . . not scrupulous about the means of success, nor very mindful of the truth," and "a contemptible hypocrite as well." [38] Yet for all that, Jefferson was to be preferred to Burr; particularly since a deal might be made with him, as it could not with Burr. (Here again was an inconsistency.) "Let our situation be improved," Hamilton suggested, "to obtain from Jefferson assurances on certain points." These he listed as the maintenance of the present system, particularly in its relation to Hamilton's financial structure; a good-sized Navy and a policy of neutrality—meaning, no war with England.[39]

Hamilton's advice and exhortations were wholly disregarded. His star had never been lower. Many Federalists believed he had been responsible for the shipwreck of their party; and not even his final desperate threat to quit the party for good shook their determination to vote for Burr when the question was put in the House.[40]

On the Republican side there was almost equal confusion and alarm. Their plans had gone awry; and they sought feverishly for some method of enforcing the election result over the avowed Federalist intention to defeat it.

At no time during the hectic weeks that followed was there the slightest suspicion in the minds of the Republican leaders that Burr was seeking to take advantage of the situation. That came only later, when every vague rumor, every third-hand report, was sedulously collected to pull Burr down in the interest of a coalition of Southern Republicans and the faction of the Clintons in New York.

Burr indeed, the moment it was known that Jefferson and he were tied, wrote an explicit waiver to Samuel Smith of Maryland, a staunch Jeffersonian in Congress, and gave him permission to publish the disavowal.[41] He also wrote directly to Jefferson himself, informing him that Burr's personal friends in Congress had been instructed to vote for Jefferson—a pledge which was rigorously carried out.[42] He wrote to Gallatin, the Republican strategist, advising him that "Livingston [of New York] will tell you my sentiments on the proposed usurpation, and indeed of all other occurrences and projects of the day."[43]

Young David A. Ogden, whom the Federalists sent to New York in an attempt to obtain certain pledges from Burr in return for their support, reported his failure and disgustedly advised that they had better "acquiesce in the election of Mr. Jefferson, as the less dangerous man of the two."[44]

On the Republican side nothing but praise was heard for Burr's stand. Jefferson himself warmly declared that "the Federalists were confidant at first they could debauch Col. Burr. . . . His conduct has been honorable and decisive, and greatly embarrasses them."[45] Senator Mason of Virginia spoke "of a variety of letters" received in Washington from Burr which were "couched in the strongest terms" and gave assurances of complete cooperation in defeating Federalist maneuvers.[46] Caesar Rodney, a Delaware Republican, thought Burr "deserves immortal honor for the noble part he has acted on this occasion."[47] Governor McKean of Pennsylvania testified to the same effect.[48]

Elbridge Gerry had straddled his friendship precariously between Adams and Jefferson and had sought Adams's election as President and Jefferson's as Vice-President, rather naïvely believing that the two men would work harmoniously together to suppress the Federalists. At the next election, so Gerry reasoned, Adams would retire and support Jefferson for the presidency. Since Gerry was in a sense impartial, his testimony must carry considerable weight. He told Jefferson of a long conversation which he had with Burr in which the

latter expressed himself forcibly on the scheme of the Federalists to
elect him President as "the acme of their perfidy, and enmity to this
country," and an attempt to promote divisions and civil war.[49] And
finally, Gallatin declared that Burr "has *sincerely* opposed the design
and will go to any *lengths* to prevent its execution." [50]

In the face of this unanimous testimony by key Republicans on the
spot, it is difficult to understand the myth which was later generated
on the basis of Jefferson's afterthoughts—when he decided to break
with Burr—and the accusations of his bitter rivals in New York that
Burr had worked secretly with the Federalists to elevate himself to the
presidency.

At the time, indeed, the Republicans were far more concerned with
the possibility that the Federalists would attempt to hold on to the
government themselves by forcing a deadlock in the balloting and
then appointing an officer of their own to administer the government.
Against such a possibility they mobilized all their forces. They declared "openly and firmly, one and all, that the day such an act passed,
the middle States would arm, and that no usurpation, even for a single
day, should be submitted to." At such a time a convention of the states
would be called to reorganize the government and write a new Constitution.[51]

In Virginia, where James Monroe was now governor, the angriest
passions ruled. Proposals were made to pass strong declaratory resolutions, to hold the legislature in continuous session for instant action
if the attempt were made, and to break the Union if it succeeded. A
chain of express messengers was established, to travel day and night
between Richmond and Washington during this "critical and alarming" period.[52]

Madison suggested that Jefferson and Burr issue a joint proclamation calling the newly elected Congress immediately into session
and have it decide the election instead of the old Congress. He acknowledged that this was not constitutionally "regular," but believed
that the emergency justified it.[53] But Gallatin would have none of the
plan. He was even more attached to legal forms than Madison. It
was his idea to oppose any usurpation by having the Republican states
refuse to recognize or obey any usurper. They would meet in consultation and adopt ways and means to cope with the situation. If
New England refused to join them, then the Union must be dissolved.[54] Hugh H. Brackenridge offered to organize a corps of Penn-

sylvania frontiersmen who would march on Washington and execute a military "coup de main." [55]

While the entire country seethed with rumors, plots and threats of force, the Federalists in Congress were working diligently to rivet their system on the nation in spite of any eventuality.

At the first indication that they had been defeated, they moved to establish themselves firmly in the federal judiciary and to extend its jurisdiction and influence. As one of their number warned them, if we do not, the enemy will at the next session; and we shall see Republican "scoundrels placed on the seat of Justice." [56]

In pursuit of this laudable aim, therefore, bills were introduced late in December 1800 to reorganize the judicial system of the United States. One provision reduced the Supreme Court from six to five Justices whenever a vacancy occurred in the present bench. This was intended to forestall a Republican appointment as long as possible. Another section laid out six circuit courts, presided over by sixteen judges, who would be immediately appointed by Adams. The circuit courts were granted original jurisdiction in all federal cases except those expressly reserved by the Constitution to the Supreme Court. In addition, provision was made for justices of the peace and other minor officials in the newly erected District of Columbia.[57]

The intention of the Judiciary Act was obvious. "I dread this above all the measures meditated," wrote Jefferson, "because appointments in the nature of freehold render it difficult to undo what is done." [58]

In spite of the angry denunciations of the Republicans, the Act was pushed through both Houses, Adams signed the bill on February 13, 1801, and it became the law of the land. Then, with a right good will, the outgoing President proceeded to appoint deserving Federalists to the powerful judicial posts, secure in the knowledge that they held tenure for life.

No measure of the defeated Federalists aroused more fury among the Republicans than this. With John Marshall as Chief Justice of the United States, with a federal bench exclusively occupied by Federalists and possessed of the power to nullify or emasculate Republican measures on the ground of unconstitutionality, the new judiciary system surpassed even the wildest expectations of its makers in acting as a brake on Republican innovations.

The next Congress repealed the Act, but could not undo its effects; just as Jefferson had feared. The new judges lived to ripe old ages;

and long after the Federalist party became just the fragment of a fragment, Federalist principles ruled the courts and shaped constitutional interpretation into paths from which there could be but little future deviation.

In the same spirit of rule or ruin the Federalists sought to renew the expiring Sedition Act. Only on the third reading in the House did the Republicans muster sufficient strength to defeat by a vote of 53 to 49 this last desperate onslaught of their unreconstructed foes.

James Platt of New York gave feeling voice to the prevailing Federalist attitude. "The House had been told," he said, ". . . that the sun of Federalism was about to set. He confessed that he viewed with horror the awful night that would follow." [59]

CHAPTER 31

The Republican Triumph

O N FEBRUARY 11, 1801, Congress opened the final act of the great struggle between Federalism and Republicanism. On that day the Senate was to make its formal count of the electoral ballots. All the prominent figures on both sides, with the single exception of Aaron Burr, who remained in Albany to preside at the wedding of his daughter Theodosia, crowded into the new capital of the United States.

Washington was a city of magnificent intentions and distances; but as yet the magnificence was not discernible to the unimaginative eye. For all the years of planning and construction, it looked like a raw, unfinished frontier town; bleak, desolate, a sea of mud in times of thaw and of iron-hard ruts in time of freeze. Both the Capitol and the President's House still resounded with the hammers of workmen and rose like gaunt skeletons on a dreary landscape. The offices of the various governmental departments were either still on paper or empty shells as yet unfloored. Almost impassable swamps cut the town into segregated sectors, and the dread malaria wasted the inhabitants and made certain sections uninhabitable. Pennsylvania Avenue ran on a causeway from the Capitol through the heart of quaking marsh. On the Potomac stood a large but empty warehouse and a wharf at which no vessel was ever seen.

Clustered about the Capitol were seven or eight boardinghouses, one tailor shop, one shoemaker, one printer, one washerwoman, one grocer, one stationery shop, one drygoods shop and one oyster house. This was the entire federal city; though a considerable distance away, on the Georgetown road, where the ground was higher and the public offices were planned, stood a few score private homes.

Members of Congress, public officials and visitors found it difficult to obtain accommodations. They crowded the available boardinghouses near the Capitol; the overflow was compelled to hunt for quarters as far away as Georgetown. The most popular boardinghouse in town was the one run by Conrad & McMunn. Here a number of congressmen, Gallatin and Jefferson huddled in cheerless discomfort. Gallatin complained over the extravagant rates. He was being charged for board and lodging, doubled up with another roomer, the sum of $15 a week. The beef was poor and vegetables nonexistent; though he admitted that the poultry and mutton were good.[1]

Jefferson hated the town. He felt himself in the heart of enemy country, where bitter-end Federalists ruled the roost. Accustomed to gracious living, he sat at the farther end of a long table in the dining room of Conrad & McMunn, where only the presence of two women prevented the place from looking like a monk's refectory. When he stirred into the open, averted glances and scowling brows burned into his sensitive soul like brands.[2]

The one comfort he hugged to his bosom was wholly illusory. He believed that John Adams was exercising his influence with Congress to have them comply with the mandate of the people.[3] Actually, the embittered President was keeping hands off. As far as he was concerned, there was no "danger of a political convulsion, if a President, *pro tempore,* of the Senate, or a Secretary of State, or Speaker of the House, should be made President by Congress." Such a procedure, declared Adams, would not only be legal but would satisfy the people. However, he added, it would simply mean that another election would have to be held; and Jefferson would again be chosen. "We shall be tossed, at any rate," he concluded gloomily, "in the tempestuous sea of liberty for years to come, and where the bark can land but in a political convulsion, I cannot see."[4]

The day of February 11th dawned in miserable cold and shrouded in swirling snow. But the air was charged with an electricity in which rumor and counterrumor moved with lightning speed. Corrupt bargains were bruited about in the most minute detail; Congress had already picked the usurper; the militia of a dozen states were on the march, converging on the beleaguered city; at a given signal all Republicans—or Federalists—would be assassinated en masse; no report was too wild to be seriously believed.

But within the unfinished Capitol there was a measure of solemnity. The two Houses gathered in joint session; the electoral ballots were opened and counted; and the foregone results were followed with breathless attention. Jefferson and Burr were tied for the presidency.

Now the House of Representatives, as provided by the Constitution, took over. Its task was to decide between the two candidates. The voting was by states. The delegation of each state first balloted among themselves; and the majority vote of the members decided the vote of the state. Each state's vote counted as one, so that tiny Rhode Island and Delaware carried equal weight with mighty Virginia, Massachusetts, Pennsylvania and New York.

The first ballot taken by the House showed the clear lines of division; though it did not disclose the dissensions within the state delegations themselves. The Republican states voted unanimously for Jefferson. The Federalist states were *almost* unanimous for Burr. But the few dissentients in the Federalist ranks were sufficient to keep Burr from being elected.

Eight states declared for Jefferson—New York, New Jersey, Pennsylvania, Virginia, North Carolina, Kentucky, Georgia and Tennessee. Six states voted for Burr—New Hampshire, Massachusetts, Rhode Island, Connecticut, Delaware and South Carolina. Two states—Vermont and Maryland—were deadlocked within their own delegations, and cast blanks.

Since nine states were necessary for a majority, the balloting continued. Seven ballots were taken in rapid succession, without the slightest change. Both sides were standing firm. But one interesting fact emerged from the voting. While Jefferson was leading on the basis of unit states, Burr had an actual majority in the total votes of individual members—53 to 51.[5]

It had been previously decided to keep on voting until a choice was made. An hour was taken to "eat a mouthful" and then the balloting again proceeded. Joseph Nicholson of Maryland, though seriously ill, had himself carried through the snow and cold to the Capitol and now lay on an improvised cot in the committee room in order to cast his vote for Jefferson. Had he not done so, the vote of Maryland would have gone to Burr. Harrison Gray Otis of Massachusetts shuddered at the sight. "It is a chance," he wrote, "that this kills him. I would not thus expose myself for any President on Earth."[6]

It grew dark and the candles were lit. The cavernous chamber echoed with drafty gusts of frigid air and the temperature dropped. At midnight the balloting went wearily into its seventeenth count. Refreshments, both liquid and solid, were brought to the shivering members. "The suspense is awful," commented a Federalist, "but the conflict of passions not yet very violent."[7]

At seven the next morning the blear-eyed men were still in session. Twenty-five ballots had been taken, and every time the result was the same. Now unanimous consent was obtained for a siesta until noon, when again some ballots were taken. Since these showed no change or sign of cracking in the determined fronts, it was agreed at one o'clock to suspend until the following day.[8]

The solitary hope held out to the Republicans was the possibility of the shift of a single vote in the Maryland delegation, which would break the deadlock in that state and throw its vote into the column of Jefferson. But as yet all the pressure they could exert was insufficient to convince the particular member on whom they pinned that hope.[9]

On February 14th, at eleven in the morning, the tired members reconvened. But three more ballots—by this time thirty-three in number—convinced both sides that it would be wise to adjourn over the week end. James A. Bayard, the single member from Delaware, was particularly urgent. He had been voting his state steadily for Burr, but now he had come to a momentous decision, which required some time to mature.[10]

Repeated attempts had been made by the Federalists to seduce Burr and obtain certain pledges from him. Had they succeeded, the few Federalists in certain state delegations who persisted in voting for Jefferson would have switched their votes and Burr would have been elected.

But, as Bayard declared angrily and with partisan injustice, "Burr has acted a miserable paltry part. The election was in his power, but he was determined to come in as a Democrat, and in that event would have been the most dangerous man in the community. We have been counteracted in the whole business by letters he has written to this place. Some of our gentlemen from an intemperate hatred to Jefferson were disposed to proceed to the most desperate extremities. Being perfectly resolved not to risk the constitution or a civil war, I found the moment arrived at which it was necessary to take a decided step. The hope of electing Burr was abandoned on all hands. I therefore considered it the time to announce my intention of voting for Jefferson. It has produced great clamor and the violent spirits of the Party denounced me as a deserter of the Party." [11]

Shortly after it was all over, Bayard again asserted that "the means existed of electing Burr, but this required his co-operation. By deceiving one man (a great blockhead), and tempting two (not incorruptible), he might have secured a majority of the States. He will never have another chance of being President of the United States; and the little use he has made of the one which has occurred, gives me but an humble opinion of the talents of an unprincipled man." [12] Certainly a strange judgment on a course of action which the ordinary person can only consider as virtuous and high-minded.

With Burr thus intractable for their purposes, Bayard and some of the more moderate Federalists now turned to Jefferson as their last chance for making a deal. What took place is clouded in charges on the one side and vehement denials on the other. But some salient facts emerge from the general murk.

Bayard went to see John Nicholas of Virginia. If certain assurances could be had from Jefferson, he proposed, three states would switch from Burr to him. He, Bayard, would cast Delaware's ballot; and Baer and Craik of Maryland, and Morris of Vermont, all Federalists, would break the deadlocks in their two states in favor of Jefferson.

The pledges Bayard demanded in exchange were three: that the Hamiltonian system of finance be left intact, that the navy be not reduced, and that no subordinate Federalist officials be dismissed from the government service.

Nicholas thought the terms reasonable, but refused to act as intermediary. Samuel Smith of Maryland was more amenable, and agreed to put the proposition to Jefferson. He returned to Bayard on the next day. He had spoken to Jefferson, he reported, and he had been authorized by him to say that the Federalist terms "corresponded with his views and intentions, and that we might confide in him accordingly." In addition, he had been instructed to give specific assurances that George Latimer and Allan McLane, the respective collectors of Philadelphia and Wilmington, in whom Bayard was personally interested, would be left in office. As a result Bayard dispatched an immediate note to McLane: "I have taken good care of you, and think if prudent, you are safe." [13]

With these concessions in his hand, Bayard called a caucus of the Federalists. The Southern group of the party were ready for instant agreement; the New Englanders proved more stubborn. But finally, as Bayard reported it, after "great agitation and much heat," they all agreed to the plan but one William Edmond of Connecticut. Because of his stubbornness, the New Englanders of four states thereupon retracted and determined to stand with him to the bitter end. Those from Vermont and Maryland, however, agreed with Bayard to vote blanks and thus clinch the bargain.[14]

Later on Jefferson was vehemently to insist that he had never entered into any bargain; that though he had been approached, he had "declared to them unequivocally, that I would not receive the government on capitulation, that I would not go into it with my hands tied." [15]

Against his denial must be placed the sworn statement of his own political lieutenant and future member of his Cabinet, Samuel Smith; as well as the hard fact that McLane was actually continued in office, in spite of a storm of protests from hungry and deserving Republicans in Delaware. Burr, too, writing from New York, declared he had heard the Federalists boasting that they had come to an agreement with Jefferson; though Burr added prudently that he did not himself believe it.[16]

The House convened after the week-end recess, but the final arrangements had not yet been consummated; and after a few ballots, adjourned again.

On the following day, February 17th, the House met again in the knowledge that the hour of decision had arrived. As the thirty-sixth ballot was taken and the roll of states was read, when the clerk came to Delaware, it was obvious that all was over. Delaware—in the person of Bayard—announced that it was casting a blank ballot. Maryland and Vermont—where the Federalists, pursuant to agreement, voted blanks in the polling of their delegations—thereupon went to Jefferson. South Carolina joined Delaware in casting a blank. Only the four diehard New England states of Massachusetts, New Hampshire, Connecticut and Rhode Island persisted in voting for Burr.

As the final total was announced—ten states for Jefferson, four for Burr, and two blank—a huge wave of relief swept the weary auditors and the country at large. "Thus has ended," commented Gallatin, "the most wicked and absurd attempt ever tried by the Federalists." [17]

But the bitterness lingered on. The last few days of the expiring Federalists were feverish in the extreme. They saw nothing but darkness and destruction ahead; and with a desperation born of fear they sought to erect barriers against the oncoming flood.

The most important of these was the extended system of courts and justices which had been rushed through during the closing days of their power. For once John Adams and the most extreme members of his party saw eye to eye. The judiciary was their single hope and prospect of salvation from the anarchy that impended.

Adams sat in his office immured and solitary, poring over lists of names from which to choose the proper men for the grim days ahead. Ability in the law and a certain breadth of vision were essential, it was true; but far more important were the political opinions and unswerving devotion of the candidates to the Federalist cause and principles.

The Supreme Court, head and front of the system, was safe. John Marshall could be counted on to withstand all the machinations and "French principles" of a Republican Congress; while the contraction of the court's membership in case of a vacancy gave Jefferson but little chance to place a Republican on the bench.

Sixteen circuit court judges had been added to extend and cement the system. A District of Columbia had been established to embrace the city of Washington and its environs. Here too was a *tabula rasa* on which the names of justices of the peace and other officials could be inscribed.

Nominations were rushed over to and confirmed in haste by an expiring Senate. Commissions were drafted, appointments were engrossed and delivered to the new incumbents of offices held for life, immutable against all but the hazard of death or enormously difficult impeachment proceedings.

Then there were the other offices in endless array—United States marshals, district attorneys, collectors of the revenues, justices of the peace. John Adams sat in his office until nine in the evening of March 3, 1801, signing commissions in his large, wavering hand, racing against time and the oncoming Republicans. When at last he affixed his name to the commission of Hugh Barclay as marshal for the western district of Pennsylvania, his task was done. He had signed the final one of his so-called "midnight" appointments.

What his thoughts were as he went to bed that night can only be surmised. Certainly they were not pleasant. He had been repudiated by the people of the nation he had served so many years and so well; he had been repudiated even by the major leaders of his own party. The man who had been his friend in the days of the Confederation and while they were both in Europe had unkindly risen against him and wrested the presidency from his hands. He could see only anarchy and convulsions ahead for the nation he had helped to build.

As the new day of March 4th dawned, in his bitterness and desolation John Adams rose, supervised the final packing of his belongings into his carriage, got in and started out on the highroad to the north. As the great coach lumbered and jolted along, he may have heard the salvos of cannon that ushered in the new day for the incoming President of the United States. He had no mind to remain—though it would have been an act of courtesy—to witness the inauguration of his successor.

Had he heard the famous paragraph which Jefferson read in an almost inaudible voice from his Inaugural Address to the newly assembled Congress, his scowl might have changed to a sardonic laugh. As Adams's coach rolled through Maryland, Jefferson was saying:

"Every difference of opinion is not a difference of principle. We have called by different names brethren of the same principle. We are all Republicans, we are all Federalists."

Notes

CHAPTER 1
(Notes refer to text pages 3-13.)

[1] Washington, *Diaries* (J. C. Fitzpatrick, ed.), IV, 7.

[2] Hamilton to Gouverneur Morris: Hamilton, *Works* (H. C. Lodge, ed.), X, 425. See also Jefferson, *Writings* (P. L. Ford, ed.), I, 184-5, 236, for further comments by Hamilton.

[3] The best general account of Washington's journey is in Rufus Griswold, *The Republican Court*, 125-34, compiled from contemporary newspapers and letters. For the Trenton episode see also Washington, *Writings* (J. C. Fitzpatrick, ed.), XXX, 291 n.

[4] *Gazette of the United States*, Apr. 25, 1789.

[5] *Republican Court*, 123. Ezra Stiles, *Literary Diary*, III, 351.

[6] Adams to Mercy Warren, Mar. 2, 1789: *Warren-Adams Letters*, II, 305-6.

[7] *Gazette of the United States*, May 2, 1789.

[8] De Moustier to Montmorin, undated, Archives des Affaires Étrangères, Paris.

[9] *Annals of Congress* (Gales and Seaton, eds.), I, 26-9. *Republican Court*, 140-1.

[10] Ames to George R. Minot, May 3, 1789: Ames, *Works*, I, 34-5.

[11] Maclay, *Journal* (1890 ed.), Apr. 27, 1789, 4-5.

[12] *Ibid.*, Apr. 30, 1789, 8-9.

[13] Washington, *Writings*, XXX, 291-6.

CHAPTER 2
(Notes refer to text pages 14-31.)

[1] Isaac Weld, *Travels through the States of North America*, I, 46-7.

[2] Rochefoucauld-Liancourt, *Travels through the United States*, I, 2-3.

[3] *Columbian Centinel*, Jan. 4, 1797.

[4] *Moreau de St. Méry's American Journey* (K. & A. M. Roberts, trans. & eds.), 118-19. *Gazette of the United States*, June 26, 1799.

[5] Weld, *Travels*, I, 114. Rochefoucauld-Liancourt, *Travels*, I, 7.

[6] Rush to Thomas Percival, Oct. 26, 1786: *Letters of Benjamin Rush* (L. M. Butterfield, ed.), I, 400-406. Anthony Trollope, many years later, noted much the same sequence of settlement in western America: *North America* (N.Y., 1951), 135-6.

[7] Timothy Dwight, *Travels: in New-England and New-York*, I, 218-19.

[8] An excellent account is given in Shaw Livermore, *Early American Land Companies*.

[9] *Moreau de St. Méry,* 165.
[10] *Notes on Virginia:* Jefferson, *Works* (Federal edition), IV, 85-6.
[11] Weld, *Travels,* I, 6.
[12] *Moreau de St. Méry,* 156.
[13] *Ibid.,* 47.
[14] (Boston) *Independent Chronicle,* Dec. 6, 1792.
[15] *Ibid.,* Apr. 5, 1792.
[16] *Columbian Centinel,* Feb. 3, 1798.
[17] Timothy Dwight, *Travels,* I, 178-9. See also I, 338.
[18] *Gazette of the United States,* Feb. 10, 1797.
[19] Weld, *Travels,* I, 192. The literature is full of similar incidents.
[20] For a complete discussion of the revivalist sects, see William W. Sweet, *Religion on the American Frontier,* 4 v. (1931-46).
[21] Rochefoucauld-Liancourt, I, 116-18.
[22] See George Turberville to Madison, June 16, 1789; Madison MSS., N.Y. Public Library.
[23] *Gazette of the United States,* Apr. 15, 1789.
[24] *The Independent Gazeteer* (Philadelphia), March 28, 1787.
[25] "A Plan for a Federal University," Oct. 29, 1788: *Letters of Benjamin Rush* (L. M. Butterfield, ed.), I, 491-5.
[26] Preface to *The Columbiad* (Philadelphia, 1807).

CHAPTER 3

(Notes refer to text pages 32-53.)

[1] To R. H. Lee, Apr. 22, 1789: Samuel Adams Papers (Bancroft Transcripts), N.Y. Pub. Lib. Lee, senator from Virginia, agreed with Adams. No error was more fundamental, he replied, than the idea "of one government, founded on the ruins of State governments." (Apr. 25, Aug. 8, 1789: *ibid.*)
[2] *Gazette of the U.S.,* Apr. 15, 1789.
[3] To Edmund Randolph, Mar. 1, 1789: Madison, *Writings* (G. Hunt, ed.), V, 325-7.
[4] To Minot, Mar. 25, 1789: Ames, *Works,* I, 31-2.
[5] The House convened on Apr. 1, the Senate on Apr. 6, 1789.
[6] G. L. Turberville to Madison, Nov. 8, 1788: Madison MSS., N.Y. Pub. Lib. Edward Carrington to Madison, Feb. 16, 1789; Madison Papers, LC. Madison to Edmund Randolph, Mar. 1, 1789: Madison, *Writings,* V, 325-7.
[7] De Moustier to de Montmorin, June 9, 1789: Archives des Affaires Étrangères, Paris.
[8] Ames to Minot, May 3, 1789: Ames, *Works,* I, 34-5. T. Lowther told James Iredell that Madison spoke "in so low a tone of voice, that I could not well distinguish what he said." (May 9, 1789: McRee, *Iredell,* II, 258-9).
[9] *Annals of Cong.,* I, 102-3.
[10] *Ibid.,* I, 106.
[11] *Ibid.,* I, 115-16. For the petitions, see *American State Papers* (hereafter given as *ASP*): *Finance,* I, 5-11.

[12] *Annals of Cong.*, I, 113-14.

[13] *Ibid.*, I, 124.

[14] *Ibid.*, I, 146-8.

[15] *Ibid.*, I, 159-67.

[16] *Ibid.*, I, 132-4, 221-5.

[17] *Ibid.*, I, 227.

[18] Ames to Minot, July 23, 1789: Ames, *Works*, I, 65-6.

[19] Ames to Minot, May 27, 1789: *ibid.*, I, 44-6.

[20] *Annals of Cong.*, I, 201-5.

[21] Phineas Bond to Lord Carmathen, Jan. 4, 1789: *Amer. Hist. Assoc. Ann. Repts.* (1896-7), I, 591-2.

[22] Bond to Duke of Leeds, Aug. 15, 1789: *ibid.*, I, 608-14.

[23] "Notes on U. S. Carrying Trade," [May, 1789?]: Jefferson Papers, LC., v. 53, p. 9035.

[24] Ames to Minot, July 2, 1789: Ames, *Works*, I, 57-60. If Ames's thesis might be dismissed as that of a political foe, the observations of George Turberville and of Edmund Randolph, both Virginians, cannot be so dismissed. Turberville's comments have already been referred to. Randolph wrote Madison on Mar. 27, 1789 that "if the peace of this country [Virginia] is interrupted by any untoward event, one of three things will have a principal agency in the misfortune: the new constitution, british debts and taxes." (Madison Papers, LC., v. 11, p. 28.)

[25] *Annals of Cong.*, I, 191.

[26] Maclay, *Journal*, 50, 53.

[27] *Ibid.*, 70-1. *Annals of Cong.*, I, 615-19.

[28] *Annals of Cong.*, I, 2129-32.

[29] *Old Family Letters*, Series A, 33-6.

[30] *Annals of Cong.*, I, 35.

[31] Maclay, *Journal*, 2, 29.

[32] To Edmund Randolph, May 10, 1789: Madison Papers, LC., v. 11, p. 59.

[33] To Patrick Henry, June 12, 1789 (transcript): Wm. C. Rives Papers, LC.

[34] To David Stuart, July 26, 1789: Washington, *Writings*, XXX, 359-66.

[35] *Annals of Cong.*, I, 783, 819-20.

[36] *Ibid.*, I, 813.

[37] *Ibid.*, I, 592-3.

[38] *Ibid.*, I, 607.

[39] *Ibid.*, I, 455-576.

[40] To Edmund Randolph, May 31, 1789: Madison, *Writings*, V, 372-4 n. To Edmund Pendleton, June 21, 1789: *ibid.*, V, 405-6 n.

[41] Adams to James Lovell, Sept. 1, 1789: Adams, *Works*, VIII, 493-5. See Maclay (*Journal*, 106-10) for a discussion of the Senate debate. Ames thought "the meddling of the Senate in appointments . . . one of the least defensible parts of the Constitution. I would not extend this power any further." (Ames, *Works*, I, 50-2.)

[42] *Annals of Cong.*, I, 425-50.

[43] *Ibid.*, I, 775.

[44] Maclay, Journal, 73.

[45] To George Walton, Sept. 25, 1789: Adams, *Works,* VIII, 495-6.
[46] To Benjamin Rush, Apr. 20, 1789: *Pa. Mag. of Hist. and Biog.,* v. 70 (1946), 100-1.
[47] William Grayson to Patrick Henry, Sept. 29, 1789: Rives Papers, LC. See also Theodoric Bland to Henry, Mar. 9, 1790, *ibid.;* and Pierce Butler to Iredell, Aug. 11, 1789: McRee, *Iredell,* II, 263-5.
[48] To Jefferson, June 30, 1789: Madison Papers, LC., v. 11, p. 99.

CHAPTER 4

(Notes refer to text pages 54-75.)

[1] "Queries on Conduct," May 10, 1789: Washington, *Writings,* XXX, 319-21.
[2] To Washington, May 5, 1789: Hamilton, *Works* (J. C. Hamilton, ed.), IV, 1-3.
[3] To Washington, May 17, 1789: Adams, *Works,* VIII, 491-3.
[4] Maclay, *Journal,* 67.
[5] *Ibid.,* 134-5.
[6] July 27, 1789.
[7] Griswold, *Republican Court,* 157.
[8] *Ibid.,* 158.
[9] *Ibid.,* 165 n. Griswold attributes the remark to a "Col. Stone"; probably Michael Jenifer Stone, member of Congress from Maryland. See also *New Letters of Abigail Adams* (S. Mitchell, ed.), 18-22.
[10] *Ibid.,* 172.
[11] William Sullivan, *Familiar Letters,* 118-19.
[12] Washington to Lafayette, June 3, 1790: Washington, *Writings,* XXXI, 46.
[13] Abigail Adams to her sister, July 12, 1789: *New Letters of Abigail Adams,* 14-18.
[14] To John Dandridge, June 24, 1790: Washington, *Writings,* XXX, 348-9. To James Craik, Sept. 8, 1789: *ibid.,* XXX, 395-7.
[15] A. Maclaine to Iredell, Dec. 22, 1789: McRee, *Iredell,* II, 275-6.
[16] St. Clair to the President [Aug., 1789]: *Territorial Papers of the U.S.,* II, 204-12. For the Spanish offer, see Gov. Miro's Proclamation, Sept. 2, 1789: *ibid.,* II, 213-14.
[17] Madison to Washington, Mar. 8, 1789: Madison, *Writings,* V, 328-9.
[18] Madison to Washington, Mar. 26, 1789: *ibid.,* V, 331-3. Tench Coxe to Madison, Mar. 18, 1789: Madison Papers, LC., v. 11, p. 20.
[19] To Washington, Apr. 2, 1791: Jefferson, *Works* (Fed. ed.), VI, 239. Dr. Ezra Stiles had adopted the same view two years before. He even optimistically foresaw that the Americans, settled on Spanish soil, would revolutionize all the Spanish possessions and convert them to Protestantism (*Literary Diary of Ezra Stiles,* III, 364-5).
[20] For the story of Wilkinson's remarkable career, see James R. Jacobs, *Tarnished Warrior* (N.Y., 1938). For his relations with Burr, see Schachner, *Aaron Burr,* chap. 19. For much unpublished material on Wilkinson's dealings in 1789, see Harry Innes Papers, LC., v. 23.

21 George Nicholas to Madison, May 8, 1789: Madison Papers, LC., v. 11, p. 57.
22 Madison to Nicholas, July 5, 1789; Harry Innes Papers, LC.
23 Wharton, *Diplomatic Correspondence of the Revolution*, IV, 743.
24 Washington Papers, LC., v. 245, pp. 32-9.
25 John Brown to Innes, Oct. 7, 1789; Harry Innes Papers, LC.
26 Grayson to Patrick Henry, June 12, 1789; Rives Papers, LC.
27 Jan. 9, 1789: *ASP: Indian Affairs*, I, 2-8.
28 June 15, July 6, July 7 (3 reports): *ibid.*, I, 12-14, 15-16, 38, 48-9, 52-4.
29 June 15, July 7, 1789: *ibid.*, I, 12-14, 52-4.
30 Washington to Senate Committee, Aug. 8, 1789: Washington, *Writings*, XXX, 373-4.
31 Washington to the Senate, Aug. 22, 1789: *ibid.*, XXX, 385-90.
32 Maclay, *Journal*, 125-8.
33 *Ibid.*, 128-9. *Annals of Cong.*, I, 69-70.
34 J. Q. Adams, *Diary*, VI, 427.
35 *Annals of Cong.*, I, 691, 694-7, 703.
36 Knox to Washington, Jan. 4, 1790: *ASP: Indian Affairs*, I, 59-61.
37 Washington to Senate, Aug. 7, 1790: *ibid.*, I, 81-2.

CHAPTER 5

(Notes refer to text pages 76-92.)

1 To Gouverneur Morris, Oct. 13, 1789: Washington, *Writings*, XXX, 442-5.
2 Washington, *Diaries*, IV, 14.
3 *Gazette of the U.S.*, Oct. 17, 1789.
4 Washington, *Diaries*, IV, 27.
5 *Ibid.*, IV, 30.
6 Boston *Independent Chronicle*, Oct. 29, 1789.
7 Washington, *Diaries*, IV, 35-6.
8 Hancock to King, Apr. 25, 1789: Rufus King Papers, N.Y. Hist. Soc.
9 Washington, *Diaries*, IV, 37-8.
10 *Ibid.*, IV, 39-50.
11 Washington to Catherine M. Graham, Jan. 9, 1790: Washington, *Writings*, XXX, 495-8.
12 To Wm. Short, Dec. 14, 1789: Jefferson, *Works* (Federal ed.), VI, 24.
13 "Commerce with France of U. S. during 1789": Jefferson Papers, LC., v. 53, p. 8983.
14 Higginson to John Adams, Dec. 21, 1789: *Amer. Hist. Assoc. Ann. Rept. for 1896*, I, 769-72.
15 J. Temple to Duke of Leeds, Oct. 10, 1789: British State Papers, G. L. Ford Transcripts, N.Y. Pub. Lib.
16 *Gazette of the U.S.*, Oct. 24, 1789.
17 "Dr. Hamilton's Grand Restorative" pretended to cure diseases "from indiscreet pleasures and juvenile indiscretions, diseases of women, consumptions, lowness of spirits, indigestion, melancholy, involuntary emissions, pains in

limbs, seminal weakness, obstinate gleets, impotency and barrenness, gout, wasting of the flesh, drunkenness," and in fact, every ill to which flesh is liable; *Independent Chronicle*, July 31, 1800.

[18] *Independent Chronicle*, Feb. 12, 1789.

[19] Christopher Gore to King, Jan. 18, 1789: King, *Rufus King*, I, 357-8.

[20] Jeremy Belknap to Ebenezer Hazard, May 8, 1789: *Mass. Hist. Soc. Colls.*, ser. 5, v. 3, pp. 123-7.

[21] Craigie to Daniel Parker, May, 1788: Craigie Papers, Amer. Antiquar. Soc.

[22] W. P. & J. P. Cutler, *Manasseh Cutler*, I, 240-1. For Duer's dealings in certificates see the Duer Papers, N.Y. Hist. Soc.

[23] Craigie to Parker, July 27, 1788; to Van Statehorst & Hubbard, June 27, 1789: Craigie Papers, Amer. Antiquar. Soc.

[24] Craigie to Parker, May, 1790: *ibid.*

[25] Bleecker to Craigie, Dec. 15, 26, 1789: *ibid.*

[26] Oct. 8, 1789: Webb Correspondence, Amer. Antiquar. Soc.

[27] Brissot de Warville to Duer, Nov. 27, 1789: Duer Papers, N.Y. Hist. Soc.

[28] Jarvis to Melancton Smith & Craigie, Nov. 1, 1790: Craigie Papers, Amer. Antiquar. Soc. When the latter taxed Duer with the transactions, Duer (then out of office) admitted the fact and merely defended himself with the assertion that he had not let Jarvis down (Nov. 20, 1790: *ibid.*).

[29] Seth Johnson to Craigie, Dec. 24, 1793: *ibid.* John Beckley to Monroe, June 22, 27, 1793: photostats, Monroe Papers, N.Y. Pub. Lib.

[30] Oct. 12, 1789: Hamilton, *Works* (Lodge, ed.), IX, 462-3.

[31] Nov. 19, 1789: Hamilton Papers, LC., 1st ser., v. 8, pp. 999-1000.

[32] *ASP: Finance*, I, 15-25.

[33] To King, June 7, 1789: King, *King*, I, 361-2.

[34] To Minot, Jan. 13, 1790: Ames, *Works*, I, 72-3.

[35] *Mass. Hist. Soc. Proc.*, 2nd ser., XV, 140.

[36] *Gazette of the U.S.*, Feb. 23, 1793.

CHAPTER 6

(Notes refer to text pages 93-106.)

[1] Washington, *Diaries*, IV, 67-8.

[2] *ASP: For. Rel.*, I, 11-12.

[3] *Annals of Cong.*, I, 1043-4.

[4] Hamilton, *Works* (Lodge, ed.), II, 283.

[5] Maclay, *Journal*, 173-5.

[6] *Ibid.*, 172-3.

[7] Jan. 24, 1790: Madison, *Writings* (Hunt, ed.), V, 434-6.

[8] Jan. 30, 1790.

[9] *Columbian Centinel*, Feb. 24, 1790.

[10] Thomas Willing, Philadelphia banker, boasted he had seen the report in manuscript before it went to Congress; or at least so Maclay reported (*Journal*, 188).

[11] Professor Charles A. Beard unearthed the record of their transactions in the Registry Books of the N.Y. Loan Office (*An Economic Interpretation of the Constitution*, 109). While Schuyler's preknowledge can only be surmised, there is definite evidence that Hamilton had previously informed Church of his plans (Angelica Church to Hamilton, Jan. 7, 1790: Hamilton Papers, LC.).

[12] *Annals of Cong.*, I, 1093-4.

[13] *Ibid.*, I, 1095-9, 1103.

[14] Maclay, *Journal*, 185, 189.

[15] To Oliver Everett, Feb. 28, 1790: Cutler, *Cutler*, I, 460-1.

[16] Madison to Henry Lee, Apr. 13, 1790: Madison, *Writings*, VI, 10-11 n.

[17] To Edmund Pendleton, Apr. 4, 1790: *ibid.*, VI, 9-10 n.

[18] *Annals of Cong.*, I, 1077-8, 1107.

[19] *Ibid.*, I, 1114, 1117.

[20] *Ibid.*, I, 1110.

[21] *Ibid.*, II, 2205-6.

[22] *Ibid.*, I, 1137-8.

[23] *Ibid.*, I, 1142-3.

[24] *Ibid.*, I, 1144, 1146.

[25] *Ibid.*, I, 1154.

[26] *Ibid.*, I, 1156.

[27] Gore to King, Jan. 24, 1790: King, *King*, I, 385-6.

[28] May 6, 1790: Rufus King Papers, N.Y. Hist. Soc.

[29] May 30, 1790: *ibid.*

[30] *Annals of Cong.*, I, 1182-6.

[31] *Ibid.*, I, 1187.

[32] *Ibid.*, I, 1197-9.

[33] David Stuart to Washington, June 2, 1790: Washington, *Writings*, XXXI, 49-50 n. See also Carrington to Madison, Apr. 7, 1790: Madison Papers, N.Y. Pub. Lib.

[34] *Annals of Cong.*, I, 1189. See also Madison to E. Randolph, Mar. 21, 1790: Madison Papers, LC., v. 12, p. 103.

[35] *Annals of Cong.*, I, 1200.

[36] *Ibid.*, I, 1202.

[37] To Jeremiah Wadsworth, Mar. 21, 1790: Wadsworth Papers, Conn. Hist. Soc.

[38] *Annals of Cong.*, I, 1192-6.

[39] MS. Memorandum: Madison Papers, LC.

[40] Maclay, *Journal*, 194-5.

[41] *Ibid.*, 197.

[42] To Madison, Feb. 5, Mar. 27, 1790: copies, Madison Papers, N.Y. Pub. Lib.

[43] To Madison, Feb. 27, 1790: Madison Papers, LC., v. 12, p. 84.

[44] To Madison, Mar. 13, 1790: *ibid.*, v. 12, p. 98.

[45] *Annals of Cong.*, I, II, 1196-7, 1205-28, 1281-98, 1345, 1354.

CHAPTER 7

(*Notes refer to text pages 107-121.*)

[1] To Madison, Mar. 27, 1790: copy in Madison Papers, N.Y. Pub. Lib.
[2] Henry Lee to Madison, Apr. 3, 1790: Madison Papers, LC., v. 13, p. 2.
Edmund Randolph to Madison, May 20, 1790: *ibid.*, v. 13, p. 31. Turberville to Madison, Apr. 7, 1790: Madison Papers, N.Y. Pub. Lib. Monroe to
Madison, July 2, 1790: Monroe, *Writings,* I, 208-9.
[3] To David Stuart, June 15, 1790: Washington, *Writings,* XXXI, 49 ff.
[4] Tench Coxe to Hamilton, Mar. 5, 1790: Hamilton, *Works* (J. C. Hamilton, ed.), V, 455-6.
[5] To King, Jan. 24, 1790: King Papers, N.Y. Hist. Soc. Gore, it seems,
had his own reasons for wanting assumption to pass. He had become rich by
speculations in the public funds and stood to lose heavily in paper values if
assumption failed (J. Q. Adams to John Adams, Sept. 21, 1790: J. Q. Adams,
Writings, I, 56-9).
[6] *Annals of Cong.,* II, 1312-13.
[7] *Ibid.,* II, 1411.
[8] *Ibid.,* II, 1342, 1387-90.
[9] *Ibid.,* II, 1395, 1418.
[10] *Ibid.,* II, 1428-32.
[11] Maclay, *Journal,* 222, 224.
[12] Ames to Minot, Mar. 23, 1790: Ames, *Works,* I, 75. Jonathan Trumbull to Wadsworth, Mar. 21, 1790: Wadsworth Papers, Conn. Hist. Soc.
[13] To John Adams, Apr. 5, 1790: J. Q. Adams, *Writings,* I, 49-54.
[14] Maclay, *Journal,* 228.
[15] *Annals of Cong.,* II, 1577-8.
[16] Maclay, *Journal,* 229.
[17] *Annals of Cong.,* II, 1587-92.
[18] Craigie to Parker, May 8, 1790: Craigie Papers, Amer. Antiquar. Soc.
[19] Craigie to Samuel Rogers, Aug. 18, 1790: *ibid.*
[20] To Thomas Dwight, June 11, 1790: Ames, *Works,* I, 79-81.
[21] Jefferson, *Works* (Fed. ed.), I, 173.
[22] To T. M. Randolph; *ibid.,* VI, 47.
[23] Maclay, *Journal,* 284-5.
[24] Jefferson, *Works* (Fed. ed.), I, 173-7. The other three members who
changed their votes were Thomas Sumter of S.C. and Daniel Carroll and
George Gale of Md. (*The Papers of John Steele,* I, 74).
[25] Ames to Minot, June 23, 1790: Ames, *Works,* I, 81-3.
[26] King's Notes, June 30, 1790: King Papers, N.Y. Hist. Soc.
[27] Maclay, *Journal,* 318-19.
[28] *Ibid.,* 344-5.
[29] To Rush, June 17, 1790: "A Survey of Benjamin Rush Papers" by Lyman
Butterfield, in the *Pa. Mag. of Hist.,* v. 70 (1946), 101-2.
[30] To T. M. Randolph, June 20, 1790: Jefferson, *Works* (Fed. ed.), VI,
75-8. To the same effect to Monroe, June 20, 1790: *ibid.,* VI, 78-81. To
George Gilmer, June 27, 1790; *ibid.,* VI, 83-4, adding as another "sweetener"

that Virginia's possession of the capital "will vivify our agriculture and commerce by circulating thro' the state an additional sum every year of half a million of dollars." To John Harvie, July 25, 1790: *ibid.*, VI, 107-9. So that it cannot be said that Jefferson did not know what he was about.

31 June 17, 1790: Madison, *Writings*, VI, 16 n.

32 To his father, June 31, 1790: *ibid.*, VI, 19 n.

33 To Thomas Dwight, July 25, 1790: Ames, *Works*, I, 86-7.

34 *Annals of Cong.*, II, 1686-7.

35 *Ibid.*, II, 1624-5, 1662, 1672, 1676, 1678-80, 1710-12.

36 July 3, 1790: Jefferson Papers, LC., v. 56, p. 9544.

37 To T. M. Randolph, Aug. 14, 1790: *ibid.*, v. 57, p. 9711.

38 *Journal of the Va. House of Delegates* (1790), 35.

39 *Ibid.*, 80-1.

40 Nov. 13, 1790: Wm. Jay, *John Jay*, II, 202. Jay to Hamilton, Nov. 28, 1790: Jay, *Correspondence* (H. P. Johnston, ed.), III, 409-10. Others besides Hamilton expressed alarm. See Benjamin Lincoln to Hamilton, Dec. 4, 1790: Hamilton, *Works* (J. C. Hamilton, ed.), V, 460-2.

41 To Monroe, Feb. 16, 1791: Monroe Papers, LC., v. 1, p. 179.

42 *Gazette of the U.S.*, May 22, 1790: quoting the *Pennsylvania Journal*.

43 *Ibid.*, Feb. 19, 1791.

44 To Monroe, July 11, 1790: Monroe Papers, N.Y. Pub. Lib.

CHAPTER 8

(Notes refer to text pages 122-142.)

1 David Stuart to Washington, Mar. 15, 1790: Washington, *Writings*, XXXI, 28 n.

2 Washington to Stuart, Mar. 28, 1790: *ibid.*, XXXI, 28-30.

3 Bond to Duke of Leeds, Nov. 10, 1789: *Amer. Hist. Assoc. Ann. Rept. for 1896*, v. 1, p. 642.

4 *Gazette of the U.S.*, June 2, 1790.

5 *Annals of Cong.*, II, 972-6.

6 To Gen. Gates, Mar. 13, 1790: Emmett Coll., N.Y. Pub. Lib.

7 To Wm. Short, May 27, 1790: Jefferson, *Works* (Fed. ed.), VI, 58.

8 Washington, *Writings*, XXXI, 93 n. Moses Seixas, head of the Newport Congregation, wrote the phrase which Washington copied practically verbatim: "A government, which to bigotry gives no sanction—to persecution no assistance." (Quoted in *Gazette of the U.S.*, Sept. 15, 1790.)

9 Adams, *Works*, VI, 233-4.

10 *Ibid.*, VI, 249-52, 277-9, 243.

11 *Ibid.*, VI, 399.

12 To Rush, Apr. 18, 1790: *ibid.*, IX, 565-7. To Sam Adams, Oct. 18, 1790: Sam Adams Papers, Bancroft Transcripts, N.Y. Pub. Lib.

13 Facsimile in Haraszti, *John Adams and the Prophets of Progress*, 82. Adams, *Works*, VI, 223-5.

14 Wm. Grayson to Patrick Henry, Sept. 29, 1789: quoted in Warren, *Supreme Court*, I, 12-13.

[15] To Iredell, Mar. 19, 1792: McRae, *Iredell*, II, 344.

[16] Aug. 9, 1792: *ASP: Misc.*, I, 51-2.

[17] *Conn. Courant*, May 9, 1791. *Gazette of the U.S.*, May 16, 1792.

[18] Warren, *Supreme Court*, I, 67-8.

[19] *National Gazette*, Apr. 16, 19, 1792.

[20] Phila. *General Advertiser*, Apr. 20, 21, 1792.

[21] Elbridge Gerry in the course of the debate on the right of the President to remove Cabinet officers without the Senate's consent. Madison, Page, Baldwin and White agreed with him: *Annals of Cong.*, I, 372-83.

[22] Feb., 1793: *Chisholm vs. Georgia*, 2 Dallas Reports, 419.

[23] Jefferson Papers, LC., v. 54, p. 9162.

[24] July 17, 1790: Misc. Letters, Dept. of State, Nat. Archives.

[25] These excerpts are taken from the Boston *Independent Chronicle*, Apr. 22, May 6, 13, 1790. But they can be duplicated from other papers.

[26] Boston *Gazette*, Sept. 7, 1789.

[27] *Columbian Centinel*, Apr. 16, 1791.

[28] Jefferson, *Works* (Fed. ed.), XII, 395.

[29] To Francis Eppes, July 4, 1790: *ibid.*, VI, 84-6. To Monroe, July 11, 1790: *ibid.*, VI, 88-90. To T. M. Randolph, Aug. 29, 1790: Jefferson Papers, LC., v. 57, p. 9756.

[30] To T. M. Randolph, May 30, 1790: Jefferson, *Works* (Fed. ed.), VI, 64.

[31] [July 12, 1790]: *ibid.*, VI, 90-5.

[32] Stephen Cottrell to Grenville, Apr. 17, 1790: *Amer. Hist. Rev.*, v. 8 (1903), pp. 78-86.

[33] Leeds to Morris, Apr. 28, 1790: Morris to Leeds, Apr. 30, 1790: Brit. State Papers, Ford Transcripts, N.Y. Pub. Lib.

[34] May 1, 1790: Washington Papers, LC., v. 246, p. 78.

[35] To Washington, Nov. 22, 1790: *ibid.*, v. 248, pp. 36-8.

[36] Washington to Morris, Oct. 13, 1789: Washington, *Writings*, XXX, 439-42.

[37] Bond to Leeds, Sept. 18, 1790: *Amer. Hist. Assoc. Ann. Rept. for 1897*, 462-4.

[38] Morris to Washington, May 29, 1790: *ASP: For. Rel.*, I, 123-5.

[39] To Thomas Pinckney, June 11, 1792: Jefferson, *Works* (Fed. ed.), VII, 104-9.

[40] Jefferson to Humphreys, Aug. 11, 1790: *ibid.*, VI, 118-20.

[41] Humphreys to Washington, Oct. 31, 1790: Washington Papers, LC., v. 248, pp. 6-7.

[42] *Annals of Cong.*, II, 1656.

[43] George Chalmers, *Opinions on Interesting Subjects of Public Law and Commercial Policy arising from American Independence* (London, 1784).

[44] *Annals of Cong.*, II, 1657.

[45] Bemis, *Jay's Treaty*, 64.

[46] Hamilton to Washington, July 8, 22, 1790: Hamilton, *Works* (Lodge ed.), IV, 296-9, 299-302.

[47] Washington, *Diaries*, IV, 139.

[48] Aug. 27, 1790: Washington, *Writings*, XXXI, 102.

[49] Bemis, *Jay's Treaty*, 76.

[50] Jefferson, *Works* (Fed. ed.), VI, 141-3.
[51] To Edward Rutledge, July 4, 1790: *ibid.*, VI, 86-8.
[52] Hamilton, *Works* (Lodge, ed.), IV, 313-42.
[53] To Washington, Aug. 27, 1790: Washington Papers, LC., v. 247, pp. 53-4. Knox's opinion was much to the same effect, Aug. 29, 1790: *ibid.*, v. 247, pp. 55-6.
[54] Washington to Hamilton, Oct. 30, 1790: Washington MSS., Letter Bk. 23, Communications with the Treasury, LC., p. 23.

CHAPTER 9

(Notes refer to text pages 143-159.)

[1] Dec. 17, 1790: Washington, *Writings*, XXXI, 172-4. Jefferson agreed in a summary report, Dec. 15, 1790: Jefferson, *Works* (Fed. ed.), VI, 167-70.
[2] To Carmichael, Aug. 2, 1790: Jefferson, *Works* (Fed. ed.), VI, 111-14. "Considerations on Navigation of the Mississippi," [Aug. 22, 1790]: *ibid.*, VI, 123-31.
[3] Beckwith to Grenville, Nov. 3, 1790: Brit. For. Off. Papers, Public Records Office, London.
[4] Abigail Adams to her sister, Aug. 8, 1790: *New Letters of Abigail Adams*, 56-7. Georgia disliked the treaty, through which 3,000,000 acres claimed by her had been given to the Creeks. Her representative in Congress, James Jackson, had violently if vainly protested the treaty: *Annals of Cong., 1st Cong., 3rd Sess.*, 1793.
[5] Act of July 22, 1790: *Annals of Cong.*, II, 2241-3.
[6] Harry Innes to Knox, July 7, 1790: Innes Papers, LC., v. 19, pp. 40 ff.
[7] Knox to St. Clair, Aug. 23, 1790: *ASP: Indian Aff.*, I, 98-9.
[8] Act of Sept. 29, 1789.
[9] Sept. 25, 1790: *ASP: Indian Aff.*, I, 115.
[10] To Knox, Nov. 4, 1790: *ibid.*, I, 104-6.
[11] Nov. 19, 1790: *Territorial Papers of the U.S.*, II, 310-11.
[12] Rufus Putnam to Washington, Jan. 8, 1791; to Knox, Jan. 8, 1791: *ASP: Ind. Aff.*, I, 121-2, 122.
[13] Scott to Knox, June 28, 1791: *ibid.*, I, 131-2.
[14] The "Yazoo" Act, Dec. 21, 1789: *ibid.*, I, 114.
[15] Report of Jan. 22, 1791: *ibid.*, 112-13.
[16] Oliver Wolcott to his wife, Sept. 7, 1790: George Gibbs, *Memoirs of the Administrations of Washington and Adams*, I, 57.
[17] To her sister, June 9, 1791: *New Letters of Abigail Adams*, 67-9.
[18] Feb. 5, 1792: *ibid.*, 77-8.
[19] Griswold, *Republican Court*, 258-60.
[20] "Additional Report on Public Credit," *ASP: Finance*, I, 64-7.
[21] *Annals of Cong., 1st Cong., 3rd Sess.*, 1842-3.
[22] *Ibid.*, 1846, 1851. Madison wrote privately to the same effect to Edmund Pendleton, Jan. 2, 1791: Madison, *Writings*, VI, 22-5 n. A month later he changed his mind and now called the whiskey tax "displeasing to me, and a greater evil than a direct tax." (To same, Feb. 13, 1791: *ibid.*, VI, 42-4 n.)

23 To Nicholas Lewis, Jan. 11, 1791 [misdated 1790]: Jefferson Papers, LC., v. 53, p. 9062.

24 Dec. 27, 1790: *ASP: Misc.*, I, 20-1.

25 *Annals of Cong., op. cit.*, 1846, 1848, 1884.

26 An excellent account of these earlier disturbances is given in Leland D. Baldwin, *The Whiskey Rebels*. It was estimated that a horse could carry two eight-gallon kegs of the precious dew over the mountains to the Eastern market. Costing fifty cents a gallon to produce, and retailing at a dollar a gallon, each trip netted a total profit of eight dollars; a sizable sum to the moneyless farmers (Hugh Brackenridge, *Hist. of the Western Insurrection in Pa.*, 17). For some unpublished documents on the troubles see the Gallatin Papers, N.Y. Hist. Soc.

27 *ASP: Finance*, I, 67-76.

28 Ames to Thomas Dwight, Dec. 23, 1790: Ames, *Works*, I, 90. Sir John Temple to Duke of Leeds, Jan. 5, 1791: Brit. State Papers, Ford Transcripts, N.Y. Pub. Lib.

29 Prices are taken from the weekly market reports in the *Gazette of the U.S.* On June 8, 1791, the newspaper exulted that "the stocks have risen beyond all experience and all parallel."

30 To Monroe, Jan. 24, 1791: Monroe Papers, LC., v. 1, p. 177.

31 Maclay, *Journal*, 390, 344-5.

32 *Ibid.*, 362-4.

33 *Annals of Cong., op. cit.*, 1891.

34 *Ibid.*, 1892.

35 *Ibid.*, 1896-1902.

36 *Ibid.*, 1903-7.

37 To George Mason, Feb. 4, 1791: Jefferson, *Works* (Fed. ed.), VI, 186.

38 Jefferson, *Works* (Fed. ed.), VI, 197-204.

39 Hamilton, *Works* (Lodge, ed.), III, 445-93.

40 To Nicholas Lewis, Feb. 9, 1791: Jefferson, *Works* (Fed. ed.), VI, 194.

CHAPTER 10

(*Notes refer to text pages 160-178.*)

1 *ASP: Commerce and Navigation*, I, 34-5. For the statistics on 1791, see *ibid.*, I, 38.

2 Voyages of the Ships *Washington* (1790-1), *Mary* (1799) and *America* (1788-90); Constable-Pierrepont Papers, N.Y. Pub. Lib. These papers are indispensable for any economic history of the period.

3 *Ibid.*, including all invoices attached.

4 Before these ventures finally made home port again, the firm of W. Constable & Co. was reorganized under the name of W. & Jas. Constable on the plea of a heavy indebtedness to British merchants (to Phyn, Ellice & Inglis of London, Aug. 4, 1791: *ibid.*). That the reorganization was merely a dodge to eliminate Robert Morris of Philadelphia, who was a silent partner in the old firm, and avoid responsibility for his land speculations as well as those of William Constable himself, may be traced in a series of letters in these Papers,

particularly in W. Constable to Morris, Aug. 22, 30, 1791; to Duer, Oct. 25, 1791. Constable angrily refused to endorse any new notes for Morris; he had done so before, he wrote, and it "nearly involved me in irreparable ruin." For himself, he continued, he had "not dared to announce the dissolution of our late house lest it might have excited people to call on me." Later on, his transactions with the shady William Duer *did* bring about his downfall.

⁵ Reports of Dec. 28, 1790: *ASP: For. Rel.*, I, 100-4, 104-5.

⁶ *Ibid.*, I, 108, 128.

⁷ Report on Cod and Whale Fisheries, Feb. 1, 1791; Jefferson Papers, LC., v. 60, pp. 10412-63. Report on Commercial Intercourse, Mar. 15, 1791; *ibid.*, v. 69, pp. 11914-26.

⁸ Feb. 14, 1791: *ASP: For. Rel.*, I, 121-2.

⁹ Feb. 21, 1791: *ibid.*, I, 128.

¹⁰ Report to Congress, Jan. 18, 1791: Jefferson, *Works* (Fed. ed.), VI, 175-84.

¹¹ Jan. 1, 1791: *ibid.*, VI, 175 n.

¹² Jan. 13, 1791: Hamilton, *Works* (Lodge, ed.), IV, 347-8.

¹³ Beckwith to Grenville, Jan. 23, 1791: Bemis, *Jay's Treaty*, 80-1.

¹⁴ Mar. 29, 1791: Amer. Letters, State Dept., Nat. Arch.

¹⁵ Report on Cod and Whale Fisheries, *supra*.

¹⁶ Bond to Leeds, Mar. 14, 1791: Brit. State Papers, Ford Transcripts, N.Y. Pub. Lib.

¹⁷ See Note 7, *supra*.

¹⁸ To Humphreys, Mar. 15, 1791: Jefferson, *Works* (Fed. ed.), VI, 218-20. To same effect to Carmichael, Mar. 17, 1791, and to Short, Mar. 19, 1791: *ibid.*, VI, 220-2, 222-3.

¹⁹ To Harry Innes, Mar. 13, 1791: *ibid.*, VI, 216-17.

²⁰ Mar. 12, 1791: *ibid.*, VI, 213-15.

²¹ To Jefferson, Aug. 23, 1792: Washington, *Writings*, XXXII, 128-30.

²² Washington to the Senate, Feb. 9, 1790: *ASP: For. Aff.*, I, 90-1.

²³ Mar. 27, 1791: Misc. Letters, Dept. of State, Nat. Arch.

²⁴ To Jefferson, Apr. 1, 1791: *ibid.*

²⁵ Washington, *Diaries*, IV, 154-5.

²⁶ To Washington, Apr. 17, 1791: Jefferson, *Works* (Fed. ed.), VI, 243-7. See also to Monroe, Apr. 17, 1791: Monroe Papers, N.Y. Pub. Lib.

²⁷ To Sir John Sinclair, Aug. 24, 1791: Jefferson, *Writings* (Mont. ed.), VIII, 230-1.

²⁸ July 28, 1791: Jefferson, *Works* (Fed. ed.), VI, 292-7.

²⁹ To Humphreys, June 23, 1791: *ibid.*, VI, 272-4. Hamilton said practically the same thing in a private letter to Goodhue, June 30, 1791: N.Y. Society Lib. MSS.

³⁰ To Washington, Jan. 24, 1790: Washington Papers, LC., v. 245, pp. 102-5.

³¹ Jefferson to Jonathan B. Smith, Apr. 26, 1791: Hanley-Smith Papers, LC.

³² May 8, 1791: Jefferson, *Works* (Fed. ed.), VI, 254-7.

³³ Lear to Washington, May 8, 1791: Washington Papers, LC., v. 250, pp. 73-4. He reported also with some relish that Jefferson's letter would start a

feud with Adams, since the latter had openly expressed his "detestation" of Paine's volume.

³⁴ J. Q. Adams, *Writings,* I, 65-110.

³⁵ *Columbian Centinel,* June 29, 1791, quoting Phila. *Federal Gazette.*

³⁶ To Jefferson, May 12, 1791: Madison, *Writings,* VI, 50-1.

³⁷ July 17, 1791: Jefferson, *Works* (Fed. ed.), VI, 282-5. Adams accepted the explanation, but tartly demanded when and where he had ever advocated a monarchy or hereditary form of government in the United States (July 29, 1791: Adams, *Works,* VIII, 506-9).

³⁸ July 10, 1791: Jefferson, *Works* (Fed. ed.), VI, 280-2.

³⁹ July 28, 1791: *ibid.,* VI, 288-91.

⁴⁰ Jefferson to Madison, July 24, 1791: *ibid.,* VI, 285-6.

⁴¹ For examples see the Anas: *ibid.,* I, 179-80; and the famous one dated Aug. 13, 1791, in which Jefferson claims that Hamilton told him: "I own it is my own opinion, though I do not publish it in Dan and Bersheba, that the present government is not that which will answer the ends of society, by giving stability and protection to its rights, and that it will probably be found expedient to go into the British form." (*Ibid.,* I, 184-5.)

⁴² Feb. 28, 1791: Jefferson, *Writings* (Mont. ed.), VIII, 133.

⁴³ Jefferson to Bache, Apr. 22, 1791: copy in Alderman Lib., Univ. of Va.

⁴⁴ July 21, 1791: Madison Papers, LC., v. 14, p. 28.

CHAPTER 11

(Notes refer to text pages 179-195.)

¹ Gore to King, June 13, 1791: King Papers, N.Y. Hist. Soc.

² Wm. Seton to Hamilton, June 20, 1791: Hamilton Papers, LC.

³ Jefferson to Madison, July 6, 1791: Jefferson, *Works* (Fed. ed.), VI, 277-8. Wm. Constable of New York, who proceeded directly to Philadelphia to subscribe, ran into the same situation and also threatened suit. Eventually he received forty shares. (Constable to Taylor, Aug. 23, 1791, and to Fitzsimons, Oct. 21, 1791: Letter Books of W. & J. Constable, N.Y. Pub. Lib.)

⁴ Jefferson to Madison, July 10, 1791: Jefferson, *Works* (Fed. ed.), VI, 279. To same effect to Monroe, July 10, 1791: Monroe Papers, N.Y. Pub. Lib.

⁵ Madison to Jefferson, July 10, 1791: Madison, *Writings,* VI, 54-6 n.

⁶ J. B. Cutting to P. Colquhoun, Oct. 12, 1791: *Historical Manuscripts Commission: The Manuscripts of J. B. Fortescue,* II, 228.

⁷ To Henry Lee, Aug. 8, 1791: Madison, *Writings,* VI, 58-9 n.

⁸ To Madison, Aug. 14, 1791: Madison Papers, LC., v. 14, p. 47.

⁹ *Columbian Centinel,* Aug. 13, 1791.

¹⁰ *Diary of Ezra Stiles,* III, 425-6.

¹¹ To Edward Rutledge, Aug. 29, 1791: Jefferson, *Works* (Fed. ed.), VI, 307-9.

¹² July 31, 1791: Hamilton, *Works* (J. C. Hamilton, ed.), V, 473-6.

¹³ To King, Aug. 17, 1791: King Papers, N.Y. Hist. Soc.

¹⁴ Aug. 13, 1791.

¹⁵ Aug. 10, 1791.

[16] To Mrs. Rush, Aug. 12, 1791: *Letters of Benjamin Rush*, I, 602-3.

[17] King to Hamilton, Aug. 15, 1791; Hamilton Papers, LC. King did not mention Duer by name, but Hamilton's letter of Aug. 17, 1791, to Duer speaks of the "innuendoes" as applying to him (Hamilton, *Works*, Lodge, ed., IX, 493-4).

[18] Hamilton to Seton, Aug. 15, 16, Sept. 7, 1791: Hamilton, *Works* (Lodge, ed.), IX, 490, 491-2, 495.

[19] *ASP: Finance*, I, 117.

[20] Seton to Hamilton, Sept. 12, 1791: Hamilton, *Works* (J. C. Hamilton, ed.), V, 480.

[21] *Gazette of the U.S.*, Jan. 25, 1792. The 6 per cent debt then commanded a premium of about 30 per cent.

[22] *Ibid.*, Oct. 22, 1791.

[23] The correspondence may be found in the Hamilton Papers, LC., vols. 11 and 12. Excerpts have been printed in Arthur H. Cole, *Industrial and Commercial Correspondence of Alexander Hamilton* (1928).

[24] *ASP: Finance*, I, 123-44.

[25] Jefferson, *Works* (Fed. ed.), IV, 85-6.

[26] *Gazette of the U.S.*, Aug. 31, 1791.

[27] The amazing story of the Society may be read in Schachner, *Hamilton*, chap. 19, and in Joseph S. Davis, *Essays in the Earlier History of American Corporations* (2v., 1917).

[28] To Jefferson, Mar. 4, 1792: Washington, *Writings*, XXXI, 495.

[29] The story of the building of the city of Washington is told in *Thomas Jefferson and the National Capital* (S. K. Padover, ed.).

[30] To Hamilton, Apr. 4, 1791: Washington, *Writings*, XXXI, 273-4.

[31] Apr. 4, 1791: *ibid.*, XXXI, 267-8.

[32] To Monroe: Monroe Papers, N.Y. Pub. Lib.

[33] To Humphreys, July 20, 1791: Washington, *Writings*, XXXI, 317-21. Speech to Cong., Oct. 25, 1791: *ASP: For. Rel.*, I, 16-17.

[34] To Washington, Dec. 4, 31, 1790: Pickering Papers, Mass. Hist. Soc., v. 61, pp. 108, 119.

[35] To Washington, Apr. 10, 1791: Hamilton, *Works* (Lodge, ed.), IX, 478-9.

[36] *National Gazette*, Feb. 2, 1792.

[37] St. Clair to Knox, Nov. 9, 1791: *ASP: Indian Affairs*, I, 137-8.

[38] Gore to King, Dec. 25, 1791: King Papers, N.Y. Hist. Soc.

[39] *Annals of Cong.*, 2nd Cong., 1st Sess., 491-4.

[40] Jefferson, *Works* (Fed. ed.), I, 213-14.

[41] Grenville to Hammond, Mar. 27, 1792: *Amer. Hist. Assoc. Ann. Rept. for 1936*, 25-7.

[42] Hammond to Grenville, June 8, 1792: Brit. State Papers, Ford Transcripts, N.Y. Pub. Lib.

CHAPTER 12
(Notes refer to text pages 196-213.)

[1] Oct. 25, 1791; *ASP: For. Rel.*, I, 16-17.

[2] To Gouverneur Morris, July 28, 1791: Washington, *Writings*, XXXI, 326-30.

[3] *Annals of Cong., 2nd Cong., 1st Sess.*, 148-9.

[4] *Ibid.*, 179, 181.

[5] *Ibid.*, 185.

[6] To Minot, Feb. 20, 1793: Ames, *Works*, I, 128-9.

[7] *Annals of Cong., op. cit.*, 244-6, 248.

[8] Jefferson, *Works* (Fed. ed.), I, 217-18: VI, 460-70. Madison to Pendleton, Mar. 25, 1792: Madison Papers, LC., v. 15, p. 22. To Breckinridge, Apr. 8, 1792: Breckinridge Papers, LC. Veto Message, Apr. 5, 1792: Washington, *Writings*, XXXII, 16-17.

[9] To Minot, Mar. 8, 1792: Ames, *Works*, I, 114-15.

[10] To Henry Lee, Apr. 15, 1792: Madison Papers, LC., v. 15, p. 35.

[11] *Annals of Cong., op. cit.*, 364, 365-6, 393.

[12] *Ibid.*, 441-2.

[13] Draft Instructions: Brit. State Papers, Ford Transcripts, N.Y. Pub. Lib. Public and Private Instructions, July 4, Sept. 2, 1791: *Amer. Hist. Assoc. Ann. Rept. for 1936*, 1-13.

[14] Hammond to Grenville, Jan. 9, Feb. 2, 1792: Brit. State Papers, Ford Transcripts, N.Y. Pub. Lib.

[15] Jefferson, *Works* (Fed. ed.), I, 191.

[16] To Edward Rutledge, Aug. 25, 1791: Rutledge Papers, Pa. Hist. Soc.

[17] To La Motte, Aug. 30, 1791: Jefferson, *Writings* (Mont. ed.), VIII, 238-40.

[18] To Rutledge, *supra*.

[19] Ternant to Hamilton, Sept. 21, 1791: Hamilton, *Works* (J. C. Hamilton, ed.), IV, 174-5. Hamilton to Washington, Sept. 22, 1791: *ibid.*, IV, 175. Jefferson to Short, Nov. 24, 1791: Jefferson, *Works* (Fed. ed.), VI, 329-34.

[20] [Nov. 1791]: Jefferson, *Works* (Fed. ed.), VI, 335-7.

[21] *Ibid.*, VI, 336 n.

[22] To Monroe, Jan. 30, 1792: Monroe Papers, LC., v. 2, p. 190.

[23] To Jefferson, Feb. 13, 1792; Jefferson Papers, LC., v. 70, p. 12242.

[24] King's Notes, Jan. 1792: King Papers, N.Y. Hist. Soc. Jefferson to Archibald Stuart, Mar. 14, 1792: Jefferson, *Works* (Fed. ed.), VI, 407.

[25] To Washington, Jan. 27, 1792: Washington Papers, LC., v. 253, p. 75.

[26] Jan. 28, 1792: Washington, *Writings*, XXXI, 468-70.

[27] Jefferson to Thos. Pinckney, Jan. 17, 1792: Jefferson, *Works* (Fed. ed.), VI, 367.

[28] Nov. 29, 1791: *ibid.*, VI, 338-9.

[29] Nov. 30, 1791: *ASP: For. Rel.*, I, 189.

[30] Dec. 14, 1791: *ibid.*, I, 189.

[31] Dec. 15, 1791: *ibid.*, I, 190.

[32] Mar. 5, 1792: Jefferson Papers, LC., v. 71, pp. 12321-86.

33 Hammond to Grenville, Jan. 9, 1792; Brit. State Papers, Ford Transcripts, N.Y. Pub. Lib. Jefferson suspected in general that Hamilton "communicated to Hammond all our views and knew from him in return the views of the British court." (Jefferson, *Works*, Fed. ed., I, 209.)

34 Mar. 6, 1792: Jefferson Papers, LC., v. 71, p. 12393.

35 Jefferson to Hammond, Feb. 2, 1792: Jefferson, *Works* (Fed. ed.), VI, 383. To G. Morris, Mar. 10, 1792: *ibid.*, VI, 403-4.

36 May 29, 1792: *ASP: For. Rel.*, I, 201-16.

37 June 2, 1792: *ibid.*, I, 237.

38 Hammond to Grenville, June 8, 1792: Brit. State Papers, Ford Transcripts, N.Y. Pub. Lib.

39 Jefferson to Madison, June 1, 1792: Jefferson, *Works* (Fed. ed.), VI, 69.

40 Hammond to Jefferson, Nov. 22, 1793; *ASP: For. Rel.*, I, 238.

41 Hammond to Grenville, Apr. 14, 1792: Brit. State Papers, Ford Transcripts, N.Y. Pub. Lib.

42 June 16, 1792: Jefferson, *Works* (Fed. ed.), VII, 111-13.

43 To Madison, June 29, 1792: *ibid.*, VII, 129-31.

44 "Report on Negotiations with Spain," [Mar. 18, 1792]: *ibid.*, VII, 414-45.

45 Gardoqui to Floridablanca, Aug. 22, 1791: Bemis, *Pinckney's Treaty*, 181-2.

46 Mar. 18, 1792: Jefferson, *Works* (Fed. ed.), VI, 411-14.

47 Anas: *ibid.*, I, 237-40.

CHAPTER 13

(Notes refer to text pages 211 229.)

1 Henry Remsen to Jefferson, Apr. 23, 1792: Jefferson Papers, LC., v. 73, pp. 12722-8. Madison to Pendleton, Mar. 25, 1792: Madison Papers, LC., v. 15, p. 22. James Watson to Jeremiah Wadsworth, Mar. 14, 1792: Wadsworth Papers, Conn. Hist. Soc.

2 Duer to Wadsworth, Mar. 12, 1792: Wadsworth Papers, Conn. Hist. Soc.

3 Wolcott to Richard Harrison, Mar. 17, 1792: Wolcott Papers, Conn. Hist. Soc.

4 Mar. 14, 1792: Hamilton, *Works* (Lodge, ed.), IX, 502-3.

5 Remsen to Jefferson, *supra*.

6 Hamilton to Duer, Apr. 22, 1792: Hamilton, *Works* (J. C. Hamilton, ed.), V, 506-7. Watson to Wadsworth, Apr. 3, 1792: Wadsworth Papers, Conn. Hist. Soc.

7 Jefferson to T. M. Randolph, Apr. 19, 1792: Jefferson, *Works* (Fed. ed.), VI, 480-1.

8 To Remsen, Apr. 14, 1792: Jefferson Papers, Univ. of Va.

9 Jefferson to Short, Mar. 18, 1792: Jefferson, *Works* (Fed. ed.), VI, 413.

10 Hamilton to Seton, Mar. 25, Apr. 4, 12, 1792: Hamilton, *Works* (Lodge, ed.), IX, 503-5, 506-7, 507. Seton to Hamilton, Mar. 26, Apr. 16, 1792: Hamilton, *Works* (J. C. Hamilton, ed.), V, 500-1, 505. Same to same, Apr. 9, 1792: Hamilton Papers, LC., v. 15, p. 2098.

[11] To Hamilton, June 10, 1792: Hamilton, *Works* (J. C. Hamilton, ed.), V, 511.

[12] *National Gazette,* Jan. 16, 26, Mar. 15, May 7, 1792.

[13] Jefferson, *Works* (Fed. ed.), I, 227-31.

[14] A copy is in Hamilton, *Works* (Lodge, ed.), VII, 229.

[15] *Gazette of the U.S.,* Aug. 11-18, 1792.

[16] Some of Hamilton's protean disguises may be conveniently examined in his *Works* (Lodge, ed.), VII, 230-301.

[17] To Jefferson, Aug. 23, 1792; to Hamilton, Aug. 26, 1792: Washington, *Writings,* XXXII, 130-1, 132-4.

[18] To Washington, Sept. 9, 1792: Jefferson, *Works* (Fed. ed.), VII, 136-49.

[19] To Washington, Sept. 9, 1792: Hamilton, *Works* (Lodge, ed.), VII, 303-6. See Hamilton to Carrington, May 26, 1792 (*ibid.,* IX, 513-35) for a much more specific and detailed account of his grievances against both Jefferson and Madison. He speaks of their "dangerous" views on foreign politics and of their "womanish attachment to France and a womanish resentment against Great Britain." If they had their way, he was convinced, the United States would be at war with England in less than six months.

[20] Hamilton, *Works* (Lodge, ed.), II, 368-407.

[21] Hamilton to Washington, Aug. 10, Sept. 1, 1792: *ibid.,* X, 11; VI, 339-41. Washington to Hamilton, Sept. 7, 1792: Washington, *Writings,* XXXII, 143-5.

[22] Hamilton to Washington, Sept. 9, 11, 1792: Hamilton, *Works* (Lodge, ed.), VI, 342-7. Washington to Jefferson, Sept. 15, 1792; to Hamilton, Sept. 16, 1792: Washington, *Writings,* XXXII, 149-50, 152-3.

[23] To Washington, Sept. 18, 1792: Misc. Letters, Dept. of State, Nat. Arch.

[24] To Thomas Clare, Dec. 18, 1792: Gallatin Papers, N.Y. Hist. Soc.

[25] Madison, *Writings,* VI, 106-10 n. Washington to Madison, May 20, 1792: Washington, *Writings,* XXXII, 45-9.

[26] July 30, 1792: Hamilton, *Works* (Lodge, ed.), X, 7-10.

[27] May 23, 1792: Jefferson, *Works* (Fed. ed.), VI, 487-95. Randolph added his plea to Washington, Aug. 5, 1792: Washington Papers, LC., v. 255, p. 86.

[28] King to Hamilton, July 10, 1792: Hamilton Papers, LC., v. 16, p. 2224. Hamilton to King, June 28, 1792: King Papers, N.Y. Hist. Soc. Same to same, July 25, 1792: Hamilton, *Works* (Lodge, ed.), X, 3-5.

[29] To Monroe, June 23, 1792: Jefferson, *Works* (Fed. ed.), VII, 127-9.

[30] To ——, Sept. 21, 1792: Hamilton, *Works* (Lodge, ed.), X, 19-20.

[31] To ——, Sept. 26, 1792: *ibid.,* X, 21-2. He wrote along similar lines to others.

[32] Breckinridge to his mother, Mar. 18, 1792: Breckinridge Papers, LC., v. 8, p. 1248. G. Thompson to Breckinridge, June 14, 1792: *ibid.,* v. 8, p. 1280.

[33] To Thomas Pinckney, Dec. 3, 1792: Jefferson, *Works* (Lodge, ed.), VII, 191-2.

[34] "Mirabeau" in *National Gazette,* Dec. 12, 1792.

[35] Joseph Jones to Madison, Dec. 24, 1792: Madison Papers, LC., v. 15, p. 108.

CHAPTER 14
(Notes refer to text pages 230-244.)

[1] Jefferson, *Works* (Fed. ed.), I, 250-1.
[2] To Thos. Dwight, Jan. 1793: Ames, *Works*, I, 126-7.
[3] MSS. Memo: Madison Papers, LC., v. 15, p. 114.
[4] Hamilton's Report, Feb. 4, 1793; *ASP: Finance*, I, 192-4.
[5] *Annals of Cong., 2nd Cong., 2nd Sess.*, 895.
[6] Draft Resolutions: Jefferson, *Works* (Fed. ed.), VII, 220-3.
[7] *Annals of Cong., op. cit.*, 901.
[8] *Ibid.*, 910-14.
[9] *Ibid.*, 955-63.
[10] Jefferson, *Works* (Fed. ed.), I, 262: VII, 252-4.
[11] To King, Oct. 11, 1792: King Papers, N.Y. Hist. Soc.
[12] *Columbian Centinel*, Nov. 7, 1792.
[13] *National Gazette*, Dec. 19, 1792.
[14] *Ibid.*, Dec. 26, 1792. *Columbian Centinel*, Jan. 9, 26, 1793. The description of the Boston festivities is a composite from several Boston papers; a convenient summary is in C. D. Hazen, *Contemporary American Opinion of the French Revolution*, 165-9.
[15] To George Gilmer, Dec. 15, 1792; to J. F. Mercer, Dec. 19, 1792: Jefferson, *Works* (Fed. ed.), VII, 194-5, 195-7.
[16] Jan. 3, 1793: *ibid.*, VII, 202-6.
[17] To Jefferson, Aug. 1, 1792: *ASP: For. Rel.*, I, 332.
[18] Morris to Jefferson, Aug. 22, 1792: *ibid.*, I, 336.
[19] To Morris, Oct. 15, Nov. 17, 1792: Jefferson, *Works* (Fed. ed.), VII, 162-3, 175-6.
[20] *Columbian Centinel*, Mar. 30, 1793.
[21] To ——, Mar. 18, 1793: Jefferson, *Writings* (Mont. ed.), IX, 45.
[22] *Independent Chronicle*, Apr. 19, 1793. *National Gazette*, Apr. 20, 1793.
[23] *National Gazette*, Dec. 26, 1792.
[24] *Boston Gazette*, Jan. 21, 1793.
[25] *Columbian Centinel*, Mar. 16, 1793. John Adams was indignant that "our countrymen are about to abandon the good old, grave, solid manners of Englishmen, their ancestors, and adopt all the apery, levity, and frivolity of the French." (Jan. 31, 1793; *Letters to his Wife*, II, 123-4.)
[26] To Humphreys, Mar. 23, 1793: Washington, *Writings*, XXXII, 398-400.
[27] "Questions to Cabinet," Apr. 18, 1793: *ibid.*, XXXII, 419-20.
[28] Jefferson, *Works* (Fed. ed.), I, 267-9.
[29] Washington to Hamilton and Jefferson, Apr. 12, 1793: Washington, *Writings*, XXXII, 415-16, 416. Hamilton to Jay, Apr. 9, 1793 (two letters): Hamilton, *Works* (Lodge, ed.), X, 38-9. Jay to Hamilton, Apr. 11, 1793: Hamilton, *Works* (J. C. Hamilton, ed.), V, 552-3.
[30] Hammond to Grenville, Mar. 7, Apr. 2, 1793: Brit. State Papers, Ford Transcripts, N.Y. Pub. Lib.
[31] Jefferson to Madison, June 23, 1793: Jefferson, *Works* (Fed. ed.), VII, 407-8.

[32] Jefferson to Morris, Mar. 12, 1793: *ibid.*, VII, 259.
[33] Hamilton to Washington, Apr. 1793: Hamilton, *Works* (Lodge, ed.), IV, 369-96.
[34] Anas: Jefferson, *Works* (Fed. ed.), I, 268. Cabinet Opinion, Apr. 28, 1793: *ibid.*, VII, 283-301.
[35] Washington, *Writings*, XXXII, 430-1.
[36] *United States: Treaties, Conventions,* etc. (W. M. Malloy, ed.), I, 468-79.
[37] Jefferson to Madison, Mar. [25], 1793: Jefferson, *Works* (Fed. ed.), VII, 250-2.

CHAPTER 15
(Notes refer to text pages 245-267.)

[1] Jefferson to Madison, Mar. [25], 1793: Jefferson, *Works* (Fed. ed.), VII, 252.
[2] Minnigerode, *Jefferson, Friend of France,* 145 ff.
[3] *Amer. Hist. Assoc. Ann. Rept. for 1896,* I, 963-7 (in French).
[4] To the French Minister, Feb. 5, 1793; *ibid.*, I, 967-71.
[5] *Passim:* George Rogers Clark Papers, Draper MSS., Univ. of Wisconsin.
[6] To Carmichael and Short, Mar. 23, 1793: Jefferson, *Works* (Fed. ed.), VII, 267-8.
[7] Viar and Jaudenes to Carondelet, Aug. 21, 1793; Blount to Robertson, Jan. 18, 1794: *Amer. Hist. Assoc. Ann. Rept. for 1896,* I, 999-1000, 1036-8.
[8] Minnigerode, *op. cit.,* 145.
[9] *Amer. Hist. Assoc. Ann. Rept. for 1903,* II, 211-13.
[10] Mar. 7, 1793; *ASP: For. Rel.,* I, 354.
[11] Morris to Le Brun, Mar. 24, 28, 1793; Le Brun to Morris, Mar. 26, 29, 1793: *ibid.*, I, 358, 359.
[12] Apr. 23, 1793; Washington Papers, LC., v. 259, pp. 95-6.
[13] Steele to Hamilton, Apr. 30, 1793: Hamilton, *Works* (J. C. Hamilton, ed.), V, 561-2.
[14] To Hamilton, July 26, 1793: *ibid.*, V, 570-2.
[15] J. Q. Adams, *Writings*, I, 135-46.
[16] To Jefferson, May 28, 1793: Monroe, *Writings*, I, 256-60.
[17] To Jefferson, June 27, 1793: *ibid.*, I, 261-7.
[18] *National Gazette,* May 15, June 1, 12, 1793.
[19] To Madison, May 19, 1793: Jefferson, *Works* (Fed. ed.), VII, 336-8.
[20] Jefferson to Monroe, May 5, 1793: *ibid.*, VII, 308-11. To J. W. Eppes, May 12, 1793: Jefferson Papers, Mass. Hist. Soc.
[21] Jefferson to Hammond, May 3, 1793: Jefferson, *Works* (Fed. ed.), VII, 306. To Ternant, May 3, 1793: *ibid.*, VII, 307.
[22] Grenville to Hammond, Mar. 12, 1793: *Amer. Hist. Assoc. Ann. Rept. for 1936,* 36-40.
[23] Jefferson to Hammond, May 15, 1793: Jefferson, *Works* (Fed. ed.), VII, 325-8.
[24] *Ibid.*
[25] To Ternant, May 15, 1793: *ASP: For. Rel.,* I, 147-8.

26 To George Wythe, Apr. 27, 1793: Jefferson, *Works* (Fed. ed.), VII, 282. To Madison, Apr. 28, 1793: *ibid.*, VII, 301-2.

27 Jefferson to Edmund Randolph, May 8, 1793: *ibid.*, VII, 315-19. But Randolph had also ordered U.S. attorneys to watch for and punish violations of neutrality (to Wm. Channing, May 12, 1793: Emmet Coll., N.Y. Pub. Lib.). Hamilton issued a second and sharper instruction to the Collectors on Aug. 4, 1793 (*ASP: For. Rel.*, I, 140-1).

28 *National Gazette*, May 22, 25, 1793.

29 Genêt to Minister of For. Aff., May 18, 1793: *Amer. Hist. Assoc. Ann. Rept. for 1903*, v. 2, pp. 214-5.

30 Genêt to Le Brun, May 31, June 19, 1793: *ibid.*, v. 2, pp. 216, 216-18.

31 Genêt to Jefferson, May 23, 1793: *ASP: For. Rel.*, I, 147.

32 Le Brun to Morris, May 26, 1793: *ibid.*, I, 365.

33 Le Brun to Morris, June 21, 1793: *ibid.*, I, 368.

34 To Monroe, May 5, 1793: Jefferson, *Works* (Fed. ed.), VII, 308-11.

35 To Madison, May 12, 1793: *ibid.*, VII, 323-4.

36 To Madison, Aug. 11, 1793: Madison Papers, LC., v. 16, p. 55.

37 Jefferson, *Works* (Fed. ed.), I, 271-3. Hamilton had already sent his views to Washington, May 15, 1793: Hamilton, *Works* (Lodge, ed.), IV, 408-17.

38 Jefferson, *Works* (Fed. ed.), I, 271-3.

39 *Ibid.*, I, 273-4.

40 *Ibid.*, I, 273 n.

41 May 16, 1793: *ibid.*, VII, 332-5.

42 Jefferson to Hammond, June 5, 1793: *ibid.*, VII, 367-9.

43 Jefferson to Pinckney, June 4, 1793: Franklin Papers, Yale Univ.

44 To Carmichael and Short, May 31, 1793: Jefferson, *Works* (Fed. ed.), VII, 348-52.

45 Genêt to Jefferson, May 27, 1793: *ASP: For. Rel.*, I, 149-50.

46 Jefferson to Genêt, June 5, 1793: *ibid.*, I, 150.

47 Genêt to Jefferson, June 8, 1793: *ibid.*, I, 151.

48 Genêt to Jefferson, June 1, 1793: *ibid.*, I, 151.

49 *Ibid.*

50 Wharton, *State Trials of the U.S.*, 4-88.

51 Jefferson to Richard Harrison, June 12, 1793: Jefferson, *Works* (Fed. ed.), VII, 380-2. Genêt to Jefferson, June 14, 1793: *ASP: For. Aff.*, I, 152.

52 June 17, 1793: *ASP: For. Aff.*, I, 154-5.

53 June 22, 1793: *ibid.*, I, 155-6.

54 June 23, 1793: *ibid.*, I, 159.

55 June 25, 1793: *ibid.*, I, 159.

56 To Minister of For. Aff., June 19, July 31, 1793: *Amer. Hist. Assoc. Ann. Rept. for 1903*, v. 2, pp. 216-18, 231-3.

57 Washington to Henry Lee, July 21, 1793: Washington, *Writings*, XXXIII, 22-4.

58 To Madison, June 9, 1793: Jefferson, *Works* (Fed. ed.), VII, 373-7.

59 *National Gazette*, June 5, 1793.

60 To Jefferson, June 19, 1793: Madison Papers, LC.

61 To Jefferson, June 27, 1793: Jefferson Papers, LC., v. 89, pp. 15316-17.

[62] To Washington, June 24, 1793: Washington Papers, LC., v. 261, p. 36. On the other hand, Gov. Henry Lee of Va. was convinced that nine-tenths of the people applauded the neutrality policy (to Washington, June 14, 1793: *ibid.*, v. 261, p. 7).

[63] Taylor to Jefferson, June 25, 1798; to Monroe, Mar. 25, 1798: *Branch Historical Papers,* v. 2, pp. 268-70.

[64] To Jefferson, June 25, 1798: *supra.* An Inquiry into the Principles and Policy of the Government of the United States (1794), *passim.*

[65] Taylor to Madison, May 11, June 20, 1793: *Branch Historical Papers,* v. 2, 253-4, 254-8.

[66] E. T. Mudge, *The Social Philosophy of John Taylor of Caroline,* 2.

[67] W. & J. Constable to Phyn, Ellice & Inglis, May 4, 1793: Constable-Pierrepont Papers, N.Y. Pub. Lib. *Gazette of the U.S.,* May 8, 1793.

CHAPTER 16

(Notes refer to text pages 268-289.)

[1] Jefferson to Monroe, June 28, 1793: Jefferson, *Works* (Fed. ed.), VII, 415-17. To Carmichael and Short, June 30, 1793: *ibid.,* VII, 424-35. To Madison, June 23, 1793: *ibid.,* VII, 407-8.

[2] June 14, 1793: *ibid.,* VII, 388-90.

[3] To Jefferson, June 20, 1793: Washington, *Writings,* XXXII, 507.

[4] June 28, 1793: Jefferson, *Works* (Fed. ed.), VII, 412-13. He also asked Pinckney to demand from the British an order to the West Indies officials putting an end to these practices (June 26, 1793: Jefferson Papers, LC., v. 89, p. 15307).

[5] June 28, 1793 (see note 1 *supra*).

[6] Reprinted in Hamilton, *Works* (Lodge, ed.), IV, 432-89.

[7] July 7, 1793: Jefferson, *Works* (Fed. ed.), VII, 436-7.

[8] To Jefferson, July 30, 1793: Madison, *Writings,* VI, 138-9 n.

[9] *Gazette of the U.S.,* Aug. 24 ff. Reprinted in Madison, *Writings,* VI, 138-88.

[10] Bond to Grenville, June 8, 1793: "Letters of Phineas Bond," *op. cit.,* 528-31. *Gazette of the U.S.,* Aug. 24, 1793.

[11] Statement by Dallas in the Phila. *General Advertiser,* Dec. 9, 1793.

[12] Anas: Jefferson, *Works* (Fed. ed.), I, 282-8.

[13] Cabinet Opinion, July 8, 1793: *ibid.,* VII, 437-43.

[14] Genêt to Jefferson, July 9, 1793: *ASP: For. Rel.,* I, 163.

[15] Washington to Jefferson, July 11, 1793: Washington, *Writings,* XXXIII, 4.

[16] "Copy of a minute given to the President, July 12, 1793": Jefferson Papers, LC., v. 90, p. 15487.

[17] July 12, 1793: Jefferson, *Works* (Fed. ed.), VII, 445-6.

[18] Anas: *ibid.,* I, 291.

[19] Hammond to Grenville, Aug. 18, 1793: Brit. State Papers, Ford Transcripts, N.Y. Pub. Lib.

20 Jefferson to Monroe, July 14, 1793: Jefferson, *Works* (Fed. ed.), VII, 446-50.

21 Jefferson to Madison, July 14, 1793: Jefferson Papers, LC., v. 90, p. 15508.

22 Memorial of York, Va., Sept. 5, 1793: Washington Papers, LC., v. 262, p. 93.

23 Resolutions of Caroline Co., Va., Sept. 10, 1793: *ibid.*, v. 262, p. 101.

24 *Daily Advertiser,* Aug., 1793: reprinted in Hamilton, *Works* (Lodge, ed.), V, 17-49.

25 Monroe to Jefferson, July 23, 1793: Jefferson Papers, LC., v. 90, pp. 15562-3.

26 Jefferson to Madison, Aug. 11, 1793 (2nd letter): Madison Papers, LC., v. 16, p. 55.

27 Anas: Jefferson, *Works* (Fed. ed.), I, 305-8.

28 Jefferson to Madison, Aug. 11, 1793: Madison Papers, LC., v. 16, p. 55.

29 Madison to Jefferson, Sept. 2, 1793: Madison, *Writings,* VI, 190-7.

30 Deforgues to Genêt, July 30, 1793: Minnigerode, *op. cit.,* 278-80.

31 Aug. 16, 1793: Jefferson, *Works* (Fed. ed.), VII, 475-507.

32 To Genêt, Aug. 7, 1793: *ASP: For. Rel.,* I, 167. To Hammond, Sept. 5, 1793: *ibid.,* I, 174-5. To the French Consuls, Sept. 7, 1793: *ibid.,* I, 175.

33 Jefferson to Supreme Court, July 18, 1793: Jefferson, *Works* (Fed. ed.), VII, 451-2, 452-6 n.

34 Jay and Justices to Washington, Aug. 8, 1793: *Correspondence and Public Papers of John Jay,* III, 488-9.

35 Washington to Cabinet Heads, Aug. 3, 1793: Washington, *Writings,* XXXIII, 35-6. "Rules governing Belligerents," Aug. 3, 1793: Jefferson, *Works* (Fed. ed.), VII, 460-1 n. "Cabinet Opinion on Prizes," Aug. 15, 1793: *ibid.,* VII, 474-5.

36 Phila. *General Advertiser,* Aug. 10, 1793.

37 *Ibid.,* Aug. 6, 1793.

38 *Ibid.,* Aug. 6, 1793.

39 *National Gazette,* Aug. 21, 1793.

40 *Amer. Hist. Assoc. Ann. Rept. for 1903,* 238-41.

41 Genêt to Jefferson, Sept. 18, 1793: *ASP: For. Rel.,* I, 172-4.

42 Genêt to Jefferson, July 4, 1797: Minnigerode, *op. cit.,* 413-25.

43 Jefferson to Madison, Sept. 1, 1793: Jefferson, *Works* (Fed. ed.), VIII, 11-14. To Duplaine, Oct. 3, 1793: *ASP: For. Rel.,* I, 178.

44 Jefferson to Gov. Lee, Sept. 13, 1793: Misc. MSS., Mo. Hist. Soc.

45 Jefferson to T. M. Randolph, Nov. 2, 1793: Jefferson, *Works* (Fed. ed.), VIII, 57.

46 Sept. 22, 1793: *ibid.,* VIII, 48-9.

47 Jefferson to Washington, Oct. 3, 1793: *ibid.,* VIII, 52-4. Cabinet Decision [Nov. 23, 1793]; *ibid.,* VIII, 74-6.

48 Dr. Rush to his wife, Aug. 21, 1793: *Old Family Letters, Series B,* 3-5.

49 Aug. 25, 1793: *ibid.,* 5-7.

50 Aug. 29, Sept. 4, 5, 1793: *ibid.,* 9-11, 15-17.

51 Sept. 6, 1793: *ibid.,* 17-19.

52 Sept. 25, 1793: *ibid.,* 44-6.

[53] Sept. 6, 1793, *supra.* Wolcott to his father, Sept. 12, 1793: Gibbs, *Memoirs,* I, 110.

[54] Rush to his wife, Oct. 27, 28, 1793: *Old Family Letters, Ser. B,* 86-8, 88-90.

CHAPTER 17

(Notes refer to text pages 290-308.)

[1] Knox to Washington, Sept. 18, 24, 1793: Washington Papers, LC., v. 263, pp. 4, 8.

[2] Washington to Jefferson, Oct. 11, 1793: Washington, *Writings,* XXXIII, 116-18.

[3] Jefferson to Madison, Nov. 2, 17, 1793: Jefferson, *Works* (Fed. ed.), VIII, 58-9, 72-3.

[4] To Congress, June 2, 1794: *ASP: Ind. Aff.,* I, 482. See also Knox to Gov. Edward Telfair, June 10, Sept. 5, 1793, sharply disapproving of Georgia's plans to invade Creek territory in force (*ibid.,* I, 364, 365-6).

[5] "Roster of U.S. Troops," Dec. 24, 1793: *ibid.,* I, 360. Wayne to Knox, Oct. 5, 1793: *ibid.,* I, 360-1.

[6] "Remonstrance of the Citizens West of the Allegany Mountains," 1793: Breckinridge Papers, LC., v. 10, p. 1603.

[7] Short to Secretary of State, Jan. 21, 1794; *ASP: For. Rel.,* I, 445-6.

[8] To Jefferson: *ibid.,* I, 238.

[9] Jefferson to Pinckney, Sept. 7, 1793: *ibid.,* I, 239-40.

[10] Hammond to Grenville, July 7, 1793: British State Papers, Ford Transcripts, N.Y. Pub. Lib. The Order of Nov. 6, 1793, completed Hamilton's disillusionment, and he now advocated fortification of the seaports and the raising of an army of 30,000 men (to Washington: Hamilton, *Works,* J. C. Hamilton, ed., IV, 506).

[11] *ASP: For. Rel.,* I, 21-3.

[12] *Ibid.,* I, 141-2.

[13] *Ibid.,* I, 247.

[14] To House of Representatives, Dec. 16, 1793: *ibid.,* I, 300-304.

[15] "Opinion on Neutral Trade," Dec. 20, 1793: Jefferson, *Works* (Fed. ed.), VIII, 120-4.

[16] *Annals of Cong., 3rd Cong., 1st Sess.,* 155-6.

[17] Constable to Hugh Goodair & Co., Jan. 17, 1794; to James Diant, Jan. 22, 1794; to Shaw & Inglis, Mar. 14, 1794: Constable-Pierrepont Papers, N.Y. Pub. Lib.

[18] *Gazette of the U.S.,* July 17, 1793.

[19] Phila. *General Advertiser,* Dec. 2, 1793.

[20] Boston *Independent Chronicle,* Mar. 1794: reporting meeting of Oct. 1793.

[21] *Ibid.,* Apr. 18, 1794.

[22] Washington Co. Democratic Soc. to Kentucky Democratic Soc., Apr. 8, 1794: Innes Papers, LC., v. 19, p. 114.

[23] At the time of the greatest excitement over the appointment of Jay as special envoy to England, the Society of Prince William Co., Va., could muster

only twenty-two members, with eighteen voting for the resolutions (June 7, 1794; Innes Papers, LC., v. 19, p. 124).

24 Jefferson, *Works* (Fed. ed.), I, 305-8.

25 To Henry Lee, Oct. 16, 1793; to R. H. Lee, Oct. 24, 1793: Washington, *Writings*, XXXIII, 132-3, 137-8.

26 *Columbian Centinel*, Jan. 22, 1794. Henry Wansey, *An Excursion to the United States of North America in 1794*, 23.

27 *Annals of Cong., op. cit.*, 177-209.

28 To Madison, Apr. 3, 1794: Jefferson, *Works* (Fed. ed.), VIII, 141.

29 Notes of "View of commercial relations of Great Britain and France in reference to U.S." [1794]; Hamilton Papers, LC., v. 23, pp. 3245-51.

30 *Annals of Cong., op. cit.*, 209-25.

31 *Ibid.*, 418-21, 425, 426.

32 *Ibid.*, 433, 436, 438, 497-8.

33 To Jefferson, Mar. 26, 1794: Madison, *Writings*, VI, 210-11.

34 To Gore, Feb. 25, 1794: Ames, *Works*, I, 135-6. He also inveighed against Hammond as petulant, imprudent and liable, with Republican cross-fire, to start a war (to Gore, Mar. 5, 1794: *ibid.*, I, 137-9).

35 To King, Mar. 2, 23, 1794: King Papers, N.Y. Hist. Soc.

36 Gore to King, Mar. 15, 1794: *ibid.*

37 J. G. Jefferson to Monroe, Mar. 22, 1794: Monroe Papers, LC., v. 2, p. 247.

38 Grenville to Hammond, Jan. 10, 1794: *Amer. Hist. Assoc. Ann. Rept. for 1936*, 47-9.

39 Hammond to Grenville, Apr. 17, 1794: Brit. State Papers, Ford Transcripts, N.Y. Pub. Lib.

40 *Annals of Cong., op. cit.*, 561, 566.

41 *Ibid.*, 566-7.

42 *Ibid.*, 89-90.

43 Randolph to Hammond, May 20, 1794: ASP: For. Rel., I, 461-2.

44 Hammond to Randolph, May 22, 1794: *ibid.*, I, 462-3.

45 Schuyler to King, Mar. 23, 1794: King Papers, N.Y. Hist. Soc.

46 To Gov. Clinton, Mar. 31, 1794: Washington, *Writings*, XXXIII, 310-11.

47 To Knox, Apr. 4, 1794: *ibid.*, XXXIII, 330-2.

48 Constable to Forsyth, Richardson & Co., Apr. 5, 1794: Constable-Pierrepont Papers, N.Y. Pub. Lib.

49 Constable to Geo. C. Fox & Sons, Apr. 16, 1794: *ibid.*

50 Randolph to Congress, Mar. 5, 1794: ASP: For. Rel., I, 423-4.

51 Shelby to Jefferson, Jan. 13, 1794: *ibid.*, I, 455-6.

52 "Cabinet Note," Mar. 10, 1794: Washington Papers, LC., v. 265, p. 136.

53 Randolph to Washington, Mar. 11, 1794: *ibid.*, v. 265, p. 139.

54 Randolph to Shelby, Mar. 29, 1794: ASP: For. Rel., I, 456-7.

55 Carondelet to Alcudia, July 30, 1794; Gayoso to Alcudia, Sept. 19, 1794: *Amer. Hist. Assoc. Ann. Rept. for 1896*, 1069-70, 1079-81.

56 Randolph to Washington, Feb. 23, 1794: Washington Papers, LC., v. 265, p. 96.

57 Randolph to Washington, Jan. 26, 1794: *ibid.*, v. 265, p. 16.

58 To Morris, June 25, 1794: ASP: For. Rel., I, 410.

[59] Morris to Jefferson, Jan. 21, Mar. 6, 1794: *ibid.*, I, 402-3, 404-5.
[60] Monroe to Randolph, Nov. 7, 1794: *ibid.*, I, 656.
[61] Monroe to Madison, Jan. 20, 1796: Monroe, *Writings*, II, 440-7.

CHAPTER 18

(Notes refer to text pages 309-332.)

[1] Henry Adams, *Gallatin*, 88.
[2] Hamilton to Washington, Mar. 24, 1794: Hamilton, *Works* (Lodge, ed.),
III, 183-4. Washington to Hamilton, Apr. 8, 1794: *ibid.*, III, 190.
[3] *Annals of Cong.*, *3rd Cong.*, *1st Sess.*, 47, 57.
[4] Feb. 23, 1794: *Letters of John Adams to his wife*, II, 143-4.
[5] To Samuel Phillips, Mar. 8, 1794: Lodge, *Cabot*, 75-7.
[6] To Gore, Mar. 26, 1794: Ames, *Works*, I, 139-41.
[7] King's Memorandum; a copy of the lost original is in Hamilton Papers,
LC., v. 22, pp. 3018-39. Printed with variations in King, *King*, I, 517-23.
[8] Apr. 8, 1794: Monroe, *Writings*, I, 291-2.
[9] Apr. 6, 1794: Washington Papers, LC., v. 266, pp. 68-9.
[10] Madison to Jefferson, Apr. 14, 1794: Madison Papers, LC., v. 17, p. 51.
[11] Randolph to Washington, Apr. 9, 1794: Washington Papers, LC., v. 266,
p. 72.
[12] Apr. 9, 1794: Washington, *Writings* (W. C. Ford, ed.), XII, 415.
[13] Monroe to Washington, Apr. 11, 1794: Washington Papers, LC., v. 266,
p. 80 (photostat).
[14] Hamilton to Washington, Apr. 14, 1794: Hamilton, *Works* (Lodge, ed.),
V, 97-115.
[15] To Jefferson, Apr. 28, 1794: Madison Papers, LC., v. 17, p. 57.
[16] To Jefferson, May 4, 1794: Monroe, *Writings*, I, 292-6.
[17] Phila. *General Advertiser*, Mar. 21, 1794.
[18] Hammond to Grenville, Apr. 17, 1794: Brit. State Papers, Ford Transcripts, N.Y. Pub. Lib.
[19] King's Memorandum, *supra*. Senator John Taylor of Virginia was convinced from private conversations with King, Izard and Smith, all Federalists,
that the Northern states intended to dissolve the Union (Taylor, *Disunion
Sentiment in Congress in 1794*, ed. by G. Hunt, 1905).
[20] King's Memorandum.
[21] *Ibid.*
[22] Apr. 23, 1794: Hamilton, *Works* (Lodge, ed.), V, 115-23.
[23] Randolph to Washington, Apr. 19, 1794: Washington Papers, LC., v.
266, p. 100.
[24] To Washington, May 6, 1794: *ibid.*, v. 266, p. 143.
[25] "Instructions," May 6, 1794: *ASP: For. Rel.*, I, 472-4.
[26] To Jefferson, Apr. 28, 1794: Madison, *Writings*, VI, 211-12.
[27] John Breckinridge's account, May 29, 1794: Breckinridge Papers, LC.,
v. 10, p. 1698. A similar ceremony was held in New York: *N.Y. Journal*,
Aug. 2, 1794.

[28] To Grenville, May 25, 1794: Brit. State Papers, Ford Transcripts, N.Y. Pub. Lib.

[29] Randolph to Hammond, May 1, June 2, 1794: *ASP: For. Rel.*, I, 450-4, 464-8.

[30] To R. H. Lee, Apr. 15, 1794: Washington, *Writings*, XXXIII, 330-2.

[31] Wansey, *An Excursion to the U.S. in 1794*, 110, 113, 118-21, 123-4.

[32] *Ibid.*, 20, 32, 36.

[33] Fauchet to Randolph, Mar. 1, 2, 1794; Randolph to Fauchet, Mar. 12, 1794; Fauchet to Randolph, Mar. 12, 1794: *ASP: For. Rel.*, I, 427-8.

[34] Accounts of the French refugees may be found in F. S. Childs, *French Refugee Life in the United States*, and in Moreau de St. Méry's *Travels*.

[35] Washington to Jay, Apr. 29, 1794: Washington, *Writings*, XXXIII, 345-6. To R. R. Livingston, May 14, 1794: *ibid.*, XXXIII, 364. Monroe to Jefferson, May 27, 1794: Monroe, *Writings*, I, 299-301.

[36] Randolph to Monroe, June 10, 1794: *ASP: For. Rel.*, I, 668-9.

[37] Fauchet to Minister of For. Aff., June 4, 1794: *Amer. Hist. Assoc. Ann. Rept. for 1903*, 372-7.

[38] *Pittsburgh Gazette*, Apr. 26, 1794.

[39] *Gazette of the U.S.*, July 25, 1794.

[40] H. H. Brackenridge, *Incidents of the Western Insurrection*, I, 86; III, 149.

[41] *Gazette of the U.S.*, Aug. 1, 1794.

[42] *Columbian Centinel*, Sept. 10, 1794.

[43] *Gazette of the U.S.*, Aug. 1, 1794. The best accounts of the "Rebellion" are in H. H. Brackenridge, *op. cit.*, and L. D. Baldwin, *Whiskey Rebels*.

[44] To Grenville, Aug. 29, 1794: Brit. State Papers, Ford Transcripts, N.Y. Pub. Lib.

[45] *ASP: Finance*, I, 280.

[46] To Washington, Aug. 2, 1794: Hamilton, *Works* (Lodge, ed.), VI, 353-8.

[47] Aug. 5, 7, 1794: *ibid.*, VI, 388, 389-94.

[48] Randolph to Mifflin, Aug. 7, 1794: *ibid.*, VI, 394-408.

[49] To Dwight, Sept. 11, 1794: Ames, *Works*, I, 149-51.

[50] *Columbian Centinel*, Aug. 23, 1794.

[51] Sept. 19, 1794: Hamilton, *Works* (Lodge, ed.), VI, 441-2.

[52] *Gazette of the U.S.*, Aug. 7, Sept. 1, 26, 1794.

[53] To Henry Lee, Aug. 26, 1794: Washington, *Writings*, XXXIII, 474-9.

[54] To Chas. H. Thornton, Aug. 19, 1794: *ibid.*, XXXIII, 464-5.

[55] To Burges Ball, Sept. 25, 1794: *ibid.*, XXXIII, 505-7.

[56] Gallatin, *Writings*, I, 4-9.

[57] To Jay, Nov. 1, 1794: Washington, *Writings*, XXXIV, 15-19.

[58] To Hamilton, Oct. 26, 1794: *ibid.*, XXXIV, 8-9.

[59] Dallas to his wife, Oct. 4, 1794: G. M. Dallas, *Dallas*, 33-5. Gallatin to his wife, Dec. 3, 1794: Gallatin Papers, N.Y. Hist. Soc.

[60] Jared Ingersoll to Jasper Yates, Nov. 1, 1794: Emmet Coll., N.Y. Pub. Lib.

[61] To King, Oct. 30, 1794: Hamilton, *Works* (Lodge, ed.), VI, 77.

[62] To his wife, Nov. 8, 1794: Dallas, *Dallas*, 45.

63 To Washington, Nov. 8, 1794: Hamilton, *Works* (Lodge, ed.), VI, 455-6.
64 Gallatin to his wife, June 1, 1795: Gallatin Papers, N.Y. Hist. Soc.

CHAPTER 19

(Notes refer to text pages 333-353.)

1 Wayne to Knox, July 7, 1794: *ASP: Indian Aff.*, I, 487-8.
2 To Jay, Aug. 30, 1794: Washington, *Writings*, XXXIII, 483-5.
3 Grenville to Hammond, Nov. 20, 1794: *Amer. Hist. Assoc. Ann. Rept. for 1936*, 71-3.
4 Wayne to Knox, Aug. 28, 1794: *ASP: Indian Aff.*, I, 491-2.
5 Campbell to Wayne, Aug. 21, 1794; Wayne to Campbell, Aug. 21, 1794; Wayne to Knox: *ibid.*, I, 493-4.
6 To Knox, Oct. 17, 1794: *ibid.*, I, 524-6.
7 Knox to Washington, Dec. 29, 1794: *ibid.*, I, 543-4.
8 Higginson to Hamilton, July 12, 1794: Hamilton, *Works* (J. C. Hamilton, ed.), V, 603-4.
9 Bradford to Secretary of State, July 5, 1794; Hamilton to same, July 8, 1794; Knox to same, July 2, 1794: Washington Papers, LC., v. 267, pp. 142, 145, 149.
10 Randolph to Washington, July 9, 1794: *ibid.*, v. 267, p. 150.
11 Hammond to Grenville, Aug. 3, 1794: Brit. State Papers, Ford Transcripts, N.Y. Pub. Lib.
12 Grenville to Hammond, Oct. 2, 1794: *Amer. Hist. Assoc. Ann. Rept. for 1936*, 67-8.
13 Jay to Randolph, July 6, 1794: *ASP: For. Rel.*, I, 476.
14 Jay to Randolph, July 12, 30, 1794: *ibid.*, I, 479, 480.
15 Jay to Washington, Sept. 13, 1794: *Correspondence of Jay*, IV, 59.
16 Temple to Carmaethen, Dec. 7, 1786: Bemis, *Jay's Treaty*, 206-7.
17 Jay to Randolph, Aug. 8, 1794: *ASP: For. Rel.*, I, 482. Grenville to Hammond, Aug. 8, 1794: *Amer. Hist. Assoc. Ann. Rept. for 1936*, 64-6.
18 Jay to Randolph, Sept. 13, 1794: *ASP: For. Rel.*, I, 485-96.
19 Professor Bemis gives the full text of this draft in Appendix III of his *Jay's Treaty*. It was never made a part of the official documents in the negotiations because, as he points out, the final treaty indicated "a stupendous retreat" from the draft, and any publicity would have embarrassed both Jay and the Federalists (*ibid.*, 243).
20 Jay to Hamilton, Sept. 11, 1794: Hamilton, *Works* (J. C. Hamilton, ed.), V, 27-8.
21 *ASP: For. Rel.*, I, 520-5.
22 Jay to Randolph, Nov. 19, 1794: *ibid.*, I, 503-4.
23 Jay to Hamilton, Nov. 19, 1794: Hamilton, *Works* (J. C. Hamilton, ed.), V, 54.
24 Randolph to Jay, Dec. 3, 15, 1794: *ASP: For. Rel.*, I, 509, 509-12.
25 Jay to Randolph, Feb. 6, 1795: *ibid.*, I, 518.
26 Monroe to Madison, Sept. 2, 1794: Madison Papers, LC., v. 17, p. 82. *ASP: For. Rel.*, I, 688.

27 Randolph to Monroe, Dec. 2, 1794: *ASP: For. Rel.,* I, 689-90.
28 Monroe to Com. of Pub. Safety, Sept. 3, 1794: *ibid.,* I, 676-8.
29 Monroe to Randolph, Jan. 13, 1795: *ibid.,* I, 691-2.
30 Randolph to Monroe, Sept. 25, 1794: *ibid.,* I, 678.
31 Monroe to Madison, Nov. 30, 1794: Monroe, *Writings,* II, 130-40.
32 Jay to Monroe, Nov. 24, 1794: Monroe Papers, LC., v. 3, p. 379.
33 Jay to Monroe, Nov. 28, 1794: Madison Papers, N.Y. Pub. Lib.
34 Jay to Monroe, Nov. 25, 1794: Monroe Papers, LC., v. 3, p. 381.
35 Monroe to Randolph, Mar. 17, 1795: *ASP: For. Rel.,* I, 700-701. Jay eventually sent his secretary to France to give Monroe some idea of the treaty terms (Jay to Monroe, Feb. 19, 1795: Madison Papers, N.Y. Pub. Lib.).
36 Gallatin to his wife, June 28, 1797: Gallatin Papers, N.Y. Hist. Soc.
37 Fauchet to Randolph, Sept. 8, 1794: *ASP: For. Rel.,* I, 601-3. Randolph to Govs. of the States, Oct. 10, 1794: *ibid.,* I, 604-5.
38 Randolph to Monroe, Dec. 3, 1794, May 31, 1795: Monroe Papers, N.Y. Pub. Lib.
39 Randolph to Monroe, July 29, 1795: *ibid.*
40 Randolph to Monroe, June 1, 1795: *ASP: For. Rel.,* I, 705-12.
41 *ASP: For. Rel.,* I, 24-6.
42 *Gazette of the U.S.,* Dec. 15, 1794 (quoting the *Newark Gazette*).
43 To Madison, Dec. 28, 1794: Jefferson, *Works* (Fed. ed.), VIII, 156-9.
44 Oct. 11, 1794: Washington Papers, LC., v. 269, p. 64.
45 *Annals of Cong., 3rd Cong., 2nd Sess.,* 794.
46 *Ibid.,* 896.
47 *Ibid.,* 895-8.
48 *Ibid.,* 899-900.
49 *Ibid.,* 901-2.
50 *Ibid.,* 909-11.
51 *Ibid.,* 914, 943-4.
52 Madison to Jefferson, Nov. 30, 1794: Madison Papers, LC., v. 17, p. 108.
53 Monroe to Randolph, Oct. 16, Nov. 20, 1794: Monroe, *Writings,* II, 69-87, 117-24.
54 Mar. 11, 1795: Madison Papers, LC., v. 18, p. 33.
55 *Aurora,* Jan. 14, 1795.
56 *Annals of Cong., op. cit.,* 1004, 1034-5.
57 Act of Jan. 29, 1795: *ibid.,* 1497-9.

CHAPTER 20

(*Notes refer to text pages 354-370.*)

1 "Report on Public Credit," Jan. 16, 21, 1795: *ASP: Finance,* I, 320-38.
2 Pickering to Wm. Bingham, Dec. 17, 1795: Pickering MSS., Mass. Hist. Soc., v. 6, p. 157.
3 Feb. 8, 1796: *Letters to his Wife,* II, 195.
4 To Grenville, Jan. 5, 1795: Brit. State Papers, Ford Transcripts, N.Y. Pub. Lib.

⁵ "Memorandum for Wm. Constable," June 1795: Constable-Pierrepont Papers, N.Y. Pub. Lib.

⁶ "Report of the Treasury Dept. on Exports," *Annals of Cong., 3rd Cong., 2nd Sess.,* 2598.

⁷ Rochefoucauld-Liancourt, *Travels,* I, 23, 65, 67-8.

⁸ *Ibid.,* I, 552-3.

⁹ Isaac Weld, *Travels,* I, 102-3.

¹⁰ Washington to D.C. Commissioners, Jan. 28, 1795: Washington, *Writings,* XXXIV, 106-8.

¹¹ *Moreau de St. Méry, op. cit.,* 211.

¹² Cobbett to Jefferson, Nov. 2, 1792: Mary E. Clark, *Peter Porcupine in America,* 7.

¹³ Priestley, *Memoirs,* I, 126.

¹⁴ "Addresses to Doctor Priestley," and "Observations on Priestley's Emigration," 1794-5: *Porcupine's Works,* I, 121-44, 147-215.

¹⁵ "A Summary View of the Politics of the United States" and "Dispute between America and Great Britain": *ibid.,* I, 343-400.

¹⁶ *Porcupine's Works,* I, 138 n., 140 n.

¹⁷ Monroe to [Randolph], Mar. 17, 1795: copy in Madison Papers, N.Y. Pub. Lib.

¹⁸ Madison to Jefferson, Feb. 15, 1795: Madison Papers, LC., v. 18, p. 24.

¹⁹ Hamilton to Wm. Bradford, June 13, 1795: Wallace Papers, Pa. Hist. Soc.

²⁰ Randolph to Jay, Apr. 26, May 30, 1795: M. D. Conway, *Omitted Chapters of History,* 234-5.

²¹ Fauchet to Randolph, May 2, 1795: *ibid.,* 247.

²² Randolph to Fauchet, May 23, 1795: *ibid.,* 247.

²³ Apr. 25, 1795: *Amer. Hist. Assoc. Ann. Rept. for 1936,* 97 n.

²⁴ Madison to R. R. Livingston, Feb. 7, 8, 1795: R. R. Livingston Papers, N.Y. Hist. Soc.

²⁵ Jefferson to Madison, Apr. 27, 1795: Jefferson, *Works* (Fed. ed.), VIII, 169-72.

²⁶ Hamilton to King, June 11, 1795: King Papers, N.Y. Hist. Soc.

²⁷ *Annals of Cong., op. cit.,* 859, 860-1.

²⁸ Hamilton to King, June 20, 1795: Hamilton, *Works* (Lodge, ed.), X, 103-4.

²⁹ N.Y. *Diary,* May 20, 1795.

³⁰ Hammond to Grenville, June 25, 1795: Brit. State Papers, Ford Transcripts, N.Y. Pub. Lib.

³¹ Washington to Hamilton, July 3, 1795: Washington, *Writings,* XXXIV, 226-8.

³² Wadsworth to Hamilton, [July] 1795: Hamilton, *Works* (J. C. Hamilton, ed.), VI, 14.

³³ Phila. *General Advertiser,* July 14, 1795.

³⁴ R. R. Livingston to Madison, July 8, 1795; to Monroe, Jan. 2, 1794: Livingston Papers, Bancroft Transcripts, N.Y. Pub. Lib.

³⁵ To Washington, July 8, 1795: *ibid.*

³⁶ July 9, 1795: Hamilton, *Works* (Lodge, ed.), V, 138-81.

[37] July 13, 1795: Washington, *Writings*, XXXIV, 237-40.
[38] Aug. 20, 1795: R. R. Livingston Papers, N.Y. Hist. Soc.
[39] July 15, 1795: reprinted in *Porcupine's Works*, II, 273.
[40] July 31, 1795: *ibid.*, II, 275.
[41] *Independent Chronicle*, July 16, 1795.
[42] Phila. *General Advertiser and Aurora*, July 29, 1795.
[43] King to Gore, July 24, 1795; Gore to King, July 27, 1795; Cabot to King, Aug. 14, 1795: King Papers, N.Y. Hist. Soc.
[44] N.Y. *Argus*, July 20, 1795. J. C. Hamilton, *History of the Republic*, VI, 225.
[45] N.Y. *Argus*, July 27, 1795.
[46] Phila. *Genl. Adv. and Aurora*, July 24, 1795. E. Randolph to Washington, July 27, 1795: Washington Papers, LC., v. 274, p. 9. Wolcott to Washington, July 26, 1795: Gibbs, *Memoirs*, I, 217-18. (Wolcott, however, thought it was Blair who threw the treaty to the mob.)
[47] Letter Book, Washington Papers, LC.
[48] Randolph to Washington, July 20, 1795: Washington Papers, LC., v. 273, p. 125. Washington to Randolph, July 29, 1795: Washington, *Writings*, XXXIV, 254-7.
[49] Phila. *Aurora*, Aug. 1, 1795 (quoting from N.Y. *Mirror*).
[50] To Randolph, July 22, 1795: Washington, *Writings*, XXXIV, 243-6.
[51] Hamilton, *Works* (Lodge, ed.), V, 189-491; VI, 3-197.
[52] N.Y. *Argus*, Aug. 19, 27, 1795.
[53] Sept. 21, 1795: Jefferson, *Works* (Fed. ed.), VIII, 192-3.
[54] To Hamilton, July 29, 1795: Washington, *Writings*, XXXIV, 262-4.
[55] Hammond to Grenville, July 27, 1795: Brit. State Papers, Ford Transcripts, N.Y. Pub. Lib.
[56] To Jay, Aug. 31, 1795: Washington, *Writings*, XXXIV, 292-4.
[57] To Grenville, Aug. 14, 1795: Brit. State Papers, Ford Transcripts, N.Y. Pub. Lib.

CHAPTER 21

(*Notes refer to text pages 371-393.*)

[1] Fauchet to Commissioner of Foreign Relations, June 4, 1794 (no. 3): Conway, *Omitted Chapters*, 312-13.
[2] Same to same, Sept. 5, 1794 (no. 6): *ibid.*, 319.
[3] Same to same, Oct. 31, 1794 (no. 10): *Amer. Hist. Assoc. Ann. Rept. for 1903* (in the original French), 444-55.
[4] Grenville to Hammond, May 9, 1795: *Amer. Hist. Assoc. Ann. Rept. for 1936*, 85.
[5] Wolcott's Notes: Gibbs, *Memoirs*, I, 232-31.
[6] "Queries to his Cabinet," Aug. 12-18, 1795: Washington, *Writings*, XXXIV, 275-6.
[7] Wolcott to John Marshall, June 9, 1806: Gibbs, *Memoirs*, I, 241-6. Conway, *Omitted Chapters*, 286-7.
[8] Wm. Ellery to Wolcott, Jan. 11, 1796: Emmet Coll., N.Y. Pub. Lib. Conway, *Omitted Chapters*, 305.

[9] Randolph's *Vindication* (1795), 84 ff.
[10] Wolcott to Hamilton, Sept. 26, 1795; to his father, Oct. 13, 1795: Gibbs, *Memoirs*, I, 247-8, 256.
[11] Washington to Wolcott, Oct. 2, 1795: *ibid.*, I, 249-50.
[12] Randolph to Madison, Nov. 1, 1795: Madison Papers, LC., v. 18, p. 71.
[13] Madison to Monroe, Jan. 26, 1796: *ibid.*, v. 19, p. 13.
[14] Charles Warren, *Jacobin and Junto*, under date of Aug. 14, 1795.
[15] Beckley to Madison, Sept. 10, 1795: Madison Papers, N.Y. Pub. Lib.
[16] Phila. *Aurora*, Aug. 22, Sept. 14, 15, 1795.
[17] To Pickering, Aug. 29, 1795: *Amer. Hist. Assoc. Ann. Rept. for 1896*, 793-4.
[18] Dec. 2, 1795.
[19] To Hamilton, Sept. 26, 1795: Hamilton, *Works* (J. C. Hamilton, ed.), VI, 39-40.
[20] To Pickering, Sept. 27, 1795: Washington, *Writings*, XXXIV, 314-16.
[21] Washington to Carrington, Oct. 9, 1795: *ibid.*, XXXIV, 331-3.
[22] Hamilton to Washington, Nov. 5, 1795: Hamilton, *Works* (Lodge, ed.), X, 129-32.
[23] Jefferson to Giles, Dec. 31, 1795: Jefferson, *Works* (Fed. ed.), VIII, 201-4. Ralph Izard to Jacob Read, Nov. 17, 1795: Emmet Coll., N.Y. Pub. Lib.
[24] John Breckinridge to Samuel Hopkins, Sept. 15, 1794: Breckinridge Papers, LC., v. 11, p. 1783.
[25] "Memorial of Fayette Co.," Aug. 28, 1795, and "Petition to the Kentucky Legislature," [Nov. 1, 1795]: *ibid.*, v. 12, p. 136; v. 13, p. 140.
[26] Randolph to Jefferson, Aug. 28, 1794: Jefferson Papers, LC., v. 97, pp. 16675-6.
[27] July 26, 1794: Bemis, *Pinckney's Treaty*, 236-7.
[28] Feb., 1795: *ibid.*, 266-7.
[29] Pinckney to Randolph, Aug. 11, 1795: *ASP: For. Rel.*, I, 535-6.
[30] Grenville to Phineas Bond, Oct. 10, 1795: Brit. State Papers, Ford Transcripts, N.Y. Pub. Lib.
[31] Bond to Grenville, Jan. 2, 1796: *ibid.*
[32] *ASP: For. Rel.*, I, 546-9.
[33] Dec. 8, 1795: *ibid.*, I, 27-9.
[34] Washington to Morris, Dec. 22, 1795: Washington, *Writings*, XXXIV, 398-403.
[35] Bond to Grenville, Jan. 2, 1796: *supra.*
[36] Adet to Pickering, Jan. 9, 1796: *ASP: For. Rel.*, I, 656.
[37] Pickering to Adet, Jan. 15, 1796: *ibid.*, I, 656-7.
[38] Adet to Pickering, Mar. 3, 1796; Pickering to Adet, Mar., 1796: *ibid.*, I, 657, 657-8.
[39] N.Y. *Argus*, Jan. 1, 1796.
[40] *Columbian Centinel*, Apr. 27, 1796.
[41] Gallatin's Memorandum: Adams, *Gallatin*, 157. "A Sketch of the Finances of the United States" (1796): Gallatin, *Writings*, III, 73-201.
[42] *Annals of Cong., Fourth Cong., 1st Sess.*, 195, 245-7.
[43] Phila. *Aurora*; N.Y. *Argus*, 1796 *passim.*

44 Grenville to Bond, Jan. 18, 1796; to Robert Liston, Mar. 18, 1796: *Amer. Hist. Assoc. Ann. Rept. for 1936*, 106-10; 112-13.

45 To Wolcott, Apr. 20, 1796: Hamilton, *Works* (Lodge, ed.), X, 161-2.

46 Monroe to Pickering, Feb. 20, 1796: *ASP: For. Rel.*, I, 730-1.

47 Washington to Hamilton, May 8, 1796: Washington, *Writings*, XXXV, 38-43.

48 Adet to Pickering, Jan. 12, 1796; Pickering to Adet, Jan. 20, 1796: *ASP: For. Rel.*, I, 645, 645-6.

49 Adet to Pickering, Mar. 29, 1796: *ibid.*, I, 644.

50 *Annals of Cong., op. cit.*, 426-7.

51 *Ibid.*, 429-30, 437-8.

52 *Ibid.*, 444-6, 465.

53 *Ibid.*, 524-6.

54 To Madison, Mar. 27, 1796: Jefferson, *Works* (Fed. ed.), VIII, 230-2.

55 Washington to his Cabinet, Mar. 25, 1796: Washington, *Writings*, XXXIV, 505. The replies are in Washington Papers, LC., v. 278, pp. 44, 46-50, 52-4, 71-3. Ellsworth to Trumbull, Mar. 13, 1796: *ibid.*, v. 278, pp. 24-26. Hamilton to Washington, Mar. 24, 28, 1796: Hamilton, *Works* (Lodge, ed.), X, 151, 152-5.

56 *ASP: For. Rel.*, I, 550-1.

57 *Annals of Cong., op. cit.*, 763.

58 *Ibid.*, 772-3.

59 John Brown to Innes, Apr. 2, 1796: Innes Papers, LC., v. 19, p. 150.

60 *Conn. Courant*, Apr. 18, 1796.

61 *Ibid.*, Apr. 25, 1796.

62 Apr. 15, 1796: Hamilton, *Works* (Lodge, ed.), X, 157-60.

63 Barlow and Donaldson to Humphreys, Apr. 5, 1796; *ASP: For. Rel.*, I, 554-5.

64 Pickering to Washington, Jan. 6, 1797; Wolcott's Report, Jan. 4, 1797: *ibid.*, I, 553-4, 555.

65 King to Hamilton, Apr. 20, 1796: Hamilton Papers, LC., v. 28, p. 3884.

66 *Annals of Cong., op. cit.*, 940, 942-3, 946, 969.

67 *Ibid.*, 979-80, 1114.

68 Apr. 30, 1796: *Letters to his Wife*, II, 225-7. Adams was one of the few Federalists to believe that the House had the right to call for the papers on the Treaty, and to express its opinion on the merits (Apr. 19, 1796: *ibid.*, II, 224). Washington considered Ames's speech "unanswerable" (to Thos. Pinckney, May 26, 1796: Washington, *Writings*, XXXV, 61-3).

69 *Annals of Cong., op. cit.*, 1280, 1282, 1289, 1291, 1295.

CHAPTER 22

(*Notes refer to text pages 394-412.*)

1 To Monroe, June 12, 1796: Jefferson, *Works* (Fed. ed.), VIII, 243-4.

2 To Jefferson, May 22, 1796: Madison Papers, LC., v. 19, p. 68.

3 Jefferson to Mazzei, Apr. 24, 1796: Jefferson, *Works* (Fed. ed.), VIII, 238-41.

[4] Washington to Hamilton, May 15, 1796: Washington, *Writings*, XXXV, 48-51.

[5] Washington to Jefferson, July 6, 1796: *ibid.*, XXXV, 118-22.

[6] Chauncey Goodrich to Oliver Wolcott, Sr., May 13, 1796: Gibbs, *Memoirs*, I, 338-9.

[7] *Annals of Cong., op. cit.*, 2905-9.

[8] Wolcott to Hamilton, June 17, 1796: Hamilton, *Works* (J. C. Hamilton, ed.), VI, 132-3.

[9] To House of Representatives, Dec. 29, 1794: *ASP: Naval Aff.*, I, 6.

[10] *Ibid.*, I, 17-18, 19-21.

[11] Grenville to Bond, May 19, 1796: *Amer. Hist. Assoc. Ann. Rept. for 1936*, 118-119.

[12] Captain H. Mowat to Robert Liston, Mar. 27, 1797: *ibid.*, 119 n.

[13] *Gazette of the U.S.*, Aug. 3, 1796.

[14] Washington to Hamilton, June 26, 1796: Washington, *Writings*, XXXV, 101-4.

[15] Hamilton to Wolcott, June 15, 1796: Hamilton, *Works* (Lodge, ed.), X, 174-6.

[16] Monroe to Minister of Finance, Apr. 7, 1796: Monroe Papers, N.Y. Pub. Lib.

[17] Monroe to Madison, July 5, 1796: Monroe, *Writings*, III, 19-27.

[18] Paine to Washington, July 30, 1796: Paine, *Writings* (Conway, ed.), III, 213-52.

[19] Pickering to Monroe, June 13, 1796: *ASP: For. Rel.*, I, 737-8.

[20] "Cabinet Opinion": Washington, *Writings*, XXXV, 123-4 n.

[21] Washington to Pickering, July 27, 1796: *ibid.*, XXXV, 156-7.

[22] *ASP: For. Rel.*, I, 741-2.

[23] Sept. 1, 1796: Monroe, *Writings*, III, 52-4. De la Croix to Monroe, Oct. 7, 1796: *ASP: For. Rel.*, I, 745. Mountflorence to Monroe, Aug. 30, 1796: Monroe Papers, N.Y. Pub. Lib.

[24] Monroe to Jefferson, Mar. 26, 1798: Monroe, *Writings*, III, 106 ff. Benjamin Vaughan to Monroe, Sept. 2, 1797: Monroe Papers, N.Y. Pub. Lib.

[25] To Hamilton, June 26, 1796: Washington, *Writings*, XXXV, 101-4.

[26] To Hamilton, May 15, 1796: *ibid.*, XXXV, 48-51.

[27] To Hamilton, Aug. 25, 1796: *ibid.*, XXXV, 190-2.

[28] "Farewell Address," Sept. 19, 1796: *ibid.*, XXXV, 214-18.

[29] N.Y. *Argus*, Oct. 21, 1796.

[30] Phila. *Aurora*, Dec. 21, 1796. Beckley to Monroe, Oct. 17, 1796: Monroe Papers, N.Y. Pub. Lib.

[31] Hamilton to ——, 1796: Hamilton, *Works* (Lodge, ed.), X, 195-6.

[32] Dayton to Sedgwick, Nov. 12, 13, 1796: copies in Hamilton Papers, LC. Sedgwick to Dayton, Nov. 19, 1796: *ibid.* Sedgwick to Hamilton, Nov. 19, 1796: *ibid.* The full story is given in Schachner, *Hamilton*, chap. 23.

[33] *Independent Chronicle*, Nov. 7, 1796.

[34] *Columbian Centinel*, Jan. 4, 18, 1797.

[35] Liston to Grenville, Nov. 17, 1796: Brit. State Papers, Ford Transcripts, N.Y. Pub. Lib.

[36] *Gazette of the U.S.*, Nov. 3, 1796.

37 Troup to King, Jan. 28, 1797: King Papers, N.Y. Hist. Soc.
38 Troup to King, Nov. 16, 1796: *ibid.*
39 Higginson to Hamilton, Dec. 9, 1796, Jan. 12, 1797: Hamilton, *Works* (J. C. Hamilton, ed.), VI, 185-7, 191-2.
40 Madison to Jefferson, Dec. 5, 1796: Madison Papers, LC., v. 19, p. 104.
41 To King, Dec. 16, 1796: Hamilton, *Works* (Lodge, ed.), X, 215-17.
42 Phila. *Aurora*, Dec. 12, 1796. Jefferson to T. M. Randolph, Jan. 9, 1797: Jefferson Papers, LC., v. 101, pp. 17286-7. Jefferson's "Summary" [1800]: *ibid.*, v. 219, p. 39161.
43 Jan. 8, 1797: Madison Papers, LC., v. 20, p. 4.
44 Jefferson to Madison, Dec. 17, 1796: Jefferson, *Works* (Fed. ed.), VIII, 254-6. See also to Rutledge, Dec. 27, 1796: *ibid.*, VIII, 256-9.
45 Dec. 19, 1796: Madison, *Writings*, VI, 296-302.
46 Dec. 28, 1796: Jefferson, *Works* (Fed. ed.), VIII, 259-61.
47 Jefferson to Madison, Jan. 1, 1797: *ibid.*, VIII, 262-4. Madison to Jefferson, Jan. 15, 1797: Madison, *Writings*, VI, 302-5.
48 Adams to T. Dalton, Jan. 19, 1797: Emmet Coll., N.Y. Pub. Lib.
49 To Madison, Jan. 8, 1797: Jefferson, *Works* (Fed. ed.), VIII, 268.
50 Phila. *Aurora*, Dec. 23, 1796.

CHAPTER 23

(Notes refer to text pages 413-431.)

1 Adet to Pickering, Oct. 27, 1796: ASP: For. Rel., I, 576-7.
2 Pickering to Adet, Nov. 1, 1796: *ibid.*, I, 578. Hamilton, however, thought the tonc of Pickering's reply too harsh (to Washington, Nov. 11, 1796: Hamilton, *Works* [Lodge, ed.], X, 215-17).
3 Adet to Pickering, Nov. 15, 1796: *ibid.*, I, 579-83.
4 To King, Dec. 16, 1796: Hamilton, *Works* (Lodge, ed.), X, 215-17.
5 To Jefferson, Dec. 5, 1796: Madison Papers, LC., v. 19, p. 104.
6 C. C. Pinckney to Pickering, Dec. 10, 11, 1796: ASP: For. Rel., II, 6.
7 Pinckney to De la Croix, Dec. 13, 1796: *ibid.*, II, 6-7.
8 Pinckney to Pickering, Dec. 15, 1796: *ibid.*, II, 7-8.
9 Pinckney to Pickering, Feb. 18, 1797: *ibid.*, II, 10.
10 Dec. 7, 1796; *ibid.*, I, 30-2.
11 *Ibid.*, I, 32, 33.
12 *Annals of Cong.*, 4th Cong., 2nd Sess., 1615-16, 1667.
13 *Ibid.*, 1694-8, 1704.
14 *Ibid.*, 1867, 1909.
15 Ames to Hamilton, Jan. 26, 1797: Hamilton, *Works* (J. C. Hamilton, ed.), VI, 198-203.
16 *Conn. Courant*, Apr. 10, 1797.
17 Grenville to Liston, Jan. 27, 1797: Brit. State Papers, N.Y. Pub. Lib.
18 To Washington, Jan. 19, 22, 1797: Hamilton, *Works* (Lodge, ed.), X, 229-31, 233-5. To Sedgwick, Feb. 26, 1797: *ibid.*, X, 339. To Pickering, Mar. 22, 1797: *ibid.*, X, 243-6.

¹⁹ To Hamilton, Mar. 31, 1797: Hamilton, *Works* (J. C. Hamilton, ed.), VI, 221-5.

²⁰ The pertinent letters are in *ibid.*, VI, 215-16, 238-46.

²¹ To Madison, Jan. 22, 1797: Jefferson, *Works* (Fed. ed.), VIII, 271-4. See also to T. M. Randolph, Jan. 22, 1797: Jefferson Papers, LC., v. 101, p. 17292.

²² To Iredell, Mar. 10, 1797: McRee, *Iredell*, II, 495-6.

²³ To King, Feb. 15, 1797: Hamilton, *Works* (Lodge, ed.), X, 237-8.

²⁴ Jefferson, *Works* (Fed. ed.), I, 334-6.

²⁵ Sedgwick to King, Mar. 12, 1797: King, *King*, II, 156-9.

²⁶ *ASP: For. Rel.*, I, 38-9.

²⁷ Adams, *Letters to his Wife*, II, 244-5.

²⁸ *Ibid.*, II, 242-3.

²⁹ Wm. Smith to King, Apr. 3, 1797: King Papers, N.Y. Hist. Soc.

³⁰ N.Y. *Argus*, Mar. 8, 1797.

³¹ *Ibid.*, Feb. 27, 1797. See also Phila. *Aurora*, Mar. 10, 14, 1797, and *Independent Chronicle*, Mar. 6, 1797.

³² To Henry Knox, Mar. 30, 1797: Adams, *Works*, VIII, 535-6.

³³ Hamilton to King, Apr. 8, 1797: King Papers, N.Y. Hist. Soc.

³⁴ Hamilton to Wolcott, Mar. 30, 1797: Hamilton, *Works* (Lodge, ed.), X, 248-9. Also to Pickering, Mar. 29, 1797: *ibid.*, X, 246-8.

³⁵ Stephen Higginson to Pickering, Mar. 25, 1797: *Amer. Hist. Assoc. Ann. Rept. for 1896*, 796-7.

³⁶ Liston to Grenville, Apr. 18, 1797: Brit. State Papers, N.Y. Pub. Lib.

³⁷ Apr. 14, 1797: Adams, *Works*, VIII, 540-1.

³⁸ Hamilton to McHenry, Apr. 29, 1797 (two letters): Steiner, *McHenry*, 213-16, 216-22.

³⁹ Tracy to Hamilton, Apr. 6, 1797: Hamilton Papers, LC., v. 29, p. 4121.

⁴⁰ Mountflorence to Pickering, Feb. 14, 21, 1797: *ASP: For. Rel.*, II, 11. *Porcupine's Gazette*, June 12, 1797, quotes a Paris letter listing the names of some of these renegade captains. They hailed from Boston, Marblehead, Cape Ann, New York, Baltimore, Charleston and elsewhere.

⁴¹ *Conn. Courant*, May 22, 1797.

⁴² S. E. Morison, *Otis*, I, 41.

⁴³ *Porcupine's Gazette*, June 6, 1797.

⁴⁴ May 16, 1797: *ASP: For. Rel.*, I, 40-42.

⁴⁵ *Annals of Cong.*, *op. cit.*, 71-3, 87.

⁴⁶ *Ibid.*, 70, 193, 233-7.

⁴⁷ June 7, 1797: *ibid.*, 239.

⁴⁸ *Ibid.*, 240-381.

⁴⁹ *Ibid.*, 385.

⁵⁰ *Ibid.*, 385-6, 390-3, 409-10.

⁵¹ To Edward Stevens, June 14, 1797: Jefferson Papers, LC., v. 102, p. 17424. To Thomas Pinckney, May 29, 1797: Jefferson, *Works* (Fed. ed.), VIII, 291-4.

⁵² Jefferson to T. M. Randolph, May 19, 1797: Jefferson Papers, LC., v. 101, p. 17384.

⁵³ Phila. *Aurora*, May 25, July 14, 1797.

[54] N.Y. *Time-Piece*, June 9, June 23, 1797. *Independent Chronicle*, June 15, 1797.
[55] To Rutledge, June 24, 1797: Jefferson, *Works* (Fed. ed.), VIII, 316-19.
[56] To Uriah Forrest, June 20, 1797: Adams, *Works*, VIII, 546-7.
[57] Létombe to De La Croix, June 7, 1797: *Amer. Hist. Assoc. Ann. Rept. for 1903*, 1028-31.
[58] June 21, 1797: Jefferson, *Works* (Fed. ed.), VIII, 313-15.
[59] Pickering's Report, June 22, 1797: *ASP: For. Rel.*, II, 28-63.
[60] Adams to Gerry, July 8, 1797: Adams, *Works*, VIII, 547-8.
[61] To Wolcott, Oct. 27, 1797: *ibid.*, VIII, 558-9.
[62] Report of David Lenox, July 12, 1797; King to Pickering, Apr. 13, 1797; Grenville to King, Nov. 3, 1796: *ASP: For. Rel.*, II, 138-40, 146, 146-7.
[63] Liston to Grenville, Mar. 16, 1797: Brit. State Papers, N.Y. Pub. Lib.
[64] Blount to Jas. Carey, Apr. 21, 1797: *ASP: For. Rel.*, II, 76-7.
[65] *Independent Chronicle*, July 27, 1797.
[66] *Ibid.*, Aug. 27, 1797.
[67] Madison to Jefferson, Aug. 24, 1797: Madison Papers, LC., v. 20, p. 61. J. D. Dawson to Madison, Aug. 13, 1797: *ibid.*, v. 20, p. 60.
[68] "Propositions of Thomas Power," July 19, 1797: Innes Papers, LC., v. 19, pp. 154-5. Wolcott to his father, July 4, 1797: Gibbs, *Memoirs*, I, 548.
[69] Pickering to Adams, July 3, 1797: *ASP: For. Rel.*, II, 66.
[70] Yrujo to Pickering, July 11, 1797: *ibid.*, II, 87-8.
[71] *Porcupine's Gazette*, July 13, 14, 15, 1797.
[72] *Ibid.*, Oct. 5, 6, 1797.
[73] Wharton, *State Trials*, 322. *Porcupine's Works*, VII, 315-407.
[74] *Porcupine's Gazette*, July 31, 1797.
[75] *Gazette of the U.S.*, Sept. 1, 1797.
[76] Phila. *Aurora*, Apr. 1, 1800.
[77] N.Y. *Spectator*, Oct. 7, 1797, quoting Boston *Mercury*.

CHAPTER 24

(Notes refer to text pages 432-446.)

[1] For American comment on Fructidor see N.Y. *Spectator*, Nov. 8, 1797.
[2] Nov. 23, 1797: *ASP: For. Rel.*, I, 44-5.
[3] To Martha Randolph, Dec. 27, 1797: Jefferson Papers, Morgan Library.
[4] To his wife, Dec. 9, 1797: Gallatin Papers, N.Y. Hist. Soc.
[5] *Annals of Cong.*, 5th Cong., 2nd Sess., 493.
[6] N.Y. *Time-Piece*, Oct. 18, 1797.
[7] To his wife, Jan. 18, 1798: Gallatin Papers, N.Y. Hist. Soc.
[8] *Annals of Cong.*, op. cit., 955, 959, 961-2. "Committee Report," *ASP: Misc.*, I, 166-74.
[9] *ASP: Misc.*, I, 174-8.
[10] Bayard to Richard Bennett, Feb. 16, 1798: *Papers of Jas. A. Bayard* (E. Donnan, ed.), 48-9.
[11] *Annals of Cong.*, op. cit., 1036, 1040, 1063, 1066-8.

[12] Feb. 15, 1798: *New Letters of Abigail Adams,* 132-3. Gallatin to his wife, Feb. 23, 1798: Gallatin Papers, N.Y. Hist. Soc.

[13] Jefferson to Madison, Jan. 25, 1798: Jefferson, *Writings* (Fed. ed.), VIII, 385-61.

[14] Jefferson to Madison, Feb. 15, 1798: *ibid.,* VIII, 368-70.

[15] To T. M. Randolph, Jan. 11, 1798: Jefferson Papers, LC., v. 102, p. 17554.

[16] To McHenry, Mar. 4, 1798: Washington, *Writings,* XXXVI, 179.

[17] To Heads of Depts., Jan. 24, 1798: Adams, *Works,* VIII, 561-2.

[18] McHenry to Hamilton, Jan. 26, 1798: Hamilton Papers, LC., v. 30, pp. 4196-8.

[19] Hamilton to McHenry: Steiner, *McHenry,* 291-5.

[20] Harper to Hamilton, Apr. 27, 1798: Hamilton, *Works* (J. C. Hamilton, ed.), VI, 282.

[21] Grenville to King, Jan. 13, 1798: King, *King,* II, 270-1.

[22] King to Pickering, Jan. 14, 27, 1798: *ibid.,* II, 271, 274-6.

[23] Gerry to his wife, Oct. 9, 1797: Gerry Letter Book, 1797-1801, privately owned by Mrs. Townsend Phillips of New York (photostats in N.Y. Pub. Lib.).

[24] Envoys to Pickering, Oct. 22, 1797: *ASP: For. Rel.,* II, 157-8.

[25] Marshall's Journal, Oct. 15, 1797; copy in Pickering Papers, Mass. Hist. Soc.

[26] Vans Murray to J. Q. Adams, Apr. 13, 1798: *Amer. Hist. Assoc. Ann. Rept. for 1912,* 394.

[27] Marshall's Journal, *op. cit. ASP: For. Rel.,* II, 157-8.

[28] This running account of the XYZ Affair is taken from the Report of the Envoys, Oct. 22, 1797: *supra,* and from Marshall's Journal, *op. cit.*

[29] Envoys to Pickering, Oct. 27, 1797: *ASP: For. Rel.,* II, 161-3. Marshall's Journal, *op. cit.*

[30] Envoys to Pickering, Oct. 29, 30, Nov. 11, 1797: *ASP: For. Rel.,* II, 163, 163-4. Marshall's Journal, *op. cit.*

[31] Oct. 31, 1797: Gerry Letter Book, *supra,* N.Y. Pub. Lib.

[32] Gerry to his wife, Nov. 25, 1797: *ibid.*

[33] To Helen Thompson, Jan. 3, 1798: *ibid.*

[34] Pinckney to King, Dec. 14, 1798: King, *King,* II, 259-60.

[35] Envoys to Pickering: *ASP: For. Rel.,* II, 167.

[36] Jan. 31, 1798: *ibid.,* II, 169-82.

[37] Marshall's Journal, *op. cit.*

[38] King to Pinckney, Dec. 24, 1797: King, *King,* II, 263-4.

[39] Talleyrand to Envoys, Mar. 18, 1798: *ASP: For. Rel.,* II, 188-91.

[40] [Undated]: *ibid.,* II, 191-9.

[41] Mar. 22, 1798: Marshall's Journal, *op. cit.*

[42] To his wife, Mar. 26, Apr. 16, 1798: Gerry Letter Book, N.Y. Pub. Lib.

[43] King to Gerry, Apr. 2, 13, 1798: King Papers, N.Y. Hist. Soc.

[44] Gerry to his wife, Apr. 20, 1798: Gerry Letter Book, N.Y. Pub. Lib.

[45] Pinckney to King, Apr. 4, 1798: King, *King,* II, 303-4.

[46] Talleyrand to Gerry, May 30, June 1, 1798: *ASP: For. Rel.,* II, 210.

[47] Hauteval to Talleyrand, June 1, 1798: *ibid.,* II, 226-7.

[48] Gerry to Miss Eliza Gerry, July 12, 1798; to his wife, July 25, 1798: Gerry Letter Book, N.Y. Pub. Lib.

CHAPTER 25

(Notes refer to text pages 447-468.)

[1] Mar. 5, 1798: Richardson, *Messages of the Presidents,* I, 263-4.

[2] Adams, *Works,* VIII, 568.

[3] Hamilton to Pickering, Mar. 17, 1798: Hamilton, *Works* (Lodge, ed.), X, 275-8.

[4] Mar. 19, 1798: Richardson, *op. cit.,* I, 264-5. Abigail Adams claimed her husband had always doubted the legality of Washington's executive order prohibiting the arming of merchant ships (*New Letters of Abigail Adams,* 146-7).

[5] Cabot to King, Mar. 21, 1798: King Papers, N.Y. Hist. Soc.

[6] Pickering to King, Apr. 2, 1798: King, *King,* II, 296-7.

[7] Jefferson to Madison, Mar. 21, 1798: Jefferson, *Works* (Fed. ed.), VIII, 386-8.

[8] Phila. *Aurora,* Mar. 20, 21, 1798.

[9] Dawson to Madison, with the circular, Mar. 20, 1798; Madison Papers, LC., v. 20, p. 94.

[10] To Jefferson, Apr. 2, 1798: Madison, *Writings,* VI, 311-14.

[11] Pickering to Hamilton, Mar. 25, 1798: Hamilton, *Works* (J. C. Hamilton, ed.), VI, 272-3.

[12] *Annals of Cong., 5th Cong., 2nd Sess.,* 1319-20, 1342.

[13] *Ibid.,* 1358, 1371.

[14] *Ibid.,* 531-2, 547, 3717.

[15] Richardson, *op. cit.,* I, 265.

[16] To King, Apr. 9, 1798: King, *King,* II, 310-13.

[17] Troup to King, June 3, 1798: *ibid.,* II, 328-30. King received letters from other Federalists to the same effect: *ibid.,* II, 331-4.

[18] To J. W. Eppes, Apr. 11, 1798: Randall, *Jefferson,* II, 383-4. To same effect to Peter Carr, Apr. 12, 1798: Jefferson, *Works* (Fed. ed.), VIII, 405-7.

[19] To Monroe, Apr. 19, 1798: Jefferson, *Works* (Fed. ed.), VIII, 407-9.

[20] "Address of the Young Men of Augusta, Ga.," July 2, 1798: printed in *Conn. Courant,* Sept. 17, 1798.

[21] Summarized in *Columbian Centinel,* Apr. 25, 1798.

[22] *Ibid.,* July 4, 1798.

[23] *Gazette of. the U.S.,* Apr. 18, 1798. *New Letters of Abigail Adams,* 164-6.

[24] Jefferson, *Works* (Fed. ed.), I, 346.

[25] N.Y. *Time-Piece,* May 7, 1798.

[26] *Annals of Cong., op. cit.,* 1440-2, 1468, 1473, 1474, 1476.

[27] *Ibid.,* 548-9, 555, 575.

[28] *Ibid.,* 1520-1, 1700, 1772, 3724-6, 3729-33, 3737-9, 3747.

[29] *New Letters of Abigail Adams,* 170-2. Jefferson to Madison, May 10, 17, 1798: Jefferson, *Works* (Fed. ed.), VIII, 417-19, 419-21.

[30] Hamilton to Washington, May 19, 1798: Hamilton, *Works* (Lodge, ed.), X, 284-6.

[31] Washington to Hamilton, May 27, 1798: Washington, *Writings,* XXXVI, 271-4.

[32] Madison to Jefferson, quoting Monroe, Apr. 29, 1798: Madison Papers, LC., v. 20, p. 108.

[33] Madison to Jefferson, May 13, 1798: *ibid.,* v. 20, p. 112.

[34] To James Nicholson, May 18, 1798: Gallatin Papers, N.Y. Hist. Soc.

[35] Jefferson to John Taylor, June 1, 1798: Jefferson, *Works* (Fed. ed.), VIII, 430-3.

[36] To Grenville, May 2, 1798 (no. 20): Brit. State Papers, N.Y. Pub. Lib.

[37] To Grenville, May 2, 1798 (no. 21): *ibid.*

[38] May, 1798: Hamilton, *Works* (Lodge, ed.), X, 283-4.

[39] *Annals of Cong., op. cit.,* 1566-8.

[40] King to Duke of Portland, Oct. 17, 1798; Pickering to King, Feb. 5, 1799: King, *King,* II, 641-2, 644.

[41] Otis to his wife: Morison, *Otis,* I, 107. Tracy to Wolcott, Aug. 7, 1800: Gibbs, *Memoirs,* II, 399.

[42] N.Y. *Time-Piece,* May 4, 1798.

[43] *Annals of Cong., op. cit.,* 1954-7, 2012, 2016.

[44] To Madison, May 14, 1798: Rives Papers, LC.

[45] To T. M. Randolph, May 3, 1798: Jefferson Papers, LC., v. 103, p. 17748.

[46] *Moreau de St. Méry, op. cit.,* 253.

[47] *Annals of Cong., op. cit.,* 3776-7.

[48] *Ibid.,* 2093-4, 2097-8.

[49] *Ibid.,* 2105, 2107.

[50] *Ibid.,* 2109-10.

[51] Hamilton to Pickering, June 7, 1798; to Wolcott, June 29, 1798: Hamilton, *Works* (Lodge, ed.), X, 292-4, 295.

[52] N.Y. *Argus,* Nov. 6, 13, 1799.

[53] The *Argus* had subjected Hamilton to vicious personal attacks in connection with the so-called "Mrs. Reynolds" incident (see, for example, the issues of Apr. 17, Aug. 19, 1799).

[54] To Pickering, June 8, 1798: Hamilton, *Works* (Lodge, ed.), X, 294-5.

[55] John Taylor, *An Inquiry into the Principles and Policy of the Government of the United States* (reprinted New Haven, 1950), 437.

CHAPTER 26

(Notes refer to text pages 469-485.)

[1] Jefferson to Madison, June 21, 1798: Jefferson, *Works* (Fed. ed.), VIII, 439-43. *Gazette of the U.S.,* June 20, 21, 1798. Claypoole's *American Advertiser,* June 20, 1798.

[2] To King, June 12, 1798: King, *King,* II, 347.

[3] June 25, 1798: ASP: *For. Rel.,* II, 204.

[4] June 6, 1798: Hamilton, *Works* (J. C. Hamilton, ed.), VI, 297-8. To same effect, July 2, 1798: *ibid.*, VI, 308-9.

[5] King to Grenville, Aug. 16, 1798: King, *King*, II, 391.

[6] Grenville to Liston, June 8, 1798: *Amer. Hist. Assoc. Ann. Rept. for 1936*, 155-60.

[7] Liston to Grenville, Sept. 27, 1798: Brit. State Papers, N.Y. Pub. Lib.

[8] Message to Cong., June 21, 1798; *ASP: For. Rel.*, II, 199.

[9] Washington to Henry Hill, July 5, 1798; to James Marshall, July 16, 1798: Washington Letter Press Copies, N.Y. Pub. Lib.

[10] Hamilton to Washington, June 2, 1798; Hamilton, *Works* (Lodge, ed.), X, 286-7.

[11] Pickering to Washington, July 6, 1798: Pickering Papers, Mass. Hist. Soc. Washington to McHenry, July 4, 1798; to Adams, July 4, 1798: Washington, *Writings*, XXXVI, 304-12, 312-15.

[12] Washington to Hamilton, July 14, 1798: Washington, *Writings*, XXXVI, 329-32. Pickering to Hamilton, July 18, 1798: Hamilton, *Works* (J. C. Hamilton, ed.), VI, 327-8. Pickering to Jay, July 28, 1798: *ibid.*, VI, 329-30. Pickering to Jas. A. Hamilton, June 14, 1821: A. M. Hamilton, *Intimate Life of Hamilton*, 323-4.

[13] Aug. 14, 1798: Adams, *Works*, VIII, 580.

[14] Pickering to Hamilton, Aug. 21, 1798: Hamilton, *Works* (J. C. Hamilton, ed.), VI, 343-6.

[15] McHenry to Hamilton, Sept. 10, 1798: *ibid.*, VI, 356. Wolcott to Hamilton, Sept. 19, 1798: *ibid.*, VI, 358-9. Pickering to Hamilton, Aug. 23, 1798; *ibid.*, VI, 351-2. McHenry to Washington, Aug. 25, 1798: Washington, *Writings*, XXXVI, 426 n.

[16] Adams to McHenry, Aug. 29, 1798: Adams, *Works*, VIII, 587-9.

[17] Sept. 7, 1798: copy in Hamilton Papers, LC., v. 32, p. 4464.

[18] Sept. 25, 1798: Washington, *Writings*, XXXVI, 453-62. Washington to Pickering, Oct. 1, 1798: Hamilton, *Works* (J. C. Hamilton, ed.), VI, 361-2.

[19] Adams to Washington, Oct. 9, 1798: Adams, *Works*, VIII, 600-1.

[20] Hamilton to Washington, July 29, 1798: Hamilton, *Works* (Lodge, ed.), X, 299-303. Washington to Hamilton, Aug. 9, 1798: Washington, *Writings*, XXXVI, 393-5. To McHenry, Aug. 10, 1798, Sept. 14, 1798: *ibid.*, XXXVI, 402-4, 441-3. Wolcott to Hamilton, Aug. 9, 1798: Hamilton Papers, LC., v. 31, p. 4388.

[21] To Col. Wadsworth, Aug. 19, 1798: photostat, Trumbull Coll., Conn. State Lib.

[22] Adams to S. B. Malcom, Aug. 6, 1812: Adams, *Works*, X, 123 ff.

[23] N.Y. *Argus*, Feb. 23, 1799.

[24] To McHenry, Sept. 30, 1798: Washington, *Writings*, XXXVI, 474-5.

[25] Feb. 6, 1799: Dreer Coll., Pa. Hist. Soc.

[26] For the Miranda story see W. S. Robertson, *The Life of Miranda* (2v., 1929) and Schachner, *Hamilton*, chap. 25.

[27] Though Adams signed a number of warrants for deportation under the Alien Act, no action was taken, since those named in them had already de-

parted (Adams to Pickering, Oct. 17, 1798: Pickering Papers, Mass. Hist. Soc., v. 23, p. 241).

[28] To Richard Harison, July 7, 1798: *ibid.*, v. 37, p. 315.

[29] Pickering to Harison, Jan. 1, 1799: *ibid.*, v. 37, p. 381. *Southern Sketches*, no. 7, p. 9 (Charlottesville, 1936).

[30] To Maria Nicholson, July 10, 1798: Adams, *Gallatin,* 196-7.

[31] Phila. *Aurora,* Aug. 3, 1798.

[32] These statistics are taken from F. M. Anderson, "The Enforcement of the Alien and Sedition Laws," in *Amer. Hist. Assoc. Ann. Rept. for 1912.* A later study of the laws is J. C. Miller, *The Alien and Sedition Acts* (1951).

[33] Wharton, *State Trials,* 333-7.

[34] Quoted in Richmond *Examiner,* Mar. 4, 1800.

[35] Phila. *Aurora,* July 24, 1799.

[36] Adams to Pickering, Aug. 13, 1799: Pickering Papers, Mass. Hist. Soc.

[37] Wharton, *State Trials,* 659-79.

[38] *Ibid.,* 688-718.

[39] *Ibid.,* 718 n.

[40] Greenleaf's *New Daily Advertiser,* Oct. 15, 1799.

[41] *Gazette of the U.S.,* Nov. 12, 1798.

[42] William Bingham to King, Sept. 30, 1798; Troup to King, Oct. 2, 1798: King, *King,* II, 425-7, 428-33. N.Y. *Spectator,* Sept. 22, Nov. 10, 1798. Wolcott to Adams, Sept. 14, 1798; Gibbs, *Memoirs,* II, 107.

[43] *Gazette of the U.S.,* Nov. 3, 1798.

CHAPTER 27

(Notes refer to text pages 486-504.)

[1] Jefferson, *Works* (Fed. ed.), VIII, 458-79.

[2] Nicholas to Jefferson, Oct. 4, 1798: Jefferson Papers, LC., v. 104, p. 17877. Jefferson to Nicholas, Oct. 5, 1798: Jefferson, *Works* (Fed. ed.), VIII, 449. Nicholas to Breckinridge, Oct. 5, 1798: Breckinridge Papers, LC., v. 16, p. 2820.

[3] Resolutions of Woodford Co., Aug., 1798: Breckinridge Papers, LC., v. 16, p. 2803½.

[4] Wallace to Breckinridge, Nov. 5, 1798: *ibid.,* v. 17, p. 2831.

[5] Kentucky Resolutions, Nov. 10, 1798: facsimile, Jefferson, *Works* (Fed. ed.), VIII, 458-9.

[6] Warfield, *The Kentucky Resolutions of 1798,* 94. Breckinridge also told Monroe that his state would publicly resist any attempt to enforce the Acts within it (Aug. 12, 1798; Monroe Papers, N.Y. Pub. Lib.).

[7] *Virginia Report of 1799-1800,* 22-3.

[8] Dec. 29, 1798: Madison, *Writings,* VI, 327-9 n.

[9] Jefferson to W. C. Nicholas, Nov. 29, 1798: Jefferson, *Works* (Fed. ed.), VIII, 483. To Madison, Nov. 17, 1798: *ibid.,* VIII, 456-7.

[10] John Taylor to Jefferson [1798]; *Branch Papers,* 277-8.

[11] Oct. 1, 1798; *ASP: For. Rel.,* II, 204-8.

[12] Du Pont to Talleyrand, July 21, 1798: *Mass. Hist. Soc. Proc.*, v. 49, pp. 65-6, 66-76.

[13] Codman to Otis, Aug. 26, 1798: Morison, *Otis*, I, 168-70.

[14] King to Troup, Sept. 16, 1798: King Papers, N.Y. Hist. Soc. To Hamilton, Sept. 23, 1798: Hamilton, *Works* (J. C. Hamilton, ed.), VI, 359-60.

[15] Gerry to Adams, Oct. 20, 1798: Adams, *Works*, VIII, 610-12. Adams to Pickering, Oct. 26, 1798: *ibid.*, VIII, 614. Pickering to Adams, Nov. 5, 1798: *ibid.*, VIII, 616. Adams to Gerry, Dec. 15, 1798; *ibid.*, VIII, 617.

[16] Murray to Adams, July 17, 1798: *ibid.*, VIII, 680-4.

[17] Murray to Pickering, Aug. 18, 1798: *Amer. Hist. Assoc. Repts. for 1912*, 457-8.

[18] Murray to J. Q. Adams, Aug. 31, 1798; to Pickering, Sept. 1, 1798: *ibid.*, 461-3, 463-5.

[19] Adams to Pickering, Oct. 29, 1798: Adams, *Works*, VIII, 614-15.

[20] D. N. Logan, *Memoir of Dr. George Logan*, 59-60 n.

[21] Murray to J. Q. Adams, Aug. 6, 7, 10, 1798: *Amer. Hist. Assoc. Repts. for 1912*, 448-50, 450-2, 452-3.

[22] Logan to his wife, Sept. 9, 1798: Logan, *Logan*, 79-80.

[23] Logan, *Logan*, 85, 86 n.

[24] To Grenville, Nov. 7, 1798: Brit. State Papers, N.Y. Pub. Lib.

[25] *Annals of Cong.*, 5th Cong., 3rd Sess., 2206, 2489, 2498-9, 2721.

[26] Phila. *Aurora*, Dec. 21, 1798.

[27] Adams to Pickering, Oct. 20, 1798: Adams, *Works*, VIII, 609-10.

[28] *ASP: For. Rel.*, I, 47-8.

[29] Otis to Hamilton, Dec. 21, 1798: Hamilton, *Works* (J. C. Hamilton, ed.), VI, 377-9.

[30] Hamilton to Otis, Dec. 27, 1798: Hamilton, *Works* (Lodge, ed.), X, 325-6.

[31] Jefferson to Pendleton, Apr. 22, 1799: Jefferson, *Works* (Fed. ed.), VIII, 65.

[32] Feb. 25, 1799; Washington, *Writings*, XXXVII, 136-8.

[33] *Annals of Cong.*, op. cit., 2429-30, 2435, 2453, 2455-6.

[34] Report to H. of R., Dec. 29, 1798; *ASP: Naval Aff.*, I, 65-6.

[35] Liston to Grenville, Jan. 16, 1799: Brit. State Papers, N.Y. Pub. Lib.

[36] *Annals of Cong.*, op. cit., 2823-5, 2883, 3804-5.

[37] *Ibid.*, 2985-93, 3001-2, 3016.

[38] Dawson to Madison, Jan. 7, 1799: Madison Papers, LC., v. 21, p. 22.

[39] Ames to Gore, Dec. 18, 1798: Ames, *Works*, I, 245-8.

[40] Washington to Murray, Dec. 26, 1798; to Bushrod Washington, Dec. 31, 1798; to Patrick Henry, Jan. 15, 1799; to Bartholomew Dandridge, Jan. 25, 1799: Washington, *Writings*, XXXVII, 71-2, 80-1, 87-90, 107-9.

[41] To Pendleton, Jan. 29, 1799: Jefferson, *Works* (Fed. ed.), IX, 27-9.

[42] Talleyrand to Pichon, Sept. 28, 1798: *ASP: For. Rel.*, II, 239-40.

[43] To Madison, Feb. 19, 1799: Jefferson, *Works* (Fed. ed.), IX, 50-3.

[44] Feb. 1, 1799: Pickering Papers, Mass. Hist. Soc., v. 10, pp. 301, 303.

[45] Pickering to Hamilton, Feb. 25, 1799: Hamilton, *Works* (J. C. Hamilton, ed.), VI, 398-9.

[46] Adams, *Works*, VIII, 626-7, 628-9.

[47] Feb. 19, 1799: Hamilton, *Works* (J. C. Hamilton, ed.), VI, 396.

[48] To Hamilton, Feb. 22, 1799: Hamilton Papers, LC., v. 35, p. 4903.

[49] Hamilton to Sedgwick, Feb. 21, 1799: Hamilton, *Works* (Lodge, ed.), X, 345-6. See also Pickering to Hamilton (note 45, *supra*).

[50] Adams to Senate, Feb. 25, 1799: *ASP: For. Rel.*, II, 240.

[51] Ames to Dwight, Feb. 27, 1799: Ames, *Works,* I, 252-3.

[52] Phila. *Aurora,* Feb. 20, 21, 1799.

[53] To Charles Lee, Mar. 29, 1799: Adams, *Works,* VIII, 629.

CHAPTER 28

(Notes refer to text pages 505-521.)

[1] R. G. Harper to his Constituents, Feb. 10, 1799: *Papers of Jas. Bayard,* 74-80.

[2] To King, Mar. 6, 1799: King, *King,* II, 548-9.

[3] Phila. *Aurora,* Mar. 11, 1799.

[4] Pickering to Liston, Apr. 12, 1798: Pickering Papers, Mass. Hist. Soc., v. 8, p. 335.

[5] *Annals of Cong., 5th Cong., 3rd Sess.,* 618-19.

[6] Phila. *Aurora,* Sept. 3, 1799; reprinted in *Letters on Various Interesting and Important Subjects by Robert Slender (Freneau),* Phila., 1799. See also the *Aurora,* Oct. 25, 1799.

[7] Wharton, *State Trials,* 458-641.

[8] Pickering to Adams, May 10, 1799: Adams, *Works,* VIII, 643-4. Wolcott to Adams, May 11, 1799: *ibid.,* VIII, 644-5. Pickering to Adams, Sept. 9, 1799: Pickering Papers, Mass. Hist. Soc., v. 12, p. 35.

[9] Cabot to King, Mar. 10, Apr. 26, 1799: King, *King,* II, 551-2; III, 7-10.

[10] Higginson to Wolcott, Mar. 29, 1799: Gibbs, *Memoirs,* II, 229-30. To same effect, Ames to King, June 12, 1799: King, *King,* III, 42-3.

[11] Liston to Grenville, Mar. 4, 1799: Brit. State Papers, N.Y. Pub. Lib.

[12] Pickering to King, June 14, Aug. 6, 1799: Pickering Papers, Mass. Hist. Soc., v. 11, pp. 434, 574.

[13] King to Pickering, July 15, 1799: King, *King,* III, 53-9.

[14] J. Lawrence to King, June 4, 1799; Troup to King, June 5, 1799: King, *King,* III, 28-9, 33-5.

[15] Stephen Van Rensselaer to Hamilton, Mar. 15, 1799: Hamilton, *Works* (J. C. Hamilton, ed.), VI, 404.

[16] Troup to King, May 6, June 5, 1799: King Papers, N.Y. Hist. Soc.

[17] N.Y. *Argus,* May 3, 1799.

[18] Hamilton to Sedgwick, Feb. 2, 1799: Hamilton, *Works* (Lodge, ed.), X, 340-2. To King, Feb. 6, 1799: King Papers, N.Y. Hist. Soc.

[19] N.Y. *Spectator,* Feb. 20, 1799.

[20] *Gazette of the U.S.,* Apr. 29, 30, 1799 (quoting the N.Y. *Gazette and General Advertiser*).

[21] Sermon of Rev. Ashbel Green: *Gazette of the U.S.,* May 6, 1799.

[22] *Gazette of the U.S.,* May 16, July 1, 1799.

23 To Madison, May 16, Sept. 30, 1799: Madison Papers, LC., v. 11, p. 63; v. 12, p. 37.

24 Phila. *Aurora*, July 24, 1799.

25 Pickering to Adams, July 24, 1799: Adams, *Works*, IX, 3-4.

26 Adams to Pickering, Aug. 1, 1799: *ibid.*, IX, 5.

27 Pickering to Adams, Aug. 1, 1799; *ibid.*, IX, 5-7.

28 "Address," June 29, 1799: Thomas Cooper, *Political Essays*, 31-9.

29 Adams to Pickering, Aug. 13, 1799: Pickering Papers, Mass. Hist. Soc., v. 25, p. 99.

30 Washington to C. C. Pinckney, Aug. 10, 1799: Washington Letter Press Copies, N.Y. Pub. Lib.

31 Washington to Jonathan Trumbull, July 21, 1799: *ibid.*

32 Aug. 20, 1799: Nicholas P. Trist Papers, LC.

33 Aug. 23, 1799: Rives Papers, LC.

34 Jefferson to W. C. Nicholas, Sept. 5, 1799: Jefferson, *Works* (Fed. ed.), IX, 79-81.

35 Warfield, *Kentucky Resolutions of 1798*, 123-6. Breckinridge to Jefferson, Dec. 13, 1799: Jefferson Papers, LC., v. 105, pp. 18094-5. "Draft Resolutions," undated; Breckinridge Papers, LC., v. 18, pp. 3011-16.

36 Jefferson to Madison, Nov. 26, 1799: Rives Papers, LC.

37 Monroe to Madison, Nov. 22, 1799: Monroe, *Writings,* III, 159-60. Jefferson to Madison, Nov. 22, 1799: Jefferson, *Works* (Fed. ed.), IX, 89-90.

38 Wolcott to Hamilton, Apr. 1, 1799: Hamilton, *Works* (J. C. Hamilton, ed.), VI, 406-7.

39 Hamilton to McHenry, June 14, July 10, 1799: Steiner, *McHenry,* 390, 397-8. McHenry to Hamilton, Aug. 20, 1799: Hamilton Papers, LC., v. 50, pp. 7999-8002.

40 Hamilton to McHenry, June 27, 1799: Hamilton, *Works* (Lodge, ed.), VII, 97-8.

41 To Uriah Forrest, May 13, 1799: Adams, *Works,* VIII, 645-6.

42 Pickering to Higginson, Sept. 27, 1799: Pickering Papers, Mass. Hist. Soc., v. 12, p. 113.

43 Murray to J. Q. Adams, Apr. 22, May 3, 1799: *Amer. Hist. Assoc. Ann. Rept. for 1912,* 542-3, 547-8.

44 Murray to J. Q. Adams, May 7, 21, 1799: *ibid.*, 549, 553-4.

45 Talleyrand to Murray, May 12, 1799; *ASP: For. Rel.*, II, 243-4.

46 Adams to Pickering, Aug. 6, 1799: Adams, *Works,* IX, 10-12.

47 Higginson to Pickering, Aug. 7, 22, 1799: Pickering Papers, Mass. Hist. Soc., v. 25, pp. 82, 109. Pickering to Higginson, Aug. 14, 1799: *ibid.*, v. 11, p. 609.

48 Troup to King, Sept. 2, 1799: King, *King,* III, 91-2.

49 King to Pickering, Oct. 11, 1799: *ibid.*, III, 122-31.

50 Pickering to Adams, Sept. 11, 1799: Adams, *Works,* IX, 23-5.

51 Pickering to Ellsworth, Sept. 16, 1799: Pickering Papers, Mass. Hist. Soc., v. 12, p. 69.

52 Ellsworth to Pickering, Sept. 20, 1799; *ibid.*, v. 25, p. 177.

53 Stoddert to Adams, Sept. 13, 1799: Adams, *Works,* IX, 25-9.

[54] Adams to Stoddert and Pickering, Sept. 21, 1799: *ibid.*, IX, 33, 33-4. To Ellsworth, Sept. 22, 1799: *ibid.*, IX, 34-5.

[55] Pickering to Adams, Sept. 24, 1799: *ibid.*, IX, 36-7.

[56] Lee to Adams, Oct. 6, 1799: *ibid.*, IX, 38.

[57] Adams to Pickering, Oct. 16, 1799: *ibid.*, IX, 39.

[58] Pickering to Murray, Oct. 4, 1799: Pickering Papers, Mass. Hist. Soc., v. 12, pp. 141-3. Same to same, Oct. 25, 1799: *Amer. Hist. Assoc. Ann. Rept. for 1912*, 610-12.

[59] To Pickering, Oct. 31, 1799: Pickering Papers, Mass. Hist. Soc., v. 25, p. 261.

[60] Sedgwick to King, Dec. 12, 1799: King, *King*, III, 154-6.

[61] Tracy to McHenry, Sept. 2, 1799: Steiner, *McHenry*, 416-17.

[62] To Hamilton, Oct. 27, 1799: Washington, *Writings*, XXXVII, 408-10.

CHAPTER 29

(Notes refer to text pages 522-539.)

[1] To Tobias Lear, Jan. 2, 1800: Hamilton, *Works* (Lodge, ed.), X, 356-7.

[2] To King, Jan. 5, 1800: *ibid.*, X, 360. See also Troup to King, Jan. 1, 1800: King Papers, N.Y. Hist. Soc.

[3] *Annals of Cong.*, 6th Cong., 1st Sess., 204.

[4] Otis to his wife, Dec. 14, 26, 1799: Morison, *Otis*, I, 140-1, 141. *Gazette of the U.S.*, Dec. 27, 1799.

[5] Quoted in *Gazette of the U.S.*, Feb. 13, 1800.

[6] Liston to Grenville, Jan. 2, 1800: Brit. State Papers, N.Y. Pub. Lib.

[7] *Annals of Cong.*, *op. cit.*, 241, 244-5.

[8] *Ibid.*, 247, 249-50, 252-3, 271, 369.

[9] McHenry to Hamilton, Feb. 18, 1800: Hamilton Papers, LC., v. 68, p. 11079. Jefferson to Martha Randolph, Jan. 21, 1800: Jefferson MSS., Morgan Lib.

[10] *Annals of Cong.*, *op. cit.*, 372-3, 277-8, 506-7.

[11] S. T. Mason to Monroe, Jan., 1800: Monroe Papers, LC., v. 6, p. 947.

[12] *Annals of Cong.*, *op. cit.*, 62-3, 111-15, 118-24, 184.

[13] Jefferson to Monroe, Jan. 12, Mar. 4, 1800: Jefferson, *Works* (Fed. ed.), IX, 90-2, 121-3.

[14] *Journal, Va. House of Delegates*, Jan. 13, 17, 1800.

[15] *Columbian Centinel*, Feb. 8, June 25, 1800.

[16] *Ibid.*, May 10, 1800.

[17] *ASP: For. Aff.*, I, 72.

[18] Jefferson to Dr. Wm. Bache, Feb. 2, 1800: Jefferson Papers, LC., v. 106, pp. 18167-8.

[19] N.Y. *Commercial Advertiser*, Apr. 23, 1800. Jefferson to Madison, May 4, 1800: Madison Papers, LC., v. 21, p. 72.

[20] Troup to King, Mar. 9, 1800: King, *King*, III, 207-9.

[21] Matthew L. Davis to Gallatin, Mar. 29, 1800: Adams, *Gallatin*, 232-4.

[22] Adams, *Works*, X, 125.

²³ For details of this vital election, see Schachner, *Aaron Burr,* chap. 13, and *Alexander Hamilton,* chap. 26.

²⁴ M. L. Davis to Gallatin, May 1, 1800: Gallatin Papers, N.Y. Hist. Soc.

²⁵ Davis to Gallatin, May 5, 1800; James Nicholson to Gallatin, May 6, 1800; *ibid.* Gallatin to his wife, May 12, 1800: Adams, *Gallatin,* 243. Dawson to Monroe, May 4, 1800: Monroe Papers, N.Y. Pub. Lib.

²⁶ N.Y. *Spectator,* May 17, 1800.

²⁷ Hamilton to Jay, May 7, 1800: Hamilton, *Works* (Lodge, ed.), X, 371-4.

²⁸ Wm. Jay, *Life of John Jay,* I, 414.

²⁹ May 10, 1800: Hamilton, *Works* (Lodge, ed.), X, 375-6.

³⁰ Hamilton to Sedgwick, May 8, 1800: *ibid.,* X, 374. Jefferson to T. M. Randolph, May 7, 1800: Jefferson Papers, LC., v. 107, p. 18277.

³¹ Dec. 11, 1799: *New Letters of Abigail Adams,* 219-22.

³² McHenry to Adams, May 6, 1800: Adams, *Works,* IX, 51-2. McHenry to John McHenry, May 20, 1800: Gibbs, *Memoirs,* II, 346-8.

³³ Adams to Pickering, May 10, 1800; Pickering to Adams, May 12, 1800; Adams to Pickering, May 12, 1800: Adams, *Works,* IX, 53-4, 54-5, 55.

³⁴ May 13, 1800: Hamilton, *Works* (J. C. Hamilton, ed.), VI, 442.

³⁵ Phila. *Aurora,* May 9, 1800.

³⁶ May 14, 1800: Hamilton, *Works* (Lodge, ed.), X, 376.

³⁷ July 1, 1800: *ibid.,* X, 377.

³⁸ Pickering to Hamilton, May 15, 1800: Hamilton Papers, LC., v. 76, p. 12324 (deleted from published version in Hamilton's *Works* edited by his son, VI, 443-4).

³⁹ To Hamilton, July 7, 1800: Hamilton, *Works* (J. C. Hamilton, ed.), VI, 447-8.

⁴⁰ Hamilton, *Works* (Lodge, ed.), VII, 309-64.

⁴¹ Duane to Monroe, Oct. 23, 1800: Monroe Papers, N.Y. Pub. Lib.

⁴² Richard Stockton to Wolcott, June 27, 1800: Gibbs, *Memoirs,* II, 374-6. More of the conspiratorial correspondence may be found in Gibbs, II, *passim.*

⁴³ R. G. Harper to Hamilton, June 5, 1800: Hamilton Papers, LC., v. 77, pp. 12581-2. Also J. A. Bayard of Delaware to Hamilton, June 8, 1800: *ibid.,* v. 77, p. 12593.

⁴⁴ Hamilton to Chas. Carroll, July 1, 1800: Hamilton, *Works* (Lodge, ed.), X, 378-80.

⁴⁵ Liston to Grenville, May 6, 1800: Brit. State Papers, N.Y. Pub. Lib.

⁴⁶ Troup to King, June 24, 1800: King Papers, N.Y. Hist. Soc. Same to same, Nov. 9, 1800; J. Hale to King, July 9, 1800: King, *King,* III, 330-2, 269-70.

⁴⁷ Troup to King, Oct. 1, Dec. 15, 1800: King Papers, N.Y. Hist. Soc.

⁴⁸ McHenry to Wolcott, July 22, 1800: Gibbs, *Memoirs,* II, 384-5.

⁴⁹ Cabot to Wolcott, Oct. 5, 1800: *ibid.,* II, 433.

⁵⁰ *Gazette of the U.S.,* June 10, 12, 1800.

CHAPTER 30

(Notes refer to text pages 540-556.)

[1] Jefferson to Madison, June 13, 1800: Rives Papers, LC.

[2] Jefferson to Gideon Granger, Aug. 13, 1800: Jefferson, *Works* (Fed. ed.), IX, 138-41.

[3] Jefferson to Dr. Rush, Sept. 23, 1800: *ibid.*, IX, 146-9.

[4] *Diary of Rev. Thomas Robbins* (I. N. Tarbox, ed.), I, 145.

[5] *Gazette of the U.S.*, Sept. 12, 1800.

[6] [John M. Mason, D.D.], *The Voice of Warning, to Christians, on the ensuing Election of a President of the United States* (N.Y., 1800). See also [Rev. Dr. Linn], *Serious Considerations on the Election of a President* (N.Y., 1800).

[7] [Tunis Wortman], *A Solemn Address to Christians and Patriots, upon the Approaching Election* (N.Y., 1800). [John Beckley], *Address to the People of the United States; with an Epitome and Vindication of the Public Life and Character of Thomas Jefferson* (Phila., 1800).

[8] Bayard to Hamilton, Aug. 11, 1800: *Papers of Jas. A. Bayard*, 112-15.

[9] Burr to R. R. Livingston, Sept. 7, 24, Dec. 9, 1800: R. R. Livingston Papers, N.Y. Hist. Soc. Troup to King, Sept. 14, 1800: King Papers, N.Y. Hist. Soc.

[10] To Theophilus Parsons, July 1, 1800: *Correspondence of Jay*, IV, 274-5.

[11] To John Trumbull, Sept. 10, 1800: Adams, *Works*, IX, 83-4.

[12] To John Marshall, July 31, Sept. 4, 1800: *ibid.*, IX, 66-7, 80-1.

[13] To King, July 15, 1800: King, *King*, III, 275-7.

[14] *ASP: For. Rel.*, II, 331-2.

[15] *Ibid.*, II, 295-343.

[16] Ellsworth to Pickering, Oct. 16, 1800: Pickering Papers, Mass. Hist. Soc., v. 26, p. 216.

[17] Troup to King, Dec. 31, 1800: King Papers, N.Y. Hist. Soc.

[18] Liston to Grenville, Nov. 6, 1800: Brit. State Papers, N.Y. Pub. Lib.

[19] Liston to Grenville, Oct. 8, 1800: *ibid.*

[20] *Ibid.*

[21] *Gazette of the U.S.*, Nov. 11, 17, 1800: quoting also from the *Aurora*. Beckley to Gallatin, Feb. 4, 1801: Gallatin Papers, N.Y. Hist. Soc.

[22] Nov. 21, 1800: *New Letters of Abigail Adams*, 256-60.

[23] Speech to Congress, Nov. 22, 1800; *ASP: For. Rel.*, I, 53-4.

[24] "Statement of the Committee": C. C. Pinckney, *Life of Thomas Pinckney*, 154-6. James Gunn to Hamilton, Dec. 13, 1800: Hamilton, *Works* (J. C. Hamilton, ed.), VI, 483-4.

[25] Jefferson to T. M. Randolph, Dec. 12, 1800: *Mass. Hist. Soc. Colls.*, 7th Ser., v. 1, p. 80.

[26] John Randolph's Diary: copy in Va. State Lib.

[27] Hale to King, Dec. 29, 1800: King, *King*, III, 357-8.

[28] Burr to Jefferson, Dec. 23, 1800: Jefferson Papers, LC., v. 108, p. 18525.

²⁹ G. W. Erving to Monroe, Dec. 17, 1800; Jan. 25, 1801: Monroe Papers, LC., v. 6, pp. 998, 1017. See also Monroe to Madison, Nov. 6, 1800: Rives Papers, LC.

³⁰ Jefferson to T. M. Randolph, Dec. 12, 1800: *supra.*

³¹ Cabot to Hamilton, Aug. 10, 1800: Hamilton, *Works* (J. C. Hamilton, ed.), VI, 454.

³² Sedgwick to Hamilton, Dec. 17, 1800: *ibid.,* VI, 491-2. Morris to Hamilton, Dec. 19, 1800: *ibid.,* VI, 492-4.

³³ Bayard to Hamilton, Jan. 7, 1801: *ibid.,* VI, 505-7.

³⁴ Sewall to Otis, Dec. 29, 1800: Morison, *Otis,* I, 212.

³⁵ To Bayard, Aug. 6, 1800: Hamilton, *Works* (Lodge, ed.), X, 384-7.

³⁶ Hamilton to Bayard, Dec. 27, 1800: *ibid.,* X, 402-4. Hamilton wrote an amazing number of letters along these lines; among others, see those to Wolcott, Dec. 18, 1800; to John Rutledge, Dec., 1800; to G. Morris, Dec. 26, 1800; to James Ross, 1801: *ibid.,* X, 392-3, 401, 404-5, 405-7.

³⁷ To Wolcott, Dec. 17, 1800: *ibid.,* X, 393-5.

³⁸ To Bayard, Jan. 16, 1801: *ibid.,* X, 412-19.

³⁹ To Sedgwick, Dec. 22, 1800: *ibid.,* X, 397-8.

⁴⁰ Troup to King, Dec. 31, 1800: King, *King,* III, 358-9.

⁴¹ Dec. 16, 1800: M. L. Davis, *Burr,* II, 75.

⁴² Dec. 23, 1800: Jefferson Papers, LC., v. 108, p. 18525.

⁴³ Jan. 16, 1801: Gallatin Papers, N.Y. Hist. Soc.

⁴⁴ Ogden to Peter Irving, Nov. 24, 1802: quoted in N.Y. *Morning Chronicle,* Nov. 25, 1802.

⁴⁵ To Mary J. Eppes, Jan. 4, 1801: Jefferson, *Works* (Fed. ed.), IX, 166-7.

⁴⁶ S. T. Mason to Monroe, Jan. 2, 1801: Monroe Papers, LC., v. 6, p. 1009.

⁴⁷ To Joseph H. Nicholson, Jan. 3, 1801: Nicholson MSS., LC.

⁴⁸ To Jefferson, Jan. 10, 1801: McKean Papers, Pa. Hist. Soc.

⁴⁹ Gerry to Jefferson, Jan. 15, 1801: Gerry Letters Books, N.Y. Pub. Lib.

⁵⁰ To his wife, Jan. 15, [1801]: Gallatin Papers, N.Y. Hist. Soc.

⁵¹ Jefferson to Monroe, Feb. 15, 1801: Jefferson, *Works* (Fed. ed.), IX, 178-180.

⁵² Monroe to Jefferson, Jan. 6, 1801; to John Hoomes, Feb. 14, 1801: Monroe, *Writings,* III, 253-5, 258-60. Nicholson to a Constituent, Jan. 15, 1801: Pa. Hist. Soc.

⁵³ To Jefferson, Jan. 10, 1801: Madison, *Writings,* VI, 410-16.

⁵⁴ Gallatin, *Writings,* I, 18-23. Gallatin to his wife, Jan. 15, 1801: *supra.*

⁵⁵ To Jefferson, Jan. 19, 1801: Jefferson Papers, LC., v. 109, pp. 18645-9.

⁵⁶ Gunn to Hamilton, Dec. 13, 1800: Hamilton, *Works* (J. C. Hamilton, ed.), VI, 483-4.

⁵⁷ *Annals of Cong.,* 6th Cong., 2nd Sess., 1534-48.

⁵⁸ To Madison, Dec. 26, 1800: Jefferson, *Works* (Fed. ed.), IX, 161-2.

⁵⁹ *Annals of Cong., op. cit.,* 916-17, 1049-50.

CHAPTER 31
(Notes refer to text pages 557-564.)

[1] Gallatin to his wife, Jan. 15, 1801: Gallatin Papers, N.Y. Hist. Soc.

[2] *Ibid.* Jefferson to Martha J. Randolph, Jan. 26, 1801: Jefferson, *Works* (Mont. ed.), XVIII, 234-5.

[3] Jefferson to T. M. Randolph, Jan. 23, 1801: Jefferson, *Works* (Mont. ed.), XVIII, 233.

[4] Adams to Gerry, Feb. 7, 1801: Adams, *Works,* IX, 97-8.

[5] R. G. Harper to his Constituents, Feb. 24, 1801: *Papers of Jas. A. Bayard,* 132-7. Uriah Tracy to Mr. Gould, Feb. 16, 1801; Pa. Hist. Soc.

[6] Otis to his wife, Feb. 11, 1801: Morison, *Otis,* I, 207-8. John Randolph to St. George Tucker, Feb. 11, 1801: W. C. Bruce, *Randolph,* I, 168.

[7] James Platt to James Kent, Feb. 11, 1801: Kent, *Kent,* 141.

[8] Jefferson to Archibald Stuart, Feb. 12, 1801: Jefferson Papers, LC.

[9] Gallatin to his wife, Feb. 12, 1801: Adams, *Gallatin,* 260-1.

[10] Gallatin to James Nicholson, Feb. 16, 1801: *ibid.,* 262.

[11] Bayard to Bassett, Feb. 16, 1801: *Papers of Jas. A. Bayard,* 126-7.

[12] Bayard to Hamilton, Mar. 8, 1801: Hamilton, *Works* (J. C. Hamilton, ed.), VI, 522-4.

[13] Bayard to McLane, Feb. 17, 1801: *Papers of Jas. A. Bayard,* 127-8. See also the depositions of Jas. A. Bayard, Apr. 3, 1806, and Samuel Smith, Apr. 15, 1806, in the case of *Gillespie vs. Smith:* Davis, *Burr,* II, 129-33, 133-7. Also Bayard, *Remarks in the Senate of the United States,* Jan. 31, 1855.

[14] Bayard to McLane, *supra.* To Samuel Bayard, Feb. 22, 1801: *Papers of Jas. A. Bayard,* 131-2.

[15] Jefferson to Monroe, Feb. 15, 1801: Jefferson, *Works* (Fed. ed.), IX, 178-80.

[16] Burr to Gallatin, Feb. 25, 1801: Adams, *Gallatin,* 246-7.

[17] To his wife, Feb. 17, 1801: Gallatin Papers, N.Y. Hist. Soc.

Bibliography

MANUSCRIPT SOURCES

American Antiquarian Society
   Andrew Craigie Papers
Archives des Affaires Étrangères: États-Unis, Paris
Archivo de Relaciones Exteriores, Mexico (D.F.)
British Public Records Office, London
Connecticut Historical Society
   Wadsworth, Jeremiah, Papers
   Wolcott, Oliver, Papers
Historical Society of Pennsylvania
   Barton, Benjamin, Papers
   Dreer Collection
   Etting Papers
   Logan, Maria Dickinson Collection
   McKean Collection
   Pennsylvania Democratic Society MSS. Minutes
   Rittenhouse Photostats
   Rutledge Papers
Library of Congress
   Breckinridge Family Papers
   British State Papers, Henry Adams Transcripts
   Genêt Papers
   Hamilton, Alexander, Papers
   Henley-Smith Papers
   Innes, Harry, Papers
   Jefferson, Thomas, Papers
   Madison, James, Papers
   Monroe, James, Papers
   Rives, William C., Papers
   Short, William, Papers
   Trist, Nicholas P., Papers
   Washington, George, Papers
Louisiana State Archives
Massachusetts Historical Society
   Jefferson Papers, Coolidge Collection
   Knox, Henry, Papers
   Pickering, Timothy, Papers
   Sedgwick, Theodore, Papers
   Smith, William S., Papers
   Washburn Papers
Mississippi State Archives

National Archives
  State Department Papers
  Territorial Papers
  Treasury Department Papers
New York Historical Society
  Burr, Aaron, Misc. MSS.
  Duer, William, Papers
  Gallatin, Albert, Papers
  Hamilton, Alexander, Misc. MSS.
  King, Rufus, Papers
  Livingston, Robert R., Papers
New York Public Library
  Adams, Samuel, Papers; Bancroft Transcripts
  Archives Françaises: États-Unis; Bancroft Transcripts
  British State Papers, Ministry to the United States, Gordon Lester Ford
    Transcripts
  Constable-Pierrepont Papers
  Emmet Collection
  Gerry, Elbridge, Letter Book, 1797-1801; Photostats
  Hamilton, Alexander, Misc. MSS.
  Livingston, Robert R., Papers
  Madison, James, Papers
  Monroe, James, Papers
  Washington, George, Letter Press Copies
University of Texas
  Bexar Archives
University of Virginia
  Jefferson Papers

NEWSPAPERS

Boston *Columbian Centinel*
Boston *Gazette*
Boston *Independent Chronicle*
Hartford *Connecticut Courant*
New London *Bee*
New York *Argus*, or *Greenleaf's New Daily Advertiser*
New York *Commercial Advertiser*
New York *Spectator*
New York *Time-Piece and Literary Companion*
Philadelphia *Gazette of the United States*
Philadelphia *General Advertiser* (later *Aurora*)
Philadelphia *National Gazette*
Philadelphia *Porcupine's Gazette*
Philadelphia *Poulson's American Daily Advertiser*
Pittsburgh *Gazette*
Richmond *Examiner*
Vermont *Gazette*

Printed Sources

Adams, Abigail, *New Letters of* (Stewart Mitchell, ed.), Boston, 1947

Adams, John, *The Works of* (Chas. Francis Adams, ed.), 10 v., N.Y., 1850-6

Adams, John, *Letters of, addressed to his wife* (Chas. Francis Adams, ed.), 2 v., Boston, 1841

Adams, John Quincy, *Writings of* (Chas. Francis Adams, ed.), 7 v., N.Y., 1913-17

American Historical Association Annual Reports
  "Correspondence of Clark and Genêt," 1896, v. 1, pp. 930-1107
  "Letters of Stephen Higginson," 1896, v. 1, pp. 704-841
  "Letters of Phineas Bond," 1896, v. 1, pp. 513-659; 1897, pp. 454-568
  "Mangourit Correspondence," 1897, pp. 569-679
  "Correspondence of the French Ministers to the United States, 1791-1797," 1903, v. 2
  "Letters of William Vans Murray to John Quincy Adams," 1912, pp. 345-708
  "Instructions to the British Ministers to the United States," 1936

American Historical Review, "Documents on the Blount Conspiracy," X, 574-606

American Philosophical Society, *Proceedings of the*, v. 1, pt. 1 (1744-1837)

American Philosophical Society, *Transactions of the*, vols. 1-5 (Philadelphia, 1789-1802)

American State Papers (Gales and Seaton, eds.): *Foreign Relations; Finance; Indian Affairs; Public Lands; Commerce and Navigation; Military Affairs; Naval Affairs; Miscellaneous* (Washington, 1832-3)

Ames, Fisher, *Works of* (Seth Ames, ed.), 2 v., Boston, 1854

Bache, Benjamin F., *Remarks occasioned by the Late Conduct of Mr. Washington*, Philadelphia, 1797

———, *Truth Will Out*, Philadelphia, 1798

Barlow, Joel, *Advice to the Privileged Orders*, London & N.Y., 1792

———, *The Columbiad*, Philadelphia, 1807

———, *Two Letters to the Citizens of the United States, and one to General Washington*, New Haven, 1806

Bayard, James A., *Papers of* (Elizabeth Donnan, ed.), Washington, 1915

Beckley, John, *Address to the People of the United States; with an Epitome and Vindication of the Public Life and Character of Thomas Jefferson*, Philadelphia, 1800

Biddle, Alexander, *Old Family Letters*, Series A & B, Philadelphia, 1892

Brackenridge, Hugh Henry, *Incidents of the Insurrection in the Western Parts of Pennsylvania in the Year 1794*, Philadelphia, 1795

Branch, The John P., *Historical Papers of Randolph-Macon College*, v. 2 (1905)

Brissot de Warville, J. P., *New Travels in the United States of America*, N.Y., 1792

Callender, James T., *American Annual Register*, Philadelphia, 1797

———, *The History of the United States for 1796*, Philadelphia, 1800

———, *The Prospect Before Us*, Philadelphia, 1800

Cobbett, William, *Porcupine's Works*, 12 v., London, 1801

Cooper, Thomas, *Political Essays*, Northumberland (Pa.), 1799

Coxe, Tench, *A View of the United States of America*, Philadelphia, 1794

———, *Strictures upon the Letter imputed to Mr. Jefferson, addressed to Mr. Mazzei*, Lancaster (Pa.), 1800

Cranch, William, *(U.S.) Reports*, 6 v., 1812

Custis, George W. P., *Recollections and Private Memoirs of Washington*, N.Y., 1860

Cutler, Wm. P. & Julia P., *Life, Journals and Correspondence of Rev. Manasseh Cutler*, 2 v., Cincinnati, 1888

Dallas, A. J., *United States Supreme Court Reports in Pennsylvania*, 4 v., 1806-7

Dwight, Timothy, *Travels; in New-England and New-York*, 4 v., New Haven, 1821-2

Freneau, Philip, *Letters on Various Interesting and Important Subjects*, Philadelphia, 1799

———, *The Poems of* (Fred L. Pattee, ed.), 3 v., Princeton, 1902

Gallatin, Albert, *The Writings of* (Henry Adams, ed.), 3 v., Philadelphia, 1879

Gibbs, George, *Memoirs of the Administrations of Washington and John Adams*, 2 v., N.Y., 1846

Graydon, Alexander, *Memoirs of a Life*, Harrisburg (Pa.), 1811

Griswold, Rufus W., *The Republican Court*, N.Y., 1855

Hamilton, Alexander, *The Works of* (John C. Hamilton, ed.), 7 v., N.Y., 1851

Hamilton, Alexander, *The Works of* (Henry Cabot Lodge, ed.), 12 v., N.Y., 1904

Jefferson, Thomas, *The Works of* (Federal Edition, Paul L. Ford, ed.), 12 v., N.Y., 1904

Jefferson, Thomas, *The Writings of* (A. A. Lipscomb, ed.), 20 v., N.Y., 1904

King, Rufus, *The Life and Correspondence of* (Charles R. King, ed.), 6 v., N.Y., 1894-9

Linn, Rev. Dr., *Serious Considerations on the Election of a President*, N.Y., 1800

Maclay, William, *The Journal of*, N.Y., 1927

Madison, James, *The Writings of* (Gaillard Hunt, ed.), 9 v., N.Y., 1904

Mason, John M., *The Voice of Warning, to Christians, on the Ensuing Election of a President of the United States*, N.Y., 1800

Massachusetts Historical Society Collections, Ser. 5, v. 3, "The Belknap Papers"

———, "Warren-Adams Letters," vols. 72-3 (1917-25)

Monroe, James, *The Writings of* (Stanislaus M. Hamilton, ed.), 7 v., N.Y., 1898-1903

Moreau de St. Méry's American Journey, 1793-1798 (Kenneth and Anna M. Roberts, trans. & eds.), N.Y., 1947

Paine, Thomas, *The Writings of* (Moncure D. Conway, ed.), 4 v., N.Y., 1894-6

Priestley, Dr. Joseph, *Memoirs of*, 2 v., London, 1806

Richardson, James D., Messages and Papers of the Presidents, 10 v., Washington, 1897-1908

Rochefoucault-Liancourt, Duc de la, Travels through the United States of North America, 2 v., London, 1799

Rush, Benjamin, Letters of (L. M. Butterfield, ed.), 2 v., Princeton, 1951

Steele, John, The Papers of (H. M. Wagstaff, ed.), 2 v., Raleigh (N.C.), 1924

Stiles, Ezra, The Literary Diary of (F. B. Dexter, ed.), 3 v., N.Y., 1901

Taylor, John, A Definition of Parties, Philadelphia, 1794

———, An Inquiry into the Principles and Policy of the Government of the United States, New Haven, 1950

———, Disunion Sentiment in Congress in 1794, Washington, 1905

Trumbull, Autobiography, Reminiscences and Letters of, N.Y., 1841

Trumbull, John, The Poetical Works of, 2 v., Hartford, 1820

United States, Annals of the Congress of the (Gales and Seaton, eds.), Washington, 1834-51

United States, Census of the Several Districts of the, 1790 and 1800, Washington, 1802

United States, The Public Statutes at large of the (Richard Peters, ed.), 8 v., 1845

United States, The Territorial Papers of the (Clarence E. Carter, ed.), 14 v., Washington, 1934-8

United States: Treaties, Conventions, International Acts, Protocols and Agreements (Wm. M. Malloy, ed.), 2 v., Washington, 1910

Wansey, Henry, An Excursion to the United States of North America in 1794, Salisbury (England), 1798

Washington, George, The Diaries of (John C. Fitzpatrick, ed.), 4 v., Boston, 1925

Washington, George, The Writings of (John C. Fitzpatrick, ed.), 39 v., Washington, 1931-44

Weld, Isaac, Jr., Travels through the States of North America, 2 v., London, 1807

Wharton, Francis, State Trials of the United States during the Administrations of Washington and Adams, Philadelphia, 1849

Wortman, Tunis, A Solemn Address to Christians and Patriots, upon the Approaching Election, N.Y., 1800

SECONDARY WORKS

Adams, Henry, History of the United States during the Administration of Thomas Jefferson, 4 vs. in 2, N.Y., 1930

———, The Life of Albert Gallatin, Philadelphia, 1879

Allen, Gardner W., Our Naval War with France, Boston, 1909

Anderson, Dice R., William Branch Giles, Menasha (Wisconsin), 1914

Austin, Mary S., Philip Freneau: The Poet of the Revolution, N.Y., 1901

Baldwin, Leland D., Whiskey Rebels, Pittsburgh, 1939

Bassett, John Spencer, The Federalist System, N.Y., 1906

Beard, Charles A., Economic Origins of Jeffersonian Democracy, N.Y., 1915

Bemis, Samuel Flagg, Jay's Treaty, N.Y., 1923

——, *Pinckney's Treaty*, Baltimore, 1926

Bowers, Claude G., *Jefferson and Hamilton*, Boston, 1925

Brackenridge, H. M., *History of the Western Insurrection in Western Pennsylvania*, Pittsburgh, 1859

Brant, Irving, *James Madison, Father of the Constitution*, N.Y., 1950

Channing, Edward, *A History of the United States*, v. 4, N.Y., 1926

Childs, Frances S., *French Refugee Life in the United States, 1790-1800*, Baltimore, 1940

Chinard, Gilbert, *Honest John Adams*, Boston, 1933

Clark, Mary E., *Peter Porcupine in America*, Philadelphia, 1939

Clark, Victor S., *History of Manufactures in the United States*, 3 v., N.Y., 1929

Clarke, M. St. Claire and D. A. Hall, *Legislative and Documentary History of the Bank of the United States*, Washington, 1832

Conway, Moncure D., *Omitted Chapters of History . . . Edmund Randolph*, N.Y., 1888

Dallas, George Mifflin, *Life and Writings of Alexander James Dallas*, Philadelphia, 1871

Davis, Joseph S., *Essays in the Earlier History of American Corporations*, 2 v., Cambridge (Mass.), 1917

Davis, Matthew L., *Memoirs of Aaron Burr*, 2 v., N.Y., 1852

Drake, Francis S., *Life and Correspondence of Henry Knox*, Boston, 1873

Dunlap, William, *History of the American Theatre*, 2 v. in 1, London, 1833

Ford, Emily E. F. (E. E. F. Skeel, ed.), *Notes on the Life of Noah Webster*, 2 v., N.Y., 1912

Ford, Worthington C., *The United States and Spain in 1790*, Brooklyn, 1890

Forman, Samuel E., *The Political Activities of Philip Freneau*, in *Johns Hopkins University Studies*, Ser. 20 (1902)

Graham, Gerald S., *Sea Power and British North America, 1783-1820*, Cambridge (Mass.), 1941

Hammond, Jabez D., *The History of Political Parties in the State of New-York*, v. 1, N.Y., 1852

Hart, James, *The American Presidency in Action: 1789*, N.Y., 1948

Haskins, Charles Homer, *The Yazoo Land Companies*, N.Y., 1891

Hayden, Ralston, *The Senate and Treaties, 1789-1817*, N.Y., 1920

Hazen, Charles D., *Contemporary American Opinion of the French Revolution*, Baltimore, 1897

Henry, William Wirt, *Patrick Henry*, 3 v., N.Y., 1891

Hibbard, Benjamin H., *A History of the Public Land Policies*, N.Y., 1924

Holdsworth, John T., *The First Bank of the United States*, Philadelphia, 1911

Howard, Leon, *The Connecticut Wits*, Chicago, 1943

Jacobs, James R., *The Beginning of the United States Army, 1783-1812*, Princeton, 1947

Jones, Howard Mumford, *America and French Culture, 1750-1848*, Chapel Hill, 1927

Kimball, Fiske, *Domestic Architecture of the American Colonies and of the Early Republic*, N.Y., 1922

Livermore, Shaw, *Early American Land Companies*, N.Y., 1939

Lodge, Henry Cabot, *Life and Letters of George Cabot*, Boston, 1877
Logan, Deborah N., *Memoir of Dr. George Logan of Stenton*, Philadelphia, 1899
McLaughlin, J. F., *Matthew Lyon*, N.Y., 1900
McMaster, John B., *A History of the People of the United States*, vols. 1-2, N.Y., 1936
McRee, Griffith, J., *Life and Correspondence of James Iredell*, 2 v., N.Y., 1857
Malone, Dumas, *The Public Life of Thomas Cooper*, New Haven, 1926
Marshall, John, *Life of George Washington*, 5 v., Philadelphia, 1805
Massachusetts Historical Society Proceedings, "Du Pont, Talleyrand, and the French Spoliations," by S. E. Morison, v. 49, pp. 63-79
———, "Convention of 1800 with France," by Brooks Adams, v. 44, pp. 377-428
Miller, John C., *Crisis in Freedom: The Alien and Sedition Acts*, Boston, 1951
Morison, Samuel E., *The Life and Letters of Harrison Gray Otis*, 2 v., Boston, 1913
Morse, Anson E., *The Federalist Party in Massachusetts to the Year 1800*, Princeton, 1909
Mott, Frank Luther, *A History of American Magazines, 1741-1850*
Mudge, Eugene T., *The Social Philosophy of John Taylor of Caroline*, N.Y., 1939
Newlin, Claude M., *The Life and Writings of Hugh Henry Brackenridge*, Princeton, 1932
Odell, George C. D., *Annals of the New York Stage*, vols. 1-2, N.Y., 1927
Paltsits, Victor H., *Washington's Farewell Address*, N.Y., 1935
Pickering, Octavius and Charles W. Upham, *The Life of Timothy Pickering*, 4 v., Boston, 1867-73
Robinson, William A., *Jeffersonian Democracy in New England*, New Haven, 1916
Schachner, Nathan, *Aaron Burr, a Biography*, N.Y., 1937
———, *Alexander Hamilton*, N.Y., 1945
———, *Thomas Jefferson*, 2 v., N.Y., 1951
Setser, Vernon G., *The Commercial Reciprocity Policy of the United States, 1774-1829*, Philadelphia, 1937
Simms, Henry H., *Life of John Taylor*, Richmond, 1932
Steiner, Bernard C., *The Life and Correspondence of James McHenry*, Cleveland, 1907
Sweet, William W., *Religion on the American Frontier*, 4 v., N.Y., 1931-46
Thomas, Charles M., *American Neutrality in 1793*, N.Y., 1931
Todd, Charles Burr, *Life and Letters of Joel Barlow*, N.Y., 1886
Treat, Payson J., *The National Land System, 1785-1820*, N.Y., 1910
Warren, Charles, *Jacobin and Junto*, Cambridge (Mass.), 1931
———, *The Supreme Court in United States History*, 3 v., Boston, 1922
White, Leonard D., *The Federalists*, N.Y., 1948
Zimmerman, James F., *Impressment of American Seamen*, N.Y., 1925

Index